THE KING FAMILY OF KIRKBY MALHAM, ASKHAM, UMBERSLADE & CHADSHUNT

&

THE KNIGHT FAMILY OF BARRELLS

WALTER KING

January 2020

1

1f.

CONTENTS

INTRODUCTION

On 7 February 1828, at St George's, Hanover Square, Edward Bolton King, of Umberslade, in Warwickshire married Georgiana Knight, the younger daughter of a Warwickshire neighbour, Robert Knight, of Barrells. The service was taken by the bridegroom's younger brother, Rev John Myers King, the recently married and also recently ordained curate of Chilton Polden, in Somerset. The witnesses were the bride's father and the bridegroom's cousin, Rev James King, vicar of Longfield, Kent, Charlotte Myddleton Biddulph, of Chirk Castle (an old friend of the bride's father), and Frances Anne Wingfield, a friend of the bride's, whose father was a trustee of the Knight family settlement and whose brother was heir to Sherborne Castle. It was a union of two very different families.

The King family were from Yorkshire. They first emerged into history during the boom time of the woollen industry in the fifteen and sixteenth centuries. The production of wool – and increasingly of finished cloth too – was making England rich, and the King family benefitted. A junior branch of the family was established at Kirby Malham by the end of the sixteenth century and this village remained their home for some two hundred years. They were – like many of their sort – independent, strongly Protestant, and supporters of the parliament during the Civil War. They were farmers, merchants, clergymen and, by the end of the seventeenth century, naval officers, surgeon-apothecaries and lawyers too. They were people of consequence in Malhamdale though not yet risen into the ranks of the gentry. A King heiress had brought her wealth into the Lister family in the early sixteenth century, but the seventeenth century Kings would not rank with the true gentry of the West Riding – the Listers, Lamberts, Towneleys and Asshetons.

The second half of the eighteenth century saw a remarkable rise in the family fortunes. Sir Fletcher Norton was a cousin and old school-fellow of Rev James King, the vicar of Clitheroe. Norton had made a great fortune in the law, and by the 1760s was Attorney General and then Speaker of the House of Commons. In 1782, he was raised to the peerage. It was he who invited James King south, and set him on the path to a succession of rich clerical livings which saw him finally as Dean of Raphoe in Ireland. It was Norton whose influence in 1776 gained James' second son and namesake a coveted position on Captain Cook's last voyage and Norton also who encouraged James' two youngest sons to pursue careers in the law. Both prospered. Edward ended up as Vice Chancellor of the County Palatine of Lancaster – the senior chancery judge in the principality. John served as Under-Secretary of State at the Home Office during a crucial period in the French wars. James' eldest son, Thomas, was a contemporary at Christ Church of Charles O'Hara, whose father was an early friend and intimate of Edmund Burke. In this way, Thomas became tutor to Burke's son and thereafter was recommended by Burke to the Duke of Marlborough, who was able to endow him with a number of rich livings, including the Churchill family's home parishes of Bladon and Woodstock. James' third son, Walker, became even closer to Burke, editing his *Annual Register,* helping to prepare his speeches and finally acting as one of his literary executors. Walker – who ended up a bishop - was a highly political clergyman, but was in all things guardian of the Burke flame before and after his patron's death.

Since those heady years of power and influence, the family's later story was almost inevitably an anti-climax. They remained prosperous through the first half of the nineteenth century, but the more difficult years of the later nineteenth century saw many struggle. Younger sons disappeared to the colonies. Many others were clergymen, but clergy incomes were shrinking fast. Daughters remained unmarried and unfulfilled. By the beginning of the twentieth century, only Walker and Edward King's descendants survived in the male line. Walker's grandson was the distinguished bishop, Edward King of Lincoln. Among his other descendants were a general, an admiral, several others who were distinguished in their professions, and the author of 'Stig of the Dump'! The fortune inherited from a maternal uncle by Edward's eldest surviving son, Edward Bolton King, raised his descendants into the ranks of the landed gentry but – like many others - they entered the twentieth century with the estate heavily mortgaged, with much gentility but little substance.

The earliest known members of the Knight family were small farmers in Beoley, on the Worcestershire/Warwickshire border. In 1554, a younger son of the family, William Knight, bought Barrells Green over the border in Warwickshire, where his descendants remained for the next three hundred years. In 1622, his grandson, another William Knight, married a local girl whose brother had left Warwickshire to make his fortune in London. London during this period was steadily expanding and the demand there for agricultural produce seemed inexhaustible. Barrells was a hundred miles away, but the less perishable agricultural produce could still be transported and sold there. To have a family member in London, able to find a market for as many goods as could be produced, was advantageous to both. In the early 1650s, William's younger son, Robert Knight, was apprenticed to his uncle and in 1658 was himself admitted a member of the Grocers' Company. This Robert Knight prospered mightily, marrying his uncle's daughter and producing a large family. He seems to have branched out into sugar refining, which was a capital intensive but lucrative trade given the sweet tooth of the late seventeenth century Londoner.

Thereafter the family's centre of gravity shifted to London. Robert's brother and nephew continued to farm at Barrells, but Robert's sons, nephews and great-nephews were in London and began to play an important part in the commercial and banking world there. It was Robert's younger son, another Robert Knight, who gained notoriety and spectacular wealth through his involvement with the South Sea Company. He fled abroad at the time of the crash and forfeited a large part of his fortune. Nonetheless he remained a rich man and his son – Robert Knight III - gained the Irish peerages (Earl of Catherlough & Baron Luxborough) that might have been his if things had gone differently.

Robert Knight III was close to his brother-in-law, Lord Bolingbroke, but drifted from that allegiance after Bolingbroke left for France. Thereafter he gravitated towards the ministry. His private life was complicated. His wife, Henrietta St John, was flirtatious and in 1736 he banished her to Barrells (which he had recently bought from an impecunious cousin). His son seems to have been a rather colourless young man. He married a rich wife and lived in some splendour in Park Lane, though died in his early thirties in 1762 without issue. His daughter, Henrietta, was the reverse of colourless. Scandal followed her, though her father adored her. She married young, but fell out with her husband and then went abroad with a man the same age as her father. A divorce was obtained, but their son was born before it was finalized. In 1760 her husband died and she went home, which resulted in her father's second wife moving out, because Henrietta was considered a scarlet woman with whom no respectable woman could consort. Two years later, Henrietta was again pregnant by a French cavalry officer and had to go abroad to have the baby. She died in childbirth in Marseilles and the child was brought back to London by the father, where both were taken in by Lord Catherlough (who had been unaware of his daughter's pregnancy).

Then, early in 1766, Lord Catherlough's eye fell upon a young girl from Henley-in-Arden. She was a labourer's daughter, but very beautiful. He took her up to London to make a lady of her and before he died in 1772 they had had four children together, with another on the way. The elder boy, Robert Knight IV, was named as his father's heir and so grew up a very rich young man, committed to the radical ideas that were around during the French Revolution. However, he made a disastrous marriage with a seventeen year-old girl who turned out to be as flirtatious as earlier Knight ladies. In 1802, when she was suspected of an affair with an army officer, they agreed to separate. Shortly afterwards, when it was clear that she was continuing to see her admirer, Robert took their two daughters from her – the younger then not much more than a year old. To defend his sister's honour, her brother challenged Robert to a duel, and was duly imprisoned in the Marshalsea. Ten years later, Mrs Knight found herself pregnant by an elderly peer and gave birth to a son. No doubt as an act of revenge, she brought up the boy as her husband's child and heir to his estates. Robert spent ten years trying to prove the boy's illegitimacy, but the law then assumed that a woman's child was her husband's, unless the husband had been abroad at the time of the conception.

An old man from the neighbourhood of Barrells remarked to one of the family that "the Knights were a lively lot" – which seems to sum them up well. Their story is not like that of the Kings and the admixture of their genes seem to have had a disturbing effect on their descendants. Nonetheless, the stories of both families are worth the telling.

Walter King
London
January, 2020

CHAPTER ONE

THE EARLIEST KNOWN DAYS OF THE KING FAMILY

Early Speculation

As in many families, the nineteenth century saw some myths established about the origins of the King family. Mrs Rodd of Chardstock House seems to have been the main culprit. Her researches – for which she did not provide any reliable evidence – suggested a knightly origin. According to her, an ancestor, Sir Ralph King, fought at Agincourt.

It is more likely that the Kings rose to comparative prosperity as merchants. Richard King (1489-1519) was a rich Bradford clothier who is said to have been born in Gisburn in the West Riding of Yorkshire. He was the son of John King, also a Bradford clothier, who was born in Halifax. Richard married Anne Cocke and, on his early death at Penkridge in Staffordshire, left an only daughter, Anne. She was the heir to lands in Manningham, near Bradford and Kingscross, near Halifax. In 1540, she married Thomas Lister, of Westby, in Gisburn. The Listers were a well-established family of Yorkshire gentry. Anne's younger son, John Lister, inherited her land in Bradford and his descendants – as Lister-Kay and Cunliffe-Lister – are still in Yorkshire.

In 1571, the will of a Robert King of Gisburn was proved at York. He seems to have been a man of some property. He left an eldest son, Richard King, and another son, Robert. One or two of the children were minors when their father's will was drawn up. It seems at least possible that the elder Robert King was a relative – possibly a nephew - of Richard King, of Manningham and - like him - a merchant.

For 200 years, the cloth industry had been developing in Yorkshire. In earlier years, wool had been the major export but, in the 14th century, the manufacture of cloth developed fast. The wool-producing areas had their own cottage industries. In the subsidy rolls of 1379, in a total population (excluding children) of 233, Malhamdale supported two fullers and two tailors. During this time also, Bradford, Wakefield and Leeds were growing fast as trading centres. The family of Richard King of Manningham seem to have ridden the wave of this prosperity.

Rev Robert King & Cambridge University
Rev Robert King is the first person with a secure place on the family tree, and he has left a tangible legacy in the form of his Bible, which is in the care of Kirkby Malham church. It is probably safe to assume that our ancestor was the Robert Kinge who was ordained simultaneously deacon and priest by Richard Barnes, Bishop of Carlisle, in St Michael-le-Belfrey, York on 24 July 1573. A simultaneous ordination tended to be reserved to the graduates at Oxford and Cambridge. This suggests that our Robert was such a graduate and may have been the "Robert of Yorkshire" who is listed as matriculating at the University of Cambridge in 1571. If our Robert was the second son of Robert King of Gisburn, who died that same year leaving a young family, then the dates would fit quite nicely.

If Robert was at the University of Cambrdge in 1571-1573, then he would have experienced some riotous times. Thomas Cartwright was a Fellow of Trinity College who had spent some time in Ireland as Chaplain to Adam Loftus, the Archbishop of Armagh. In 1569 he was appointed Lady Margaret Professor of Divinity and was gaining a reputation as an eloquent preacher and persuasive lecturer. People said that the windows of Great St Mary's Church had to be taken out to allow those outside to hear him preach. He was however one of those who wanted the English Church to move on in a more Genevan direction from the 1559 Settlement. He used service books and psalters from Geneva rather than the Book of Common Prayer, and argued for the imposition of a Presbyterian church order. In this he was strongly opposed by John Whitgift, recently appointed Vice-Chancellor and Master of Trinity. Even the otherwise sympathetic Archbishop Grindal of York felt that Cartwright was going too far.

Despite protests, Cartwright was deprived of his professorship in December 1570 and, in September 1571, Whitgift also deprived him of his fellowship. Cartwright thereupon left Cambridge and for a time joined Theodore Beza in Geneva. He had however left a glowing reputation behind him and the cause of a Presbyterian church order was by no means dead. In 1572 the *Admonition to Parliament* was anonymously published, and presented to parliament by two Puritan clergymen, John Field and Thomas Wilcox. They were imprisoned in July 1572 and, when Cartwright (who had returned from Geneva) attempted a defence, he was forced to leave the country again to avoid arrest. Nonetheless, Archbishop Parker certainly thought that episcopacy's days were numbered and that he might be the last Archbishop of Canterbury. Towards the end of his life Parker became morbidly depressed and anxious about the lack of support for episcopacy to be found in the Queen's Council. Robert Dudley was an avowed Puritan, and carried no candle for bishops. It was the Queen who guaranteed an episcopal future for the Church, but her power to do so could not be taken for granted in the early 1570's.

Kirkby Malham, 1569-1575

When Elizabeth succeeded to the throne in November 1558, she had wanted a broad religious settlement. She hoped for a return to the situation as it had existed at her father's death, but too much had happened in those eleven years. The Commons demanded the return of the 1552 Prayer Book, while the bishops held to Mary's Settlement. Elizabeth imposed her own Settlement that pleased neither the returning exiles, Mary's Bishops nor many of the parish clergy. In the North, she pursued a cautious policy. She was careful not to alienate the conservative grandees, and had every confidence in Archbishop Thomas Young, President of the Council of the North and of the Ecclesiastical Commission for the Province of York. When Young died in 1568, the equally conservative Earl of Sussex succeeded him as President of the Council.

Things could not however be kept quiet indefinitely. In the summer of 1568, after an enforced abdication, Mary Stuart escaped from her Scottish prison and arrived in England. She was Elizabeth's natural heir, though Elizabeth would not recognise her as such. The seizure of a treasure ship later that year alienated Spain and Elizabeth's support for the Huguenots in the French wars alienated France. Cautious souls wanted peace with a Europe that was becoming increasingly polarized between Protestant and Catholic. They also wanted a settlement of the succession, with Mary being recognized as Elizabeth's heir. They planned to get rid of Cecil, who was thought to be putting the realm in danger. In the event, neither Spain nor France moved against Elizabeth and in October 1569 Cecil was able to isolate his enemies. The Earl of Leicester refused to desert the Queen and the Duke of Norfolk was sent to the Tower.

This didn't stop the Northern Rising. People had gone too far to draw back, and on 16 November 1569 the banner of insurrection was raised at Brancepeth Castle. The leaders were the Earls of Westmoreland and Northumberland. Thomas Percy, 7th Earl of Northumberland, was the son of the 6th Earl's younger brother, Sir Thomas Percy, who had been executed for his part in the Pilgrimage of Grace in 1536. He had regained much of the Percy inheritance, mainly during the reign of Mary, and was critical of Cecil's policies. His solution was to put Mary Stuart on the throne, and to bring about reconciliation with Rome.

Northumberland seems to have been able to gather his tenants together in the old way, and these tenants included several in Craven – who in turn brought along their own tenants. Leonard Metcalfe, Lord of the Manor of Kirkby-in-Malhamdale, Hanlith and Thorp, was summoned. He took with him Thomas and John Lawson and Robert Parkinson of Kirkby and William Lawson and William,

Roger and John Sergeantson of Hanlith. This was typical of the wider reality. Several Yorkshire squires sent sons to fight under the banner of the Five Wounds. Mass was heard in Durham Cathedral, English service books were burned on many village greens, and the army began the march south. They got as far as Clifford Moor, near Wetherby, when they found themselves facing an army under the Earl of Sussex, with another under Sir George Bowes behind them. They retreated to Raby, while Bowes garrisoned Barnard Castle and Sussex holed up in York. The insurgents were hoping for Spanish support, which did not materialize. What did materialize was an army of 12,000 men under Lord Hunsden and the Earl of Warwick that arrived in the north before Christmas. The rebels fled in all directions, with the grandees escaping into Scotland. The Earl of Northumberland was captured, but most of the others escaped abroad.

Reprisals began immediately. Sir George Bowes, as Sheriff of York, was required to tour the counties that had been implicated in the Rising, and a victim was required from each town or village that had contributed to the rebel army. Richard Kaley was chosen from the village of Rilston – where the Norton family had been implicated. William Sergeantson was chosen from the village of Hanlith. He was condemned to be hanged – probably on Sheriff Hill, in Malham – with William Lawson, his friend and partner in the rebellion, acting as hangman. The Lord of the Manor, Leonard Metcalfe, was condemned to death at Durham in March, but was eventually pardoned. He left prison in September 1571, and two years later was able to lease back his former lands from the crown. It was one rule for the rich and another for the poor!

There is no record of where Robert King went to minister after his ordination. Archbishop Grindal was struggling. The villages were wedded to their old superstitions, which had become deeply embedded in community life. They were suspicious of the "new religion" and many of the gentry were openly hostile. In an area that was already short of priests, there was an acute shortage of priests with any education, who could be trusted to preach a sermon. Sermons had not been a priority in the old days, when all a priest had to do was to mumble the Mass and go home. During Grindal's rule – 1570-1575 - Oxford and Cambridge graduates were often ordained to a roving ministry. They might be based in the Archbishop's household at York or elsewhere, but would exercise a kind of travelling Pauline ministry, seeking to encourage and support church life wherever even a flicker of a light seemed to be burning. However, this practice came to an end when Grindal left for Canterbury and it seems likely that Robert King then settled down at Kirkby Malham – if he was not already there. He would have come to a traumatized community.

Kirkby Malham, 1575-1585
The reign of Elizabeth was a time of considerable achievement in the life of the English church – particularly in the calibre of the priesthood. An educated priesthood which had seemed a distant dream in 1570 was a reality by the time of Elizabeth's death. Even the "reformation of manners" – the centrepiece of the Elizabethan crusade - had made some progress. Drunkenness and a general bawdiness was no longer the accepted norm in the life of most village communities. There were however continuing tensions. The new, educated priesthood wanted to study and their studying often took them in directions with which the Queen was not happy.

The old arguments about episcopacy and dress codes still raged, but some of the younger priests were looking beyond those old issues. The writings – both "Catholic" and "Protestant" (this division was still not well-established) - of continental thinkers from the 14th and 15th centuries were circulating. These men had been writing at a time when the papacy was at a low ebb and when the civil authority itself was ineffective. They were exploring a spiritualized Christianity that stood lightly to the organization, but laid great emphasis on prayer and healing.

Such a one was Giles Wigginton, a native of Oundle, who was presented by Trinity College Cambridge to the benefice of Sedbergh in 1579. His ministry was hugely valued, and not only in Sedbergh. He became known throughout the surrounding area, but his zeal and popularity resulted in his deprivation in 1585. When not imprisoned in London, he continued to hold meetings in his house in Sedbergh until 1592 when he was restored. It was no accident that Wigginton had been deprived soon after John Whitgift had succeeded Grindal as Archbishop of Canterbury. Whitgift started a countrywide campaign against those clergy he regarded as "non-conformist" and Wigginton was one of the casualties. It is interesting is that the Queen appointed a certain Thomas Squire to Kirkby Malham in the year that Wigginton was deprived, thus bringing Robert King's ministry to an end. Was King's deprivation part of Whitgift's purge? The family's later links with the religious radicals suggest that this was a possibility.

Robert King was named as the vicar at the time of his death in 1621 – enabling Sir Thomas Wentworth to appoint his successor. This suggests that – like Wigginton – his deprivation was temporary. Once Whitgift's ardour had been cooled by increasing age and ill-health, it seems that a much more sympathetic Archbishop of York was able to settle things down. Religious radicalism in the Craven district was to flourish for a while longer.

Later Years
Robert King was clearly embedded in the parish. His only son, Thomas King, married as his first wife Margaret Sergeantson of Hanlith – they were an established local family. His daughter married William Preston, of Malham, who is said to have refused a knighthood on the accession of Charles I. Preston was regarded as a "gentleman", if not an "esquire". The couple were childless, but Preston's nephew and heir, Henry Wallock, was to act as guardian of Robert's grandsons after their father's death – and one of them married one of Wallock's daughters.

Robert was well off, and certainly not dependent on whatever small stipend was attached to the benefice of Kirkby Malham. In 1620, Josias Lambert, the squire of Carlton (and father of the parliamentary general), gave Robert his bond for £142, to secure repayment of a loan of £71 0s 8d. £71 is more than £17,000 in today's values, so perhaps Robert acted as a kind of banker, besides possibly maintaining his links with his family's mercantile business. This link between clothiers and an early form of banking was becoming increasingly common in the provinces. However, Josias Lambert was famously impecunious, so I don't know how valuable his bond was.

Robert King died at a good age in 1621, and his will details various bequests to his children and grandchildren. By this time, the tensions that had existed in his youth had increased. The generation that had flourished under the old Queen - Burghley and Leicester, Raleigh and Sidney - had supported reform and seen England as a bulwark in a Protestant Europe. But they had now passed away. James I and those round him had no time for either reform or for Protestant heroics. Still, it was left to his son Charles I to tip dissatisfaction into open revolt – and the King family would have no trouble deciding which side they were on.

CHAPTER TWO

THOMAS KING, OF KIRKBY MALHAM (ca 1578-1634)

In 1600 Thomas King married Margaret Sergeantson, who lived just up the hill in Hanlith. His sister was married to William Preston, who came from a similar local family. Prestons had been vicars in Giggleswick, Long Preston and Broughton in the 16th century, and a Preston gave a bell to Long Preston church. Later, in 1618, Thomas' elder daughter Alice was to marry a Richard Preston.

When his father died, it was natural that Thomas should want to build a new, modern house. During Elizabeth's reign there had been a great re-building. People were no longer prepared to live in their humble, medieval homes. Thomas' initials - TK 1622 - still show over the door of the house he built. Church End was certainly something more than the usual cottage-cum-barn that was home for most people in 16th century Craven. With such a fine house, he was proclaiming to the world a certain status.

The trouble was that the wool trade was entering a difficult period. The wool from Malhamdale was still either made up into undressed cloth locally or sent down to the Leeds, Bradford and Halifax. It was then shipped out through Hull to the markets in the Baltic States and in Germany. The selling though was not now as easy as it was. There was much political upheaval in Europe, and the German markets were shrinking. More important, Dutch Republic was becoming extraordinarily powerful and engrossing to itself the cloth-making industry and shipping. It was a long crisis for English wool producers that, in the end, would produce a new kind of trade and a new and much more varied kind of cloth production. However, in the 1620's and 1630's, all people understood was that there was a major contraction of trade. It affected Thomas King. He had built Church End, but he doesn't seem to have lived there long. After his first wife's death in 1615, he had married again. At his death, his young sons by his second wife were minors, much of his land was mortgaged and his family seem to have gone through a lean time. The life of Thomas King the elder does not seem to be a success story in the annals of the family.

Changes in the Church
Church life in Craven continued to be lively in his day. One of the liveliest figures was Roger Brearley (1586-1637), curate at Grindleton from around 1615-22 and thereafter at Kildwick 1622-30. He was an independent preacher, influenced by the German mystics like Johann Arndt and Jacob Boehme, who travelled around a good bit. He had a following – known as the Grindletonians – and George Fox was to find in the survivors a receptive audience. Brearley led a reaction against the closely argued doctrinal orthodoxies of Calvinism - what he called "forensic Christianity". He offered instead personal renewal, individual growth in holiness and religious experience. Brearley's thinking was free-ranging and he found many in his locality who thought like him – and not least John Lambert of Calton, later to be a radical leader in the civil war. In 1628 he was summoned before the Archbishop's Court to answer charges of unorthodox teaching, but Archbishop Mathew was still alive and he was acquitted. From 1631 until his death he was vicar of Burnley. No one could say that life was dull in the Craven district at the beginning of the 17th century.

But the atmosphere was changing in the York diocese. In the last years of Archbishop Matthew a new generation was growing up around the old archbishop which was less sympathetic to the Puritan tradition. Arminianism was in the air. Richard Neile, who was Archbishop from 1632-1640, wanted the churches tidied up, with pews removed from the chancel and an altar along the east wall. He also didn't want too much preaching. More clergy were brought before the archdeacon's court, and fewer Puritan clergy found recognition. Gradually clergy of independent or Puritan sympathies came to see themselves as a persecuted minority. Although not all Puritans were on the parliamentary side in the Civil War, there was now a tendency for them to drift that way, in the hope that a parliamentary victory would bring about the changes they were looking for.

Laudianism seems to have touched Kirkby Malham early. In 1623 Sir Thomas Wentworth sold the presentation to the parish to his sister, Lady Savile. She thereupon appointed the young Nicholas Walton as vicar, and Walton seems to have been a High Churchman of the new school.

Legal Matters
Legal problems however sat at the centre of the gathering storm. The King had always reserved the right to intervene in disputes if something was wrong, and to transfer a case to his own court. The trouble was that Charles I was using his prerogative or conciliar courts to gain convictions in unpopular cases. Thus, when Parliament was finally recalled, the prerogative courts were for the chop. The Court of the Star Chamber, the chief court used for ecclesiastical prosecutions, was abolished early on in the Long Parliament. The Court of Delegates and the Court of High Commission were also abolished in 1641. The Archdeacons' Courts - which were the Bishops' main instrument in enforcing religious conformity – didn't last much longer.

Parliament and the Common Law marched together, and made an enemy of the ecclesiastical courts.   Their leader was Sir Edward Coke. Under his guiding hand, the Common Law gradually rose to supremacy. What the Common Law actually said was often unclear, and its early principles were not altogether appropriate for an increasingly urban and commercially based community, but under Coke's guiding hand it came to express what a liberal and propertied gentleman thought it ought to express. The judge now expounded the Law as the priest expounded the Gospel – and both revealed what was in the heart of God.   Coke was the Calvin of the law courts, and came to be more powerful than Calvin in the understanding of Law. He was the first Whig, the forerunner of Locke, and maybe also a hero of the King family. He cultivated the myths about the Common Law that were to prove powerful weapons in the political struggle. In Coke's understanding, the common law had evolved from time immemorial as the bulwark of the freeborn Englishman against oppression. It was Anglo-Saxon in inspiration, surviving the Norman Conquest, but needing constant vigilance lest it be overturned or traduced. By the time Coke died in 1634 there was one more influence that challenged the thinking of Charles I and resonated powerfully with the increasingly articulate and propertied families of Yorkshire. In fact, Coke's achievement became part of the national myth – and lawyers became powerful defenders of that myth. Bishops however were part of the demonology. England has been suspicious of Bishops ever since.

CHAPTER THREE

THOMAS KING, OF KIRKBY MALHAM (1623-?1681)

Not a great deal is known about Thomas King, but he lived through the
momentous events of the Civil War, in which Yorkshire played its part.

The Upheavals of 1640-2

During the 1630's things were going from bad to worse for the King.
The National Assembly of the Church of Scotland rejected the 1637
Prayer Book that had been issued on the King's authority. So keen
was he on his project to make a thorough unity of his kingdoms that
Charles decided to force the Prayer Book on them. However, after
one abortive attempt at invasion, he had to recall Parliament in
order to raise the money to pay for a second attempt. Parliament
then became the focus of all the discontents that had grown up
during the time of his personal rule. The most dramatic of the
parliamentary initiatives was the impeachment of the Earl of
Strafford[1]. Strafford had built up a power base in Ireland in the
King's interest and was thought to be intent on enforcing the King's
will in England through his Irish Army. In May 1641 Strafford was
executed. At the beginning of November there came news of the
Irish rebellion, and London was filled with rumours of a Catholic
invasion – in the King's interest. The parliamentary leaders under
Pym seized the initiative with their Grand Remonstrance. The King
retaliated by attempting to arrest them, and failed. In January 1642
he decided to leave London to seek help in the north. He arrived in
York in March.

---

[1] Sir Thomas Wentworth (1593-1641) of Wentworth Woodhouse, near
Rotherham & M.P. for Yorkshire, had bought the glebe lands from Lady
Shrewsbury in 1617. However, in his attempts to discover where they were, he
had not made himself popular locally. In 1621 he also purchased from Lady
Shrewsbury the right of presentation to the living – and appointed Asher Tench
as vicar, who seems to have formerly been attached to Leeds Parish Church.
Tench, didn't stay long for two years later Wentworth sold his rights to his sister,
Lady Savile, and she appointed someone else..

The people of Yorkshire had shown reluctance to rally to the King in the summer of 1640 when he had wanted their help to attack the Scots. Two years later, they showed no desire to enlist on the King's side against the elected Parliament. A major deputation of gentry and freeholders arrived in York in May 1642, headed by Sir Thomas Fairfax. Fairfax had been born at Denton Hall, just east of Skipton, and so was a local man and well established among the substantial gentry of Yorkshire. Among the signatures on the petition handed in by Fairfax was that of John Lambert of Carlton in the parish of Kirkby Malham[2]. He was then only twenty-two years old but already keen to make his mark. Only more pressure persuaded him to attend a huge gathering a few weeks later on Heworth Moor, near York when Fairfax presented a petition on behalf of the farmers and freeholders of Yorkshire, asking the King to make an accommodation with parliament. The King had been prepared to receive the gentry and their petition, but he was not prepared to receive the freeholders. This slight of Fairfax and of the freeholders for which he spoke did no good to the King's cause.

The King was keen to secure one of the coastal ports, in order that reinforcements and relief supplies from the Queen could be landed. On 10 July he lay siege to Hull where Sir John Hotham had refused him entry. Later in the month, he left Yorkshire to establish himself at Nottingham. He raised his standard there on 22 August – the traditional date for the start of the Civil War.

The Opening of the First Civil War, 1642-3
Within weeks of Charles declaring himself, Parliament had appointed Lord Fairfax commander of the Parliamentary forces in Yorkshire, with his son, Sir Thomas, as his second in command. However, despite the general support for the Fairfax family in Bradford and Halifax and the nearby mill towns, things didn't get off to a good start. In December 1642, the Earl of Newcastle marched

---

[2] For Lambert and the account of these times, see David Farr, *John Lambert, Parliamentary Soldier and Cromwellian Major General, 1619-1684* (2003)

into York with a considerable force and continued down to meet Sir Thomas at Tadcaster. Here they were checked, but were nonetheless able to occupy the town due to Fairfax's enforced withdrawal to Selby. He had run out of ammunition and powder.

Newcastle then moved south to garrison Pontefract, while Sir William Savile went west, taking Wakefield and Leeds without a fight and expecting to do the same at Bradford. Bradford however stood out against him and he was forced to withdraw. Sir Thomas then arrived with reinforcements, strengthened his force and counter-attacked. On 23 January 1643 he drove Savile out of Leeds, and the next day took Wakefield. Savile and Newcastle thereupon withdrew to York.

On 22 February 1643 the Queen landed at Bridlington with foreign reinforcements, and proceeded to York. Her arrival had the effect of strengthening the royalist presence in east Yorkshire, and Lord Fairfax found himself vulnerable in Selby. In March, Lord Fairfax withdrew to Leeds, while his son covered his withdrawal. Unfortunately, Sir Thomas was pursued by a considerable mounted force under Colonel George Goring, and soundly beaten. Hundreds of prisoners were taken – which provoked an outcry in the parliamentary strongholds of Halifax and Bradford.

Newcastle wanted to escort the Queen south, to join the King, but he was reluctant to leave Yorkshire to Lord Fairfax. In the event, the Queen went south to Newark with a strong force, while Newcastle decided to strike a major blow at the Fairfaxes in their headquarters. On 30 June 1643, Newcastle's army of 10,000-12,000 men roundly defeated the parliamentary forces of around 4,000 men at Adwalton Moor, near Bradford. Newcastle advanced to Bradford, forcing the parliamentarians to abandon this loyal town – and Leeds and Wakefield too. Lord Fairfax and his son escaped to Hull, which had driven out the Hothams and remained loyal to the parliament. Outside Hull, the whole county was in Newcastle's power. It was the low point of the war.

The Parliamentary Recovery, 1643-5

In September, in response to these reverses in the north, Parliament finally agreed the Solemn League and Covenant with the Scots and a Scottish army prepared to invade England. This tilted the balance of power against the royalists and the parliamentary forces began to enjoy some success again. At the end of January 1644, Newcastle had to go north to face the Scots, and Fairfax and his son were commanded to take the opportunity of seizing some of the key places in Yorkshire. This they did – finally storming Selby on 11 April, and then moving up to York. Newcastle was forced to race back to hold York, hotly pursued by the Scots – who met up with Lord Fairfax at Tadcaster. The siege of York began ten days later.

Prince Rupert was however marching north and gaining a considerable force in Cheshire and Lancashire. Some parliamentary horse were sent to check his advance through the southern passes of the Pennines but the Prince outwitted them by marching further north and coming down through Skipton. By the beginning of July he had reached York and relieved the city. The combined Scottish and parliamentary army was not getting on and might have disintegrated, were it not for Prince Rupert's determination to fight them. The Battle of Marston Moor on 2 July 1644 could have been a great royalist victory – and Sir Thomas Fairfax and the Earl of Manchester thought that it was so when they left the field. However, victory was snatched from defeat – chiefly by Cromwell's horse. Newcastle left for Hamburg – not to return until the Restoration. Prince Rupert returned to Lancashire where he attempted to build another army but, when the city of York fell on 16 July, he left the north for good. The war was over in the north.

Young John Lambert of Calton was already close to Sir Thomas Fairfax. In July 1643 he is known to have been with Fairfax in Lincolnshire, where the parliamentary armies were beginning to have better success[3]. By the end of the year he had been given

---

[3] Leaving his father in Hull, Sir Thomas had escaped by sea with a considerable

command of a cavalry regiment, and it was in this capacity that he returned – as 'Colonel Lambert' - to Yorkshire. By the beginning of March 1644, he regained Bradford for the parliamentary cause. In July he was at Marston Moor, probably with Cromwell.

The rest of 1644 was spent in various sieges. Knaresborough fell in November. Helmsley fell after a long siege early in 1645. Lord Fairfax remained in general command in the north while his son moved south to take over from the Earl of Essex as Lord Commander of the parliamentary forces, with Cromwell as Lieutenant-General and cavalry commander. The two of them were in command at Naseby on 14 June 1645, which effectively brought the first Civil War to an end. Fairfax then went on to reduce Oxford and the West Country, returning to London in November 1645. Lambert returned north to triumphantly reduce Lady Anne Clifford's stronghold of Skipton Castle in December 1645. This brought to an end the surviving sign of royalist power in Craven.

Seeking a Settlement, 1646-1653
After the fall of Oxford in the summer of 1646 there should have been peace. The trouble was that the Army had not been paid and was not prepared to disband before it had been. It was also unclear what kind of political settlement was to be established. Some of the Army Leaders had strong views and were happy to use the Army to impose them. Ireton and Lambert produced their Heads of the Proposals, which would have established a good, constitutional government – balanced between King and parliament. They were rejected by the King and by Parliament in August 1647. By then, Lambert had been sent north as Major General of the five counties of the Northern Association (perhaps to get him out of the way), and he stayed there until the spring of 1649. He was not implicated in the death of the King, and was never an anti-royalist.

Sir Thomas Fairfax too was a moderate, though we went along with much of the business during the confusing years of 1645-50. He

force and joined the Earl of Manchester in Lincolnshire,

was placed at the head of the judges who were to try the King, but withdrew when he realised that the intent of the court was to sentence Charles to death. He finally resigned his commission rather than lead the army in a pre-emptive strike against Scotland, which was now ruled by Charles II and the Presbyterians[4]. Scotland, in Fairfax's view, was an independent nation that had every right to go its own way. Cromwell took his place, with Lambert as second in command. Together they crushed the Scots at the Battle of Dunbar in September 1650. Lambert then went from strength to strength. In 1650-3 he effectively ruled Scotland, preparing the country for the 1654 Act of Union.

The Protectorate, 1653-1659
Lambert was at Cromwell's side when the Rump was dissolved in April 1653 and was appointed to the Council of State. His only rival in power was General Harrison, but Harrison was discredited by the failure of Nominated Parliament of July-December 1653. The Rule of the Saints had not been a success and Lambert was less into that sort of thing than Harrison – or indeed Cromwell. The new Constitution - the *Instrument of Government* - was drawn up by Lambert and from 1654 to 1657 he was recognised as Cromwell's natural successor. It was not a good time though. The rule of the Major Generals was remembered as the climax of Cromwell's personal rule and Lambert was forever associated with that failed experiment. Cromwell now had his eye on a more conservative, hereditary settlement. The Cromwell family were gradually emerging into political prominence. There was then another Parliament and another Constitution - the *Humble Petition and Advice* - and in July 1657 Lambert resigned all his offices.

Cromwell's death made little difference and things went on pretty steadily until the Army and the Parliament again fell out. The parliament elected in January 1659 was a conservative force that realised the unpopularity of raising any money for the Army. By

---

[4] He retired to his home at Nun Appleton, near York and stayed there until the last days of 1659.

April, the Army was demanding its dissolution. Richard Cromwell acquiesced and a Council of State was put in place (as in 1653) to carry on the government. Money however was required and that needed a parliament. The Council gave in and recalled the Rump – thus negativing everything that had happened since its dissolution in 1653. Richard Cromwell went quietly and the Commonwealth was restored. Unfortunately for the army, the Rump proved itself as hostile to the interests of the army as it has been in 1653. In October 1659, as in 1653, the army leaders (now Lambert and Fleetwood) dissolved it and established a Committee of Safety to govern the country for the time being.

The army did not however have general support. Cromwell had understood the way things were going before he died. The old army and its radical leadership were no longer loved. People were tired of politics. Lambert took an army north to negotiate with Monck who, with the Scottish Army, had declared for the Rump. Lord Fairfax came out of retirement and joined Monck, who was rightly suspected of wanting to restore Charles Stuart. Without Lambert by his side, Fleetwood crumbled and recalled the Rump - which met on 26 December. Haselrig took control, in alliance with Fairfax and Monck. Lambert was isolated and his army melted away. Just before the Rump was dissolved, Lambert was committed to the Tower on suspicion of plotting against the settlement. Monck was now assembling behind him the substantial gentry and traditional ruling class. The Militia Act of March 1660 destroyed the old army and put the power firmly back into the hands of the landed gentry and their volunteer supporters. In April, Lambert escaped from the Tower and attempted a last heroic stand for the Republic. It was hopeless. When the new "Convention Parliament" assembled at the end of the month, they were the real and only power in the land. The "Presbyterian Knot" was outmanoeuvred and the decision was for the return of Charles II.

The Rage of Satan & His Instruments, 1660-9

The bodies of Cromwell, Ireton and Bradshaw were dug up and hung at Tyburn. The regicides were hunted down and executed. However, for the most part, Charles did his best to act as a mediator between those who had supported the Parliament and those who had remained loyal to the monarchy. Fears of a radical rising in January 1661 did however influence the elections of the following March. Fairfax himself lost his seat. The new "Cavalier" Parliament worked hard to draw a line on everything that had made the years since 1642 so interesting. They had Sir Harry Vane and John Lambert in their sights. In June 1662 Vane was executed and Lambert - aged only 43 - condemned to life imprisonment. It was, as Edmund Ludlow wrote, "the rage of Satan and his instruments".

Church matters were immediately an issue. Parish churches now looked set to lose their independence with the return of the Bishops and the lay patrons. Richard Baxter was one of the strongest voices that tried to preserve something of the status quo. He could not understand how the Bishops of huge, unwieldy dioceses could possibly exercise any real ministry in their many parishes. He wanted each parish priest to have "the power of keys" in his congregation, though he was prepared to investigate a sort of presiding role for a restored episcopacy. The spirit of the time was against him. The debates on a church settlement drew to a close at the end of 1661, and Parliament - against the desire of the King - demanded the ejection of all who would not accept the reimposition of the bishops and the Prayer Book. In August 1662 many sincere ministers left the Church of England, thereby immeasurably impoverishing it.

Vane's execution, followed so soon by the ejections, caused a deal of grumbling. Yorkshire had never been keen on the Scots and saw no need to have this "Scottish King" on the throne. In November 1663 a rising in Yorkshire was squashed before it happened, but it encouraged Parliament to move again against the Dissenters. The Conventicles Act of 1664 – though sparingly enforced - only served to make martyrs of those who felt excluded from the new settlement. Still, moderate Presbyterians at least still looked to comprehension - to the discovery of some means whereby they could be included within the Established Church, or at least tolerated alongside it. Archbishop Sterne of York was particularly slow to move against Dissent. His fear was of the Roman Catholics, not of Protestant dissent. Good sermons might still be heard in church, not always preached by the vicar (if there was a vicar). If they weren't heard in church, they could be heard in the houses of the gentry - or at a gathering not too far away.

It's interesting that there is no record of an incumbent being instituted to Kirkby Malham after the Restoration until 1681. It could be that the Archbishop had no desire to upset an established way of life, in what was after all General Lambert's home parish. There were enough horror stories of empty parish churches and overflowing chapels for a sensible Bishop to exercise caution. Then, when Clarendon gave way to Shaftesbury in August 1667, there was new hope for those who still couldn't accommodate. Attempts were made to bring a bill to the Commons in the autumn of 1667 and in early 1668, but Parliament was not ready. When Thomas King died, there were many issues still unresolved but hope was still strong. The monarchy was a parliamentary one. The Church might still work under a moderate episcopacy that would allow for a lively, biblical faith and considerable local discretion. The good old cause was not dead, despite some of the excesses of Parliament. The darker days lay ahead.

The Economics of Yorkshire in the mid-17th century

The politics of these years are so overwhelming that it's easy to ignore the underlying economics. Through all the upheavals, how did people make a living? The Dutch remained the chief threat to our livelihood. However, the Dutch threat was now known and measures were being taken to restrict their power. In 1651 imports via Holland were forbidden - all imports had to come from their place of origin and be carried in English boats. These laws, followed by the Dutch War of 1652-4, struck a heavy blow against

Dutch prosperity. When they were succeeded by the war against Spain in 1656, there was a new sense of confidence and expansion in England. The Second Dutch War of 1665-7 ended in humiliation for Britain, but by then Louis XIV was about to give them the knock-out blow. After 1672 the Golden Age of Dutch expansion was over. The world was opening up to English trade and England was beginning to play a leading part. There were no immediate returns that would have been noticed in Malhamdale, but the times were changing. The long depression of the early part of the century was drawing to a close.

Domestic issues
At the time of the great upheavals, the fortunes of the King family are uncertain. If our ancestor is Thomas King "the younger" who married the daughter of Henry Wallock of Bordley, then he was a young man of nineteen at the outbreak of the Civil War. He and his brother were minors at their father's death and they had automatically become wards of Court. Their father's lands included lands that had formally belonged to the old monastic houses and these were held by knight service. The king was therefore able to sell his right of care to whoever applied. It may be that Henry Wallock purchased the wardship. He was a kinsman, so it would have been natural.

By the time of his father-in-law's death in 1653, Thomas was married with a young son. He seems to have settled in a house in Scosthropp that may have been his father-in-law's. Was he caught up in the war?

The King Family and Presbyterianism in Kirkby Malham
In the opening years of the 19th century, when Revd John Whittaker was assembling his "History of Craven", Edward King of Askham told him that "the first of the family had garrisoned the Church for Parliament". It is not clear what this "garrisoning" involved.

We might find a hint in the fate of the Laudian vicar of Kirkby Malham, Nicholas Walton. Walton had been appointed vicar by Lady Savile of Thornhill Hall, near Wakefield in 1623[5]. He immediately started keeping the registers in Latin, and this was no doubt part of a general move to make the church there "higher" – and maybe to make a greater reality of the control of church affairs by the gentry. Lady Savile and her brother, Sir Thomas Wentworth, were both keen to impose their claims on the community.

Walton later claimed to have been ejected from his living on 30 November 1643. Episcopacy had been formally abolished in January 1643 and Parliament appointed committees to remove ministers who were incorrigibly royalist. Many were ejected. It is said that 2000 ministers were ejected for various reasons during these years. No doubt Walton, who had been appointed by Lord Strafford's sister, was accounted incorrigibly royalist. In September 1643, the Solemn League and Covenant was agreed with the Scots – and a parliamentary Presbyterianism was established in England. In October 1644 County Committees were established, in order to provide for the ordination of new ministers. In 1645, with the Prayer Book banned, the Directory for Public Worship was issued – though it's not clear how widely it was used.

Walton doesn't say who ejected him, but it seems likely that it was a movement of the leading inhabitants – which would certainly have included the King family. It was a brave move. The Parliamentary cause was under threat at the time – which was why Scotland's help was needed. Walton was replaced by John Wallock[6].
   Wallock was presumably a Presbyterian or Independent preacher,

---

[5] Walton was ordained deacon in Rose Castle by the Bishop of Carlisle, by letters dimissory from the Archbishop of York on 22 December 1622, and was ordained priest by the Bishop of Carlisle in the same way on 21 December 1623. He was therefore most probably a young man – though not a graduate.
[6] John Wallock was surely related in some way to Thomas King's father-in-law, Henry Wallock. .

for there is no record of his episcopal ordination. He was ministering during years of considerable uncertainty.

Whether or not the Prayer Book?
Walton regained his living on 2 August 1646, after the end of the First Civil War – and presumably in his turn managed to eject Wallock. National sentiment had changed since the early days of the conflict. Royalism was projected as a creed of sociability and civility – of the old values and old stabilities. There were many who now expected an accommodation between the King and Parliament. In the end, this didn't happen. The Army intervened and the King was executed. The country was now embarked on an uncertain course – and was deeply divided.

Judging by the Latinized registers, Walton seems to have continued in his old way at Kirkby until at least early 1651. How did he manage this? He had the support of the widowed Lady Savile – who is reported to have augmented his income in 1650. Lady Savile had been in Sheffield Castle when it surrendered to the Parliamentarians in August 1644, and had acquitted herself well – despite giving birth to her posthumous youngest child the day after the Castle fell. Her husband, Sir William Savile, had been appointed Governor of Sheffield in May 1643 after the royalists had taken the castle, but he had died later that year. Maybe Lady Savile – by this time a royalist hero - was not the person to see the rightful vicar kept out of his living, though her home at Thornhill was in ruins and she must have had a rough time of it.

By 1652, even Lady Savile couldn't keep Walton in post. The newly established Triers and Ejectors – part of whose job was to remove unsatisfactory parish priests – would have made short work of him. Presumably Wallock returned?

Other Local Clergy
There was however good local support for the parliamentary cause amongst the local clergy. John Webster [7] had taken over as parish

priest at Kildwick within a few years of Roger Brearley's departure, and then moved down to Clitheroe in 1643 to take on the Grammar School there. After that he was a noticeably radical chaplain in the Army, before returning to Craven as pastor of the church at Mitton (the parish that included Grindleton). Edward Price was vicar of Carleton-in-Craven (the neighbouring parish to Kildwick) for thirty-six years, from 1638-1674. He was said to be "a constant preacher" and "the best in these parts". From his parish came Thomas Taylor, the leader of the "people in white raiment" who greeted George Fox in Sedbergh and was an early Quaker leader. Craven was fertile soil for the new ideas that were gaining ground now.

---

[7] John Webster (1610-1682), born in Thornton-in-Craven, and graduated at the University of Cambridge. He was preaching at All Hallows in Lombard Street in 1653, perhaps through the influence of General Lambert. An admirer of Jacob Boehme. He had always been skilled in medicine and, after 1662, he seems to have given up the ministry and practised medicine in Clitheroe instead.

CHAPTER THREE

JAMES KING, OF SKELLANDS (ca 1650 - 1708)

The question of James King's parentage has perplexed family historians for many years and it remains a question that still cannot be answered with certainty. However, on a balance of probability, it seems likely that his father was Thomas King of Skellands – a farm house just outside Kirkby Malham but still in the parish – and that his mother was Elizabeth, the daughter and co-heir of Henry Wallock of Bordley. He grew up to be counted among the leading inhabitants of the village at a time when people generally were working hard to heal "our late unhappy divisions". It is a pity that we have no idea what Skellands looked like, but it may well have been one of the many stone built houses that went up in the 1670s, in which so many of James King's friends and relatives lived.

According to the parish records at Kirkby Malham, James married Ann Carr at Long Preston Church in 1675. In Whittaker's History, she is described as "daughter and heir of ... Carr of Langcliffe, near Settle". In the Carr family tree, found in Whittaker's, she is described as the daughter of Roger Carr, but the generations are mixed up and the information doesn't look reliable. The difficulty is that the Carrs were an extensive family in Giggleswick and it is impossible to disentangle the relationships from the registers. However, it is clear that Ann King was closely related to Leonard Carr, who built Manor Farm in the centre of Langcliffe in the 1670s and whose initials are still to be seen over the door. Leonard's nephew and heir, William Carr of Langcliffe, was later to be lent money by his kinsman, Thomas King of Skellands – James and Ann King's son.

Life in Malhamdale from the 1680's to 1700's
The only specific record of James King's activities I have so far discovered relates to the local school in Kirkby Malham. In the old

days there had been a school in the church, known as the Charity School of the Rood. However, in 1606, the school was reconstituted. Benjamin Lambert of Calton Hall – the leading local landowner – set up a board of six trustees. The owner of Calton Hall was ex officio trustee; the others represented different parts of the parish. In 1706 Stephen Proctor was appointed teacher at the school. The trustees were then Rev Francis Bryer, William Serjeantson, Sir John Middleton, James King and Robert King. Bryer was the curate at Kirkby Malham[8]. Sir John Middleton had married the Lambert heiress. Robert King was probably the son of Henry King of Kirkby Malham and a cousin of James King's. The appointment of Stephen Proctor turned out to be a bad one and in 1711 (after James King's death) the trustees were petitioning Archbishop Sharp for his removal on the grounds of drunkenness.

It would be interesting to know more of what was happening in Malhamdale during these years. John Lambert's arrest and imprisonment could not have gone down well. His wife and children seem to have continued at Calton, and there is a tradition that Mrs Lambert walked across the Dales to an independent congregation more to her liking[9]. It is unlikely that the reimposition of the Prayer Book was received happily by many people. It is interesting that there is no record of an incumbent being appointed to Kirkby Malham before 1681, which might suggest that this remote parish was allowed to go more or less its own way[10]. These were years for keeping quiet and hoping for better times.

---

[8] In the 1690's he had been the curate at the Halton Gill Chapel in the parish of Arncliffe, so maybe Kirkby Malham was a better position for him.

[9] John Lambert's property was held by trustees for the benefit of his wife and then for his eldest son, another John Lambert, who married Barbara Lister of Arnoldsbiggin in 1672 and had an only daughter. This daughter married Sir John Middleton of Belsay Castle, Northumberland, and her son and heir sold the Yorkshire estates in 1727. Mrs Lambert died in 1676 and the General in 1684 – still under arrest in Plymouth.

[10] A William Hardwicke was preaching at Kirkby Malham from 1666 and Lionel Holmes from 1671, but neither seems to have been instituted. Just before he left to become vicar of Wrawby (on the way to Grimsby, in Lincolnshire), Holmes

Dark Days, 1669-1688

In 1672 Charles issued another Declaration of Indulgence, without recourse to Parliament. There was a public outcry. The following year the Declaration was withdrawn, Shaftesbury [11] was dismissed from his posts and Danby [12] took over. Archbishop Sheldon's [13] Church of England and the Cavalier Parliament were now in charge, and toleration for either Catholics or Dissenters was a dead letter. Things went on steadily for a while, but there was increasing suspicion of the King, of his links with France, and of his sympathy for Roman Catholicism. The Duke of York's Catholicism had become public in 1672 and it rapidly became the focal issue in politics. Louis XIV stood as an example of what a Catholic monarch could be like - suppressing all dissent, both political and religious. It was widely believed that a Catholic King James would surely reign like Louis XIV. In the end, there was an explosion.

The marriage in 1677 of Princess Mary and William of Orange reassured people for a while, but there was continued distrust of Charles, and increasingly of Danby and his ministry. From the

---

married Ann Sergeantson of Airton, a first cousin of William Sergeantson, of Hanlith. George Robinson was apparently instituted on Holmes' departure in 1681.

[11] Anthony Ashley Cooper, 1st Earl of Shaftesbury (1621-1683), a Puritan who was originally close to Cromwell but was among those who devised the arrangements for Charles II's return. One of those who made up the Cabal, the group who came into government after Clarendon's fall - until the parliamentary revolt of 1673. Passionate for comprehension and patron of Locke. Fled after the Rye House Plot of 1683 and died in exile.

[12] Thomas Osborne, Earl of Danby, 1st Duke of Leeds (1631-1712), High Church Anglican, anti-French royalist, who came in because Parliament trusted him and fell in 1678, engulfed in the fury of the Popish plots. He was among those who invited William of Orange in 1688 and headed up that King's first administration.

[13] Gilbert Sheldon (1598-1677) Fellow & Warden of All Souls', Oxford and an ardent supporter of William Laud. Ejected in 1648 and spent the Commonwealth in retirement. Restored to his wardenship in 1659, he became Bishop of London in 1660, and Archbishop of Canterbury in 1663. Worked hard to re-establish Laudian principles in the Church.

autumn of 1678 Popish plots were discovered everywhere. People were convinced that the Catholic powers of Europe and their English allies were bent on the assassination of Charles II and the succession of his brother. In 1679 Stephen Tennant of Broughton Hall and his aunt were tried for treason at York, suspected of plotting Charles' assassination. Two Catholic priests working in the West Riding were executed. People were demanding that James be excluded from the succession. Finally, in 1681, Charles II called a halt to the Exclusion Crisis by dissolving Parliament. Some of his opponents took this opportunity to try other means of ensuring either a Protestant succession or a Republic. The 'discovery' of the Rye House Plot in 1683 resulted in the deaths of Lord Russell and of Algernon Sidney. They both became martyrs for the Good Old Cause.

The intellectual energy behind the drive towards comprehension – Locke, Shaftesbury, Sidney, Russell – was impressive, but it hadn't carried the country during Charles' lifetime. The discovery of the Rye House Plot meant the end of that group as a political force for the time being. However, the disaster of James' reign seemed to prove them right.

The Cause of Liberty, 1689-1708

The accession of William of Orange did not change as much as some people had hoped. William was jealous of his prerogative and was happy to work with those who had supported his uncles. For many, he seemed to betray the principles of freedom and accountability that he had apparently come to save. There was however a different feel. Parliament had made William III and Parliament was able to assert its power in a way it had only occasionally managed to do under Charles II. The Toleration Act of 1689 guaranteed the rights of Protestant Dissenters (though not of Roman Catholics), and so brought to an end one long difficulty from Charles' reign. The Triennial Act guaranteed regular parliaments. A new England was being formed.

The intellectual back-up for Commonwealth ideas in William's day was provided by a remarkable series of re-publications between 1696-1702. The writings of the heroes of the Commonwealth – Sidney, Milton, Ludlow, Harrington – were edited and reproduced by John Toland in order to provide an underpinning for the new monarchy. The climax and achievement of this movement was the Act of Settlement of 1701, which settled the crown on the nearest acceptable Protestant heir, the Electress Sophia.

Yet it was not all democracy and progress! The power of government increased during these years. Most of William's reign was taken up with the expensive and inconclusive war with France. The first one lasted from 1689 to 1697 and attempted to reduce the power of the France of Louis XIV. In this it did not succeed. When the war broke out again in 1701, the task was clearly one that would take some while. The Bank of England came into being, to organise the national debt. The resources of the government increased and with it the government's ability to bribe. The concern was now not so much the power of the Crown over against Parliament, but the growth of patronage and placemen[14]. "Parliaments which in all preceding ages… have been the place of our liberty… are now become the instruments of all our oppressions"[15]. Most people of whatever party now felt excluded, even if - on the whole - they were behind the war.

Death and burial
James King's will is dated 24 July 1708. It is quite detailed. His wife Ann is left £20 a year "in full satisfaction of what my wife may claim as her jointure/dower"[16]. However, this was on condition that she

---

[14] Lady Suffolk commented to Horace Walpole in 1765 after an appointment was made to the Royal Household, that such posts "had no salaries before King William's reign.. the salaries of the present great offices were formerly very small.. it is plain that salaries were not the great object as now".
[15] "The Honourable Algernon Sidney's Letter Against Bribery and Corruption", published in 1697. Quoted in Blair Worden, "*Roundhead Reputations*" (2001).
[16] In present day (2019) terms, perhaps around £50,000

released to her son the land that that had been willed to her. If she did not do this she forfeited £6 a year. Does this mean that Ann, said to be her father's only child, only brought to the marriage land of that amount? There was also a house in Kirkby Malham that Ann was to have if she didn't want to continue to share the house at Skellands with her son.

Three grandchildren were left five pounds each and a godson was left twenty shillings. Forty shillings was left to the poor of Kirkby Malham.

James' executors were John Waddington, John Paley and Ron Newstead. I know nothing of Newstead. Waddington is a local name. John Paley however is no doubt John Paley of Langcliff, the grandfather of Dr William Paley, who was Master of Giggleswick School for over fifty years and was the father of the celebrated theologian, Dr William Paley.

CHAPTER FOUR

THOMAS KING OF SKELLANDS (1686-1727)

Life in Malhamdale in the 1710's and 1720's

Thomas was only twenty-two when he took over the farm. He was twenty-eight when he became the second of his line to marry into the Sergeantson family. He would have brought her home to Skellands. Thomas seems to have had a secure place among the leading local families, and was related to the local parsons and grammar school teachers of Craven and beyond. Two of his Carr cousins (his slightly younger contemporaries) were at Christ's College, Cambridge. One of them went on to become Headmaster of Giggleswick School; the other was rector of Bolton Abbey[17]. As the only son, Thomas would have been required to farm the land. The generations between Robert King of the Civil War and James King of Clitheroe and Raphoe are very quiet.

Things were however changing. A chief influence was the development of the navy. In the old days, the navy was something of a private enterprise, with individuals or naval ports getting ships together for various purposes, which might then be hired in time of war. However, by the end of the 17th century the navy was becoming a national force, maintained out of the taxes levied by parliament. Some progress was made in Cromwell's time, but the main work was done in the reigns of Charles II and James II. Concerns that army officers should be drawn from the ranks of those who had a stake in the country were extended to the navy, and steps were taken to establish an "officer class". As David Hannay says in the 1911 edition of the Encyclopaedia Britannica, "lads of gentle birth were sent on board ships in commission with a letter of service - from which came their popular name of "king's letter boys" - to the captain, instructing him to treat them on the

---

[17] Rev John Carr (1688-1745) was Headmaster of Giggleswick School. Rev James Carr (1691-1745) was Rector of Bolton Abbey.

footing of gentlemen and train them to become officers". Then, by the end of Queen Anne's reign, such trained naval officers were entitled to permanent pay, even in peacetime[18].

The navy this became a career for younger sons, and it is interesting that Thomas King's brother-in-law, Richard Sergeantson, had enlisted in the navy towards the end of Queen Anne's reign. Richard was a younger son, and the navy gave him a respectable occupation and income - other than that which came from schoolmastering or preaching. Other members of his family followed his example in the following generations.

The reign of Anne, 1702-1714

Queen Anne was a very ordinary woman, but she presided over an extraordinary time. The long war against Louis XIV enhanced English power and prestige. On the home front, increased wealth meant cultural change. There was a reaction against the aristocratic profligacy of Charles II's time. The middle classes were coming through. People wanted decency and decorum. There was to be a reformation of manners. The High Priest of this movement was Joseph Addison[19], and his chief weapon was The Spectator - a journal that ran during 1711 and 1712 and had a huge circulation and an enduring impact on English culture. Addison made fun of the old fashioned Tory squires - represented by Sir Roger de Coverley, his most famous creation - and looked instead to the money men and the sturdy yeomen of England. It was from these sturdy yeomen that the Kings descend, and from them that they derive their particular characteristics.

There was a concern for "freedom", and this included freedom to think. The despotic European regimes were a constant threat, and

---

[18] This was the beginning of the half-pay system, whereby officers who were surplus to peacetime requirements nonetheless received some pay. It only worked for officers.
[19] 1672-1719, he was the son of a Dean of Lichfield and an important person in the Whig governments, apart from his literary work.

Jacobitism meant absolutism. Locke was the thinker who stood behind everything, and in matters of Christian orthodoxy Locke had flown quite close to the wind in his later years. Yet there was nothing of the freethinker about Locke, despite what later writers would have us believe. Freedom could be compatible with Christian believing. A responsible freedom opened the way to truth. That is not to say that there was not heterodoxy in these days - and on a major scale. John Toland[20] was the most notorious of the freethinkers and yet his views - albeit in extreme form - continued the mid-seventeenth century concerns for freedom and decency into as new, more complex age. Moral concerns were major concerns, and explain the increasing concern of Christian writers for moral issues.

The Early Hanoverian Church, 1714-1727

King William's accession had established England as a Protestant state, and the monarchy as a firmly constitutional one. King George's accession a quarter of a century later reinforced this. The intellectual world in which the Kings would have been in sympathy is probably best found in the work of William Whiston, Samuel Clarke[21], Benjamin Hoadly[22]and George Berkeley[23], all men who had come out of the moderate Whig world of Joseph Addison and the Spectator.

---

[20] John Toland (1670-1722), an Irish Catholic, turned Protestant, turned Deist. Gained notoriety with his "Christianity not Mysterious" (1696), and continued to develop his thinking on religious and political matters into the Hanoverian period.
[21] Samuel Clarke (1675-1729), a leading theologian who was deeply influenced by Isaac Newton and sought to develop a Christian theology that was sustained by reason. Hoadly was a friend, and edited his Collected Works.
[22] Benjamin Hoadly (1676-1761), a much maligned church leader of the first half of the 18th century. He conducted a lifelong struggle to make the Church more comprehensive and was a conspicuous defender of nonconformists.
[23] George Berkeley (1685-1753), in England and on the Continent from 1713; an absentee Dean of Derry from 1724; Bishop of Cloyne from 1734. A distinguished theologian.

It was a controversial time. In 1717 Hoadly preached his famous sermon on the nature of the Kingdom of Christ. For him "no man had the power to prescribe laws and to tyrannise over other men's opinions in religious matters. Christ himself was the sole lawgiver of his kingdom and it was the duty of man to know, each for himself, the true meaning of Christ's commands". Hoadly had immediately to face the wrath of the High Churchmen, but found a doughty ally in Dr John Balguy[24]. Dr Henry Stebbing had attacked Hoadly, by arguing that a Church couldn't exist without a teaching authority to say what that Church believed. Balguy denied that an identity of opinion was necessary for the existence and well-being of a Church. He wanted comprehension.

However, Hoadly was keen to defuse the controversy and asked Balguy to cool it. Balguy thereupon turned to the safer realm of moral theology. He took on the deist, Francis Hutcheson, who had argued against Samuel Clarke that moral judgements were simply instinctive, like animals guarding their young[25]. Balguy argued that, though instinct helps, yet the higher moral good is that achieved by reason seeking the heart of God – in whom all good subsists. He developed that idea in his "Divine Rectitude". He sought to make Rectitude the underlying principle of his theological system, holding on to the doctrine of redemption against the deists through an argument for the meritorious sufferings of Christ.

A generally admired but hitherto forgotten work was "The Religion of the Protestants a safe way of salvation", by William Chillingworth[26].

---

[24] John Balguy (1686-1748), the son of the master of Sheffield Grammar School. On his father's death in 1696 he remained a pupil at the school, until going to St John's College, Cambridge in 1702. Graduated in 1706 and taught for a while before being ordained in 1711 and working as a tutor. In 1727 Dr Hoadly made him a Prebendary of Salisbury and, by the Bishop's influence, he accepted the vicarage of Northallerton in 1729 where he remained until his death. His major works were "The Foundations of Moral Goodness" (1728) and "Divine Rectitude" in two parts (1730 & 1741). His son Thomas was a contemporary and friend of Dean King's and a highly respected and learned clergyman.
[25] "Enquiry into the Original of our Ideas of Beauty and Virtue" (1725)

Chillingworth had argued for free enquiry, based on the bible. The argument was all for the greatest possible comprehension and a playing down of the High Church doctrines that had caused such division in the reign of Charles II. It is easy to see how he appealed to people at the beginning of the eighteenth century.

Sympathy with the concerns of the Civil War period remained strong, linked to a suspicion of France and of European Catholicism. The military triumphs of Queen Anne's reign gave reassurance that the love of liberty was the surest way to national security. After her, the Hanoverian settlement ensured a safe future.

Early Hanoverian Politics

The sensation of the 1713 London season had been the success of Addison's play, *Cato*. The model had been Cato the Younger, who had killed himself rather than live under the corrupt rule of the Caesars. Withdrawal from public life in the interests of virtue became a dominant theme. 'Happiest of all men, to me, seems the private man'. *Cato's Letters,* published in 1720-1724, in the wake of the collapse of the South Sea Bubble, was a very influential collection of writings that went on being reprinted into the mid-century. It pays homage to the 'old Whig' cause, though it moderates the old radicalism – the demands for a republic and land redistribution. *The Independent Whig* linked the cause of the marginalized country gentleman with the Whig cause, and brought both into opposition to Walpole's monopoly of power by the use of places and sinecures. There was a strong sense that the Revolution of 1688 had been betrayed – and yet there was a reluctance to criticize too strongly for fear of the Jacobites[27].

Family Matters

Thomas was a substantial man in his community. Shortly before his death, he seems to have joined with a Carr kinsman, Charles Nowell of Cappleside, in lending money on security to a Carr cousin and

---

[26] William Chillingworth (d. 1644)
[27] See Blair Worden's remarkable book, *Roundhead Reputations,* Penguin, 2001

contemporary, William Carr of Langcliffe. This didn't bring William Carr's problems to an end. In 1731 he was to mortgage Manor Farm, his main house in Langcliffe, to Richard Lawson (probably also a relation). In 1738 this mortgage was transferred to Charles Nowell, and three years later to Dr John Cookson – Thomas King's future son-in-law.

Thomas and Alice King had six children - James, Ann, Jane, William, Elizabeth and Mary - before Thomas died at the age of 41 when their eldest child was only twelve years old. Alice's sister Elizabeth Norton had been left a widow with two young children in 1720 and her half-brother, Robert Serjeantson of Hanlith, had been widowed with four young children in 1722. Robert himself died two years later, aged 34, just after marrying again. Premature death – probably from tuberculosis - seems to have been the order of the day. Alice married again, in 1729, to Rev Henry Wilkinson, the curate at Kirkby Malham, but was widowed for the second time three years later.

It would be interesting to know where Henry Wilkinson came from. James King's calling to the priesthood might have had something to do with his stepfather. Although various kinsman were or had been clergymen, it had been some generations since any King was ordained. There was emerging out of the upheavals of the Civil War a Yorkshire world that was close-knit, intellectually able, and liberal in inspiration.

CHAPTER FIVE

DEAN JAMES KING 1715-1795
A country clergyman for thirty years and the father of a generation of able sons.

Background
When he died in 1727, Thomas King left everything in trust for his eldest son until he reached the age of twenty-one. £1500 was set aside for William and the four daughters, and his wife Alice was to have £25 a year. James' trustees were the men of the family – his mother's cousin, John Walker of Hungerhill, his maternal uncle, John Sergeantson of Hanlith, his paternal uncle by marriage, Henry Wilcock of Thornton, and a Carr kinsman, Charles Nowell of Cappelside in Giggleswick[28]. They seem to have done a good job by him.

The early years of the eighteenth century were pretty dire for agriculture. Charles Wilson wrote, "the twenty years from 1730-1750 constitute a virtually continuous agricultural depression". The years before then were little easier. This depression had a double effect. Smaller landowners left the land, and large landowners – with the necessary capital – enlarged their holdings and improved their methods. It was the age of Jethro Tull and Turnip Townshend – and of the gentrification of the countryside. The Kings wisely seem to have left the land – or at least ceased to look to it as their only source of income. It was take-off time for them – and for many like them in the Yorkshire Dales.

William Norton, James' younger cousin, joined the navy in the 1730's. A member of the King cousinhood in Malhamdale also

---

[28] In the History of Giggleswick School, Charles Nowell is recorded as kin to the second founder of the school – Rev John Nowell - and he had served as a Governor of the School. However, in April 1745 he was removed because 'he had been long imprisoned in Lancaster Gaol'. The offence is not specified. Was it debt?

joined up around this time. Naval power was becoming the centrepiece of British policy. Liverpool - not so far from Malhamdale - was becoming a major international port and many young men from farming backgrounds were making a career as sea captains. If British interests were to be defended against the Spanish and the French, it would be through a dominance of the seas. In 1740 James Thomson wrote "Rule, Britannia!" and it sums up the spirit of the age. A patriotic war was fought against Spain from 1739 that had become a war against France before it came to an end in 1748. Things started up again in 1756 under Pitt, and there were some notable triumphs – Wolfe at Quebec and Hawke at Quiberon Bay. It was a good time to be a sailor.

Early Influences

But not everyone was cut out for the armed forces. Thomas Paley of nearby Langcliff had a clever son who graduated from Christ's College, Cambridge in 1733. After a spell in the Peterborough diocese, young William Paley returned to Giggleswick in 1745 as master of the Grammar School[29]. He was to be there for fifty years. Teaching in the grammar schools or universities, the parish ministry or the law all offered a good living to able young men. James King and William Norton's older brother Fletcher both received a good education at the Grammar School at Ripon – then just establishing itself as a boarding school, and so able to take boys from outside the city's immediate environs. University was the next step. In June 1734 they travelled south, to be admitted as pensioners of St John's College, Cambridge[30].

---

[29] His son was William Paley, the distinguished theologian.

[30] Other Ripon men starting at St John's at the same time were Thomas Balguy, Zachary Suger and John Dering. Suger went on to serve in parishes in Lincolnshire and York and was to develop a considerable reputation as a preacher. Balguy was elected fellow of St John's in 1740. He was something of a scholar. Bishop Hoadley made him Archdeacon of Winchester and in 1781 he was offered the bishopric of Gloucester (which he refused on health grounds). His father, John Balguy, was a Fellow of St John's before his marriage, and was then Rector of Northallerton. He was a friend and early defender of Bishop Hoadley. John Dering, the son of the Dean of Ripon, had matriculated at St John's in 1732. He

At the time of their arrival, St John's was a Tory stronghold under the leadership of Dr Robert Lambert, a Yorkshireman himself and master since 1727. However, in February 1735 Lambert died and there was a heavily contested election. The victor was Dr John Newcome, Lady Margaret Professor of Divinity, and a strong Whig. As a protégé of the Duke of Newcastle, Newcome was felt by the old guard to stand for all that was corrupt and wrong in the running of the country. He didn't have an easy time of it during his opening years.

From the point of view of theology, the 1730's are chiefly notable for strenuous efforts on the part of orthodox Christian scholars to defeat the claims of the deists. An important moment was the publication in 1736 of "Analogy of Religion" by Joseph Butler, then a country clergyman and a favourite of the Queen's. From 1738 he was Bishop of Bristol and then moved on to Durham. Butler was writing in defence of orthodox Christianity against the Deists, and the quality of his writing has been appreciated more and more over the years. Some would say that Butler is an early example of reason giving way to feeling and experience in religion – but at the time he would have been seen as a respectable defender of the reasonableness of Christianity.

At the time of James King's university career it is more likely that a young man looking to ordination would be reading Locke (with a bit of a health warning), Jeremy Taylor on "The Liberty of Prophesying", and 17th century divines such as Edward Stillingfleet[31] and William Chillingworth[32]. A more contemporary theologian was

---

was the rector of Hilgay in Norfolk for over thirty years until his death in 1774. His grandfather was John Sharp, Archbishop of York 1691-1714, spiritual adviser to Queen Anne – which means he was a first cousin of Granville Sharp (1735-1813), the emancipationist, whose father Thomas Sharp, Archdeacon of Northumberland, was the Archbishop's youngest son.

[31] Edward Stillingfleet (1635-1699), Dean of St Paul's from 1678 and Bishop of Worcester from 1689. A moderate, who was yet unhappy with Locke's "*Essay concerning Human Understanding*".

William Warburton, who was much read in the 1750's and who enjoyed famous controversies with the later Deists – particularly Lord Bolingbroke.

Yet all this was rather dry. There were other more exciting things going on in Oxford. John Wesley had gone up to Christ Church in 1720 and had run his Holy Club from 1729-1735 while he was a Fellow of Lincoln. George Whitefield had come to faith under Wesley's influence at Easter 1735 and was startling people in London, Gloucester and Bristol through 1736 and 1737 with the eloquence of his preaching. How much of all that reached Cambridge? More interestingly, how did James King react to the growing influence of Methodism during his later ministry?

After graduation, James King was ordained by the Bishop of Lincoln to a curacy at Hamerton, assistant to the vicar, Rev William Robinson. Bishop Reynolds was, I think, the visitor of St John's and Hamerton was in his diocese and not far from his palace at Buckden. Two years later James was ordained priest to the more substantial village of Barrow-upon-Soar, near Loughborough. This was another parish in the Lincoln diocese and he would have acted as curate to Rev Vere Foster, the vicar. In 1741 he took his M.A. and in 1743 was appointed by Sir Nathaniel Curzon of Kedleston to the perpetual curacy of Clitheroe, near to his home territory, within the parish of Whalley Abbey and just across the county border into Lancashire.

The Clitheroe Years, 1743-1772
Clitheroe was a township of some 1400 people, had its own grammar school and returned two members of parliament. It was a typical Lancashire town, with its main street climbing up the hill to where the old church stood[33].

---

[32] William Chillingworth (1602-1644), best known for his "Religion of the Protestants a Safe Way to Salvation". Argued that "the Bible only is the religion of the Protestant" and was all that was needed.

[33] James King's church was pulled down and replaced with something grander at

The old parsonage could well have been on the site of the present one, a short walk from the church, and looking out onto the main street. Clitheroe was then in the diocese of Chester and the deanery of Blackburn. In modern terms, Blackburn was a huge deanery, stretching from the Yorkshire borders to the east to the outskirts of Preston in the west, and from the Forest of Bowland in the north to Darwen and Rossendale in the south. Clitheroe and Colne were substantial settlements but they were both "perpetual curacies"[34]. It was a bit anomalous, but it worked reasonably well at a time when middle management in the church barely existed. The perpetual curate at Colne was an ex-Roman Catholic who was getting up the noses of his parishioners and had no idea of how to deal with dissenters. This mattered, because he was surrounded by them. Colne had been the centre of revival since Benjamin Ingham[35] and William Batty had started preaching there in the 1740's. It is interesting that, though chapels and meeting houses sprang up all about, there is no mention of one being built in Clitheroe. It would seem that the ministry of James King was such that there was no need for the gospel to be preached by anyone else.

It was a good place to work in. James King was twenty-eight years old and this was to be his home for nearly thirty years. In 1744 he married his cousin, Ann Walker, and settled down to bring up their family of one surviving daughter and five sons. They were quiet, steady years and it is clear that their children looked back on their Clitheroe childhood with considerable affection. They were comfortably off by the standards of the day - but it is not easy to get any feel for the life. Everyday life in the Yorkshire and Lancashire towns of the 1750's and 1760's has not been much chronicled, but

the beginning of the 19th century.
[34] Whalley Abbey was the mother church, responsible for staffing the parish during the middle ages. After the dissolution of the abbey, the right of presentation to Clitheroe and Colne fell to the rector
[35] Benjamin Ingham was married to Lady Margaret Hastings, sister-in-law of Selina, Countess of Huntingdon. The Inghamites were close to George Whitefield and seceded from the Church of England in 1754.

it is generally true that there was a great development in general "politeness" in middle class society in the eighteenth century. England was becoming more prosperous. The professions – doctors, lawyers, school-teachers and clergymen - were coming into their own. The middle classes, put firmly centre stage by Addison and his Whig allies, were growing in confidence. Life on the Lancashire borders in the 1750s and 1760s was still largely untouched by the Industrial Revolution. That would develop after James King's departure – and then only in the south of the area. Clitheroe and Downham were never industrialized

M.F. Snape writes about the importance of football in eighteenth century village life[36]. The Declarations of Sports of 1618 and 1633 had sanctioned football as a Sunday recreation, as long as it didn't start until evensong was over. It was in accordance with these regulations that the Downham preaching day developed. Sir Ralph Assheton had commissioned a memorial sermon to be preached at Downham every 30 January – the anniversary of the execution of Charles I – accompanied by a distribution of alms. Since he did this in the midst of the 'Popish plot' crisis and fears for the succession of a Catholic King, Assheton had no doubt a desire to strength Tory-style allegiance to the Crown in his part of Lancashire. As it turned out, the crowds that turned out for the distribution soon found a more exciting focus in the game of football that followed – traditionally against the men of Newchurch-in-Pendle.

It is said that on one occasion the preacher confiscated the football, in order to ensure that the game didn't start until the service was over. He then kicked it down the churchyard steps to enable the game to begin. This became something of a tradition and James King was known in Clitheroe as the 'keeper of the football' – which he would kick from the church gates on winter Sundays after the afternoon service.

---

[36] M.F. Snape *The Church of England in Industrialising Society, pp 31-32*

The only family anecdote that survives of James King dates from Victorian times and may or may not be reliable, though it fits with the football anecdote. Oliver Bolton King says, "The story is well-known in the family of how, on his wedding day, James was riding from Clitheroe to the church at Bolton when he encountered hounds in full cry. Carried away by excitement he joined the field in a stiff run right on to the kill. As a result a mud-bespattered bridegroom arrived at the church so late that the clock had to be put back an hour". Fox-hunting to hounds was in its infancy at the time. The traditional sport of the aristocracy had been the hunting of deer, and in Elizabeth's day no man of breeding would have demeaned himself by hunting vermin. Deer however were less plentiful during the seventeenth century. In any case they were never accessible to the country gentry, who were becoming more prosperous and looking for a sport of their own. During the first half of the eighteenth century fox-hunting with hounds was becoming their sport, and the caricature of the provincial fox-hunting squire was gradually established in London political circles. It is possible that there were hounds near Clitheroe, but there is the feel of an anachronistic Victorian invention. Foxhounds were not as plentiful in 1744 as they were to be a century later.

James and his wife were honoured for providing a safe and godly (though perhaps not too uncomfortably godly) home, from which their children went out to take their place in the great world.

James King's Politics
Where did James King stand? The 1740s and 1750s was a conservative time. The Civil War era was not well regarded and there was a general fear of slipping back into those divisions. Equally, there was a fear of the resurgence of Jacobite absolutism. One of the key developments in the mid-century was the rise of the 1688 Revolution to a position of eminence. Earlier in the century, people were more aware of what had not been achieved by that revolution and of all that had been left undone as the aristocracy took over. However, as Walpole's hold on power weakened, Tories

and excluded Whigs drew together in their defence of 1688 – and even of the ideals that had caused the Civil War.

The rising of 1745 came close to Clitheroe. Prince Charles Edward had relied on French support, which for various reasons did not materialize. He raised his standard in the Highlands in August 1745 and moved down to take Edinburgh. In September he defeated the Hanoverian force at Prestonpans. On 15 November he took Carlisle and then marched south to Lancaster, where he hoped that the Lancashire Jacobites would join him. Not many did, although a regiment drawn from the north of England was assembled under the leadership of Francis Towneley of Towneley – a major estate, about 18 miles south of Clitheroe. This was the 'Manchester Regiment' that welcomed the Prince at the end of November when he arrived in Manchester to the ringing of bells and much celebration. The Prince then continued down to Derby but there he became concerned about his supply lines. The French were nowhere to be seen and he was persuaded to return to Scotland to await their arrival. The retreat gave the Hanoverian forces time to regroup. The Prince left the Manchester Regiment at Carlisle – to hold at least one English city until he returned – and continued north. On 21 December the Duke of Cumberland reached Carlisle and laid siege to the city. It fell a week later and the leaders of the Manchester Regiment were taken to London. On 30 July 1746, Colonel Towneley and his lieutenants were hung, drawn and quartered on Kennington Common – the last time such a barbarous punishment was ever inflicted in this country. By then, on 21 April, the Prince had gone down to defeat at Culloden.

No one much loved the government in London, but the 1745 Rising had little chance of success. The old Whig cause needed something to get its teeth into, and that didn't materialize until the early years of the reign of George III. Then the old anxieties about an over-mighty Crown were re-ignited, and it was James King's sons who were ready to join the fray.

Mrs Cookson in Clitheroe

Sometime in 1759, Mrs Sarah Cookson arrived in Clitheroe. James King's widowed sister, Jane, had married Dr John Cookson of Wakefield. Dr Cookson was a cousin of Mrs Sarah Cookson's late husband, who had been Lecturer at Leeds Parish Church. Mrs Cookson was childless, but she had with her a nephew, William Tatham – a boy of the same age as Walker, whose badly off parents were divorcing. Mrs Cookson seems to have been quite a powerful lady. She was the younger sister of Henry Marsden of Wennington Hall in Westmoreland. On her brother's death in 1762, she took it upon herself to keep an eye on her two young nephews (one of whom was mentally defective) since she felt she had a surer hand with them than their mother. She was not likely to have been the easiest parishioner.

In 1768, when Walker King went up to Oxford from Sedbergh School, young William Tatham left the Lancaster Free School and was placed with a cotton planter in Virginia. No doubt there were links between the cotton spinners of Leeds and the planters of Virginia. James King left Clitheroe soon afterwards, so he was spared the gossip that was circulating after Mrs Cookson also left Clitheroe and set herself up permanently in Wennington Hall with her surviving (feeble-minded) nephew and a young steward, to whom she was said to be closer than she ought[37].

Sir Fletcher Norton, 1771-1776

James King's cousin Fletcher had been called to the bar in 1739 and gradually built up a reputation as a formidable advocate. He became attorney-general for the county palatine of Lancaster and a KC. He entered parliament in 1756, was knighted and in 1762 was appointed solicitor-general by Lord Bute. In the autumn of 1763, at the height of the Wilkes controversy, he was promoted attorney-

---

[37] The story is well told by Emmeline Garnett in "John Marsden's Will", Hambledon Press, 1998. Coincidentally, the Tatham brothers were the heirs of the Sandford family of Askham Hall – though all the Sandford money had gone by now.

general in George Grenville's administration[38]. John Wilkes had been harrying both Bute and Grenville in the *North Briton* and Norton won the respect of both by his efforts against Wilkes in the courts and in parliament. In January 1764, mainly through Norton's legal skills, Wilkes was expelled from the House of Commons and fled to France. However, Grenville was gradually losing the King's support and when the Grenville ministry fell in July 1765 Norton too lost his position. He didn't re-emerge until 1769, when he accepted an appointment as privy councillor in the Duke of Grafton's administration. Then, with the opening of the parliamentary session of November 1770, he was elected Speaker of the House of Commons. As far as the opposition were concerned, this was a low point[39]. The King and the Court carried all before them. As far as Lord North was concerned – and no doubt Norton also – the King's government needed to be carried on by the best people available.

Then began the five years that saw James King gathered out of his obscure Lancashire parish and moved upwards from place to place in the ecclesiastical hierarchy. It mattered in those days who you knew and in the early 1770's Sir Fletcher Norton was a good man to know. As Speaker, he was able to invite his cousin James to be his chaplain and then in 1772 presented him to the parish of St Mary's and Holy Trinity, in his own power base at Guildford in Surrey[40]. Two years after that the Guildford parishes were exchanged for the pleasant village of Dunsfold, with a canonry at Windsor thrown in[41].

---

[38] In succession to Charles Yorke who had held the post since 1757. He was the younger son of Lord Hardwicke and was confidently tipped as a future Lord Chancellor. Yorke had made a mess of the Wilkes business and had gone under pressure. He was restored to his post in 1765. In January 1770, when Lord Camden (who had been Lord Chancellor since the beginning of Chatham's administration in July 1766) had to give up the seals, Yorke became Lord Chancellor - but died three days later.

[39] Currently then focused on Lord Rockingham and Lord Chatham

[40] He had sat as MP for Guildford since 1769.

[41] In June 1774 Edmund Burke wrote to Walker King - then at Goodwood with the Duke of Richmond - of "the great good fortune that has happened to your father". Burke estimated that with a canonry worth up to £600 a year and with £240-£300 from his living, James King ought to be clearing over £800 a year.

At this point, James resigned his living at Clitheroe and managed to hand Downham to his son, Thomas[42]. Finally, in 1776, James exchanged his canonry for the deanery of Raphoe in Ireland. It was all a remarkable example of the power of 18th century patronage.

However, in the following year, Norton fell foul of the King and so the source of patronage dried up. When presenting the bill for the increase of the civil list to the king, he told George III that parliament has "not only granted to your majesty a large present supply, but also a very great additional revenue; great beyond example; great beyond your majesty's highest expense". George III did not forgive him. In 1778 when the Lord Chancellor's job was available, it went to Norton's younger rival, Edward Thurlow. After the general election of 1780, Lord North withdrew his support from Norton in the election for the Speaker's chair, alleging that his health was not equal to the task. Norton stood nonetheless, and was defeated. His change of mind was common during the 1770's when the imminent loss of the America colonies was sending the King's reputation to an all-time low. Fox had begun the decade as a general supporter of the King's and ended it a staunch critic. The same thing seems to have happened to Norton. All his life he had supported the King's administration, but by the mid-1770's he was alienated. In 1782, during the brief ministry of Lord Rockingham, Norton was promoted to the Lords as Lord Grantley. If Thurlow had been prepared to resign as Chancellor (which he was not), Norton might have come in then as Lord Chancellor. He deserved something from his new allies. Dr Johnson remarked of Norton, "Much may be done if a man put his whole mind to a particular subject. By so doing, Norton has made himself the great lawyer which he is allowed to be".

Ireland & Raphoe
Raphoe, the new home of James and Ann King, was an ancient centre. The original community dated back by tradition to the time

---

[42]There were fifteen applicants for the Clitheroe living. Thomas only held Downham for a year.

of St Columba, himself a native of what was later county Donegal. There were bishops at Raphoe from very early times, but there was never any town there outside the monastery. The area had been part of the territory of the O'Donnell family and was pretty much untouched by English or Scottish influences. However, in 1607, with the flight of Rory O'Donnell, lately Earl of Tyrconnell, the Ulster Plantation got under way. The Church of Ireland was treated generously and Andrew Knox, Bishop of Raphoe 1612-1633, encouraged settlers to take up tenancies on land that now belonged to him. A town did gradually grow up, with the result that the best of Raphoe's buildings today are from the eighteenth century. Nonetheless, it is likely that even in Dean King's day the life was in neighbouring Derry. It may well be that the Kings lived in Derry rather than in Raphoe.

The state of the Church of Ireland at this time was not as bad as nineteenth century historians would have us believe. However, the eighteenth century saw a revival in the fortunes in of the Roman Catholic Church in Ireland that was not shared by the Church of Ireland. As the Catholic Church grew, it became an increasing cause of scandal that the Church that absorbed the ancient endowments commanded the allegiance of barely 10% of the population.

Early Years in Ireland, The Volunteer Movement 1776-1783
James King arrived in Ireland shortly before the news of the British defeat by their American subjects at Saratoga. The news had a transforming effect on the situation there. A Franco-American treaty was concluded in March 1778, which meant that France and Britain were at war and Ireland was vulnerable to invasion. If the French landed, how would the Irish Catholic population respond – and if the Americans could win against the English, might not the Irish? The Catholic Relief Act of 1778, which repealed one of the most effective of William III's penal laws, was a clear attempt by the government in London to conciliate the Catholic community in the face of this threat. The response of the Irish Protestant community was the formation - also in 1778 - of the Irish Volunteers, a

militantly Protestant initiative that had the partial and grudging support of the Catholic gentry.

The Volunteer movement had remarkable success. Their numbers by the end of 1779 were very large and they had become a political as much as a military force, with which the government had to deal. The political opposition in England supported them because they were an embarrassment to Lord North's government. They supported the Americans while attacking the French, and had adopted the Opposition cause of dismantling the barriers to increased Irish trade with England. Their political leader was Henry Gratton (1746-1820) and freer trade with England was his first achievement. Legislative independence was now the goal of the Movement and this was achieved in 1782. This was then followed by the demand of Henry Flood - a new star in the Irish political firmament – for complete independence. By 1783 there was also a proposal – put forward by the radical Bishop of Derry - for the extension of the franchise to include the Protestant middle class and even some Catholics. Neither Gratton nor Flood nor indeed many of the delegates to the Volunteer Convention of November 1783 were keen on Catholic inclusion. As result of these dissensions, the Irish Parliament was able to ignore the Convention's resolutions on extending the Protestant franchise and the momentum disappeared. The war with America and France was over now, Free Trade and legislative independence had been achieved. There was nothing to keep the Movement together and in business. A genuinely united and independent Ireland had never been on their agenda (despite what Irish Nationalists since then would like to think).

Later Years in Ireland, from 1783
Things in Ireland were relatively quiescent after 1783 until the outbreak of the French Revolution. It then became clear that the disenfranchisement of the Catholic community could become an issue for those radicals – mainly from the Belfast Presbyterian community - who could sympathise with the Revolution. The

leading light was now the Protestant hero, Theobald Wolfe Tone (1763-1798), who in October 1791 founded the Society of United Irishmen – to include anyone of French sympathies, whatever their religious affiliation. The radicalism of Wolfe Tone and his friends did not appeal to Burke, but their openness to the Catholic cause did. As a result, Burke stood quietly behind them and he used all the influence he had with Pitt to bring about the Catholic Relief Act of 1793 – which removed almost all the remaining Catholic disabilities. However, the recall of Lord Fitzwilliam in March 1794 for having been prepared to admit Catholics to Parliament was a major setback. Irish society was becoming deeply divided, with Jacobin influences increasing against a background of government repression, supported by what was now being known as the Protestant Ascendancy. The 1798 Rising and its tragic aftermath was becoming inevitable.

Conclusion

It's very easy for the Dean to be overshadowed by his sons and for him and his wife simply to be seen as the parents of a talented brood. However, after 1772 – and especially after 1776 – he had his own position and in the early days of his time in Ireland he was young enough to be active and involved.

I don't know what the Dean did during his time in Ireland. One assumes that his sympathies would have been with Burke and that he would have been quietly looking to find ways of breaking the Protestant ascendancy and of bringing the Catholic gentry into government. It was early days then and Catholics were not as active in politics as they were to be in the 1790's. However, the need for a greater degree of Catholic emancipation in Ireland was something of which both Pitt and (especially) Grenville were convinced, if only the King and the Irish Protestant community could be persuaded to grant it. The 1800 Act of Union – which was meant to go side by side with Catholic emancipation - was part of Pitt's attempt to bring peace to Ireland. If the Protestant community could not be persuaded to bring the Catholic community into Government, perhaps it could be done from London. The plan foundered on the King's refusal to countenance emancipation. For Pitt and Grenville this was a resignation issue. Grenville resigned again in 1807 for the same reason. Walker King himself was one of the few bishops (the only one?) to vote consistently for Catholic emancipation.

CHAPTER SEVEN

DR THOMAS KING, RECTOR OF BLADON (1748-1801)
From the age of 26 his life was tied up with that of the Duke and Duchess of Marlborough at Blenheim. A quiet, rural idyll that seems to have suited him.

In January 1764 the eldest son Thomas, known as Joe, went up to Christ Church, Oxford where he graduated in 1768[43]. Then, by May 1769, he was established as tutor to the young son of Edmund Burke. Burke was just beginning to establish himself as a landed gentleman and as a force in Westminster politics. A tutor like Joe would have gone with his new status. From Joe's point of view, it was usual for a young graduate to spend some time in a great house or accompany a young gentleman abroad. All young men needed patrons and this opening gave Joe the opportunity of making some useful contacts. Joe was a friend and Oxford contemporary of Charles O'Hara[44], whose father was one of Burke's closest Irish friends, and this may have been where the contact came from. It was the beginning of a lifelong friendship that encompassed both families.

In 1774, when young Richard Burke began his studies at Oxford, Burke arranged for Joe to transfer to Blenheim, as tutor to the Duke

---

[43] Matric Christ Church - 19 1 1764. BA 1768. MA 1772. BD 1783. DD 1785

[44] Charles O'Hara (1746-1822), elder son of Charles O'Hara of Annaghmore, co Sligo and of Lady Mary Carmichael (d 1759), daughter of 2nd Earl of Hyndford and sister of Dr William Carmichael, Bishop of Clonfert (1753-8), Ferns (1758), Meath w Clonmacnoise (1758-65) and Archbishop of Dublin (1765-6). Charles junr was at Christ Church from 1763 and then studied for the bar in London. Called to the bar in Dublin ca 1772. M P for co. Sligo. In 1780, he married Margaret, daughter of Dr John Cookson of Wakefield. Mrs Cookson was Dean King's sister. They had four children - Mary, Jane, Charles and Charlotte. Charles King O'Hara (1785-1860) of Annaghmore died unmarried, and left his property to his sister Jane's younger son, Charles William Cooper, on condition that he took the name of O'Hara. Charles O'Hara's younger brother William was a Captain in the Navy and died unmarried in 1792. See also R J S Hoffman *"Edmund Burke, New York agent, with the letters to Charles O'Hara, 1761-1776"* American Philosophical Society 1956, and in *"The Great Melody"* by Conor Cruise O'Brien

of Marlborough's heir[45]. He was, according to Burke, on £200 a year, with his own post-chaise, a servant and all found. Blenheim was then under the careful stewardship of the 35-year old 4th Duke, who was the first of his family to really live in the place. He had been an early friend to King George III but was increasingly reluctant to be involved in the great world. In 1774 Capability Brown had just completed his transformation of the grounds at Blenheim. Brown was at the height of his fame, and many people came to admire the great lake, the island and the tree plantings. The Duke also had other properties - Marlborough House in London[46], Syon Hill House in Brentford, Marlborough House in Brighton and Langley Park in Buckinghamshire[47] - so Joe's life was not confined to Blenheim alone. Reynolds painted the magnificent portrait of the Duke and his family in 1778, and so one gets a good idea of the people with whom Joe was living. They were a fine looking bunch. There are however differing accounts of what life was like. Some said that the Duchess was cold and difficult, and some that life was very boring. Archdeacon Coxe[48] has left a jaundiced account of his stay at Blenheim in 1773-5, but the young children presumably made life fairly lively and they were certainly enthusiastic about their amateur theatricals. Theatricals were the great rage of the 1780's.

Burke had in mind for Joe the career of one of the Duke's former tutors - John Moore, recently appointed Bishop of Bangor, and later Archbishop of Canterbury. He thought that the same way might

---

[45] George, Marquess of Blandford, later 5th Duke of Marlborough (1766-1840), married 1791 Lady Susan Stewart, had five surviving children and settled at Whiteknights, near Reading in 1798. Here he created a beautiful garden, but he was spendthrift and disreputable. His marriage failed and he and the Duchess lived apart from 1819. Mary Soames wrote a biography, *The Profligate Duke* (1987).
[46] Old Duchess Sarah's town house.
[47] The house that had been the 4th Duke's parents' home and where he had been brought up.
[48] Rev William Coxe (1747-1828), subsequently with Lady Pembroke at Wilton (Lady Pembroke was the Duke's sister). A noted historian, and later Archdeacon.

open up for Joe. In the event it didn't. Joe liked the Duke and Duchess and the Duke and Duchess liked Joe. In January, 1778 he was appointed to the family's parish of Bladon with Woodstock. He spent the rest of his life there, though in May, 1785 the Marlborough influence added two Oxfordshire benefices - Great Hampden & Great Kimble[49]. In August 1795, by the gift of Archbishop Moore, Joe became Chancellor of Lincoln Cathedral. I believe that the Strawberry Gothic rectory that was built for him at Bladon is still there. The Duke and Duchess were well known for their retired style of living, going rarely to London. Joe's quiet life with them was a bit of a joke in the family.

There is a memorial to the old Dean in Woodstock church[50]. Joe's own memorial in Woodstock church speaks of him as "a pious and faithful pastor, of primitive simplicity of character, and exemplary innocence of life". He married Mary Manby (whose brother taught at Eton) and they had three surviving daughters, all of whom seemed to have died unmarried or at least childless. A Miss King was in the Warwickshire area in the 1840's, and in 1844 was one of Bolton King's party at the first Warwickshire Yeomanry Ball.   This may have been one of Joe's daughters and it may have been from her that Bolton King inherited the portraits of the Dean and his wife and of Capt. James King.

---

[49] These parishes were actually in the gift of Lord Hampden
[50] The dean and his wife retired to live with Joe and his family at Bladon. As eldest son, Joe was the chief beneficiary of his will.

CHAPTER EIGHT

CAPT JAMES KING (1750-84)

The sailor whose early death robbed the family of a future Admiral.
Hero of the South
Seas expedition of 1776-80.

The first of the children to leave home was the second son James. He had attended the Clitheroe Royal Grammar School, but left early. In 1762 he joined the navy under the patronage of his father's cousin, Capt William Norton. The navy was the thing of the moment. Britain's wealth had been steadily increasing over the previous hundred years thanks to the increase in trade, and from the 1750's the country was enjoying something of a boom. Shipping was central to this increasing wealth and shipping did not just mean London. Since the beginning of the century, the western ports had been growing at the expense of London. Bristol, Whitehaven and Liverpool were expanding rapidly, and Liverpool especially was central to the economy of the Lancashire towns. But there was stiff competition for the world's trade, and many believed that the navy was the key to Britain's continued place in the sun. William Pitt was the most bellicose of the politicians. He declared, "Our trade depends upon a proper exertion of our maritime strength: that trade and maritime strength depend on each other.. that riches, which are the true resources of the country, depend upon commerce".

And for Pitt, the chief weapon of war was the navy and the chief threat was France. In America France was determined to pen the British in along the Atlantic seaboard by linking her colony at Quebec with her Louisiana territory, and mounted an attack on British settlers in Ohio. In Europe she took a first step in excluding Britain from the Mediterranean by taking Minorca. Thus began the Seven Years War, the most expensive of the century - but for Britain the most momentous.

It was an exciting time. British fortunes steadily improved. Horace Walpole spoke of 1759 as an "annus mirabilis", when "our bells are worn threadbare with ringing for victories"[51]. Pitt resigned from the ministry in October 1761, in protest against the refusal of his colleagues to declare war on Spain. However, war with Spain was inevitable and Pitt's policy went on without him - at least for a while.

War and Peace, 1762-1772

On 19 November 1762, James appeared on the muster role of *Assistance* as a midshipman, under his father's cousin, Capt William Norton. However, the following day Capt. Norton gave up his command and a few weeks later James' status changed from midshipman to able seaman. The most likely explanation is that James presented himself for duty and so qualified for the muster roll, but there was no expectation that he would sail on *Assistance*. By qualifying for the muster roll, he was able to date his service from November 1762 when seeking promotion to lieutenant, for which a minimum of six year's service was required. He would most likely have been 'demoted' to able seaman (a legal fiction) because the succeeding captain would have his own candidates for the limited number of openings for midshipmen. In all likelihood, from November 1762 to the end of the following year, James was probably safely on land under Capt Norton's care. He next appears in December 1763 on the muster roll of the *William and Mary* – a royal yacht, to which Capt Norton would have been honoured to be appointed. It was a grand ship to serve on, but it would have spent most of its time at anchor in the Thames. Again, James would have been ashore much of the time.

His first real service was in March 1766 when he appears on the muster roll of the *Gibraltar* under Capt. Richard Braithwaite[52]. He

---

[51] quoted in John Ehrman *"The Younger Pitt: The Years of Acclaim"* 1969 p 3
[52] Capt Richard Braithwaite (1725-1805), from a Newcastle family, had entered the navy under the patronage of his uncle, Adm. Sir Challoner Ogle. He was the

was involved in a routine peacetime mission, policing the waters around the valuable Newfoundland fisheries. *Gibraltar* returned to England in January 1767 and two months later, at the request of Capt. Norton, he was transferred from the Gibraltar to Capt. Braithwaite's new ship, *Liverpool*. It was a repeat performance of his tour on *Gibraltar*. He was back in England and paid off in March 1768. Later the same month, he was taken on the muster roll of *Guernsey* under Capt. Chads. They were again in Newfoundland but *Guernsey* was back by the end of the year. It was during this tour that he met William Young, a fellow midshipman, who was to be with him when he died. James then transferred back to the *William and Mary* for his examination as lieutenant in March 1769 – just after he had completed his six years.

In a letter to Edmund Burke dated 8 November 1784, Thomas King wrote that James "lived as one of their children in the family of Agethorps and Trestwicks at Boston when he served on the Newfoundland station. I think he stayed behind one or two winters when the fleet returned to England..". This anecdote gives one a sense of what it might have been like to be a teenage midshipman in the 1760s. Barlow Trecothick was an influential merchant in the City of London, with close ties to Burke and the Rockingham group. He had been apprenticed to Charles Apthorp, one of the richest merchants in Boston, and had married his daughter. It may be that James had letters of introduction to the Apthorp family, through the Norton family link, which would have opened the way to the best circles in Boston. We do not need to think that James spent his teens simply toiling away on ships.

Passing his exam did not mean that James was immediately promoted lieutenant. In the summer of 1769 he joined *Antelope* under Captain George Gayton and again visited Newfoundland. Antelope was back by the end of the year and but when it returned

---

uncle of Cuthbert Collingwood (later Admiral), who joined his ship as a boy in 1761. He was possibly a relation of Capt. Norton's late sister's husband, John Braithwaite of Sharow, near Ripon.

there in March 1770 James was transferred back to *William and Mary*. Finally, on 10 January 1771, he was commissioned lieutenant on *Cambridge,* when it was brought back into service during a diplomatic stand-off with Spain. Spain backed down and four months later Cambridge was laid up again and James was on half-pay. However, in June 1771 he was appointed Lieutenant of the *Ferret* which was bound for Jamaica and Hispaniola, via Madeira. In November he was beached, but picked up another commission as 2nd Lieutenant of the *Carysfort* in June 1772 which seems to have been on anti-pirate patrol along the North American coast. In August, *Carysfort* was caught in a major storm of Florida, in which her main mast was carried away, together with four men drowned (one of which was the 1st Lieutenant). In November 1772, he was back in Port Royal, Jamaica and transferred as 4th Lieutenant in the much larger *Achilles*, with whom he returned to England.

The Great Adventure, 1772-1781

The peace that had been signed in 1763 endured and the inevitable manpower cuts finally hit James. He was put on half-pay in April 1773. However, this gave him the time and leisure to visit Paris and then to join Thomas King and young Richard Burke who were at Auxerre. On his return, he picked up the fact the peacetime preoccupation of the Royal Navy (in partnership with the Royal Society) was exploration. In 1764-6 Captain John Byron made a circumnavigation of the world, while mapping some of the Pacific islands. A further circumnavigation took place under Capt Samuel Wallace in 1766-8. Capt James Cook's first voyage was in 1768-71, with the object of observing the transit of Venus at Hawaii and to collect plants. In 1772-5 Cook was on another voyage, continuing his mapping of the Australia.

It may be that it was Sir Fletcher Norton who suggested that James study astronomy, in order to be better qualified to take part in one of these expeditions. Norton was on the Board of Longtitude, which administered the prizes being offered to anyone who could discover a method of accurately establishing a ship's position at sea.

In any case, it seems that James was at Oxford in 1773-5, attending the lectures of Dr Thomas Hornsby, Savilian professor of Astronomy[53] and it was the Board of Longtitude who recommended James to Capt James Cook[54] as a nautical and astronomical observer. Cook had just returned from a three-year voyage in which he had been trying to discover a "southern continent". There had been no southern continent to find, but Cook had come back a celebrity, was promoted captain, and elected a Fellow of the Royal Society. Now he was a ready for another expedition - to find the Northwest Passage from the Pacific end. There was much competition to get on the expedition. Cook took officers that had been with him before, but also accepted some others with particular qualifications. King was one of the latter.

James received his commission in February 1776 and the expedition set sail in July. There were two ships - *Resolution*, under Cook's command, and *Discovery*, commanded by Charles Clerke[55]. John Gore and James Burney[56] were the 1st lieutenants, and James King and John Richman were 2nd lieutenants. William Bligh[57] was Ship's

---

[53] Thomas Hornsby (1733-1810), Savilian Professor of Astronomy from 1763, in succession to James Bradley. Began the Radcliffe Observatory, and observed the transit of Venus in 1761 and 1763, from which he deduced the solar parallax. Edited Bradley's *"Astronomical Observations"*.

[54] Capt James Cook (1728-1779), was with the Baltic trading ships until 1755 when he volunteered for active service under Capt Palliser, who remained his patron. He studied mathematics and astronomical navigation, and was appointed marine surveyor of the coast of Newfoundland and Labrador in 1762. The results were published in 1766-8. In 1768-71, on Palliser's recommendation he commanded an expedition to the Pacific to observe the transit of Venus. In 1772-4 he was exploring the coast of Australia. The 1776 expedition was his last.

[55] Capt Charles Clerke (1741-1779) was with Commander John Byron on his round-the-world trip in 1764-6, and was master's mate with Cook on his first expedition in 1768-71. He was 2nd Lieutenant on the second expedition in 1772-4 – when young George Vancouver was of the company. Vancouver also served with him now.

[56] Rear Adm. James Burney (1750-1821). Entered the navy in 1764 and was with Cook on his second expedition. Saw some later service in North America, but retired in 1783. Like his sister, he was a writer and he produced his own account of the expeditions in "South Sea Discoveries".

Master on the *Resolution*[58]. They reached the Hawaiian Islands by January 1778 and then crossed to the American coast to look for a passage. In August they finally passed through the Baring Straits and into the Chukchi Sea. They were then stopped by pack ice, and Cook decided to return to the Hawaiian Islands for the winter, to try again the following year.

In February 1779, Cook was killed. Clerke took command of the expedition, with King as his first lieutenant on the *Resolution*. Clerke was already ill with tuberculosis, but was determined to have another shot at the Northwest Passage. In July, they were in the Chukchi Sea again but again pack ice drove them back. Clerke died a few weeks later. Gore then took command of the expedition and James King took over the *Discovery*. On their return in August 1780, they were celebrities. It was the late eighteenth century equivalent of having been to the moon. James was promoted post captain[59], and elected a Fellow of the Royal Society. At the end of the year, he went with Walker and his parents to Ireland, where he donated some of his Pacific artefacts to Trinity College, Dublin – for which he was granted the degree of Doctor of Letters. He returned to active

---

[57] Capt William Bligh (1754-1817), who is best known for his leadership of the next South Seas expedition. He commanded the *Bounty* in 1787-9, charged with bringing back Hawaiian breadfruit for the West Indian plantations. Then came the famous Mutiny and Bligh's heroic journey.

[58] They were not incommunicado. In November 1776 James King sent a letter to Burke from the Cape of Good Hope, commending Maj. John Cartwright to him. Cartwright had been with King on the Newfoundland Station. He retired from the navy in 1771 and had been appointed Major in the newly formed Notts. Militia the year before. With the American Declaration of Independence in July 1776 and the outbreak of war, Cartwright was on the side of the colonists. Burke - then influential in the opposition to Lord North - was known to be sympathetic and James King's friendship with Burke would have been known through his naval acquaintants. Cartwright was at the beginning of his career as a leading radical and parliamentary reformer. His views were far beyond those of Burke. He died in 1824, aged 84. Cartwright Gardens (off Euston Road) is named after him – and there is a bust of him there.

[59] Jack Aubrey was a couple of years younger when he was made post. It meant that from then on you advanced steadily to the rank of Admiral. All you had to do was survive.

service in March 1781, being given command of a frigate that was part of the Channel fleet[60]. It was not too arduous a work and Steve Ragnall quotes from letters from James Trevenen that tell of a visit to Lord Inchiquin at Rostellan House near Cork, where James King was staying[61]. During his tour of duty he managed to recapture an English ship from the French, which brought him some prize money. Then, in April 1782, he transferred to a larger frigate that left for the West Indies in November.

War, Illness & Death, 1781-1784

The peace established in 1763 did not long survive the outbreak of the War of American Independence. France declared war on Britain in 1778, to be followed by Spain in 1779 and the Netherlands in 1780. King was recalled to active service and appointed to *Crocodile*, a new ship of 24 guns, 519 tons, and with 160 men[62]. He sailed on 11 June 1781, captured a French privateer off the coast of Guernsey and generally distinguished himself. He returned early in 1782, and in March had another command. He was commanding the *Resistance*, a 44 gun frigate of 879 tons and 300 men, and conveying some merchant ships to the West Indies. It's said that he

---

[60] The account of the voyage - *"A Voyage to the Pacific Ocean"* was the best seller of 1785. It was put together by Dr John Douglas, who used Cook's diaries for the first two volumes and King's for the last one. In 2002, a London bookseller advertised a first edition for sale at £10,000. Oliver Bolton King says that James King's personal log of the South Sea voyage was sold in 1923 for £385. 1923 was a year of financial difficulty for my father, so he could have been the vendor. OBK also says that a picture of Capt. James King hangs in the Greenwich Maritime Museum – presumably a copy of the picture Edward sold to the National Library of Australia in Canberra.

[61] Murrough O'Brien (1726-1808), 5th Earl of Inchiquin had succeeded his uncle in the Irish title in 1777. In 1753, he had married his first cousin, Lady Mary O'Brien, who succeeded her mother in 1761 as Countess of Orkney and in a Buckinghamshire estate that included Cliveden and Taplow Court. This made the Inchiquins neighbours and friends of the Burkes. Lady Mary was deaf and dumb. She died in 1791 and Lord Inchiquin then married Mary Palmer, Sir Joshua Reynolds' niece and heiress.

[62] from *"Captain James King"*, a pamphlet by Reginald Rurson, in the Clitheroe Public Library. Good on the naval details

escaped a strong force of French warships by sailing through a stormy night to the safety of Jamaica. In the then state of navigation, this was quite a feat. It is said that he encountered Horatio Nelson[63] while in the West Indies.

By the autumn of 1782 the war was winding down and peace terms were being discussed in Paris. James was staying with his brother at Bladon, and with the Burkes at Beaconsfield. In October he wrote to Dr John Douglas[64], "I kissed the King's hand last Wednesday, and the Queen's on Thursday. When I meet you I shall communicate what passed".

The peace treaty was finally signed in 1783 but James was not to enjoy it long. He had contracted tuberculosis. He was nursed by Jane Burke at Beaconsfield, but died late in 1784 in Nice, where he had gone in an attempt to regain his health. Burke wrote of him, "In truth James King was made and singularly formed to inspire confidence and attachment. His temper was admirable. He reconciled himself to people wherever he went". William Bligh, who was Ship's Master under James King on his South Sea voyage, had another view. Arthur Barker, in his life of Bligh says, "For Bligh King was an intellectual, too clever by half... He was polite, urbane, a smooth young gentleman, but he became Bligh's bête noire on the voyage. To Bligh, King was a mealy-mouthed weakling, with a flair for ducking out of dirty or dangerous jobs". But Bligh had a large chip on his shoulder.

James King was from the great generation of naval heroes. Rodney, Cook, Jervis, Hood were legends of British greatness. They were part of an outward push from Britain dating back to the second half of the 17th century which succeeded in wresting the leadership in world trade from France and the Netherlands. The sad thing was that the trade through which Europe was growing rich - the trade

---

[63] Baines gives details of some of his feats of navigation while serving in the West Indies in his *History of the County Palatine of Lancashire*
[64] Dr John Douglas, Bishop of Salisbury 1791-1807

by which Britain was growing rich - was based on the slave trade. The naval encounters in the West Indies were in defence of the slave plantations and to gain more benefits for the plantation owners. There is a deep moral ambiguity at the heart of this "great" period and about the activities of this hero of the family.

James King's portrait, done by Webber - the ship's artist in 1776-80 - was sold by Edward in 1968 to the National Library of Australia in Canberra. In 1939, a memorial to James was unveiled in Clitheroe Grammar School by Edward Bolton King, then a Fellow (Student) of Christ Church, Oxford. More recently a plaque was put up on the site of the old vicarage in Clitheroe. King Lane and King Street in Clitheroe are, according to one of King's biographers, named after the family.

The search for the North West Passage – that would connect the Atlantic and Pacific Oceans – continued after the end of the war. Capt George Vancouver – a veteran of Cook's last two expeditions – surveyed the north western coastline in great detail during 1791-5. He decided that there was no north-west passage, but his detailed maps of this coastland opened it up the settlers and traders. There were tensions with the Spanish – who claimed exclusive rights – but these were eventually settled. The American-Canadian frontier wasn't agreed until the 1840s.

During his surveying, Vancouver was exploring a channel north of what is now Vancouver Island. He called the channel 'Burke Channel' and the island north of it 'King Island'. As the channel continued east of King Island it became 'Dean Channel' and then 'Dean River'. Along the way there was also Edmund Point, Raphoe Point, and Port John, Walker Point and Edward Point after the King brothers. The namings are catalogued in his published journals[65]. An island in the Behring Sea, close to the Alaska coast, was also named after James King.

---

[65] Hakluyt's edition of Vancouver's Journals, edited by W. Kaye Lamb, Vol. 3, pp. 924-9.

1f.

CHAPTER NINE

DR WALKER KING (1751-1827)
BISHOP OF ROCHESTER

*The Whig politician, who looked back to his family's Parliamentary allegiance during the Civil War
and - with his patron and mentor Edmund Burke - was a lifelong warrior against the influence of the Crown.*

Walker went up to Brasenose College from Sedbergh School in February 1768, but soon changed to Corpus Christi College[66]. Joe King was with the Burkes, and Edmund Burke seems early on to have interested himself in the career of the younger brother. On his graduation in 1771 Burke was thinking of Walker as a tutor for Charles Lennox, the Duke of Richmond's heir. Nothing came of it and Walker stayed on in Oxford. However, in April 1774 Walker did accept an invitation to go to Goodwood to read with the Duke[67]. He arrived in June, and found he was spending most of his time

---

[66] Corpus Christi was then under Dr Thomas Randolph (1701-1783), who had been elected master in 1748. His patron had been the moderate High Churchman, Dr John Potter, who was at Oxford as Fellow of Lincoln, Regius Professor of Divinity and Bishop until 1737, when he became Archbishop of Canterbury. In 1744 Randolph published, "The Christian's faith a Rational Assent". From 1768 he was also Lady Margaret Professor of Divinity. He is said to have "possessed a mildness of temper that made him generally beloved by his young students". "Randolph, by his large connections, both lay and ecclesiastical had probably contributed to bring to the college a much more desirable type of young man than that which had most frequented it during recent years". There is a bust of Bishop Walker by Chantry in the Common Room at Corpus. The Bishop sent his own sons to Oriel, probably because Dr Eveleigh, the master, was a canon of Rochester. However, his nephew, Bolton King, went to Corpus in 1819.
[67] Burke had written to his father, who had suggested some headings for his son's reply to this invitation. He told Walker (31 March 1774 - letter in the De Morgan Library) that Burke thought he might go for it for a short while, but said he needed to look as though he wanted it. "I spoke of your attributes which at your time of life were very great, but said that a scholastic idleness and sensibility made you hide your Talent in Company, and he spoke of the great difficulty of "showing one's parts without assurance". "I would not have the name of Duke carry you away in any shape, in altering your manners, etc"

with the Duke's heir, Mr Lennox. Things didn't run altogether smoothly - the Duke had fixed ideas on how his nephew's education should go. Though offered the job on a permanent basis, Walker didn't stay after the summer.

The Annual Register, 1774-1782

Soon after this he seems to have got involved in Burke's project, The Annual Register[68]. Burke had started this in 1758 as a general review of contemporary politics and literature. Its principle feature was a long article reviewing events in British and Europe during the previous year. It counted as journalism - not considered a proper occupation for a gentleman - so Burke never mentioned his involvement in it, and nor did Walker King. It is however probable that for ten to fifteen years after 1775 the main article was written by Walker and that this was one of the main focuses of his work during that time. He had become in effect a political columnist and, as Burke's right man, a central part of the Rockingham movement in politics.

Walker came in to The Register at the moment that the Rockingham opposition was again taking up the cause of the American colonies. In 1767 Charles Townshend had introduced new duties on America imports which, in December 1773, led to the Boston Tea Party. Lord North's government were tough in their response and when Walker was writing up the events of 1774-5 for the 1775 edition of the register[69] he made much of the opposition's attempts to bring about reconciliation. The 1776 and 1777 editions were devoted to American affairs to the exclusion of almost everything else. The 1777 edition was the twentieth since The Register's foundation and, Walker remarked, a celebration might have been possible "if the awful aspect of the times had not forbidden every emotion bordering on levity". Perhaps this was written after December 1777 when the news of the defeat of General Burgoyne at Saratoga

---

[68] See Thomas W Copeland *Edmund Burke - Six Essays* (1950), Chapter Three - A Career in Journalism
[69] which confusingly didn't come out until 1776!

reached London. Until then, Burke and the Rockinghams had led a lonely opposition to the war that was going well for the British, aided only by occasional dramatic speeches by the ailing Lord Chatham. Now the tide seemed to be turning. In February 1778 the Commons debated Lord North's Conciliatory Propositions and it was really only George III who kept the war going.

George III was lucky. The gloomy mood didn't last. After Saratoga - and despite the intervention of France - the war continued to go well for the British[70]. Lord North would like to have strengthened his government by the accession of the Rockinghams, but the King was able to insist on a general commitment to pursue the American war until the colonists were defeated. The capture of Charleston in June 1780 served to reinforce his determination. It's therefore interesting that the 1779 edition of The Register has gone quiet on America and that the 1780 edition is concerned with something quite else - the abolition of sinecures.

The power of the crown under George III had depended on the King's ability to bribe Members of Parliament with sinecures. Patronage which under George II had been mainly in the hands of ministers, was under George exercised by the King himself. It made it easy for George to get rid of governments of which he had grown tired - in 1765 and (especially) in 1766. The Rockinghams were determined that when they returned to the office they would make sure the King's wings were clipped. Hence Burke's plan for "Economical Reform" which he introduced in the Commons in February 1780, and which featured largely in The Register. Had it passed, the King would have lost about sixty placemen. Burke lost - but narrowly. The following month, John Dunning moved his famous resolution that "the influence of the Crown has increased, is

---

[70] The Franco-American Treaty of March 1778 had left Ireland vulnerable and resulted in the repeal in 1778 of some of the disabilities suffered by the Catholic population there - noted with approbation by the Register. There was a real threat of a French invasion of England in the summer of 1779 which had however receded by January 1781 when the 1779 edition of The Register came out.

increasing and ought to be diminished". Lord North wanted to give up, but George III refused him and he was saved - for the moment - by the Gordon Riots and the news of Charleston.

North was still working for a coalition and George III would have been happy to have Burke onside. However, the American War still stood in the way. George III was determined on victory; the Rockinghams were determined that the Americans should be given their independence. In February 1781 Burke brought in another Bill to reduce sinecures - duly reported in the Register - but this failed, as did a motion to make peace in America. Then, in November 1781 came the news of the defeat of Lord Cornwallis at Yorktown. The King was still hot to continue the war, but the public mood was gathering against Lord North's administration. In March 1782 Lord North insisted on going, and George III pondered abdication. In the event, the King didn't abdicate. He accepted Lord Rockingham - with bad grace - even on the condition that he gave up his veto on the independence of America. All this was carefully reported in the Register for 1781 and 1782.

Other Activities

Walker kept up his links with Oxford. In Burke's *Correspondence* it is said that he obtained a Fellowship at his college after graduation, but elsewhere it is said he didn't obtain it until 1778. Had he obtained it in 1771, his ordination at Raphoe in 1781 would be more easily explained[71]. A Fellow had to be ordained within ten years of obtaining his Fellowship.

In July 1779 Walker was back at Goodwood. Burke was nursing Richmond. He needed his support in his struggle on behalf of the American colonies. Richmond had influence in the party and in the Irish parliament. Burke wanted him onside, especially as Rockingham himself was lukewarm on much of what Burke cared about. Burke wanted someone at Goodwood who could keep Richmond on side, while trying to calm his more extreme ideas and

---

[71] He was ordained deacon on 7 January and priest on 21 October 1771.

Walker was that person. This time round Walker was more of a success with the family than he had been in 1774. He even joined the Sussex militia alongside his noble charge. Lady Sarah wrote that Mr King was "trying to be as military as possible and looking very well in his red coat". Richmond was an odd chap, a real drawing room radical. Walker reported to Burke a conversation he had had with the duke in October 1779 when Richmond trotted out the full radical agenda of manhood suffrage, annual parliaments and new constituencies as the basis for an Opposition agenda - stuff to send Rockingham into a spin should he hear about it.

At the end of 1780 Walker had left Goodwood to join his father in Londonderry. His service as his father's curate was however short-lived. In March 1782, the Rockinghams were finally back in power. Walker was brought back from Ireland to take up the post that Burke had himself held before - the job of private secretary to Lord Rockingham. The sky was now the only limit to his ambitions. He had constant access to the Prime Minister and he was the friend and protégé of the most influential member of the government after Rockingham himself.

The Administrations of 1782 & 1783

One of the first acts of the new administration was to grant legislative independence to the Irish parliament. Burke had no love for this Protestant-dominated assembly, but acquiesced. He did not acquiesce in the plans to extend the franchise to property owners of both denominations – no doubt because the Protestant middle classes would be the main beneficiaries and their demands were for a completely independent Protestant Ireland.

Apart from that, there was little time to do anything much. The King was implacably hostile. He wanted the Rockinghams out as soon as possible, and worked unceasingly with Lord Shelburne to bring this about. His chance came in July 1782 when the ailing Rockingham died. The King immediately appointed Lord Shelburne to head the administration. This meant that Fox and Burke resigned. Both of them now plotted Shelburne's downfall. They achieved this in March 1783 in what was considered an extraordinary alliance with their old enemy, Lord North. The succeeding Fox-North coalition was in fact the Fox-North-Burke coalition and continued the influence of the Rockinghams a bit longer. The King however was not defeated. Despite a large parliamentary majority behind the Coalition, he managed to dismiss it in December and persuaded William Pitt to head up a minority administration in the King's interest.

The immediate cause of the fall of the Coalition was the India Bill - Burke's composition and crusade. From the mid-70's Burke had been troubled by the corrupt administration in Bengal and from January 1781 he had been a leading light in the Select Committee that had been set up to investigate the situation there. When he came to power, stricter parliamentary control of the East India Company's activities in India was his chief priority. The Bill that was intended to bring this about was introduced into the Commons in November 1783 and passed comfortably. The King however would have none of it. Parliamentary control in India was not what he wanted. He preferred the status quo to any increase in Parliament's power. The Lords were told that anyone voting for the Bill would be regarded as an enemy to the King. Inevitably the Bill was defeated in the Lords and the King was able to dismiss his ministers. Pitt grimly but skilfully held on until the following March, by which time he could risk a dissolution and was able to establish a majority at the elections. It was an extraordinary achievement for such a young man, and a triumph for the King. But neither was forgiven by the Rockingham Whigs - or the Foxite Whigs, as they were becoming now. For the King to dismiss an administration that had a large majority in the Commons was held (understandably) to be unconstitutional. For Pitt to agree - at the King's request - to head up an administration that did not have parliamentary support, and then to use the influence of the Crown to achieve a parliamentary majority was unacceptable. Fox never forgot the outrage of 1783-4. Walker King grew into political maturity when the translation into England of a continental-style despotism was considered a real possibility. Throughout his life, the undue influence of the Crown in political life was his main concern. The memory of the 17th century Good Old Cause, in which his family had been involved, was close to his heart.

The Impeachment of Warren Hastings

The loss of office did not prevent Burke persevering with the Indian cause. He now had Warren Hastings in his sights and throughout 1784-6 struggled manfully - and finally successfully - to unite the opposition behind him in a demand for Hastings' impeachment. Remarkably, by June 1786 even Pitt himself was prepared to make impeachment no longer a party issue. In December 1787 the Commons passed the motion that "Warren Hastings Esq. be impeached of High Crimes and Misdemeanours". When Burke opened the case in February 1788 he occupied, according to Conor Cruise O'Brien "a more central position within the British political order than he had ever before occupied, or ever would again". It was a vital year and an exhausting one - for Walker as well as for Burke. Walker was his chief support - collecting information, drafting speeches, organising witnesses. People were soon bored, and by the beginning of 1789 Burke's persistence in his struggle for the people of India was becoming an embarrassment to his friends. Yet it was a great campaign on behalf of an abused people, and the hearts of both men were in it - and would remain in it for the rest of their lives.

Burke's Last Years, 1790-7

The struggle for India ended the close friendship and alliance between Fox and Burke, even before the dawn of the French Revolution. Then, with Burke's declaration against the French Revolution in January 1790, his membership of the parliamentary opposition and his long campaign against the encroachment of royal power was effectively over. In November 1790 he published his "Reflections on the Revolution in France", and the following spring was working with Walker on "An Appeal from the Old to the

New Whigs". These were major works that marked the end of Burke's part in the official opposition. He was now in effect in alliance with Pitt, though his friends did not actually join the government until July 1794. This alliance with the man who had been the King's means of getting rid of the Coalition in 1783 was a strange turn of events, but it made sense in the conditions of the day. It seemed to promise an Indian summer of Burke's influence in government. Burke's greatest triumph was to gain the vice-royalty of Ireland for his closest disciple, Lord Fitzwilliam, and Lord Fitzwilliam's arrival in Ireland in January 1795 promised new hope in Irish affairs – even of Catholics gaining the vote. These hopes were not realised. There was no question in Pitt's mind of Catholics being admitted to government. In March 1795 Fitzwilliam was recalled and the 1798 Rebellion became inevitable. However, the Coalition survived, thanks at least partly because of Burke's continuing commitment to it, and Pitt was grateful - as far as he had it in him to be.

Burke was now getting old and he was concerned for his faithful right hand man who now, with French Laurence, was working on his master's Collected Works. The first three volumes came out in May 1792. As long ago as 1769 when talking of Joe, Burke had worried that his extended period of opposition meant that he was not in a position to help his friends. That was all the more true now. With only two brief spells in power – in 1765-6 and 1782-3 - Burke's chief protégé was now in his early forties with very little to show for twenty years of devoted service. In November 1783, while the administration was still in power, Archbishop Markham had given Walker the benefice of Easington in Yorkshire, but nothing else appeared for some while. In 1787 he accepted the post of Preacher at Gray's Inn. In September 1792 Sir Joshua Reynolds' heiress, Miss Palmer, married Lord Inchiquin. Walker had been spoken of as a possible suitor and had clearly been thinking of marriage, but marriage would mean the end of his fellowship and could therefore only be afforded if his wife had money or if he received some preferment. Sarah Dawson, who does seem to have had some money of her own, became his wife in the year of Miss Palmer's marriage - and gradually more was to come. The Coalition had changed things. Thanks perhaps to the direct intervention of Pitt and the King during an episcopal vacancy, Walker received a prebendal stall at Peterborough. Had Lord Fitzwilliam stayed in Ireland, Walker would have been sure of an Irish bishopric. Burke had paved the way with a reference to "our excellent Dr King who, having been several times in Ireland with his father the Dean of Raphoe, has very just notions concerning that country".

Neither his marriage nor his prebendal stall meant that Walker was any less at Burke's side. He was the chief moving force in Burke's campaign to help the French émigrés, and had raised £20,000 for them by January 1793. He was a close support when young Richard Burke died in August 1794 - the greatest and final blow in Burke's life. He worked hard to get Burke a government pension - which was granted soon after Richard's death - and he was subsequently the chief architect of the campaign to get Burke's debts cleared (Walker estimated them at £30,000 in August 1795). After Burke's death in July 1797, Walker was one of his literary executors and began the work of gathering all relevant papers and letters together at Lord Fitzwilliam's house (whence they were later transferred to the Library of Sheffield University). The Collected Works came out slowly. Volume 6 was published in 1813; Volume 7 in 1821; Volume 8 in 1827. At least the task was completed by Walker's death, although it was many years before a definitive edition was possible[72].

After Burke, 1797-1809

---

[72] Burke's inkstand, cane and despatch box - together with a bust of the great man - descended through Walker's daughter, Mrs John King of Cutcombe Rectory, to his great-grandson, Walker King of Barley House, Exeter. Oliver Bolton King says that this Walker King left them to his son and grandson, and - failing their issue - to his father, Bolton King. A considerable collection of the Bishop's letters was also at Cutcombe, which have been coming onto the market in recent years.

Walker became Burke's literary executor, editor of his Collected Works, and was generally guardian of the flame. In his introduction to Volume 7 of the Collected Works, he wrote that "the principles of Whiggism had been more philosophically developed, and more accurately defined, more systematically arranged, and applied with more profound wisdom and practical object, by him than by any other person..."

He continued to gather benefices and positions after the pattern of the day. A good patron was Bishop Moss of Bath & Wells whose daughter was married to his brother John. In 1794 Walker was presented by Bishop Moss to a prebendal stall at the Cathedral and five years later to the benefices of Burnham and Aller in Somerset[73]. There is a memorial to Walker in the cloisters of Wells Cathedral, which suggests that Wells and that diocese was a real home and that it remained important to him. In 1803 he got a third stall - at Canterbury - which must have made his existence rather peripatetic if he was to fulfil the requirements of residence. Then, in 1806, with the death of Pitt, Lord Fitzwilliam returned to government. Walker wrote to him, to remind him of the hopes he had had of preferment in earlier years. He was one of many. The Foxites had been in opposition since 1783 and were desperate. The Grevillites had been out since 1801. Nonetheless, Lord Fitzwilliam took his obligations seriously. Though the ministry was dismissed in March 1807, Fitzwilliam wrote in July of that year to his old adversary, the Duke of Portland, to press Walker's claims. Fitzwilliam and Portland had been barely on speaking terms since the debacle of 1795, but what they shared was a reverence for the memory of Edmund Burke. Both of them would have wanted to honour Burke through Walker. When Bishop Dampier was translated to Ely in 1809, it was the Duke of Portland who gave Walker the bishopric of Rochester. It was an interesting testimony to the way that Burke was owned by a broad spectrum of political opinion in England then - and since.

---

[73] Oliver Bolton King says that it was at this time that he moved from Marylebone to Somerset and made his home there.

Bishop of Rochester, from 1809

Rochester was a poor diocese, which was traditionally held with the Deanery of Westminster in order to provide a decent income. Walker did not get Westminster, though he held on to some of his benefices and to his prebendal stalls. What is clear that Walker was a lonely voice on the episcopal bench. He remained a Burkeian or Rockingham Whig at a time when very few of the Bishops had any sympathy at all for a liberal voice. Lord Liverpool's administration endured, and Walker clearly remained close to Lord Fitzwilliam in opposition. With the end of the war the opposition ranks were split over the reaction to the public unrest. Lord Grenville supported Sidmouth's repressive measures. Lord Grey objected, supported by Fitzwilliam and also (surely) by Walker King. The times were changing. Catholic emancipation in Ireland seemed to be finally on the horizon, and parliamentary reform was the other chief concern of the new generation. In some of the early votes, Walker was to be found in the liberal Whig camp. In his person he linked the liberal Whiggery of Burke's early career with the liberal Whiggery of the Reform period.

It would be a pity if we only remembered Walker's episcopacy for the way in which he provided for his family in the last years of his life. His son-in-law was given a parish in the diocese, which was followed up with a prebendal stall at Wells. He presented his eldest son to the rectory of Stone on his ordination in 1822, and also gave him Frindsbury – mainly to keep it warm for his younger brother. When James was ordained in 1825, he had Stone (and later Henley-on-Thames as well), so Frindsbury went to a cousin. The Bishop went blind in his last years and his elder son was a much needed right hand man. When the Bishop was close to death, the Archdeacon of Rochester died. He had been archdeacon for sixty years and had been ineffective for a long time. The Bishop made a deathbed request for his son to be appointed archdeacon – which he duly was. Very few emoluments were attached to the post. Archdeacon Law's income had derived mainly from the prebendal stall he had held with the archdeaconry. However, during the episcopal vacancy, the stall was given to someone else. Archdeacon King had to go to law to establish his right and to eject his rival.

The only casualty of the bishop's death seems to have been his younger daughter, Sarah. A few weeks after his death, she married her cousin John King. Fat livings were now no longer available and John and Sarah struggled through several curacies before getting a couple of remote and run down parishes in Somerset. Here they lived for over 50 years – a blameless and reflective couple – but far less well provided for than their relations. Walker's widow retired to Burnham-in-Sea, where she died in 1852.

It had been a period when patronage was normal, and it opened links that continued in the Rochester diocese into the next century. Archdeacon King's influence secured for his eldest son the rectory of Leigh-on-Sea (then in the Rochester diocese), and that benefice descended to his son who died in office (a canon of Chelmsford cathedral) in 1950.

CHAPTER TEN

EDWARD KING 1755-1824

The least remembered of the brothers. He became a lawyer and ended up as a Chancery judge, the senior legal officer in the courts of equity in the county of Lancaster.

Edward - otherwise Ned - was the fourth of the Dean's sons and the only one who remained close to his northern roots. He is the only one who sounds northern, and who died close to the increasing energy of northern industry. He was about sixteen years old when the family left Clitheroe, thanks to the patronage of his father's cousin, Sir Fletcher Norton, a former Attorney General and now the Speaker of the House of Commons. His father was appointed the Speaker's Chaplain in 1771 and the following year Norton presented him to the living of Holy Trinity, Guildford, near his own home at Wonersh Park. In 1774 this living was exchanged for that of Dunsfold, with a canonry at Windsor. Two years later Windsor and Dunsfold were exchanged for the Deanery of Raphoe, in Ireland. Sir Fletcher Norton was a very important person and James King was the recipient of his cousin's bounty.

London & Westminster Politics, 1774-1780

In 1774, when the family was moving from Guildford to Windsor, Edward entered Gray's Inn. It would be very interesting to know to whom he was articled, but clearly a relative of Sir Fletcher's would have been a favoured pupil. He had every opportunity to follow the political scene. Visits to the Houses of Parliament were considered an integral part of a young lawyer's training. They were expected to listen to the speeches and in this way hone their own budding oratorical skills. For Edward, there would have been real reasons for listening. His patron, Sir Fletcher Norton, presided over the proceedings in the Commons. His brothers' patron, Edmund Burke, was a key member of the Opposition there.

During the 1770s, Parliament was preoccupied with the American colonies. The Boston Tea Party, in December 1773, had signalled a new phase in the deteriorating relationship between the colonists and the mother country. Burke did all that he could to bring about an accommodation and in this he had the support of the ailing Chatham[74]. Throughout 1775 he was arguing for a series of measures that might have enabled the colonists to maintain a link with England, but his arguments were not well received. George III was determined to hold America within the Empire by force – and the country was behind him. Most people liked to think that the Empire was top dog and unbeatable. Initial British successes reinforced these prejudices. However, in January 1777, Washington crossed the Delaware and the fortune of war changed. In November came the news of the defeat of General Burgoyne at Saratoga. In the following March the French made an alliance with the colonists – to be closely followed by Spain.

The concern was now not only for the security of mainland Britain, but for Ireland as well. The government believed that an invasion of Ireland might result in a Catholic rising. In the summer of 1778 they lifted some of the most objectionable of the penal laws against Catholics. However, the main threat was coming from the Protestant Irish nationalists who were providing for their own safety through 'the Volunteers' – a huge military force that soon developed its own agenda. Under the leadership of Henry Grattan – and clearly influenced by the American experience - they were looking for free trade with the mother country and legislative independence. The government was struggling against France, Spain, America - and now Ireland. By the summer of 1779 a French invasion of the English mainland was a real possibility. After the glories of Chatham's wars, it wasn't a very cheerful time.

---

[74] Chatham's last years were spent arguing strenuously for an accommodation. This architect of empire couldn't stand by and see a third of the Empire lost. His last and most dramatic intervention was in April 1778 when he collapsed in the Lords while pleading for continued attempts at conciliation - against the Rockingham party's motion for withdrawal.

The Gordon Riots

And then – from 2-11 June 1780 – came the Gordon Riots. The British government had long been suspected of Catholic sympathies. The Quebec Act of 1774, which had granted freedom of worship to the Catholic Church in Quebec, had not been popular in the American colonies. No popery was an early cry of the supporters of the American Rebellion – though swiftly crushed by Washington. Then the Catholic Relief Act made it possible for Catholics to serve in the British armed forces, and some people feared that a Catholic soldiery would align itself with France to suppress this country's freedoms. Early in 1780, the Protestant Association was formed under the leadership of Lord George Gordon. On 2 July, Gordon led a great procession to the Houses of Parliament to demand the repeal of the legislation. Things got out of control. Newgate prison was set ablaze – held to be a symbol of the oppressive state[75]. Slogans about liberty and equality were shouted round. Houses were plundered and burned. The chaos of those days, when the mob seemed to rule in London, gave Burke a horror of demagogy and seems to have gone far in shaping his response to the French Revolution.

Sir Fletcher's eclipse

Sir Fletcher had supported Lord North's government at its formation in 1770, but like many people he was getting disillusioned with the war. There was then no expectation that the Speaker should be politically neutral and by the mid-1770's Norton was not. In 1777, in a debate to increase the civil list, he came out with his famous remark that parliament has 'not only granted to your majesty a large present supply, but also a great additional revenue; great beyond example; great beyond your majesty's highest expense'. The King didn't forgive him for that. By the general election of 1780 Norton was definitely associated with the opposition to the war and to the King. At the beginning of the new

---

[75] It was remarkably similar to the storming of the Bastille in 1789 – and at that time was thought to be so by many.

session, there was a contested election for the Chair and Norton lost.

It was clear to many people that the King had got the country into this disastrous war, and that it was the King alone who was demanding that it continue. There was a general feeling – both in government and in opposition – that the power of the King to control policy must be curtailed in the interest of a more thoroughly parliamentary government.   Royal power depended on the King's ability to bribe members through places and salaries, and so it was through these that the attack on royal power needed to come.   In February 1780, Burke introduced his bill for the reform of the civil list and the reduction of sinecures. Later on, he was to campaign for more parliamentary (as opposed to royal) control of the East India Company. It was to be a long campaign[76].

Big Ideas

 There were not too many big ideas around in London in the 1770's. Tom Paine cut his teeth in radical propaganda with his best-seller, *Common Sense,* in 1776. He was putting forward the anti-monarchical claims of the Good Old Cause – which didn't really endear him to the more conservative elements in the American Rebellion. The Rebellion was not about radical politics. Its outcome was really the working out of the inevitable tensions of governing across such a distance – hastened by the obduracy of George III and his compliant ministers.

Legal Life in the 1780's and 1790s

In March 1777, at Sefton in Lancashire, Edward married Henrietta Lang of Leyland, near Preston. He was only twenty four years old, with his living still to make, so it was a bold move. The Langs see to

---

[76] For Opposition Whigs like Lord Shelburne, this campaign was ill-conceived. Shelburne believed that George II had been reduced to the status of a Venetian doge, and that the royal prerogative needed some restoration. He was picking up the ideas of Lord Bolingbroke, that were later to be espoused by the one –time radical, Sir Francis Burdett, in the 1820's.

have been business people in the Preston area – but of no great wealth. The new Mr & Mrs King first settled in lodgings near the Inns of Court, and worshipped at St Clements Dane[77]. In 1778 Edward was appointed a Commissioner for Bankruptcy. This involved administering the estate of bankrupts – a post that was in the gift of the Lord Chancellor[78] - and it would have provided Edward with some well-needed income. In 1780, he was called to the bar. This meant that he was now free to practice. By 1783 he had moved his growing family to Sydenham – then a popular area for London professionals.

The administration of criminal law in the 18th century has had a bad press. E P Thompson[79] particularly has encouraged people to think that the law was administered harshly in the interests of the landed aristocracy, and Lancaster Gaol is full of grisly reminders of how executions were carried out in those days, including the execution of children. More balanced interpretations have appeared in recent years[80]. Most justice was administered in the magistrates' court, when the magistrate would know the accused and the accused the magistrate. There was a great deal of discretion in the way the law was enforced here that reflected this intimacy, which the regular assize courts underpinned.

Discretion was however taken too far. The rulings of strict judges at the assize courts could often be greatly at variance to those given by more lenient men. Statute law badly needed revising and liberal minds were applying themselves to the work in Edward's day.

---

[77] The parish of St Clement Danes was a natural place for a young lawyer to take up residence – with the Inns of Court nearby. Dr Johnson lived in Inner Temple Lane, and regularly worshipped at the church until his death in 1782. .

[78] I do not know if the appointment was from Lord Bathurst, who resigned in July 1778, or his successor, Lord Thurlow. Thurlow was always deeply hostile to Burke and everything he stood for, but probably the intermediary was Sir Fletcher Norton, then still in the Speaker's chair.

[79] In "*Whigs and Hunters*" - a study of the effects of the Black Act of 1723.

[80] especially J M Beattie "*Crime and the Courts in England, 1660-1800*"

The Debates on Law in the 1780's

Montesquieu had published his influential *De l'Esprit des Lois* in 1748. It was a hugely influential work that looked at human society from a moderate rationalist viewpoint. Montesquieu had no time for utopians who believed in laws framed from first principles that could be imposed on every age and in every place. Context for him was all-important. He also believed in a gentler treatment of criminals. This theme was taken up by Cesare Beccaria[81], who published *Dei Delitti e delle Pene* in 1764. Beccaria argued for the reforming rather than retributive element in punishment. He also believed that capital punishment he did nothing to deter criminals. Both these works had had a great influence throughout the continent, though fear of public disorder prevented their application in England. In 1771 the twenty-six year old William Eden[82] had published *Principles of Penal Law*, which drew much of its inspiration from Montesquieu and Beccaria.

In 1785 the evangelical hymn-writer, Martin Madan, published his *Thoughts on Executive Justice*[83]. He advocated a strict imposition of the legal code as it then was as a way of improving society. At the request of his patron Lord Shelburne, the young Samuel Romilly answered Madan with a plea for a change in the legal system – to deal with the anomalies and to make it more enforceable. Though little read, it reinforced Romilly's growing reputation as a lawyer

---

[81] Cesare, Marchese di Beccaria (1738-94). This was his one major work. He was chronically shy and couldn't cope with the notoriety it brought him.

[82] William Eden (1744-1814), cr. Lord Auckland (I.1789, E.1793) younger son of a co. Durham family. He entered Lincoln's Inn, but then went on to an administrative and political career in which his desire to provide for his family came before principle. He served as Under Secretary of State for the Northern Department 1772-8, and as M.P. for the Duke of Marlborough's seat at Woodstock 1774-93. He was a Northite who supported the coalition in 1783-4.

[83] Martin Madan (1726-1790) was a lawyer, who was converted through the influence of John Wesley. William Cowper was his first cousin. He was a poet and hymn-writer – his best-known hymn being *Lo! He comes, with clouds descending*.

and increased the invitations he received to the homes of influential liberals.

The early years of the French Revolution were also a very important time for law reform. Romilly continued to defend the Revolution until September 1792. He published a pamphlet in 1790 – *Thoughts on the probable influence of the French Revolution in Great Britain* – in which he forecast that the French experience would help forward the cause of reform in Britain. He also attempted a reply to Burke's *Reflections* – eventually published in 1792 as *Letters containing an account of the late revolution in France, and observations on the laws, manners and institutions of the English, written during the author's residence at Paris, Versailles and London in the years 1789-90. Translated from the German of Henry Frederic Groenvelt.* It contained a criticism of the English laws of the time. However, with the September massacres, Romilly gave up on France. Mirabeau had died, and he knew none of the new leaders.

The Northern Circuit

Edward seems to have kept his links in the north, and to have developed them now. Maybe work in the Chancery courts was slow in coming after he qualified. Maybe he wanted to go north anyway – it was easier to shine away from London and a northern town was a healthier place to bring up his family. Either way, it seems likely that he joined the Northern Circuit, and got some experience of court work in the assizes as he travelled from northern town to northern town.

He had friends and relations in the north who might be able to help him to work. Sir Fletcher Norton's mother (and his great aunt) was living in Preston in 1764, and may have still been there when she died in 1774. This town of lawyers would have remembered the mother of one of the north's most powerful lawyers. Edward's recently widowed aunt Cookson was in Wakefield[84]. Another aunt,

---

[84] Her elder daughter was married in 1780 to a family friend, Charles O'Hara of Annaghmore.

Mrs Skirrow, may still have been alive in Bingley. And then in the old heartlands, Aunt Shuttleworth was at Hungerhill, while his father's Tempest cousins were still at Chapel House in Kilnsey.

Edward also seems to have taken on his mother's family home at Hungerhill – at least after the death of his mother and her sisters. He is sometimes referred to as "Edward King of Hungerhill" and his mother-in-law died there. In 1807 he put up a memorial to Rev. Josias Dawson, the young curate at Bolton – which suggests a close involvement with the affairs of the parish.

The Courts of Chancery

Like Romilly, Edward was engaged in the courts of chancery. Chancery work is concerned with business matters, and legal work would have grown in the north with growing prosperity and the expansion of trade, but it had a bad reputation. "For two centuries before Dickens wrote Bleak House, the word "Chancery" had become synonymous with expense, delay and despair"[85]. The courts of chancery had begun life in the later fourteenth century as personal courts of the Chancellors of the County Palatine, charged with sorting out business not covered by the Common Law. They were meant to be flexible, and to operate according to "conscience" or "equity", without all the paraphernalia of precedent that governed the operation of the common law courts. However, in London anyway, the fiction that everything depended on the Lord Chancellor's personal ruling resulted in the delays that so discredited the courts of chancery. A politically active Lord Chancellor didn't have time to discharge the duties of his office. Furthermore, precedent had over the years become as binding in chancery as in the common law courts and the courts became very reluctant to vary their judgements. Lord Eldon, who reigned as Lord Chancellor from 1801-6 and 1807-27, remarked in 1818, "Nothing would inflict on me greater pain in quitting this place than the recollection that I had done anything to justify the reproach that the equity of this court varies like the chancellor's foot"[86].

---

[85] J H Baker "*An Introduction to English Legal History*" p 128

Proud Preston

Preston was always a legal centre for the north-west. It was however a business centre too. These two worlds were increasingly challenging the traditional alliance of the Established Church with the landed gentry. The political interest in Preston was shared between the Earls of Derby and the Hoghton family of Hoghton Tower[87]. The vicar of Preston from 1782-1809 was Prebendary Humphrey Shuttleworth, who had been presented by Sir Henry Hoghton and was married to his sister. However, this old alliance was gradually wilting in the face of the advance of trade. The world that Adam Smith eulogized, of equal relationships instead of feudal deference and inequality, was fast becoming the real world of the north-west.

London Life

Edward and Henrietta moved from the Inns of Court to Perry Hill, Sydenham during the summer of 1783[88]. This would be their home

---

[86] quoted in Baker p 128. John Scott, 1st Earl of Eldon (1751-1838) was Edward's contemporary but they had little in common. Eldon entered the Middle Temple in 1773, having first thought of a career in the church and was called to the bar in 1776. He prospered mightily under the patronage of Andrew Bowes of Gibside and of Lord Chancellor Thurlow, becoming an M P in 1782, and then following Fletcher Norton's career steps as first solicitor-general (1788) and then attorney-general (1793). He gained notoriety as the prosecutor of those believed to have Jacobin sympathies, and thereafter was ferociously anti-reformist and anti-Catholic.

[87] In 1971, while I was at Kirkby, I remember visiting Hoghton Tower with Anthony Blond. He was a friend of Sir Anthony de Hoghton, who was busy selling off the heirlooms and ended up "as a beggar in Sloane Square" at the time of his death in 1978. His stepmother, Mrs Addams, who married the 64 year old Sir Cuthbert de Hoghton in 1944 at the age of 20, was not delighted to see any friend of her stepson. She was trying to hold things together – sometimes by simply blocking the drive, to prevent the vans getting through. She died in 2008 and it's her son who is there now.

[88]Sydenham was not then the built up area it is now. It was a popular place for city folk to build large villas, to enjoy a rural retreat and it was part of the very large parish of Lewisham.

for the remainder of Henrietta's life and where their children were brought up.

Oliver Bolton King had seen letters and diaries from this time telling of family trips. "In 1793 for example they set out in a post chaise and complete with mother-in-law for the Sussex coast. The following year they visited Hampshire and were much impressed with the New Forest. That year the fishing was very successful. The trip of nine days cost twenty guineas. Next year it was Shropshire, and the servant on the return journey shared his horse with a pannier of fish taken from Mr John Dyke's stream". These trips must have been quite like the tour in Derbyshire that Elizabeth Bennett and her aunt enjoyed in "Pride and Prejudice".

Edward and Henrietta had eight children together, but only three daughters survived to adulthood. Two daughters – Ann and Mary died as infants. However, in the three years from October 1794, Edward suffered a whole series of bereavement. First, his eldest child, Lettice, died at the age of sixteen. Then, in March 1796, his younger son, Edward, died at school in Denbighshire aged nine. Two months later, Henrietta herself died. And finally, in November 1797, Edward's eldest and only remaining son, James King, died at the age of sixteen. All were buried in Lewisham churchyard. It is hardly surprising that, after all this, Edward left Sydenham with his three surviving daughters and returned to the north for good.

Promotions, 1797-1800

In 1797, Edward became a Bencher of Gray's Inn. This is an honour granted to barristers of at least ten years standing, by which they become part of the governing body of their Inn. He was Treasurer in 1799 - the chief position of honour in the society[89]. In October 1798, he married again. His new wife was Dorothea Myers, the only child of a long dead mayor of Preston, whose mother (who had

---

[89] The shields of the Treasurers of Gray's Inn are in the stained glass windows of the Hall - it would be good to see the King shield there.

remarried) lived at Croston in Lancashire. Their first two elder children were born there in 1799 and 1801.

In January 1800, he was appointed Vice-Chancellor of the County Palatine of Lancaster. This was a post dating back to 1491, when the Chancellor of the Duchy was first thought to need a deputy. The post of Chancellor had become mostly a sinecure, given to a member of the government[90]. The Vice-Chancellor did at least do some work. In legal terms, Lancashire was then – like Durham – a sort of miniature kingdom. The courts that sat in Westminster Hall had no authority in Lancashire, thanks to this survival of the claims of the powerful medieval earls (now merged in the crown)[91]. As Vice Chancellor, Edward was the presiding judge in the chancery court of the county, sitting in great state in the splendid new courtroom in Lancaster Castle. The office was in Preston and the court sat there once a year, but was at Lancaster for the rest of the year. Edward could have continued his work as a barrister outside the county palatine, but it seems likely (at least after the move to Askham) that he now concentrated on family life and his work as a judge.

In 1805, The Bishop of Durham appointed Samuel Romilly to be Chancellor of the County Palatine of Durham. This post also enjoyed great state, but the court tried only four or five cases a year – and its writ didn't run beyond the County of Durham. It was not a powerful organization and Romilly – who had no connections in the county - had a frustrating time. Nonetheless, he didn't want people to think he was only interested in making money, and felt it was time that he accepted judicial office. He also wanted to see how he

---

[90] The Chancellor of the Duchy from 1786-1803 was Charles Jenkinson, Lord Hawkesbury, and (from 1796) Earl of Liverpool. His loyalties were first and foremost with the King.

[91] The independent court at Lancaster did not survive the great legal reorganisations of the 1870's when the by then redundant distinction between equity and law was phased out and the chancery courts disappeared into the courts of common law. However, there is still a Vice Chancellor of the County Palatine - a chancery division judge in the north western circuit.

might acquit himself as a judge. Maybe Edward, with less ambition than Romilly, had similar motives?

A legal plum like the Lancaster Vice-Chancellorship was - like a bishopric - the result of political patronage in London. Fortunately for Edward, the Lord Chancellor was from his world and would have smiled on his credentials. Alexander Wedderburn[92] was a school-friend and intimate of Henry Dundas, Lord Melville[93] - also in those early days a Northite. With the fall of Lord North, Loughborough was one of the strongest supporters of the Coalition of 1782-3[94], while Dundas had followed Pitt. They remained however moderate Whig conservatives and were happy to be together again in government in 1792 when Loughborough became Lord Chancellor in a reconstructed administration. In the later years of Pitt's administration, with the Portland Whigs in leading roles, it did no harm to be a friend of Mr Burke's (or the brother of John King). Edward King was in any case a senior advocate worthy of promotion.

At the time of his appointment, Edward was only forty-five years old. If he had been ambitious, he might have looked for a seat in parliament and sought political office. It's not clear that he wanted this. He had a new marriage and a growing family. To obtain a seat in parliament would have involved him in much expense – and he had probably not got the profile in London of the sort that he would need to succeed.

---

[92] Alexander Wedderburn had started out as a Rockingham Whig but had defected to Lord North, to become Solicitor-General in 1771 and Chief Justice of the Common Pleas in 1780.

[93] Henry Dundas (1742-1811), Treasurer of the Navy 1783, Home Secretary 1791-4, Secretary of State for War 1794-1801. Cr Lord Melville 1802. 1st Lord of the Admiralty 1804-5. Tried for misappropriation of naval funds in April 1805, but acquitted. Joined the Duke of Portland's administration in 1807. A Pitt loyalist, and former chief of John King.

[94] Thurlow would not stand down as Lord Chancellor, and so the post was held in commission with Loughborough the senior commissioner. It was no secret that he badly wanted the job, if Thurlow could be got rid of.

However, it was soon very clear that in the current climate lawyers who were not safely conservative would go no further. Pitt's resignation in March 1801 over Catholic emancipation meant the end for the moderate Whigs. Pitt made a brief return in May 1804, but it was a broken-backed administration. When he died, Fox and Grenville – with Edward's brother John a part of the government - lasted only a minute before the issue of Catholic emancipation did for them too[95]. There were one or two attempts at coalitions – in 1809 and 1812 – but they were half-hearted. The Whigs would have to wait a long time.

Legal Campaigns

This didn't mean that people didn't try to reform the Law. The best-known champion of reform was Sir Samuel Romilly[96]. He had a difficult run. In 1808 he managed to repeal the Elizabeth statute that made stealing from the person a capital offence. His success however raised opposition, and further attempts on other equally grim statutes in succeeding years failed in the House of Lords – which was then dominated by Lord Ellenborough. His efforts did however bring him some fame and he was recognised as a leader of the responsible, liberal opposition to the very conservative governments that remained in power for twenty-five years after March 1807.

As Vice Chancellor

It's good to think that Samuel Romilly and Edward King might have had much in common. Public executions in Lancaster became less of a spectacle after Edward's appointment. Branding was discontinued in 1811.

---

[95] It was all the more remarkable that brother Walker got his bishopric in 1809.
[96] Sir Samuel Romilly (1757-1818), the son of a London watchmaker of Huguenot descent. He entered Gray's Inn in 1788; was called to the bar in 1783, and went on the midland circuit – mainly concerned with chancery practice. A friend of Mirabeau. He committed suicide after his wife's death.

Life at Askham, 1803-1815

Young Edward Bolton King was baptized in what was then a chapel at ease at Tarleton, in the parish of Croston, in Lancashire. Dorothea's mother, Mrs Porter, may have been renting Bank Hall, a beautiful Jacobean manor house in Bretherton[97]. Bretherton had no church in those days.

However, there were greater things to come. Dorothea King's uncle was the rich and childless Edward Bolton of Askham Hall in Westmoreland. Bolton had been a banker in Preston where his family had been established for many years. He did well. Preston was prospering in those years and had a high reputation as a centre of fashionable society. Cotton manufacturing came with John Horrocks in the last decade of the century, but linen and woollen cloth making were well established. Mr Bolton seems to have given up his business in the 1770's and retired to the beautiful Askham Hall. Several relations no doubt courted him. When Edward and Dorothea had their first child, she was named Susan after Mrs Bolton[98]. Then, in 1801 a son was born - named of course Edward Bolton. In 1803 Mr Bolton died and the infant Edward Bolton King became the owner of Askham Hall, some land and £125,000 in consols[99]. However one assesses wealth, the little boy was seriously rich. After old Mr Bolton's death, the family seem to have settled in Askham. John King was baptized there in February 1804, Henrietta was married there and Dorothea baptized there in 1805, and Ann was married there in December 1806. It looks as though Askham was their home for a little over ten years. In later years, John King published a volume of poetry that tells of a boyhood spent 'where Lowther's stream with sparkling wave descends, and

---

[97] In 1775, Mrs Myers had married Henry Porter of Croston. He was buried at Bolton-by-Bolland on 30 March 1803, aged 79. She was buried there in 1822, aged 86.

[98] Although apparently Edward Bolton had a sister also called Susan – who was unmarried. She worked a damask tablecloth that descended to Jane Formby.

[99] The equivalent of £460 million, according to The Times in 2000 - for what such comparisons are worth!

in broad Eamont's statelier current ends'[100]. It evokes an idyllic, rural life in what is still a very beautiful part of the world.

Askham had been the home of the Sandford family for hundreds of years, but they had fallen on bad times and Edward Bolton eventually purchased the property after some heavy mortgaging had gone wrong. Most of the surrounding territory was in the hands of the Lowther family. The architect of the Lowther family's fortunes was Sir John Lowther who at the end of the seventeenth century managed to acquire the major part of the coal producing land in Cumberland and Westmoreland, while also developing and controlling the port of Whitehaven and the associated trade with Ireland. His heir, Sir James Lowther, died in 1756. He left a fabulous fortune to a cousin, another James Lowther, who was made Earl of Lonsdale in the 1790's. Sir William Lowther – who inherited the property shortly before old Edward Bolton's death – was Lord Lonsdale's cousin. He succeeded as Viscount Lowther through a special remainder and in 1807 was advanced Earl of Lonsdale. Between 1806 and 1811 he built Lowther Castle on the burnt out remains of the old Lowther Hall, just outside Askham village. This huge place remained the home of the Lowther family until it was shut up in 1936. In the 1950's, the seventh earl moved in to Askham Hall and Lowther Castle was reduced to a ruin[101].

The Bolton Legacy & the Shadow of Slavery

There was a curious undercurrent during the Askham years. Edward's brother John seems to have disagreed with the way that he and the other trustees were managing the estate. He believed that Edward and the other trustees - John Gorst, Thomas Langton and William Fielding[102] - "did possess themselves of such parts of

---

[100] *The Parson's Home,* by J.M.King, 1849

[101] In 2006 it was announced that the family was planning a new house, designed by Craig Hamilton, to be built in the park. They also have plans to turn the ruined castle into some sort of theme park. Askham Hall is now a hotel.

[102] Names that are redolent of business life in Preston and district at the beginning of the nineteenth century. John Gorst built himself a house in fashionable Wincley Square, Preston in 1802. His grandson, Sir John Eldon Gorst,

the Testator's Estate and effects not specially bequeathed to him [i.e Edward Bolton King]". The estate was put in Chancery and the case dragged on until young Edward Bolton King came of age[103]. It seems likely that Edward did use the property as his own, and was not strict about what was in fact his son's. For a chancery lawyer, he seems to have been cavalier about such things. A cousin left him some property in 1821 in trust for the children of his first wife. Edward happily left it by will to his younger son by his second marriage.

It is not clear how exactly Mr Bolton came by his millions. It was an uncomfortable question that might have caused Edward King some unease. It was well known that much of the wealth of the north-west was dependent on the slave trade. London and Bristol were involved but, after the hiatus of the American War of Independence, Liverpool had become the slave capital. Bankers very often had shares in slave ships. Huge fortunes were made, and the Liverpool merchant class stood strongly by their profits. Manufacturing in the northern towns depended on a ready supply of raw cotton. This was produced with slave labour. The abolition of the slave trade in British territories could result in a declaration of independence by the planters, or in their transferring allegiance to countries that were not abolitionist. The supply of cotton might then be cut off and the manufacturing industry collapse. There were plenty of economic arguments for delay.

By the 1780's however quiet disapproval was giving way to a strengthening opposition. Thomas Clarkson, Granville Sharp and William Wilberforce set up a committee, but it was not until Lord Grenville's access to power in 1806 that anything was achieved.

---

was a distinguished Tory politician – and founder of a political dynasty. Thomas Langton was a flax merchant of Kirkham, whose children continued in business. A grandson was a Manchester banker. Another grandson, John Langton, fell on hard times, emigrated to Canada in 1837 and had a successful career there.
[103] By 1818 Edward Bolton King's fourteen year old brother had been added to the list of defendants.

The trade in British owned possessions was abolished in 1807, though slavery itself was not abolished in British possessions until 1834. It took a long while, but at no time would people like Edward King have expected to profit by such a trade. Suspicions that the Bolton fortune was slave based embarrassed Edward's son in the 1830's. And yet slavery had been part of British trading practice since the days of Sir John Hawkins in the sixteenth century. This was the price paid for the dramatic rise in British prosperity during the eighteenth century.

Last Years at Kirkham, 1817-1824

Ill health may have prompted a move further south. It's said that Edward sold Askham Hall to Lord Lonsdale in 1815. It may be that it was let – which would have been more proper, given that it belonged to his son. Edward was referred to as "of Askham Hall" in the notice of his death in the Gentleman's Magazine. When he made his will in May 1816 it says that he is 'now residing at Croston'. He may have returned to the house they had before the move to Askham.

However, by February, 1819 – when he added a codicil to his will – Edward had moved to the other side of the Ribble estuary at Kirkham and this was to remain his home for the rest of his life. Kirkham was an ancient borough, mid-way between Blackpool and Preston, and with several substantial houses owned by local business people. The parish church served a population of some 10,000, as well as two or three chapels of ease for the outlying settlements.   Edward had a large house built there - known as Carr Hill House - and he presumably moved in sometime during 1816-1818.

The old parish church was in a bad state of repair. Between 1817-1822 the nave and part of the chancel were demolished and completely rebuilt, with galleries in the north and south aisles and an organ at the west end. It was a church rebuilt after the fashion of the day, and still looks much as it did at the end of Edward's life.

1f.

The church in the background of his picture may be Kirkham Church from the east before the rebuilding, and it may be featured in the portrait because Edward's was the guiding hand in its rebuilding. However, the church in the picture also looks very much like Croston church.

Edward established the Kirkham Harriers in 1822, the joint property of himself and Hugh Hornby of Ribby Hall[104].

Edward and the Faith

Edward had lived through a time of spiritual revival in the Church of England. He had received from his father a liberal education. The presiding genius had been Edmund Law, Master of Peterhouse, Cambridge and (1768-87) a rather absentee Bishop of Carlisle. William Paley took over from the Bishop's son John as Archdeacon of Carlisle in 1782, effectively running the little diocese for the old master. The theology was gently latitudinarian - a word they hated - without being heterodox.

However, despite the sane and intelligent thought, it could all become formal and distant. In the face of the intellectual challenges of the later eighteenth century, the tendency was to drift from this into Unitarianism or atheism. As in the 1730's, some people looked to warm the faith up - while steering clear of anything too weird. Charles Simeon[105] was the guiding light and the

---

[104] It seems hardly likely that he himself hunted at this stage in his life. However, it's interesting that he was involved with harriers - then used just for hunting hare, and on foot. It was a different, quieter and more subtle sport - with none of the social ambitions that came later with the hunting of the fox with hounds. At this date, fox hunting was not as dominant a sport as it was to become a few years later. The Hornby family made their fortune by making sailcloth – see E S Shaw, *Kirkham in Amoundernes*, Preston: R Seed & Son, 1947.

[105] Charles Simeon (1759-1836), vicar of Holy Trinity, Cambridge from 1783, where he was influenced by Henry Venn, formerly vicar of Huddersfield, but later retired to the rectory of Yelling. He played a major part in establishing the Evangelical Revival in the Church of England, was one of the founders of the Church Missionary Society, and encouraged young men into the mission field.

men of the Clapham Sect a famous expression. The first two decades of the nineteenth century saw a group of highly gifted young man take up the faith with renewed vigour - Henry Martyn[106] and Reginald Heber[107] chief among them. People were beginning to care about mission - at home and abroad - with a new vigour. The old dean would have been sympathetic. Edward King surely was too.

He was buried under a large altar tomb[108] in the south-east corner of the churchyard at Kirkham, to be joined by Dorothy over twenty years later[109]. Since his elder son was generously provided for, he left his property to be divided between his younger son and five daughters. Dorothy eventually sold the house to Thomas Langton Birley[110]. The Birleys were a long-established Kirkham family who

---

[106] Henry Martyn (1781-1812), a talented scholar and one of Simeon's disciples. He was inspired by Simeon to consider missionary work, and went out to India in 1805. A hero of the evangelical movement, though rather more "wild" than Heber.

[107] Reginald Heber (1785-1826) came from a long-established Craven family, from the parish of Marton, a few miles west of Skipton. His father was Rector of Malpas, and his daughters eventually inherited the family estates. One of them married a son of Bishop Percy of Carlisle and founded the Heber Percy dynasty. Heber himself was vicar of a family living at Hodnet, Shropshire from 1807 where he wrote his hymns (published in 1827, after his death). He took over as Middleton's successor at Calcutta in 1823. An attractive, informal man, deeply committed to ecumenical co-operation with William Carey and the Baptist missionaries, but keen to distance himself from any party in the church.

[108] With the inscription "Reader enquire no more, but go do thy duty".

[109] Dorothy seems to have spent her old age in the home of her younger daughter, at Dalemain in Cumberland

[110] Birley married in 1836, so maybe she sold it to him in that year. He was an ancestor of the painter, Sir Oswald Birley, and the club-owner, Mark Birley. One of my great-grandfather's first cousins, Dorothea Myers Formby (d 1906), the eldest daughter of Rev James Formby by Edward and Dorothea's daughter Alice, married Richard Moore, son of Rev Richard Moore (1789-1886) who from 1815 was one of the Kirkham curates. Richard Moore senr. had particular responsibility for the church at Lund from 1820 and supervised the rebuilding of the old church during the 1820's. Lund became an independent parish in 1840, with Moore as its perpetual curate. Richard Moore junr., who died in 1870, was a solicitor in Kirkham.

continued in the town to the end of the twentieth century – though Carr Hill House has now been demolished.

Edward was remembered as a man of probity. His younger son wrote some beautiful verses on the death of his elder sister in 1872, in which he thinks of his parents waiting to welcome her into heaven. This is the verse about his father,

> Nor absent he, who through long space of time
>
> In painful struggle strove to slow decay
> Like good old Simeon daily on his knees
> in God's own temple, not an old man now -
> eternal youth effulgent on his brow[111].

---

[111] The full poem:
Thee thine own weep, and in the soft lament

We join, who all a sister's virtues knew:
Humble thou wast; close-knit in love with those
Who watch beside thee, marvelling at thy faith,
Which mastered the strong agony of death

Nor rest thou needest now, nor sympathy
A spirit-choir sang round thy parting soul;
Flowers ever fresh thy path through Eden strew
While with their guerdons at the golden gate,
Palm, crown and harp expectant angels wait.

Among them one - thou scarcely know'st her face,
For she is young and radiant now
as when Her eyes drunk in thy smile - her first born's smile:
E'en then she prayed this glorious hour might come
Of souls united in a Saviour's home.

Nor absent he..

O Father, Mother, Sister, when shall I,
Infirm in purpose, incomplete in acts,
Release and pardon through the Saviour gain,
And in the shelter of his wounded side
My shame, my weakness, and my sorrows hide.

Edward King had been an older parent - nearly fifty when this younger son was born. In those days, he would have been an old man as the boy grew up. He was only 69 when he died, but clearly struggled with something like arthritis and his son remembered him as old. However, his prayerfulness was also remembered - a godly, professional man, from a godly, upright family. It was a good heritage to pass on and it might enable this son to survive the temptations that came with his prosperity.

The Family

If the early editions of the Landed Gentry are anything to go by, Edward Bolton King was closest to his brother and his two sisters of the second family. He was happy to acknowledge his eldest half-sister and her children, who inter-married with other members of the family. The links with the Sunderlands and Radcliffes seem however to have been less secure. This may have been because Ann Sunderland died comparatively young and Mary Radcliffe fell into seriously reduced circumstances. Whatever the reason, their descendants disappeared from the scene and the business-dominated world of Kirkham was no more.

Edward King was apparently a friend of James Northcote (the pupil of Joshua Reynolds) who painted the beautiful portrait of his mother in 1789. Northcote painted Edward's portrait in 1802 –

25 August 1872

which shows him in simple dress, with a church on the background. He could have been painted in full judge's robes, but this was clearly not Edward's way. This is presumably the portrait that was at Chadshunt and which was left by Bolton King in his will to his younger brother. It was sold at Christie's on 31 March 1967. The engraving that appears in Arthur Carden's book is of this portrait.

CHAPTER ELEVEN

JOHN KING, OF THE HOME DEPARTMENT (1760-1830)

The brother who stayed near the seat of power, and to whom both Burke and the other brothers would address themselves, was the youngest, John King. He had gone to Eton when his father was appointed to Windsor in 1772 and had been a contemporary there of William Pitt and of Pitt's cousin, William Grenville. Here began the friendship with Grenville that was to shape the rest of his life. In July 1777, he followed Grenville to Christ Church where he had been elected a canoneer student[112]. On graduating in 1781, he again followed Grenville to Lincoln's Inn[113]. He was later to transfer to Gray's Inn - on 4 June 1790 - and was called to the bar five days later.

William Grenville entered parliament for a family seat in February 1782 and – in accordance with the Grenville family line – supported the ministry of Lord Rockingham. When Rockingham died in July 1782, Lord Temple – and Grenville – agreed to serve under Lord Shelburne. With the collapse of Shelburne's administration in March 1783, the Grenville family left office – only to return the following December when the young William Pitt was appointed first minister. There followed some six years during which time Grenville's role in Pitt's government became steadily more important. Finally, in June 1789, he took over as Secretary of State at the Home Department. He had long coveted the job and it was during his tenure – 1789-91 – that he came to be acknowledged as Pitt's second in command. In January 1791 he invited John King to

---

[112] The Canoneer Students were those who were nominated by either the dean or one of the canons of Christ Church. John's patron could well have been the Dean of Christ Church, Dr Markham, who was an old friend of Edmund Burke.
[113] Matric Christ Church 16 7 77. BA 1781. MA 1784. Student of Lincoln's Inn 1781. Migrated to Gray's Inn 4 6 90. Barrister at Law 9 6 90. Bencher 10 2 13. Treasurer 1815.

join his office as a law clerk on £300 a year. It does not seem to have been a full-time post and King continued his work at the Bar.

Under-Secretary of State at the Home Dept.

Grenville was persuaded to leave the Home Office in June 1791 to take over from the Duke of Leeds as Foreign Secretary. Pitt's great friend, Henry Dundas, took over as Home Secretary – but he and Grenville were increasingly to work very much in tandem. In December 1791, Evan Napean, the hardworking Under-Secretary of State at the Home Department, needed a rest. Someone had to fill the gap *pro tem*. King was asked to take over, which he agreed to do – on condition that he received 'a pension equal to what he might have made at the bar'. This was agreed at £1,500 p.a. There were two under-secretaries – one tended to come and go with the ministry, whereas the other was more permanent, though this distinction took some time to be made official[114]. King's colleague was another of Grenville's friends and nominees, Scrope Bernard, M.P. for Aylesbury. The generous income no doubt made possible his marriage in April, 1792 to Harriet Moss, daughter of the Bishop of Bath & Wells. In August 1792, on the resignation of Scrope Bernard, King's post was confirmed, even though Evan Nepean was by then back in harness.

What might have seemed a comfortable and lucrative berth in December 1791 very soon became something very different. Already there was considerable debate on the issues arising from the French Revolution. Tom Paine's *Rights of Man* had been published in March 1791 and had become an immediate best-seller. Many similar pamphlets followed. Nonetheless, the government – and Pitt in particular – was happy to let the debate continue. They

---

[114] Edmund Burke was delighted. He wrote to John's brother, Walker, "Grenville has done nobly indeed". A contributing cause to John's promotion may have been Grenville's sympathetic response to Burke's *Reflections* (November 1790) and – even more so – his *Appeal* (August 1791). Pitt was more laid back about the French threat until the summer of 1792; Grenville much less so. It was Grenville who led the rapprochement with Burke that ultimately led to the Portland Whigs coming into government.

sensed no threat to the stability of the kingdom. This mood changed very quickly during the course of 1792. Since his accession to power, Pitt had presided over a remarkable economic boom. This suddenly came to end in the autumn when a bad harvest and a general crisis in business confidence were allied to some remarkable military triumphs on the part of the French revolutionary army. "Constitutional Societies" were springing up in the major cities. The membership of the radical London Corresponding Society exploded during the winter of 1792. And all the while France threatened to move into the Netherlands and take over the Dutch Republic. When England finally declared war on France in January 1793, it was in the context of a real fear of radical unrest – and even revolution – at home.

When government wanted to check on the extent of unrest in the three kingdoms, they looked to the Home Office – which meant John King and his little band of clerks in their makeshift offices. Yet there was little that King could do. Government in the eighteenth century was decentralized. It relied on the aristocracy and on the gentry, working through the assizes and magistrates' courts. Any interference with the local J.P.s – or indeed with the juries – would have met with stiff opposition. Any kind of centralized police force – indeed, any police force at all – was out of the question. The system worked reasonably well in the countryside, but in the cities – and the cities were growing quickly at this period – it was not working. There were various stratagems. Barracks were built in strategic regions, the militia were mobilized, the distributors of seditious libels were to be prosecuted, and an Aliens Act was passed in January 1793, requiring all foreigners to register. Neither King or Napean could speak French, and so the young William Huskisson was appointed Superintendent of Aliens with two clerks lodged in the attic at the Home Office.

One thing that King could do – and did – was to encourage prosecutions. Sometimes these were instigated through a small network of agents, but more often through a general encouragement of local magistrates to act when dangerous activity came to light. These prosecutions were not always successful. Magistrates were mindful of local opinion and in some areas – Derby, Nottingham, Sheffield – it was very difficult to get convictions. A high point in King's attempts at bringing prosecutions was the prosecution of the leaders of the London Corresponding Society at the Old Bailey in October 1794. There were fears of a French invasion at the same time as an increase in the activities of the societies. The government believed that they had to act. Thomas Hardy, Horne Tooke, John Thelwall and Thomas Holcroft and others were tried, but were defended very skilfully by Thomas Erskine[115]. All were acquitted – to the government's embarrassment. Thereafter, the power of the societies waned, but the government's concerns did not reduce. It is estimated that the cost of living rose by some 30% between 1790 and 1795, with the rate of increase doubling from 1793. From the summer of 1795 large public protest meetings were held in London, Norwich, Sheffield, Leicester and the towns of the West Riding. The Prime Minister's windows in Downing Street were smashed by a mob. In October 1795 George III's carriage was pelted in St James' Park. This was followed by Pitt's "Reign of Terror". Habeas Corpus was suspended from May 1794 until July 1795, and in December 1795 the Treasonable Practices Act and the Seditious Meetings and Assemblies Act were promulgated.

Much of the enforcement of these new laws fell on John King and his staff at the Home Office – and the pressure was growing. In July 1794, Henry Dundas left the Home Office to become Secretary at War, and he took Evan Napean with him. Until William Wickham was appointed to the other secretaryship in 1798, King was left without effective support[116]. He was on his own, with a new Home

---

[115] The same lawyer who had successfully defended Count Duroure when he was on trial for his life in 1784.

[116] Pitt had suggested George Canning, newly an M.P. and a devotee of Pitt, as the other Under-Secretary, but Canning was not keen to serve under the Whig Duke of Portland and nor, it seems, was Portland prepared to appoint him.

Secretary – the Duke of Portland. The new laws had the effect of driving discontent underground – and making its aims more radical. A link was opened up with an increasingly disaffected Ireland and much of King's concern in the years immediately preceding the Irish Rebellion of 1798 was taken up with tracking down the leaders of Irish disaffection. Arthur O'Connor[117], James Quigley[118] and John Binns were key people. Quigley and others were arrested in Margate in February 1798, while seeking a passage to France to encourage a French invasion. It was not possible to prove conspiracy and only Quigley – on whom incriminating evidence was found – was found guilty and executed. O'Connor had large numbers of opposition Whigs testifying to his good character. John King headed the list of witnesses at the trial at Maidstone in May, which was quite a sensation. The execution of Quigley and several arrests in London, Manchester and other centres had its effect. The failure of the Irish rebellion however resulted in many Irishmen fleeing to England, where they continued a danger. Some of the leaders were spared the gallows on condition of making a confession, which allowed King to gain some useful intelligence. By mid-1799, the underground movement was effectively broken. With the coming of peace in 1802, the security services as they had functioned from the Home Office were quickly dismantled. They did not function again when the war was resumed in 1804 – and indeed Britain was to have no security services again until the First World War. John King's spy network was a one off!

Though his official capacity did not dictate it, King aspired to a seat in Parliament. Other under-secretaries had found this a way to advancement and King was clearly ambitious. On 5 Aug. 1800 John

---

[117] Arthur O'Connor (1763-1852), sat in the Irish House of Commons from 1790-5 and joined the United Irishmen in 1796. Arrested immediately after his acquittal, he was in prison in Ireland and in Scotland until 1802, when he was banished. He went to France where he was (briefly) a general in the French army. He married the only child of the Marquis de Condorcet, the philosopher.
[118] James Quigley (1762-1798), from county Armagh, trained as a priest in France but escaped in 1789, and was active in the Defenders and in linking the Defenders and the United Irishmen. Latterly active in England.

King reported to Pitt that he had had an offer from Lady Portsmouth. Her third son, Coulson Wallop, had come in for the family seat of Andover in May 1796 – his uncle retiring to give him a place. However, the young man seems to have been a bit simple. King told Pitt that he was "little better than an idiot, in addition to which he has spent all his money, and his mother does not think him a proper person to continue to represent [Andover]. At the same time she is anxious to obtain some provision for him (to the extent of about £400 per annum) and provided I can be the means of effecting this, I am to be considered as the family Member". King left this matter to Pitt's determination and it appears that Pitt decided against, as Wallop remained in the House until the dissolution, when he was replaced by his brother Newton. At this time, Pitt was exhausted and the stage was being set for his resignation a few months later. John King's ambition for a parliamentary seat and the desire of the Wallop family for a pension could not have been high on the Minister's agenda.

Addington's Ministry, March 1801 - May 1804

Pitt resigned on 14 March 1801, after a delay caused by a brief recurrence of the King's illness. Grenville and Dundas went with him, though not the Duke of Portland - King's then chief at the Home Department. Addington, the new Minister, had wanted Thomas Pelham as Home Secretary but Pelham, who had been ill, was unsure. However, by July he was ready to accept the post and Portland became Lord President of the Council. King – who had got on well with Portland – was not best pleased. It would be interesting to know what King's view was of Robert Emmet's Dublin rising of July 1803[119]. Contemporaries accused the Irish government of being unprepared, but they had no support from the

---

[119] Robert Emmet (1778-1803), the son of prosperous Protestant family in Dublin and the younger brother of the nationalist, Thomas Addis Emmet. He fled to France in 1798 to escape the arrests that preceded the 1798 uprising but returned afterwards to reorganize the United Irishmen. He planned to seize Dublin Castle and stage a coup. The attempted failed. He was caught and hanged.

Home Office in London, now that the spy network had been run down on Addington's instructions.

Pitt's Second Ministry, May 1804 – January 1806

Pitt returned to power on 10 May 1804, but without Grenville who - now allied with Fox - refused to come in without him. Portland, who continued as Lord President, evidently applied to Pitt to make King a joint secretary to the Treasury with William Sturges Bourne[120], but Huskisson was preferred[121]. King remained at the Home Office for the duration of Pitt's second ministry.

George Rose reported in his diary that George Canning disagreed with King's plans to prevent the authority of the Irish government from being undermined by John Foster, formerly Speaker of the old Irish House of Commons, and now sitting in the new united parliament as M.P. for Lowth. King believed that the solution would be to restore Home Office control over the Irish chief secretary 'compelling the Irish secretary to a more intimate and constant correspondence with him [King] ... *thus* arming [the chief secretary] with power to combat Foster and all his host in Lord Hawkesbury's name'[122]. Canning could not stomach this and noted that it was quite different from King's former 'fine plans'. A supporter of Pitt in and out of office, Canning was currently serving rather discontentedly as Treasurer of the Navy – though Pitt did offer him the post of Chief Secretary for Ireland in January 1805 (though was refused)[123].

---

[120] William Sturges, from 1803 Sturges Bourne (1769-1845) was a close friend of George Canning and served as Home Secretary during Canning's short-lived administration. He had sat as M.P. for Hastings from 1798 but this was his first government post.

[121] William Huskisson (1770-1830) was much admired by Pitt and had served as Under Secretary of War in 1795-1801. He was to have a distinguished political career.

[122] Robert Jenkinson, Lord Hawkesbury, later 2nd Earl of Liverpool & long serving Prime Minister, was serving as Home Secretary in Pitt's administration.

[123] George Canning (1770-1827), from an impoverished background, he went to Eton & Christ Church, and was accounted a brilliant scholar. The French

Addington's friend, Nicholas Vansittart, was eventually appointed Chief Secretary – but he only lasted until the autumn. He was replaced by Charles Long, a loyal Pittite – though in November it was 'whispered' that King was to replace Long[124]. This didn't happen.

In Lord Grenville's Ministry, February – September, 1806

When Pitt died, the King wanted the ministry to continue with as little alteration as possible, but the ministers – led by Lord Hawkesbury – decided that they did not have sufficient support. The King was constrained to invite Lord Grenville to come in – and to abandon his veto of Fox. Grenville brought in Addington and Ellenborough, but "Mr Pitt's friends" were excluded. Among these, Canning, Portland, Camden and Bathurst were much in agreement, but Hawkesbury and Castlereagh played from a different sheet. There wasn't much love lost in the Pittite camp.

Grenville seems to have decided early on to make King Joint Secretary at the Treasury, with a seat in parliament. However, Grenville's brother, Lord Buckingham, wanted his own man – W.H. Fremantle - in the post, in order to bind his brother more closely to him. Grenville, who was under pressure from the Prince of Wales to choose one of the Prince's friends, wrote on 4 February, 1806, "This persecution obliges me to adhere to the arrangement for putting King there. I had almost settled it so as to make room for Fremantle, but I must now close it as soon as I can. Possibly some means may arise hereafter of giving King his retreat, and putting the

---

Revolution pushed him to the right of the Whig party and in 1793, with Pitt's help, he became M.P. for Newtown on the Isle of Wight. He was briefly Prime Minister before his death. He was not always so hostile to King. On 5 Dec. 1793, he noted in his journal, 'I dined with King—one of the under-secretaries of state for the Home department, and one of the worthiest and friendliest and best sort of men in the world'. Harewood mss, Canning jnl., quoted in http://www.historyofparliamentonline.org/volume/1790-1820/member/king-john-1759-1830, accessed 16 Feb 2012.

[124] Buckingham, *Court and Cabinets*, ii. 456.

other there, which I believe would be the better arrangement, but which I cannot hazard now". King needed a seat in Parliament. Thomas Grenville offered his Buckingham seat, while Lord Buckingham was prepared to bring him in for St. Mawes if the sitting member were provided for, but it was for the Irish borough of Enniskillen that he was returned, the vacating Member having offered the seat to Lord Wellesley, who placed it at government disposal. King did not vacate an office he held in Jamaica on taking his seat.

King did not enjoy his time as Secretary to the Treasury. A political opponent, Lord Lowther, maintained that he was 'very unfit for his office'. On 3 July 1806 Lord Grenville informed the Irish secretary, William Elliot: 'An opportunity has occurred which John King seems disposed to embrace of exchanging his present situation ... for one of a different description'. Grenville thought King would be difficult to replace and wondered whether Marsden, the Irish under-secretary, would fit the bill, but it was Fremantle who succeeded to King's office and seat in Parliament. King's brother-in-law Charles Moss (soon to be made Bishop of Oxford by Grenville) commented, "Finding his health suffer very much from his attendance at the House of Commons, King signified to Lord Grenville some time ago that it was his wish to give up his office as soon as his services could be dispensed with and as he preferred a place which would give him some occupation to a pension to which his long services fairly entitled him, it was determined that he should be one of the comptrollers of army accounts. Nothing can have been more friendly than the whole of Lord Grenville's conduct towards him, and his disposition to promote his views with respect to his future establishment". Lord Buckingham wrote triumphantly to Fremantle that he hoped to see "the fair influence of the crown fairly used to the support of government and not indirectly turned, as it was in repeated cases by King's mismanagement, against us, a fact which Lord Grenville never would credit, though Lord Melville and George Rose, who were the principal agents upon King's mind, could not keep their secret". Buckingham clearly thought that King was too close to Mr Pitt's friends. Maybe King found the internecine squabbling impossible to cope with and simply wanted out.

Comptroller of the Army Accounts, 1806 - 1830

On 7 October 1806 he was made third Comptroller of the Army Accounts[125]. He became second Comptroller by succession in July 1811 on the death of the first Comptroller. In October 1823 he became first Comptroller – which post he held until his death. It was not a sinecure, and he was in the office the day before he was found dead in his bed in March 1830[126].

His was a remarkable career that has been all but forgotten. He is rarely mentioned in the key works of the period and – when he is – is often confused with others of the same or a similar name. Perhaps there are no personal papers that would enable someone to write a proper biography, but it would be good if somehow he could reclaim his place in history. For better or worse, King's work at the Home Office was vitally important to the war effort and to the security of the county as a whole. He deserves not to be forgotten.

Family Life

John and Harriet King had thirteen children. Two daughters died in infancy, the youngest of the four sons died as a young naval officer, and all but one of the seven surviving daughters died as young women. One, Elizabeth, died at the age of nineteen when she was engaged to be married. The others were all married and left some fourteen motherless children behind them. Presumably, the reason was tuberculosis, which was particularly prevalent during this

---

[125] This office was created in 1703. Appointments were made by the crown by letters patent under the great seal. Until 1806 two comptrollers served with a salary of £1500. In that year the number was increased to three, the first comptroller being granted a salary of £2000, the other two salaries of £1500 each. Between 1815 and 1817 a fourth comptroller served, also with a salary of £1500. On the death of King, the first commissioner, his place was not filled, his two remaining colleagues serving until the abolition of the office in 1835.
[126] *Gent. Mag.* (1830), i. 282.

period and was known ass the "romantic disease" – though there was nothing very romantic about so many early deaths.

Harriet King was the daughter of one bishop and sister to another. Bishops were rich in those days and Harriet was her father's and her brother's eventual heir. Her brother died in 1811 and around that time the family rented the beautiful Aldenham House, in Hertfordshire, from the Huck family. The Hucks were wealthy brewers, but the current heir was confined in an asylum, so had no use for the place. The King family remained at Aldenham until at least John King's death. The house eventually returned to the Huck family, in the shape of Henry Huck Gibbs, who became Lord Aldenham. It is now home to Haberdashers' Aske's Boys' School.

John had many descendants, though his male line has died out. His eldest son, John James, had an only son, John Henry, who died childless. Presumably John Henry would have inherited any papers left by his grandfather, and maybe these went to one or other of his three sisters. These sisters all had daughters, who married into various interesting families, so that probably the memory of John King died out fairly soon.

Some of John's descendants in the female line were grand – a great-great-grandson was the 10th Duke of Beaufort, and there were a few barons and several baronets. Several grandchildren and great-grandchildren married into the peerage. However, as in all families, some fell on hard times and needed to seek a better life abroad. His descendants are in Canada, the United States, New Zealand, South Africa, and Australia.

CHAPTER TWELVE

BOLTON KING 1801-1878

When he came of age he came into a substantial fortune which he used - and to an extent used up - in politics. He was committed to liberal reform but in the context of traditional community life. He had no taste for the extension of parliamentary rule and central government bureaucracy that so marked the mid-nineteenth century.

PART ONE: Early Years & Early Activity, 1801-30

Edward Bolton King was born into a steady, responsible, professional world[127]. His sisters and half-sisters married into the professional and landed world of the north-west. There is a regional feel to the young man before he established himself further south. His mother lived into the 1840's and there are memories of her as "severe and prim", suggesting something of the ambiguities of the social status of Preston's professional classes in the eighteenth century. The chief among these classes looked down on the trades people, yet they were not quite on a level with the county families. Young Bolton had some useful connections, and his uncles had certainly played their part in the big world – yet in his youth he may have lacked a certain southern polish. Thanks to his great uncle, Edward Bolton, he was rich and his long minority must have seen a considerable accumulation of income[128].

---

[127] He was born at Croston in Lancashire – the home of his grandmother, Mrs Porter, some ten miles south west of Preston. He was baptised in St Mary's Church, the chapel of ease at Tarleton. St Mary's is now redundant. It has a beautiful, unchanged eighteenth century interior.

[128] Neither he nor his brother seem to have been sent to one of the major public schools, even though the Bishop's sons went to Westminster and uncle John's sons were at Eton. His *Times* obituary says that he was educated at Eton, though the school records do not mention him. There was at the time a continuing debate about the relative merits of private and public education, and his father may have decided that private was better.

Politics in the 1810's

The years of Bolton's growing up were lively. The governments of the time were conservative. The triumph of Waterloo in 1815 didn't help the Opposition, much of which had been opposed to further interference in France. Then came a whole series of Acts that seemed to be allying this country with the repressive European regimes that had emerged from the wars – and had the effect of damning up the demands for change until it burst out in 1831-2 and swept away much that need not have been swept away[129]. Lord Grey was the leader of the Opposition Whigs in the 1820s and he led them – from the Lords - with increasing caution. Real opposition was in the hands of the radicals, whose leader in the Commons was Sir Francis Burdett.

It was the age of the great Reviews. The Edinburgh Review had been founded in 1802 and in 1818 reached a high point in its circulation. It was the forum for the newly confident Whig- Radical opposition – whose then darling was Henry Brougham. The Quarterly Review had followed it in 1809, to provide a more conservative approach to issues.

Oxford & Lincoln's Inn, 1819-26

On 25 March 1819 young Bolton matriculated as a gentleman commoner at Corpus Christi College, Oxford[130]. The master for the previous 36 years was the 85-year old Dr John Cooke, known for his mild rule. John Keble had studied there and Thomas Arnold had left four years previously. It would be interesting to know who his friends were during those years, and whether he was affected by the politics of the time. The Peterloo Massacre took place in August 1819 – when the yeomanry cavalry (commanded by Thomas

---

[129] This at any rate was Disraeli's view.

[130] Corpus Christi College was the college of his uncles, Bishop Walker and Capt James. Gentlemen Commoners were the rich and/or aristocratic ones. They wore different gowns, dined on a table by themselves or with the dons on the high table, and were not expected to read for a degree (unlike the "reading men"). His brother John came up to Balliol the following year.

Trafford) had been called in to violently disperse a peaceful gathering. It was an event that radicalised many young people. In the Six Acts of 1819-20 the government brought in more repressive legislation. A new generation was growing up that had not known the French Revolution, and was beginning to question the anti-Jacobin assumptions that had become entrenched through the long war and the invasion scares. During 1820 the radical anger found a focus in Queen Caroline and in the struggle to prevent a Bill of Pains and Penalties being moved against her. They succeeded in November 1820, but things quietened down after that.

Bolton didn't graduate from Oxford. In 1821 he entered Lincoln's Inn[131]. Reginald Heber was elected Preacher at Lincoln's Inn in April the following year[132], though one imagines that Heber's Tory sympathies were not those of Bolton King – even at this time. The Inns of Court were one of the natural routes to follow after university, and he may have had some thoughts of a career at the bar. He may at any rate have been looking for a lawyer's training – like his father. The law – like the church - was part of the cultural background of the 19th century King family.

I have no idea what he did with himself in London during the busy years from 1821. With his straight-laced, serious-minded Lancashire background, he presumably didn't become a young man about town. 1821 was the year of the publication of *Life in London* by Pierce Egan. The account of the doings of Corinthian Tom and his country friend, Jerry Hawthorn, gripped the London world – and presented the accomplished man about town as one caught up in gambling, drinking, cock-fighting, boxing, fencing and fox-hunting[133].

---

[131] The same year that John Henry Newman left it, abandoning the idea of a legal career and deciding instead to be ordained.

[132] Heber had a distinguished career at Oxford (Brasenose) where he had gone in 1800. On graduating, he was elected a Fellow of All Souls, and – after ordination in 1807 – was instituted to the family living at Hodnet. The appointment at Lincoln's Inn was his first major bit of recognition. In December 1822 he was offered the diocese of Calcutta. He left England in June 1823 and died in India on 3 April 1826, aged 43.

The book was dedicated to King George IV. It stood for everything a later generation was to abhor about the Regency years and their aftermath, and I don't think that young Bolton King would have lost himself there. Nonetheless, such things were part of a young man's life in those days. Bolton King was a lifelong huntsman and he would have known his way around the great boxers of his day.

The young Bolton had a lot of family in and around London. His uncles had children of his age – and uncle John particularly had a large family who were gradually marrying at this time[134]. He seems to have been particularly close to the Bishop's younger son, James King, who married the daughter of Bolton's much older half-sister in 1825. Bolton himself was said to have been keen on the Bishop's younger daughter, but she preferred his younger brother. John King and Sarah King were married in June 1827 from Sarah's sister's house some three months after the Bishop's death.

There was interest in politics. The mood was gradually becoming more open to change. Free trade ideas were everywhere. People were reading political economy – Ricardo, Malthus and James Mill. In 1823-5 Frederick Robinson – "Prosperity Robinson" – was presiding over a booming economy as Chancellor of the Exchequer. George Canning, who had taken over as Foreign Secretary in August 1822 after the suicide of Lord Castlereagh, was providing a focus in government for several left-leaning Tories[135]. If Bolton King was one

---

[133] They were the original Tom & Jerry. Pierce Egan (1772-1849) was the son of an Irish road mender who made his name as a sports journalist. In 1812 he published a history of boxing – Boxiana.

[134] Three of uncle John's daughters and the Bishop's elder daughter were already married by the time Bolton arrived in London. Then Anne married Col. Eustace in 1821; Katherine married Henry Adeane of Babraham in 1822; John junr. married Charlotte Wyndham of Petworth in 1823 and the Bishop's elder son, Walker junr, married Anne Heberden the same year. 1825 saw three weddings: Uncle John's second son, William King, married Elizabeth Coddington; the Bishop's younger son, James, married Maria Carleton, the daughter of Bolton's half-sister; and uncle John's daughter Emily married W.H. Harford of Bristol.

[135] Notably William Huskisson and Frederick Robinson (later Lord Goderich).

of those who were moving away from their parents' liberal conservatism and finding a home amongst the radical Whigs, then he was very much a child of his time.

Umberslade & Marriage 1826-30

Old Edward King died in 1824 and, though Bolton's mother seems to have continued at Kirkham for a while, it was time for Bolton to find a home of his own and settle down. In 1826 he bought Umberslade Park from the earl of Plymouth. It was a derelict mansion, near Tamworth on the outskirts of Birmingham,[136]. The house had come to Lord Plymouth through his mother, heiress to the Archer family, but he had never lived there. About 1700 acres went with the house. He clearly didn't intend to pursue a legal career. Maybe even then he had the intention of going into politics?

The confident time of the early 1820's had given way after a series of bank failures in December 1825. 1826 was a year of economic stagnation and then, in February 1827, Lord Liverpool had a stroke. His long tenure had to a large extent held the Whig, reformist influences at bay. There was no-one to take his place. His successor, George Canning, was a conservative at home but a liberal abroad. He put together a government without the Tory right wing, but with a number of Whigs. This alliance survived Canning's death in August 1827, and even Goderich's fall in January 1828. However, Wellington gave up on the Whigs in May 1828 and formed a thoroughly Tory administration. There was nonetheless a feeling during the 1828 session that parliamentary reform would have to come – and that Catholic Relief would be the sign of its coming. In March 1825 Sir Francis Burdett had introduced a Catholic Relief Bill, which got voted down[137] – and the 1826 election

---

[136] Oliver Bolton King says that he sold Carr Hill House in Kirkham in 1825, but Carr Hill House belonged to his father – and his father's property was divided between his brother and sisters. He bought Umberslade for £75,000 and then went on to spend £13,000 on renovations.

[137] Apart from Bishop Henry Bathurst of Norwich, Bishop Walker King of

was won on a no popery ticket. Nonetheless, the Whigs and the radicals were gaining in confidence. Frederick Lingard had written a pro-Catholic history of England in 1819, which William Cobbett popularised in 1824-5 with his "History of the Protestant Reformation". They helped to disseminate the romantic idea that the Protestant Reformation was the source of everything bad about the present age, and that the middle ages were a bit of a pastoral paradise. They helped to lay the foundation for the movement that finally got rid of Catholic disabilities.

It has been suggested that Bolton King already had a political association with Robert Knight. Knight had been a radical since as a young man he had stood at a bye-election in Warwick to defend the Revolution in France. His views were vastly different to those with which Bolton King would have been familiar during the years of his growing up. Whatever the circumstances, Umberslade was next door to the Knights' country house at Barrells – and in February 1828 Bolton married Robert Knight's younger daughter at St George's, Hanover Square.

PART TWO: The Campaign for the Reform Bill & its Aftermath, 1830-7

It was a public life. Reading the Warwickshire papers gives one a pretty clear idea of how it all unfolded and what he was involved in - and it started with a bang. In January 1830 Bolton King was appointed a Justice of the Peace, and a few weeks later he became High Sheriff of Warwickshire. This largely honorific post brought him more than usually into the public eye because the High Sheriff presided over the borough and county elections that followed the death of George IV in June that year. Since Birmingham was in the county of Warwick, and had no representation of its own, Warwick election meetings were always lively. At the election of the county

---

Rochester was the only Bishop to vote for the Bill.

members on 6 August, Bolton King had to address the members of the Birmingham Political Union and "desired them, as gentlemen and Englishmen, to hear every one quietly and patiently".

Then, in November 1830 Wellington's government fell and Lord Grey came in on a Reform ticket. Throughout that winter there were extraordinary scenes as huge gatherings throughout the country petitioned the government for a reform of parliament. Sir Charles Greville[138], one of the members for the borough, declared himself against any measure, but it was clear that Grey was soon going to request a dissolution and to seek a mandate for a reform measure. A vast gathering on Warwick race-course in April 1831 showed that the movement to some sort of reform was overwhelming. Three days after the gathering, Bolton King announced that in the expected elections he would be standing as a reformer against Sir Charles Greville and alongside John Tomes, the other member for the borough[139]. Parliament was dissolved on Saturday, 23 April. Canvassing in Warwick started in earnest the following Monday. King's colours were pink, and his motto "Whole Bill" and "King and Reform"[140]. The declaration took place on Friday – elections happened quick in those days. John Tomes and Bolton King were declared elected, with Sir Charles Greville trailing in third place[141].

King made his maiden speech in the House on 1st July 1831, arguing for the removal of the tax on cotton imports. Lord Althorp[142]

---

[138] Maj. Gen. Hon Sir Charles Greville (1780-1836), M P for Warwick 1815-30, 1832-3 & 1835-6. Younger son of the 2nd Earl of Warwick, and a rather more respectable version of his uncle and namesake who kept Lady Hamilton before she became Lady Hamilton!

[139] For more detail, see under Robert Knight IV, Bolton King's father-in-law. Warwick in those days was a town with a population of around 6500.

[140] William IV was at that stage thought to be sympathetic to Reform (for no very good reason) so there was a happy ambiguity in the motto.

[141] The voting figures were Tomes 698, King 523, Greville 505.

[142] John Charles, Viscount Althorp & (1834) 3rd Earl Spencer. Leader of Grey's party in the House of Commons since 1830. Not a great debater, but more

responded. King seems to have made a mark, because on 18th July he was called to wind up the debate on the reduction of pensions. Then, on 30th August, he made quite a long speech in criticism of the £10 Householder clause in the proposed Bill. Already he could see that the number of new electors in Warwick on this basis would be very small, and would do nothing to curb the Castle's control of the town's parliamentary interest. However, he got nowhere with Sir Thomas Denman, the Attorney General, and the £10 Householder qualification remained. After much difficulty the Reform Bill finally passed into law in June 1832, and Bolton King looked forward to another contest in December.

It was an unhappy six months. Canvassing started at the beginning of October. Very early on it was clear that the Castle was going to do all it could to get Sir Charles Greville back and, since the electorate had changed very little as a result of the Reform Bill, they stood a good chance. By mid-November the town was bitterly divided. Bolton King had to deny that he was a slave owner or had any property in the West Indies. Clearly people wondered where his money came from, and thought his Lancashire origins told against him in this respect. The declaration for the Borough was due on Tuesday, 11th December. On the previous Friday, a meeting in the Market Square was disturbed by supporters of Sir Charles Greville carrying clubs. By Monday the Army had to be called in to keep order. When the result was announced, Sir Charles Greville had topped the poll and Bolton King only got back because John Tomes gave way to the younger man[143].

Tensions and Splits, 1832-1837
The fall out from the Election continued. After an enquiry, a committee of the House declared Sir Charles Greville not elected, and the writ for the borough was suspended pending re-organisation. The idea was to add Leamington to Warwick[144] - an

---

acceptable to people generally than the more brilliant Henry Brougham.
[143] The voting figures were Greville 701, King 553, Tomes 463.
[144] Leamington had grown from a village of 300 people in 1801 to a town of over

idea that did not delight Leamington people. They didn't want the upsets from Warwick to spread into their quiet streets. It was however the obvious answer, if the electorate was to be large enough to prevent bribery in the future. In July 1833 it was said that Lord Warwick would be dismissed from his Lord Lieutenancy as a result of his interference in the election, and the noble Lord had to vigorously protest his innocence in the House of Lord at the end of August[145]. In March 1834 a Bill for the extension of the Warwick franchise was sent up to the House of Lords. It was, as the Warwick Advertiser noted, "the only Bill for the prevention of bribery that has passed without a single division – a pretty convincing proof of the opinion entertained by a very large majority of the House with respect to the delinquencies of our "independent" Borough". However, the Lords threw out the Bill in August and the bells of St Mary's Church Warwick rang out in celebration[146]. Then, in November 1834, the King dismissed the government. Lord Althorp had gone to the Lords and the King would not have Lord John Russell as Leader of the Commons. The Dissolution soon followed.

The writ for Warwick was granted and the canvassing went on throughout December. Bolton King was rumoured to be looking elsewhere – possible to one of the county seats. Sir George Phillips had announced that he would not be seeking re-election in the Southern Division of the county and that seat would certainly have suited Bolton King better. He didn't have an easy relation with the Warwick Radicals and they would have preferred one of their own - William Collins - to represent them[147]. However, someone else

---

6000 in 1831, thanks to its reputation as a spa town.

[145] Henry Richard Brooke, (1816) 3rd Earl of Warwick (1779-1853), elder son of the 2nd Earl by his second wife. Married the widowed Lady Monson in 1816 and had an only child, Guy, Lord Brooke.

[146] The vicar of St Mary's, Rev John Boudier, was a strong anti-Reformer and a Churchwarden, Mr Oram, had been disqualified from holding any public office after being found guilty of bribery in the election of December 1832. Mr Oram was summoned to give evidence before the House of Lords, but failed to turn up.

[147] William Collins (1793-1859) was the son of Thomas Collins, an alderman of the Borough, and son-in-law of the former M. P., John Tomes.

came forward to represent the Reform interest in the Southern Division[148]. Bolton King faced a second anti-Reformer besides Sir Charles Greville and on New Year's Eve got an undertaking from his supporters that he would campaign "free of expense". By now the expense of repeated elections was taxing his resources. In the country as a whole, the Tories under Sir Robert Peel were expected to recover a lot of the ground they had lost at the rout three years before[149]. In Warwick Sir Charles topped the poll, but Bolton King again got in.

The new Corporation Act came in and at the first Corporation elections of January 1836 William Collins topped the poll. He was then elected Mayor. Clearly Collins was an able and popular man. Then, in August 1836, Sir Charles Greville resigned his seat on the grounds of ill-health[150]. Local Tories brought in Charles John Canning, the able son of the famously liberal minded Prime Minister[151]. Canning won the seat, but not by such a margin as might have been expected in the current pro-Tory climate. It was increasingly clear that Bolton King and the Warwick Radicals were parting company. That summer the *Advertiser* published lists of every division since the beginning of the current Session in February, to show how the Warwickshire members voted – or whether they voted. Bolton King didn't show up too well. And the paper said,

---

[148]Edward Sheldon (1782-1836) of Brailes House – a friend and political ally of King's. A Tory, Sir John Mordaunt, had already declared. The other Reformer from the previous Parliament, Sir Grey Skipwith, took a long time to declare, and lost out to Sheldon and Mordaunt. When Sheldon died in June 1836 the Tories were quick off the mark and E. J. Shirley, who lost to Skipwith in December 1832, captured the second seat for the Tories.

[149] The Tories did well, but the main thing about this election was the resulting strength of the radical vote in the Commons, allied to the Irish under Daniel O'Connell.

[150] He died 2nd December following.

[151] Charles John Canning (1812-1862), Earl Canning. Was Governor General of India from July 1855, and First Viceroy after the reorganisation. Tipped as a possible successor to Lord Palmerston, but died young. His opponent was H. W. Hobhouse (1791-1868), brother of John Cam Hobhouse. The voting was Canning 464, Hobhouse 434.

"Readers may draw their own comparisons and conclusions". In October placards appeared all over Birmingham saying that Bolton King had sat in judgement as a magistrate on someone accused of trespassing on his father-in-law's land. The local paper saw this as an attempt at character assassination.

Then, in March 1837, Lady Canning died and her son went to the Lords. There was a bye-election and William Collins stood. He came in over his Tory opponent by 457 to 422. It was the personal triumph of a popular candidate, made possible by several Tories changing their votes. Clearly at the next election they would return to their allegiance and Collins wouldn't be the loser. Bolton King's days as Warwick's M.P. were numbered. Ten days after the election the *Advertizer* published an article, "We had yesterday an opportunity of inspecting a very beautiful Mezzotinto engraving, by Mr S. Angell, from a portrait painted by that eminent artist, Mr Gill[152], of Mr Bolton King, one of the liberal members for Warwick. It is a delightful specimen of art, equally creditable to the painter and the engraver, and one of the most striking likenesses we have ever seen. We can have no doubt that the electors, who are desirous of *seeing the face* of their worthy representative, will be anxious to possess copies of this exquisite production"[153]. In June that year William IV died and sure enough, at the ensuing election Collins was in and King was out[154]. He had fought four elections in seven years. It had been a tough, thankless and expensive time.

---

[152] Probably Edmund Ward Gill (1794-1854). The portrait is lost but the mezzotint is in the Warwickshire County Library. I had a copy made. It was not considered by the family a good picture (which it isn't) nor a good likeness.

[153] A copy of the engraving is in the Warwickshire Record Office and a photo of that copy hangs in my study.

[154] The voting figures were Collins 498, Douglas 468, King 439. Sir Charles Douglas, the Tory candidate, was like Canning a moderate man. He had been secretary to Lord Goderich when Lord G had sat in Grey's government. It was well known that Lord Goderich had left the Government over the threats to the Irish Church and that he was now close to joining Sir Robert Peel.

There was a testimonial dinner in November when many nice things were said and King was presented with a splendid "central ornament or candelabra"[155]. In his speech King said, "My object always was to support liberal measures, to extend civil and religious liberty, and to give as far as possible equal rights and equal privileges to men of all religions, of all classes and every state in the country". There were great attempts at unity, but the Tory *Leamington Courier* asked "Where were the Dormers[156], the Leighs[157], the Philips'[158], the Skipwiths[159], the Wests and the usual attendance of Radical assemblies in this district?" And they reported a rumour that Bolton King would stand for South Warwickshire now. "Surely such a report is unfounded. The annoyance of another defeat (and it is inevitable) would effectively disturb that placidity of temper for which the Squire of Umberslade has ever been distinguished"[160].

---

[155] The candelabra was left to his eldest son in his will, but was said by Oliver Bolton King in 1953 to belong to his brother Edward. I didn't see it when I went to Catworth.

[156] Joseph Dormer (1790-1871), only son of Hon. John Dormer by a Hungarian lady. In 1826 he succeeded a cousin (who was Mrs King's uncle) as 11th Lord Dormer. He lived at Grove Park, and was married to the eldest daughter of Sir Henry Tichborne (which meant that he was involved in the affair of the Tichborne claimant)

[157] Chandos Leigh (1791-1850) cr. 1839 Lord Leigh. His father had inherited Stoneleigh from the last (mad) Lord Leigh in 1806, though his inheritance was constantly questioned by distant (putative) cousins. His mother was the daughter of Lord Saye & Sele. A younger son was Dean of Hereford 1894-1919. He and his eldest son were close political allies of Bolton King.

[158] Sir George Philips of Weston House, M P for the Southern Division 1832-4. Bought his estate with money made in business in Manchester. His granddaughter and heiress was the mother of Lord Duncan (later Earl of Camperdown) who stood unsuccessfully as a Liberal for the Southern Division in 1865.

[159] Sir Grey Skipwith (1771-1852), M P for the Southern Division on the Reform side 1831-5. Tried unsuccessfully for the Northern Division in 1837. Had eighteen children (including ten sons) by one wife!

[160] If he was known for his quick temper, he was also known to be very ready to air his views. Hence (apparently) his nickname "Bellows". "My keeper, who I took with a high character from Mr Boulton King (Bellows) gave me just at this time, in consequence of having discovered him to be a very great rascal, being in league

PART THREE: Middle Years, 1837-1857

Agriculture & Protection - The Background, 1837-44

In June 1838 Bolton King and Georgiana were presented to the young Queen Victoria and then in August they and the family[161] left for the continent. After all the expenses of the elections, this was probably an exercise in retrenchment. A fifth daughter, Isabella, was born in Paris in April 1839, and the family then headed home. For the next two years King seems to have been preoccupied with agricultural matters. This encouraged him to focus on what was to become the next great controversy of the day. This country had always controlled the price of grain in the interests of producers, but after the end of the War corn prices were set high. There had been fears of a recession, and the measure was intended to protect the farmer. In fact, the recession never came and the result of the 1815 Law was to make the landowners rich and very unpopular. The radicals saw it as the landowners legislating in their own interest. The industrialists – newly empowered after 1832 – saw it as a subsidy that was unfair to the manufacturing arm. Free Trade was in any case becoming an increasingly powerful rallying cry. Richard Cobden had written a pamphlet on it that was published in 1835 and in 1838 he formed an association in Manchester to campaign for the repeal of the Corn Laws. The anti-Corn Law League was founded in 1839.

Bolton King was clearly not persuaded by the Manchester campaign. In May 1839, at the meeting of the Warwickshire Agricultural Society, he said that England would remain superior to

---

with a notorious poacher, and sweeping away all my game. He also pursued other game by carrying off my cook. I was obliged to discharge them both at an hour's notice". *Dyott's Diary*, ii, 303. The diarist was General William Dyott (1761-1847) of Freeford Hall, Staffordshire, ADC to King George III and a strong Tory.

[161] Georgiana, with two boys (Bolton 9 & Edward 4) and four girls (Georgiana 8, Frances 6, Jane 3 & Catherine 6 months)

all other nations as long as its agriculture was supported and as long as it was recognised as "the first and most important interest in the country". He was clearly looking for an opportunity to return to Parliament. His name was among those suggested in December 1839 when Attwood stood down as M. P. for Birmingham[162]. In the event G. F. Muntz was elected.

In October 1840 his health was drunk at the meeting of the Warwickshire Association for the Protection of Agriculture[163].

He was specifically asked not to contest the borough of Warwick in the General Election of June 1841. The Tories had taken control of the town in November 1840 and the Liberals feared for Collins' seat. They were in no mood to try for both.

Early in 1841 King was hearing rumours of Peel's conversion to Free Trade. King was committed to the traditional patterns of country life and he wanted both a strong agriculture and a strong manufacturing base. He was convinced that the end of Protection would mean the end of security for the working man, be he involved in agriculture or manufacturing. The Chartist riots of 1839 had been frightening and King's constant theme when he spoke at agricultural meetings was the interdependence of landowner, tenant and labourer. In April 1842 he was one of only three gentlemen present at a meeting of the Warwickshire Association for the Protection of Agriculture, which had been called "for the purpose of considering the propriety of taking steps to oppose the measures recently introduced into Parliament by Sir Robert Peel"[164]. King began to distance himself from the radicals and the

---

[162] Thomas Attwood had retired to Jersey. He was depressed by the Chartist agitations and never again took any interest in politics. He died in 1856.
[163] Douglas Hurd claimed that the Essex branch was the first when it was formed in November 1843. A central office was established in London in February 1844 (*Robert Peel: A Biography,* London: Weidenfeld & Nicholson, 2007, p. 329.
[164] Peel introduced a Corn Bill in February 1842 that reduced the level of protection, and followed this up with a Bill that would allow live and carcass imports with very little duty payable.

Birmingham people, who were of course hot for the Anti-Corn Law League. His was a lonely voice. The Conservative Association continued to give Peel general support through 1842, and to keep this former Reformist at bay. However, the young Lord Brooke[165] was beginning to listen. Brooke, the heir to the Earl of Warwick, was then a key figure in the Conservative politics of Warwickshire. What Brooke thought mattered in Warwickshire because of who he was. It was the time of Disraeli's Young England and maybe he was influenced by King's vision of a Carlyle-style alliance between conservative Liberals and liberal Conservatives in the interests of the poor.

Agriculture & Protection - Climax & Collapse, 1844-7

In January 1844 a special meeting of the Agricultural Association was called "against all changes that may be brought forward tending to the violation of the protective principle, and to the depreciation of the native industry in any of its branches". Bolton King laid further emphasis on "the national industry in general" in his speech at the meeting. He went out of his way to argue that Protectionism was not just a self-interested campaign by the landowners, but one genuinely concerned for society as a whole. He supplied the moral backbone for the movement and was recognised as a key part of it, despite the cross party divisions. Over the next twelve-month he and Lord Brooke were working very closely together against Sir Robert Peel and I think Bolton King must have been hoping for a realignment of politics around the issue. In November 1845 things came to a head. After several discussions about the Corn Laws in the Cabinet, and with Peel unable to carry his colleagues - above all Lord Stanley[166] - he resigned. Russell

---

[165] Lord Brooke, and (1853) 4th Earl of Warwick (1818-1893), married in London in Feb. 1852 Hon. Anne Charteris (d 1903), granddaughter of the Earl of Wemyss. It was their son and heir who married the notorious Daisy.

[166] Edward Stanley, Lord Stanley & (1851) 14th Earl of Derby. Prime Minister February-December 1852 & June 1866-February 1868. He was originally a Canningite who went into Lord Grey's government in 1830 but left early. He was the dominant figure among those who abandoned Sir Robert Peel in 1845-6, and led the re-constructed Conservative party for over twenty years.

wanted Palmerston to come in, to construct a government that was as much Canningite as Whig and might pick up others among the more liberally minded members of Peel's government. Prejudice against Palmerston on the part of Lord Grey[167] and Edward Ellice[168] prevented this, and it was left to Peel to bring in the Act for Abolition. It was a sad, missed opportunity for the Whigs – and the end of the Conservative Party for a generation..

In Warwick, there was another huge meeting in December, at which Bolton King took the leading role after Lords Aylesford[169] and Brooke. I think he was hoping to capture one of the South Warwickshire seats at the general election that was then expected, but the parliamentary struggle was a long one and in the end it was not the Corn Laws vote that got Peel out. The debate began in the Commons in February and the final vote wasn't taken there until May. It went through the House of Lords the following month with Whig, Irish and Radical support. Peel was then defeated on the Irish Coercion Bill and went as the Corn Laws passed the Lords. Lord John Russell took over without an election, with Palmerston now on board. The Conservative candidate in the county[170]

---

[167] Henry Grey, Lord Howick & (1845) 3rd Earl Grey (1802-94), son of the Prime Minister & a standard bearer of the old Foxite Whig tradition. Under-Secretary for the Colonies 1830-4, Secretary at War 1835-9, Secretary for the Colonies 1846-52. Colonial affairs were his chief interest. Had given up on the Liberal Party by 1880. He had a reputation for being difficult.

[168] Edward "Bear" Ellice, MP for Coventry - a self-made man and prominent Whig politician. He followed the pro-French traditions of the Foxite Whigs and disliked Palmerston's "taking on" the French during his first stints as Foreign Secretary in 1830-4 and 1835-41. His son, Rt Hon Edward Ellice, married Lady Jane Bouverie, half-sister of my gt. gt. grandmother, Lady Catherine Buckley.

[169] Heneage Finch, 5th Earl of Aylesford (1786-1859). He succeeded in 1812 and was married to the Earl of Warwick's sister, Lady Augusta Greville. At his death the Warwick Advertiser said, "The late Earl was of a retiring and unobtrusive disposition and for many years past occupied himself chiefly with agricultural pursuits".

[170] Evelyn John Shirley (1788-1856) of Eatington Park, failed for the Southern Division in 1832, came in at the bye-election in July 1836 and went on until May 1849, when he made way for Lord Warwick's nephew, Lord Guernsey. His son, E J Shirley (1812-82), sat as Tory M P for the Southern Division 1853-65 – for two

reconciled himself to the Protectionist cause and, though King challenged the Peelite Sir Charles Douglas in the borough at the General Election of July 1847, he had no real support there and resigned before the poll.

However much King argued to the contrary, Protectionism was seen as an aristocratic cause that had little to say to business people. Disraeli indeed argued that the agricultural interest needed special protection - over against the manufacturing interest - because England had "a territorial constitution". This was not King's argument. He disliked the harshness of the Free Traders and dreaded the kind of society their enthusiasm was likely to create. However, he was more committed to Liberal principles than he was to Protection and knew that the Protectionists were not the people he wanted to stay with now. At the county elections in August 1847 W. H. Leigh [171] stood against Newdegate and Spooner in the Northern Division. Leigh had been – like King – a Protectionist, but he now considered the matter settled and was happy to stand as a Liberal, giving broad support to the Government of Lord John Russell. He was seconded by Bolton King. The Protectionists were now dominated by the diehards. The appalling Charles Newdegate [172] was heading up the Warwickshire Association for the Protection of Agriculture.

In his rest from parliamentary matters, Bolton King had time to think through his political creed. The "Conservatives" and the "Liberals" may have set out their stalls in the aftermath of the

---

years as Bolton King's partner.

[171] William Henry Leigh (1824-1905) 2nd Lord Leigh of Stoneleigh. Developed into a strong supporter of Gladstone's, staying a Liberal after the splits of 1885-6.

[172] Charles Newdegate (1816-1887) P.C., D.L., J. P., of Harefield & Arbury, Tory M P for North Warwickshire 1843-85. As an increasingly influential county member and member of the Anti-League (the Central Agricultural Protection Society), he was among those who brought down Sir Robert Peel in 1846. A Party Whip, who expressed the deep suspicion of many of the county members to the possibility of Disraeli taking over as Leader in the Commons after the death of Lord George Bentinck in 1848.

Reform agitation, but things were by no means as clear-cut as they appeared. Sir Robert Peel was a strange person to lead a party to which the landed interest looked for leadership – and many believed that the coalition he had built up could never hold. On the other side, Lord Melbourne was hardly the person to inspire the Radicals, and the Whigs showed every indication of being tired out. King must have listened to the arguments of Sir Francis Burdett, and he certainly knew about Disraeli's arguments for a National Party that combined respect for the ancient institutions, the Church and the landed interest with a real radical zeal[173]. And then there was Carlyle. Thomas Carlyle[174] was becoming the sage of the time. His "Chartism" was published in the first days of 1840 and clearly deeply influenced Bolton King. It was a work directed equally, as Carlyle told John Sterling, at "Girondin Radicals, Donothing Aristocrat Conservatives and Unbelieving Dilettante Whigs"[175]. It spoke for where Bolton King was, especially after his bruising encounter with the radicals of Warwick. "Chartism" and Thomas Carlyle were central to his future action.

A mid-Victorian Liberal 1847-57

It was a muddled time. In Parliament, Whigs, Liberals, Radicals and the Irish combined to keep Lord John Russell's ministry afloat. The Protectionists (led by Lord Stanley) and the Peelites made up the Opposition. Increasing prosperity meant that the concerns for Protection or Free Trade as a means of defending local industry or

---

[173] *Coningsby* came out in 1844 and *Sybil* in 1845.

[174] Thomas Carlyle (1795-1881), an early enthusiast for the German Romantics - Schiller and Goethe. Gradually established a reputation as a sort of Tory radical. His *Past and Present* (1843) established an idealistic view of the Middle Ages, in contradistinction to the harsh, industrial world of England in the early 1840's. His *Oliver Cromwell* (1845) established the Protector as a Victorian hero.

[175] It is interesting that Rev. John King published his translation of the Georgics of Virgil in 1843. The Georgics are a didactic poem on farming, written in 37-30 bc. It hoped for a stable order after the Civil War that would be based on a restoration of agriculture and of the traditional way of life associated with it. This might suggest that John King was closer to Disraeli's New England romanticism than his brother.

protecting the poor seemed out of date. Domestic issues slipped on to the back burner, and people became more interested in foreign affairs. England was developing its role as the defender of Liberty – in Portugal, Spain, Hungary, Poland, Greece and Italy. It was standing firm against lesser powers and the person who came to represent this ascendant liberalism was Lord Palmerston, Foreign Secretary in Lord John Russell's government of 1846-51. Palmerston was a Canningite, heir to that tradition of "liberal measures abroad, conservative measures at home" which had been the first stage away from the universal reaction of 1793-1822. In his later years, he was becoming the darling of the patriotic middle class while steering clear of too close an identification with the Whigs. He and Disraeli had a lot of time for each other and, when Palmerston was instrumental in bringing down Lord John's government in 1852, Derby and Disraeli both hoped that he would take a leading part in the new Conservative government. That government didn't last long. When it fell, the Irish would not have Lord John Russell back, so the usual Whig-Peelite-Irish coalition was led by the Peelite leader, Lord Aberdeen. It did not have much to commend it and the Crimean War destroyed it. In February 1855 Lord Aberdeen gave way to Lord Palmerston – the Churchill of his day[176]. The Palmerston years had begun.

Palmerston's first task was to prosecute the War and to bring it to a honourable conclusion. This he managed to do. An Armistice was signed in February 1856 and the Treaty of Paris was signed at the end of the following month. Then, in October, came the capture in Canton waters of a pirate ship, under the orders of the Chinese Commissioner for Canton, Yeh Ming-chin. The pirate ship was flying the British flag. Sir John Bowring, the Governor of Canton, demanded an apology and the release of the prisoners. When the apology was not forthcoming he ordered the bombardment of Canton. The Government felt they had to stand by Bowring. A

---

[176] It took a while though. Aberdeen resigned on 25 January and the Queen sent in turn for Lord Derby, Lord Lansdowne, Lord Clarendon and Lord John Russell before she sent for Palmerston!

union of High Church and those with a Nonconformist conscience stood against them. In the debate in the Commons in March 1857 a vote of censure was passed. Palmerston decided to go to the country.

M P for South Warwickshire, 1857-1859

This was the occasion of Bolton King's return to the Commons after twenty years in the wilderness. As soon as the dissolution was agreed one of the sitting members, E. P. Shirley, declared himself a candidate and "opposed to the unjust and cruel war with China". A week later Bolton King declared himself, in support of Lord Palmerston. Three days after that Lord Guernsey[177] announced his withdrawal for health reasons. King had the mood of the moment. He said, "I believe it was in great measure owing to the courage and firmness of Lord Palmerston that the late war was brought to an honourable conclusion". He argued for the rightness of Palmerston's firm stand in China, but also made it clear that he would be looking for further reform measures on the domestic front. He was advocating non-denominational education, based on "the plain, undisputed truths of the bible". The Advertiser remarked, "The explanation of his views and intentions, though not very specific, is likely to be deemed satisfactory as far as it goes, by moderate men of both parties". His proposer, Sir Francis Shuckburgh, described him as "no radical, but a Whig Conservative". He was returned unopposed on a patriotic ticket, the only non-Tory to be returned for the county between 1836 and 1885. In the country as a whole Lord Palmerston received a massive endorsement. Cobden and Bright both lost their seats. Palmerston had a majority of 85 over all his opponents. As Jasper Ridley remarked, "It was the greatest electoral victory that a party leader had won since Lord Grey's victory in the first election after the passing of the Reform Bill in 1832"[178].

---

[177] Heneage Finch (1824-71), Lord Guernsey & (1859) 6th Earl of Aylesford. Elected in 1849 on the retirement of E. J. Shirley the Elder. Married a substantial heiress, Jane, only child of John Knightley of Offchurch Bury, Warwicks. A rather colourless figure who died young.

Palmerston thereupon lost momentum. Through the summer of 1857 news of a "sepoy rebellion" in India was coming through, accompanied very soon by accounts of atrocities against British people, including women and children. The British Army regained the initiative, and committed its own atrocities - but Palmerston had seemed too laid back. In September and October the papers had contained little apart from Indian news, and there were calls for vengeance on the Indian population. In November, Bolton King chaired the Annual Meeting of the Warwickshire Auxiliary Bible Society, and called for the conversion of the people who had committed such acts. "No religion, if it could be so called, after the atrocities which had been committed, could be so cruel or abominable as that of the Hindoos". He was four square behind the Government of India Bill, which passed the Commons in February 1858, and transferred the government from the East India Company to the Crown.

Then in January 1858 an Italian named Orsini attempted to murder Napoleon III and his Empress. Orsini was found to be a supporter of Mazzini, and to have links with refugees in London. The Emperor's Foreign Minister, Count Walewski, sent a note of protest to Palmerston and in February Palmerston brought in a Conspiracy to Murder Bill. It made it a felony rather than just a misdemeanour to plot in England to murder anyone abroad. After initially supporting the Government, Disraeli and the Conservatives decided to support the Radicals[179]. Palmerston misjudged the mood of the house. He had seemed slow to respond to the needs of British subjects in India. Now he seemed prepared accept a ticking off by an autocratic Emperor in France, and to compromise Britain's reputation as a haven for freedom lovers escaping the European despotisms. Conservatives, Radicals, Peelites and Lord John

---

[178] Ridley, *Lord Palmerston* p.469

[179] It was Disraeli's first attempt to out-Palmerston Palmerston. It was to pay off later.

Russell's Whigs combined to put his Government out. In February, Lord Derby came in, at the head of a minority administration.

I wish I knew how Bolton King voted in the division. There had been rumblings about Palmerston's inactivity. Bolton King had already declared himself in favour of further measures of Reform. It could well be that he was less solid behind Palmerston now and more inclined to look to those prepared to bring in Liberal measures more energetically. In March 1859 Lord John Russell brought in a Bill for Parliamentary Reform. Bolton King voted for this, with the other Liberal groups. Now it was Lord Derby's turn to be in a minority. He was defeated and unexpectedly decided to go to the country. The dissolution was announced on 4 April. The election was to begin on 29 April. The election changed little. The Conservatives remained a minority, and the question was now whether the various Liberal groupings would unite to defeat them. Disraeli tried to get Palmerston and his people to join a continuing Conservative administration. Palmerston however was not playing. After a great gathering in London in June 1859, the followers of Lord John Russell, Palmerston and John Bright all pledged themselves to work together. A few days later Lord Derby's Government fell[180]. Palmerston was again Prime Minister, but this time in a united Liberal rather than Palmerstonian administration.

Bolton King was not in the thick of all this. Georgiana had died in May 1858, leaving him with four unmarried daughters[181]. As soon as Lord Derby announced the dissolution, Bolton King had announced that he would not be standing again. The seat returned to the Tories[182]. Three months later King was married. The

---

[180] The meeting is generally held to mark the beginning of the Liberal Party in Victorian politics.

[181] Frances, Catherine, Isabella and Henrietta. Henrietta had her sixteenth birthday only five days after her mother's death.

[182] Sir Charles Mordaunt (1836-1897) was the new member, and he sat until 1868. It was a peaceful election. Much talk of the "late respected member", and of the close relationship between Sir Charles and Lord Leigh. Sir Charles married Harriet Moncrieffe in 1866 – they figured in the celebrated divorce case in 1875

tradition among the descendants of this second wife was that, as she lay on her deathbed, Georgiana told her husband to "marry Louisa". If this is so, it would do something to explain his marriage to a woman thirty years his junior, barely older than his eldest children by Georgiana, and without any delay to start a second family[183].

PART FOUR: Elder Statesman, 1859-1878

Warwickshire Politics, 1859-1874

From then on, Bolton King began to act as a sort of elder statesman of the Liberal cause in Warwickshire. He had been a Palmerstonian in 1855-9. However, there is every reason to believe that he stood four square behind the accord of June 1859, and that from then on he was a committed Liberal with a capital "L" - albeit a Palmerstonian sort of Liberal rather than a radical or a Whig. In the run up to the General Election of April 1865 he was the key mover in bringing in Lord Duncan[184] as a Liberal candidate. There hadn't been a contested election for some years and Bolton King was accused of sowing dissension. His reply was that, "There shall not be an election in South Warwickshire without a contest until we have a fair share in the representation of the county". Liberal organisation was ropy and no match for the efficiency of the Conservative machine, but at least they were in business. Duncan

---

that involved the Prince of Wales.

[183] His second wife was the daughter of Rev Charles Palmer, vicar of nearby Lighthorne. Lighthorne Vicarage was and is a splendid house. Louisa' mother was the eldest daughter of the 4th Earl of Aylesford. Bolton and Louisa were married by Louisa's uncle, the Revd. & Hon. Charles Finch. Lady Charlotte Palmer was one of sixteen children, yet only she and the 5th Earl had children. The Finch family were a shy lot in that generation! Bolton's second marriage produced a son and two daughters (who didn't marry).

[184] Robert Duncan-Haldane, Lord Duncan & (1867) 3rd Earl of Camperdown. His mother was the daughter and heiress of Sir George Philips of Weston Park. He had got a double first at Oxford in 1863 and went on to be a supporter of the Liberal Party in the Lords. He was later a Liberal Unionist. Never held any ministerial position. Unmarried.

lost out, and Bolton King called for an extension of the franchise in the county areas. He was high-lighting the general sense that a Second Reform Bill had to be brought in.

The sudden death of Lord Palmerston in October 1865 made this inevitable and opened up long hidden divisions in the government. "The Liberal Party" was still a fragile coalition that had needed Lord Palmerston to hold it together. Palmerston's successor, Lord John Russell, did not command the same allegiance. In March 1866, when he introduced his Reform Bill, the Government was defeated by an alliance of Conservatives and dissident Whigs[185].

There was then some thought of a Conservative-Whig coalition, with Lord Stanley[186] as Leader in the Commons, and some neutral person being Prime Minister in the Lords. However, Derby nor Disraeli was prepared to stand down, and a purely Conservative government was formed. This Government then went on to bring forward its own Reform Bill on the basis of household suffrage. This received the Royal Assent in August 1867. It was a radical Bill, and a remarkable achievement on the part of Disraeli. At Christmas 1867 Russell retired as Leader of the Liberals and Gladstone took over. In February 1868 Derby retired and Disraeli took over as Prime Minister. The stage was set for the famous duels between two major personalities. Then in March 1868 Gladstone brought in a proposal to disestablish and disendow the Church of Ireland. Disraeli's Government had been thinking through its own proposals to provide some endowments for the Roman Catholic and Presbyterian churches in Ireland. Gladstone's proposals however divided them, while they re-united the Liberals. Everyone was now looking for the General Election, to be fought on the new register.

---

[185] Known as Adullanites. They included Robert Lowe, Lord Elcho, Lord Grosvenor.
[186] Edward Stanley, Lord Stanley & (1869) 15th Earl of Derby (1826-1893), M P from 1849, Under Secretary at the Foreign Office Feb-Dec 1852, Foreign Secretary 1866-8 & 1874-8. Always on the liberal wing of the Party and invited to join the Government in 1855 and 1865. Resigned from the Conservative Party in 1880. Married the widowed Lady Salisbury - step-mother to the 3rd Marquess.

Liberal hopes were high. It was universally believed that the extension of the franchise must benefit them. In August 1868 Bolton King presided at the meeting that decided to run two Liberal candidates at the ensuing General Election. The chief issue was Irish Church Disestablishment, which Bolton King favoured. It was a close run thing, but in Warwickshire the Liberals lost out[187]. In the country as a whole the Liberals triumphed, and Gladstone became Prime Minister. For three and a half years there was ceaseless activity. The Irish Church was disestablished and disendowed in 1869. The Education Act and the Irish Land Act were both passed in 1870. The first greatly increased government support for Church Schools and also created Board Schools[188]. The second gave extraordinary security to Irish tenants as long as they paid their rents. Purchase was abolished in the Army by royal decree in the same year. The Licensing Act of 1872, which laid down fixed opening hours, was felt to be a serious curtailment of liberty - but was popular with the nonconformists. There was further reform of the Civil Service and a radical reform of the law courts in the Judicature Act of 1873.

Gladstone was certainly busy, but he upset people - partly for doing too much and partly for doing too little. There was no social legislation, and nothing that cost anything much. Government expenditure was no higher in 1874 than it was in 1868. That at least was popular at Chadshunt.

It was the Irish problem that divided Bolton King and Gladstone. The Irish Land Act had given extraordinary security to tenants there.

---

[187] Sir Robert Hamilton and Lord Hyde were the Liberal candidates. H. C. Wise and John Hardy (brother of Gathorne Hardy, Disraeli's Home Secretary) were the Conservatives. The figures were Wise 2580, Hardy 2498, Hamilton 2465, Hyde 2452. Hamilton was a soldier who served in India during the mutiny and had retired into the county. Hyde was the son and heir of Lord Clarendon who was Foreign Secretary 1865-7 and again under Gladstone until his death in 1870.
[188] The nonconformists had assumed that the Board Schools would be the main thing and were angry at the support offered to denominational schools.

The trouble was that it was not clear why the radical legislation Gladstone introduced to deal with the particular problem of Ireland should not eventually be introduced in Scotland and England. Ireland was certainly radically disaffected, but there was also unhappiness in Scotland and in England. Landowners were increasingly not the flavour of the moment. People had been murmuring about the increased concentration of land ownership and the House of Lords commissioned a great survey of landholding in Britain. When it was published in 1874, it showed that the concentration was greater than anyone had realised and there were new cries against the evils of "landlordism". Surely this aristocratic take-over of agricultural land must be reversed? Why should not tenants be able to gradually buy their holdings? Putting this on to the Liberal Party's agenda was certainly a possibility, given the increasing radicalism of tenants and farm labourers, and the support they found amongst urban voters. Joseph Arch started his National Agricultural Labourers' Farm Union in 1872 on Bolton King's doorstep, at Wellesbourne. Within a year it had a membership of 100,000.

The long agricultural depression of the late nineteenth century had now begun. In 1868 Gladstone had opened a Pandora's box by his reformist vigour, and he could not control the result. His government was increasingly unpopular. In March 1873 he was defeated in the Commons, but Disraeli refused to take office. He wanted Gladstone to dig himself deeper into the mess - which he did.

Whither the Liberal Coalition, 1874-1878?
1868 was the last election in which Bolton King seems to have taken part with any enthusiasm. As Robert Blake has said of the Gladstone's first Government, "It was the first avowed and vigorous reformist Government since Grey's, and its legislation had annoyed almost as many groups and interests as the Whigs had managed to offend between 1830 and 1834." Bolton King had always been a conservative liberal, but conservative liberalism had come to an end

with the death of Palmerston. It looked now as though a choice had to be made. On the one hand, there was Gladstone busy, interfering liberalism that seemed to be opening the way to a dangerous radicalism that had no time for Church or Crown or the agricultural interest. On the other hand, there was Disraeli who had somehow come out from under the diehards of the 1840's to offer Palmerstonian principles in foreign affairs and Canningite principles at home. With agricultural revenues shaky, and unrest growing, it took all Bolton King's liberal principles to keep him loyal to Gladstone at the next election.

On 24 January 1874 Gladstone unexpectedly dissolved Parliament and went to the country. Bolton King chaired the meeting at the Warwick Corn Exchange when Sir Robert Hamilton was again adopted as the candidate for South Warwickshire. There was no thought of bringing in two candidates and Bolton King had not much to say. He wanted expenditure kept down, and thought this was more likely under Gladstone. He wanted the farmer let alone. The Advertiser reported, "For himself, the Chairman candidly admitted that he was not very much in love either with Mr Gladstone or with the members of his ministry, but he was convinced that they were a much better Government, generally speaking, than could be framed by Mr Disraeli"[189].

Hamilton lost, and so did Gladstone. In May 1875 Bolton King had a heart attack and there were fears for his life. He recovered, but it was clear he hadn't long to live. The political world he had known was changing fast, and the changes were difficult and painful ones. His elder son took over at a dark moment for landlords.

Bolton King stood in a fine political tradition, which was consonant with that of his family through the generations. He loved the world of old England, the hunt and the yeomanry. He supported non-denominational Christian education, but he had doubted the power of free trade to protect the things that were good and the people

---

[189] The result in South Warwickshire was a Conservative triumph.

who were vulnerable. Victorian prosperity seemed to prove him wrong but in fact the destruction of agriculture in the 1880's and the Americanising of English life were in the end to prove him right. It was a tragedy that no-one managed to construct a gentle Protectionist party out of the confusions of politics in the 1840's. It could have provided an alternative to socialism; it might have prevented the dominance of the Free Trade ideology in England during the last 150 years.

PART FIVE - THE LANDOWNER

When he came into the county, Bolton King wasn't dependent on his rents. With only 1700 acres, producing an income of something over £2000 a year, he couldn't have been. On the other hand, he did interest himself early in agriculture. In March 1831, in the midst of the all the agitation for parliamentary reform, he sat on the committee of the recently formed Warwickshire Agricultural Society. While he was in parliament he wasn't very active, but on his return from France in the spring of 1839 he went to the Annual Meeting. He had his health drunk there as "a gentleman of the county who has filled the duties of a county gentleman so as to command the esteem of all his neighbours". Two years later he was Chairman of the Central Finance Committee. He seems not so much interested in the practical details of farming as the social context. It was during these years that Bolton King became a thorough country gentleman. Outside Parliament, his commitment was now to agriculture. He saw agriculture as his business and landowning as his calling.

In practical terms, this meant building up an estate that would give him a sensible income. While his father-in-law lived, Bolton King had the management of over 6000 acres of fine Warwickshire farmland. There was also his own mansion at Umberslade, the house that Mr Knight had built at Chadshunt and the house at Barrells (which was boarded up). In the 1840's and early 1850's Bolton King must have carried considerable influence. After Mr

Knight's death, however, the situation changed and King became a much smaller landowner. The situation was further complicated by his wife's death in May 1858 and by his decision to marry again (to a lady with no fortune) and to start another family. Since he already had six surviving daughters, besides my great-grandfather (who now needed to marry and set up on his own), this inevitably put a further strain on the family finances. The house at Umberslade was already let and in 1858 was sold[190]. Life in the 1860's and 1870's was not quite what it had been and Bolton King was not the big noise he had been. In October 1858, when he was chairing the annual meeting of the Wellesbourne Ploughing Society, he remarked, "I have been an occupier of land all my life, and for some time to a much greater extent than I am at present". This was now certainly true. The glory days were over.

Question Marks against the Landlord System
The radical tradition in the English countryside had been dormant for a while, but it hadn't gone far below the surface. Events in Ireland kept rural issues on the agenda. The failure of landlordism to prevent the disaster of the 1845-9 had put a question mark in some minds against the rights of Irish landlords – and even in some places of landlords in general. During the 1860's people were realising that sooner or later strong measures would have to be taken in Ireland. Gladstone's first priority was to redistribute the property so controversially held by the Church of Ireland. He knew that the Church's supporters in Parliament were few. In July 1869 he got Parliament's agreement to take away something like half the Church's property and to apply it for the relief of poverty. The Roman Catholic Church was delighted. The Liberal landlords (like Bolton King himself) seemed not to understand that if Parliament

---

[190] It was leased to a Dr Edward Johnson in 1849 and used as a spa – or hydrotherapy centre. Florence Nightingale stayed there with her father in 1851-2 when he had something wrong with his eyes. In 1855 it was leased to G. F. Muntz (1794-1857) who made a fortune from an alloy used to coat the bottom of ships. It was his son, G. F. Muntz junr. (1822-98), who bought the freehold. The family continued to live there into the 20th century, though the house is now flats.

could confiscate the Church's property, it could as easily confiscate theirs too. The landlords were indeed next on Gladstone's list, but in their case he was thinking not of confiscation but of reform – and only in Ireland. What his radical supporters had in mind was another story.

Landlordism in Ireland operated on different principles to landlordism in England – though few people realized this. Irish landlords had none of the responsibilities that English landlords had towards their tenants. Irish tenants had to drain their land, put up and maintain buildings and fences and generally act as freeholders, but without any of the security enjoyed by the freeholder. The Irish Land Act of 1870 granted to Irish tenants just this sort of security, together with the right to assign or will their tenancies. It was a fair provision in some respects, though it was the well-off farmers of the post-famine world who benefited – not the poor. The landlords were the chief casualties. They had large debts and low rents and they were now unable to dislodge their tenants in order that they might farm the land themselves. The writing was on the wall for them.

The Irish Church Act of 1869 and the Irish Land Act of 1870 were two remarkable pieces of legislation. The government seemed to believe that the mandate it had received from the increased electorate after the 1867 Reform Act gave it the right to intervene far more radically than any government before it. The dire state of Ireland gave it an excuse, but powers exercised in Ireland could later be exercised in England. After 1870, the face of the agricultural industry in Ireland was transformed as a result of a government decree for the benefit of the poor. Some English landowners feared that the next move would be to introduce similar laws in this country. Gladstone did not intend it, but his radical supporters did. Men like John Bright wanted to see a considerable extension of tenants' rights in England, including a right to buy. In the aftermath of Gladstone's first administration it looked as though their day might come. When central government had once enjoyed such an exercise of power, there would be no stopping it.

Unrest in Warwickshire

Agricultural workers had a pretty poor deal in the mid-nineteenth century. They were poorly paid and poorly housed. Since there was a plentiful labour market, employers had no incentive to pay more. Since they were poorly paid, they were not able to pay economic rents if their cottages were improved. And there was not a way out for them. In 1833, when agricultural workers attempted to combine to gain higher wages, their leaders were rounded up and transported to Australia. The fate of the "Tolpuddle Martyrs" was well known in rural areas. However, another of Gladstone's innovations in his first administration was to relax the laws against combination. Workers no longer faced prosecution if they tried to obtain better wages and conditions

In the early 1870's it was clear that some parts of rural Warwickshire were looking for just such legislation from Parliament in support of their interests. In February 1872, just down the road at Wellesbourne, there was a strike of farm labourers. They were complaining about tied cottages and low wages. The Daily News took up the cause in London[191]. At Easter 1872 Joseph Arch[192] inaugurated the Warwickshire Agricultural Labourers' Union at Leamington, and this soon became the National Agricultural Labourers Union. In July, Arch addressed a large meeting at Tysoe[193], where men were enrolled in the Tysoe branch. They were asking for more at a time when agricultural was still doing well. They understandably felt they wanted a share in agriculture's prosperity. The trouble was that they became active on the eve of agriculture's

---

[191] The *Daily News* had been a champion of Liberalism since its foundation in 1846 – and was at the time the only major national newspaper committed to the Liberal cause.
[192] Joseph Arch (1826-1919)
[193] See M K Ashby *Joseph Ashby of Tysoe* pp 59-62. Isabella was there with her husband, the Vicar, and the Marquess of Northampton's agent. Mr Francis had the courage to address the meeting and to challenge the points made by Arch.

collapse, and their actions were to hasten the end of the small landlord – though after Bolton King's death.

Gladstone's legislation is no doubt the origin of Bolton King's remark in 1874 that he wanted the farmer let alone. It is unlikely that he had any sympathy for Joseph Arch. It is equally unlikely that he had any sympathy for the Birmingham radicals like John Bright who wanted all tenancies gradually transformed into freeholds.

PART SIX: THE YEOMANRY

Bolton King was a lifelong supporter of the Yeomanry Cavalry. The Yeomanry had their origins during the Napoleonic wars, when there were fears of a French invasion. Troops were formed by prominent landowners from farmers and others who owned their own horses and could afford to buy their own uniforms. The government supplied the arms and some instructors. After Waterloo, the Yeomanry played an important part in supporting the magistracy during the social and economic upheavals of those years. They received pay when they were called out.

In May 1839, the family returned from their visit to France. A few weeks later, Chartist riots were breaking out in Birmingham. On 4 July, two thousand Chartists assembled in the Bullring – to be dispersed by a band of the "new police" from London. The next day the Yeomanry were called out. On 23 July, Bolton King's Second Troop was called up in relief. At the end of the month Bolton King was part of the Grand Jury sworn to try the rioters, and three of them were sentenced to death[194]. It was at this time that Bolton King was presented with a sword by his Troop – which sadly was later sold[195].

---

[194] They were later reprieved.

[195] It turned up again at auction in the United States in 2004 – described as "A Victorian Pattern 1822 light cavalry officer's sword, presented to Captain Edward Bolton King, Warwickshire Yeomanry, circa 1839. Slightly curved 34.5 inch blade

151

The Yeomanry's role declined during the more peaceful middle and later years of the nineteenth century, to find a new role when recruits were needed to support the regular army during the Boer War. During the Army Reforms initiated by Lord Haldane, yeomanry regiments found themselves merged in various infantry regiments – though often looking back to their origins in the original yeomanry.

PART SEVEN: THE HUNT

Bolton King seems to have hunted since he first came into the county. The Warwickshire Hunt was a proud thing[196]. The 16th Lord Willoughby de Broke was Master from 1845 until his death in 1852. He was, I think, succeeded by Spencer Lucy of Charlecote. Then the 18th Lord Willoughby de Broke took over from 1876 until his retirement in 1900 (when he was succeeded by his son, the 19th Lord). The Hunt needed a grandee because it cost a fortune to run, and Lord Willoughby de Broke owned 18,000 acres. There was a crisis in 1852 on the death of the 16th Lord Willoughby de Broke. This Lord Willoughby died childless, but was found to have provided generously for his much younger widow. The new Lord Willoughby seems to have thought himself penniless and felt he would have to

---

etched overall with elaborated scrollwork, panoplies, VR and crown, Royal coat of arms, the King coat of arms, and inscription "Presented December 1839 to Captain Edward Bolton King/By the Non-Commissioned Officers and Privates of the /Second Troop of the Warwickshire Yeomanry Cavalry as a Small Testimonial/of the High Estimation He is Held in as their Commanding Officer". Steel three bar hilt of standard pattern. Fishskin and wire-wrapped grip. Iron two ring scabbard. Condition: Blade with some scattered patches of staining/light pitting. Hilt fine. Scabbard cleaned and showing light pitting overall". Although the inscription says it was presented in December 1839, there is a report in the Warwick Advertiser saying that, "On 7 January 1840 a very beautiful sword was presented to Capt. Bolton King at Hockley by the N.C.O.s and privates of his Troop".

[196] It would be good to consult *The Annals of the Warwickshire Hunt* by Sir Charles Mordaunt and Rev Walter Verney.

give up hunting the county. An emergency meeting was held on 16 March 1853, with Bolton King in the chair. It was decided to ask Lord Willoughby to continue - which on second thoughts he duly agreed to do. At the annual meeting of the Yeomanry Cavalry in August 1854 Lord Leigh proposed the toast of Bolton King as "a friend to fox-hunting".

Horses mattered to Bolton King. He had good stables and entered some of his horses at the spring and summer meetings. He was a country gentleman who enjoyed country sport at a time when fox hunting was central to the social life of the county.

PART EIGHT: THE POLICE

Since about the middle of the eighteenth century, there were mutterings about the efficacy of the forces of law and order in the country. The concerns were mainly about the fast growing capital, but they were not exclusively directed there. Some of the concerns seem to have come from the evangelicals, who deplored the drunkenness and rough sports of the lower orders – which local magistrates were held not to take seriously enough. Some of the concerns were from those – mainly on the conservative wing of the political spectrum – who feared the increasing radicalism of the poor during the 1790s and the riots that accompanied food shortages during and after the war.

The drive for a centralized police force in the metropolis was a pet project of the Duke of Wellington and his acolyte, Sir Robert Peel. Several attempts were made to introduce one, but it was only in 1828 that Peel was successful. His success did not mean that concerns about this undermining of local freedoms suddenly went away and the pressure from government to introduce London-style forces in the country were fiercely resisted by those who felt that the system of local magistrates and parish constables was a central part of a properly local moral economy[197].

---

[197] See *The English Police: A political and social history,* by Clive Emsley (1991).

The County Police Act of 1839 enabled (but did not require) magistrates to provide for a professional police force. Some counties did make arrangements. Some counties did not. In Warwickshire, several major boroughs – Birmingham, Coventry, Leamington, Warwick, Stratford – had their own arrangements. In February 1840, in the face of protests by Bolton King, the magistrates of the Quarter Sessions in Warwickshire decided to make arrangements for a constabulary in one of its four hundreds – the Knightlow hundred (covering the north east of the county). Commander George Baker R.N. was the first Superintendant and the hundred was divided into five districts (Rugby, Kenilworth, Bedworth, Southam, Milverton) which were placed under Police Inspectors. A year later Baker was replaced as Superintendant by James Isaac, one of the District Inspectors, who went on to serve as Chief Constable when the County Constabulary was formed in 1857. Inspectors and the local constables were poorly paid and worked hard. It was not easy to recruit quality men – but the system struggled on and was eventually accepted. Later, a constabulary was established in the hundred of Barlichway (in the south west) in 1855 which immediately merged with Knightlow[198].

Bolton King's opposition to the introduction of a police force shows a Burkean regard for traditional institutions that hide within them the structures whereby liberty is preserved. The fact that a centralized, professional police force was a French invention was a further reason for him to be suspicious. However, whatever the less than noble intentions of Sir Robert Peel and the Duke of Wellington, the end result has not been too bad. In recent years, the police have increasingly seen themselves as heirs of the old parish constables, locally accountable and locally controlled. The Home Secretary's power continues to be limited and the police themselves continue to be accountable to the County Councils – in

He is the acknowledged authority on police history and has a view that is sympathetic to Bolton King's position.

[198] See the Quarter Sessions Records (QS/7) in the Warwickshire Record Office.

this respect the heirs to the old County Magistrates in their Quarter Sessions.

PART NINE: PRISONS

The treatment of juvenile offenders had been an issue since the publication in 1838 of Dickens' "Oliver Twist". As High Sheriff in 1830, Bolton King had been introduced to local prisons – and he remained concerned. Lord Shaftesbury had led the movement to reform rather than to punish the young, and a separate prison for young people was opened at Parkhurst on the Isle of Wight. Then came Palmerston's Reformatory Schools Act of 1854.

PART TEN: CHURCH AFFAIRS

Bolton King's father was clearly a more than ordinarily devout man. To have himself painted against the background of Kirkham church implied a devotion to the place. The poem by his son spoke of him

>Like good old Simeon daily on his knees
>in God's own temple..

which suggests a devotion to Morning and Evening Prayer said daily in church. This had certainly been Cranmer's ideal at the time of the Prayer Book composition. The many monastic offices were to be simplified. They were however to be continued in the two daily offices and these would be said by a devout laity assembled in church. It was a way of being which his son's contemporaries might have thought a bit dry. He was though clearly a sincere Christian man, with a faith learnt at the parsonage house in Clitheroe.

This would have provided the atmosphere for Bolton King's upbringing. His grandfather and two of his uncles were clergymen. His elder sister married a clergyman in 1821, his younger brother was ordained in 1827[199]. The only book to have survived from

---

[199] Rev John Myers King (1804-1887), Scholar of Balliol, 1821-7, BA 1824, MA

Umberslade is a book of Family Prayers, which show the intense and anxious evangelical faith common to that period. This was the background, though the indications are that Bolton King was never given to much spiritual reflection himself. He liked to present the character of a man of action, active in the hunt and yeomanry - though certainly too a man of moral and spiritual integrity. He seems to have been impatient with the Christian infighting which characterise this period, and did his best to steer a middle course - in the best moderate Liberal way.

The Church at Nuthurst

He did contribute the main cost of rebuilding the ruined church at Nuthurst, close by Umberslade. Hitherto, the family had gone to the church at Tanworth-in-Arden for baptisms and funerals, although Nuthurst itself was a detached part of the parish of Hampton. The rebuilt church was consecrated in January 1835 by Bishop Henry Ryder of Coventry & Lichfield[200] and became the family's main place of worship. It was not though a parish church and the children's baptisms were still recorded in the Tanworth church registers. The VCH even describes Nuthurst as a mortuary chapel, which is hardly what Bolton King intended at the time of the restoration. Its chequered later history was due to the Baptist allegiance of the Muntz family, the later occupants of Umberslade. They built a substantial Baptist chapel across the field. Then in 1879 a new Anglican parish was created at Hockley Heath and a new church was built there. Nuthurst chapel was included in the

---

1827. Vicar of Cutcombe from 1832. Author of the Georgics of Virgil, trans into English verse 1843, 2nd ed 1871. The Aeneid of Virgil 1847, 2nd ed 1875. The Eclogues & Georgics 1882.

[200] In 1802 Bishop Ryder had married Sophia, daughter of Thomas March Phillips of Garendon, Leicestershire, who sister Susan was married to Edward Dawson of Whetton, one of Mrs Walker King's nephews. Bishop Ryder was made Bishop of Gloucester in 1815. At the time he was known as the only evangelical Bishop on the bench. His son George was a contemporary and friend of Manning, Newman and Wilberforce. He was ordained and married the youngest of the Sargent sisters - thus becoming a brother-in-law to Manning and Samuel Wilberforce. He became an RC in 1846.

new parish and as a result lost its reason for being. When I first saw it, the boarding around the little sanctuary was in place and it was possible to see the pews at the front of the church, with a tiled floor behind - for the ordinary folk to stand on, or sit on chairs. A vault underneath the chancel was used for the burial of Bolton & Georgiana's infant children and, later, of Georgiana herself. There was a large stone slab outside marked "Chadshunt 1835", presumably placed there after Georgiana's death and the move to Chadshunt.

Church Reform in the 1830's

In his early political life, Bolton King showed a Liberal attachment to church reform. At the general election of January, 1835 he spoke in the support of Edward Sheldon of Brailes House, who was standing as a candidate for the southern division of the county. He said approvingly, that Sheldon was "a strenuous advocate of Church Reform and decidedly opposed to Pluralities. He will vote for an equalisation of Church property and for a proper remuneration of the working clergy. In the same spirit he will vote for a fair commutation of tithes..". These were the issues of the election. The things that Bolton King was supporting were part of a shared Whig-Tory agenda for the reform of the church, to prevent the radical disendowment and disestablishment required by the radicals. The Ecclesiastical Commissioners were set up in May 1835.

Bolton King was never a radical, which was of course part of his problem in Warwick. Anglicans generally were not popular in Liberal circles in the boroughs. Free Churchmen and Anglicans were beginning to find themselves on opposite sides of a political divide. Already there was beginning that alliance between radicals and Free Churchmen against the Church of England (whether in England, Wales or Ireland) that was to prove so effective during the nineteenth century. At the turn of the century there had been a remarkable spirit of co-operation. Partly no doubt because of the then dominance of the evangelical party in the Church, some of the great missionary enterprises started as collaborative undertakings.

The London Missionary Society, launched in 1795, began as a partnership between Congregationalists, Anglicans, Presbyterians and Methodists. The British and Foreign Bible Society had a governing body that was half Anglican, half Free Church, when its constitution was drawn up in 1804. The Committee of the Protestant Dissenting Deputies, the official body representing the interests of Congregationalists, Baptists and Presbyterians, was a moderate body in the 1830's, seeking only to effect change in areas in which few but diehards would disagree.

The Church Rates Controversy
The trouble was that the 1830's and 1840's saw the Church facing new challenges. The huge increase in the population of the great industrial cities demanded a speedy extension of church building programmes and the creation of new parishes. Dissenters however refused to allow that the costs of building new Anglican churches should be a charge on the Rates, as the then law allowed. A development of this was the refusal in some big cities to accept that Dissenters owed an obligation to the Established Church at all. The question of compulsory Church Rates - used to support the local parish church - was a major issue from the 1840's and a dividing issue in a way it never had been before.

It was a division that Bolton King deplored and it is interesting to see him taking the chair at a meeting of the County of Warwick Auxiliary Bible Society in November 1848. He clearly was not used to such gatherings and it was remarked that the clergy and ladies "were surprised to find themselves chaired by the commander of the Yeomanry". Bolton King remarked how good it was to see all Protestants co-operating together. He clearly deplored the divisions caused by the radicals and the High Churchmen. As a moderate Liberal, he held to the old-fashioned evangelical ideal of a nondenominational Christian State and society. However, his non-denominationalism stopped short of a sympathy with Roman Catholicism. In the previous generation there had been a general sympathy for the Roman Catholic Church in France when it fell victim of the Revolution. There had been a concern for the rights of Roman Catholics in Ireland (at least in Liberal circles). There had even been sympathy for the Pope himself when he had been a prisoner of Napoleon. Now however the situation was different. Gregory XVI had shocked English liberal opinion in 1832 in his encyclical, *Mirari vos,* which was aimed at Lacordaire and the Liberal Catholic movement in France. Rome was already identifying itself with the forces of reaction, even before the shutters finally came down in reaction to the upheavals of 1848. The two forces were lining up against each other, and Bolton King was firmly on the liberal side.

No Popery

It is against this background that we can understand the "papal aggression" furore of 1850. No one objected to the reorganisation of the government of the Catholic Church in this country; the argument was rather with the language and the claims. They stirred ancient fears of foreign domination. Lord John Russell had taken the occasion to publicly knock the Puseyites and certainly in Warwick the concern was with the Puseyites as much as with the Catholics. The Roman Catholics were assumed to want a return to spiritual subjection, much as those who had fought against parliamentary reform had wanted to maintain a political subjection. The Puseyites were suspected of wanting to Romanize the Church of England and to lead it in a similar direction. There was as huge meeting in the Shire Hall at Warwick in December 1850, at which Bolton King moved a successful amendment to the main motion calling on Her Majesty's Government to *do* something about the Puseyites. It went as follows, "and we further pray that your Majesty will take into consideration the best means of effectually discouraging the many Popish errors and innovations, both in ceremonies and doctrine, which have lately been introduced by certain Clergy in the Church of England, and not sufficiently discouraged by some Bishops, and which, if allowed to continue, will be productive of greater danger to our Protestant faith than any interference by the Pope of Rome". I don't know whether he would have wanted the unliberal proceedings against Puseyism which followed during the next twenty-five years and which culminated in the Public Worship Regulation Act of 1874. It does however show that Bolton King had no sympathy with the assertion by the Puseyites of the Church's rights over against the State. For him, as for so many of his compatriots, clericalism and priestly power was profoundly un-English. He no doubt also feared that the firm alliance between Puseyism and the forces of reaction (as in Pusey and Liddon's opposition to the opening up of Oxford and Cambridge Universities to non-Anglicans from 1854) would only hasten the day when the Church would be disestablished.

In 1857 Bolton King again showed his impeccable Protestant credentials. He was standing for the county as a Palmerstonian liberal, and remarked in his election speech that "he supported Lord Palmerston's episcopal appointments". It was well known that since Lord Palmerston had come to power in February 1855, appointments to senior posts in the Church of England had been in the hands of the leading evangelical layman, Lord Shaftesbury. A succession of these appointments in 1856-7 had been of hard-working evangelical clergy, of no special academic distinction. They were controversial and Palmerston had been criticised. Bolton King however allied himself with Palmerston and called for further measures of church reform. It would be interesting to know what he meant by "further measures of church reform". He *may* have meant the abolition of church rates, which some optimistic free churchmen and some liberal Anglicans hoped for from Lord Palmerston's government. If they did, they were disappointed.

PART ELEVEN: EDUCATION AND CHURCH SCHOOLS

For most of his life, education for working people was provided - for the most part - through the village schools. These were supported from the rates, levied by the vestries. This of course meant that the vicar and churchwardens had control of them. Various efforts were made at the beginning of the century to establish a national system, but these always foundered on the inability of parliament to agree whether these should be denominational schools or not. The Church of England took an energetic lead in 1809 with the foundation of the National Society, to establish Church Schools in those communities that didn't have one. Various other voluntary bodies did the same, on a smaller scale and in 1832 they received their first parliamentary grant.

In the 1850's the pace of education reform quickened. With the steady pressure for an extension of the franchise, there was a recognised need - in Robert Lowe's words - "to educate our masters". The parliamentary grants to the voluntary schools quadrupled between 1851-1858, but there was an increasing sense that something more had to be done. A commission of enquiry was up in 1858 under the leadership of Sir John Pakington and the result was the Education Act of 1870. It was the achievement of Gladstone in his first government to establish a compromise whereby the voluntary schools (mainly the Church schools) were guaranteed a continuing place, while non-denominational National Schools were to be set up in those communities which were not otherwise served. Bolton King was already advocating non-denominational schooling in 1856, so it would be interesting to know whether he thought that denominational church schools had any place. Possibly not. His generation had an optimistic view of the State's continued preparedness to guarantee the general Christian character of its schools, and Bolton King himself remained to the end convinced of the essential partnership of church and chapel in the service of the gospel

1f.

CHAPTER THIRTEEN

REV JOHN MYERS KING

Vicar of Cutcombe with Luxborough, Somerset from 1832 and
translator of Virgil

He was born at Askham Hall on 16 February 1804, and baptized in the church a few weeks later. He was named for his long dead maternal grandfather, John Myers of Preston. The beautiful Westmoreland countryside seem to have played a major part in his formation – though the family moved back to Lancashire when he was eleven years old. He seems to have been educated at home, but studied with the young Thomas Arnold to ensure that he qualified for Oxford. He matriculated at Balliol College on 12 June 1820 and was admitted a Scholar there the following year. He took his degree in 1824 – the year of his father's death.

On 9 June 1827, John married Sarah King, the younger daughter of his uncle, Rt. Revd. Walker King, Bishop of Rochester. The Bishop had died just three months previously, so Sarah was married from Norton Rectory, near Faversham, the home of Sarah's elder sister, Anne, and her husband, Canon Thomas Wodehouse. They acted as the witnesses to the wedding, together with Sarah's brother, James King, the Rector of Longfield, who was married to Maria Carleton, the daughter of John's much older half-sister.

Less than a month after his marriage, on 5 July 1827, John was ordained priest by Bishop Law of Bath & Wells to a curacy at Chilton Polden, near Bridgwater[201]. Sarah had spent much of her youth in Somerset. Her father held a canonry at Wells Cathedral, which he

---

[201] In 1825, Bishop George Henry Law had ordained Sarah's brother, James. Law was the son of Edmund Law (1703-1787), whose family came from Askham, and who was successively Archdeacon of Carlisle and Rector of Greystoke from 1743-1754, Master of Peterhouse from 1754 and Bishop of Carlisle from 1768. He was a noted friend of religious liberty. Bishop George Law had been Bishop of Chester from 1812-1824. He died in 1845, aged 84.

retained after he was made a bishop, together with the living of Burnham-on-Sea – whither Sarah's mother retired on her husband's death. Two years later, on 8 June 1829, John also took responsibility for the neighbouring village of Edington. However, he resigned Chilton Polden & Edington on 12 July 1830, and on 15 October 1831 he was licensed to a curacy at Badgworth, near Axbridge – on the A38 just east of the M5.

Finally, on 8 December 1832, John was instituted to the parish of Cutcombe, in the Exmoor National Park, off the A396 near Dunster. The living was in the gift of the Lord Chancellor who at that time was Lord Brougham. Brougham's home – Brougham Hall – was only five miles from John's childhood home at Askham[202]. John built the modest house that was used as the vicarage at Cutcombe until the early 1970s – and extended & 'improved' the little church. It was a tiny village. The lord of the manor in his time was Philip Pleydell-Bouverie of Brymore. Luxborough, with which Cutcombe was linked, was nearby. In the 1820s John Lethbridge lived there with his first wife - at Chargott Lodge – when the village was owned by his father. I'm not sure that he still owned it in John King's time.

King arrived at Cutcombe with his two eldest children. Two more followed – in 1834 and 1839. He was a classical scholar, and seems to have spent much of his time doing translations and educating his children. His daughter's blindness came on around 1846.

King's decision to publish his translations during the 1840s may have been linked to the campaign for the abolition of the Corn Laws. The Corn Laws were held to protect the institutions of rural life – and the Protection campaign aimed to protect the nation's

---

[202] Henry Brougham, Lord Brougham & Vaux, was Lord Chancellor in Lord Grey's government from 1830-4, and as such the patron of various livings. He was an able lawyer and campaigner for several progressive causes, especially the abolition of slavery. Brougham was excluded when the Whigs returned to power in 1835 and never again held office, so that source of possible preferment dried up.

industry. King's elder brother was active as a Whig in their defence.
King himself might have seen his translations of Virgil's work as a
contribution in the same cause.

According to John's daughter Alice, life at Cutcome Rectory didn't
change much through the more than fifty years that the family lived
there.

John died at Cutcombe on 25 May 1887.

The Georgicks of Virgil
Undated, but probably published in the early 1840s
It is the second major work by the Latin poet Virgil, probably
published in 29 bc., following his *Eclogues* and preceding the
Aeneid. Dryden's 1697 poetic translation sparked a renewed
interest in agricultural poetry and country life amongst the more
educated classes during the eighteenth century. In England, poets
wrote their own Virgilian styled georgics and country themed pieces
with an emphasis on withdrawal from city life, the rustic arts, and
the embracing of a happy life on a country estate.

The Aeneid of Virgil
translated into English Verse by the Rev. J.M. King, Late Scholar of
Bal. Coll., Oxford, Vicar of Cutcombe, Somerset, and Chaplain to the
Lord Dorchester[203].
London: Francis & John Rivington[204], 1847

---

[203] Lord Dorchester was the son of his half-sister, Mrs McNamara, but it was
curiously old fashioned for him to have appointed a domestic chaplain. It may
have been granted him in order to facilitate his holding another benefice.
According to an act of 21 Henry VIII, the domestic chaplains of peers were
permitted to hold more than one benefice (See *The Parson's Counsellor*, by Sir
Simon Degge & Charles D. Ellis, 7th Edn. London: Charles Hunter, 1820). King
never found another benefice. The mood of the time was very much against
pluralities. In 1852, his brother-in-law was required to give up Henley-on-Thames
by Bishop Wilberforce.
[204] A publishing firm founded in 1711 and specializing in theological and
educational literature. It had links with the High Church party – having published

There is a dedication to Lord Brougham and Vaux.
My Lord, As I am indebted, for the only preferment I have obtained in my profession, to your Lordship, who, when raised, by the energy of your own talents, to the highest civil station in this kingdom, did not forget those who had been honoured by your earlier friendship, it is natural that I should wish to present to you the best offering that my ability will permit: *Me tener solvet vitulus*. And as Poetry and Oratory are but two different streams that gush from the same full and sparkling fountain, it cannot be otherwise than becoming, to dedicate a version of the noblest Poem of Antiquity to the greatest Orator of Modern Times, however unworthy that version may be, both of its subject and its object[205].

"The *Aeneid* was written in a time of major political and social change in Rome. The fall of the Republic and the final war of the Roman Republic having torn through society and many Romans' faith in the greatness of Rome. However, the new emperor, Augustus Caesar, began to institute a new era of prosperity and peace, specifically through the re-introduction of traditional Roman moral values. The *Aeneid* was seen as reflecting this aim, by depicting the heroic Aeneas as a man devoted to and loyal to his country and its prominence, rather than to personal gains, and going off on a journey for the betterment of Rome. In addition, the *Aeneid* attempted to legitimize the rule of Julius Caesar (and by extension, his adopted son Augustus) by renaming Aeneas' son, Ascanius (called Ilus from *Ilium*, meaning Troy), *Iulus* and offering him as an ancestor of the family of Julius Caesar". *Wikipedia*

King states in his preface that the Aeneid was undertaken "like its predecessor of the Georgicks", "solely for the purposes of my own family". "It cannot, I think, be denied, that the works of Virgil contain a more perfect union of imagination and judgement, of

---

'Tracts for the Times'.
[205] A hint in this dedication that King – now aged 43 - was feeling overlooked in his small and remote Somersetshire parish.

poetical inspiration and chastened elegance, and correctness and delicacy in taste, with melody in sound, and harmony in numbers, than any other composition which the human intellect has produced". He believed that a new translation was required if Virgil was to become a popular English poet – and Dryden's translation was wanting (being the product of old age and sickness). Pope made it sound as though we are "wandering over the flowery lawns of Richmond, than through the groves of Argos".

The Georgics of Virgil
Translated by the Rev. J.M. King,
Vicar of Cutcombe, Somerset, Late Scholar of Ball. Coll. Oxford
London: Hurst and Blackett, Publishers, 1871

To Henry Blackett, Esq.
"Dear Mr Blackett, As this reprint is issued mainly with a view to those, who, from kindly recollections of social intercourse or from a stronger tie, have expressed a wish to have some memorial of me, I have, not without your permission, placed your name upon the title page, in token that I enjoy the privilege of counting you amongst that number"[206].

To Henry Morley, Esq., Professor of English Literature, University College, London
"Dear Mr Professor, To you I am under an obligation which your ability only could have enabled, and your kind heart have prompted you to lay upon me. I allude to the encouragement which you have given my child, who, beneath the crushing weight of perpetual blindness, has struggled to win for herself an honourable name in English literature. If to any degree she may succeed, to you very principally she will owe her reward. To the world your generous aid can never be known: by me it can never be forgotten. To you, a

---

[206] Henry Blackett (1826-1871) was the son of John Blackett, who founded the publishing firm of Hurst and Blackett in about 1824. He steadily expanded the business and they were the publishers of Victor Hugo's *Les Miserables*. The firm was eventually incorporated into Hutchinsons.

1f.

master of the Saxon tongue, I offer this attempt to display the flexibility and copiousness, and, in some instances, I hope, the terse comprehensiveness of our country's language. To me one of the greatest pleasures throughout life, certainly not grown less keen in old age, has been to grapple with words and mould them to my purpose; specially, to draw up before me a word-army of vigorous Saxons, and drill them to keep step with the German "phalanx or Roman cohort"[207].

The Eclogues of Virgil
Undated - possibly an issue or a reprint in 1879?
A celebration of rural life, written during the civil war after the murder of Julius Caesar in 44 BC.

The Eclogues and Georgics of Virgil
translated into English Verse by The Rev. J.M. King, Vicar of Cutcombe, Somnerset; late Scholar of Balliol College, Oxford improved edition, uniform with 'The Aeneid'
London; Edward Stanford, 1882[208]

To the Right Honourable and Right Reverend The Lord Arthur Charles Hervey, Lord Bishop of Bath and Wells
My Lord, Your Lordship's reputation as a scholar opens to me this way of expressing my sense of your kindness to me as my Bishop, during the latter years of a long pastoral life passed entirely in your Lordship's Diocese, and during the last fifty years in the same retired West-Country Parish, remote from all the appliances and advantages, if advantages they are, of the nineteenth century.

---

[207] Henry Morley (1822-1894) was the son of an apothecary/doctor in Hatton Gardens. He trained as a doctor, but later transferred to literature. In 1851 he joined the staff of *Household Words*. He taught at King's College from 1857-65 and from 1865-1889 he was Professor of English Literature at University College, London. UCL had run extra-mural lectures in association with the London Ladies Educational Association since 1868, and in 1878 admitted ladies to the University on the same terms as men. A Hall of Residence was built at UCL in 1882.
[208] Edward Stanford (1827-1904) founded the firm in 1848 and ran it until he passed it on to his son in 1882. It still exists – as a specialist map publisher.

But needs it is, that each one loves his home:
He who says, No, but babbles with his tongue:
Home and it faces haunt his memory still[209].
I am, my Lord, Very gratefully and respectfully, your faithful and obedient servant,
J.M. King, Cutcombe Vicarage , Christmas Day, 1882.

Letter prefacing The Eclogues...
Dear Sir Thomas Acland, When you called at the Vicarage in the Autumn, after showing your kindly interest in Alice by asking what new bee was buzzing in her bonnet, you added, "Tell your father I am expecting some more from him." Now, there was nothing more in the grove at Mantua save a few shrubs that grew at the entrance, and I am Yours very sincerely, An Used-Up Vicar, Cutcombe Vicarage, January 1st 1879[210]

Letter prefacing The Georgics..
The same letter to Henry Morley that prefaced the 1871 edition, with the added note to "has struggled to win for herself an honourable name..." "That name has now been attained. The signature of Alice King is valued for the brightness of fancy which colours, and for the high religious tone which affixes the stamp of pure gold to all she writes".

Ars Poetica
An English Version
Dedicated, by his permission, to The Very Rev. The Dean of Llandaff[211]

---

[209] Euripedis, *Phoenissae*, 361. The Greek comes first, followed by the translation.
[210] Sir Thomas Dyke Acland, 11th Bt. (1809-1898), Tory M.P. for Somerset West from 1837, but followed Peel on Free Trade and didn't stand in 1847. He sat as a Liberal from 1865, but was defeated as a Home Rule Liberal in 1886. He was active in educational reform and in agricultural issues, a friend of John Ruskin and an early admirer of Millais.
[211] C.J. Vaughan (1816-1897), the son of a vicar, who was educated at Rugby and Cambridge. In 1839 he was elected fellow of Trinity College, Cambridge, and for a short time studied law. He took orders in 1841, and became vicar of St Martin's, Leicester. Three years later he was elected headmaster of Harrow

1f.

Clifton: E. Austin and Son, 1887

A poem by Horace. King's name is not give, but in the dedication, the address given is "Cutcombe Vicarage, January 1st, 1887" – less than six months before his death. "I thank you for having permitted me to decorate my title leaf with a name which has been printed in such bright colours on the pages both of ancient and modern literature. I do not, I trust, step over the line of sound judgement and good taste in affirming the strength and comfort which throughout a long life I have derived from observing your steady and unobtrusive adherence to the simple faith and ritual of the Protestant Fathers of our Church, and your charity towards those who differ from us. "Admiratione te potuis tempralibus laudibus, et, si natura suppedilet, aemulatione decoremus". Tacitus in *vita Agricolae*.

School, where he had a distinguished career. He married in 1850 Catherine Maria Stanley, youngest daughter of Edward Stanley, Bishop of Norwich. He resigned the headship in 1859 and accepted the bishopric of Rochester, but afterwards withdrew his acceptance. It has been said that he was required to do so by the father of J.A. Symonds who had been told of a passion the headmaster had for one of the boys.

He was appointed master of the Temple in 1869, and in 1860 vicar of Doncaster. He was made dean of Llandaff in 1879, a post he held until his death. In 1894 he was elected president of University College, Cardiff, in recognition of the prominent part he took in its foundation. Vaughan was a well-known Broad Churchman, an eloquent preacher and an able writer on theological subjects, his numerous works including lectures, commentaries and sermons. He died in 1897. One of King's nieces was married to the vicar of Llandaff, so this may have been the link.

CHAPTER FOURTEEN

EDWARD RALEIGH KING 1833-1900

A golden youth that ended in the chaos of the Crimean War, his mother's death and his father's second marriage. Life at Chadshunt could not survive the collapse of British agriculture in the 1880's – but his life is central to an understanding of how someone with liberal antecedents responded to the social and intellectual upheavals of the second half of the nineteenth century

PART ONE - The Background

Growing Up

My great-grandfather was born at Umberslade and spent his early childhood there. He had an elder brother, five years his senior, who died in November 1840 - a few weeks short of his twelfth birthday. It was a major tragedy for his parents. Edward was not quite seven years old and was now the heir. I suspect that he grew up in the shadow of his brother's memory?

In 1847-50 he was at Eton. Edward Hawtry was just coming to the end of his successful, reforming rule and Eton was becoming the high quality, socially exclusive place that it has since remained. Despite the intellectual traditions of his family, Edward doesn't seem to have been a scholar. In his holidays Edward would have seen his father and mother at the height of their fortunes. During the Protection controversy in 1841-7, his father was centre stage in Warwickshire politics. Though he never gave up his Liberal allegiance, Bolton King was making common cause with the Tory leadership in Warwickshire in what he believed was a defence of the English way of life - both in town and country. He found himself allied with the Tory grandees against the men of Birmingham. He believed that this Free Trade brigade wanted to take away every protection from British agriculture and British manufacturing. It was a heroic battle, which he lost. Free Trade was becoming the corner stone of high Victorian thinking, and there was nothing that King or anyone could do about it. Nonetheless, he put up a good fight and he seems to have been well respected for his views.

The Political Climate
Liberalism meant different things through the nineteenth century, and during Edward's formative years - from the mid-1840's to the mid-1850's - it had a particular character. The domestic concerns of the 1830's and early 1840's became less important as prosperity increased.   Foreign affairs instead were moving centre stage. Her wealth was making of Great Britain a major player on the world stage, and liberals of Bolton King's sort believed that Britain's wealth and influence should be used to further liberal principles in the despotic states of continental Europe and beyond. It was Lord Palmerston who was the focus of this attitude. In November 1846 Palmerston condemned the seizure of the Republic of Cracow by Austria, which had been done with the agreement of Russia and Prussia. In the Portuguese crisis of 1846-7, Palmerston was instrumental in persuading Queen Maria da Gloria to restore the Constitution - thus undermining the influence of right-wing Spain. In the Swiss crisis on 1846-8 he was similarly on the side of the radicals, though could do less for them against the combined interests of France and Austria. In March 1848 he said in the Commons, "I hold that the real policy of England.. is to be the champion of justice and right;.. giving the weight of her moral sanction and support wherever she thinks that justice is, and wherever she thinks that wrong has been done".

It was an extraordinary time. In February 1848, Louis Philippe fell, and Lamartine took over in France as head of an extreme radical government; in March revolution broke out in Madrid and in Vienna Metternich fell; in April the Chartists held their great demonstration on Kennington Green and Sardinia invaded Austrian-held Lombardy and Venetia. In May the Magyar leader, Kossuth, declared Hungary's independence from Austria. In Germany, the Liberals were out in force. In November, Pius IX fled from Rome. Some of these movements were so extreme that British public opinion was not fully behind them. On the whole though, Britain was seen as the only European state that had sympathy for the forces of change that were rushing through Europe, and the government of Lord John Russell - and in that government especially Lord Palmerston - managed to maintain this reputation.

In August 1849 Kossuth and the Polish General Bem escaped across the frontier into Turkey. The Russian and Austrian governments demanded their extradition, but Britain stood with Turkey to resist the demand. We were becoming the arbiter of Europe, able through our huge and increasing wealth to stand up to any government in Europe. The climax came in the summer of 1850. In January 1850, Palmerston had ordered the blockade of Piraeus in order to enforce compensation claims against a British citizen, David Pacifico who had been roughed up in an obscure incident in Athens in 1847. France made a formal protest, the Conservative opposition under Lord Stanley carried a vote of censure in the House of Lords, and the Queen pressed Lord John to sack Palmerston. Instead, Russell and Palmerston stood together and in June secured a tremendous vote of confidence in the House of Commons.

Palmerston asked the House to decide, "whether, as the Roman, in days of old, held himself free from indignity when he could say *Civis Romanus sum;* so also a British subject, in whatever land he may be, shall feel confident that the watchful eye and the strong arm of England will protect him against injustice and wrong".

In his biography of Palmerston, Ridley says of him in 1850, "Palmerston's critics were limited to a small number of educated people, most of them members of his own class, and many of them his personal friends; his supporters were the country squires and country parsons, the solicitors and doctors in the towns, the City of London, nearly all the Jews, the business men - even those in Manchester - and the great mass of the working class who talked about Palmerston in the inns".   Palmerston was the "Minister of England", and Edward's father was certainly one of those country squires who stood four-square behind him. It was against this background that Edward left Eton and received his commission in the 13th Light Dragoons.

Sporting Interests in the 1840's

But life was not all politics. Old Bolton King was just as keen on horses as he was on politics. His son was to grow up a great deal keener on horses – and indeed sport generally - than he was on anything else. He grew up during the first golden age of the sporting gentleman, and it was in that role that he was remembered.

In February 1848 Lord Aylesford was succeeded as Colonel of the Yeomanry by Lord Brooke and Bolton King took over as Lt. Colonel, with Lord Guernsey being promoted Major. This meant that, since Lord Brooke was not yet married, Mrs Bolton King was the senior lady on all important Yeomanry occasions - which included the presentation of the new standards in May 1848 and the review by Lord Cardigan. She opened the dancing with Lord Brooke at the Yeomanry Ball in January 1849, which young Edward attended aged just fifteen. He was then described as a private in the 2nd Troop of the Yeomanry Cavalry. The Yeomanry was his father's pride and joy. He liked the idea of the yeomen of England gathering in defence of civil order, to back up the parish constables. It had all worked well in 1839 when the Yeomanry had been called out to deal with the Chartists riots in Birmingham. Bolton King hated the idea of a centralised police force and saw no need for it. He led the opposition at the Quarter Sessions of July 1849. If there was trouble - and it was usually in Birmingham - the Yeomanry could cope.

The other love of his father's life in those days was the Warwickshire Hunt. At a Hunt dinner in 1868 Lord Camperdown spoke warmly of him. Mr Bolton King, he said, was "a keen sportsman who had been much in the field during the season; and he would go further and say that for the past thirty years Mr King had hunted more with the Warwickshire hounds than any other person in the county".

It would be interesting to know what other sports interested old Bolton King. Cock-fighting, bear-baiting and bull-baiting had all flourished in his youth – but the reforming Whig Government had declared them illegal in 1835. There were still gentlemen around in the 1850's who kept fighting cocks, but all these sports were gradually dying out. However, there was one illegal sport that refused to die out – despite it having been illegal since 1750 – and that was prize-fighting.

At the end of the eighteenth century and the beginning of the nineteenth century, prize-fighting had enjoyed royal patronage from the Prince of Wales and his brothers. A string of heroes enjoyed public acclaim – John Jackson, Richard Humphreys, Daniel Mendoza, Jem Belcher and so on. In the late 1840's the big name was William Thompson – known as Bendigo. He was quite a showman, and was very popular. Fights were very much part of the culture of this country in those days. Sir Henry Hawkins tells the story of a fight he attended at Six Mile Bottom. It had to be over the border into Cambridgeshire because the Essex magistrates didn't approve. The Cambridgeshire magistrates were apparently less hostile. People of all sorts came from all over, with gentlemen rubbing shoulders with the roughest members of the criminal classes. Very probably young Edward would have seen attending a fight – and enjoying a few bouts of fisticuffs himself – as part of his growing up and becoming a man of the world.

A Young Man's Books
A few of Edward's books survive. They give a glimpse of what he was reading – and an insight into the reading culture of his boyhood and young manhood. In his father's day, novels were considered generally unsafe. Jane Austen and Sir Walter Scott were challenging those prejudices, but they would still have been there –

especially in so godly a household as Vice Chancellor Edward King's. Few ladies read novels in those days, and men thought of it as an indulgence. However, by the 1840's the novel – now generally in three small volumes (like bound Penguins) - had arrived as the dominant literary form. Not many people actually bought them. Prices were high and the preferred option was to have them from a circulating library. They were however read by everyone – young and old.

The earliest of Edward's surviving books is *The Life of a Sailor* by Capt. Frederick Chamier (1796-1870), published in 1832. This is the first edition, but the book was to remain popular with boys throughout the nineteenth century. Another book, *Peter Simple*, by Capt. Frederick Marryat (1792-1847) was published in three volumes in 1834. This is the first edition, but only the first volume. Capt. Marryat is now best remembered as a writer of children's books – *Children of the New Forest* and *Masterman Ready* – but his first books were for adults and this was one of the first. *Peter Simple* is a sort of early Jack Aubrey novel – a story of a sailor during the Napoleonic wars. With Chamier, Marryat started a vogue for nautical novels. He had been a sailor, retiring in 1830 after a distinguished career.

Jack Brag, a novel by Theodore Hook (1788-1841), was first published in 1837. Hook was a Tory journalist and wit who was popular in the 1820's and 1830's. With Bulwer Lytton, Disraeli and Lady Charlotte Bury he was known as a writer of "silver fork novels". It was a style that was later to be sent up by Thackeray, who ridiculed middle class writers (like Hook) who wrote about the upper classes without actually knowing a lot about them. He was not quite in the same league as the others, and I don't imagine it was a book that Edward would have read as a boy.

Another of his surviving novels is a first edition of *Jack Hinton, the Guardsman*, by Charles Lever (1806-1872). Lever was an Irishman, the best known of the Irish writer genre that was popular in those days. He first became known in 1837 with the serialized publication of *Harry Lorrequer* in the Dublin University Magazine. *Jack Hinton*, published in 1843, was Lever's third book and I think is one of his best. Another book that belongs to Edward's boyhood is Capt. the Hon. Henry Keppel's *The Expedition to Borneo of HMS Dido* for the suppression of slavery. It was first published in 1846 – this is a later (3rd?) edition of 1847. Keppel was engaged in a humanitarian clean-up, subsequent to the passing of the anti-slavery laws, though he was also dealing with Malay pirates who were harassing trading ships in the area. It was good derring-do stuff for a 13-year old boy.

These books are a good reminder that boys who were growing up in the 1840's had something more than Scott and the Pickwick Papers to entertain them. Papa remarked that he had never got into Dickens, and this could well have been a family prejudice. Young gentlemen read a different kind of fiction – and a lively young man like Jack Hinton had more to say for himself than all the socially anguished people of Dickens' novels.

PART TWO - The Cavalry Officer

In the 13th Light Dragoons, 1850-4

In November 1850, just before his seventeenth birthday, a commission was purchased for Edward in the 13th Light Dragoon Guards[212]. Commissions were always obtained by purchase in those days - to ensure that the army was in the hands of men of property rather than of military adventurers (as, it was believed, in the days of the Commonwealth). However, with or without money, it still required an amount of influence to obtain a commission in a smart cavalry regiment and it would be interesting to know who approached whom to obtain this commission.

---

[212] The going rate for a cornetcy in 1856 was £840 – or something like £75,000 in today's money. It was a major investment. When Edward's lieutenancy was purchased, the price was over £100,000 in today's money.

1f.

The regiment had served in India from 1819-1840, and was not well known in England in those days. When it returned, it needed reconstituting. Very many officers and men who were committed to life in India had simply exchanged into regiments that were staying. None of the serving officers in 1850 had seen service in India in the pre-1840 days. Maj Charles Doherty had joined the Regiment in 1840, and the senior Captain, William Ormsby Gore, had joined soon afterwards.   There was the usual establishment of six troop captains and twelve subaltans. One at least among the junior officers, Cornet Peter Purcell, was to become Edward's close and lifelong friend.

The regiment had been stationed in Scotland since the spring, with the troops variously in Edinburgh, Glasgow and Piershill. In the spring of 1851 they moved south to York. After a year in York they came down to Hounslow. There was a General Inspection by the Inspector General of Cavalry, the Duke of Cambridge, in July 1852. Then came the major event of the Duke of Wellington's funeral on 18 November 1852. Pretty well the whole British Army was involved in this, and the 13th Light Dragoons were certainly on parade. Edward doesn't seem to have been in Warwickshire much between 1850-2, but in 1853 he had a horse running in the Warwick Spring Meeting, ridden by Lieut. Purcell. The horse was called Bendigo and Purcell ran him to a photo finish in the Grand Military Steeplechase. The horse was subsequently sold for 150 guineas. Edward had a filly running the next year, called Beckbury Lass. She didn't do so well. This involvement in local races didn't count as holiday, and it certainly wasn't shirking. Cavalry officers were expected to take their horses seriously and to take part in events like this.

In July 1853 there were some military manoeuvres at Chobham. The long years of peace had given the Army very little idea of battle and manoeuvres had been an idea of the Duke of Wellington. After his death, they finally became a reality. These were the first manoeuvres ever staged by the Army, and they involved 8,000-

10,000 men in a pretend battle. The Queen was there, with other distinguished guests, and everything was thought to have gone well. After this, the regiment moved off to the Midlands. Headquarters, with Lt Col Doherty and Edward, went to Birmingham and the other troops variously either to Birmingham, Coventry, Nottingham or Newport. At another time this would have seemed like a cushy billet, close to home. However, there were rumours of war and the following spring the regiment was commanded to hold itself in readiness for service in the Crimea.

Edward had seen three years of not a very arduous life as a young officer in a fashionable regiment. The mood is evoked in the arrival of Cornet Codrington at the regimental headquarters in Richardson's "The Charge of the Light Brigade". Cecil Woodham-Smith wrote, "The dash of British cavalry officers was never greater than at the opening of the Crimean campaign in the spring of 1854. These aristocratic horsemen were, in the idiom of the day, "plungers", and "tremendous swells". They affected elegant boredom, yawned a great deal, spoke a jargon of their own, pronouncing "r" as "w", saying "vewwy", "howwid", and "sowwy", and interlarded sentences with loud and meaningless exclamations of "Haw, haw". Their sweeping whiskers, languid voices, tiny waists, laced in by corsets, and their large cigars were irresistible, frantically admired and as frantically envied". Short hair was the order of the day, but cavalry officers were allowed "moustachios and whiskers", and Dundreary whiskers were common. The life was the life of a gentleman, with Waterloo and the other Napoleonic campaigns only distant memories.

Yet it is easy to caricature the life. There was a tough, underlying reality. The cavalry was the offensive arm of the army. The infantry marched into battle, and got mown down. The cavalry charged, with swords drawn, and the constant drilling and practice was aimed in the end at perfecting the tactics of the cavalry charge. In the 1850's there was a general belief that there was nothing that a charge of cavalry could not defeat. At the end of the charge, the sword - point forward - was intended to thrust into the body of the enemy. In Napoleonic times, the Dragoons' swords had been sabre-shaped, designed for hacking. Now, the longer point was favoured, although a great deal of hacking still went on in hand to hand fighting. The main trouble was the bluntness of the swords. The army insisted on steel scabbards. The sword rattled around in them and was blunted before use. The wooden or leather scabbards used in India were not considered. The tendency of the sword to blunt and rust was a continuing problem.

It was real soldiering. The Yeomanry was alright, but not the real thing. When Edward returned home in uniform, he would have looked a fine sight. He had a double-breasted blue jacket with white (officially buff) facings, and grey trousers with a double white stripe down the sides. On his head he had the tall, black beaver-skin shako, with its gilt and silver cross plate and regimental badges. Sadly, the practice of wearing one's uniform all the time had been discontinued after the Napoleonic wars, but there would certainly have been private shows of his finery for the family when he was at home - which was often.

The Crimean War - the Early Stages, March-August 1854
The army hadn't fought a war since Waterloo and it wasn't much prepared for it. Still, at the end of March 1854 the regiment had its orders to prepare to leave for the East. Lord Raglan was in command, with Lord Lucan in charge of the Cavalry Division and Lord Cardigan in command of the Light Brigade - which included Edward's regiment. The commanders were an elderly lot and, if they had seen active service (which Cardigan at least had not), it was now a very long time ago. On 12 May the regimental headquarters embarked from Portsmouth under Col. Doherty. Six weeks later they had arrived at Varna in Bulgaria, and a couple of days later marched out to join the rest of the Brigade at Devnya. It had been a tough journey, with the horses suffering worst from the cramped conditions and the heat. Edward was still only twenty years old.

Almost as soon as they arrived they had news that the Russians had withdrawn across the Danube. Since the French and British had come to defend the Turks against a Russian advance in the Danube provinces, it wasn't at all clear what they were meant to do, now that the Russians were no longer there. All they could do was to wait for instructions. However, waiting in Bulgaria in the intense heat, with inadequate supplies and no medical provision was no easy thing. An epidemic of cholera had hit southern Europe that summer and on 19 July struck the French camp. Three days later it had spread to the British lines. In an attempt to escape the disease, the Brigade was moved further inland to Yenipazar, but cholera travelled with them. 10,000 men died in Bulgaria before a shot was fired. The officers would have been protected from some of the worst deprivation, but the heat and disease got to them also. With no one to fight and nothing to do except watch their friends sicken and die, morale in the army was low.

Lord Cardigan did his best to keep the men occupied with a rigorous, daily routine of inspections, drills and field days. Amongst the soldiers, the drills were followed by drinking bouts, which were followed by prosecutions for drunkenness and floggings. The officers indulged in wild dog hunting. Captain Portal of the 4th Light Dragoons wrote: "The men and officers are getting daily more dispirited and disgusted with their fate. They do nothing but bury their comrades; they have no excitement to relieve the horrid monotony of camp life. There is nothing in the world to do but listen to growls and grumbling, from the highest to the lowest, of the dreadful mortality that is decimating our once magnificent army".

In the Crimea, September 1854

Finally, at the end of August, the decision was taken to invade the Crimea with the intention of seizing Sevastopol, the Russian port, fortress and naval base from which she controlled the Black Sea. This at least would give the French and British governments something to show for this now apparently unnecessary expedition. When Captain Weatherall, of the DQMG's staff, brought the news to the Brigade it was greeted with "the gloomy silence of men with sickness and death uppermost in their minds".

Embarkation took far longer than anticipated. Some of the units were on board by 24 August, but no one disembarked until 14 September. This meant that some men were to spend three weeks on board rolling ships in miserable, unsanitary conditions. Most of the 13th embarked on a steam transport on 1 September, but they too suffered terribly from disease during the crossing. When disembarkation started at Yevpatoriya, it was discovered that all kinds of hospital transport – litters, carts – had been left at Varna. The sick that had been carried off the ships, had to be carried back again to wait on board until they could be taken down to the hospital at the Allied Base at Scutari.

Among the sick – according to Captain Tremayne - were Major Gore, Captain Jenyns and Lieutenants Purcell and King. If Edward was among those who were carried down to Scutari at this point, it is difficult to understand how he managed to gain his medal and clasp. It seems likely that these officers did indeed fall ill before the descent on Balaclava and the beginning of the siege, but that they were not all hospitalised on landing.

If Edward was still around, the Army set off south for Sevastopol on 19 September. It was a terrible march, in intense heat, without water, and with soldiers already weakened by disease. Lord George Paget, in command of the 4th Light Dragoons who provided the rear guard, wrote: "The stragglers were lying thick on the ground, and it is no exaggeration to say that the last two miles resembled a battlefield". When they reached the Bulganek River there was pandemonium. "Regiment after regiment broke ranks and rushed down the slope to hurl themselves to the water alongside the horses of the advance guard". Lord Cardigan led the Advance Guard, made up of the 11th Hussars and the 13th Light Dragoons.

They were ordered to cross the river and to explore Russian dispositions beyond the high ground south of the river. As they reached the high ground, they found Cossack troops ready for them, and they entered the first engagement of the war. However, before very much could happen, Lord Raglan had seen a much larger Russian force behind the Cossacks. Fearful for his cavalry, he ordered them to withdraw – which they did, to the jeers of the Cossacks. It didn't do a lot for the morale of the cavalry – nor (since he got the blame) for Lord Raglan's reputation.

A few miles on, the Army came to the Alma River and here indeed the Russian Army was drawn up, on the high ground on the south side of the river. The cavalry was held back as the infantry advanced across the river and up the slopes. It was a tremendous display of coolness under fire, and the Russians in the end fled. The natural thing would have been for the cavalry to pursue them, but Raglan held them back. The cavalry were to be "kept in a bandbox". After the Affair at the Bulganek, and with the relationship between Lords Cardigan and Lucan at a low ebb, this did nothing for the morale of the cavalry. Alma however opened the way to Sevastopol and the Army might have marched straight there and benefited from the surprise. Raglan however was cautious and marched round the town, taking the port of Balaclava on 26 September without a fight and setting up for a siege.

And so things stood until the early morning of 25 October 1854. It was an odd siege. Raglan hadn't the manpower to enforce it properly, and the camp outside Balaclava was very vulnerable to attack. Cholera and dysentery continued to weaken the forces and it could have been now that Edward's health broke down. All that is certain is that he was not with his regiment on 25 October, for he was not among those engaged in the famous Charge. News travelled slowly, and Edward's sickness wasn't reported in the Warwick Advertiser until the issue of 1 November. Given the four to six weeks it seems to have taken to get news home, this keeps open the probability that Edward was at Alma (20 September), but it remains possible that he was amongst those already ill by the time of the landings (14-16 September). In the issue of the Warwick Advertiser for 2 December 1854 it is said that he was in hospital at Scutari. Curiously, it was later reported that Edward's dog – who he had painted on his return – was at Balaclava and Inkerman (fought on 5 November) and was in Sevastopol at the end of the year. This suggests that he was not sent home until early in the New Year at the earliest.

The End of the War
In January 1855, Lord Aberdeen resigned and Lord Palmerston took over. Gradually Palmerston gained the initiative. People felt that the war was being prosecuted with more energy and that Russia was being pressed harder. Czar Nicholas I died in March, and his son - Alexander II - was eager for peace. However, Palmerston wanted to be sure that Turkey was safe from any future Russian threat. The war continued through another sweltering summer, and into another Crimean winter. The last major British engagement was at Redan in June 1855. It resulted in a defeat with heavy losses. At the same time the French had a victory that resulted in the fall of Sevastopol. A British defeat and a French victory were not the best basis on which to end the war. However, Napoleon III was now keen to make peace with Russia in order to form an anti-Austrian alliance with Russia, with a view to pressing French influence in Italy. Britain couldn't go on alone, and the peace was finally concluded in March 1856.

The Crimean War was some kind of watershed. Before 1854 the old order of the conservative, élitist Duke of Wellington had held sway in the army. Senior officers were aristocrats, career soldiers were looked down on, and Indian officers were avoided. It was an excessively caste based world that was due for reform. One of the results of the disasters in the Crimea was a campaign - directed at the aristocracy - to abolish purchase in the army, and to promote only on merit. When Palmerston came to power he set his face against such as revolution. He held to the old idea – that was now looking distinctly old-fashioned - that an army led by properly professional soldiers would be a threat to the Constitution. But the writing was on the wall and the abolition of purchase was one of the first acts of Gladstone's administration in 1868-74, when Edward Cardwell was Secretary at War. It was at this time that Col. Garnet Wolseley was recalled from Canada, made KCMG and CB, and appointed Assistant Adjutant General at the War Office.

PART THREE - Marriage & the West Country

In Warwickshire, 1855-61

Edward was by then long out of it - like so many of his contemporaries. He probably did not get back to England in time to see his grandfather before his death on 5 January 1855, in the middle of one of the coldest winters on record. His grandfather's death - though long anticipated - meant a marked change of circumstances for his family. According to a prior arrangement, the Barrells estate of 3000 acres was sold and the proceeds divided between the two claimants. The King family was now reduced to farming rather less than 3000 acres around Chadshunt.

In September 1855 Major Ormsby Gore retired, thus making it possible for the senior captain in the regiment to purchase his promotion, and opening up a troop captaincy by purchase for the senior lieutenant – which was Edward. There was however no likelihood of Edward ever re-joining his regiment in the Crimea and he retired from the army a few weeks later. He and Major Ormsby Gore were the first of the officers of the 13th to leave the army, but several more were to follow in the months ahead. As papa wrote in a note about his grandfather, "Although never actually wounded, the muddle and rigours inseparable from the Crimean campaign had impaired a constitution never very robust".

From now on Edward seemed to settle down into a gentle country round. The army and its concerns were behind him. In October 1855, his sister Jane married Capt. Charles Carden at St James'

Piccadilly.   In December, Edward was a Steward at the Ladies' Charity Ball in Warwick, and was also at the Warneford Hospital Ball, the Warwickshire Hunt Ball and the Yeomanry Ball - all in January 1856. Also in January 1856, he received his commission in the Yeomanry Cavalry. At the Spring Meeting in March 1856, he was riding his own horse, *Beggar Boy*, with no huge success. In the same week he was at his eldest sister's wedding at St George's, Hanover Square. Georgiana was marrying Capt. Henry Cotton. Capt. Cotton came from Shropshire. He was part of old Robert Knight's Shropshire world and rather grand. Then there was another autumn of race meetings, another winter of hunting and hunt balls, and in January 1857 the marriage of his aunt, Frances Knight, to Colonel Gooch.

Old Bolton King was still heavily into politics. Lord Guernsey, the member for South Warwickshire, was not very active. There was quite a lot of muttering about his failure to show up in the Commons. Thus, when Palmerston unexpectedly went to the country in the spring of 1857, Bolton King put up, Guernsey withdrew and he got in. A role seemed to be opening up for Edward - now just twenty three years old. He could be of use at home, looking after the estate while his father busied himself in London.   But then, in May 1858, his mother died and everything changed. His three youngest sisters were unmarried. Someone had to run the house. His father decided to marry again and to retire from parliament. After the summer of 1859, Bolton King was at Chadshunt full time, and starting a second family. Proper provision was made for Edward – presumably out of the sale of Umberslade (which had been leased out for some years) - but it must have been a shock. Certainly it does not appear that relationships with the second Mrs Bolton King and her children were ever close or easy. Edward had now to strike off on his own, no longer the son of a man who farmed 6000 acres of Warwickshire land, and no longer the only son. This new family would need providing for eventually. Edward's prospects as a Crimean veteran in 1860 were not quite what they had been in 1850 when he first gained his commission.

However, life went on. Edward and his father were at the Autumn Race Meeting at Warwick in 1859, although the feel of that was a bit different now. It was now more than just a local thing. The railways meant that the great swells could travel in and mix with each other. Country society was changing. Things were less local. In the old days the grandees didn't mix much with each other. They lived within their locality, often speaking with a local accent, and mixing for the most part with the local gentry in a social and political partnership. Now everyone was becoming more mobile and expensive. One effect of this was the development of house parties and race meetings that called together grandees from all parts of the country. They were now mixing with each other, uninvolved in their local affairs and with their pastimes becoming increasingly purposeless and extravagant. Relationships with the local gentry became distant.

The Young Sportsman
The aristocracy was beginning to withdraw from public life - or beginning to be pushed out. The middle class and the university men were taking over. The role of parliament and central government was increasing. And during the 1860's the radicals were once more finding their voice. Edward either wasn't interested or wasn't wanted in public life. He remained the young swell of the pre-Crimean War days, very proud and a stickler for style and dress. His energies seem to have been focused on sport – and especially on his horses. What had been a relaxation for his father, as he engaged in a myriad of local and national government issues, was for Edward life itself.

One gets a sense of how he was known locally in these days from the *Annals of the Warwickshire Hunt*. From the early 1860s, Sir Walter Palk Carew wrote that "in all his Melton days he never saw three such young fellows ride better or straighter to hounds than Mr W.H. Chamberlaine, Capt. E. Raleigh King and Mr Spencer Lucy used to do with the Warwickshire"[213]. On 7 January 1860, Sir

Charles Mordaunt wrote in his diary, "Capt E. Raleigh King, who was one of the few who got to the covert in time from this side of the county, went very well in this run on his chestnut horse, Don Quixote. Capt. King was at that time one of the best riders with the Warwickshire hounds, and he had another good chestnut horse called Zouave"[214].

It mattered enormously how you looked on a horse – whether man or woman. Surtees made this clear in his very popular novels in the 1850s and 1860s. The talented horsewoman, Lucy Glitters, was one of his great creations. The success of Catherine Walters – known as 'Skittles' – was due to her superb horsemanship. This beautiful Liverpudlian courtesan took London by storm in 1861-2. Crowds assembled to see her ride in Rotten Row and her lovers included the greatest and the best.

In November 1859, Edward had the idea of reviving the Warwick and Leamington Steeplechase. They say the original steeplechase was run in Ireland in 1752, but such things are difficult to date. Races between hunters over a stretch of country became gradually an extension of the social life that surrounded the local hunt - especially after the end of the Napoleonic Wars. There were a lot of cavalry officers looking for excitement after 1815. Then, during the 1830's, some racing entrepreneurs looked to get a slice of the action, and things started to become commercial. In 1830, Thomas Coleman organised the St. Albans' Steeplechase. The Leamington Steeplechase was established by 1837. In 1839, William Lynn, an hotelier with an eye for business, set up the Grand Liverpool

---

[213] I'm not sure who Mr Chamberlaine was, but Spencer Lucy (1830-1890) lived at Charlecote. He had no sons, so his eldest daughter inherited. She married a Fairfax, which is why the present family at Charlecote is called Fairfax-Lucy.
[214] This was Sir Charles Mordaunt (1836-1897), of Walton Hall, a typical Warwickshire gentleman only interested in hunting and fishing, who made a disastrous marriage with Harriet Moncrieff in 1866. Sir Charles threatened to cite the Prince of Wales in his highly publicized divorce case in 1870 when, to avoid the scandal of divorce, Harriet was declared insane. She remained in institutions until her death in 1906.

Steeplechase - which was to become the Grand National. These highly organised commercial events began to push out the small local events, and I can't believe that Edward stood much of chance. If the Warwick and Leamington Steeplechase was to be revived, it would need more expertise than he and his friends could provide.

Still, it was a good idea, to get local gentlemen and farmers riding against each other in the old way, even if it didn't really come off. The weather was foul, which didn't help, and Edward himself came in last in both his races. He doesn't seem to have tried again and in fact organised steeplechasing generally went through a low period in the early 1860's. It needed the formation of the National Hunt Committee in 1866 to restore its fortunes. What Edward was really looking for in 1859 was what today would be called a point-to-point. As steeplechasing developed in a commercial and professional direction from the 1870's, so point-to-pointing became the preserve of the amateurs in the local hunt - who had really done some hunting.

Marriage & Torquay 1861-64
Then, in July 1861, Edward married the seventeen-year old Susan Lethbridge in her local parish church at Bishop's Lydeard, near Taunton in Somerset. Her sister was married to his great friend, Peter Purcell, and her father was a Somersetshire baronet. She was from his world and it was all quite satisfactory - though as one of fifteen surviving children, she had no money.

Marriage doesn't seem to have made much difference to Edward's lifestyle. People didn't think in terms of buying a house and settling down in those days. Edward and Susan may have stayed at Sandhill Park for the hunting season, but their first child and only son was born within a year of the marriage in Weymouth. He was baptized on 28 June 1862 at St John's Church, Melcombe Regis, a newly built church at the end of the Esplanade. George III had enjoyed taking the waters at Weymouth at the end of the eighteenth century, and his patronage had put the town on the map. In 1850, Susan's mother had been buried there (in the churchyard of Weymouth's mother church – St Mary's, Radipole), which is presumably where the family were living at that time. Weymouth was also then the home of one of Susan's older sisters, Alda, who was married (not very happily) to Capt. Purcell Weston.

During the 1863-4 season Edward was hunting in Somerset, and was at Sandhill for Christmas 1863. Then, early in 1864, he took a house in Torquay. It was called Castell à Mare on the Middle Warbury Road - a new road of substantial villas, high up above the Bay. Their arrival was announced in the Torquay Directory of 3 February 1864. They remained there for the summer - and it was here that Susan gave birth to her elder daughter, Violet Frances.

Torquay was then a remarkable place. It was established as a watering place at the end of the eighteenth century, but its reputation had steadily grown. In 1842 Thomas Stephens of Exeter published *The Climate of South Devon and its Influence upon Health*, in which he commended the balmy air to the gentry. In 1854 it was said "an unusually large proportion of the inhabitants consist of gentry, many of whom are invalids resorting to Torquay for the sake of the climate". Bishop Phillpotts, the 86-year-old Bishop of Exeter, had his main residence in Torquay. Angela Burdett-Coutts had a house there from 1859-1877 and married a local boy several years younger than she was. Disraeli had regularly visited Mrs Brydges Williams there until her death in November 1863. The chief landowner and developer in Torquay, Sir Laurence Palk, was married to one of Susan's many West Country cousins.

Torquay at this period was most alive during the winter. It was then that a succession of balls and modern plays were staged at the Theatre Royal. When the Kings arrived, Tom Taylor's *The Ticket of Leave Man* was showing. It had proved a great success in London and the Prince and Princess of Wales were said to have seen it twice. The theatre was popular at this time. Dion Boucicault and Charles Reade were also established as popular dramatists and in

April 1864 Tom Robertson gained his first success with the staging of *David Garrick* at the Theatre Royal, Haymarket. In the spring of 1865 Marie Wilton took on the Prince of Wales' Theatre in London and began a legendary career in the theatre, in partnership (from 1867) with her husband, Squire Bancroft. The theatre was fast becoming respectable, actors were beginning to aspire to some gentility, and the plays being shown bore some relationship to normal life. Edward and Susan were always keen on the theatre, and it is said were friends of Sir Charles Wyndham.

But there were other things to do in Torquay. In the summer particularly there was yachting. The Torquay Yacht Club was established in 1863, and the building of the Haldon pier in 1870 "brought the country's greatest yachtsmen to the town for the first time". I don't know whether Edward sailed, but his brother-in-law, Wroth Lethbridge, was always a keen sailor, as was Dammy Foster – R. Baynton Foster - his friend and executor.

And there was France - the France of the Second Empire. From the time of the Great Paris Exhibition of 1855, Offenbach's music had been all the rage. He had a striking success in 1858 with *Orpheus aux enfers*, but with *La Belle Helene* (1864), "Europe was at Offenbach's feet". The Jockey Club in Paris was the centre of fashion and one of its patrons, Sir Henry Hoare of Stourhead, was Susan's first cousin. Her half-brother also lived in Paris. Two of Peter and Agnes Purcell's children were born there in 1857-60. In that eventful year - 1864 - Susan's youngest brother, Walter Lethbridge, aged only nineteen, married Eleanore Boyer, a Parisian actress.

Apart from Paris, there was the Normandy coast. Deauville developed during the early 1860's as a fashionable seaside resort, with a race course and miles of sand. Napoleon III and the Empress Eugenie patronized it, and painters painted it. It would be interesting to know if my grandfather's and father's love of the Normandy coast had anything to do with my great-grandparents.

Whether or not they were keen on Deauville during its brief flowering, the France of the Second Empire figured large on my great-grandparent's horizons.

Edward kept his horses, and entered *Best Man* for the Torquay Steeplechase, for horses that had been regularly run with a hunt in one of the four west of England counties in 1863-4. He was unplaced. They had left Torquay by the end of August, and Edward seems to have hunted in Warwickshire in the 1864-5 season, but in the spring of 1866 they were back in Weymouth for the birth of their third child, Adeline Agnes.

PART FOUR – Ottowell House, Lillington - in waiting, 1864-81

Edward and Susan were at the Warwickshire Hunt Ball in January 1865, with a large family party. Edward was also in evidence when the Yeomanry Cavalry was on parade in May 1865. He was a Lieutenant in the 4th Troop, with Lord Willoughby de Broke as Captain. By 1868 they had settled in Ottowell House, a small manor house at Lillington, on the outskirts of Leamington. It's difficult to get a handle on the quiet, provincial life that Edward and Susan lived at Lillington. He and Susan appear in the list of those who attended the annual Hunt Balls in January. He was invariably on the Yeomanry exercises that took place each year in May. He was a magistrate and sometimes seems to have joined his father on the bench. There was a Tennis Club in Leamington and Edward and Susan were members. In 1875, when his father was ill, he was acting major in the Cavalry - and then in February 1876 he took over as Major.

My great-grandfather seems to have done his best. He was happy with his horses and his books. To begin with there was no real difficulty. Gladstone's flirtation with the radicals during his first administration of 1868-74 did not promise well for the future. But agriculture was doing well in the 1860's and early 1870's and things seemed on an even keel. It wasn't to last. On the one hand the rural areas in this county were being slowly but surely radicalised. On the other, the Age of Prosperity was coming to an end. When Edward took over, he was to face a murderous combination of radical demands and collapsing farm prices.

Contemporary Events – The Tichborne claimant

Mrs Frances Knight, Edward's wayward grandmother, was first cousin to Lord Dormer, who lived at Grove Park. Lady Dormer was the eldest daughter of Sir Henry Tichborne, a considerable landowner in Hampshire. Sir Henry's heirs (since he had no sons) were his brother and his brother's son, Roger. Roger however had gone abroad in 1853 and was reported drowned. Thus, when Sir Henry and his brother died, the next baronet was Roger's younger brother, who succeeded as Sir Alfred Tichborne. Sir Alfred lived a very rackety life and died young in 1866, leaving an infant son. Should this lad die, Lady Dormer was among the presumptive co-heirs.

However, Roger Tichborne's mother had never accepted that her elder son was dead. She was half-French and lived most of her life in France. She hadn't got on with her husband – and didn't get on with her husband's family. Soon after Sir Alfred's death, the family learned that someone in Australia was claiming to be Roger Tichborne and that Lady Tichborne had accepted him as such. The man – known as Thomas Castro – met Lady Tichborne in January 1867 and from then on became her protégé. The family did some research but, for as long as the claimant did not threaten the estate, they did not want to upset the dowager. However, in March 1868, Lady Tichborne died and two months later the claimant put in a formal claim to the Tichborne estates. Battle began.

It was an extraordinary case. There was never any real proof that the claimant was Roger Tichborne. However, the family had thoroughly alienated an increasingly democratic age by suggesting that it was impossible that a young aristocrat should have so thrown over his origins that he could reappear as a rough, working class guy from the Australian outback. Ordinary people thought it was a wonderful story and they wanted to believe it. Many of the old staff at Tichborne Hall said they did, as did the local tradespeople. Some representatives of the gentry also gave their support. Only the family stood out - Lady Dormer and her sisters foremost among them. The case opened in May 1871 and dragged on for nearly a year. The jury found against the claimant.

There then began a second trial, with the claimant accused of perjury. This trial began in 1873 and by the time the verdict was given – in February 1874 – legal fees had stacked up to the tune of £200,000. The defence team was no match for Henry Hawkins, known to be the best cross-questioner of his day. However, Dr Keneally – a fiery Irish barrister – milked the class issue (and the Roman Catholic issue) for all it was worth. He made the legal mistake of trying to prove that the claimant was Roger Tichborne (with the implication that the infant baronet should be deprived of his property). He should have aimed at proving that there was some reasonable doubt about his identity. In the event, the claimant was condemned to fourteen years penal servitude. He went to prison under escort, an angry crowd being prepared to free him by force.

Other events – The Poulett heir
When Frances Knight's illegitimate son was trying to raise loans after his mother's death, he approached his first cousin, Lady Poulett, hoping that she would affirm his legitimacy. Lady Poulett had however passed the request on to her elderly mother, Mrs Berkeley Portman. Though Mrs Portman knew full well that Robert and Frances Knight had been separated from 1802 onwards, she nonetheless perjured herself in affirming that they had been happily married until Mrs Knight's death. Lady Poulett may have remembered this episode when her two surviving sons died unmarried within a few months of each other in 1857. The heir to the earldom and the estate in Somerset was Lord Poulett's nephew. Unfortunately, in 1849 this nephew had made an unsatisfactory

marriage with a lady who gave birth to a son six months after the wedding. Her husband denied paternity, but in law the child was his. It was not until the nephew's death in 1903 that the matter came to trial and this child, known as William Turner, was declared illegitimate and barred from the inheritance. It was the first time that a child born in wedlock was declared not to be the child of the mother's husband, even though that husband was alive and living in this country. This was something that Robert Knight had attempted but not achieved!

Edward's Books
Edward's surviving books from his middle years give some interesting insights. It may be significant there are no novels published after 1850. From about that time, the fashion in popular novels was changing – from novels that were mainly about the very poor or very rich to novels that dealt with middle class life. Edward was not into middle class life, and it might be that his contemporary novel reading tailed off. This absence of modern novels from his surviving library may be a sign of a growing alienation from the dominant culture of his middle years.

There is an 1852 edition of Smollett's works. Tobias Smollett was a very popular novelist of the mid-eighteenth century, and his *Roderick Random* (1748) and *Peregrine Pickle* (1751) are still very readable. They were however not for children, so it would not have been until he was already a soldier that it would have been proper to put Smollett in his hands! A sporting classic is the fourth (1869) edition of Nimrod's *Life of John Mytton*. First published in 1835, this was an account by a top journalist of a major sporting character. The special interest was that the first wife of Edward's father-in-law, Sir John Lethbridge, was Mytton's sister – and there were other family connections. The other absolutely standard book amongst his collection was of course Captain Gronow's *Reminiscences*, published in 1860. Edward's is the 1865 edition that he had rebound in 1871. Later on, the Irish theme is continued in *Realities of Irish Life*, published in 1868. It is an account of the difficulties of Irish life by an agent who worked with some of the great Irish landowners. W. Steuart Trench is an enlightened employer, and presents a moderate view of Irish life. Irish issues were a dominant concern in mid-Victorian England. Another book from this time is *The Cruise round the world of The Flying Squadron, 1869-70* by Rear Admiral G. T. Phipps Hardy. This was another story of derring-do on the high seas. Edward's interest in French affairs is revealed in *The War Correspondence of the Daily News*, covering the period from 5 December 1870 to 2 May 1871. This period included the first siege of Paris by the Prussian forces after the defeat at Sedan, and also the second siege by French republican forces after the establishment of the Commune. Since one of Susan's sisters was trapped in Paris at the time, with her family, there was an obvious reason for concern. Perhaps the best glimpse of the mature man comes through *Life as I have found it* by General de Ainslie (a connection of Susan's) and published in 1883. De Ainslie presents his life as one of many disappointments and failures. Things didn't go well for him. My great-grandfather could have been cast in the same mould.

The fact that these particular titles descended through papa rather than through Aunt Ethel suggests that they were of interest to my grandfather also, otherwise he wouldn't have taken them from Egerton Gardens to his own place after his father's death.

PART FIVE – Politics and the Crisis of Agriculture, 1878-92

Agrarian Reform & Local politics in the 1880's

The fears raised in landowning circles by Gladstone's Irish Land Act of 1870 were not allayed by further legislation aimed at the Irish landowner but which could easily cross the Irish Sea at a future date. The Irish Land Act of 1881 sought to make up for the deficiencies of the previous one. The tenant was to pay a fair rent, whose fairness was to be fixed by a tribunal. He was to have fixity of tenure for as long as he paid his rent. He was to be able to sell his interest in the land. These were called the "three f's" and it was hoped that they would ease the situation. They didn't. Unrest in Ireland in 1882 – the year of the murder of Lord Frederick Cavendish – was worse than ever.

Scotland was not far behind. In Skye, the crofters petitioned to have their traditional grazing rights restored. They backed up their demands by demonstrations and rent strikes. The following winter of 1882-3 was thought to be the worst since the disasters of the 1840's. There was great economic distress and strong sympathy for the crofter' cause. Landlords could not act as they had done in the 1840's – with confiscations and evictions. The political climate was hugely different. In 1883 Alexander McKenzie published *A History of the Highland Clearances*. The Highland proprietors were portrayed as heartless tyrants who had ruthlessly betrayed their responsibilities and their people. On the urging of the Home Secretary, Sir William Vernon Harcourt, a Royal Commission was appointed and legislation introduced in 1885 – the Crofters' Act – that introduced some of the restrictions on landed property already introduced in Ireland. The landlord was not to enjoy complete freedom of ownership. With the widening franchise, it was no longer possible to ride roughshod over the rights of tenants.

Ireland was special and the Highlands were recognized as a special case also, but the political mood of the 1880's was universally hostile to landowners everywhere. English landowners were certainly not let alone. The radicals had great plans for the reconstruction of the English countryside and they seemed to be gaining the ear of the Liberal Government. In 1882 Lord Elcho set up The Liberty and Property Defence League. It served as a lobby group for industrialists and land-owners who were alarmed by trade unionism, socialism, and elements in the Gladstone administration, but also attracted many liberals and philosophical individualists. There wasn't any longer a place for the likes of Edward Raleigh King among the supporters of Gladstonian Liberalism. The great split that happened in 1886 was becoming inevitable.

The Liberal Advance in Warwickshire, from 1880
The collapse of agriculture during the 1870's is often given as a
reason for the resounding defeat of Disraeli's administration at the
General Election of 1880. One problem was the emergence of
"farmer candidates" who stood to highlight the state of agriculture
but tended to split the Conservative vote. In December 1879, Sir
John Eardley Wilmot, one of the Conservative candidates for South
Warwickshire, announced that he would not be standing as a
candidate at the Election. He had heard that a John Lane had put
up as the Tenant Farmers' candidate and he was probably
concerned about a split vote that would let the Liberals in.
However, on 11 March 1880, three days after Disraeli had
announced a dissolution, Lane withdrew and Wilmot re-entered the
contest with Lord Yarmouth, his partner from the 1874 Election. On
20 March, there was an angry meeting of the Warwickshire Tenant
Farmers' Association. John Lane tried to justify his withdrawal on
the basis of lack of funds and the swell of support for Sir John
Wilmot. Clearly his colleagues were not best pleased and when
Gilbert Leigh declared his candidature in the Liberal interest two
days later, it was thought that he would be taking up the interests
of the Association. Polling was on 6 April. Sir John headed the poll,
but Lord Yarmouth went down to Gilbert Leigh. The Liberal leaning
Warwick Advertiser was ecstatic. It was hailed as the first break in
the Conservative monopoly of the constituency since 1837, with the
single exception of Bolton King's tenure in 1857-9. It was sad that
old Bolton King had not lived to see the day[215].

The South Warwickshire results were repeated through the country,
giving the Liberals a substantial majority. However, in Warwickshire
it was generally accepted that the Liberal success had been due to
the tenant farmers' switching from the Conservatives to the
Liberals. Hitherto they felt that the farmers had hardly given the

---

[215] Hon Gilbert Leigh (1851-1884) was the eldest son of the 2nd Lord Leigh, of
Stoneleigh Abbey. The Leighs were strong Whig-Liberals and political associates
of Edward's father. Gilbert was killed in a shooting accident in the U.S.A.

Liberals a fair chance. Now Lord Hartington had his chance to do something for agriculture.

Lord Hartington didn't of course. Gladstone was regretting his decision to retire after his defeat in 1874 and made it clear that he would like to lead the government. In the circumstances, Hartington could only acquiesce and decline the Queen's invitation. Gladstone came in as Prime Minister. His second ministry was not a success. The agricultural depression deepened but he would do nothing about it. There was some agitation from Fair Trade groups to bring in protection for agriculture against subsidized foreign goods, but Free Trade dogma made this impossible. In any case, in those days economic conditions were held by most to be as uncontrollable as the weather. Then came the Third Reform Bill of 1884 that extended voting rights to country householders. The Warwickshire electorate was vastly increased, and the constituencies were reorganized.

Lord Salisbury took over after Gladstone's resignation in June 1885. This government only lasted six months, but at least it appointed a royal commission to look into the causes of the agricultural depression. It was a chance for the advocates of protective tariffs to put their case, but it is highly unlikely that Salisbury would have done anything, even if he had survived. He was too clever a politician for that and too committed to wooing the middle class Tory vote in the provinces. Agriculture would have to sink or swim under its own strength, whatever party was in power. Then came the General Election of December 1885, with the new franchise. The Liberals swept the board in Warwickshire. Before the dissolution there had been six Conservative members and five Liberal members in the county. After this Election, there were twelve Liberal members and only two Conservatives. It was a result that could only have been dreamed of in Bolton King's later years, but what it meant to Edward Raleigh King was that the tenant farmers and the labourers now held power. As the depression continued, it would be the landlords who would be squeezed.

There had been some radical legislation for Ireland in Gladstone's Second Administration, but the main thing was the perceived growth of anti-landlord opinion in his government. It was believed by many that, after destroying landlordism in Ireland, the radical Liberals would turn their attention to England. It was this that provided the background for the Home Rule crisis of 1886.

Despite Liberal gains in Warwickshire and in other rural constituencies in the election of December 1885, Conservative gains in the boroughs resulted in a hung parliament. Conservatives and Liberals both needed Parnell's support to achieve a workable majority. Salisbury dithered and then handed over to Gladstone early in February 1886. Gladstone thereupon brought forward an Irish Home Rule Bill. In doing so, he lost Hartington, Chamberlain and several other talented MPs. There were feverish plots and negotiations. Hartington would have liked to revive the Palmerstonian alliance, and to come in at the head of it. Salisbury was happy to serve under a government led by Hartington, but expected that it should be a Conservative one. In the event of a General Election, it was agreed that Constituency Associations should be asked not to put up Conservative Candidates against incumbent Liberal Unionists.

The Conservative & Unionist Alliance, July 1886

In the end, ninety-two Liberals voted against the Government. Gladstone dissolved in July 1886 and went to the country. The Liberals of the Stratford Division split in two. Lord William Compton, who had won the new seat the previous December, stayed loyal to Gladstone. A Mr Townsend came in as a pro-Union Liberal. He won, though with 1200 fewer votes than had been cast in December. The Stratford Division Conservatives presumably voted Unionist - which kept their figures up. The Liberals however seemed to have stayed at home. Did my great-grandfather vote Unionist? I have no evidence either way, but it seems likely.

It was not an easy time. Conservatives found it very difficult to overcome generations of opposition in order to work with Liberals. The Liberal Unionists likewise insisted that they remained Liberals. Lord Hartington made it clear that his chief concern was for an eventual reconciliation with the Gladstonian Liberals. He was not interested in being absorbed into the Conservative Party, nor was he interested in a coalition. The relationship between the two constituency associations was difficult. However, what emerged in 1886-7 was a sort of Palmerstonian alliance of the sort that Bolton King himself would surely have approved. The difference was that Palmerston's government had left the Tories out, while Salisbury's left out the radicals. Perhaps the closer parallel was Pitt's government after 1794. Either way, it was entirely appropriate now for a member of the King family to find Lord Salisbury's team more palatable than Mr Gladstone's.

There was no coalition in 1886-92. However, when Salisbury came in again in June 1894, after the Liberal interlude, it was at the head of a Coalition Government. It was the Unionist Party that won a huge majority at the General Election in 1895, and a Liberal Unionist continued to sit for the Stratford Division until the Liberal landslide of 1906.

The Great Depression, 1878-92

Old Bolton King died at the right moment. Agriculture was on the brink and his son had a difficulty legacy. In April 1875, at the time of old Bolton King's illness, new trustees were appointed to the 1850 Settlement. Then, within a few months of his father's death, Edward had to raise a mortgage of £10,000 on the estate to cover the cost of his sisters' portions – and especially the various generous portions allotted to his young half-brother and half-sisters. When Ernest married in 1892, new trustees were appointed, and a further loan of £4000 had to be raised[216]. Before

---

[216] £14,000 works out at around £2 million at 2019 prices, which was a big loan to service at about 4-5%. I don't however know the full value of the Chadshunt estate.

Edward even tried to make a go of the estate in adverse circumstances, he was struggling with heavy encumbrances.

The figures speak for themselves. In 1877, the year before Edward took over at Chadshunt, wheat prices in England stood at 56/9 per cwt. They had been climbing steadily since the early 1850's and now stood at the level they had held for the last quarter of the previous century. Two years later the price was reduced by well over 20% and by 1893 it was down to less than 50% of pre-slump levels. This was nothing to do with an increase in home production. It was because of the flood of cheap imports. Home production had supplied 80% of food consumption in 1868. By the early 1900's it was supplying less than half what was needed. Foreign wheat was cheaper - and by foreign wheat was meant American & Russian wheat. In America the early settlers had decided that the prairies were desert. They decided to plough them up and to grow wheat and maize. Thanks to humus deposits accumulated over centuries the initial crops were huge, but it didn't last. By the 1930's the degraded prairie soil was simply blowing away and required government sponsored irrigation and liberal doses of fertiliser and pesticides. By then it was too late for the old prairies. A rich and delicate ecosystem had been destroyed. It was too late also for British agriculture. The old style, ecologically sensitive mixed farming was now giving way to intensive, chemical-dependent agribusiness. Yet in the 1870's it was politically impossible for food to be anything other than as cheap as possible. Thanks to the radical campaigns of the 1840's, anything else was believed to be the result of a conspiracy among the landowners against the poor.

And it was this that provided the political background to the economic problems of agriculture. The Corn Laws were fixed in popular mythology as a landlord conspiracy against the poor to keep food prices high. Politically food prices had to be kept low. Even if this meant the collapse of agriculture, food prices had to be kept down. And it was not only prices that were a problem. In the period of the price slump, the wages of an agricultural labourer rose by nearly 20%. Trades Unions were being established in the agricultural industry. In any case, farm-workers were leaving for better-paid jobs in the towns. And all the while there was a growing prejudice against landlordism. Gladstone was determined to solve the problem of Ireland and among his solutions was a scheme whereby tenants were able to buy their freeholds at favourable rates. People were asking why such schemes couldn't be extended to Scotland and to England. A Royal Commission on landholding reported in 1874 that showed just how high a proportion of land in England was concentrated in very few hands. Gladstone had appointed the Commission to allay the anxieties of the radicals and had expected a different report. Everyone was startled to see just how concentrated the landholding was. It was an experiment in information gathering that has not been repeated to this day. Landlords were nowhere the flavour of the month.

The last quarter of the nineteenth century was economically not a happy time. In agriculture particularly, but in almost every part of the economy, there was this squeeze on prices, rise in wages, and downward pressure on profits. The only people who could survive were those who had sufficient free capital to invest in their business and adapt to changing patterns. Capital was something that Edward didn't have. Once the jointures for his six sisters had been paid and - more significantly - the very generous provision made for the three children of his father's second marriage, there was little capital left. The 1880's were a grindingly difficult time for small landowners like my great-grandfather. They tried to live quietly (and my great-aunt testified to just how quietly they did live), but rents were falling steadily and their income was insufficient for even basic needs.

The political commitment to Free Trade was however absolute. Alone among the major industrialized nations of the world, Britain held to its free trade ideals at a time when everyone else was putting up tariffs to protect their home producers. We could afford to do this because of the enormous overseas investments built up in the years of our prosperity (estimated at £1.5 billion in 1885), because of the surplus of trade with India, and because of invisible earnings in shipping services, insurance and banking. We were becoming the universal buyer of the manufactured goods and agricultural produce of the rest of the world, running up a phenomenal balance of payments deficit in merchandise, but thereby sustaining the world economy. It was politically possible to do this because of the strong emotional investment in the free trade principle and because the agricultural interest, which was the most obvious casualty (though by no means the only one) of continuing free trade, was politically impotent after manhood suffrage was introduced in 1880. The continuing difference today between subsidized continental agriculture and the more self-sufficient agriculture of this country is a legacy from these days.

PART SIX - The Pattern of Change, 1878-92

Changing Patterns of Government
The 1870's and 1880's were not only a time of crisis and change for landowners. They also a saw a profound change in the way the country was governed. During the first part of the nineteenth century, the landed gentry governed the county. "Government" in those days was limited to three main areas: assuring there were sufficient funds to govern the country, administering justice and keeping order.
Providing the king with sufficient revenue had been a parliamentary responsibility since the thirteenth century, and Warwickshire gentry had their say through the county representatives they elected to serve. When local town life went through low periods, they also managed to control the elections of representatives from the local boroughs.

The administration of justice was the sheriff's responsibility. It was he who presided in the county court, supported – since Tudor times – by justices of the peace. The sheriff was always a local landowner and so were the justices of the peace.

In the sixteenth century, the business of keeping order was transferred from the sheriff to the new office of lord lieutenant. However, in choosing men to lead the militia the lord lieutenant called on the same men of substance who were already active as justices of the peace and members of parliament. Government at the beginning of the nineteenth century was a cosy, comfortable arrangement that gave due dignity to the gentlemen of the county as leaders of the community of the county. It was a way of working which kept too much power being vested in central government and it worked rather well.

Times were however changing. It first showed in the cost of government. This was increasing steadily throughout the nineteenth century as central government became busier and as the bureaucracy continued to grow. Old Bolton King returned again and again to the theme of the need for economy and retrenchment in government. It was an ancient cry and very much the cry of the gentry who instinctively saw in a prodigal government the first creeping tentacles of centralism and oppression. Pitt first introduced income tax in response to the demands of the French wars, but the income tax continued after peace was established and was never cut back. Tax revenues gave enormous power to government and to an increasingly confident parliament. Parliament's democratic mandate made it unassailable. It could levy more or less what taxes it liked, and make more or less what demands it liked. After all, Parliament and an increasingly meritocratic civil service were sure to know better than people on the ground what was best for them.

The Decline & Fall of the Quarter Sessions
A similar change was coming in local government and in the administration of justice. The Quarter Sessions were an ancient institution and a much-enjoyed time for the local gentry to get together to exchange news and ideas. However, with fast increasing instructions coming from central government, the quarter sessions were being used for things well beyond the

administration of justice. Furthermore, the tradition of recruiting just the local gentry to the bench was being questioned from the 1850's. There was resentment that the landowners held an effective monopoly in the administration of the law. After all, most law was designed to defend property (and, most controversially, to protect game) and so they were rarely disinterested judges. Gradually, the composition of the bench started to change, to include more substantial townsfolk and yeoman farmers. Edward was admitted a magistrate shortly before his father's death, but he doesn't appear to have sat very often.

Eventually, the Local Government Act of 1888 replaced the self-perpetuating oligarchy of the quarter sessions for governing purposes (though not for the administration of justice) by an elected council. Government in the county had in effect been taken away from the gentry and, although many of them continued to serve on county councils (and one or two grandees even continued as Chairmen of County Councils), it was the beginning of the end. The gentry no longer had an automatic role, beyond collecting their rents and racing their horses.

The Militia, the Yeomanry and the Police
The history of the local militia was a patchy one. Sometimes it had worked; sometimes (as against the Young Pretender in 1745) it was thought to have failed. After the Peace of 1815 it had fallen largely into disuse. Then in 1871, with the reorganization of the army, authority over it was removed from the lord lieutenant and vested in the crown. This was an early example of the engrossing of authority by the sovereign-in-parliament.

After 1815, it was the Yeomanry cavalry that for most practical purposes had taken the place of the militia and which continued the tradition of the country gentry offering military service with their tenants and other small freeholders. This was the force which kept order during the civil disturbances of the 1830's and which was always available in the background if the parish constable felt things were getting out of control. Then, during the peaceful middle years of the nineteenth century, the Yeomanry cavalry was not much used. In Bolton King's early days there was a full turnout. By the time of his retirement in 1875, only a few troops could be fielded. It wasn't now clear what they were for. Edward was promoted Major in the Cavalry in early 1876, but four years later he retired. After its swan song during the Boer War, the Warwickshire Yeomanry Cavalry quietly died.

The Police Act of 1856 required a professional police force to be established in every county and this increasingly took the place of the Yeomanry cavalry. During the 1860's and 1870's, the role of the gentry in the preservation of order was taken from them and handed over to a semi-independent, professional body, supported by taxation. Vitally, the police were locally and not centrally accountable – thus at least preserving the role of the county in this key function – but they were locally accountable to elected councillors and not to landed proprietors. The contrast between the apparent indolence of my great-grandfather and the urgent activity of my great-great-grandfather cannot therefore just be attributed to an innate indolence and an innate energy. In the 1830's and 1840's there was a clear job to be done and Bolton King was there to do it. In the 1880's there was nothing to be done. People didn't want my great-grandfather and his kind to get involved. It was a different, more hostile world and things got steadily worse.

The Church of England
If it seemed impossible to do anything about the way things were going in the country as a whole, there seemed a better hope in Church affairs. The Tractarians had started off in the 1830's in response to the wave of radical Whig reforms. The Church's position as the state in its spiritual aspect seemed threatened as the state's self-understanding changed. Pusey, Newman and the rest fought hard to develop an understanding of the Church that would enable it to stand in its own strength - if need be - against the vast

changes that were affecting society. They had caused a stir - in the intellectual world. However, the Tractarians' early university based phase was giving way by the 1860's to something less highfalutin, more parish-based, and much more widely noticed.

A representative figure was Charles Wood, 2nd Viscount Halifax. He was the grandson of Lord Grey of the Reform Bill. His father has served in the governments of Lord John Russell and Lord Palmerston. Wood might have been expected to take up a career in Liberal politics. However, in 1868, when asked by Dr Pusey to take on the Chairmanship of the English Church Union, Wood had to explain to his father why he felt Church politics the better way for him. The Conservative Party, he believed, was a broken reed - and in any case was closed to him for family reasons. The Liberals were hostile to the Church, despite Gladstone's best efforts. The great work of his generation was "the restoration of the Church of England". It was to this cause that he was to devote himself.

There was a lot for this conservatively minded young man to do. The English Church Union had been founded in 1860 to bring together different regional associations that had been founded in response to the different upsets in the Church during the 1840's and 1850's. Initially the issues were theological. German theology and philosophy were challenging the traditional creeds. This new thinking was liberating to the likes of Thomas Arnold, John Sterling and others. To more cautious churchmen, this "Broad Church" movement was the beginning of a slippery slope into atheism. In 1847 Lord John Russell had offered the see of Hereford to a prominent Broad Churchman, Renn Dickson Hampden. Hampden and his friends were favoured by the Queen, and were an increasingly powerful force. They were behind the publication of "Essays and Reviews" in 1860, which seemed to question many of the fundamentals of the Christian faith. Archbishop Tait, Bishop Temple and Dean Stanley were all influential figures and were all Broad Churchmen. The Church Union was there to register a protest against the action of such men and to mobilize public opinion.

Unfortunately, it was easy for people to see in this conservatism an aping of Rome. Rome had been quick to set itself against the modern world – in politics and in intellectual enquiry. For conservative Anglicans now to question Broad Church views and non-denominationalism seemed simply Roman. Yet a desire for orthodox teaching and for a faith that went beyond mere form did not necessarily spell Rome.

There were other issues, to do with the Church's accountability to a Parliament that was no longer necessarily Christian or Anglican. In 1848 the Judicial Committee of the Privy Council had overruled the Bishop of Exeter, who had refused to institute the Rev G. C. Gorham to a living in his diocese, because he felt he was unsound on the question of baptismal regeneration. In 1865 the same committee ruled on the question of the deposition of Bishop Colenso of Natal - who seemed to hold heterodox views - by the Bishop of Capetown. The climax came in 1874 with the passing of the Public Worship Regulation Act. This resulted in the imprisonment of several Ritualist priests. The English Church Union was spirited in their defence, and Charles Wood was so strong in his defence of Rev Arthur Tooth in 1877 that he almost lost his position in the household of the Prince of Wales.

There was also the general secularizing effect of different legislation. In 1854 Oxford and Cambridge universities ceased to be Church of England places of education. In 1857 Parliament had laid down civil proceedings for making divorce and remarriage possible. In 1868 compulsory Church Rates were abolished, thus making the cost of the maintenance of the parish churches a congregational rather than a community matter. In 1869 the Irish Church was finally disestablished and disendowed. Chamberlain and Dilke were keen to move on to the Church of England.

But, in response to all this, there was a renewed vigour and
determination in the Church of England to stand over against this
new parliamentary state. Inevitably this involved looking back to
the days when the Church of England had the Pope as an ally
overseas in its struggle with powerful kings. It also involved
"restoring" a liturgy and a spiritual discipline that people felt had
been lost during the eighteenth century. Wood had known Pusey
and Liddon at Oxford, but he had also seen the efforts of Robert
Liddell to restore some Catholic faith and practice at St Paul's
Knightsbridge. As Chairman of the Church Union he was active in
the defence of Fr. Mackonochie, who was at St. Alban's Holborn for
twenty-five years from 1862, and who also fell victim to mobs and
protests. Fundamentally though these young Anglicans found in a
reformed Church a counter-culture that could not be found any
longer in the increasingly non-denominational state. In this they
were following Rome. This had been Rome's programme since the
beginning of the century
What evidence there is - and there is not much - suggests that
religion at Chadshunt in the mid-century was of a dull, matins style.
There was dutiful Sunday attendance, but not more than that.
There were no innovations at St George's Hanover Square, nor at St
James' Piccadilly - the parishes in which Bolton King had his town
house. However my great-grandparents were not untouched by it
all. In 1865 my great-grandmother's first cousin Georgina Hoare
(sister of the rampaging Sir Henry Hoare of Stourhead) was
professed to the Community of St John the Baptist that had been
founded in 1851 by the Rector of Clewer. Throughout the 1870's,
as Sister Georgie, she was heading up a band of sisters working at St
Alban's Holborn under Fr. Mackonochie. Edward's second cousin,
Edward King, later a High Church Bishop of Lincoln, was enjoying his
happiest days at Cuddesdon from 1858-1873. People may have
found it difficult, but there was an authenticity and a power about it
all. As in his grandfather's days, when the evangelicals were waking
people to faith amidst the atheism and rationalism of the late
eighteenth century, so now men and women of the High Church
movement was waking people amidst the materialism of the

nineteenth century.

PART SEVEN - Last Years 1892-1900

The move to London

The expense of keeping up Chadshunt proved in the end too much. Ernest had to marry, and he couldn't be expected to get a job, so there had to be further retrenchment. In 1892, Chadshunt was let and the family moved to London. Edward, Susan and their daughters took a house in Brompton Square. Old Bolton King had always had somewhere in Mayfair, but Mayfair was too expensive now.

Papa described his grandfather's life there. "I believe that the years from 1893 to 1900 were the happiest of his life. He would potter out into the Brompton Road in top hat and tailcoat carrying an enormous green umbrella (green with age), and leading a brindled Irish terrier, and keeping a wary eye on passers-by. If he saw anyone advancing whom he did not wish to meet he would open the umbrella and putting his head down, would advance like Duncan's army behind the trees at Dunsanane. Impertinent and seedy strangers who asked him if he were saved would receive a curt injunction to go away. Thus Edward Raleigh King and his dog Mike would reach Harrods stores. Here, more trouble was in store. After passing through the doors he was politely but firmly told that dogs were not allowed not even on a lead. My grandfather knew this perfectly well because he would have tried before to gain admittance at several doors on a number of occasions. It was a good joke and the technique never varied. He would draw himself up to his full height and announce, "Where I go, my dog goes" and stalk out with his head in the air, making tracks for Rotten Row, where for a hour or so he would gaze critically at the riders, disapproving not only of their equestrian prowess but of their clothes as well. Mike would then be let off the lead and allowed to proceed under his own steam as far as the Achilles statue. There followed a gentle stroll in the direction of Marble Arch where he would meet a number of cronies who shared his rather jaundiced view on life..."

He remained interested in life in Chadshunt and Gaydon. In May 1899 he conveyed the school house and land at Lighthorne Heath to trustees – presumably to give the school a more independent existence. He had made his will in March 1899, when he was living at 20 Egerton Gardens, leaving the contents of his London house to his wife. He died a year later in a rented house in Norham Gardens, Oxford. Chadshunt was then sold. Susan, Violet and Ethel returned to London, and settled at 46 Egerton Crescent for the remainder of Susan's life.

Conclusion
The second half of the nineteenth century was not a good time for landowners. First they had become politically unpopular – increasingly a lost cause in parliament after the failure of the Protectionist campaign and the Conservative conversion to Free Trade. Then they were economically torpedoed. Nothing like it happened anywhere else in Europe. It was though the price that England was happy to pay for its industrial pre-eminence. A detached view would suggest that after making their fortunes in the professions in the 18th century – and after two generations of financially prudent marriages – the family would have been wise to have got out of land while the going was good and to try something else. This was not an option for my great-grandfather. He was brought up in the country as a way of life, committed to a network of responsibilities and duties that were more than just a source of income. His golden years had been in the 1840's and 1850's when things looked pretty steady and you would have needed remarkable understanding to see the direction in which things were going. Only in the 1870's and 1880's was the drift clear, and then it was too late for him to get out.

He didn't leave his son an easy legacy. "At least my son will never have to work", he is alleged to have said. In his youth he had learned a distaste for earned money that his father and grandfather would not have understood. The upper class of the 1850's had a distaste for earning money. In 1853 the correspondence of Gustave de Beaumont and Alexis de Tocqueville illustrates a gentleman's "extreme, not to say insurmountable, repugnance" for a job, even the directorship of a railway company: "Whoever takes it on, demeans himself". They ignored or forgot the labours of their forebears that had enabled them to be sufficiently not in need of money to indulge in this view. But they did condemn their children and grandchildren to narrow means, and limited horizons. Unable to work by class constraints, their energies lacked productive focus.

Papa remarked that his grandfather had a very jaundiced view of life in his last years. Many disinherited gentry did. They were in spiritual exile in their old age, with no clear understanding of where things were going. No one owed the small landowners a living of course. Yet today, after a century of commercial farming, we are looking again at stewardship of the soil. Stewardship may be as significant a criterion in the care of land as food prices. The small landowners didn't have a divine right to rule. Yet elected local government has proved itself pretty powerless in the face of an ever more powerful central government and civil service. At the local level, democracy has not delivered the sort of mandate that property conferred before 1850. It's possible that a sort of controlled "privatisation" will be a better answer.

CHAPTER FIFTEEN

BOLTON KING 1860-1937

Bolton King was my grandfather's doppelganger. I don't know what my great-grandfather thought about his father's second marriage - his stepmother, Louisa Palmer, was a neighbour and friend, but she was only a year or two older than he was. Umberslade was sold and my great-grandfather was given enough to marry on, but these things don't often work out very well. The settlement made by Bolton King on his second family was very generous and the financial difficulties at Chadshunt during the 1880's were blamed at least partly on that. Things cooled. When my great-grandfather died, my grandfather buried him within the same churchyard, but as far from old Bolton King's grave as possible. My grandfather did not live far from his young half-uncle for most of my father's growing up, but my father was adamant he knew nothing about him - apart from the fact that he was a socialist. That in itself was enough to make knowing him an impossibility in the tense world at the beginning of the nineteenth century.

Young Bolton King went to Eton in 1874 and did well, staying on until 1879 as Captain of R. A. H. Mitchell's House, and becoming Captain of the Oppidans and a member of Pop. He was at Balliol under Jowett[217] - "the best historian of his year", as Jowett told Mrs Barnett. Jowett was a great influence on him, as were T. H. Green [218]

---

[217] Benjamin Jowett (1817-93), Fellow of Balliol from 1839, Master from 1870. From 1860 a valued friend and confidante of Florence Nightingale. Dr Jenkyns (Master 1819-54) had been a high and dry churchman who had got rather out of his depth in the religious controversies of the 1830's and 1840's. Jowett navigated them better. He offered "a careful interpretation of personal experience as our one clue to the nature of man, the world and God" in opposition to the temptations of Roman absolutism.

[218] T H Green (1836-1882), Fellow of Balliol from 1860, influenced by Fichte, Hegel, Wordsworth, Carlyle & Maurice. Admired Jowett and John Bright. A great inspiration to his students, as he reinterpreted the creeds in a moral way. "A divine life or spirit pervading the world, making nature intelligible, giving unity to

and Arnold Toynbee[219]. Bolton was a member of "The Inner Ring", an undergraduate group founded by Arthur Acland [220] to discuss social and economic questions. Other members included Michael Sadler, later Master of University College, Oxford, Cosmo Gordon Lang, later Archbishop of Canterbury and Anthony Hope Hawkins. Bolton graduated in 1883, having got a double first in Classical Mods and History.

Toynbee Hall, 1883-1892

That same year, while his nephew and contemporary was checking horseflesh at Epsom and Newmarket, Bolton was deep in discussion about what Oxford's response should be to the social needs of East London. In January 1884 he and his friends decided that there had to be a settlement, where Oxford men would go to work alongside the poor and to help improve their lot. Their allies in this were Samuel and Henrietta Barnett. Mr Barnett had recently been made vicar of St Jude's Whitechapel, and Mrs Barnett was a friend of Octavia Hill. Bolton King was the driving force behind it and its first secretary. He didn't waste time and within a year lectures were being given in the new establishment.

In his memoirs Tom Okey [221] gives an interesting insight into the mood of London in the late 1870's and early 1880's. The earlier

---

its history, embodying itself in states and churches, and inspiring individual men of genius" (Works of Thomas Hill Green, ed. R.L. Nettleship, Cambridge: Cambridge Univ. Press, 2011, Vol. 3, Memoir).

[219] Arnold Toynbee (1852-83), son of an aural surgeon who campaigned for better conditions amongst the poor. Toynbee came up to Balliol in 1875 and was very influenced by T. H. Green. A college tutor from 1878. Lectured on the industrial problems of the day to working class audiences in the big towns.

[220] Arthur Acland, later Sir Arthur Acland, 13th Bart., (1847-1926), the youngest son of Sir Thomas Acland, 11th Bart, who was a contemporary and friend of Gladstone and one of Susan Raleigh King's West Country cousins. He served as an M.P. from 1885 and was an intimate of Asquith, Sir Edward Grey and Haldane. He was Vice-President of the Board of Education 1892-5. His niece married Archbishop William Temple.

[221] Tom Okey (1852-1935) *A Basketful of Memories*. A journeyman basket-maker from the East End who became a lecturer at Toynbee Hall and from 1919 held the

years had been dominated by Charles Bradlaugh and Mrs Besant, who preached republicanism and secularism at the Hall of Science in Old Street. However things were now hotting up. H. M. Hyndman - a recent convert from Tory radicalism - founded his Democratic Federation in 1881 and recruited William Morris in January 1883. Marx was being read and understood. Some exceptionally gifted working men - including John Burns and Tom Mann - were coming into prominence. E. P. Thompson wrote that "it is possible to date the effective birth of modern Socialism in Britain from 1883"[222]. Like many working class youths, Okey's education had been dominated by a narrow Protestant piety. He was now discovering an intellectual world that was much more liberating. It was one that was rooted in and normally respectful of Christian morality, but that was critical of Christian dogmatics and of the privileges of the Established Church. The Church of England was for Okey the Tory party at prayer, while Robert Owen, Tom Paine and the radical traditions of the French Revolution were variously an inspiration.

It was into this world that Bolton King came, full of the idealism he had learnt at Oxford, ready to open the minds of the poor. He lived at Toynbee Hall from the end of 1884 until 1892.   He worked full-time to develop the vision, organising lectures and taking the local working men on trips to Italy to see the sights. The library at Toynbee Hall was built up from a nucleus of Bolton's own works on social and political subjects. It was an exciting golden time.

The Cause of the Agricultural Labourer, from 1883
In 1892 Bolton settled permanently in Warwickshire. Despite the departure of his mother and sisters for London after his father's death, he had remained active in the area and his involvement was growing. His half-brother was giving up the big house and moving to London, so there was not the embarrassment of his presence. It

---

first chair of Italian Studies at Cambridge. He was a close friend of Bolton King, William Morris and Bernard Shaw.
[222] E. P .Thompson, *William Morris: Romantic to Revolutionary* (1955)

made sense to move on from Toynbee Hall and to make his permanent home in Warwickshire. While still at Oxford he had attended a Co-operative Congress and had returned much impressed by the idea of a co-operative principle in agriculture. Under his father's will, his mother had a life interest in some local farms and she agreed to rent him one of these - Radbourne Manor Farm - some 150 acres. Bolton established the Radbourne Manor Farming Association whereby an association of the labourers working on the farm rented it from him and aimed to put by a proportion of the profits so that eventually they would corporately own it. It was a lovely idea, but it didn't work. By 1890 the scheme was defunct, despite help and support from Arthur Acland and Joseph Arch.

At the same time as he was setting up the Farming Association, Bolton was also building decent and affordable housing for labourers. In 1883 - 1886 he bought forty-eight acres of land in Gaydon and built thirteen cottages on it - one of which he retained for his own use. It became his home in 1892, and it was where he began his married life in 1895[223]. His experience in this convinced him that proper housing for labourers could only be built with a subsidy from the rates - a revolutionary idea in the 1880's! Besides the cottages, Bolton also built a Reading Room in the village that was a place for lectures - like Toynbee Hall - as well as for general entertainment.

---

[223] His wife Lydia was a local labourer's daughter, who had been in service in London. He had four children - all of whom were educated in Warwick, and all of whom made their careers in education. Oliver was at Manchester University and then worked for the Birmingham Education Department. It's said that he never quite reached his potential, but he was keen on the theatre and an authority on family history. Edward went up to Balliol, and was a Fellow (Student) of Christ Church where he worked with Lord Cherwell on guided missiles and stuff during the war. He was later with the British Council. I met him when he was living at Catworth in Huntingdonshire in the 1970's. He was also keen on family history. Ralph was also at Balliol and became a teacher - latterly as Head of Buxton College (a Grammar School in Derbyshire). Lettice went to Oxford and also became a teacher - latterly as Head of the Harris Institute in Blackburn (?or Preston).

Historian of Italy

It was when he settled in Gaydon that Bolton began putting together the material for his magisterial history of Italy. *A History of Italian Unity* was the first study in English of the struggle for a united Italy and it has remained a foundation work. The divisions in Italy made no economic sense and it was a dream since the Napoleonic era to unite the country and for Italy as a whole to play its part in the life of Europe. However, the Papacy, Austria and the reactionary regime in Naples were almost insuperable obstacles. Bolton King charted the hopes raised and then dashed through over fifty years to the final entry into Rome in 1871. He admired Cavour, but his main hero was the flawed dreamer, Guiseppe Mazzini. He published a separate study of Mazzini in 1903, which said as much about Bolton King's hopes and dreams as it did about Mazzini's. Bolton King wanted to see Christianity remade as a sort of moral system, free of its old creeds.

In this he was part of a liberal movement in and out of the church. Within the church, the Modern Churchman's Union, founded in 1898, best represented the mood. One of its first high-priests was Hastings Rashdall, whose "The Idea of the Atonement in Christian Theology" (1919) argued for an exemplarist understanding of the Atonement. He believed Christ's death was a supreme moral example, and wanted people to approach religion as rational people, seeking moral guidance. Canon Glazebrook of Ely was a friend of the Barnetts. In *The Faith of a Modern Churchman* (1918), Glazebrook argued against the Virgin Birth and the empty tomb, and drew down on his head the wrath of Bishop Chase. Glazebrook was in the same league as Bishop Barnes of Birmingham, who presided at Bolton King's funeral at Chadshunt in 1937. Bishop Chase argued that these ideas would reduce Christianity to "a nerveless altruism", and certainly a purely moral gospel has lacked power. The Ethical Societies of the late nineteenth century are long gone.

Warwickshire Politics, 1889-1902

In 1888, while still at Toynbee Hall, Bolton was appointed a Justice of the Peace for Warwickshire. The next year he stood in the first County Council elections but went down to an easy defeat. Three years later he stood again - against Lord Willoughby de Broke [224]. He was asking that men of other classes and backgrounds should come on to the council, to moderate the dominance of the old landed gentry. He also believed that the Council should more actively use the powers it had to improve conditions locally. He was then narrowly defeated but was immediately elected an Alderman, and took his place on various key committees - on allotments, rates and technical education. He was elected Chairman of the last committee at a key period. During the 1890's people were increasingly aware of being overtaken by Germany in technological studies. J. S. Haldane and the Webbs were working hard to make the University of London and the new universities being established in Birmingham, Leeds, Liverpool and Manchester great centres for applied science. Even at the humbler level at which Bolton King was working in Warwickshire, efforts were made to develop a practical education after the age of thirteen, relevant to the work in which the young people were to be engaged. A lot of seeds were sown that would take Bolton King away from his first concerns about farming and rural housing and make him a thorough going educationalist. Haldane used to argue that "mind", not labour or capital, created wealth. Education was the most important thing of all. This became Bolton King's creed also.

In 1896 Bolton was elected President of the Warwick Liberal Club and was increasingly a heard and respected voice in Liberal circles. He was strongly opposed to the South African War, which broke out in 1899 - which didn't help him when he was adopted as the Liberal candidate to fight South Warwickshire at the bye-election of 1901.

---

[224] This was Henry Verney (1844-1902) 18th Lord Willoughby de Broke, a local grandee with 18,000 acres, Master of the Warwickshire Foxhounds and Colonel of the Warwickshire Yeomanry. His son was one of the Diehards in the Lords dispute in 1911.

He had the support of his party leader, Sir Henry Campbell-Bannerman, but Asquith, Grey and Haldane were all pro-Boer. Bolton King saw a replay of the American War of Independence, and quoted Burke's views on how an empire should be held together. It was a rowdy election, and he went down to defeat at the hands of the Liberal Unionist. Liberal Unionists held the seat at every election between 1886 and 1910 - except in the Liberal landslide of 1906.

After the defeat of 1901, in the seat for which his father had sat in 1857-9, Bolton turned from parliamentary politics into another direction. As Chairman of the Technical Education Committee, Bolton King had been a key part of the development of technical education in Warwickshire and he had developed a good grasp of the educational needs of the country. With the Education Act of 1902 the Technical Education Committee ceased to exist, to be replaced by the County Education Committee. Bolton King was Vice-Chairman, and was expected to succeed J. S. Dugdale as Chairman in a short while. However, in 1904, he decided to make the unusual change from alderman to official, and was appointed the first Director of Education for Warwickshire. It was a controversial appointment. Bolton had a high political profile, he was known as a radical. He started work, it is said, "amid a storm of prejudice and unreasoned opposition".

Director of Education, 1902-1928
The setting up of a central bureaucracy was a controversial part of the 1902 Act, but Bolton King guided it through. Local vicars could now sit on the governing bodies of their local church school, but they were now answerable to the County Education Committee. Head teachers also were responsible to the county - both in board schools and voluntary schools. This was all new. Bolton King was careful to treat teachers as partners rather than subordinates, and gave them their own representative committees. A first priority was to sort out the many small and often sub-standard voluntary schools in the small villages. Some were closed; some were

improved. Otherwise, his chief concern was to extend education for most children beyond the then age of thirteen. There were very few grammar schools, and nothing within reach of most labouring children. The Fisher Education Act of 1918 raised the school leaving age to fourteen and gave hope, through providing for the possibility of continuation classes, for education to go on until sixteen. Sadly, this didn't happen. Bolton King worked hard to provide continuation classes in village halls, by the use of local or peripatetic teachers, but there was much opposition from employers - who didn't want to release their young employees. By the time he retired, he was arguing for the school leaving age to be raised to fifteen. It was a slow progress.

Conclusion

He had loved and admired his elderly father who was already sixty when he was born, and died when he was seventeen. His life was very much in his father's tradition. One of old Bolton King's Warwickshire friends was Mark Phillips, the bachelor, Unitarian squire of Welcome. Phillips' niece and heiress married Sir George Trevelyan of Wallington and produced the talented family that included G. M. Trevelyan. They were admirable people, increasingly serious minded advocates of social reform, high minded liberals of great probity. They were Bolton King's people and represented the best of this side of the King tradition. What he lost was faith. His "remaking of Christian doctrine" just didn't work.

One of his poems:

Still it is true, though God is gone,
it is our work to do his will,
to fight for Him till life is done,
to stand upon his holy hill.

Though God is gone, and where he stood
the dust of ruin hangs a shroud,
another God, more great, more good,
looms up behind the clearing cloud.

Raleigh King v Bolton King

Bolton King the younger was full of good works and post-Christian ethical aspirations. He claimed the Liberal mantle that was now changing into a socialist one. He had been admirable in the 1880's and 1890's, and he was still in tune with how things were going in the world. He had not experienced the exile. This division between Ernest and Bolton King was deeply entrenched – and had been since they were boys. Bolton studied and engaged with the thinking of his day. He wanted to improve things – and change things. Ernest wasn't particularly interested in either. He was committed to a way of life, to a tradition, to the old way of doing things.

It is not now so obvious that Bolton King had followed the better way. In the end, liberalism itself has come under attack. Its confidence in the march of history seemed misplaced after the Holocaust. Its moral confidence – linked to its neglect (at best) of the religious inheritance (or any other inheritance) – seems now more like arrogance. It had worked for a more centralized, more monochrome state, but the state that was being delivered was not the Promised Land. The humbler, less articulate approach of the defeated conservative has now begun to look more attractive. You don't have to be a thorough going post-modernist to appreciate a certain shyness about those old liberal truth claims.

Yet in the days when they enjoyed power, they were indeed powerful. Czarist Russia had its Communist take-over; people think that this country escaped. In fact, the revolution that took over the country from 1880 to 1920 was almost as thorough, and my family in its way suffered an experience not unlike the uprooted gentry of Russia. The Kings were not died in the wool Tories and never had been, but Liberal Unionism didn't mean much once the Home Rule Liberal Party had bounced back in 1906. Liberalism after 1906 meant secularism and radicalism. The old Liberal families, whose roots were on the Parliamentary side in the Civil War, who had opposed James II and welcomed William III, who had struggled for an inclusive church and state in the eighteenth century, and had been the first to move on the work of reform, once the shock of the French Revolution and the struggle of the wars was over - were now in exile in their own country, written out of history, irrelevant to the great secular-socialist tradition that was now taking everything over. They weren't sent to the Gulag. They weren't knocked down in the streets or sent for re-education in the factories[225]. Yet they and their inheritance was as effectively – more effectively - rubbished. Given how thoroughgoing the defeat of the liberal gentry was at the beginning of the last century, it is remarkable that the Church has survived as well as it has done. It is remarkable too that today it is possible in some way to rehabilitate a life like my grandfather's.

Bolton King's Publications:
Mazzini's Essays (1894)
A History of Italian Unity 2 vols (1899)
Italy Today (with Thomas Oakey) (1901)
Mazzini (1902)
as "Walter Ray" Poems of Yesterday and To-day (1921)
Schools of Today: Present Problems in Education (1929)
Mazzini's Letters (1930)
Fascism in Italy (1931)

---

[225] See *Celestial Harmonies* by Peter Esterházy (2001) for a moving account of his family's destruction after communism arrived in Hungary in the 1940's – and of the brutal treatment suffered by his father, Mátyás Esterházy.

CHAPTER SIXTEEN

ERNEST RALEIGH KING (1862-1920)

When my grandfather was born in Weymouth in the summer of 1862, the old way of life still seemed reasonably secure. His father retired from the army aged 21, after gruelling service in the Crimea, with enough money not to need to pursue a career. He was heir to an estate of nearly 3000 acres of good Warwickshire farmland and when his father remarried and sold Umberslade Hall, a settlement was made that enabled him to marry. In the early years of the marriage, he stayed near his young wife's West Country family, only settling in Warwickshire in the later 1860s. Ernest's childhood home was in Lillington, near Leamington Spa. I imagine he spent his time there riding and hunting. He was always a countryman and no doubt learnt these things as a boy.

The census of 1871 shows Ernest lodging with the Vicar of Kenilworth, the Rev. William Bickmore, who was vicar there from 1856-1875. Bickmore was married to Gertrude Hyde Villiers – a niece of the Bishop of Durham – and had a family of nine young children. Presumably in order to augment his stipend, he took in pupils. There were two other pupils at Kenilworth Vicarage in 1871 – Thomas Innes and John Don Wauchope[226]. Innes was thirteen and Wauchope was eleven. Ernest was unusually young to be away from home[227].

---

[226] I haven't identified Thomas A.M. Innes. John Don Wauchope (1859-1951) was the eldest son of Sir John Don Wauchope Bt. of Edmonstone, Midlothian, who had succeeded a cousin in the title a few years before. The cousin had been an actor – specializing in drag roles – who bankrupted himself and sold up everything, including the family estate at Newton Don. John Don Wauchope went up to Trinity College, Cambridge and did a spell in the Scots Guards. He didn't marry, was a magistrate in Midlothian – but I don't think did much else. His younger brother, Andrew Don Wauchope, was a distinguished international rugby player.

[227] Great uncle Alfred Buckley was thirteen when he went to be coached by a

The tradition is that Ernest didn't go to school, because he didn't want to. He appears in the Eton Register, so may have been admitted there in 1874, but the further details confuse him with his young uncle. Probably he went to Eton, wasn't happy there, and was withdrawn.

PART ONE - THE ARMY 1878-1884

Ernest and the Late Victorian Army, 1878-1884

in 1878, when he was sixteen, Ernest was gazetted a second lieutenant in the Renfrew Infantry. His father had entered the 13th Light Dragoons in 1850 at the same age, so Ernest was following in his footsteps.

In other respects things were different to what they had been in his father's day. His grandfather had just died and was found to have provided very generously for the children of his second marriage. The provision was so generous in fact that the only way the legacies could be paid was by mortgaging the estate. Money was very tight. There was no question of Ernest trying for a cavalry regiment, where a substantial private income would be required to cover the expenses of the mess, sport and social recreation. The expenses of an infantry officer were less – he might get by on a private income of £100 to £150 a year[228]. For this, he enjoyed at least six months leave, while spending much of his time on duty, hunting, shooting and playing cricket.

In 1850, Edward Raleigh King had his commission bought for him. After 1871 this was no longer possible. The purchase of commissions was brought to end by Royal Warrant. Ernest had therefore to sit one of the twice-yearly exams and, once passed, to

---

vicar in 1842 (while living in the vicarage) before going on to Eton the following year.
[228] See Edward M. Spiers, *The Late Victorian Army*, Manchester U.P., 1992, esp. ch. 4.

wait to be allocated to a regiment. In the event, he was allocated to the Renfrew Infantry, with which he had no conceivable links. His Scottish career in a regiment of line was however short-lived for he resigned this commission on 18 October 1879.

On 29 November 1879 Ernest was re-commissioned as a second lieutenant in the 5th (West Yorkshire) Militia. The Militia was a volunteer force made up mainly of farm labourers, miners and other men, who went through some basic military training at a local depot, in return for pay. After the Napoleonic Wars, it had been allowed to decay but the French invasion scare of the 1850s resulted in its being revived.   It was popular with working men since it provided a sort of paid holiday for people in seasonal work who could sometimes get away. The middle classes, on the other hand, preferred to serve in the Volunteer Battalions. Militia officers (who had little or nothing to do with training the recruits) were often those who had failed the entrance examination required for regular commissions and who later hoped to transfer to a line regiment. Many of those with regular commissions came through the Militia, though efforts were always being made to increase the number of those with a Sandhurst or university background. Sometimes Militia officers intended simply to spend a few years in the army before pursuing a different career.

In 1881, under the Childers reforms, the infantry of the line were reorganised. The regular regiments of foot lost their numbers, instead taking on a territorial or county title, and amalgamating with the militia battalions and rifle volunteers in their designated regimental districts. Thus, the 19th Regiment of Foot (the Green Howards) was amalgamated with the 5th West Yorkshire Militia (which became the regiment's 3rd Battalion) and the North York Rifles (now the 4th Battalion) to become the Princess of Wales's Own (Yorkshire Regiment), with its recruiting area continuing to be the North Riding. I'm not sure that the ancient Green Howards really believed that the West Yorkshire Militia guys were up to their standards, but they had to lump it. The effect for Ernest was that he was no longer just an officer in the Militia, but in the 3rd Battalion of the Princess of Wales's Own (Yorkshire) Regiment – which must have sounded better.

On 28 June 1882 Ernest gained a commission at home, as Lieutenant in the Warwickshire Regiment. He is then described as "late Lieutenant in the Princess of Wales's Own (Yorkshire) Regiment". The Gazette does not specify which battalion he was attached to, but presumably it would have been to the 3rd Battalion – the militia. The Warwickshire Regiment had originally been the 6th Foot. In 1778, at the height of the American War, it was recruiting in Warwickshire and four years later became the 6th (1st Warwickshire) Regiment of Foot – probably in accordance with General Conway's desire to see regiments establish a territorial link. In 1832 William IV granted it the title of "Royal". The Regimental Depot was established at Warwick in 1873 and (after Childers' reforms) the name was changed again to the Royal Warwickshire Regiment[229].

Ernest resigned from the Warwickshire Regiment on 30 April 1884, a few weeks before his twenty second birthday.

PART TWO - THE TURF, 1880-1920

Being Young in the 1880's

It was a darkening time for English agriculture and a difficult time for his father. Old Bolton King's improvidence meant that, after paying the legacies, there was no capital available to make necessary improvements. In the wider world, farm tenants and farm labourers were flexing their muscles just as farm prices were on the verge of collapse. The Liberal triumph in Warwickshire at the 1880 election and the Liberal landslide (on the new franchise) in 1885 raised serious questions for landlords - and for landlordism as a way of life. Still, at the beginning of the decade it was probably possible to believe that things might improve in a year or two.

---

[229] The regimental museum is at St John's House, Warwick, CV34 4NF

1f.

Despite falling incomes, Ernest seems to have been able to live as a smart young man. As his younger sister was later to testify with some bitterness, whatever money was available was reserved for Ernest and his horses. She and her sister had to make do with a parcel of books from Mudie's[230].

In his memoirs, George Lambton gives a good impression of a young man starting off in the 1880's [231]. Lambton was the fifth of the eight sons of the 2nd Earl of Durham, so he wasn't rich in his world. He says he had around £800 a year, which he didn't seem to think was very much. He spent a year at Cambridge, and another few months with a crammer for the Army. He didn't fancy army life. He was already buying horses and putting them with trainers – and riding. In 1880 he decided to be a gentleman rider. He did a bit of steeple-chasing and a bit of flat, and gradually got known. He ended up a successful and well-respected trainer – one of the first generation of gentlemen trainers. Did my grandfather try the same road?

There were many riding heroes in the 1880's. Capt Bay Middleton was an older man, but still well known as a rider. He was killed in a steeplechase on Lord Willoughby de Broke's estate at Kineton in 1892 [232]. Capt Roddy Owen was a soldier, but rode seriously until he won the National in 1892[233]. He died of cholera in Egypt in 1896,

---

[230] Mudie's Library was established by Charles Edward Mudie (1818-90) in 1842. The development of the railways enabled him to send boxes of books all over the country – which he did to great effect. The Library died out at the beginning of the 20th century with the development of the free libraries.

[231] *Men & Horses I have known*, Hon. George Lambton (1924)

[232] Capt. W. G. "Bay" Middleton (1846-92) of the 12th Lancers, developed an unmatched reputation as a steeplechaser during the 1870's and was escort to Empress Elizabeth when she visited England. When he visited her in Austria however, he was not well received. He had an affair with Lady Blanche Hozier (one of many) and was the reputed father of Clementine Hozier, who married Winston Churchill. His nickname came from a Derby winner of 1836 of the same name.

[233] There's a memorial window to him in St Michael's, Chester Square. I've often wondered whether Roddy Owen was my father's godfather. Why was papa called Roddy? He never said and I never thought to ask him.

aged 40. His brother Hugh was almost equally well known as a rider, but was killed in a fall from his horse while still a young man. Count Kinsky[234] was a romantic figure – and a great mate of Lambton's. He had first come to this country as a young man in the late 1870's. The Empress Elisabeth was visiting Aintree and he was in her party. This began a lifelong love affair with England and the English way of life. He was a daring rider and in 1883 won the Grand National.

Peter Purcell Gilpin

Nearer home was my grandfather's first cousin, Peter Purcell-Gilpin. Gilpin was the only son of my great-grandfather's close friend and brother-in-law, Capt Peter Purcell[235]. He trained as a soldier and then settled down as a trainer at Dollanstown in co Kildare[236]. When a horse of his won the Cesarowitch stakes in 1900, he was able to build the Clarehaven stables in Newmarket[237] - which are

---

[234] Count Karel Kinsky (1858-1919) was from an aristocratic family in Bohemia (then in the Austro-Hungarian Empire, now in the Czech Republic) long renowned for its love of horses. Count Oktavian Kinsky had introduced point-to-point racing in Bohemia in 1846 and in 1874 had introduced a form of the Grand National – which is still run. Count Karel served as the Austrian Ambassador to this country for many years and was much loved by society. Lady Randolph Churchill was a close friend, though Count Kinsky was barred by his father from marrying her on Lord Randolph's death in 1894. He married someone else the following year. The First World War destroyed his world. It is said that he died a broken man.

[235] He was born in France in 1858 and married the Gilpin heiress, Amy Louisa Meux-Smith, in 1883. They settled in Ireland and had a family of five sons and two daughters – so there are a lot of Purcell-Gilpins around (in the USA, Zimbabwe and South Africa). The eldest son, Peter, married Beatrice Hope-Clarke, had children and divorced. Geoffrey (d. 1971) married Hon Aline Beaumont, had two daughters by her, divorced and married again. Amy married Frank Faber and was left things by aunt Ethel – together with her sister, Mrs Farmer. Another son, Val Purcell-Gilpin, was on the same staff as papa in 1917-18. Purcell Gilpin died at Dollanstown in 1928.

[236] In 1890 he was living at Hockliffe Lodge. Hockliffe is a village on the A5 north of Dunstable. He was also a magistrate. Hockliffe Grange was the home of Col Sir Richard Gilpin Bt, who died there in 1882. He left his estate to his nephew, Capt Henry Meux-Smith.

[237] It was something of a centre in the racing world. Lord Randolph Churchill was there in the early 90's – and Churchill took his horses seriously. It is still a going concern.

still there. He did well and made a good living. His greatest horse was a mare, Pretty Polly. Lambton (as a rival trainer) is a trifling grudging in his praise of this wonderful mare, choosing to recount at length the story of her defeat in the race for the Ascot Cup in 1906. However, that defeat was one of her few and Vanity Fair was describing her in 1908 (when they published a cartoon of Peter Gilpin by Spy) as "Empress among racehorses. In the history of racing, no female has matched Pretty Polly's record". My grandfather and Gilpin seem to have been close. In 1885 he stood godfather to Gilpin's eldest son Peter.

The Racing Scene
Lambton wrote, "If I were asked to name the most memorable period in the history of the turf within my record I should turn to the years between 1880 and 1890". Matt Dawson was one the great trainers of the day, and Fred Archer the greatest of the jockeys. Archer was a young man of 5ft 10in in height, who would naturally weigh in at between 10st and 11st, but rode at 8st 10lb. His discipline was extraordinary, but the constant starving undermined his constitution and he committed suicide in 1886 at the age of twenty-nine[238]. In the ten years before his death he won the Derby five times, the Oaks four times and the St Leger six times.

This was the world of my grandfather's youth. Newmarket was his spiritual home and horses his life. Yet he wasn't a betting man. He was known as 'Half-crown King' because he never put more than half a crown on anything. It's a pity then that he didn't take up riding for a living. From all that I've heard about him, he would have enjoyed the life of a trainer. Maybe there just wasn't the money. My grandfather was far from having Lambton's £800 a year, and Peter Gilpin had married his heiress before he started out at Dollanstown. My grandfather would have needed some capital and he didn't have it. This was a pity, because horse breeding and

---

[238] though, in the manner of those days, this was never mentioned. People spoke of "typhoid fever" or of "a breakdown in health".

training was a growing industry at the time, and one for which he was eminently qualified[239].

PART THREE - THE ATTRACTION OF FRANCE

Early Married Life, 1892-1900

When his father wanted to marry, Umberslade had been sold and enough money was realized to give him a sufficient income. It was not so clear what Ernest could do. His father was not yet sixty, but Ernest was coming up to thirty and needed to find a wife. The Chadshunt estate was heavily mortgaged and barely supported the family as it then was. Two establishments were out of the question, given the expense of maintaining the big house. In the end, his father decided to take out a second mortgage, let the house, and he and his son each took a house in town.

These arrangements enabled my grandfather to marry Dorothy Buckley in 1892. Her family weren't keen. My grandfather had no job and not much income. They may well have been doubts about his moral character. My grandmother was packed off to India to be with her cousin Hilda Spencer, in the hope that she would fall in love with some suitable Indian Army officer. She didn't. On her return, she married my grandfather at St Mary's, Bourne Street[240]. They settled in Montpellier Square – just down the road from his parents. My father was born there on Christmas Day 1893[241].

---

[239] Investment in bloodstock doubled between 1891 and 1913, and by 1913 stud fees of 300 guineas were not unusual. See G.R.Searle p. 550, quoting W Vamplew, *The Turf: A Social and Economic History of Horse Racing* (London, 1976)

[240] My grandmother's parish church was in fact Holy Trinity, Sloane Street - but the church was undergoing repairs at the time. Aunt Emmeline said that marrying my grandfather was the stupidest thing my grandmother ever did. She liked to tell a favourite Buckley family story about my grandfather throwing a shoehorn at my grandmother when they were staying at New Hall. Yet, despite difficulties, they were devoted. My grandfather would style my grandmother's hair and supervise the buying of her clothes.

[241] In the popular TV series of the 1970's "Upstairs, Downstairs", Lady Marjorie

France in the 1890's

However, money was tight. My grandmother had no money, and my grandfather's wasn't going very far. Much of their early-married life seems to have been spent in France, where living was cheaper. My father certainly always felt at home there. My grandfather loved France - though he spoke no French[242]. There were the memories of his family's links with the Second Empire. The 1860's had been a golden time in Paris. Many legends had grown up around the great figures of those days, played out to the music of Offenbach. In contrast, the Third Republic of the 1890's was a dull and bitter affair. The upper classes had never reconciled themselves to the 1871 settlement. Whether Legitimist, Orléanist or Bonapartist in their sympathies, they had all gradually withdrawn from public life. This left the Republic free to pursue its secularist agenda, which it was more than happy to do.

The French Church and the French Army made up a sort of unofficial opposition. They shared the aristocracy's contempt for the Republic and most of them looked for the restoration of the Catholic monarchy. Leo XIII was anxious. In 1890 he asked Cardinal Lavigerie, Archbishop of Algiers, to encourage faithful Catholics to rally behind the republic. Two years later the Pope issued an encyclical, *Au milieu des solicitudes,* with a similar theme. But the *Ralliement* was a failure. The conservative and monarchist right remained angry and alienated.

This was the background for the unjust conviction of Dreyfus in 1894. The campaign to free Dreyfus that was begun in 1898 by the secularists and radicals ended in defeat for the right wing forces that had rallied around the Army and the Church. The division of

---

lamented their move from Mayfair to Kensington in about 1900. People like her had always lived in Mayfair. Robert Knight and Bolton King had lived in Mayfair - but in the 1880's and 1890's their children migrated further west.

[242] One of his surviving books, "My Paris Note-Book" is a book of memoirs from the Second Empire and the early years of the Republic.

Church and State and the secularisation of the Republic - which persists to this day - was the fruit of this period.

England was fortunate in having Lord Salisbury to manage the conservative forces here in such a way that the upper classes remained to some extent engaged in mainstream politics. The bitter political divisions – which intensified here in the first decade of the 1900's - could so easily have resulted in a polarization like that that took place in France. I suspect my grandfather would not have been sad if they had. He was very alienated by the *bien pensant* radicalism of those days.

PART THREE - STRUGGLES AT HOME

The Struggle to Survive 1900-1915

On Christmas Eve 1900, my grandfather transferred Chadshunt Hall and some lands in Chadshunt and Gaydon to Thomas Augustus Motion of Maidwell, Northants., who was to serve as High Sheriff of Warwickshire in 1907[243]. Motion doesn't seem to have lived there long. Within ten years he had sold it on to the Dunne family - who are still there[244].

My grandfather seems not to have sold the land at that time. The land probably consisted of around 2500 acres, from which his father might have cleared around £800 a year in the 1870's, before the interest on the mortgage and the jointure due to his step-mother[245].

---

[243] (1866-1942), son of Richard William Motion, of Carlisle House, Clapton, Essex. In 1927, he married Lady Elizabeth Hesketh-Prichard, widow of Maj. H.V. Hesketh-Prichard and dau. of the 3rd Earl of Verulam. T.A. Motion was brother to Andrew Richard Motion, Chairman of the Cannon Brewery from 1889 and great-grandfather of Sir Andrew Motion, Poet Laureate from 1999-2009 (see his *In the Blood* – Faber, 2006)

[244] The papers relating to the Chadshunt estate from the time of Lord Catherlough's purchase of the estate are lodged in the Shakespeare Centre Library & Archive in Stratford on Avon. They are listed under "Papers relevant to the Verney family of Compton Verney".

[245] And that is before the cost of the £14,000 mortgage is taken into account

By the time he took over, my grandfather would have been lucky to get half that – with the same deductions. The answer would have been to farm it himself. My maternal grandfather had barely 1000 acres (some of which he rented). He had an adequate – though by no means princely – income, but only because he farmed it himself. If my King grandfather had done the same with even some of his land he might have survived. However, getting rid of a tenant was difficult. Perhaps getting rid of the landlord mentality was even more difficult.

The perambulations in France came to an end after 1900, and my grandparents bought a modest house at Appletree, a village just across the county border in Northamptonshire, but close to Chadshunt[246].

Money was always tight. When my father was sent away to his prep school in 1902, he was never certain that his next term's fees would be paid. My father used to joke that his mother took in washing and that his father would embarrass his neighbours by commenting on their wives' underwear which he had seen hanging on the line. "Taking in washing" was jokingly thought of as the end of the line among the declining gentry. Whether my grandmother was actually reduced to doing it or not, papa's story does however give some idea of the pressures under which they lived. Long visits by my father and his mother to her aunt at Nunton were "rest times" in a tricky marriage but were also part of an attempt at saving money.

The Radical Attack
The dominance of the Conservative Party in government from 1886-1906 disguises the fact that from the beginning of the Gladstone's second administration in 1880 until the beginning of the Great War the political agenda was set by the radicals. After the introduction

---

[246] My father and I visited the village in the summer of 1966. My father found the house but there was no one in. I remember little of it. It couldn't be seen from the road, and it had no name that I can discover.

of manhood suffrage in 1884 there was a general sense of helplessness among the country gentry. The aim of the Conservative Party under Lord Salisbury was to try and hold the line for as long as possible, and they managed this with remarkable success. However, after Salisbury's retirement in 1902 it was clear that something else was needed if the forces of conservatism were not to be swept away altogether.

Joseph Chamberlain and the Tariff Reform Campaign (launched in 1903) was an attempt to develop a non-socialist ideology that stood some chance against the overwhelming power of the socialist left. Tariff reform was an attempt to bring back a sense of common purpose to agriculture and business, and to beat back the class conflict that was beginning to dominate politics. The idea was that agriculture and business would both be helped by the imposition of tariffs on cheap foreign imports, thus giving them the same protection in their home market that their chief rivals enjoyed abroad. The resulting income might then be available for social reforms, without recourse to penal levels of taxation on the rich. It was a good idea, but it didn't win the Conservatives any elections. For one thing, it was difficult to counter the suspicion that the landowners wanted to keep the price of food artificially high, as they had in 1846. For the mass electorate, the landowners were a universal aunt Sally. Agriculture in this country was dispensable. You could buy cheaper from abroad. After two defeats in 1910, Bonar Law dropped his proposals for tariffs for most agriculture goods, thus excluding landowners from any benefit that tariff reform might bring.

By that time, landowners were feeling so bruised they probably couldn't care. Lloyd George had introduced his "People's Budget" in 1909. It was said to be a Liberal ploy. Balfour had been using the Lords to moderate the radical legislation of the early years of the Liberal government. Now the government was daring the Lords to reject the Budget so that they could go to the country to obtain a mandate to remove the Lords' veto on legislation and so give the

Commons a free run. If this was indeed the government's intention, it succeeded. The Budget introduced a series of mainly uncontroversial social reforms, but these reforms were to be financed by punitive taxes on land. The main one was a capital gains tax levied at 20% to be paid when the land was either sold or inherited. It was a clear attack on landowners and on the whole system of landholding and, although it was modified in committee and repealed in 1918, it gave some indication of what the Liberal party thought of the landed gentry. Balfour wrote to his niece, "They have chosen a particular section of the community, and a particular kind of property which they think both unpopular and helpless, and have proceeded to mulct it – demagogism in its worst aspect". The Lords knew that they risked their future if they opposed the Budget. They knew also that, without the Veto, a Home Rule Bill for Ireland would be the first piece of legislation to be introduced and passed. Yet they felt they had no option.

It was a desperate time and a thoroughly depressing one for the old fashioned landed gentry, and especially those with small estates and little capital reserves. And it only got worse. In October 1913 the government launched its Land Campaign, aimed at giving county councils the right to fix rents and wage rates, to reduce working hours and to acquire land, if necessary by compulsory purchase, to purchase smallholdings. Everything was being done to aid the labourer and even the farmer; nothing was being done for the landowner. It was that year too that the Conservative party finally caved in and abandoned its plans to introduce tariffs on food as part of any future tariff reform.

PART FOUR - THEMES OF DESTRUCTION

Church Matters
I don't know that my grandfather was anything other than a loyal churchman of the straightforward kind. My father once said that his habit of carrying lavatory paper in his pocket (because he didn't like the stuff provided in public lavatories) could prove

embarrassing in church, when he was looking for a handkerchief or for his collection. That is the only thing that connects him with the Church of England, though their destinies were entwined. His younger sister was more clearly involved - at least after her mother's death. This may have been because of her move from Kensington to Tedworth Square in Chelsea. I think that Holy Trinity, Brompton was in those days mainstream Church of England. Belgravia and Chelsea however was a different thing. St Paul's Church, Knightsbridge had been consecrated in 1843, the first parish after St Peter's, Eaton Square to be carved out of St George's, Hanover Square. It had had a succession of high-church vicars[247]. Three more churches were then built - St Barnabas Pimlico, Holy Trinity Sloane Street, and St Mary's Bourne Street. All of them were increasingly shrines of high church devotion and Aunt Ethel was faithful to St Mary's, Bourne Street over many years.

The work in this prosperous part of London did not have the resonance of the East End missions. C. F. Lowder was vicar of St Peter's London Docks from 1866-1880 and was something of a legend. Fr. Mackonochie, vicar of St Alban's Holborn from 1862-1887 and his successor, Fr. Stanton (1887-1913) were even better known. It was all part of the same thing. In some sense it was a sign of a church feeling itself at best unsupported by the state, and at worst under attack. The church – in its Anglo-Catholic aspect - was reaching into its own resources in order to survive. It could no longer underpin the nation and the nation's increasingly non-denominational, increasingly secular culture. As a result, it aimed to provide an alternative world in which to live – a counter-culture – with its own language, assumptions, belief-system and authority. The Assize Sermon of 1832 - when the church was certainly under attack - was never far away from Anglo-Catholic thinking at the beginning of the twentieth century.

---

[247] W. J. Early Bennett (1847-1851), Hon. Robert Liddell (1851-1881), and Henry Montague Villiers (1881-1908).

In all this, the Anglo-Catholic wing of the Church of England was very close to the Roman Catholic Church. That too was disengaging from the culture of the modern world and becoming a sort of counter-culture. Liberalism/modernism challenged all tradition and the controls that came with tradition. It gradually grew to dominate the schools system and the universities. Conservatives – and conservative Christians in particular – were becoming an angry and defensive enclave in a sea of all-confident liberalism.

Disestablishment

The Church had always been in the sights of the radicals. The Irish Church had been disestablished in 1869 as one of the first acts of Gladstone's first administration. The argument was that, since most of the population of Ireland was not Anglican, there were no grounds for maintaining the Church of Ireland's privileged position. Once that principle was accepted, it was a small step towards looking at the Established Church in other parts of the United Kingdom. Though a Churchman, Gladstone's Anglo Catholic position meant that he saw the Church as a voluntary association separate from the state. He held no candle to establishment, either in Wales, Scotland or England. Wales was the obvious next candidate. The Church of Wales claimed the allegiance of only about a quarter of those who claimed any denominational allegiance at all; the free churches had made huge strides from the middle of the eighteenth century when the Church there had been at a low ebb. By the end of the nineteenth century, the free churches wanted blood and Lloyd George made sure they would get it. Legislation for the disestablishment of the Welsh Church was a piece of unfinished business from Gladstone's second administration. The writing was on the wall though and in his fourth and last administration the legislation was drafted, though the Liberal government fell before it could go through Parliament. Inevitably Welsh disestablishment was part of the agenda when the Liberals came back to power after 1906 and was only second in the queue after Home Rule for Ireland once the Lords' veto had been abolished. It was on the Statute Book by the time War came, though to be implemented after the end of the war.

As far as the Liberal government was concerned, Welsh disestablishment was a practice run for the disestablishment and disendowment of the Church of England. It was known that the numbers of active Anglicans, Roman Catholics and Free Churchmen were roughly similar. Despite the strong presence of the Church of England in the life of the country, an increasingly influential Roman Catholic Church and very powerful Free Church forces within the Liberal Party were aiming for disendowment. Had the war not happened and had the Liberal-radical alliance endured, they would have achieved their objectives.

Education

The other major battle was Education. At the turn of the century the Free Churches were very powerful indeed. Their hope was clearly for a non-denominational state and an end to Anglican privileges. They saw the Church of England on the defensive and nowhere more so than in its schools. The Church of England had worked hard in the first part of the century to establish schools and very many Voluntary Schools were the fruit of that labour. State aid had been available to these since 1832, and was extended to Methodist, Catholic and Jewish schools later on. In 1870, when board schools were set up, Christian education if given was required to be non-denominational. This pleased the Free Churches. They were also glad that those schools which could not prove a specifically Anglican foundation were required to become board schools – thus removing many apparently church schools from the authority of the parish priest[248]. In the years after 1870 the board schools flourished with generous local support from the rates, very

---

[248] When I went to Clifford in 1979, there were still memories of the days when the school had been "liberated" from the vicar's control. The farmers of a chapel allegiance were influential on the Board of Governors and the Church of England was kept firmly at a distance. I was only invited to become a Governor shortly before I left – and when I already had three daughters in the school.

much at the expense of the voluntary schools that had no such support. By the mid-1890's the Voluntary Schools were tottering and the Free Churches would have been glad to see them fall. However, in 1896 the Conservative Government brought in a Bill to put the Voluntary Schools on an equal footing – with support from the rates. There was a huge outcry and the Liberal opposition talked the Bill out. In 1902 Balfour was determined to try again and this time he drove it through. The passing of his Education Bill contributed significantly to the defeat of his government in 1906.

The new Liberal Government was set on humiliating the Church of England and in 1908 sent a Bill up to the Lords that was intended to abolish rate support. The Lords refused to countenance it and rate support survived. Today, Free Church families are happy to take advantage of the Christian education available in church schools, now that non-denominationalism has become secularism!

PART FIVE - CONCLUSION

The Dark Side

My grandfather died on 2 February 1920. The announcement said that it was "after four months illness" – so the illness had first shown itself at the beginning of October 1919. The place of death was given as 46 St George's Road in the Registration Sub-District of Victoria. There is now no St George's Road in Victoria – possibly this was the street now known as St George's Drive. His residence was given as 69 Egerton Gardens. The place in St George's Road/Drive may have been a nursing home. My father registered the death on the same day. The cause of death was given as "Locomotor Ataxy – 12 years".

My father said that his father died of the effects of an old hunting accident. He may well have believed that. However, if the diagnosis on the death certificate was correct, my grandfather died of advanced syphilis. Locomotor ataxia is a syphilitic infection of the spinal column that develops in the final stages of the syphilis. It typically shows itself in a shambling gait and finally results in complete muscular collapse. The link with syphilis had been recognised within the medical profession for some years, though doctors would not always have told the patient of the link. It is just possible that my grandfather himself did not know that he had syphilis.

The doctor states that the disease had been present for twelve years. The average time from the onset of the disease until death is ten years, so that makes sense. My grandfather is likely to have felt shooting pains in his legs from around 1908, and might then have assumed that it was simply rheumatism. Deterioration advances at different rates. My father said that his father helped train horses for the front at the beginning of the war[249]. However, some time during the course of the war he moved to London – and possibly a deterioration in his health was the reason. Syphilis, which may have been contracted years before, often surfaces in middle age[250].

Syphilis
My father said that he had been introduced to a woman by his father at a young age – and this was something that Victorian fathers often did. The son would be warned about STDs and about the general need to be careful. It is almost certain that my grandfather – who was 30 when he married – was sexually experienced, and the anxieties of my grandmother's family may well have been linked to concerns about his moral character – and indeed about his general health. Doctors were known sometimes – when asked – to give warning hints about prospective fiancés to the fathers of their intended brides.

The chief difficulty was that the early symptoms of syphilis can be so fleeting. It was very easy for a young man either not to notice, or

---

[249] Cavalry horses were central to Sir John French's understanding of war, and remained important to Sir Douglas Haig
[250] Edouard Manet died of syphilis in 1883, aged 51, after several years of acute pain.

– if he did notice – to block it from his mind and wish it away. In the 1880s and 1890s much less was known about the disease – which was then incurable. Doctors might advise against marriage for a year or two, but there was rarely a suggestion that a young man should refrain from marrying.

My grandfather could have been infected before his marriage. The latent period – when no symptoms would be apparent and when he was not infectious – could easily have lasted for twenty years or more. If he knew that he had the disease but refused to think about it, he would have been like many others of his generation who managed to live into a reasonable old age and die of something apparently completely unrelated. On the other hand, my grandfather could have been infected after his marriage. When this happened, a man might have sex with his wife before he was fully aware of the infection or when he was in denial about it. In such cases the wife herself could be infected. This happened in middle class homes of those days far more frequently than is realized. Sometimes, the wife might be unaware of the onset of the disease. Sometimes she would be treated (though there was no effective treatment before 1905) without being told the nature of her condition. The doctor's responsibility to his patient didn't always extend beyond the husband. My grandfather might have infected my grandmother without either of them knowing. They might both have gone to their graves without knowing anything. On the other hand, my grandfather might have known of his infection, but not told my grandmother of the risk to her.

There remains the possibility that both my grandparents knew what had happened. There were no more children after my father. The explanation I heard was that my grandmother had a difficult birth and my grandfather didn't want to risk another pregnancy. This may have been the case. However, marital relations may have been discontinued after my grandmother's discovery of her infection or of my grandfather's discovery of his infection. My grandparent's marriage was not an easy one. If this shadow hung over their relationship, then it is easier to explain the unhappiness of my father's childhood. The further dimension is the attitude of his family. Syphilis was not spoken of in those days – and certainly not in the presence of women. It was however a major issue, and the subject of suffragette campaigning. The risk to women was well known. Was Aunt Ethel's dislike of her brother linked to her knowledge – or suspicion - of what was wrong with him? More interestingly, was Aunt Emmeline's rooted dislike of him - which clearly reflected the general attitude of my grandmother's family – linked to Uncle Basil's suspicion or knowledge of his brother-in-law's illness and the effect it had on his much loved sister?

In the end, I think mainly of the sadness of it all. My grandparents' life was over-shadowed, and my father's growing up deeply affected. He needed the steadying hand of his parents when he came back from the war. He needed his mother, to whom he was devoted. As it was, he had neither.

My grandfather was buried with his wife (and by his father and sister) in Chadshunt churchyard. His mother followed him a few months later. He left behind an only child – my father - and an unmarried sister. His grandfather's widow died that same summer at a great age – and was buried on the other side of the churchyard, under a large white marble slab to match her late husband's.

KNIGHT BIOGRAPHIES

CHAPTER SEVENTEEN

ROBERT KNIGHT OF BREAD STREET (1632-1715)

William Knight purchased Barrells in Warwickshire from the Bolton family in 1554. His father and grandfather were from just over the border in Worcestershire and he and his family seem to have been reasonably well-off farmers and trades people. His eldest son by his second marriage, Nicholas Knight, died in 1652 at a great age. He had survived his eldest son and had farmed Barrells for over seventy years. It was his grandson, John Knight, who took over. He was the father of William Knight (1657-1733) who married Anne Raleigh, and of Elizabeth Knight, who married William Martin, of Evesham. William and Elizabeth Martin were the parents of the talented brothers who founded Martin's Bank – and established a very prosperous banking dynasty.

John's younger brother Robert had gone off to London to make his fortune. It was a boom time in London. The population was growing fast and there was a growing need for food from the country. Robert Knight's connections in the fertile valleys of Worcestershire helped him to meet these needs and to make his fortune.

In 1649 he was apprenticed to his uncle, Thomas Randall, a member of the Grocer's Company. At the completion of his apprenticeship in 1658 he was himself admitted a member of the Company and set up in business on his own account in Bread Street. About that time he married his cousin, Elizabeth Randall. From his will, it is clear that he had become a substantial businessman, with several leased properties, one at least of which was a base for sugar baking. He served as a Governor of Christ's Hospital, as Common Councillor for the Bread Street Ward and in 1710 was Master of the Grocers Company.

1f.

Robert Knight had two surviving sons. The elder son, Thomas[251], married the daughter of Sir Leonard Robinson[252], a member of a prolific and wealthy City family. Their son, Robinson, was a member of the Goldsmith's Company, went bankrupt and died in West Ham in 1780 leaving two daughters. Robert Knight's daughters were married to City men: Elizabeth to Edmund Bayley, a mercer of St Mary-le-Bow; Sarah, to Philip Surman, a draper of St Clements Danes[253];and Anna to Arundell Wastfield. Philip and Sarah Surman's son Robert did well. He was a banker, bought the Valentine's estate in East Ham, and married his daughter to the younger son of a peer. Anna Wastfield had a pious son, Robert Wastfield, who died childless in the Mile End Road in 1776, leaving several legacies to dissenting charities, with many expressions of Christian resignation.

---

[251] Erith describes Thomas Knight as a man of little ambition, who was happy to live quietly on his (and his wife's) ample fortune. In 1772, their son Robinson was left £20 for a mourning ring by his cousin, the Cashier's son.

[252] Sir Leonard was the younger brother of William Robinson of Rokeby Park, Yorkshire. William was the father of Archbishop Richard Robinson of Armagh and of Knight the Cashier's second wife, Anne Robinson. In the absence of other heirs, the Rokeby estate descended to William Frend, Dean of Canterbury, who was married to William's younger daughter Grace. He took the name of Robinson in 1793. The Robinsons who were ennobled as Lord Grantham, Viscount Goderich and Marquess of Ripon were another branch of the same family.

[253] They were the parents of Robert Surman, who began life as Clerk in Martin's Bank and went on in 1715 to the Sword Blade Bank - then closely allied to the South Sea Company in its hostility to the Bank of England. In 1718 he became Deputy to his uncle, the South Sea Company Cashier, and prospered mightily until the crash. His assets were estimated at £158,262 in 1721. He recovered and in 1724 bought the Valentines estate in Great Ilford. This had been built in 1702 by her son-in-law for Mrs Elizabeth Tillotson, widow of Archbishop Tillotson. The house still stands, amid the present urban sprawl, though has been under Local Authority control since 1912. Surman was a Partner at Martin's Bank (where his cousin, James Martin was senior partner) in 1730 and in 1748 was senior partner in his own bank of Surman, Dinely & Cliff. He founded a distinguished City family and died at Valentines in 1759. Under the will of his uncle the Cashier, he was guardian of the young William Knight.

Mrs Robert died in 1684 and Robert is then said to have married Jane Barkham, whose father, Sir Edward Barkham 2nd Bt. (1631-1669), came from a long established city family and also had property at Waynfleet in Lincolnshire. By the time he died, he was married to a third wife

CHAPTER EIGHTEEN

ROBERT KNIGHT, THE CASHIER (1675-1744)

Early Career

Robert Knight was the youngest child and he seems to have continued to live with his father in Bread Street. He seems never to have become a Freeman of the City, which suggests that he didn't finish the apprenticeship that he had undertaken in 1691. In February 1702, at St Mildred's, he married Martha Powell, the daughter of Jeremiah Powell. Powell was a wealthy merchant of the parish of St Michael Bassishaw, who went on to become a Governor of the Bank of England[254]. Powell had no sons, so Martha and her sisters were his co-heirs. The estates in Powys which descended in the Knight family came from the Powell family. Rather oddly, young Robert seems to have continued to live with his father in Bread Street during this time, while developing a reputation as an able financier.

It was certainly the time to be a financier. The French wars had resulted in huge Government borrowing, and so urgent was the need that they had to borrow where they could. People were growing fat on the interest. In 1694 the Bank of England was established. They were now responsible for raising the money that was then lent to the Government at a generous (though not exorbitant) 8%. But the Government had other means of raising money. There were taxes, levied mainly on landowners. There was also the lottery - which involved people lending money to the government, in exchange for fixed term annuities, but with the

---

[254] The had three children, all baptised at St Mildred's Bread Street. Robert was baptised on 17 December 1702; Catherine on 9 August 1704; Margaretta on 11 April 1713. St Mildred's had been rebuilt after the Great Fire but was destroyed again in 1941 and was not rebuilt. It was on the east side of Bread Street, on a site now occupied by 30 Cannon Street.

added attraction of prizes for the lucky few. The money was flowing in, but as year succeeded year the Government went further into debt. When the Queen dismissed the Whig Government in August 1710 and Harley took over as Chancellor of the Exchequer more than £8 million was owed[255]. The borrowing had to go on, but the Bank of England, with its continuing Whig allegiance, was not the best organisation for Harley to approach. There was an alternative. The Sword Blade Bank had begun some twenty years earlier as a business that made French sword blades. Rather soon, under the influence of John Blunt, its company secretary[256], it left this manufacturing past behind it and started lending money. Harley was interested and used the Company to manage a couple of lotteries in the spring of 1711 - which raised the huge sum of £3.5 million for the Government.

Very soon after that, John Blunt decided to form a trading company. It was to be no ordinary trading company. Notionally it was formed to trade in the South Seas - hence its name - but the heart of the matter was that the Government's creditors were to be invited to exchange the money owed them for shares in the company. The National Debt was in other words to be taken over by the South Sea Company and the Government would be free. By 1719 two-thirds of the Government's creditors had taken up the offer and the Company's capital had risen to £12 million.

It was a remarkable success story, and Robert Knight was in there from the beginning. In September 1711 he had been appointed Cashier - a sort of Chief Executive of the Company. What is not clear is whether he had already been with Blunt at the Sword Blade. Erith and Carswell seem to assume that he was not, but Balen suggests that he was. Certainly Knight was first and last a banker.

---

[255] Malcolm Balen, *A Very English Deceit* (2002), p. 18
[256] John Blunt (1665-1733) was of a humble family, but he made good in the City at an early age. He was one of the main architects of the Bubble. Arrested and questioned, he had most of his property confiscated and retired to Bath. One of his descendants was Anthony Blunt, the spy.

His thinking was that of a Sword Blade man and, given the dominance of the Sword Blade team at the South Sea Company, it seems likely that he had already proved his metal there.

Young Robert Knight was now firmly established as a major City financier. He had successfully made the transition from Tory to Whig, while retaining the friendship of Henry St John, Viscount Bolingbroke whose agent in England he became. Bolingbroke had fled to France in March 1715, to become Secretary of State to the Old Pretender (and an Earl of the Pretender's creation). The alliance lasted less than a year. The Pretender had no intention of turning Anglican and, without that, his return was an impossibility. Bolingbroke became an opposition leader abroad, eager to make his peace and to return. His pardon was achieved early in 1723, though he didn't settle in England until April 1725.

The Bubble

I do not pretend to understand the complex financial realities of those days. Broadly speaking, it was a time of huge expansion in the European economy and there was a demand for money that could not be met in the ordinary way. Credit – or paper money – had to be increased and this in its turn depended on confidence. The idea was to increase credit in order to enable and encourage growth. John Law, the great financial genius of the time, was active in Paris and Robert Knight with John Blunt, his main patron on the South Seas Board, was active along the same lines in London. 1719 was an extraordinary year and 1720 still more extraordinary. In March 1720 Parliament more or less voted the Bank of England out of public finance, leaving the South Sea Company in control. In Plumb's words, "A huge financial monopoly had been created, in close association with the state, and trading on its credit".   At first things went well. Credit seemed to be infinitely extendable. As each new issue was made, people subscribed – persuaded not to take their profits, because yet new heights of credit seemed about to be scaled. In June 1720 Blunt was made a baronet "for his extraordinary services in raising public credit to a height not known before". On the other hand, in the summer of 1720 substantial profits were taken. The best known examples are of Thomas Guy and Sarah, Duchess of Marlborough. Guy sold out in a rising market through April to June and built his hospital with the proceeds. Duchess Sarah sold out in June. However, the politicians, the directors and the employees of the Company were doing the same. For men without a stake in the country, the attraction of a landed estate was too great to resist. Robert Surman, Robert Knight's nephew and the Deputy Cashier, reportedly spent £180,000 on buying land during that summer. Robert Knight himself bought a small estate called Luxborough in Chigwell, where he pulled down the old house and built himself something new and modern[257]. John Gay, the writer, was dreaming of a buying an estate in Somerset with his profits, but was too late.

The Bubble began to burst in August and by mid-September there was a general crisis. In November the King returned from Hanover and Parliament was recalled. Sunderland, Stanhope and Walpole struggled to save the Ministry and indeed the Hanoverian dynasty itself. There was a general clamour for a thorough investigation that those in power knew would only compromise the entire political establishment. The Commons wanted revenge for all the lost fortunes and a committee none too friendly to the Ministry was set up early in January 1721 to investigate the affairs of the South Sea Company. Robert Knight was the first person to be examined but, after two days of cross-examination, he fled abroad. All hell broke lose in the Commons and demonstrations took place in London. Lord Stanhope, the effective head of the ministry, dropped dead; James Craggs, the Postmaster General, killed himself; Aislabie, the Chancellor, resigned shortly before being sent to the Tower.

---

[257] This wasn't all that he bought. In 1717, he bought the manor of Shepton Malet in Somerset from Lord Lisburne. Lisburne had it with his wife, Lady Malet Wilmot (d 1709), who in 1682 had inherited it on the death of her mother, Lady Rochester, the Malet heiress. Robert Knight junr. bought it on the sale of his father's property, but subsequently sold it. Knight also had bought from Lord Lisburne estates in Montgomeryshire that remained in the family until the early nineteenth century.

However, the very excess of the outcry frightened people, and gradually the government, now headed by Sunderland, began to reassert its authority. There was going to be no investigation. The Commons concentrated on wrecking revenge on the Company, its directors and officers. Walpole defended those who had stood by the government but Sir John Blunt and Robert Knight couldn't be saved. Property in Knight's name amounting to £300,000 was confiscated. It doesn't sound much, but it would have made him a billionaire today.

The French Exile
When the Elections finally came in April 1722 the government survived. However, Sunderland died as the votes were coming in and Walpole then took over as first minister. He was not popular. The King didn't like him. People in general believed that he had organised a cover-up for the guilty men of 1720. And yet he was able and he survived for over twenty years. Through all that time Robert Knight remained in exile. His exile became the official reason why a thorough investigation could not be mounted. Had he been allowed to return, there would have been no excuse for continuing the cover-up. It was therefore in no one's interests to let him back. When he did return, in December 1742, it was a sign to the opposition that Walpole had gone – but it was an empty sign. Pulteney and Carteret continued Walpole's system and had no intention of going further in the pursuit of "corruption".

Robert Knight's exile was a prosperous one - notoriously so. He settled in the Faubourg St Honoré, where he was known for his rather over lavish entertainments,. He also had a country estate at La Planchette in Bercy, near the Bois de Vincennes. To begin with, he had his daughters to keep house for him. Catherine married in May 1727[258], but Robert junior married two months later and his

---

[258] On 1 May 1727, Catherine married John Page (1696-1779) and died 15 Oct 1736 leaving an only daughter who died unmarried. Page was an employee of the South Sea Company who had contested Grimsby unsuccessfully in the Company interest in 1722. In 1726, he bought the manor of Donnington, Sussex -

wife then did the honours. Robert's two children were born in Paris in 1728 and 1729. In 1732, old Robert's younger daughter married[259] and Robert himself had married again. His wife was Anne Robinson[260], the elder sister of Sir Thomas Robinson of Rokeby. Their son William was born in 1732.

France in the 1720's and 1730's was an exciting place to be. The gloomy last years of Louis XIV had given way to an explosion of self-indulgence under the regency of the Duc d'Orléans. His rule is chiefly memorable for John Law's adventures in 1716-20, but it was also notable for the creation of the Triple Alliance. In 1716 the Regent (and his able minister, abbé Dubois) threw over the Old Pretender and enlisted English and Dutch support against the Spanish. This arrangement lasted until his death in December 1723. The regency then fell to the Duc de Bourbon, supported by his mistress, Mme de Prie. That lasted until June 1726 when Louis XV took over the reins of power, in partnership with his old tutor, the seventy-three year old abbé Fleury. For seventeen years, until Fleury's death in 1743 at the age of ninety, France enjoyed peace and stability. There was plenty of opportunity in Fleury's France for financiers like Robert Knight to enjoy life. It was a time of growing

---

his local village - and was returned for Grimsby in 1727. In 1734 he resigned Grimsby to his brother-in-law, Robert Knight, and contested Chichester in the Duke of Richmond's interest - coming bottom of the poll. However, in 1741 he stood there again, this time as an independent Whig, against the Duke's candidate, and won. He sat as M. P. for Chichester until his death. His heiress was his daughter by his second wife, who married George White Thomas. White Thomas won his father-in-law's old seat from the Duke of Richmond in 1784 and held it for thirty years.

[259] On 29 February 1732, Margaretta married Hon Morgan Vane, younger son of Lord Barnard. Vane's elder brother was married to a daughter of the Duke of Southampton & Cleveland (a natural son of Charles II) and was created Earl of Darlington. Margaretta died on 6 May 1739 leaving a son and daughter. Her descendants eventually succeeded to the Barnard title and to the estates of the Vane family.

[260] After the Cashier's death, Anne married again - to James Cresset - but seems not to have had any more children. She did not come back to England in 1742. Her son died unmarried in Rheims in 1767

prosperity, thanks particularly to the West Indian trade, but people like Robert Knight were not concerned with that. Their business was making money with money, and there was a lot of opportunity for doing that in France.

Return from Exile

On 17 August 1742 a pardon under the Great Seal was granted to the Cashier, on payment of £10,000. He settled in Great Russell Street, and negotiated a settlement with his South Sea creditors. This was finally achieved shortly before his death, with a further payment of £10,000. He also contracted to buy back Luxborough House from the trustees of Sir Joseph Eyles for £20,000, and was living there at the time of his death on 8 November 1744. His hatchment is still to be seen in the parish church at Chigwell, but it is probable that he was buried in the family vault at St Mildred's, Bread Street. Luxborough was sold, once his grandson (who had the reversionary interest) came of age. A monument was erected by his son in Wootton Wawen church[261].

CHAPTER NINETEEN

ROBERT KNIGHT (1702-1772)
LORD LUXBOROUGH & EARL OF CATHERLOUGH

We first hear of this Robert Knight in a letter from Lord Bolingbroke to his half-sister, Henrietta St John. Henrietta was devoted to her half-brother and seems to have kept every letter he wrote to her over a period of thirty years. These letters remained at Barrells and were then at Chadshunt. They might easily have then disappeared with everything else had not one of my great-grandfather's younger sisters gathered them up. She left them to a son who emigrated to Canada and he sent them to a cousin, Octavia Higgon, who gave

---

[261] R Erith's *Robert Knight, Builder of Luxborough* was published in 1987 by the Woodford Historical Society. It is in parts a rather fanciful piece of writing, and contains inaccuracies, but he unearthed some fascinating stuff.

them to the British Museum in 1943. They are a vital resource for the life of Lord Bolingbroke.

Early Life

He was admitted to the Inner Temple in August 1719, in the days when the Inns of Court were regarded as finishing schools for young gentlemen. There is no suggestion that he was thinking of a legal career. Robert Knight and Lord Bolingbroke's half-brother, Jack St John, were contemporaries and friends. In July 1720, when the Bubble was at its height and the Cashier at his most influential, they were in Paris. They visited Lord Bolingbroke and his wife and Lord Bolingbroke records that "he is a very pretty youth". It is clear that Henrietta was keen on him, though by November – when the Knight fortune was no longer as established – Bolingbroke is warning his sister against any precipitate action. In February 1721 young Robert - still only eighteen years old - was with his father on the flight to Brabant. We then hear nothing more of him until June 1727 when he and Henrietta were married. He was twenty-four, and had a generous settlement from his father[262]. She was twenty-eight and of an age when marriage to an old friend from home – albeit one from the merchant class - was more advisable than risking no marriage at all.

Marriage to Henrietta

The first months of their married life seem to have been spent with Robert's father in Paris. Their son was born here and named Henry for his uncle. They returned to England in August 1728 and took a house in the newly built and fashionable Grosvenor Street, although they were also using Ruckholts in Essex – a house bought by his father in 1720 in the name of his sister-in-law Elizabeth Collier and her husband. In 1730 Robert bought the family home at Barrells from his impecunious cousin, Raleigh Knight, but seems to have made no effort to improve it or to live there. They were often at

---

[262] Young Robert had £34,000 settled on him by his father, and Henrietta had a dowry of £6000. The resulting income of £1,000 - £1,500 a year would have left them comfortably off.

Dawley, where Lord and Lady Bolingbroke had settled on their return to England in 1725 and so were close to that extraordinary centre of political and literary life that included Pope, Gay and all those who wished ill to Sir Robert Walpole and his ministry. They continued to go backwards and forwards to Paris, where Henrietta's behaviour in her father-in-law's house caused some comment. In 1735, when Lord and Lady Bolingbroke left England, Lord Bolingbroke hoped that Robert would take Dawley. He and Henrietta seemed to have been attracted by the idea, but it would have needed some more financial help from Mr Knight in Paris and this was not forthcoming. Mr Knight had by now remarried and had a son. He had other priorities for his capital.

Then, in the early spring of 1736, there was a major crisis in Robert and Henrietta's marriage. They seem to have been staying with the Earl and Countess of Hertford at their home in Marlborough, Wiltshire – and were there at the time of Lady Hertford's birthday on 10 May. It is said that Robert discovered there compromising letters to or from Lord Beauchamp's young tutor, Rev. John Dalton. Robert left their home for his father-in-law's house in Albermarle Street, taking their daughter with him. Little Henry was away at school. Henrietta was given the choice of house imprisonment in London or a retreat in the country. She chose the country – Barrells - whereupon Grosvenor Street was sold. By June, the news was public property. and it is interesting that both Lord Bolingbroke and Jack St John (though kind to Henrietta) seem to have sympathised with Robert. There seems to have been too much gossip for too long. Robert was staying with the Bolingbrokes in Paris in December 1736 and he continued for a while to be identified with him politically. However, in August 1738, Bolingbroke was writing to Henrietta, "Your husband is got into new measures of conduct, and under a new influence, since I left England.."

Politics
In an analysis of members taken in February 1742, just before Walpole's fall, Robert Knight is listed as a supporter of the ministry.

He had entered parliament in 1734 as member for Great Grimsby (following his uncle and brother-in-law, who had held the seat since 1722)[263]. He was taking Bolingbroke's advice on parliamentary issues in 1736 and was clearly personally close to him, but there is no reason to believe that he shared Bolingbroke's vision or his politics. Probably he was a typical merchant, keen to support the present administration as long as it seemed able to govern effectively. He would have had no difficulty in transferring his allegiance in the reshuffle that followed Walpole's fall, particularly in the light of that administration's recall of his father from exile. But neither would he have been unhappy with the establishment of the Broad-Bottom ministry which Bolingbroke helped to engineer in November 1744 and which brought together Walpole's supporters with the remains of Bolingbroke's Patriots. He seems to have managed to remain friendly with both sides – Lord Chesterfield, a Bolingbroke protégé, was one of his long-term political allies.

Robert Knight received an Irish peerage in July 1746, taking the name of his father's house. It no doubt would have been his father's title had things gone differently in 1720. Then, in the 1747 General Election, he failed to hold on to Great Grimsby and was returned for the Walpole pocket borough of Castle Rising. It seemed odd to some people that the son of someone whom it was believed Sir Robert Walpole had driven into exile, and the brother-in-law of Lord Bolingbroke, should sit for a Walpole family borough.

---

[263] In its day, Grimsby had been a great port but it was stagnating by the end of the 17th century with a population of something under five hundred people. However, it retained the right to return two members to parliament. During the 18th century it was this that provided the electors (perhaps a quarter of the population) with their main means of livelihood. In 1695 Arthur Moore (1666-1730) was the first of the London merchants to get himself returned. He was a Director of the South Sea Company - though fell out with his colleagues in 1713. The South Sea Company people however kept control of the seat, which was managed for them by various members of the Clayton family. Christopher Clayton (1687-1737) was confidential clerk to Knight the Cashier at the time of the Bubble. Clayton's great nephew and heir, George Tennyson, was the grandfather of Lord Tennyson, the poet. See Edward Gillett *A History of Grimsby* (1970) and Sir Charles Tennyson's *The Tennysons*.

Horace Walpole said it was because his brother shared the same mistress[264]. But in the political situation of the mid 1740's it wasn't that odd. Knight was now a solid supporter of the government and a useful person to have onside in parliament. He served throughout the parliament of 1747-54, but then failed again in Grimsby and didn't then get a pocket borough in compensation. That might have meant the end of his influence, but it is interesting that in March 1758 he applied to the duke of Newcastle for a commission in the army for a cousin. This was granted the following year and Knight was full of gratitude. When he finally regained Grimsby in 1762, it was as a supporter of Lord Bute's ministry. Bute had come to power in October 1761 on Pitt's dismissal with the express intention of bringing the war to an end. It was a deeply unpopular policy, but he persevered and in March 1763 the Treaty of Paris was ratified. Thereupon Bute resigned and, since Henry Fox declined to take over, George Grenville became the new leader of the administration. At the end of April, Knight was raised a couple of ranks in the Irish peerage as Earl of Catherlough and Viscount Barrells. Not surprisingly he was thereafter known as a supporter of George Grenville until the end of that administration in 1765 and the accession of the Marquess of Rockingham. He was then in opposition, and lost the Grimsby seat in 1768. When he returned to parliament in 1770, it was for a government seat. He was then gratified to receive a K.B. from Lord North's administration.

---

[264] On 26 June 1747 Horace Walpole wrote to Sir Horace Mann, "My brother chooses Lord Luxborough for Castle Rising. Would you know the connection? This Lord keeps Miss Horton, the player; we keep Miss Norsa the player; Rich the Harlequin is the intimate of all, and to cement the harlequinity, somebody's brother (excuse me if I am not perfect in such genealogy) is to marry the Jewess' sister. This *coup de théatre* procured Knight his Irish coronet, and has now stuffed him into Castle Rising". Christiana Horton was a celebrated actress at Covent Garden, but now around fifty years old and close to retirement. Hannah Norsa was a Jewess actress who was Lord Orford's mistress from 1736 and lived at Houghton Hall until Orford's death in 1751. John Rich (1692-1761) was the proprietor of the Covent Garden theatre, producer of Gay's Beggar's Opera, and was well-known for playing a harlequin in pantomime. His wife, Priscilla, was the brother of Edward Wilford, who married Rachel Norsa – Hannah's younger sister and also an actress.

Family Matters

Though there are many portraits of Robert Knight[265] and several letters, it's not easy to grasp the person. He was certainly an affectionate father, devoted to his daughter. He also cared about behaving properly and was not someone who pursued the smart life. After his separation he moved to quieter quarters in Golden Square[266], where he lived until his death. Possibly he was a bit out of his depth. His father's financial skills had opened doors into the great world and he was related by blood or friendship to all the great City families who were rising to power through the eighteenth century. Yet he seems often to have been a figure almost of fun, old-fashioned and easy to take for a ride. He seems to me an attractive person, who didn't have an easy life.

Old Lord St John died unlamented in 1742. In July 1744 Lord Bolingbroke returned from France and settled at Old Battersea House. Jack – as the presumptive heir - seems to have settled at Lydiard. He had married a rich wife and was able to beautify it. The present house is a testimony to his good taste - and hers. Lady St John died in 1747 and Jack married again in June 1748. Five months later he died in Naples, aged only forty-six. He left three little boys - Frederick, aged fourteen, Henry, aged ten, and John, aged only two. Robert seems to have taken an interest in them, although Frederick went to live with his uncle at Old Battersea House[267]. Sadly

---

[265] The one that belonged to my father, then said to be by Thomas Hudson, was sold by Edward at Christie's in the spring of 1973. It was resold at Christie's in December 2009 for £4,000. It was then said to be by George Knapton – a portrait painter fashionable in the 1740s and 1750s.

[266] He settled at 22 Golden Square in 1739 and stayed there until his death. No 21 had belonged to Lord Bolingbroke in 1702-14 and had then gone to Lady Masham in 1714-15. The houses had been developed for the gentry in the reign of Charles II but had declined in fashion once Mayfair was built. In 1839 its reputation was such that Dickens made it the dismal home of Ralph Nickleby.

[267] The arrangement was not a success. Lord Bolingbroke remarked of Frederick that he "has not only the vices of a young fellow, that may be overcome or moderated, and in the meantime laughed at, he has all those of a good for nothing fellow of forty confirmed in moroseness, and insensibility to friendship,

1f.

Frederick grew up to squander the inheritance he had from his father and uncle. As 2nd Viscount Bolingbroke and 3rd Viscount St John, he regularly spent beyond his means and in 1763 had to sell Battersea Manor. Two years later his wife left him[268] and a few years after that he was certified insane. His son, George, 3rd Viscount Bolingbroke, was an even bigger disaster. Henry St John (the 2nd Viscount's younger brother) was steadier. Known as "The Baptist" in London circles, he was a soldier, and managed to do what younger sons had to do - marry someone with money. He died in 1818, at the age of 80, leaving no children.

Much of the surviving correspondence deals with arguments between Robert and Henrietta about a settlement. The St John family was well-off and Henrietta benefited from the death of her brother Holles in 1738 and of her father. There were arguments about the allowance that Robert Knight was now reluctant to pay, and further arguments about Henrietta's spending. Some economies had to be introduced in 1751. Their son Henry seems to have been a quiet young man. He was married young to the only child and heiress of one of Robert Knight's business partners and they lived in a grand house in Upper Brook Street [269], with a drawing room overlooking Park Lane. They had no children and Mrs Henry Knight married Lord Deloraine after his death[270].

---

to gratitude, and to ever notion of honour". By the end of 1749 young Lord St John was in Caen with a tutor. Two years later Bolingbroke wrote to his sister, "Your nephew has set out at Caen as ill as he finished here. It was so bad that his Governor gave him but one day to resolve, and determined to return next day to England if he had not sufficient assurance of reformation. Since that he has behaved a little better and M. Freigneau takes some hope, which I cannot do so soon".

[268] She was Lady Diana Spencer (1735-1808), eldest daughter of the 3rd Duke of Marlborough. She married her lover, Topham Beauclerk, in 1768 and had three further children. See Carola Hicks *Improper Pursuits: The Scandalous Life of Lady Diana Beauclerk,* 2001.

[269] The house (after several rebuildings) eventually became the London home of Sir Ernest Cassel, and was then inherited by Lady Mountbatten.

[270] The marriage took place at St Anne's Soho on 16 November 1763. Henry Scott, 4th Earl of Deloraine did not have a good character and Lord Catherlough

It was their daughter Henrietta who made most of the running. She was married at the age of eighteen to Charles Wymondesold, the son of another of Robert Knight's business partners. The marriage fell apart and in February 1752 they agreed to lead separate lives, though apparently they didn't live apart because young Charles didn't want to tell his father. Then in January 1753 Charles refused her entry to his house and a writ was served on Josiah Child at his house in Conduit Street for criminal conversation. Henrietta had been causing quite a bit of gossip for some while, as Lady Hertford[271] told Lady Luxborough by letter a few weeks later. Henrietta and Josiah Child then went abroad, where Henrietta gave birth to a son in January 1754[272], some three months before the divorce came through and they were able to marry. A daughter was born the following year, but she died two years later. In March 1756, with the outbreak of war, the Childs had to leave France for Germany. Little Joe was sent back to England, to be brought up by his uncle, Lord Tylney, at Wanstead Park. Had he been legitimate, the little Josiah would have been next heir to the earldom and to the Child millions. As it was, he was dependent on Lord Tylney's goodwill for his future and his parents were very conscious of the hostility of Sir Robert Long, whose son was set to inherit if Josiah senior died without issue. Then in May 1759 Josiah senior developed a cough that proved consumptive. In January 1760 he died at Lyons, leaving

---

warned his daughter-in-law against the marriage. She resented his interference, though Lord C replied "I shall always have the inward satisfaction of knowing I acted a kind and friendly part by Mrs Knight". They made up later, but Lady Deloraine died in a French convent in February 1782 after a short and disastrous second marriage.

[271] Lady Hertford, later Duchess of Somerset, was a close friend of Lady Luxborough's, and always took her part against her husband. Several letters from her survive in the British Museum collection.

[272] Little Joe was born 27 January 1754 and baptised at the Church of St Sulpice in Paris on 27 February, with Henry Knight and Mary Child (Josiah's sister) as absentee godparents. Josiah & Henrietta were married at Lord Albemarle's Chapel in Paris on 3 May 1754.

Henrietta distraught. She begged to be allowed to come back to her father.

His consent seems to have cost him his marriage[273]. His second wife had a daughter by her first husband and it would not have been suitable for that daughter to be in the same house as Mrs Child. So, when Henrietta arrived in Golden Square in April 1760, Lady Catherlough moved out[274]. The parting seems to have been amicable. However, poor Henrietta was not able to live without admirers and within two years was pregnant by a French officer on half pay. In November 1762, when six months gone, she left for France – telling her unsuspecting father that she wanted to travel. In March 1763 she died at Avignon, a few days after giving birth to another son. The father, Count Duroure, brought the baby to London, with its mother in her coffin, and was apparently received

---

[273] On 18 June 1756, three months after the death of his first wife, Lord Luxborough had married Lady Lequesne of Bruton Street. She had been a Knight and was thought to be a cousin. She had married Sir John Lequesne in April, 1738 and there is a kettle & stand made by Paul de Lamerie for their wedding that is currently in the V & A. He was a Director of the Bank of England and an Alderman of the City of London. On 4 September 1742 her sister, Miss Knight "of Southampton", was married at Woodford, Essex to Edward Bacon of Earlham, for many years MP for Lynn. Woodford was the parish next to Chigwell, where Luxborough Hall was – so that she was far more likely to have been of "West Ham".

[274] She retired to Twickenham. "On the opposite side of King Street in Twickenham stood an old
house, in which resided " the Right Hon. the Countess Catherlough, widow of Robert Earl of Catherlough, in Ireland (son of Robert Knight, Esq., cashier of the South Sea Company in the year 1720), previously
relict of Sir John Lequesne, Knt, and alderman of the city of London ; " and before him William Rider, Esq. This lady, says Miss Hawkins, was " related to that Lady Luxborough whose name is often associated with that of Shenstone, and was the correspondent of the worthily celebrated Countess of Hertford." She was a most intimate friend of Mr. Sydenham, who is mentioned elsewhere. Mrs. Cole, and then Mrs. Gell, succeeded Lady Catherlough, and next, the house became the residence of Mr. Beauchamp, who, early in the century, and for years afterwards, was the principal medical man of the village. His daughter, the last surviving member of his family, lived here till her death, after which the house was taken down". Richard Stutely Cobbett, *Memorials of Twickenham*.

kindly by Lord Catherlough. In so doing he was the cause of some waggish tales going the rounds in London, about original ruses whereby half-pay officers could guarantee an income for themselves[275].

There are letters from 1765 and 1769 that show Lord Catherlough did his best to establish the identity of the child that had been brought to him. How he intended to leave his property is not clear. He may have been attempting to bring in a bill to legitimise Josiah at the time of Henrietta's death. Whether it went through I do not know, but Josiah predeceased Lord Tylney and so the question became academic. (Sir Robert's son succeeded after all – and much good it did his family. His daughter and heiress became one of the most spectacular bankrupts of the early nineteenth century). Lord Catherlough could never have been quite sure about young Louis' identity (he forbade him in his will to make any claim on his mother's estate). Then, early in 1766, he fell in love with a young farmer's daughter and spent his last years in a romantic idyll[276].

---

[275] Miss Mary Townshend to George Selwyn, 23 June 1763. "The most remarkable event I have heard of since your departure is the arrival of a French officer with a leaden coffin and a young child, who went directly to Lord Luxborough's house, and told him that the coffin contained his child, who had married him since she left England, and had died in childbed of the child he had brought with him. Lord Luxborough, though he had never heard of the marriage, without further enquiry has taken officer, leaden coffin, and child into his house and is very fond of them all. I doubt that none of our poor, half-pay captains will find such an ingenious way of providing for themselves". For his daughter's sake, Lord Catherlough was prepared to collude in the fiction that Duroure had married his daughter in May 1762, but - as the price of this - he was careful to get him to sign an undertaking renouncing all interest in Henrietta's estate

[276] For an account of this liaison, see W Cooper op cit & Town & Country Magazine, March 1771. Apart from the caricature in the magazine, there are no extant likenesses of Jane. In his will, her son directed that the picture of "my mother" be taken to Chadshunt for his daughter Georgiana. Its present whereabouts are not known. In her book, "The Merry Wives of Battersea", Mrs Stirling says that it was in the USA. She would have had her information from Aunt Ethel, so it seems that my father sold it (possibly privately) in the 1920's. In Octavia Higgon's "A Forgotten Peer" (reproduced in Arthur Carden's "The Knights of Barrells") there is an illustration of a miniature that belonged to aunt Ethel and

Indeed he seems to have been genuinely happy, and at his death had four little children with another on the way.

CHAPTER TWENTY

LOUIS HENRY SCIPION, COUNT DUROURE (1763-1822)

Background, Birth & Upbringing

His background was lively. His mother had been married young and had divorced in 1754, shortly after she had given birth to a son by Hon. Josiah Child, the man she subsequently married[277]. She and Mr Child had to live abroad because of money problems. Then, in January 1760, he died of tuberculosis. His widow returned to England, to live with her father at his house in Golden Square[278]. In October 1761 she drew up a will in which she left all her property to her son Josiah and his heirs. Should young Josiah die without issue, her property was to go to her father, then to her brother, then to

---

is said to be of Jane Davies. The hair and dress style however are those of the early 1790's and suggest that it is in fact a picture of her elder daughter. She has the look of Lord Catherlough, with the long straight nose of the Knights, and looks actually very similar to my daughter Alice Jane!

[277] He was the younger brother (and presumptive heir) of John Tylney Child, 2nd Earl Tylney of Wanstead Park in Essex. Henrietta had been discussing a separation from her first husband in February 1752, but things dragged on until he shut her out of their house in January 1753. Henrietta and Mr Child then went abroad, and were married in Paris in May 1754. Their son, another Josiah Child, was born the previous January.

[278] The second Lady Luxborough had a young daughter by her first husband. Mrs Child's reputation was such that they couldn't live in the same house. Accordingly she moved out and Lord Luxborough's second marriage came to an end.

her "right heirs". By November 1762, she had left for France[279]. She hadn't told her father that she was six months pregnant. He only discovered this the following May when a Count Duroure arrived in London, with Henrietta's coffin and a child. He claimed that the child was his son, Louis Henry Scipio, who had been born to Mrs Child in Marseilles that February. Lord Catherlough (as he had become a few weeks earlier) received Count Duroure and the child into his house.

Though a Frenchman, with strong links to his family base in Languedoc, Duroure was serving in the British army – and came from a Huguenot family who had also served in the British army. He was the younger son of Col. Ange-Urbain de Grimoard de Beauvoir, Comte du Roure, who had been killed in 1745 (aged 63) at the Battle of Fontenoy during the War of the Austrian Succession[280].

In November 1763 Lord Catherlough's settled his daughter's property on the infant Louis but this settlement was revoked and declared null and void[281]. Lord Catherlough may have intended to

---

[279] From a letter in the Brit Mus. However, in the case of Duroure v Jones it is said that Mrs Child left the country in October 1761, and that she was married in Brussels the following May. The date of the letter would need to be double-checked. One could also check the signature of a further letter written to her father in January 1763, to see if she was acknowledging herself as Countess Duroure. I think it unlikely.

[280] The French wikipedia says that "Les ancêtres de son grand-père, Scipion du Roure, qui appartenait à la branche calviniste de cette famille, s'exilèrent après le pillage du château familial par les troupes du duc de Nemours". This was during the Wars of Religion during the 16th century when the dukes of Nemours were close to the Guise faction.
The great-grandson of Col. Du Roure' elder brother, the Marquis du Roure, was Marie Francois Scipion, Marquis du Roure, who married a daughter of the Duc de Noailles. They both died young, before the Revolution, when the family of the Marquise du Roure was nearly wiped out.

[281] Count Duroure the elder had renounced his rights in the estate of his putative wife (a legal opinion on this renunciation was obtained in September 1770 - see papers in the Brit. Mus.). Lord Catherlough acted presumably because he felt that young Josiah's uncle, Lord Tylney, would provide for him and he was working on the assumption that Louis was Henrietta's legitimate child and so took

adopt him as his second heir, after his other grandson. There are certainly copies of letters that were sent to France, and replies, that tried to get clear proof as to the child's identity. However, with the birth of Lord Catherlough's children by Jane Davies, these grandsons moved down the order of inheritance. Lord Catherlough's own illegitimate children took precedence of his daughter's legitimate or illegitimate children. In his will, he left the young Duroure £3000 at the age of twenty one, to be used to buy him an annuity, on condition that he didn't contest his mother's will. Lord Catherlough presumably didn't want lawyers - or the public - probing into the difficult circumstances of his daughter's life.

Young Louis was only nine when his grandfather died. His father seems to have been on terms with the old man, and was left £20 for a mourning ring in the will. The great challenge was when his half-brother, Josiah Child, died in Florence two years later. Despite his illegitimacy, young Josiah had been named in his mother's will and so had inherited her considerable property. Mrs Child's will had been drawn up before young Duroure came on the scene and so, unless he was acknowledged to be her legitimate son, he would not inherit. The next "right heir", Lord Bolingbroke, Mrs Child's cousin, clearly thought Duroure was not legitimate. He took possession of and sold the Park Lane house that had been Henry Knight's home. Duroure's guardians entered a protest, but they don't seem to have followed it up[282].

It is not at all clear where Louis was brought up[283]. He was bi-lingual, which suggests regular contact with this father. His

---

precedence of young Josiah. However, Henrietta's intentions had been clear - Josiah was her heir, illegitimate or not.

[282] Frederick St John, 2nd Viscount Bolingbroke (1732-1787), Lady Luxborough's nephew and Mrs Child's first cousin. He was always short of money and sold off a lot of family property from 1763 onwards. Taking his late cousin's property as his own would have been in character. He was separated from his wife from 1765 and was ill and finally out of his mind from 1779. This – and the fact that the 3rd Viscount's affairs were profoundly confused at this time – no doubt helped Duroure's case. He would not have faced a very active opponent.

266

guardians seem to have been Lord Catherlough's executors – but they don't seem to have pressed his interests very hard while Lord Bolingbroke was around. Fortunately for Duroure, Lord Bolingbroke's health was giving way and his desperate search for money was coming to an end. It was surely not a coincidence that in December 1778, some five years after young Josiah's death[284], letters of administration in respect of Henrietta's will were granted at Doctors Commons to the executors, Rev Daniel Collins and Thomas Lloyd[285]. According to Henrietta's will, with the death of young Josiah, her father and brother - the estate would now go to her "right heirs". Her right heir was judged to be – not Lord Bolingbroke – but young Duroure, now fifteen years old, 'the natural and lawful Son and only Child of the said deceased'. Messrs Collins and Lloyd were said to be his legal guardians. Count Duroure senior is not mentioned. It would be interesting to know how much St John property they were able to claim for young Duroure.

The Newgate Years, 1784-1789

In about 1780 Duroure's guardians bought him a commission in the army, and by 1784 he was a Lieutenant in the fashionable Royal

---

[283] The French Wikipedia says that he passed some of his youth in Martinique, where he had inherited some plantations and that he returned to France in October 1779 on the same ship as Rose de la Pagerie (1763-1814) - later Josephine de Beauharnais, wife of the Emperor Napoleon. She was imprisoned from 21 April until 28 July 1794, suspected of being too close to the counter-revolutionary financial circles. Duroure was friendly with Josephine, so there may be some truth in this.

[284] According to Horace Walpole (*Correspondence 24:23)*, Joe died from consumption in Florence in July 1774, a few months before coming of age. He had clearly inherited the weakness in his father's constitution.

[285] Thomas Lloyd of 15 Great James Street, Bedford Row seems to have been a lawyer. In the Durham University Library there is a collection of letters from his nephew, Robert Wharton. In 1775 Wharton was travelling on the continent and in October was in Avignon where he did some business with Count Duroure senr. on his uncle's behalf. Rev Daniel Collins (ca. 1718-1802) was from 1768 until his death Vicar of Claverdon with Norton Lindsey & Bearley, villages just outside Henley in Arden and a short distance from Barrells.

Horse Guards Blue . However, the following report appeared in the *Annual Register* for 1784:

"The following extraordinary affair came before the Bow-Street magistrates : Count Duroure, who has made so much notice about town, some little time since got acquainted with a gentleman of the law, who lent him his assistance to extricate him from difficulties he was involved in : having access to his friend's table, who was married to a young lady of some accomplishments, the Count, by his attentions, insinuated himself so far into her affections, as to prevail upon her to elope with him to France. He sent off his baggage to Dover, whither he was to follow in a day or two. The husband, by a laconic letter from the lady, received the first intimation of her infidelity. After a very minute enquiry, he discovered, that the lady and her paramour were at a bagnio in Leicester-fields[286], whither he went on Sunday night, accompanied with a friend, and being guided to the room, desired admittance, which was refused; upon this he forced open the door, and the moment he entered the Count fired upon him; the ball went through his hat without doing him any mischief. The Count's conduct appeared in so extraordinary a light to the magistrates, that for the purpose of more security he was committed to Newgate".[287]

A fuller account appears in *The Political Magazine* and *The Hibernian Magazine* for 1784. Apparently the aggrieved husband, who had lent Duroure the money, was a Mr Huxley Sandon[288]. His wife was staying with her parents and apparently left them to get in a chaise with Duroure. Sandon pursued them to Dover, but they escaped him there and got to Folkestone on foot in the middle of the night (with Mrs Sandon dressed as a boy). Thence they got to

---

[286] A place where rooms were for hire – no questions asked. Sometimes just a name for a brothel.

[287] Annual Register 1784, pp. 90, 96, 97, 103.

[288] A Captain Huxley Sandon was one of Mrs Clarke's 'agents' in the business of selling commissions – presumably a relation. He was in the marines, and is said to have died in about 1810.

Rye, where a boatman refused to take them to France (because Duroure wouldn't have his luggage searched). They thereupon returned to London where Mr Sandon caught up with them at the Royal Hotel in Long Acre. The maid said that Mrs Sandon, still dressed as boy, was brandishing the pistols and threatening to shoot herself rather than go with her husband. A pistol then went off.

Shooting at a person was a capital offence in those days, but Duroure had the brilliant young lawyer, Thomas Erskine, as his counsel and he got off on a technicality[289]. Unfortunately the next day he was arrested for the debt and this time was not so lucky. He was sent to Newgate. *The Political Magazine* remarked that Duroure "has very much the countenance of a foreigner, with prominent lips and a flat nose"[290].

Duroure's trustees were continuing to claim parts of Henrietta's estate for the young man. They obtained a further grant on 28 June 1786 and, after that grant had been revoked, another one in August 1789[291]. This may mean that a settlement was reached that

---

[289] Erskine was later to shock the establishment by his defence of several radicals prosecuted during the French Revolution. He was Lord Chancellor in the Ministry of the Talents.

[290] The French wikipedia says that Duroure had "une jeunesse dorée qu'il passa en partie dans les colonies où il avait hérité de plantations. Il revint, dit-on, de la Martinique en France, sur le même bateau que Joséphine de Beauharnais, avec laquelle il avait des liens de société". It is at least possible that this is the story that Duroure told to explain away his Newgate years. La Grande Encyclopédie says, "Il passa sa jeunesse en Angleterre où il mena une vie fort déréglé". Michaud, who was good on gossip though not always reliable, says that he had to leave England because he had shot his doctor, whose wife he had seduced – which doesn't seem to have been far from the truth – although he didn't make it out of England. Maybe it was in Duroure's interests to let a bit of confusion reign on his whereabouts during the second half of the 1780s.

[291] The 2nd Lord Bolingbroke had finally died in 1787, but his elder son, the 3rd Viscount, was just as big a disaster. In 1789 he left the country to live under an assumed name with his half-sister, Mary Beauclerk, by whom he had already had two children. He was hardly in a position to chase property at Doctors' Commons , so this may have been the occasion of the action of Duroure's trustees!

enabled the unfortunate young man to get out of prison. This ruling in Doctors' Commons opened the way for Duroure to claim his mother's property. Presumably there was enough to get him out of Newgate because he was free by the middle of September 1789.

Paris, 1789-90

Later litigation shows that the day after his release Duroure took possession of the Park Lane house which had once belonged to his uncle. Lord Bolingbroke had taken it on Josiah Child's death, and sold it to a Mr Jones. However, either Mr Jones was out or he had left it empty, for Duroure is listed in the records as being resident there in 1790-1. *La Dictionnaire de Biographie Française* says that Duroure was in Paris in 1789, a member of *L'Association de bienfaisance judicaire*, which worked for victims of what they regarded as miscarriages of justice. He was clearly backwards and forwards across the channel.

The French wikipedia reveals that on 27 January 1790 he married the fifteen year old Jeanne-Adrienne de Maleyssie. The girl's father was long dead, but her mother had re-married to the comte de La Chabeaussière. The wikipedia entry continues, "Mme de La Chabeaussière, sa belle-mère, était une femme intelligente, célèbre pour son salon et son goût immodéré du théâtre: elle donnait à jouer dans son petit théâtre privé de la rue de Bourbon, entre autres les pièces écrites par son mari. À la belle saison, le couple recevait dans son château de Margency[292], et on y voyait des hommes et femmes de lettres parmi lesquels la comtesse de Beaufort, elle-même femme de lettres[293], Sophie de Jaucourt, née

---

[292] Then just outside Paris.

[293] Anne-Marie de Montgeroult (1763-1837), from a literary family, married the comte de Beaufort as his second wife in 1780. She was something of a poetess, though was also known to have had an affair with Jean du Barry, a high class procurer, who had married Jeanne Bécu to his brother in 1768 and installed her as Louis XV's last mistress. At the revolution, the comte de Beaufort emigrated, but Mme de Beaufort stayed. She narrowly escaped arrest in 1793 and retired into private life.

de Chaponay, poétesse[294], le chevalier de Cubières et Fanny de Beauharnais[295]. Cette société, gagnée aux idées nouvelles, ne jurait que par les bienfaits d'une démocratie bien comprise et d'un libéralisme sans entraves".

Litigation – and more Litigation, 1790-1791

In July/August 1790 at the Guildford assizes, Duroure brought a suit against a Mr Jones (presumably the same Mr Jones who had bought the house in Park Lane) in respect of a property in Peckham which Jones had bought from the late Lord Bolingbroke. He was represented by Mr Erskine – his champion in 1784 – "for a fee of three hundred guineas", supported by Mr Serjeant Bond, Mr Garrow[296], and Mr Marryat. The only question that the jury was required to answer was that of Duroure's legitimacy. Mr Erskine argued that his legitimacy had been taken for granted in many settlements that had been made since his birth, that the Court of Chancery had granted him "a very large property", the Court of the King's Bench had granted him a property in Middlesex, "which was tried at Guildhall, before Lord Kenyon, about a month ago". He argued movingly that not only the Peckham property but his whole patrimony was dependent on the jury's verdict. The defending counsel, Mr Rous, argued that "all the solemn acts that established the plaintiff's legitimacy, were a fraudulent conspiracy on the part of the whole family, to cover the plaintiff's illegitimacy". The jury found for Duroure "to the universal satisfaction of a crowded and brilliant Court".

---

[294] Sophie de Chaponay (1750-), married Alexandre Charles, Marquis de Jaucourt and was known in the early 1790s for some light poetry.
[295] Michel de Cubières (1752-1820), writer, secretary of the Paris Commune, wrote a eulogy of Marat after his murder. He was the lover of Fanny de Beauharnais (1737-1813), also a poet and the hostess at a celebrated salon. She was great aunt (by marriage) of the Empress Josephine, and grandmother of Stéphanie, Grand Duchess of Baden, the adopted daughter of the Emperor Napoleon.
[296] The same Mr Garrow who was the hero of the TV series – Garrow's Law – in 2009-2011

The arguments however continued. Even if he was legitimate, could he inherit? Mr Jones continued to defend his property and contested ownership was the origin of the case of Duroure v Jones that was heard before Lord Chief Justice Kenyon at the Surrey Assizes on 28 June 1791. The court report states that the day after his release, on 17 September 1789, "he (Duroure), claiming title to the premises in question[297], made an actual and personal entry thereon in due form of law to avoid the fine, and ejected the defendant". There were two issues to be decided. The first was whether Duroure (as the son of an alien father born abroad to an English mother) was able to succeed to his mother's property in this country. Lord Chief Justice Kenyon, sitting with Mr Justice Ashhurst and Mr Justice Grose, was clear that he was not. The second question was whether the Statute of Limitations was in force in this case. Although more than five years had elapsed between Duroure's coming of age and his entry in to the property, he claimed that his imprisonment had prevented his entry any earlier than September 1789. Lord Chief Justice Kenyon ruled that, once the five years allowed to an infant come of age has begun, the time continues to run, notwithstanding any subsequent disability. This judgement – the first part of which was an important and ground-breaking ruling – was a bad set-back. However, apart from the Park Lane house and other property sold by the late Lord Bolingbroke to Mr Jones, it may be that Duroure was allowed to continue in the quiet possession of other parts of his inheritance.

There was a further property that would cause dispute. Old Lord St John had left his house in Albemarle Street to his daughter, Lady Luxborough. After her death, it was to go to her daughter, Henrietta Knight and her heirs and thereafter to Henry Knight and his heirs. Little Henrietta seems to have lodged with the old man after her parent's separation, and he may have grown fond of her. On her father's death in 1742, Lady Luxborough duly inherited. On her death in 1756, it went to Henrietta. In 1760, an agreement had

---

[297] 36 Upper Brook Street – the rather splendid house in Park Lane that had come to his mother from heruncle, Holles St John.

been reached between Lord Luxborough and his children that young Josiah should inherit on his mother's death (despite his illegitimacy). On Henrietta's death, it would seem that this is what happened but, on Josiah's death, Lord Bolingbroke moved in. There is a record of an action for wrongful possession of goods by Duroure against Sir Harry Burrard, William Snell & Oliver Cromwell, relating to the documents to do with Albemarle Street that they held and refused to give up[298]. Sadly it is undated, but the lawyers were required by the court to give up the documents. It would be interesting to know whether Duroure was able to establish his right to Albemarle Street.

It seems clear that, Lord Kenyon's judgement notwithstanding, Duroure emerged from the litigation of 1790-1 very comfortably off. French wikipedia says that he had very smart lodgings in the rue de Buffon, in the faubourg Montmartre.

The French Revolution - the early stages, 1789-1792

It is not clear what Duroure did after his unsuccessful court case in June 1791. Arnault says that he joined the Club of 89 when he arrived in Paris and soon transferred to the Cordeliers. Others say that he was founder member of the Jacobins. The person who wrote his obituary in the New Monthly Magazine obviously knew him well. "Although the Count's name has not appeared to any literary publication of consequence, he has not the less contributed to enhance the value of the labour of others, and during the period of the Revolution a multiplicity of anonymous writings, as well as the harangues delivered by many public characters, were the production of his pen"[299].

---

[298] *A complete system of pleading,* John Wentworth, George Townshend & James Cornwall (1798), 638.

[299] New Monthly Magazine, vol.6, 1822.
http://books.google.co.uk/books?id=BH5HAAAAYAAJ&pg=PA522&lpg=PA522&dq=Count+Duroure&source=bl&ots=MF0H64zYRM&sig=1msnyCgESc31F3o3Z76Y-PvyXos&hl=en&sa=X&ei=bXJxT7GJF4nn8QOZn-Q – accessed 27 March 2012.

His wife's family seem to have gone with the flow of the revolution, sympathizing with the Girondin leadership. French wikipedia however says that Duroure early on fixed his colours to the ultra-revolutionary group that opposed not only Brissot and the Girondins, but also the statist plans of Robespierre and the Jacobins. This seems to make sense. Duroure's power base seems always to have been in the Paris Commune.

The Commune was originally set up in July 1789 to serve as a municipal governing body for the city of Paris. In May-June 1790, its electorate was restricted to "active citizens", which meant people of a certain age and owners of property. Its character was "moderate" under mayor Bailly (July 1789 - Nov 1791). Bailly had to resign because of growing pressure from the left, but even under the more radical Mayor Pétion, the Commune was broadly supportive of the Girondin establishment. However, by July 1792 a movement was growing to abolish the distinction between active and passive citizens and to allow the whole population to take part in the city government. On the night of 9 August, the sections took possession of the Hotel de Ville and the following day the existing Commune was replaced by an "insurgent commune". The crowds marched on the Tuileries, demanding the King's abdication. Louis XVI took refuge with his family in the Legislative Assembly, but that was dissolved. Effective power was now lodged in the Commune, which took Louis and his family into "protective custody" at the Temple prison. In Paris, there was chaos – with the insurgent commune doing nothing to restrain the mob. The "September massacres" took place during this time.

When the National Convention met on 20 September, its first act was to abolish the monarchy. New elections were also held for the Paris Commune, on the basis of universal male suffrage. There were 48 sections in Paris, each of which sent three delegates to the General Council of the Commune of Paris. Duroure seems already to have been active in his own section, Faubourg-Montmartre. Every citizen was supposed to be active in his section under the new arrangements, but in fact of the average of three thousand citizens who lived in a section, only about fifty or sixty turned out for meetings. Duroure was typical of the kind of person who got involved, and on 27 October 1792, he was elected onto the General Council to represent his own section[300]. He was then known as Scipion Duroure. The title and the collection of aristocratic-sounding names were suspended for the present, in the interest of his revolutionary zeal.

There is however evidence to suggest that Duroure was early on involved in some shady financial deals, linked to the sale of the property of the church and the emigrés. Properties were bought off the state at low prices and sold on at a considerable profit. His friend, Jean Julien – known as Julien of Toulouse – was known to be involved. It's said that he was an enthusiastic gambler and frequented the fashionable gambling salon run by Mme de Sainte-Amaranthe. He entrusted large sums of money to the banker/businessmen André Guzman, the Count de Pestre de Séneffe and Édouard de Walckiers – all of whom were known to be involved in speculation.

Scipion Duroure and the Paris Commune, October 1792-June 1793
Duroure was one of those who quickly gained influence in the General Council and who was able gradually to bring back some sort of order to the city. Very soon after his election he was elected a Vice President of the Commune. French Wikipedia says that he was *officier municipale,* but there seems no other evidence of this. Pierre Gaspard Chaumette was early elected President of the Commune. Jean-Nicolas Pache was elected mayor in the following February. Pache had been Minister of War in the Girondin government, but was pushed out by his colleagues. He was in

---

[300] Listed as Louis Henry Scipion Grimoard-Beauvoir, dit Scipion-Duroure, 506 rue Buffaut, homme de lettres, sect. du Faubourg-Montmartre. Nommé le 27 Octobre a remplacé Jircourt. If Duroure was already calling himself Scipio in October 1792 he was anticipating by a year the practice of exchanging Christian names for names from the classical age. Thus, Georges Couthon became Aristide.

consequence hostile to Brissot and his colleagues and helped to establish the Commune as the main focus of opposition to them. Duroure and Pache were close.

The Girondin leadership was not keen on executing Louis, but the political pressure was irresistible. The trial began on 11 December 1792 and the sentence was communicated to the King on 17 January. He was executed on 21 January. Michaud records that Duroure later claimed to have had responsibility for the royal family, and to have had several conversations with Louis XVI, whose last will he witnessed[301]. As a leading member of the Commune, it seems quite likely that Duroure was at the Temple.

In February 1793 Duroure was appointed First Commissioner for Finance. Duroure's wealth clearly contributed to his importance. French wikipedia says that wealthy people like him were taking control of the commune, and that was certainly a suspicion from fairly early on in the new Commune's life. However, wikipedia says that he and Pache covered their tracks by supporting *un certain nombre d'individus sur l'habileté démagogique,* among whom was René Hébert.

The representatives of the Sections were in touch with the people and saw themselves as champions of the poor. There was considerable distress among the poor in Paris. The expense of the war intensified inflation, and this meant food shortages. People were demanding some control over the price of bread. There was extensive rioting in February 1793, and the unrest continued into the spring. The Convention, dominated by the Girondins, was thought unsympathetic to the needs of the poor and was fast losing support among the radicals. The Paris Commune - as leader of a network of Communes throughout the country - was ready to step into the breach as the guardian of the Revolution.

---

[301] "Il racontait, dans les dernières années de sa vie, dans une manière originale et piquante, les conversations qu'il avait eues alors avec le prince".

At the beginning of April 1793, the French General Dumouriez defected to the Austrians and there was a renewed panic in Paris. The sections suspected treachery in the National Convention itself. Delegates from the more militant sections (Duroure among them) gathered in the Archbishop's Palace, and petitioned the Convention for the expulsion of several of its members. A revolutionary council was established at the Evêché that took over the initiative from the General Council of the Commune and challenged the authority of the Convention itself. This was the Comité Central Révolutionnaire and Duroure was one of its members. Robespierre was nervous, but realised that he needed the support of the delegates at the Evêché if he was to gain control of the Convention. When the Convention ordered the arrest of Hébert[302], Varlet[303] and some others, this was the moment for the Sections to flex their muscles. They demanded the release of their heroes, and one of the most strongly worded of the demands came from Faubourg Montmartre, Duroure's section. On 2 June, a revolutionary militia, summoned by the Comité Central, surrounded the Tuileries[304]. The Convention was cowed; the leaders of the Girondins were placed under house arrest.

Triumph and Defeat - June 1793-March 1794
During the short time of power enjoyed by the Comité Central Révolutionnaire, Duroure was one of those who was delegated to examine Roland de la Platière.[305] As Minister of the Interior after

---

[302] Jacques René Hébert (1757-1794), from a middle class family in Alençon, went to Paris in 1780-1 and started publishing his journal "*Père Duchesne*" around June-July 1790. A great gift for reproducing the thought and language of ordinary people.

[303] Jean-Francois Varlet (1764-1837), from a well to do family in Paris, active in the Revolution from the early days and advocate of direct democracy through the communes. Represented the Droits-de l'Homme section and was the darling of the *sans culottes*. He later supported Bonaparte.

[304] The Faubourg Montmarte was well represented in this citizen's army (Rudé, p.123). Michaud says that Duroure was charged with writing the account of these events.

[305] or so says Michaud in his Biographie Universelle. Jean Marie Roland de la Platière (1734-93) came to Paris from Amiens in December 1791 and became one

10 August 1792, Roland was alleged to have taken several decisions that had penalised the poor - above all, he had insisted on maintaining the price of bread, even in face of a collapsing currency. Duroure seems not to have had the opportunity to question Roland. Roland was not at home when the police arrived and seems to have fled to Rouen. Vengeance was taken on his wife instead.

The events of 2 June 1793 did not immediately result in a control of food prices. Danton still dominated the Convention and he was no friend to price controls or poor relief. However, in mid-July Danton was voted off the Committee of Public Safety and things changed dramatically. A state machine was put in place, dedicated to winning the war and providing the necessary supplies for the capital and the army. To this extent Robespierre, Saint-Just, Couthon and the rest were the friends of the Commune and the sections. To this extent, July 1793 and the beginning of "The Terror" should have been the beginning of a grand alliance between the three of them. Hoarders and profiteers were the focus of general hostility. *Père Duchesne* seemed to be the mouthpiece of those in power. Yet the Committee of Public Safety had grown wise. They were learning how to control the Commune and the sections, and from now on the real power was steadily returning from the streets to the government.

It was an extraordinary time. In July 1793 the Dauphin was taken away from his mother to be "re-educated". Marie Antoinette suffered a campaign of character assassination that was to end with her execution in October. The new revolutionary calendar was introduced. In November 1793 Notre Dame became the Temple of

---

of the leaders of the Left. Became Minister of the Interior in March 1792, but was soon dismissed by the King. He was reinstated after 10 August, but soon disagreed with the direction of affairs. He resigned two days after the King's execution and only avoided arrest after the Insurrection of 31 May by escaping to Rouen. His wife was arrested and executed on 8 November. Two days later Roland committed suicide.

Reason. Mass executions took place in Lyons, Marseilles, Bordeaux and Toulon. The Vendée was laid waste, and it is said that during the winter of 1793-4 that one third of its population was killed. But Robespierre and the Committee of Public Safety had to fight hard to defend their particular vision for the Revolution. Danton was working to bring it and the war to an end. Desmoulins launched a new journal - the *Vieux Cordelier* - at the beginning of December 1793 expressly to win over Robespierre from his sympathy with the radicals. Hébert and the Commune, knowing themselves unloved both by Robespierre and the *Indulgents*, were on the defensive. Both sides were accusing the other of peculation.

The alliance between the Sections and Robespierre, apparently established in the passing of the law of the Maximum, had been short lived. The growers, producers and middlemen very soon found ways of evading the maximum. The law was regularly evaded, and prices rose again. The newly established revolutionary militia did its best, egged on by Hébert and his friends, but the government was lukewarm. Then there was the issue of wages. The government was meant to control these too and was enforcing them in those areas that lay under its control. The Paris Commune and the sections would however have nothing to do with any controls. Robespierre - though still the darling of the *sans culottes* - was thought to be sympathetic to controls, and Hébert began calling him "the leader of the moderates". It was not a sensible move. Robespierre was still all-powerful, and it was not wise to criticise him. From October 1793 he had the radicals at the Commune in his sights.

Fabre d'Eglantine's revelation of a 'foreign plot' in October 1793 marked the beginning of the end for the Hébertists.

Robespierre was ill for most of February and the first part of March 1794, just as the competition between the radicals[306] and the

---

[306] The radical focus was the Club des Cordeliers, which had led the mourning for Jean-Paul Marat.

moderates intensified. In early March Duroure and his colleagues from Section Marat[307] showed conspicuous bravery in being the only representatives from the Paris Commune to dare to go to the Convention to demand food for the people of Paris and the punishment of the counter-revolutionaries. It was meant to be a replay of the events of 31 May-2 June 1793 but circumstances were now very different. The government was much more powerful, and did not take kindly to threats of insurrection. On 10 March Fouquier-Tinville was required to prepare a case against the Hébert, Vincent[308], Ronsin[309] and Momoro[310]. He had plenty of material to hand. Saint-Just had already denounced the leaders of the Commune as "men impatient for offices", jealous of the power of the Convention. Robespierre had identified anti-revolutionary intrigue as being rife amongst the foreigners in Paris - among whom were many of Hébert's friends, including Duroure himself.

Duroure had stood "godfather" to Hébert's only child.[311] Hébert was always short of money, and it seems likely that Duroure

---

[307] They had renamed their section "Mont-Marat" after the murder of Marat by Charlotte Corday in July 1793.

[308] François Nicolas Vincent, exercised great influence at the Ministry of War and was implicated in the excesses in the Vendée. Guillotined with Hébert and his friends in March 1794.

[309] Charles Philippe Henri Ronsin, a playwright who became a *sans culotte* militant. He was the commander-in-chief of the *armées revolutionnaires* in the Vendée, where he had acquired a terrifying reputation. Arrested in December 1793 and then freed, he was re-arrested in the purge of the Hébertists and executed.

[310] Antoine Francois Momoro, a printer-publisher who as one of the original band of revolutionaries. Called himself "The First Printer of Liberty". In November 1793, his wife had played "Reason" in the dechristianizing fête in Notre Dame - now renamed the Temple of Reason.

[311] Scipion Virginie Hébert (1793-1830). She was meant to be a boy - but was called Scipion nonetheless. She later married a Protestant pastor and had two sons. It was a "lay baptism". Hébert was one of the leaders of the de-christianizers. He wanted churches closed, priests and bishops laicized, and the Goddess of Reason enthroned in Notre Dame. In November 1793 the Commune ordered the closure of all the Paris churches - much to Robespierre's horror. However, Hébert's wife was a former nun who still held on to her faith

bankrolled him. Whatever the nature of their friendship, it was enough for Duroure to be arrested with the other Hébertists. On 18 March, they were sent to the Saint-Lazare prison and soon afterwards were brought before the Revolutionary Tribunal. At the trial, Duroure was accused of unrevolutionary activity - it was said that he travelled in a coach. He argued that he was lame, and so needed some form of transport[312]. He further argued that Hébert was simply a colleague on the Commune at a time when everyone regarded him as a true patriot. Apparently people believed the accusation of counter-revolution being levelled at Hébert, so it is understandable that Duroure seems to have believed them too. He certainly did his best to distance himself from Hébert and to present himself as a simple, patriotic member of the Commune. In this he was being ingenuous. Duroure's politics of *action direct* was no longer acceptable in Robespierre's one party state. Though he remained in prison, he was lucky to escape with his life[313]. It's not clear why he wasn't executed. Hébert and the rest – Ronsin, Vincent, Proly, Anacharsis Cloots[314] – went to the guillotine on 24 March 1794.

---

[312] Apparently he suffered from gout – he was very young for that (Mathiez, 328).
[313] Palmer says those arrested with Hébert included 'someone described as a man of letters' – which was how Duroure described himself at his election to the Commune in 1792. However, Palmer also says that all those arrested with Hébert were executed, apart from a pregnant woman and a police spy. R. R. Palmer *The Twelve who Ruled,* Princetown U.P., 1989, pp.292-3
[314] Thomas de Kloots (1755-94) was from an aristocratic Dutch-Prussian family. Came to France in the 1770's and mixed in intellectual enlightenment circles. With the outbreak of revolution he dropped his aristocratic name and took that of a classical philosopher. Elected to the National Assembly in 1790, and to the National Convention in August 1792. A utopian, who dreamed of a world republic – and a passionate enemy of religion. The high point of his career was his organisation of the Festival of Reason at Notre Dame in November 1793. However, after that he fell foul of Robespierre, who claimed to believe that he was plotting with Prussians against the Republic. His wealth and foreignness told against him. At the end of December 1793 he was expelled from the Convention and arrested.

The Paris Commune was purged and the revolutionary militia was disbanded. In many ways - though the Hébertists have not found support from later historians - their defeat marks the end of the real French Revolution.

Six Months in Prison: March-September, 1794

Their defeat solved nothing and nor did the subsequent execution of Desmoulins and Danton and the rest of the *Indulgents*. The food riots continued and the wage-earners threatened strike action. The now Robespierrist Commune could threaten all it liked, but the people had put their trust in Hébert and people like him. They had found it hard to believe in his treachery, and now they were beginning to lose faith in Robespierre. In any case, they were neutered. When the crunch came, Robespierre had little support in Paris. His rule had depended on the support of the *sans culottes* but he had destroyed them. When he was denounced in the Convention in July 1794, the sections stayed silent, and the National Guard refused to move. Robespierre was arrested and executed, together with several of his supporters.

Predictably, his successors moved to abolish the Maximum laws. Prices were allowed to rise, and even the control of wages was eased. The result though was not favourable to the poor.

Until the Events of 12th Germinal, Year III (1 April 1795)

Duroure was released from prison on 28 September 1794 at the request of Robert Lindet. Lindet was remarkable as one who had refused to condemn Danton and who (while not supporting Robespierre) opposed the Thermidorean reaction. It would be interesting to know what Duroure did with his new-found freedom. The prisons of the Convention were emptying that autumn and many former revolutionaries who had somehow escaped Robespierre's guillotine were prowling the streets of Paris – eager to avenge themselves on anyone associated with the old regime.

These were the *muscadins,* the *jeunesse dorée,* known for their exotic clothes and their experience in street violence.

By the beginning of 1795 the repeal of the Maximum laws and steady inflation were bringing working people out on the streets again. Finally, on 1 April 1795 (12 Germinal) serious rioting broke out and the people marched on the Convention. Duroure's old section – Montmartre – was to the fore and one wonders whether Duroure was back in his leadership role there. They didn't stand a chance. They were greeted by the National Guard, now firmly on the side of the government, and dispersed with some bloodshed. There were several arrests. The old terrorists who had survived Thermidor were executed or deported to Guyana – Carrier, Collot d'Herbois, Billaud-Varenne, Barère and Fouquier-Tinville among them[315]. Duroure escaped the roundup, but he was clearly aware that the Revolution was entering its authoritarian phase – which was to end with the dictatorship of Napoleon.

It was at this moment that the restoration of the monarchy was a real possibility. The brothers of Louis XVI had ruled themselves out by their public demand for the re-imposition of the old regime. However, the young Louis XVII was the hope of the constitutionalists and they were working towards his restoration when, on 8 June, he died. The Convention thereupon worked to perpetuate itself and succeeded for the time being. A new constitution was promulgated and a conservative uprising in Paris was crushed with the help of the army under General Bonaparte. It would be four more years before Bonaparte came to power, but the crushing of the Vendémaire uprising was the shape of things to come.

In England and/or Avignon – until the Fructidorian Terror, 1797

---

[315] Robert Lindet was also denounced, but escaped condemnation in the amnesty of October 1795. He was later implicated in Babeuf's uprising of May 1796 but was acquitted.

1f.

In 1795, Rev William Macritchiue, minister of Clunie in Perthshire, set out upon a tour of Great Britain. In his diary for 2 July 1795, he notes that he visited his old friend, Mr Fisher at Blackheath and there met "Count Duroure, a French gentleman of the army, one of the many French refugees now in Great Britain"[316]. A sojourn in England might have been a wise course for him at this moment.

However, Roman d'Amat says that after Germinal, Duroure left Paris and went south, that he went to Avignon and was elected *officier municipale* - a town councillor. According to d'Amat, he remained in Avignon until 1797 – despite the fact that the town doesn't seem to have been a very welcoming place for a Hébertist. Maignet, the Robespierrrist leader, had been replaced by the more moderate Goupilleau in August 1794. Then, the following December, the Committee of Public Safety decided that Goupilleau was too much of a Jacobin sympathiser and replaced him with Jean De Bry. De Bry had a hard job, trying to get enough grain with a collapsing currency and the situation got steadily worse through 1795. The need in Avignon as in Paris was for enough food. Politics itself was uncontroversial. Commitment to the early ideals of the Revolution remained strong in Avignon. It was only Robespierre's Terror that was denounced.

However, people needed food, and the government was jumpy. The Prairial uprising in Paris was replicated in and around Avignon. The *jeunesse dorée* who had created such havoc in Paris were active also in Avignon. So called terrorists were killed in the prisons and hunted down in the streets. There then came an uprising that resulted in October 1795 in the brief occupation of Avignon by royalist troops. This however was succeeded by an anti-royalist reaction, and mainstream politics was re-established. From then on, things settled down. The radicals remained a threat - as did the

---

[316] The editor of the diary (published by Elliott Stock in 1897) suggests that this may have been the young Count Duroure – or possibly his father (but Duroure's father had died the previous year). Interesting that Duroure was now presenting himself as a military man.

royalists - but Avignon was no longer the cause of anxiety it had been in the early 1790's. People wanted peace - and in the end they were to look for the restoration of the monarchy as the only hope for peace.

In September 1795 a new Constitution was voted in Paris. The Convention was disbanded, to be replaced by a parliamentary system of two houses. The executive power was entrusted to a Directory of five. The revolutionaries were guaranteed their places in the new government, to prevent their falling victim to a conservative reaction, but these guarantees could not give them credibility – and the Directory was never popular. It was a new kind of France, very far from the ideals of 1792-4.

Last Days of the Revolution, 1797-1800
The elections of April 1797 saw the return of a large number of moderate republicans – which didn't please the Directory. On 4 September 1797 (18 Fructidor), the Directory claimed that there was a threat of a royalist uprising and imposed a new terror, supported by the army. Since the crackdown was just as much against the left as against the right, it's not surprising that it's said that Duroure was arrested as a dangerous agitator. Then, curiously, the Directory gradually moved to the right. The 1798 elections brought in a phalanx of anti-government Jacobins which the Directory tried to purge, with some success[317]. Jacobins were excluded from civil and military employment. The 1799 elections then brought in a varied group that shared nothing much in common apart from hostility to the Regime.

By the coup of 18 June 1799 (30 Prairial) the five-man Directory was effectively brought to an end and Sièyes emerged as the dominant figure in a government that is known as the "Second Directory". Robert Lindet emerged from the shadows to become Minister of Finance, and General Bernadotte was Minister of War. There was

---

[317] Two of these were Joseph & Lucien Bonaparte – Lucien at least being a convinced Jacobin.

something of a Jacobin upsurge. For a moment, the press regained its freedom, in the tradition of Hébert and Marat. Duroure was among the radicals who gathered old Jacobins together in the *Réunion d'amis de l'égalité et de la liberté*, which had its headquarters in the Salle du Manège of the Tuileries, and was thus known as the Club du Manège. It was patronized by Barras, and some two hundred and fifty members of the two councils of the legislature were enrolled as members, including many notable ex-Jacobins. It published a newspaper called the *Journal des Libres*, proclaimed the apotheosis of Robespierre and Babeuf, and attacked the Directory as a *royauté pentarchique*.

But public opinion was now moderate or royalist, and the club was violently attacked in the press and in the streets. The club had to change its meeting-place from the Tuileries to the church of the Jacobins (Temple of Peace) in the Rue du Bac. Sièyes installed Fouché as his Chief of Police, and one of his first acts was to close the club after barely a month's existence. Bernadotte was dismissed as Minister of War, ostensibly because he was plotting with the Jacobins.

For a moment it had looked as though Sièyes was becoming more sympathetic to the radicals, but it was only for the moment. He was in fact looking for a strong man to help him bring the Revolution to a final end. He found it in Napoleon Bonaparte – although in Bonaparte he found more than he bargained for. On 9 November 1799 – again against the threat of a Jacobin plot - Bonaparte, Sièyes and Ducos were named provisional consuls. Three months later, Bonaparte assumed the position of First Consul and began his march to absolute power. By the end of the year, as a result of a royalist attempt on his life, Bonaparte seized the opportunity to crush the republican opposition. The remaining revolutionaries were sent to Guyana and the Seychelles.

It was the end of press freedom and the final end of the radicals for a very long time. D'Amat says that Duroure was among those proscribed as a "dangerous agitator" and condemned to deportation to Guyana - but there is no record of his arrest. In the *New Monthly Magazine* obituary, the writer said "no overtures whatsoever could shake the honest integrity of his mind; though the Prefecture of Department and the dignity of a Senator, would have been the recompense of an abandonment of principle, on the coronation of the Emperor". Bonaparte was voted Consul for life in May 1802 and the Senate voted to proclaim the empire in May 1804. Bonaparte's coronation followed in December. The Senate in the new dispensation was a collection of nominees, with no real power. The Departments had been set up by the Constituent Assembly in 1790, and the Prefects were an invention of Napoleon's in 1800. They were local government officers.

It seems that Duroure left for England sometime between 1800 and 1804. The days of Duroure and his friends were gone now. The left wing was no longer any real threat and subsequently Duroure disappears from view in France. By the time the radical dreams were being dreamed again, he was long dead - and long discredited.

In England, after 1800
Michaud says that Duroure returned to England "to recover a considerable fortune" – presumably reference to his continuing efforts to recover his mother's fortune. He was clearly low on funds – and he was listed as a resident alien in 1810. Mahul says of him, "Il a vécu dans la retraite, assez maltraité de la fortune, mais fidèle à ses principes politiques et s'occupant surtout de la langue et de la legislation anglaise, dans lesquels il était profondément versé".

He certainly remained committed to the radical cause, and a study of his life during these years would throw up quite a lot about London life in the first and second decades of the nineteenth century. It was a hard time to be a radical. People like William Cobbett were increasingly looking to the long term, since the short term was so depressing. Cobbett dedicated himself to the education of the poor and with this in mind wrote his "Grammar of the English Language". "The long-imprisoned, the heavily fined, the banished William Prynne, returning to liberty, borne by the people of Southampton to London, over a road strewed with flowers could never have performed any of his acts against tyranny and injustice without a knowledge of grammar", he wrote in his introduction. Such knowledge was an indispensable prerequisite for anyone struggling against tyranny and misgovernment, and so the poor had to learn how to express themselves - but in their own idiom. Cobbett had no time for flowery aristocratic language. The English language had to be reclaimed for the people. This was what Hébert had been trying to do in *Père Duchesne,* and it is no surprise that Duroure translated Cobbett's Grammar into French as "Le Maitre anglais", to bring the insights of the English revolutionary into post-revolutionary France[318]. In 1819 Duroure showed his continuing interest in law in a translation of a standard English work on the jury system, "Des pouvoirs et des obligations des jurys" by Sir Richard Phillips[319]. His companion in the translation was Charles Comte, a liberal lawyer[320].

---

[318] What seems to have been the first edition was published in France in 1803. A fifth edition of *Le Maitre anglais,* published in Paris in 1816, is kept in the British Library, "revue et corrigé avec soin par L.H. Scipion, Count Duroure". Phillips' edition of *Le Maitre anglais* was warmly praised by Sir Richard Phillips in his *Monthly Magazine & British Register* in 1816.

[319] "On the powers and duties of juries and on the Criminal Laws of England" by Sir Richard Phillips, published in 1811. Sir Richard Phillips (1767-1840) was a fascinating chap – an educational entrepreneur with radical links. According to Feller, it was said that Duroure was working on an edition of the philosophical works of his great uncle, Lord Bolingbroke, and on the family letters of his sister, Lady Luxborough - but nothing appeared. If he hoped to work on Lady Luxborough's letters, he must have been in touch with the family at Barrells.

[320] Charles Comte (1782-1837) was a French lawyer, journalist and political writer. In 1814 he founded, with Charles Dunoyer, *Le Censeur*, the liberal journal. In 1820, he was found guilty of attacks against the King and went into exile in Switzerland where as professor of natural law, he taught at the University of Lausanne in Switzerland. Following comments made by Fredric Jean Witt, a revolutionary, to the Bavarian police, and an intervention by the French police, Comte was forced to leave Switzerland. He took refuge in England for 18 months where he became acquainted with Jeremy Bentham, and in 1825 he returned to France and began contributing to the *Revue Americaine*. In 1827 he

In 1820 Duroure enquired whether he was owed anything from his father's estate. It was stated that his father had married again - to the Marquise de Roux - and that everything had gone to her on his death in 1794.

Duroure died in Arundel Street, London (just up from Embankment tube station) on 24 September 1822[321]. Michaud says that his illegitimate son died a few days later in the same house - and "it was thought they had been poisoned". Whether or not that was true, it is interesting that Michaud had picked up this gossip thirty years later. Duroure received a laudatory obituary in the *New Monthly Magazine*.

Isabella Francis, one of Robert Knight's granddaughters, recorded that "a Count Douroure was brought over to Barrells to be buried, having left orders in his will that he was to be buried by his mother, the Countess Douroure (*sic*). The funeral was ridiculously grand, the hearse all covered with coats-of-arms, not much to the satisfaction of the family, who doubted his really being the Countess' son"[322]. This may have been how Duroure was remembered in the family a generation later when Isabella was a girl - as a bit of an embarrassment, a stranger who was not really a relation. On the other hand, Frances Stapleton – Isabella's elder and bloomer-wearing sister – called her youngest son (born in

---

published *Traité de législation* (4 volumes, in-8) which outlined laws governing the development of companies and the reasons why development might be held back. The book established his reputation and earned him a Montyon Prize. As an economist he followed the doctrines of Jean-Baptiste Say whose daughter he married. He was active in the opposition which led to the July Revolution of 1830 and was elected a deputy in the Sarthe in 1831 and again in 1834. In 1832 he was elected to the *Académie des Sciences Morales et Politiques*.

[321] Michaud says 1824 and John Gorton's Biographical Dictionary follows him, adding that he died in Arundel Street, just off the Strand. This date comes from the plaque in Ullenhall Church.

[322] From the manuscript history of Isabella Francis (1839-1922), 5th daughter of Bolton & Georgiana King, quoted by her niece, Octavia Higgon, and included in Arthur Carden's "The Knights of Barrells".

1f.

1874) "Louis Henry", which suggests at least interest, or even admiration.

Michaud said of him, "C'était un homme assez spirituel et qui ne manquait pas de savoir, mais sa loquacité était fatigante". He had been caught up in a great enterprise. It was his misfortune that, after its failure, few people remembered the dreams that had been dreamed.

CHAPTER TWENTY

ROBERT KNIGHT IV (1768-1855)

Early Years

Robert Knight was born on 3 March 1768[323]. He was the second of the five children born to the Earl of Catherlough by Jane Davies. His father was sixty-five years old when he was born. There was an elder sister, Jane, and there would be a younger brother and sister, Henry and Henrietta. Lord Catherlough died in March 1772, when Jane was four months pregnant with her fifth child. Lord Catherlough had left directions in his will that Jane should change her name to Knight – which she duly did a few weeks after his death. She also moved her little family out of Golden Square, Lord Catherlough's long term residence in crowded Soho, across Oxford Street to a new house with more air in Holles Street. Little Caroline was born on 20 July, was buried at Barrels a month later – on 22 August. Then Jane herself fell ill. She had wanted to be buried at Barrels with her baby and Lord Catherlough but in fact was buried in the new churchyard of St Marylebone Church in Paddington Street on 9 November. Her elder daughter, young Jane, was a month short of her sixth birthday. Little Robert was four and a half years old; Henry was just three; little Henrietta was a week off her second birthday. Only Jane might have had a hazy memory of their mother, to share with her brothers and sisters later. "The portrait of my mother" - which was taken to Chadshunt from Grosvenor Square on Robert's death over eighty years later – must have been the focus of their remembering. What vague memories have been passed down are of a beautiful, good, loving and much loved lady.

---

[323] According to the memorial board he put up in the parish church at Chadshunt

They needed such a memory for it was not easy to be illegitimate in those days – particularly when there was no father to defend your status and no close relations who would take your side. It must have been a strange little household. Lord Catherlough had appointed Jane guardian to their children, so new arrangements had to be made and it's not clear what they were. Perhaps there were just nurses and housekeepers, paid for by and accountable to the executors. The infant children had few relations, and what few there were had no reason to be friendly to the little brood that had snatched their inheritance[324]. Young Josiah Child might have expected to inherit, but at least he had been named in his mother's will as her heir – which meant that he had his own means to compensate for his illegitimacy. In any case he was dead not much more than a year later. Little Louis Duroure was remembered in his grandfather's will, but his hope of Josiah's fortune was dependent on his proving his legitimacy – which was contested by the St John family. The children of Lord Catherlough's sisters – who were their nearest relations on their father's side – were unlikely to have had any reason to look kindly on them.

The first we hear of the family is in January 1785, when Robert was admitted fellow commoner at Queen's College, Cambridge. He was nearly seventeen - the usual time for going up to university in those days. The following year, his younger brother joined the army - becoming an ensign in the 22nd Foot[325]. After Cambridge, it is possible that Robert did the tour, for in 1788-9 the records of the Sir John Soane Museum show that a Mr Knight of Portland Place got John Flaxman to do a marble version of a relief in the Borghese Palace. He may have been living in Portland Place then, though Jane was married from Clapham in February, 1791[326]. When Robert

---

[324] I've no idea what sort of contact they had with their mother's brothers and sisters in Henley-in-Arden. I've not seen evidence – either in fact or fiction – of what was usual in these circumstances.

[325] He was promoted Lieutenant in the 13th Light Dragoons in 1789

[326] Jane was married at St George's Hanover Square to Benjamin Bond Hopkins (1745-94) of Pains Hill, Surrey, with Robert Knight and George Chamberlaine as witnesses. Rev George Chamberlaine of Burwood House, Surrey, was married to

came home and settled at Barrells[327], he employed Joseph Bonomi to remodel the house for him[328]. This meant that it was ready in June 1791, when he married Hon Frances Dormer[329]. Robert was

---

Hopkins' sister Elizabeth. In 1772, on the death of his grandfather, John Hopkins (who had a life interest), Bond Hopkins inherited the considerable fortune of "Vulture" Hopkins (who had died in 1732). Benjamin Hopkins' first wife (who he married in her home church of St John's Church in Hackney on 8 March 1770) was called Elizabeth Chamberlaine (the same name as B's mother – a cousin?). She died in 1771, leaving an only child – Elizabeth – who died on 11 July 1781, aged 11. Hopkins' second wife, Alicia Tomkins (who died on 28 Sept 1788, aged 37), gave him an only surviving legitimate child, Caroline (1774-1850). There was also an illegitimate son, Henry, who was left well provided for. Hopkins had built a very impressive villa at Wimbledon (much of the land on which the houses off Southside Common were built was bought by Vulture Hopkins in 1720). However, he sold his villa to M. de Calonne soon after his marriage to Jane and moved to a new built house at Pains Hill (which he had bought from Charles Hamilton soon after his grandfather's death). Hamilton had made a beautiful garden there, part of which is still a well-known beauty spot. At the time of his death in January 1794, he was building East Cliff Lodge in Ramsgate (where he died, I think) – sold after his death. Hopkins' portrait is in the Fitzwilliam Museum. See "Benjamin Bond Hopkins at Pains Hill" by Michael Symes in *Garden History*, Vol. 27, No. 2 (Winter 1999), pp. 238-243.

In April 1795 Jane married Charles Fuller as her second husband, with Robert Knight and Elizabeth Chamberlaine as witnesses. Fuller came from a banking family, though is said to have sponged on his wife. In 1797 Caroline Hopkins married Commander Richard Mansel Philipps of Coedgaing (second son of Sir William Mansel 9th Bt of Iscoed by Mary Philipps of Coedgaing), with Charles Fuller and George Chamberlaine as the witnesses. Pains Hill was sold in 1795 but the Philipps family lived off the proceeds of the Wimbledon lands (which were gradually sold off to developers after Caroline's death). Caroline is buried in Wimbledon churchyard, with her mother and other members of her family. Henrietta married Michael Impey at St George's Hanover Square in June 1792. Michael was the eldest son of Sir Elijah Impey (1732-1809), a Westminster school friend of Warren Hastings. He was Chief Justice of Bengal where he controversially insisted that English law was binding on the Indian population. He used this in 1775 to achieve the death of Maharaja Nandakumar, who had brought charges of bribery against Warren Hastings (at the instigation of Hastings' enemies on the Council of Bengal). The Impeys were a prosperous business family.

[327] Lord Catherlough's will had stipulated that Barrells be let during his son's minority.

[328] Joseph Bonomi (1739-1808)

also concerned with his Montgomeryshire estates, based on the village of Kerry, close to the English border. His grandfather had bought the land from Lord Lisburne in 1717. Robert began serving as a magistrate in Montgomeryshire in 1793, when he was "of Gwernygoe". The house at Gwernygoe, near Kerry, was built in 1792 on the site of a grange that had belonged to the abbey at Cwmhir, so he presumably built it for his own use when he was there. In 1802, when he served as High Sheriff of Montgomeryshire, he was still described as "of Gwernygo" – as also in 1808 when he again served as High Sheriff.

The French Revolution - The Early Years, to 1792

The fall of the Bastille in July 1789 was greeted with a mixture of enthusiasm and indifference. The sixteen-year-old Coleridge broke into verse at Christ's Hospital. Wordsworth at Cambridge later recalled the excitement, "Bliss was it in that dawn to be alive". Poems and articles abounded from people like that. Otherwise there was more measured appreciation. As far as the Opposition Whigs were concerned, France lived under a despotic monarchy that they suspected George III wanted to transport to England. They had no reason to condemn anything that might change things there. For Pitt, anything that might weaken France must be good. His Secretary of State, William Grenville, remarked in the late summer of 1789, "The main point seems quite secure, that they will not for many years be in a situation to molest the invaluable peace which we now enjoy". The Revolution however did change the political climate. The movement to Reform slowed and then ground to a halt. It was becoming clear that no measure for even moderate Parliamentary Reform would be countenanced. And the Church was also to be defended. Repeal of the Corporation and Test Acts[330] had been in discussion since 1787. Two votes - in 1787

---

[329] She was the youngest daughter of Lord Dormer of neighbouring Grove Park by his second wife. The Dormers were a Catholic family, but the children of Lord Dormer's second marriage were brought up as Anglicans. Robert and Frances had three children: (Elizabeth) Frances, born in 1793 and baptised at Ullenhall; Henry born in May 1795 and baptised at Ullenhall; and Georgiana, born in 1802.

and in May 1789 - had only been narrowly lost. However, when Fox introduced the Bill for Repeal in March 1790, it was lost by a large majority. Dissenters were already being identified with a wilder radicalism. The Church of England - hitherto quiet and non-political - was beginning to be the focus of stability in the face of radical change. When the rioting started - in the summer of 1791 - "Church and King" was to be the rallying cry[331]. Without really meaning to be, Pitt and the Church were being pushed into a conservative corner that was to embarrass both them and their allies in the years ahead.

Not least among those who would be embarrassed was Edmund Burke. Burke was preparing his broadside during 1790, and finally published it in November 1790[332]. He was answered by Tom Paine in March 1791 with his *Rights of Man*. Burke then followed in August 1791 with *An Appeal from the New to the Old Whigs*[333], which clearly distanced him from the Foxites in the Opposition and opened the way for a rapprochement between some at least of the Rockingham Party and the government. The second part of the *Rights of Man* came out in February 1792, gaining a circulation that exceeded even that of the first part.

The flight of the French royal family in June 1791 and the advent of the more radical Legislative Assembly in September had done nothing to shift Pitt in his determination to stay aloof from events in France. However, Pitt was having to face a more radical domestic agenda. Political debate, fired by Burke and Paine, intensified during 1792. Charles Grey helped to establish the Association of the Friends of the People in April 1792 as focus for the

---

[330] The Corporation Act (1661) required all members of Municipal Corporations to be communicants. The Test Act (1673) required all holders of office under the Crown to be communicants.

[331] See John Ehrmann *"The Younger Pitt"* Vol 2, pp 53-73. And also E P Thompson *"The Making of the English Working Class"* pp 28-58 on the role of Dissent in challenging the establishment.

[335] *Reflections on the Revolution in France*.

[333] Walker King was closely involved in its preparation.

Parliamentary Opposition, and Robert Knight was one of its founder members[334]. Debating Societies were established in numberless country towns, and included in their membership working men and tradesmen on an unprecedented scale. People of all classes were coming together in a way they wouldn't again for nearly forty years. In May 1792 there was a Royal Proclamation against seditious meetings and writings. The reaction was beginning in earnest[335].

The Warwick Bye-Election of 1792

This was the climate against which the Warwick bye-election of 1792 was played out. As an ancient borough, Warwick had returned two members to Parliament since earliest times[336]. By the end of the 17th century there was a convention that the Corporation and the Castle returned one member each. However, at the 1774 election, Lord Warwick brought in both his brothers. In so doing he over-reached himself. A movement started in the town to get its own candidate back. At the next election, in 1780, the town's candidate topped the poll, much to Lord Warwick's chagrin. However, the radical moment passed and in the more conservative climate of 1790 Lord Warwick was again able to appoint both candidates. The gentlemen of the Corporation were firmly behind Mr Pitt and they didn't even bother with an election.

In October 1791, Maj. Henry Gage, one of the members for Warwick, succeeded an uncle in his peerage and so gave up his

---

[334] Charles Grey (1764-1845) was the future Lord Grey of the Reform Bill. He was emerging as one of the leaders of the younger generation of Foxites, though this initiative had Fox's only half-hearted support and it certainly didn't get the support of the Foxite party.

[335] Paine was arrested but his trial was postponed to December, by which time he had fled to France. He had been granted French citizenship in August, and took up the seat he had been given in the National Assembly. In June 1792 the order was given to build new barracks for cavalry in the major towns, including Birmingham and Coventry. These were all completed by October.

[336] For this section, see *Victoria County History of Warwickshire*, Vol 8. Styles "*The Corporation of Warwick*", and T Kemp & A B Beavan "*List of Members of Parliament for Warwick*"

seat. A bye-election was held on 18 January 1792. Lord Warwick sold his interest to Hon. George Villiers, a younger son of Lord Clarendon, and a strong supporter of the ministry. However, John Tomes[337], a politically active townsman, came forward and recruited Robert Knight as the independent candidate. Knight was defeated by 231 votes to 160. He had the support of the voting gentry (by 29 to 19) but the remaining voters were won over by the Castle interest, Villiers family money and the influence of the ministry. Knight challenged the qualifications of the many electors, but judgement was given against him and the electorate was confirmed as all the ratepayers of Warwick (resident and non-resident). It had been a brave try, and Knight had cut his political teeth. He would certainly have thereby come to the notice of Dr Parr[338], and it may have been through Parr that he was introduced to Horne Tooke – who was to remain a close friend. Knight was now known as a Foxite Whig. In the enemies eyes he would have been known as a Jacobin.

The diaries of William Godwin show Robert Knight moving in radical circles after this bye-election. In September 1792 Godwin recorded that he "dined at Holcroft's with Mr & Mrs Knight". Thomas Holcroft was an actor and writer who was an early sympathizer with the aims of the Revolution. He had been involved in the publication of Paine's *Rights of Man* in 1791. The following year, he joined the

---

[337] John Tomes (1760-1844), MP for Warwick 1826-31. His son-in-law, William Collins, sat as MP for Warwick 1837-52

[338] Dr Samuel Parr (1747-1825), Headmaster of Norwich Grammar School 1778-85 and from 1783 vicar of Hatton, near Warwick. When the Bishop of St Asaph died in December 1788, it was said that only the King's recovery prevented his rise to the bench. He was a strong supporter of C.J. Fox. He hung Burke's portrait upside down, and regarded Britain's entry into the war as a disturbance of the peace of Europe. He hoped for Napoleon's triumph at Waterloo (as did Robert Knight). In 1802 Sir Francis Burdett offered him the living of Grafham, in Huntingdonshire, writing 'I believe that I cannot do anything more pleasing to his friends, Mr Fox, Mr Sheridan, and Mr Knight and I desire you, Sir, to consider yourself obliged to them only,' A pupil and close friend of Dr Parr's was Rev John Bartlam (1770-1824) who Robert Knight presented to the parish of Studley in 1800. There is a long obituary of Bartlam in the Gentleman's Magazine.

Society for Constitutional Information, which had been founded
some years before by Major John Cartwright, and in which Horne
Tooke was a leading light. In March 1793 Robert Knight was again
with Godwin at dinner with the Holcrofts. This was the year that
Godwin published his *Political Justice*, which proved popular and
offered a middle way of understanding the French Revolution,
between that of Burke and Paine. His novel, *Caleb Williams,* came
out the following year.

The Warwick bye-election of 1792 was recalled in November 1837,
at the dinner to commiserate with Bolton King on his defeat at the
election called on Queen Victoria's accession. Robert Knight's
health was proposed by the Chairman, Joseph Sanders, as "a
gentleman of the olden times, the counterpart of Mr Tomes, their
political connection commenced with this borough". Those times
were commonly recalled in the 1830's. The years in between had
been difficult, but the days of the early 1790's were bathed in a rosy
glow[339].

The Hard Years, 1792-1802
The radicals were gaining ground and were open to calls from
France for solidarity in the face of the reactionary forces. The bad
harvest of 1792 had an unsettling effect and in the winter of 1792-3
Pitt feared some kind of uprising more than at any other time. The
declaration of war in February 1793 was caused by fears for the
independence of the Low Countries, but no one much desired it.
For Fox and his followers, it was an unnecessary war, fought only
because it suited George III and Pitt in their desire to establish a
European style despotism here. Though Pitt claimed that he was
not intent on restoring the Bourbons, it still seemed wrong to Fox
and his friends for Britain to ally herself with the autocratic powers
of Russia and Austria against revolutionary France.

The repressive measures taken by the government and the refusal
to countenance any kind of parliamentary reform continued to

---

[339] The battle for Warwick didn't end in 1792.

rankle and resistance built up. In November and December 1793 a British Convention was assembled at Edinburgh that called for universal male suffrage. The SCI started rooting for a Convention and dropped its concern for parliamentary reform. This was further than many previous supporters wanted to go and some more moderate reformers began to draw back. Robert Knight was among those who resigned from the 'Friends of the People' in April 1794. In May 1794, Thomas Holcroft, Thomas Hardy[340], John Thelwall[341] and Horne Tooke[342] were all arrested and the last three brought to trial. The prosecutions failed, but it felt bad. People were leaving for France or the United States. The future for liberal England looked bleak.

Prices were rising fast and harvests continued bad. There were food shortages, felt most acutely by the very poor. By the autumn of 1795 there was again rising discontent. The Habeas Corpus Act, suspended in May 1794 but lifted in June 1795, was suspended once more. A Treasonable Practices Act was introduced and a Seditious Meetings and Assemblies Act - the notorious "Two Acts". It was Pitt's "Reign of Terror". And the war dragged on. The problem was now no longer the revolutionaries in Paris. The establishment of the Directory in November 1795 meant that

---

[340] Thomas Hardy (ca 1750-p.1815), a Scottish shoemaker who came south as a young man, and was fired for politics during the American War after reading Dr Richard Price's pamphlet "Observations on the Nature of Civil Liberty". The "founding genius" of the London Corresponding Society in January 1792, retired from active politics after the trial, but was honoured into old age as one of the earliest of the decent, upright working men to ask for the right to be heard in government.

[341] John Thelwall (1764-1834) a popular orator and member of the LCS. Self-educated, he was known for his lectures on the grievances of the poor. However the Two Acts of December 1795 brought his campaigning career to an end and he retired into private life.

[342] Rev John Horne Tooke (1736-1812), son of a fairly prosperous market trader in London, was ordained after Cambridge, but after getting involved in politics during the Wilkes troubles, didn't look back. Fell out with Wilkes in 1771 and was never a favourite with Fox. Best known for his hospitable home in Wimbledon after his retirement.

France was no longer revolutionary. Instead the problem was French arms and their threat to English interests - especially with the advent of Napoleon.

In 1796, came another General Election. The mood was sombre. There were few contests. Fox and the radicals were quiet. In Warwick, the Earl's candidates were unopposed[343]. The Administration was strengthened, but it was for them an empty victory. Early in 1797, according to Dr Parr's diary, a meeting of the county of Warwick 'for the purpose of obtaining a change of men and measures' was convened, under Robert Knight's authority as High Sheriff. It was so well attended that it had to move from the Shire Hall to the race course. A petition to the King, stating the causes of complaint and praying for the dismissal of ministers, was moved by Sir John Throckmorton[344], seconded by Bertie Greatheed and supported by other gentlemen 'and particularly by Sir Francis Burdett who, on that occasion, almost for the first time assumed that public character, which he has since sustained, with so much honour to himself, and so much benefit to his country.'

---

[343] Dr Samuel Parr, was working hard to bring in an independent. A wealthy East Indian man and banker, with local connections - Charles Mills - came forward in 1802 as "freedom's darling son" and forced Mr Gaussen, one of the sitting candidates, to withdraw. From then on Mills and the Castle shared the borough – though Mills wasn't noticeably active, or even very radical. He sat until his death in 1826. Mills was the uncle of Arthur Mills, who came forward as a candidate for the constituency in a crowded field at the General Election of 1847 - citing "an earlier parliamentary connection with Warwick". He got his candidature in a day before Bolton King. Sir Charles Douglas (Peelite) and William Collins (Liberal) were the successful candidates. Arthur Mills withdrew before the poll, followed by Bolton King. The following year Mills married the daughter of Gladstone's great friend, Sir Thomas Dyke Acland, and went on to become MP for Exeter and a member of Gladstone's circle.

[344] Sir John Throckmorton, of Coughton (1753-1819) was a founder of the Catholic Committee in 1782, a leading member of the Cisalpine party and an advanced Whig. Said in the *History of Parliament* to have been 'a headstrong wilful man'. Bertie Greatheed, of Guy's Cliffe (1759-1826) was a gentleman poet and slave-owner – it seems that you could believe in liberty and yet own slaves.

Then, in April 1797, Austria signed a separate peace with France - leaving Britain alone. Pitt's Reign of Terror now intensified, to reach its peak during the invasion scares and arrests of February - May 1798. More people were escaping to France, rather than risk languishing in one of Pitt's unpleasant prisons. In July 1799 the Combinations Act was passed into law, "for the more effectual Suppression of Societies established for Seditious and Treasonable Purposes; and for better preventing Treasonable and Seditious Practices". The London Corresponding Society had to be disbanded and almost any debate became illegal.

The Knight family in France - 1800
The mystery is that little Henry Knight died in France on 14 November 1800 What were the Knight family doing in France in 1800, when Britain and France were at war? The Austrians had been defeated at Marengo in June 1800 and the British government was in disarray. Pitt was in poor health and losing his grip on events. There were some abortive talks on a naval armistice in the autumn, but a further Austrian defeat at Hohenlinden in December meant that Austria was out of the war. Russia, Denmark, Sweden and Prussia had formed the Armed Neutrality and Russia was treating for an alliance with France. By the spring of 1801 peace negotiations were under way, but the peace was not concluded until a year later.

The Knights has been at Barrells in May 1795 for young Henry Knight's baptism, and Robert Knight served as High Sheriff for Warwickshire in 1797-8. In the diary of William Godwin, there are references to meetings with Knight as late as the end of January 1800, but silence thereafter. In October 1793, all English people in France had been interned. In February 1795, there was a general gaol delivery, but those let out of prison were not allowed back to England. English people were in France and continued to travel to and from France, but it was dangerous. Had the family gone to France some time in 1800, because Robert Knight could no longer live with political conditions in England? Did he leave because he risked prosecution? Were they interned in France? Were they allowed home on compassionate grounds? Or was the visit something to do with Count Duroure, whose political views were far from that of Napoleon and who seems to have left France during 1800 to escape arrest? And why did the Portmans go too?[345] It's difficult to see why France under the Consulate should have been an attractive proposition – yet Robert Knight himself seems to have remained sympathetic to the French cause.

The Middlesex election of 1802

Times were however changing. There had always been unease about the repression. Pitt himself disliked the way his government was being characterised, and he had never been set against Parliamentary Reform. In May 1797, Charles Grey had brought in a motion for reform and people were surprised by the supporting vote. Wyvill and Cartwright were stirring again, with a view to the next General Election.

In the General Election of July 1802 Sir Francis Burdett was invited to stand as candidate for Middlesex. Burdett had entered parliament in 1796 and had consistently been a critic of Pitt's oppressive policies, of the continuing restrictions on Roman Catholics and of the Government's actions in Ireland. He had however come to prominence through his campaign against the conditions in which mutineers and civil offenders were kept in Cold Bath Fields Prison. His eloquence had very effectively embarrassed the Government and was the reason for the invitation from the Middlesex electors in 1802. It was a poisoned chalice in some ways. There were huge disturbances and many challenges after the results were declared. In 1804 there had to be a re-run of the

---

[345] In her declaration on the later Henry Knight's illegitimacy, dated 20 April 1843, Mrs Portman (Frances Knight's sister) said that she had been present at the death of this little Henry Knight. Yet from what little evidence there is, her husband (who died young, aged 35) was apolitical. With an income of £13,000 a year, besides his property in London, he maybe had enough to do. I have always suspected that Jane Austen modelled Mr Darcy on him – and the Bennett girls on the Dormer sisters.

election, but his opponent wasn't confirmed as the successful candidate until February 1806, a few months before the end of the Parliamentary session.

Robert Knight was active in this Middlesex election. There is a letter dated 18 July 1804 to Burdett from his agent saying that "Mr Knight of Grosvenor Square is the Agent for the triumphal decorations, State Coach, Horse Trappings etc etc". In years to come Knight counted himself among Burdett's oldest friends. Clearly their friendship, which had begun at Horne Tooke's house in Wimbledon during the 1790s, was strengthened during these political campaigns.

Pitt died in January 1806 and was succeeded by Lord Grenville, with Fox as Secretary of State. It was a strange coalition, but its purpose was to make peace. For both parties this seemed to be the best way to curb the power of the King and to disentangle Britain from its despotic allies in Europe. Maybe it was this hope and the accession of Charles James Fox to office after over twenty years of opposition that persuaded Robert Knight to stand for parliament. Maybe he had tried before and failed to get a seat. In any event, at the General Election of November 1806 Robert Knight entered Parliament for the first time as M. P. for Wootton Bassett[346]. It was

---

[346] This was a seat in the gift of Lord Bolingbroke, so there was a family link and they may have known each other in earlier years. George St John had fallen in love with his tutor's daughter in 1780 and married her in 1783. By 1787 they had three children and George had succeeded to the title and a small income. As Lord Bolingbroke he then fell in love with his half-sister, Mary Beauclerk, by whom he had four children before leaving her in 1794 for a German lady - by whom he had nine more children - some born before marriage and some afterwards. They lived in the United States. In the summer of 1806, after the death of his first wife (who had been living at Lydiard in great poverty), Lord Bolingbroke returned to England from America and settled at Lydiard. His uncle and former guardian, General St John (the son of Lord Catherlough's friend, and Lady Luxborough's nephew), seems to have managed the family interest. He was Colonel of the 36th Foot and a member of the royal household until his death in 1818 aged 80. The General sat for Wootton Bassett himself from 1761-84 and again from July - December 1802.

a short-lived session. Fox had died in September and Grenville
resigned in March over Catholic emancipation. He was succeeded
by a conservative coalition under the nominal leadership of the
Duke of Portland, but in fact dominated by Canning, Perceval and
Castlereagh. They went to the country again in May 1807 to the cry
of Church and King and "No Popery" and triumphed. It was not a
cry with which Robert Knight could sympathise. Sir John Murray,
the Tory candidate, captured the Wootton Bassett seat. The brief
honeymoon was over.

The Mary Anne Clarke Scandal

Robert Knight may not have had great success in his parliamentary
career, but Sir Francis Burdett was going from strength to strength.
He lost the Middlesex seat at the 1806 General Election, but in May
1807 he was triumphantly returned for Westminster - the old seat
of Charles James Fox. He was to hold Westminster for thirty years.
He continued to harry the government and made himself deeply
unpopular.

Then, on 20 January 1809, a radical M. P.[347] gave notice that he
would introduce a motion "relative to the conduct of the Duke of
York". Mary Anne Clarke had been dropped as the mistress of Duke
of York (the Commander-in-Chief) and was not happy. She was now
prepared to say that she had been selling commissions in the Army
with his full knowledge and approbation. It was a move that
delighted the radicals, but deeply embarrassed the government,
already reeling from defeats in Spain. On 27 January Wardle
brought his motion, citing six cases. The second was the case of Lt
Col Henry Knight, Robert's younger brother. The House decided to
go into committee and met on 1st February. The Knight case was
the first to be heard, and Robert himself was called to give
evidence. The previous witness, Dr Andrew Thynne, described as a
physician to Mrs Clarke and to Mrs Knight, testified that he had
been approached by Robert Knight and asked to take a message to
Mrs Clarke. Mr Knight desired an exchange for his brother and

---

[347] Mr Wardle, the Member for Okehampton

£200 was the price mentioned. In his evidence, Robert Knight agreed with Dr Thynne's evidence and said that he had visited Mrs Clarke in September 1805 in order to thank her, and that she had entreated her to keep the matter a secret from the Duke. He further said that "my brother was in a very bad state of health at the time and I was very desirous that he should exchange to the infantry, for the purpose of going on half-pay, that he might recover his health. I believe he had served as long as any man in the country of his age and suffered by it; he had served 23 years, and I believe he has been in every battle during the French Revolution, and it was my anxiety to serve him, that has placed me in this distressing and painful situation". Robert was anxious to affirm that the Duke had no knowledge of the transaction, although Mrs Clarke claimed that he did.

On 19 March the government managed to carry a motion negativing Wardle's motion, but the damage was done and the Duke resigned the next day. It was embarrassing for Sir Francis Burdett. As a radical leader, he should have been in the thick of it. In fact, he stayed away - apparently laid low by gout. People were not slow to question this and to wonder, if his friend had been so involved with Mrs Clarke, maybe he had been too. However, Burdett bounced back. On 15 June he introduced the first serious motion for a measure of Parliamentary reform since 1787. In 1810, on being accused of bringing the House of Commons into disrepute he had the distinction of being imprisoned in the Tower for some two months[348].

The Congress of Vienna

---

[348] Gale Jones, an apothecary, had posted broadsheets objecting to the Government's whitewash of their bungling of the Walcheron expedition. He was arrested and Burdett wrote an open letter of protest to his constituents. Folkestone, Romilly and Whitbread stood by him, but on the motion of Sir Thomas Lethbridge he was committed to the Tower - though not before the Sergeant at Arms had to break into his house. There was much rioting, and Sir Thomas had his windows broken. Nice to think I descend from Lord Folkestone, Sir Thomas and Burdett's mate.

Robert Knight got back into Parliament at a bye-election in Wootton Bassett in 1811, but again his tenure was short-lived. A local barrister, James Kibblewhite, had been building up an interest in the borough. He had got his own candidate in – ousting the Hyde family – at the 1808 election[349]. That candidate was expelled from the house in March 1812 for embezzlement, so Kibblewhite decided to stand himself. At the General Election of October 1812 Kibblewhite was in and Knight was out.

Great things were happening in Europe. In June 1812 Napoleon invaded Russia and reached Moscow. But the Russians would not give in, and the Grand Army was forced to retreat. A fragment returned to France. Throughout 1813 his regime was tottering, but Napoleon could not bring himself to compromise. In the end, in March 1814, the Allies entered Paris and a few days later Napoleon abdicated. On 3 May 1814 Louis XVIII entered Paris. Pitt had always argued that the war was not being fought to restore the Bourbons, but here we were doing just that – in close alliance with the despotic governments of Russia, Prussia and Austria. It was a dark day for Robert Knight and his friends. When Napoleon landed in March 1815, there were hopes that something could be saved from the wreckage of revolution. The Foxite Whigs and the Radicals argued that there was no need for Britain to interfere with the internal arrangements of France. The Government of Lord Liverpool however was not prepared to compromise. Wellington gathered his army. Robert Knight told a friend that if Napoleon was defeated he would leave England for America. Waterloo was fought in June 1815, and Napoleon was defeated. But Robert Knight stayed put!

In Permanent Opposition? 1815-1822

It was a depressing time. The harvests were consistently bad and food prices were high. Reaction was everywhere - at home and abroad. Lord Liverpool's government was becoming increasingly paranoid. The Home Secretary, Lord Sidmouth, was introducing

---

[349] He apparently paid £4000 for the seat.

legislation fit to rival Pitt's during his Reign of Terror. The Habeas Corpus Act was suspended in March 1817. Political Unions mushroomed to press for Reform, and in August 1819 the regular cavalry were called in to disperse a crowd of 80,000 that had gathered to hear Henry "Orator" Hunt in Manchester. This was the famous "Peterloo Massacre". Then came the Six Acts of 1819-20, which included increased taxation on cheap publications[350].

It seemed that England had forgotten her old commitment to freedom and democracy. The French Revolution had resulted in an unbending commitment to "the old constitution" that has lasted twenty years. It had been a long repression, without – as far as the Foxite Opposition were concerned – any real justification. And now even the Foxites were losing their voice. By the time of Napoleon's fall, they were led by Lord Grey who preferred to spend his time at home in Northumberland and believed that no change was likely during his lifetime. The real opposition was coming from the Radicals – known as "The Mountain"[351] – amongst whom were Burdett, Hobhouse[352] and Folkstone[353]. Without them, it seemed, Great Britain would be just like any other continental despotism.

---

[350] Cobbett's "Tuppenny Trash" was one the publications that went to the wall as a result of these Acts. It had been a cheap edition of his Political Register that introduced political issues to the working man - just what Liverpool's government didn't want.

[351] Ironically named after the party of Robespierre in the National Convention.

[352] John Cam Hobhouse (1786-1852), cr Lord Broughton. He was a friend of Byron's at Cambridge and an early supporter of Sir Francis Burdett. In 1814, Hobhouse recorded in his journal a dinner he enjoyed with Burdett, Kinnaird, Lord Byron and Robert Knight. He was Secretary at War in Lord Grey's government, but out of sympathy with what he regarded as the fudging of the Whig grandees and resigned in May 1833.

[353] William Pleydell-Bouverie (1779-1869), Viscount Folkestone & (1828) 3rd Earl of Radnor. The Bouveries were part of the Foxite Whig connection and Folkestone took that tradition into a later generation of radical opposition. In 1800 he had married Lady Catherine Pelham-Clinton, heiress of the Pelhams, who ran things in the reign of George II. Their only surviving child married General Buckley, and was my great-great-grandmother.

Burdett was not in sympathy with Hunt and the other wilder radicals, and in 1817 he broke with Cobbett. However, he continued to support the radical cause in parliament and he remained M P for Westminster with full radical support. After the suicide of Sir Samuel Romilly in November 1818, Burdett supported Hobhouse for the other Westminster seat, but the Whigs put forward William Lamb - who won. This event encouraged Burdett to rethink his political loyalties. He saw the Opposition Whigs as a whole lot of grandees whose main concern was to dominate government in the narrow interest of the landed aristocracy. That was their purpose in 1819 and to Burdett's thinking that had been their interest since 1688. He had no sympathy with the new style radicals, but he did care about the country gentlemen. This, he believed, linked him to Lord Bolingbroke and the Tories of Queen Anne's time. In July 1819 he said, "The principles of those who were called Tories in the reign of Queen Anne forms the substance of my political creed". It didn't mean that he was any less soft on the repression and reaction of Lord Liverpool's Government. He continued to push for Parliamentary reform and for Catholic emancipation. He was for a time an intimate of Daniel O'Connell, though he later revised his opinion. But he was not a Whig. After the Peterloo massacre of 1819 he faced a Government prosecution, and he was a staunch ally of Queen Caroline.

It was the beginning of a rethink in politics. Since the middle of the 18th century everyone in Parliament was a variety of Whig. Pitt always regarded himself as a Whig, and Lord Liverpool was in the same tradition. Every appeal was to the principles of 1688 – whether it was made by Fox, Burke or Pitt. Now however some people were beginning to question the events of 1688. For Sir Francis Burdett, the so-called "Glorious Revolution" of 1688 was the beginning of an aristocratic conspiracy, when the ordinary landed gentleman was excluded from politics and when the monarchy was taken over by the aristocracy. For Burdett, the first two Georges had been little better than Venetian doges. The balance of the constitution had been upset and what was now needed was for the aristocracy to hand back to the monarchy and the people some of the powers it had taken to itself during the last hundred years and more. His argument was very similar to that of the Rockingham Whigs in the late 1750's and early 1760's, before they had become obsessed with the power politics of King George III. They were arguments that held a good deal of truth and they were to be influential among those who were seeking to re-discover a Reforming Spirit in politics that was distinct from the "first principles" style radicalism of Paine and Bentham.

The Run up to Reform, 1822-31
Robert Knight was out of the House until he purchased the pocket borough of Rye at a bye-election in 1823[354]. He failed to find a seat at the General Election of 1826, but that December came in for Wallingford at a bye election. He then sat continuously until the dissolution of 1832, voting steadily with the Opposition[355]. At long last the political climate seemed to be changing. In 1820 a military coup d'état in Spain overthrew the absolutist regime of Ferdinand VII that the Allies had imposed in 1814, and restored the Constitution that Napoleon had proclaimed in 1812. Ferdinand appealed for help and in 1822 the French invaded. The Liberal leaders were rounded up and shot and British opinion was finally outraged in the Liberal cause. In August 1822 Lord Castlereagh, the Foreign Secretary, committed suicide. He had dominated the government for twelve years and was thought (probably unjustly) to have worked too closely with the despotic European powers. His successor, George Canning, marked a definite change. From now on Britain was to detach itself from the reactionary powers. The Navy was sent to protect the revolutionaries of Spanish South America from Ferdinand VII, and troops were sent to Portugal to

---

[354] He contested the Clive pocket borough of Bishop's Castle at the General Election of 1820 with his friend, Douglas Kinnaird. The result was challenged and the other two candidates (both Clive family supporters) were declared elected. It was a noble attempt to challenge the Clive interest in Bishop's Castle.
[355] He sat for Rye until the dissolution of 1826, and then was returned for Wallingford in 1826, 1830 & 1831. At the last two elections he was unopposed. They were both of course pocket boroughs.

defend the constitutional monarchy of Queen Maria da Gloria against a Spanish inspired attack. It was the beginning of the liberal, second phase of Lord Liverpool's long administration.

Then, with Lord Liverpool's stroke in February 1827, the Government split. In April, Canning took over as Prime Minister, but Wellington, Eldon & Peel resigned. Canning constructed his government with some help from the Whigs - notably William Lamb - and even Burdett was sympathetic. Burdett thought Canning might turn into the sort of Tory of which he approved - someone to speak for the country, and to save the King. However, in August 1827, Canning died, to be succeeded by Lord Goderich[356]. This didn't work - mainly due to the weakness of Goderich' leadership - and in January 1828 the Duke of Wellington came in with Canningite support. This shaky alliance only lasted until May, when the Canningites left. Still, Wellington battled on until in April 1829 (in the face of the threat of all out revolt in Ireland) he - and George IV - finally accepted Catholic Emancipation. Then, on 26 June 1830, George IV died and a few weeks later Charles X of France lost his throne. These were hopeful signs. At the county and borough elections held at Warwick in August 1830, the Birmingham Political Union was out in force. Everyone was now expecting a generally agreed and moderate programme of Parliamentary Reform until at the beginning of November Wellington unaccountably declared himself against anything[357]. The Canningites and Whigs

---

[356] Sir Frederick Robinson Bt (1782-1859) cr April 1827 Viscount Goderich & (1833) Marquess of Ripon. He was a successful Chancellor of the Exchequer in 1822-7. He served under Canning and was eventually known as a Canningite. As such he served under Lord Grey, but with increasing unhappiness. Resigned in May 1834 with Sir James Graham and Lord Stanley. In December 1837 he finally joined Peel and served under him in 1841-7. He remained a loyal Peelite until his death.

[357] It was an attempt to rally the High Tories to him after the trauma of Catholic Emancipation, but it backfired badly.. He did not carry all his colleagues with him. His Foreign Secretary, Lord Aberdeen (1784-1860) who, as a ward of William Pitt's, was recognised as the guardian of the Pittite flame, believed some measure was necessary.

immediately united to defeat him, and Lord Grey came in at the head of a Whig-Canningite administration, committed to a much more radical programme of Parliamentary Reform than anything the Duke of Wellington would have countenanced.

The Upheavals of 1830-1832

In January 1831 the Mayor of Warwick called together a meeting of burgesses and townsfolk to petition the Government for Reform. This was the prelude to Lord John Russell's introduction of his measure in the Commons on 1st March. Then the Mayor called together an even bigger meeting, to which the gentlemen of the county were invited, to take place at Warwick Race Course on 4th April. This was a huge event[358], with people of all classes gathering in support of the Government measure. Robert Knight was among those who spoke and the Warwick Advertiser reported, "in the concluding part of his speech he regretted that his friend Sir Francis Burdett had been prevented by a severe attack of gout from attending the meeting"[359]. By that time, Sir Charles Greville[360], had voted against the second reading of the Bill and had declared himself "unalterably opposed to it" in a letter to Advertiser. Three days after the Race Course meeting, Knight's son-in-law, Bolton King, had declared his readiness to stand as a Reform candidate, should an election be called.

Parliament was duly dissolved on 22 April. When Robert's son-in-law, Bolton King, was elected as M.P. for Warwick shortly afterwards, he must have enjoyed the triumph. Forty years on, the earlier reverse was avenged and Lord Warwick's brother was turned out of his seat. He himself was unopposed at Wallingford.

---

[358] It was said that 10,000-12,000 people were there.

[359] The gout didn't prevent Sir Francis from presenting his friend to the new King, William IV, on 13 April.

[360] Maj. Gen. Hon. Sir Charles Greville (1780-1836), younger son of the 2nd Earl of Warwick, M P for Warwick 1815-31, 1832-3 & 1835-6. He was unmarried, and both his sisters – Charlotte & Louisa – were unmarried too.

The Whigs in Office

The Radicals were for the most part united behind Lord Grey in the campaign for the Reform Bill, so that Burdett and Knight were quite happy to stand four square behind the Government in the upheavals caused by the Lords' rejection of the Bill in October 1831. The King was now under great pressure to create enough peers to enable the Bill to be passed, and there is a tradition that Robert Knight refused to let his name go forward lest his title should be claimed by his wife's son[361]. On 7th May 1832 the Political Union called a great meeting at Birmingham in support of the Bill that was attended by Robert Knight and his elder daughter, and by his younger daughter and her husband. That night the Lords postponed a decision to disenfranchise the rotten boroughs. Lord Grey thereupon asked the King to make enough new peers to pass the Bill. The King refused and on 9th May the Government resigned. The Duke of Wellington thereupon attempted to construct an alternative government that might bring in a compromise Bill, but by 18th May he had to admit failure. Lord Grey came in again. On 4th June, the Lords passed the Bill and three days later the King gave his consent. It had been a traumatic time.

Robert Knight's seat at Wallingford was one of those which was disenfranchised and – aged 64 – he did not stand again. He now focused his interest entirely on affairs in Warwick where Sir Charles Greville had in October announced his intention of contesting the seat under the new franchise. In the country as a whole the Whig-Radical alliance swept the board. In Warwick though it was a different story. There was a bitter and divisive battle that resulted in the army being called in to keep the peace. The result – when order was restored – was that Sir Charles came in at the top of the poll, and John Tomes had to concede in order to leave the field free for Bolton King. There were allegations of misconduct that resulted in Sir Charles being suspended, and the arguments went on until the dissolution of December 1834.

---

[361] See later.

The Whig-Radical alliance didn't long survive the passage of the Bill. After June 1832 there was no need for the two groups to stand together and after the landslide of December 1832 they didn't. The Radicals looked again at Lord Grey and saw a tired old man unready for any real change. The supporters of Lord Grey looked at the Radicals and saw untidy and uncouth middle class people with whom they preferred not to deal. Sir Francis Burdett continued with his own line of thinking, and was now making disciples for a new generation. The chief of these was the young Benjamin Disraeli.

Disraeli first started looking for a career in politics in early 1832, soon after his 27th birthday. He then described himself as a Radical and argued for the secret ballot, triennial parliaments and a greater economy in government expenditure. It was a perfectly reasonable platform. He had been a man about town in the late 20's and two of his mates then – Count d'Orsay[362] and Bulwer Lytton[363] – also called themselves Radicals. He didn't succeed in High Wycombe – either at the bye-election in June 1832 or at the General Election in December. In fact, he didn't get into Parliament until 1837, when he came in for Maidstone. By then he had developed an

---

[362] Alfred, Count d'Orsay. A favourite of Lord Blessington and of his second wife. Lord Blessington settled his fortune on whichever of his daughters d'Orsay married. D'Orsay married the 15 year old Harriet in 1827, but in fact was her stepmother's lover. When Lord Blessington died in 1829, D'Orsay set up house with Lady Blessington (while Harriet left him and contested her father's will). Through the 1830's their house at Seamore Place was a centre of slightly risky fashion. The two fled to France in 1849 to escape their creditors and Lady Blessington died there soon after. D'Orsay was a lifelong friend of Disraeli's. He died in 1852 - just after he had been able to congratulate Disraeli on becoming Leader of the Party in the Commons and Chancellor of the Exchequer in Lord Derby's short-lived government.

[363] Edward Bulwer (1803-1873), cr Bart 1838, Bulwer-Lytton 1843 (on succeeding to his mother's estate at Knebworth), cr Lord Lytton 1866. M P from 1831 as a Whig, but fell out with Lord John Russell over the Corn Laws and sat from 1852-66 as a Conservative. Secretary for the Colonies in 1858. Known best as a popular novelist. His son entered the diplomatic service, was Viceroy of India 1875-80, and was created an Earl.

understanding of politics very similar to Burdett's, which he expounded in his "Vindication of the English Constitution" which was published in December 1835. The aristocratic Whigs had unbalanced the constitution by engrossing all power to themselves. What was needed was a national party that defended the rights of the crown and of the Church and that preserved the interests of agriculture.

It was a time of very great fluidity in politics. Burdett himself had long given up on Lord Grey's government and was quite happy when the King asked the Duke of Wellington to accept interim responsibility for the government when Melbourne resigned in November 1835. He felt that the old Administration had become simply "a heterogeneous mix of Whigs, Radicals and O'Connell's tail". He was sad when Melbourne came back in, because Melbourne was now Prime Minister by courtesy of Daniel O'Connell, and Burdett couldn't stand O'Connell. He made his views very public, and in April 1837 he was asked to resign by his Westminster constituency. He did so, fought the bye-election as a Tory, and won[364].

I think Robert Knight did not follow Burdett into Peel's new party[365]. In January 1836 he sat down at a great Reform dinner in

---

[364] His radical opponent was J.T. Leader, and Leader was given support by William Collins of Warwick. A few weeks before Collins had won a bye-election in Warwick and he now sat as the colleague of Robert Knight's son-in-law. There was bad blood between the two of them, and King realised that his days as a Warwick MP were numbered.
"Burdett belonged to the old England, of which agriculture, the rearing of stock, and country life were the distinctive features. He had a profound distrust of fund-holders, stock jobbers and international financiers. His main passion was the hunting of the fox with the Quorn or elsewhere". M W Patterson "Sir Francis Burdett and his Times" 1931
[365] Though he remained a close friend. J C Hobhouse recorded in his diary for 4 March 1841, 'Burdett had written to tell me that all his old friends were coming to dine with him on March 4th and asked me to meet them. I went very gladly, and met [Edward Bolton] Clive and Lord Sudeley and his daughter, Robert Knight and his daughter. [Edward Wynne] Pendarves, one of his oldest friends, was also

Birmingham with Daniel O'Connell, Joseph Hume, the luminaries of the Birmingham Political Union and William Collins of Warwick. In September 1836 he was prominent at the meeting to establish an "Association of Electors in the Southern Division in the Liberal Interest". A Conservative Association for the Southern Division had been set up in May 1835, so this was the Liberal response. Already "Conservative" and "Liberal" were the titles used to describe the new alignments in politics. At the testimonial dinner given in November 1837, in reply to the toast to his father-in-law, Bolton King said, "no man is more anxious for the independence and the prosperity of the liberal interest in Warwick". After the defection of Sir Francis Burdett, this probably needed saying. Bolton King significantly didn't identify the defence of "the liberal interest" with the Whigs – let alone with Lord Melbourne's administration. He himself went on to flirt with the party of Protection and then settled down very happily as a supporter of that strong Canningite, Lord Palmerston. He died faithful to Gladstone's Liberal Party, but not enthusiastic. His career is easier to understand when one understands better the career of Robert Knight.

Private Life

When the family returned from France in late 1800 or early 1801, Robert Knight set about finding a new London house. Some time in 1801 he decided to take over a lease on 44 Grosvenor Square from the Dowager Lady Pembroke. Lady Pembroke had taken the house in 1799 and had commissioned Sir John Soane to make some alterations. These were not in fact carried out, and Knight took up the work with same architect, spending a good deal more on his alterations than he had on buying the lease. He was still inspecting drawings in the spring of 1803, and Soane continued to do work on the house until 1820. Grosvenor Square remained Robert's home for the rest of his life, and he died there. He did go down to the country, but the impression is of a man more at home in London[366].

---

there.'

[366] His house was no. 44, later renumbered as 49. It was on the corner of Carlos Place (then Charles Street), with its entrance in Carlos Place, but its windows

It did not become a happy family home. After the birth of Henry, the heir, in May 1795, there were no further children until the child conceived in France – shortly before little Henry's death in November 1800. In the event of Robert dying without male issue, the property went to his younger brother, Colonel Knight.[367] Since the child born in the summer of 1801 was a daughter, Robert and Frances would have needed to try again, but this was not going to happen. Some time in the following year, Frances seems to have begun an affair with Lt. Col. Joseph Fuller - the brother-in-law of Robert's sister, Jane. The result of this was a separation. Frances was to have £2000 and £800 a year, but on condition that she gave up Colonel Fuller. By October 1802 it was clear that she had not given up Colonel Fuller and Robert thereupon halved the allowance and had his daughters removed from Frances' care. This resulted in his brother-in-law, Evelyn Dormer, challenging him to a duel. True to his Enlightenment principles, Robert's response was to report Evelyn to the authorities. Evelyn was arrested and served a term of imprisonment in the Marshalsea Prison. Finally, in April 1805, Robert Knight brought an action for Criminal Conversation against, Colonel Fuller[368]. The split with Frances had become acrimonious –

---

looking into the Square. He bought a reversionary lease to 1865 for £1,614. Work began in the spring of 1802, with an estimate of £2,380. In the event Knight spent £4,405 on the work. In 1856 the house was taken by Sir George Dashwood. The last tenant was E. A. Strauss, a prosperous hop and grain merchant who moved there in 1892 and stayed thirty three years. The house was then pulled down and redeveloped, but you can still get an idea of how the original house would have looked. See *Survey of London* XL *The Grosvenor Estate in Mayfair*, and the original drawings kept at the Soane Museum in Lincoln's Inn Fields.

[367] Colonel Knight was a bachelor, but only in his early thirties in 1802 and so quite likely to marry. If he died without male issue, then Robert Knight's daughters would inherit on the deaths successively of Robert Knight, of the Colonel and of Mrs Fuller.

[368] A report appeared in the Salopian Journal for 24 April 1805, and is reproduced in Arthur Carden's History. Robert Knight asked for £10,000 damages, and was awarded £7,000. In the absence of a male heir, his wife's adultery was doubly serious. Joseph Fuller joined the 2nd Foot Guards in 1792 as an Ensign and, after

and these proceedings would have made it more acrimonious – with serious repercussions later on. It is interesting that only three months later Robert Knight visited Mrs Clarke to arrange his brother's transfer on half-pay. Clearly he had it in mind to resettle the estates, with a view to his brother's marriage.

Colonel Knight married in 1808, at the time the resettlement was being arranged[369]. Robert had already consulted lawyers about the heirlooms and had an opinion in 1806 that as the heir to his deceased son, the next heir of the entail, he had now an absolute right to the heirlooms. All the pictures and silver now belonged to him, for his daughters. Next a careful review was then made of those who had any interest in the estate, but only the descendants of Lord Catherlough and Jane Davies were mentioned. Count Duroure's interests were ignored. Perhaps they were felt to be too remote. An inventory had been made of all the land held under the terms of Lord Catherlough's will, and it was then divided into two schedules. On the grounds that they were too widely spread, it was agreed that the lands in the first schedule could be sold, in order to consolidate the holdings around Barrells House itself. In the event, the Warwickshire lands from the first schedule[370] were bought by Robert Knight himself in his private capacity, while the Montgomeryshire lands[371] seemed to have been sold altogether. At Robert Knight's death, the land round Barrells had increased from 1,400 acres to over 2,500 acres, but everything else had gone.

---

service in Flanders and Ireland, rose to become Lt Col of his regiment in 1801. He was in Spain in 1808-9 and was a Major General in 1813. In 1815, he married Miranda Floyd, whose sister married Sir Robert Peel. They had an only daughter, Juliana, who inherited Highgrove House, Ruislip – which General Fuller had bought in 1834. Fuller became Colonel of the 96th Foot in 1824 and was appointed Equerry to the Duke of Cambridge in 1825. He was clearly a distinguished soldier.

[369] In the House of Lord Record Office, Local & Personal Acts, vol 29, 48 Geo III 1808 Cap 105 Cap 157. I studied it in January 1985.

[370] Amounting to 2700 acres, and including Studley, Chadshunt and Edstone, giving a rent of £2,017

[371] Amounting to 3000 acres in the parishes of Kerry and Llandinam, giving a rent of £1,796

Clearly Robert Knight was committing himself for the rest of his life to putting money aside each year to buy property from the estate for his daughters. He was also providing for the interests of his brother and two sisters[372].

In the event, everything was thrown into confusion when Frances Knight gave birth to a son in 1813. Since she and Robert were still married, the child was technically heir to the estates – and apparently Frances made it clear that she intended to assert his claim on Robert's death. To counter this, in the summer of 1814, Robert Knight and his immediate family filed a Bill, alleging criminal conversation against Lord Middlleton. It was stated that Robert had not seen his wife since 1804 and that therefore the child was not his. Various witness statements were included. The case was reported in the Annual Register of 5 December 1814. It was alleged that Lord Middleton had visited Mrs Knight at her house, Hampton Cottage, in Warwickshire and at her house in Manchester Square. But other gentlemen had also visited her and Lord Middleton's counsel argued that the evidence against him was slender and the jury agreed. Clearly adultery had taken place but there was no proof that it involved Lord Middleton.

They followed this up in January 1819 with an attempt at filing another Bill that would include further submissions to prove the case. This Bill was not allowed by Sir John Leach, the Vice Chancellor, on the grounds that the procedures were misconceived. The proper course would have been for an application to be made for permission to examine the new witnesses. I do not know if such permission was asked for – or obtained. In 1822, Robert Knight wrote a letter to the *Morning Post* stating the facts of the case and protesting this attempt to rob the family of their inheritance[373]. The

---

[372] Jane was childless and well-off, but still had a reversionary interest during her lifetime. Henrietta's husband had been killed in 1801, leaving her with five surviving children.

[373] He effectively accused Lord Middleton of being the father. Henry Willoughby, 6th Lord Willoughby (1761-1835) of Wollaton House, Nottingham was a rich and

following year, on 23 May 1823, Lord Middleton arranged for an annuity of £900 to be paid to Mrs Knight.

There is an interesting reference to Mrs Knight in the letters of Walter Savage Landor (1775-1864). He wrote 'When I was a very young man I met [Dr Parr] in London, but he conversed only with the lady of the house – Mrs Knight – a lady silly enough in speech but sillier in conduct. She was the daughter of Lord Dormer and had been educated in France. Ten years afterwards she was divorced from her husband . Her preference was for Lord Middleton, a swain of sixty five. She was then about thirty one. Her half-brother, who succeeded to the title, was my friend.'

In February 1828, Robert's younger daughter, Georgiana, married Edward Bolton King of Umberslade. This was the beginning of what seems to have been a happy marriage, with King becoming part of the family in Grosvenor Square and a close companion of his father-in-law. One of Georgiana's wedding presents from her father was a fine picture of him by John Partridge[374], which descended in the family until sold by my brother Edward. Partridge also did a companion picture of Georgiana, which hung in Grosvenor Square[375].

As the King family increased, Robert seems to have concentrated on ensuring a proper settlement for his daughters. In 1833 William Wingfield, the surviving trustee of the 1808 Settlement[376],

---

childless peer. His widow put up a monument in Wollaton church in which she describes him thus, "Inflexible integrity dignified his public life, in private he was endeared by his social qualities, his friendship was sincere and his benevolence noble without ostentation".

[374] John Partridge (1790-1872). He had studied in Italy and in 1828 settled in Brook Street, where he built up a successful business. He flourished until the mid-1840s – when Queen Victoria turned to Winterhalter. After that his popularity declined.

[375] This descended via Mrs Gooch to Catherine Bolton King and then from her to Rev Gilbert Stapleton and his daughter. Miss Stapleton left it to Arthur Carden.

[376] William Wingfield (1772-1858), of Orsett Hall, Essex, married Lady Charlotte

appointed George Digby Wingfield and Richard Baker Wingfield trustees of the manor of Chadshunt and associated lands. Three years later these lands were transferred to Robert Knight himself, and in 1838 he began the work of enlarging and improving the manor house for his own occupation[377]. Then, in June 1844, Knight settled his lands in Studley, Ipsley, Chadsunt and Gaydon for the benefit of his daughters and grandchildren. This settlement was revoked in March, 1850 and he drew up a new settlement that referred only to the Chadshunt and Gaydon lands. It would seem that Frances Elizabeth was to be left in independent enjoyment of her lands in Ipsley and Studley[378].

After his mother's death in 1842, the young Mr Knight[379] seems to have lived off borrowed money, secured against his expectations. In order to raise the money, he had to prove that he did have expectations. Accordingly, in April 1843, Lady Poulett was asked to make a declaration that he was the son of Robert and Frances Knight. Lady Poulett suggested that her mother would be the person to make such a declaration – which she duly did. Various certificates were then obtained and an attempt was made to value the estate, but it appears that Henry Charles was advised that his best course would be to seek an accommodation with the next heir to the entail, Charles Raleigh Knight. In January 1844 an agreement was reached between the two of them that, when Robert Knight

---

Digby, sister of the last Lord Digby of Sherborne Castle. On Lord Digby's death in 1856, George Digby Wingfield inherited Sherborne and started the Wingfield Digby dynasty. Richard Baker Wingfield (1801-1880) inherited Orsett.

[377] In 1839 he presented magnificently bound copies of the Book of Common Prayer and the Bible to the church at Chadshunt. They were still there when I visited in 1980.

[378] She seems to have left these to her eldest niece, Georgiana Cotton.

[379] Henry Charles Knight (1813-1887) came under the influence of Charles Simeon and was ordained, though he doesn't seem to have held an incumbency. He married a widow but had no male children – so the estate would have reverted to Colonel Knight's descendants on his death anyway! One of H.C. Knight's descendants is Canon David Marshall, one time chaplain to Archbishop George Carey.

died, £15,000 would be paid to Charles Raleigh Knight, and that the remainder would be divided equally between the two of them.

There was further family disagreement in 1842. At the time of his sister Jane's marriage to Charles Fuller in 1795, £36,000 was held for her by three trustees – Robert Knight, Richard Fuller and George Chamberlaine. Fuller was to receive the income as Jane's husband, but it was recognised as her money. In 1805, £15,517 of this stock was sold, raising £9,000, in order to buy the lease of the manor of Philberds in Berkshire (which seems already to have belonged to his father). It was said that £7,000 of this money was regarded as a loan to Fuller, on security of the leasehold estate. By 1842 it had become clear to Robert that Fuller had come to regard Philberds as his own property, to be left by him to whom he will, and he went to law to establish the legal status of the property. It was noted then that the original loan was a breach of the trust and should never have been made, but it appears that Robert failed to carry his case. In 1843, Fuller made his will leaving everything to his 'adopted son', Charles Fuller junr. It is likely that Charles Fuller junr. was his illegitimate son – and certainly a Charles Fuller was in possession of Philberds in the 1860s. I don't know what Aunt Jane thought about this, but the episode would not have improved Fuller's already low reputation in the family.

Robert Knight died of liver failure on 5 January 1855. The next day, Charles Raleigh Knight entered a formal claim to the estate. Three days later, Henry Charles made his counter-claim, and in April the agreement of 1844 was put into effect. The saleable value of the estate in February 1856 was declared to be £108,464, with an annual value of £3273[380]. The lease on Grosvenor Square was given up on Robert's death.

Old Robert Knight's executors were Col. Robert Myddelton Biddulph of Chirk Castle[381] and his brother, Sir Thomas Biddulph, Keeper of

---

[380] The Knight family papers are lodged in the Shakespeare Library & Archive.
[381] His father's family were from Ledbury, but his father, Robert Biddulph (1761-

1f.

the Privy Purse to Queen Victoria (who was in attendance on the Prince Consort when he died). They were neighbours in Powys.

1814), married Charlotte Myddleton, the heiress of Chirk Castle. Biddulph was a Foxite Whig, which explains the friendship with Robert Knight. Mary Ann Clarke claimed that she had first met Robert Knight "in company with Mr Biddulph". We met the present Myddletons (the Biddulph has been dropped) when we were in Herefordshire in the 1980's.

KING GENEALOGY

Robert King, of Gisburn[382], made his will 14 June 1571, which was proved at the York Registry 19 July 1571. He had six children,

1. Richard, who may have been the father of

(1) Richard King, of Kirkby, who was associated with Robert & Thomas King in Sir Thomas Wentworth's complaint of 1620, and may have been the father of

    1a.Richard, of Scostropp, m. Agnes, dau of N.. (bur at Kirkby Malham 12 Aug 1656) and was bur at Kirkby Malham 30 June 1656, having had issue[383],

        1b.John, of Scosthropp & later of Crakemoore, Churchwarden of Kirkby Malham in 1669, bapt. at Kirkby Malham 10 July 1631, m. at Kirkby Malham 5 Feb 1659/60 Alice Husband of Kirkby Malham (bur. there 10 Oct 1660). He m. 2ndly Elizabeth, dau of N... (d.s.p.s.[384] & bur at Kirkby Malham 9 April 1671). He is presumed to have m. 3rdly and died in 1709, having had surviving issue[385],

            1c.Thomas, bapt. at Kirkby Malham 20 April 1673

            2c.Richard, bapt. at Kirkby Malham 8 April 1677

        1b.Jane, bapt at Kirkby Malham 23 Oct 1634 & bur there 13 April 1666 unm.

        2b.Anne, bapt at Kirkby Malham 18 May 1637

    2a. William, m. and had issue,

        1b.Thomas, bapt at Kirkby Malham 23 Aug 1629

        1b.Jane, bapt at Kirkby Malham 22 April 1627

        2b.Issabell, bapt at Kirkby Malham 15 Feb 1634/5

---

[382] If he was the father of Rev Robert King of Kirkby Malham, he would have been born around 1520. Was he maybe related to – nephew? - of Richard King (1489-1519), a wealthy clothier of Kingscross, Halifax and Manningham, Bradford who was reportedly born in Gisburne – though he died in Penkridge, Staffordshire. Richard's father, John King, was born in Halifax, and he had a brother George who also lived in Halifax. Halifax at this time was famous for its flourishing cloth trade – 'one of the wonders of the Tudor age'. It was later strongly Puritan.
Richard King's daughter and heiress, Anne King (ca 1515-1571), married Thomas Lister of Westby some time before 1540 and was ancestress to the Ribblesdale Listers of Gisburne Park and the Cunliffe Listers of Manningham.
[383] With five other children who died young: William bapt 4 Oct 1622 & bur 22 March 1624/5; Thomas bapt 6 Jan 1623/4 & bur 14 April 1625; Robert bur 25 July 1629; Ellin bapt 15 Feb 1628/9 & bur 20 July 1629; Margaret bur 9 June 1648.
[384] She had four infant children, all buried at Kirkby Malham unbaptized on 2 Nov 1665, 12 Jan 1665/6, 20 Oct 1669 (a son), and 3 April 1671 (a son).
[385] His will was proved at the York Registry 3 Aug 1709 fol 66 vol 5 (987)

2. Robert, of whom presently

3. N...

1. Elizabeth, unm at her father's death

2. Katherine, unm at her father's death

3. N...

The second son may have been

Rev Robert King, of Kirkby Malham,b. ca 1549[386], may have matriculated at Cambridge in 1571[387], and was ordained deacon & priest at St Michael-le-Belfry, York 24 July 1573 by Richard Barnes, Bishop of Nottingham. He ministered in Kirkby Malham where in 1620, with Thomas & Richard King, he was the subject of a complaint to the Countess of Shrewsbury by Sir Thomas Wentworth. Wentworth claimed that the Kings were encroaching on his land. He was bur at Kirkby Malham 13 May 1621[388], leaving issue,

    1.Thomas, of whom presently

    1. Agnes, m. William Preston (will dated 7 June 1636), of Hill Top, Kirkby Malhamdale[389] and d.s.p.

---

[386] A Robert King, son of John King, was baptized at St John the Baptist, Halifax on 28 April 1549. Could this have been this Robert? Another indication of the possible early links with Halifax.

[387] In the Alumni Cantab there is reference to a Richard or Robert Kyng, who may have been "Robert of Yorkshire" who matriculated from the Queen's College as a sizar in 1571. If he had been at Cambridge, it explains his ordination at York as deacon & priest on one day.

[388] He was clearly a man of means, and perhaps not always a parish priest. In those days the lines were blurred between a clerical and a business vocation. In June 1620, Josias Lambert (father of General Lambert, and well known for his debts) gave his bond in the amount of £142 (£35,000 in today's money) to secure a payment of £71 0s 8d. Robert's will was made on 7 May 1621 and proved in the York Registry on 26 Oct (vol 36 fol 563). It is long and (to me) illegible. His granddaughter Alice and her daughter get a special mention.

On 3 November 1619 Alice Dodgson, single woman of Kirkby Malhamdale, was buried. She made her will on 20 October 1619, naming Rev Robert King and Thomas King, his son, as her residuary heirs. She also made several legacies among which were: to Richard King for his wife [was this Rev Robert's brother?] a flannel petticoat, to Agnes, daughter of Thomas King [who was she?] £20, and two coverlets to Ann and Margaret King [who were they – presumably this was the Margaret King who married Richard Verley a few months later], and £10 to Robert & Ellen, the children of Thomas King [who are they?]. Above all, who was Alice? She was presumably a near relation of the King family. The Dodgsons were a Gisburne family.

[389] William Preston built Hill Top in Kirkby Malham in 1617. In May 1597 he and his future brother-in-law, Thomas King, took on a 100 year lease of lands in Kirkby Malhamdale from John Metcalfe. Preston is listed immediately after Josias Lambert of Calton in a list of 24 men appointed in 1617 to "order all things concerning the church". Lambert is described as "Esq", Preston as "Gent", the rest (including Thomas King) have no description. On Charles I's accession, Preston refused the honour of knighthood – so he was a man of

2. Elizabeth, unm. at her father's death

The only son,

Thomas King, of Kirkby Malham, who built the house, Church End, which has his initials over the front door and the date 1622. b. ca 1575, m. 31 Jan 1600, Margaret Sergeantson (bur. 10 Dec 1615) and had surviving issue[390]

    1. Alice, bapt at Kirkby Malham 7 Nov 1602, m 28 Oct 1618 Richard Preston, of Airton in Kirkby Malhamdale, and had issue,

        (1) Margaret, mentioned in her great-grandfather's will.

    2. Margaret, bapt at Kirkby Malham 18 August 1611[391],

He married 2ndly ?Elizabeth[392], dau of N... and was bur 9 July 1634[393], having had further issue,

    1. Robert, of whom presently.

    2. Thomas, bapt. 9 Feb 1622/3[394]

    1. Elizabeth, bur 4 Aug 1623, [?m. 1stly James Simms]

    2. Jane, bapt at Kirkby Malham 31 Aug 1631 & bur there 28 July 1662, unm

---

means. For his will, see Wallock site: http://www.northcravenheritage.org.uk He seems to have had a brother, who left a daughter, Grace, who was unmarried in 1643. He also had four sisters. Mrs Wallock was the eldest and had two children – Henry (the chief beneficiary), and William. Henry (1597-1650) had four children – Myles (who was illegitimate), Elizabeth (m. to Robert King), Frances and Anne (one of whom married Allan Towson). Mrs Elizabeth Lawson had Christopher, William, Margaret and Elizabeth. Mrs Maud Young had William and John. Mrs Margaret Garforth doesn't have any children mentioned. He mentions Myles Wallock and leaves Henside in Langcliffe to 'Elizabeth, the wife of Robert King' and her sisters.

[390] With others who died young: John, bur. at Kirkby Malham 30 Sept 1614, and an infant son bur. with his mother.

[391] A Margaret King married Richard Verley of Gisburn in Kirkby Malham church on 8 April 1620, but it could hardly have been this same Margaret.

[392] An Elizabeth Kinge of Kirkby, widow, is mentioned in Henry Wallock's will as one of his debtors. "Old Elizabeth King of K-M widow" was buried on 28 Feb 1668/9. The second wife of Thomas King would have been in her 70's then so could have been described as "old" – and "old" could have distinguished her from daughter-in-law if she also was Elizabeth.

[393] A grant of administration was made on 18 July 1634 and there was a report to the Courts of Wards and Liveries 10 Carolus (vol 55 no 139). This suggests that his heir was a minor at his death – which Robert and Thomas were. The Court of Wards had been set up by Henry VIII to receive the income from the estates of minors and Charles I collected it energetically during the time of his personal rule in 1629-40 – which did not make him popular.

[394] Thomas King features in the 1649 will of Henry Wallock as one of his sons-in-law (with Allan Towson), which is deeply mysterious. Wallock seems to have held the mortgages on his father's lands and returned much of them to him as part of his wife's jointure. Was he married to another of Henry Wallock's daughters? If so, why does Wallock ignore Thomas' brother Robert in the will? According to William Preston's 1636 will, Robert was married to Elizabeth Wallock.

The elder son,

Robert King, of Kirkby Malham, bapt at Kirkby Malham 29 November 1618, m. *ante* 1636[395], Elizabeth, dau. and coh. of Henry Wallock, Malham & Bordley[396] & was bur at Kirkby Malham 13 June 1669, having had issue[397]

1. Thomas, bapt at Kirkby Malham 4 Oct 1636[398]
2. Henry, of East Malham, bapt at Kirkby Malham 4 Apr 1638, Churchwarden of Kirkby Malham in 1669, m Margaret (bur 14 June 1674) and had issue[399],

    1a Robert, bapt. at Kirkby Malham 11 July 1667, Trustee of the local Grammar School in 1706, ?the Robert King, a freeholder of Kirkby Malhamdale who voted for the Tory candidate at the Yorkshire election of 1741

---

[395] They were already married when William Preston, Elizabeth's great uncle and Robert's uncle by marriage, made his will in June 1636.

[396] Henry Wallock married at Burnsall, on 22 June 1615, Ann (bapt at Rylstone 24 Aug. 1588), dau. of Thomas & Elizabeth Procter, of Rylstone. His will is dated 30 June 1649 and was proved in October 1650. Besides legacies to his three daughters (Elizabeth, Frances & Anne) he also remembered his illegitimate son, Myles. The Procters were a large and prosperous local family. Sir Stephen Procter (1562-1620) built Fountains Hall and a Geoffrey Procter of Hanlith was hanged at York in 1550 after an affray.

[397] With other children who died young: Mary, bapt 1 Nov & bur 13 Dec 1639; Mary, bapt 31 March 1641, bur 24 March 1656/7; an unbaptized infant bur 12 Sept 1647; an unbaptized infant bur 2 Jan 1649/50; Miles, b 3 Sept 1654 (named for Elizabeth King's brother, Miles Wallock?), bur 29 Aug 1656; John (was he named in honour of the local hero, General John Lambert?), b 29 Sept 1657, bur 8 Aug 1674. His widow may have been the "Widow King" who was assessed on one hearth in 1672.

[398] He may have been the Thomas King of Skellands whose servant was buried in 1674 – and who about the same time (as "Thomas King senr. of Skellans, yeoman") figures in a document preserved in the Arthur Reistrick papers. He may have been the Thomas King of Kirkby who was bur there on 20 Nov 1681.

[399] With a daughter Elizabeth bur at Kirkby Malham 2 Feb 1672/3 and a son James, bapt at Kirkby Malham 4 Oct and bur there 12 Oct 1673. That the second son was called Henry (the first after Robert's father) is a further suggestion that Elizabeth Wallock was his mother.

He may have been the "H.K." who built Middle House, high up on the Moor in East Malham and whose initials over the headstone of the doorway were still visible to Mr Morkill when he was researching his book in the 1920s.

Whittaker suggests that he had a descendant, Henry King, who was in the navy "and accompanied Lord Anson in 1745" (according to W E King, of Donhead). His descendant was James King of Finsthwaite who left land to his cousin Edward King of Hungrill.

W.E. King of Donhead met an old watchmaker in Bowness ca. 1890? who remembered a commercial traveller from his youth ca. 1830? called Henry King. He "was always well dressed and the jeweller considered him to be a gentleman and above his then position in life. He also had a permanent grievance, viz that James King of Finsthwaite did not leave that property to him"

2a Henry, ?of Thorneyslack, Skelsmergh, near Kendal[400], bapt. at Kirkby Malham 21 Nov 1669, ?the Henry King, a freeholder of Kirkby Malhamdale who voted for the Tory candidate at the Yorkshire election of 1741, m. Alice.... & had issue,

    1b Richard, a merchant of Idle, near Bradford, b. 23 Sept., 1721 & baptized at Thorneyslack, 8 Oct., 1721, m. & d. in Liverpool, 1800[401], having had issue,

        1c John, b. 28 Nov. 1762 & bapt 2 April 1762 at Leeds

        1c Mary, b. 22 Jan 1757 & bapt 20 February at Idle, m. 3 September 1793, in Liverpool Parish Church (when living in Liverpool), John Bateman, a servant, of Liverpool, & d. 29 Feb 1795 having had issue,

            1d. Mary, b. ca. 1795[402], m. Mr Armstrong (and was left the family bible by her aunt Alice) & had issue,

                1e. Alice Margaret, b. ca. 1820, left the family bible by her mother

        2c. Sarah, b. 3 March 1759 & bapt. 2 April 1759 at Idle

        3c. Elizabeth, b. 5 Oct 1760 & bapt at Idle

        4c. Alice, b. 14 Oct 1770 & bapt 11 Nov 1770 at Skelsmergh, d. unm at Woolston, nr. Warrington, Lancs., 7 May 1845 & bur. in Huyton churchyard.

    2b. Robert, b. 26 Sept. 1723 & bapt. at Thorneyslack 13 Oct 1723

    3b. John (Capt), b. 27 Oct. 1725 & bapt. at Kirkby Malham 24 Nov. 1725

    4b. James - possibly the same as the naval surgeon, who latterly practised as a surgeon & apothecary in Castle Street, Liverpool[403], bapt. at Kirkby Malham, 12 November 1727, m. at Cartmel, 1751, Isabel (bur. at Finsthwaite, 4 Dec. 1766), dau. of Clement Taylor, of Finsthwaite[404], & d. 1782 (probate granted, 27 Dec.), having had issue

        1c. James, of Finsthwaite House, which he inherited from his maternal uncle, Edward Taylor, b. 1755. In 1797, on the summit of a hill, north

---

[400] A Henry King, who was living in Skelsmergh (then in the parish of Kendal) in the 1720s is said to have owned the old bible that belonged to Robert King in the 1570s – which suggests that he would have represented the senior branch of the family. The information about his children comes from the bible. The link with Skelsmergh suggests a link with James King of Finsthwaite.

[401] A "Richard King, of this parish" was buried in Huyton churchyard on 8 August 1800, aged 78. Since his unmarried daughter was buried there, it seems likely that it is the same Richard King.

[402] Mary, dau of John Bateman, of Ebenezer Street, Leeds, was born on 17 January 1794 and baptized at St Peter's, Leeds on 16 February 1794. But this would have made her mother five months pregnant when she was married.

[403] At a time when the surgeon-apothecary was becoming a sort of G.P. to the emerging middle classes. The aristocracy were looked after by their physicians – who had been to Oxford or Cambridge and might be the younger sons of the gentry.

[404] His account book for the years 1712-53 has been published by the Lancashire & Cheshire Record Society.

of the inn at Newby Bridge, he erected a tower or observatory, 'from which are obtained delightful and extensive views'. He was bur. at Finsthwaite, 30 June, 1821, s.p., leaving an estate at Campfield, Bowness to the daughters of his distant cousin, Edward King, of Hungerhill, by his first wife [but Edward left it to John Myers King, his son by his second wife] and the bulk of his property to Roger Taylor, of Stockport.

2c. Edward, described as of Bolton-le-Moors, Lancs. in his aunt's will in 1802, d. 30 November 1809 and was buried in Finsthwaite churchyard, aged 47, leaving his property to his brother.

1c. Mary, of Liverpool, d. unm. 1802??

1b. Elizabeth, b. at Kirkby Malham

2b. Margaret, b. at Kirkby Malham

3. **James**, of whom presently

1. Anne, bapt at Kirkby Malham 2 May 1660

The third son,

James King[405], of Skellands, bapt at Kirkby Malham 22 March 1651, m. at Long Stanton 29 April 1675[406] Ann, dau and heir of N... Carr of Langcliff (who survived him) and d. 1708[407] having had issue,

1. **Thomas**, of whom presently

1. Elizabeth, bapt. at Kirkby Malham 14 May 1677, m. at Kirkby Malham, 23 December 1697, Thomas Simms of Thorpe, near Burnsall[408] and had issue,

(1) Robert, living in 1708

(2) James, bapt. at Burnsall, 12 September 1703, living in 1708

2. Mary, bapt. at Kirkby Malham, 4 September 1679, bur. at Kirkby Malham, 23 August 1700

3. Anne bapt. at Kirkby Malham, 8 May 1682, m. 25 November 1703, as his 2nd wife Henry Wilcock, of Thornton-in-Craven (who was 1st m'd to Elizabeth, dau. of John Knowles, of Kettlewell[409]), and had issue[410],

---

[405] Whitaker says that he was the son of Thomas King who first settled at Skellands, and says that his mother was the coheir of Henry Wallock. On 28 January 1680 James received a further grant of administration in respect of the estate of Henry Wallock and of his mother, Elizabeth King of Scosthrop. On the other hand, the later entry of his marriage in 1675 is set against the name of "James King fillii Robti", baptized in 1651.

[406] Whitaker's pedigree of the Carr family says that Anne, only dau & heiress of Roger Carr of Langcliff was born in 1673 and married James King of Skellands in 1694.

[407] His will was made 24 July 1708 and proved at the York Registry 22 November 1708. A "Mr James King, a stranger" was buried at All Saints, Wakefield on 28 July 1708. This could have been him.

[408] He was baptized at Burnsall on 2 April 1671, the son of Robert Simms – the name variously spelt. There is a ruined farmhouse in the hamlet of Thorp known as "Simms Farm".

[409] according to Whitaker, although Whitaker says that John Knowles, Elizabeth's father,

(1) Margaret, living in 1708

(2) Anne, b. 1707, m. at Thornton-in-Craven, 23 May 1733, Rev. Matthew Topham (d. 24 December 1773, aged 67), vicar of Emley, near Huddersfield, and then from 1754 of Withernwick with Mappleton, near Hull, 5th son of Christopher Topham of Caldbergh and Withernswick, and d. 18 November 1785, having had issue,

 1a. Christopher, a merchant of Leeds, b. 1736, m. Anne Shippen, of Seacroft & d. 1811, having had issue

  1b. Christopher, b. 1766, d.v.p & s.p. in the West Indies

  2b. Godfrey, b. 1773, d.s.p.

  3b. Richard, d.v.p. & s.p.

  4b. Henry, d.s.p. 9 June 1839

  5b. John, in the army, d. at Chatham or Canterbury ca. 1811

  1b. Barbara, b. 1771, d. unm.

  2b. Ann, d. unm.

  3b. Dorothy, d. unm.

 2a. Henry, of London, b. 1744, d.unm. 28 November 1817 & was bur. at Withernswick[411]

 3a. John, F.R.S. & F.S.A., Bencher of Gray's Inn, Keeper of the Lambeth Palace Library, b. at Emley, 6 January 1746, m. 1794, Mary Swinden, of Greenwich & d.s.p. at Cheltenham 19 August 1803 & was buried in Gloucester Cathedral.

 4a. Matthew, of London, b. 1750, d. 18 May 1823 & is bur. at Withernswick[412]

 1a. Margaret, b. 1740, m. Samuel Stocks, mercer, of Wakefield

 2a. Dorothy, b. 1742, m. John Smith, of Great Hatfield, near Hull

 3a. Elizabeth, b. 1748, m. George Gibson, of Sigglesthorne, near Hull & d. 1821

 4a. Ann, b. 1755, m. at All Saints, Wakefield in 1788 Thomas Rayner, of Wakefield

 5a. Barbara, d. young

 6a. Jane, d. unm. 11 Aug. 1773

---

was the son of James Knowles of Thorp, who was the second husband of Anne Wilcock's sister, Elizabeth – so, unless Henry Wilcock's first wife was the great niece of his second, there is some confusion here!

[410] A John Wilcock was Churchwarden at Thornton in 1759.

[411] The inscription on his monument in Withernswick Church reads, "After a period of upwards of fifty years residence in London, respected for his unblemished integrity as a merchant. Beloved for his candour and mildness of temper. And above all estimable for the purity and piety of his manners. Departed this life in the humble hope of a better".

[412] The inscription on his monument in Withernswick Church reads, "He was distinguished for uniform uprightness, strict veracity, great judgement and strong attachment to his family. And after a peculiarly trying and painful illness born with great fortitude, departed this life in Verulam Buildings, Gray's Inn (London)".

(3) Elizabeth, m. at Gargrave, Yorkshire, 24 June 1773 her sister's brother-in-law, Godfrey Topham (d.s.p. 7 April 1776, aged 67), of Caldbergh, Yorkshire & d. *post* 1783

The only son,

Thomas King, of Skellands, bapt.at Kirkby Malham, 22 June 1686, m. at Kirkby Malham, 24 Feb 1714 Alice (who m. 2ndly 1 Nov. 1729 Rev Henry Wilkinson, curate at Kirkby Malham since 1719 (who was bur 12 June 1732, aged 36), dau. of William Sergeantson[413], of Hanlith and had issue,

1. **James**, of whom presently
2. William, bapt. at Kirkby Malham, 27 Dec. 1720, d. at Skellands, 23 Oct. 1739.
1. Anne, bapt. at Kirkby Malham, 26 Nov. 1717, d young[414]
2. Jane, bapt. at Kirkby Malham, 21 August 1719, m. 1stly at Kirkby Malham, 19 April, 1742, Robert Baynes (d. July, 1743), eldest son of Ralph Baynes, of Mewith Head Hall, Bentham [415]. She m. 2ndly, at Bentham, Yorks., 19 August 1745 Dr John Cookson, of Cliffe House, Westgate, Wakefield (d. 4 May 1779)[416], and d. at Spennithorne, 1 June 1810, leaving issue,
    (1) John, bapt at All Saints, Wakefield, 12 Sept 1747, d. an inf.
    (1) Margaret, bapt at All Saints, Wakefield 28 August 1746, m. at All Saints, Wakefield 4 July 1780[417], Charles O'Hara, of Annaghmore, M.P. for co Sligo[418]. He d. 1822, aged 76. She d. leaving issue

---

[413] For the Serjeantson family, see www.serjeantson.com
[414] According to Oliver Bolton King p.26
[415] The Baynes family were a well-established local family – and continued at Mewith Head into the 19th century. Jane probably did not have had any children by her first husband since Mewith Head descended to his brothers' descendants, but she had property in Bentham and Clapham for her life.
[416] He practised as a doctor in Wakefield, and was a Governor of the Grammar School there from 1739-71 – together with William Serjeantson, who was also in Wakefield. Cookson had taken over William Carr's debts in 1741. He is buried in Wakefield Cathedral. The Cooksons were originally a Giggleswick family, though they moved to Leeds and prospered there in the 17th & 18th centuries.
[417] Her cousin William Sergeantson, and her sister, were the witnesses.
[418]http://www.historyofparliamentonline.org/volume/1790-1820/member/o8217hara-charles-1746-1822 - 'A young lawyer—has an estate in Sligo—lately married a good fortune—was brought in by Lord Harcourt's means, paying only £1,000, yet he has always opposed—a very dull, tedious speaker.' This was how O'Hara was described in 1782. A year later he transferred from Dungannon to the representation of his county and retained it for the rest of his life. The official hope, expressed in 1791, that he 'might be got over, at least softened' proved misplaced, for he remained in opposition and was a sturdy opponent of the Union. Nevertheless, having married a niece [cousin] of the Duke of Portland's secretary, John King, and finding ex-Chief Secretary Pelham in power when he was returned to Westminster, he could think of at least two occasions when he had risked unpopularity to serve the Castle, even if 'I certainly made no sacrifice of principle or duty in any support I ever gave you'. He evidently looked to Pelham to provide him with an

1a Charles Edward, b. 16 September 1784 & bapt at St Marylebone 11 October 1784, d. an inf.

2a Charles King, of Annaghmore, b 1785, d unm 1860

3a Henry William, b. 18 April 1796 & baptized at St Luke's Chelsea, 30 June 1796, d. young

1a Mary

2a Jane Frances, b 4 Nov 1783, m 1810 Arthur Brooke Cooper (d 4 Dec 1854) of Coopershill, co Sligo, and d. at Annaghmore, 21 July 1874, leaving issue,

    1b Arthur Brooke, m. Elizabeth Truelock (d. 21 July 1859), and d. 12 June 1845, having had issue,

      1c. Katherine Jane, m. J. Cole

    2b Charles William, of Coopers Hill, succeeded his uncle at Annaghmore, and assumed the name of O'Hara, DL, JP, MP for co Sligo 1859-65, b 30 Oct 1817, m 28 Oct 1858 Annie Charlotte (d 12 March 1882, aged 45) dau of Richard Shuttleworth Streatfield, of The Rock, Uckfield, and d 5 April 1898, having had issue,

      1c Charles Kean, Maj., of Annaghmore, 3rd York & Lancs, Regt., last Lord Lieut. of co. Sligo, 1902-1922, b. 10 December 1860, d. unm. 4 August 1947[419]

      2c Arthur Cooper, of Ballina, co. Mayo & latterly of Coopers Hill, b. 8 February 1862, d. unm. 27 June 1934

      3c Richard Edward, of Newpark, co. Sligo, b. 1863, & m. 21 February 1911, Ethel Fisken & d. 28 May 1948, having had issue,

        1d. Sheila Charlotte, b. 20 January 1912

      4c William Henry, b. 14 March & d. 5 May 1866

      5c Henry Streatfield, b. 26 February 1870, d. 14 October 1878

      6c Alexander Perceval, emigrated to Chicago, U.S.A., b. 16 May 1871, m. Alice.. & d. 1949

      7c Frederick William, Land Agent, b. 13 February 1875, m. 26 November 1903, Muriel Isabella Helen Rice (d. at Annaghmore, 22 December 1966,

---

opening, for as his friend Dr Walker King [brother of John King] assured Pelham, 'in one very important article of life few men have been more unfortunate, and in my conscience I believe no man ever more undeservedly'.

The fact was that O'Hara's estate, worth nearly £4,000 p.a., had been heavily encumbered, and his assets being in the hands of receivers, it was difficult for him to qualify as a county Member. He chose to ignore the problem but he was evidently muzzled by the fear of exposure. O'Hara's attendance tailed off after 1813, though minority votes were reported in April and May 1814, May 1815 and April and May 1816. His last recorded vote before 1820 was against Catholic relief, 21 May 1816. He was advised by a committee of his supporters to retire in favour of his son in 1818, but declined to do so and retained the seat until his death, 19 Sept. 1822

[419] "Uncle Charlie" – who lived in Annaghmore when it had 20,000 acres around the sprawling mansion and a full staff.

aged 85), dau. of Francis Henn & d. at Cooper Hill, 8 March 1949, having had issue,

    1d Donal Frederick, of Annaghmore, b. 5 November 1904, m. Elizabeth Linnel & & d. in Buntingford, Herts. 28 November 1977, having had issue,

        1e. Dermot Charles Donal, of Annaghmore, b. 1938, m. & had issue,

            1f. Durcan, of Annaghmore, m. Nicola

      2e Errill

      1e Maeve

    2d Francis Cooper, a tea planter in Sri Lanka & latterly of Coopers Hill[420], b. 21 September 1906, m. 2 December 1933, Joan Moore Bridgman (d. 2008, aged 95) & d. 2 February 1982, having had issue,

        1e. Bryan Cooper, of Coopers Hill, b. in India, 24 September 1934, m. Lindy & had issue,

            1f. Paul, of Hong Kong, m. Katy & has issue,

                1g. Megan

                2g. Lucy

            2f. Simon, of Coopers Hill, has issue,

                1g. Kian O'Hara *Zapata*, of Mexico City, b. 2001

            He m. Christine & has further issue,

                1g. Finn, b. 2012

            3f. Sean, m. Julia & has issue,

                1g. Seamus

                2g. Rory

        2e. Timothy Errill, b. 20 February 1941, m. Jane & has issue,

            1f. Mark

        1e. Bridgid Jane, b. 1945

        2e. Kathryn E.., b. 1953

    3d Kean William, Chartered Electrical Engineer, b. 6 June 1912

    1d Rosaleen Muriel, b. 24 November 1914, m. John Logan

    2d Marian Emily, b. 24 November 1914

8c Errill Robert, Col., b. 6 September 1879, m. 25 February 1911, Moneen Bond & d. in Andover, Hants., 5 June 1956, having had issue,

    1d. Charles Errill, Capt., Royal Inniskilling Fusiliers, b. 5 April 1912, k'd 11 March 1941

1c Charlotte Jane, b. 1859, m. at Rathbaron, 3 February 1878, Alexander Perceval (d. 22 July 1887), of Temple House, Ballymote, co. Sligo & d. 19 August 1921, having had issue,

    1d. (Alexander) Ascelin Charles Philip Spencer, Major, Irish Guards, of Temple House, b. 29 December1885, m. Nora & had issue,

        1e. Alexander, of Temple House

---

[420] They were the first of the family to rake in paying guests to make ends meet. Simon O'Hara currently runs the business.

2e. John

3e. Philip Richard, Odlum Brown Investment Management, b. 12 December 1926, m. 1stly in Montreal in 1958 (Florence) Irene Payce. He m. 2ndly Lin Copithorne & d.s.p. in Canada, 23 December 2018.

1e. Moira

  1d. Sybil Annie, b. 17 July 1882, d. 22 January 1884

2c Mary, b. 6 November 1864, d. 16 September 1879

3c Annie Frances, b. 31 March 1867, d. unm. in Germany, 10 September 1882.

4c Emily Margaret, b. 8 August 1868, d. unm. 8 July 1897

5c Jane Marian, b. 23 October 1872, m. 8 May 1901, Ceely Maude (d. 4 January 1929, aged 58) & d. 24 November 1949, having had issue,

  1d. Kathleen Lisalie, b. 11 May 1903, m. 25 July 1928, Francis Mervyn Cook (d. 1979) & d. 1991, having had issue,

    1e. John Patrick Mervyn, b. 23 July 1941, m. 1stly 8 June 1963 (div. 1980) Margaret Susan, dau. of Michael Hoare, of Pyrton, Oxon. & had issue,

      1f. Nicholas John Mervyn, b. 20 March 1964

      2f. Julian Michael Patrick, b. 15 March 1966

      1f. Lucinda Margaret Venetia, b. 1973

    He m. 2ndly in 1984, Jennifer Wendy, dau,. of Joseph Ellison, O.B.E.

    1e. Ann Veronica, b. 4 June 1929, m. 9 January 1960, Michael Kenneth Maurice Spackman & had issue,

      1f. Henrietta Louise, b. 17 November 1960, m. 27 May 1995, Peter Sleeman, of Westerham, Kent & has issue,

        1g. Imogen Sophie, b. 29 March 1996

        2g. Freya Clare, b. 9 November 1999

        3g. Phoebe Juia, b. 9 November1999

      2f. Catriona Venetia, b. 19 December 1962, m. 11 June 1993, Angus Stovold & has issue,

        1g. Alexander Jack Francis, b. 20 November 1993

        2g. Finn William Frederick, b. 11 June 2000

        1g. Harriet Louise Francesca, b. 25 December 1995

  2d. Venetia Marian Cely, b. 1906, d. 1994

6c. Kathleen, b. 27 June 1876, m. 5 January 1901 Bertram Phibbs & d. 2 February 1931, having had issue,

  1d. Patrick William O'Hara, b. 13 January 1902, d. 1975

  2d. Arthur Alured, b. 1 March 1904, m. Katherine... & d. 1986, having had issue

1b Margaret Sarah, d. unm. at Coopershill, 19 February 1888

2b Mary Jane Caroline, d unm at Coopershill, 21 February 1877

3b Jane Henrietta, m February 1850 Lt Col Alexander M'Kinstry, and d in the USA 8 February 1867, leaving with other issue[421],

1c. Arthur
4b Charlotte Anne, b. 1819, m 19 February 1852 Christopher Carleton
L'Estrange (d. 11 February 1889) of Kevinsfort, co. Sligo (d 11 February
1889), and d. 22 October 1887, leaving issue,

    1c Christopher Arthur Carleton, of Woodville, co. Sligo, b. 1 July 1856, m.
    1887, Annie Kathline Victoria, dau,. of Roger Dodwell Robinson, of
    Wellmount, Sligo & d.s.p. 21 May 1900

    2c. George Gray, b. 1857, d. 1865

    3c Charles William, b. 1862, d. 1865

    4c Arthur Henry, of Kevinsfort, b. 8 July 1865, m. at St George's, Hanover
    Square, 11 January 1900, Mabel, widow of A.J. Neville, of N.S.W.,
    Australia & dau. of Montagu Newton, of Earls Court Square, London, & d.
    1920

    5c Edmund Carleton, b. 14 August 1867, d. in Queensland, Australia 26
    December 1909.

    6c Henry George, of Lisnalurg House, co. Sligo, b. 1869, m. 24 July 1901,
    Evelyn Mary (d. 15 October 1952, aged 76), dau. & coh. of Owen Wynne,
    of Hazelwood House, co. Sligo & d. in 1929, having had issue,

        1d. Christopher Carleton, Capt., of Lisnalurg, b. in co. Sligo, 30
        September 1909, m. 1939, Betty Florence (d. 1994, aged 85), dau, of
        Sir John Lumsden & d. 19 April 1984, having had issue,

            1e. Stella Evelyn Brigid, of Lisnalurg, b. in Dublin 2 September 1942,
            m. Rev. Sir Dickon Durand, 4th Bt. (d. 24 October 1992, aged 58),
            Rector of Youghal, & has issue,

                1f. Edward Alan Christopher Percy, 5th Bt., of Lisnalurg, radio
                producer and writer, b. 21 February 1974, m. 1st 5 June 2004, N... &
                had issue,

                    1g. Mary Magdalena Sophia, b. 7 April 2005

                He m. 2ndly Amanda Anara Ashwood, & has further issue,

                    1g. Ezra Solaris Amairgin Nehemiah Ashwood, b. 27 September
                    2016

                    2g. Yemaya Hathor Athena Lavannah Rosa, b. 5 August 2013

                2f. David Michael Dickon Percy, b. 6 June 1978

                1f. Rachel Elizabeth Marion, b. 6 July 1972, m. 22 September 2000,
                Grant Schofield

                2f. Madeleine Eleanor Marion, b. 3 November 1980

            2e. Caroline Mary, b. 21 February 1945, m. 9 September 1964, John
            Blayney Cole Hamilton & has issue,

                1f. Eva Cicely, b. 23 May 1966, m. James Fielder & has issue,

                    1g. Alexander John S. Cole, b. 2000

                    1g. Emily Caroline de Graves, b. 1997

---

[421] In 1911 a Marie McKinstry (b. 1856) was visiting Arthur O'Hara at Cooper Hill, with Lilah
McKinstry (b. 1890)

  2f. Louise Henrietta, b. 14 June 1967, m. Alistair Burns & has issue,
   1g. Oliver William L., b. 2000
   2g. Arthur Harry, b. 2004
  3f. Nichola Elfie, b. 12 April 1973
 2d Henry Owen, Cmdr., D.S.C., R.N., b. in Dublin in 1912, m. 1964, Janet Gough & d. in Singapore, 5 December 1972, having had issue,
  1e. Guy Henry, b. 1966
  1e. Fiona Evelyn, b. 1967
 3d. Arthur Henry, d. 1920
 1d Stella Muriel, b. 18 July 1903
 2d Elizabeth Charlotte, S.R.N., b. 1907, m. Oliver Philip Wagstaff & d. 1974
 3d Mary Evelyn, b. 1913
1c Janette Frances, b. 1853, d. 1931
2c Elisabeth Mary, of Kevinsfort House, b. 1854, d. unm. 17 April 1920
3c Charlotte Louisa, b. 1859, d. 3 February 1885
4c Margaret Alice, b. 1864, d. 1946
3a Charlotte, m 1812, Robert Digby (d. 1817), son of Very Revd William Digby, Dean of Clonfert, by his second wife and cousin, Mary, dau. of Rev Benjamin Digby, of Oswaldstown & had issue[422]
 1b. William John, of Moat Lodge, Moylough, b. 1813, m. 1859, Sarah Rebecca, dau. of William Le Poer Trenchard, rector of Moylough, & d. 1886, having had issue,
 1c. Robert Kenelm, of Moat Lodge, b. 1862, d. 1910
 2c. William, b. 1866
 1c. Charlotte Kathleen, b. 1863, m. 1890, as his second wife, John Kenelm Wingfield Digby (d. 25 December 1904, aged 45) of Sherborne Castle, Dorset, & d. 1935, having had issue,
  1d. Kenelm Essex Digby Bosworth, Maj., b. 24 March 1891, m. 1stly, at St Michael's, Chester Square, 2 March 1916, Mary Ranee (d. 20 December 1933, aged 39), dau, of Brig Gen Wellesley Paget & had issue,
   1e. Robert Kildare, b. 17 February 1921, m. 1943 Grace Kathleen Deary & d. 2008
  He m. 2ndly, in 1950, Augusta Jonasdottir Magnus (d. 1972, aged 57) & d. 28 October 1972, having had further issue,
   2e. Kenelm George, b. 4 May 1952, m. 1977, Belinda, dau, of Andrew Foster-Melliar & d.in Beer Hackett, Dorset, 7 January 2004, having had issue,

---

[422] Dean Digby – who married three times (the last time in his sixties) and died in 1812 - was quite a character. He was descended from a younger brother of the 1st Lord Digby and was the grandson and great-grandson of Irish Bishops. His youngest son, Kenelm, converted to Catholicism and became a noted medievalist.

1f.

        1f. Patrick

        2f. Nicholas

        1f. Lydia

    2d. John Reginald, M.C., b. 1896, m. 1930, Margaret Betty Holford (d. 1980, aged 74) & d. 1988, having had issue,

        1e. John Michael, b. 1938, d. 2008

        1e. Margaret Jane, b. 1935, m. 1959, Lt Col Nigel Charles Purdon Winter (d. in Chard, Somerset, 26 February 2011, aged 70) & d. 2003, having had issue,

            1f. James

            1f. Joanna Claire (Mimi)

            2f. Amanda

    3d. Robert Almarus, b. 1901, m. Mary Macdonald (d. 1974, aged 74), dau. of Donald Ross, & d. 11 August 1974, having had issue,

        1e. Robert Donald, b. 1931, m. & d. 2004 having had issue,

            1f. Mark, d.

            2f. Peter

            1f. Patricia

            2f. Mary

    1d. Kathleen Venetia, b, 1892, m. 1stly in 1914, Maj. Reginald Charles Walker (k'd 1916, aged 38). She m. 2ndly in 1918 Lt Col David Maitland Griffiths, DSO (d. 1960, aged 88) & d. in 1982, having had issue,

        1e. Anna, b. 1928, m. 1951 (div. 1959) as his second wife, (Julian) Roy Beddington[423] (d. 31 May 1995, aged 85) of Esseborne Manor, Hurstbourne Tarrant, & d. in 1967, having had issue,

            1f. Philippa

            2f. Rosa Susan Penelope, developmental biologist, b. 23 March 1956, educ. Sherborne & Brasenose Coll., Oxford, m. as his second wife, Rev. Robin Denniston (d. 6 April 2012, aged 85), publisher at O.U.P., & d.s.p. 18 May 2001

    2d. Dorothy Charlotte Edith, b. 1894, d. 1918

(2) Henrietta Maria, bapt at All Saints, Wakefield 29 May 1753, m. 28 April 1788, as his second wife, Lt. Col. (Marwood) Turner van Straubenzee, of Spennithorne, DL, JP, 52nd Foot, who served in America and India. She died 16 Aug, 1803. He d 6 April, 1823, having had issue by her[424]

    1a Casimir Turner, b. January & d. 23 March 1790

    1a Henrietta Maria, b. 1792, d. unm. 5 March, 1818[425]

---

[423] Formerly Moses, from a Jewish family. A noted water-colourist and fisherman. Anna committed suicide.

Dr Cookson had made his will in May 1769, when Henrietta was still a minor. Her guardians were to be her mother, Sir Fletcher Norton and Rev James King

[425] She made a very long will leaving what appears to be considerable property (after her father's death) divided between her Straubenzee and O'Hara cousins.

3. Elizabeth, bapt. at Kirkby Malham 22 Oct. 1722, m. at Kirkby Malham, 25 June, 1749, William Lockwood, a wine merchant of Kirkgate, Leeds[426]. He died in 1774, aged 49. She died in Easingwold, 17 March, 1801, having had issue,[427]

(1) William, a solicitor, who built "the Villa" at Easingwold, b. 15 Aug. 1752, m. 10 July, 1775 Ann, dau. of John Mitton, of Badsworth (d. 1782, aged 28), and d. at Easingwold, 17 June, 1821, leaving issue,

1a. John, a wine merchant in York, b. 1777, d at Easingwold, 31 Oct. 1805

2a. William, solicitor, of Easingwold, b. 1 April, 1778, m. 1stly 3 Feb 1802 Jane (d. 9 May, 1808, aged 29), dau. of William Key, of North Holme, & had issue,

1b. William, Rev., vicar of Kirkby Fleetham, Yorks., b. 28 August 1804, m. 1stly at Easingwold, 17 December 1827, Jane Smith (d. 29 November 1829, aged 25). He m. 2ndly 28 June 1831, Elizabeth Glaister (d. in Warlaby, Yorks. 20 October 1878, aged 78) & d. in Croft on Tees, Yorks., 29 May 1854, having had issue,

1c. William, b. 21 January 1840, m. in Prescot, Lancs. Mary Jane (d. in Ripon in 1916, aged 77), dau. of Rev. Joseph Saville Roberts Evans & d. in Ripon, 7 January 1908, having had issue,

1d. William, b. in Liverpool in 1868, d. in Northallerton, 11 June 1903

1d. Agnes, b. in Rainhill, Lancs., 27 August 1869

2d. Mary, b. in Rainhill in 1874, m. in 1942 Frederic Stockton Gowland & d. in Hutton Mount, Ripon, 21 March 1953

1c. Elizabeth, b. 1832, d, in Kirkby Fleetham in 1844,

2c. Jane, b. 15 December 1833, d. in Sidmouth, 25 March 1862

3c. Fanny, b. 2 August 1835, m. in Huyton by Roby, Lancs. 28 April 1864, Thomas Christopher Booth (d.in Warlaby, Yorks., 7 September 1878, aged 45), of Warlaby Hall, a farmer & cattle breeder, & d. in Ovingham, Northumberland, 18 April 1919, having had issue,

1d. Richard Booth, of Warlaby Hall, b. 6 January 1869, in Coniston Cold, 26 April 1900, Mary Elizabeth, dau. of Thomas Hirst (d.15 January 1942, aged 45) & d. 18 July 1958, having had issue,

1e. Thomas Calvert, emigrated to South Africa, b. 4 August 1901, m. Joyce Blampied

2e. William, b. 13 November 1902, d. 22 May 1995

3e. Richard, b. 1906, m. in Argentina, Yolanda … & had issue,

---

[426] He was apparently bankrupted by the reconstruction measures brought in by the Marques de Pombal after the Lisbon earthquake of 1755. There were several major port importing house in the 18th century – chief among them the firms now known as Croft's and Warre's. The French wars had interrupted the flow of the wines of France and the British developed a taste for the stronger wines of Portugal. After her daughter-in-law's death in 1782, Elizabeth Lockwood lived with her eldest son and helped bring up the children.

[427] Info from webpage on the Lockwood family.

1f. Lillian

1e. Fanny, m. Geoffrey Gregory & d. 1999

2e. Dorothy Jane, b. 23 January 1908, m. Arthur Dodd & d. 1999

3e. Kathleen Mary, 23 January 1908, m. 1st in Orange Free State, RSA, John Jenner. She m. 2ndly Dirk Uys & d. in 2000

2d. Thomas, b. 4 November 1870, m. 1stly in South Africa, 14 March 1913, Selina (d. 1932, aged 64), dau. of Hugh Hamilton & had issue,

1e. John Hamilton, Flt. Lieut., b. in South Africa, 1917, k'd at El Alamein, 26 April 1942

He m. 2ndly 1 February 1935, Mary Louise, dau. of Ernest Carus-Wilson & d. in Carolina, South Africa in 1936.

3d. John, Rev., b. 21 June 1872, m. 1stly, 16 October 1902, Evelyn (d. 19 February 1909, aged 30), dau. of Edward Clarke Porter & had issue,

1e. Christopher Edward, emigrated to South Africa, b. 5 May 1907, m. Connie… & d. in Durban, RSA, November 1997

1e. Marion, b. 1905, d. in East Leake, Lincs., 1st September 1970

He m. 2ndly in Lincoln, 25 January 1912, Ethel Mary Beatson (d. 16 July 1966, aged 87), dau. of Canon Frederick Beatson Blenkin & d. in Hilton, 3 May 1958, having had further issue,

2e. John Frederick, M.B.E., Treasury Dept, Canberra, Australia, b. 12 February 1921, m. Kathleen Marion, dau, of David Spencer-Jones & d. in Coffs Harbour, Australia, 25 April 1998, having had issue,

1f. David J.. S..

1f. Angela K.. R..

2e. Wilfrida Margaret, b. 2 January 1913, m. 1948, John Henry Kirk (d. in Taunton, 2 December 1995, aged 87) Chief Economic Adviser to the Min. of Ag. & Professor of Marketing at Wye College, London, & d. in Taunton, Somerset, May 1996

3e. Grace Mary, b. 21 October 1915

4d. Wilfred, Rev., b. 22 June 1872, m. in India, 17 February 1904, Constance Magdalena Lechmere, dau. of Henry Wilkins Clift, Public Works Dept., India (ret'd) & had issue,

1e. Godfrey Calvert, b. 4 December 1913, m. 29 July 1939, Mildred Ellalaine Mortimore (d,. in Lewes, in November 2003, aged 92) & d. 17 March 1979

1e. Eleanor, b,. 1915, d. 1992

1d. Jane, b. 20 February 1865, m. 13 September 1894, Rev Charles Fenwick Thorp (d. 20 February 1935, aged 77) & d. in Warkworth, Northumberland ca. 1948, leaving issue,

1e. (Charles) Arthur Robert, Lt., Sub-mariner, b. 26 June 1899, m. Ann Campbell, dau. of Rev. C.B.R. Hunter & was drowned 12 November 1925.

2e. John Christopher, emigrated to South Africa. b. 1903, m. Ione Duarring

1e. Frances Victoria, b. 7 August 1901, d. in Hexham, 10 June 1991

2d. Frances, b. 4 May 1866, m. 20 July 1895, Frederick John, son of Rev George Richard Dupuis & d. in Wylam on Tyne ca. 1950 & had issue,

    1e. Richard Dudley, Lt. Col., East Manse, Muckhart, b. 1898 in Warlaby, m. in Dundee, 18 October 1927, May Milner Brewer Jobbens (d. 22 November 2000, aged 99) & d. 27 December 1977, having had issue,

        1f. Richard, m. Theresa... & had issue

            1g. Robert

        1f. Joan, m. Robin Dodds & had issue,

            1g. Nicola

            2g. Tracey

    2e. (John) Caesar, Rev., b. in September 1903, m. in Newcastle-on-Tyne, 25 April 1928, Marjorie Brooks

3d. Elizabeth, b. 20 September 1867, m. 8 June 1893, Hon. Henry James Hepburne Scott (d. 4 June 1926, aged 60), 2nd son of the 8th Lord Polwarth & d. 2 April 1940

4d. Honoria, b. 1 August 1875, m. 19 September 1905, Rev (Frederick) Wilmott Bennitt, & d. 23 February 1960, having had issue,

    1e. (Albert) John, Rev. Canon, b. 8 June 1907, m. Nora Evelyn Richardson (d. 1981) & d. in Bury St Edmunds in January 1985

    2e. Mortimer Wilmott, m. 28 August 1910, m. Cecilia Maud Coote & d. 18 November 1995

    1e. Margaret Honoria, M.D., b. 19 March 1918, m. Wladyslaw Markiewicz & d. in 1987

4c. Mortimer Sarah, b. in Easingwold in 1837, d. unm. in Rugby 1 November 1923

5c. Laura Sophia, Mother Superior of St Wilfred's Convent, Exeter, b. 1841, d. in St Leonards on Sea, 10 February 1882[428].

6c. Elizabeth Glaister, b. 1845, m. in Prescot in 1867 William Lee (d. in Prescot, Lancs. 1887, aged 54), son of Rev. Joseph Saville Roberts Evans. She m. 2ndly in London in 1895 Lt Col Thomas Reid Waugh Davidson & d. in Hereford, 1914

He m. 2ndly, 29 May, 1819, Rachel (d. 18 April 1828, aged 41), dau. of Jonathan Chrispin & d. 31 March, 1836 having had issue,

2b. Jonathan Chrispin, a merchant in Liverpool, b. 1820, d. unm. 25 June, 1845.

1b. Ann, b. 1822, m. at Kirkby Fleetham, 27 April 1848, Dr Thomas Laycock (d. 21 Sept. 1876, aged 64), then apothecary to the York County Hospital, and from 1855 Professor of the Practice of Physical and Clinical Medicine

---

[428] It is said that her fiancé had died of typhoid fever and that she entered this new community – dedicated to the care of the poor of Exeter – soon afterwards. It was much against her mother's wishes.

at Edinburgh University, and Physician in Ordinary to the Queen when in Scotland and d. in York on 4 Oct. 1869, having had issue,

    1c. Edmond, b. 7 October 1853, d. 24 December 1860

    2c. George Lockwood, M.B. CH.M., b. 15 June 1855, emigrated to Australia & d. in Melbourne 24 May 1926

    1c. Beatrice Rachel, O.B.E., b. May 1857, m. 16 June 1881, Patrick James Stirling, son of Sir Thomas Jamieson Boyd, Lord Provost of Edinburgh & d. in Edinburgh 17 July 1934, having had issue,

        1d. Thomas Jamieson Laycock Stirling, Chief Justice of Sarawak, b. 23 October 1886, d. in Edinburgh, 1 January 1973

  2b. Ellen Tabitha, b. 1826, d. unm. at Prescot, 18 Aug. 1890.[429]

3a. Thomas, a merchant/flax broker of Hull, b. 21 April, 1781, m. 20 Feb. 1806, Caroline (d. 28 Feb. 1842, aged 58), dau. of Francis Haworth & d. at Kingston-upon Hull, Aug 1828[430], having had issue,

  1b. William Francis, b. 25 Dec. 1808, d. unm. in London in Jan. 1849

  2b. Thomas, b. in Hull in 1811

  1b. Ann, b. in Hull in 1807, m. 12 March, 1827, Joseph Nell Watson (d. 1853, aged 54), a master blockmaker of Bilton & d. in Hull in 1841, having had issue,

    1c. Thomas Lockwood, b. in Hull in 1828

    2c. William Lockwood, b. in Hull in 1833, m. 1858, Emma, dau. of Thomas Crosby & had issue,

      1d. James Joseph, b. 1863

      2d. Joseph Crosby, b. 1867

      3d. William Lockwood, b. 1872

      4d. Charles, b. in Hull 1877

      1d. Clara Ann, b. 1859, m. 1891, John William Scott & had issue,

        1e. Walter

        1e. Clara

      2d. Emma, b. 1861, m. 1881, Anderson Banks & had issue,

        1e. William Watson, b. 1881

        2e. George Anderson, b. 1886

        3e. Harry, b. 1888

        4e. Joseph Watson, b. 1896

        5e. Robert, b. 1898

        1e. Edith Hannah, b. 1882

---

[429] She moved in with her brother-in-law on her sister's death to care for the children. She latterly made her home with her nephew, William Lockwood, at Prescot in Lancashire.

[430] According to his great niece, Mortimer Sarah Lockwood, Thomas was bankrupt by 1814 "more by his own neglect of business than anything else" and had his affairs settled at "great expense." She quotes a letter from his father at this time which exhorts him to "become sober and economical and assures him he can support his own family by his own industry, if he will but make a total reformation of his conduct."

2e. Ethel, b. 1884

3e. Clara, b. 1890

4e. Emma Alice, b. 1892

5e. Annie, b. 1894

3d. Alice, b. 1865

3d. Marian, b.1868

4d. Sarah, b. 1870

5d. Elizabeth Caroline, b. 1871

3c. John Francis, a professional singer, b. in Hull in 1836

1c. Caroline, b. in Hull in 1829, m. 1849 Henry Curtis & had issue,

1d. Henry Edmund

2d. Harry

3d. Herbert

4d. Frank Lockwood

5d. Ernest

6d. Harold

1d. Caroline, m. 1878, Kenneth Stewart Baine & had issue,

1e. Charles Kenneth Stewart

2e. Kenneth Stewart

3e. Harold Stewart

4e. Herbert Stewart

1e. Florence May

2e. Edith Lillian

3e. Katie Gladys

4e. Mabel Jessie

2d. Florence, m. 1877 Alfred Dry & had issue,

1e. Francis Henry

2e. Stuart

3e. Alfred Leonard

4e. Leonard

5e. Donald Leslie

1e. Ethel Beatrice

2e. Ada Gertrude

3e. Edith Mary

4e. Kathleen

3d. Lucy Ann, m. Thomas Cook

4d. Amy Beatrice

5d. Frances Edith

6d. Kate Maria

7d. Emmeline, m. 1884 George Tranter

8d. Jessie

2c. Ann Eliza, b. in Hull in 1831, m. 1853 John Loyns & d. in Manchester in 1902, having had issue,

1d. George

2d. Charles

3d. Thomas

1d. Ann Ellen, m. in Leicester, 30 October 1881, Samuel Davis

2d. Maria, m. James Beaumont

3d. Eliza Gertrude, d. a in inf in Leicester in 1872

2b. Caroline, a milliner, b. 1810, m. in Hull, 18 April 1833, Thomas Hartley (d. 1890, aged 91), a portrait painter, & d. in Lambeth in 1888, having had issue,

1c. Thomas Lockwood, M.D., b. in Brighton in 1839, d. in Armedale, Penmaenmawr, 9 December 1923

2c. Walter Noel, K.B., F.R.S., Professor at the Royal College of Science in Dublin, b. 3 February 1847, m. Mary (d. 23 June 1916, aged 67), dau. of Michael Laffan of Dublin[431] & d. 11 September 1913, having had issue,

1d. Walter John, Capt., a bacteriologist, b. in Dublin, 24 April 1889, k'd at Gallipoli, 16 August 1915.

3b. Mary, a dressmaker, b. 1813, m. in London 10 February 1838, Thomas Martin (d. in London in 1881, aged 74) & had issue,

1c. William Lockwood, Rev., vicar of Bettisfield, Salop., b. 4 June 1846, m. in Clifton, Bristol, 10 July 1884, Mary Edith, dau. of Rev. Edward Olivant & d. in Oxford, 14 March 1935, having had issue,

1d. Christopher Lockwood, b. 4 December 1885, d. 19 March 1886

1c. Mary, a milliner, who became a nun, b. in St Pancras, 1841,

2c. Caroline, a dressmaker, b. 28 May 1843, m. at St Anne's, Soho, 19 September 1867, Rev Edmund Husband-Smith (d. in Queensland, Australia, 20 June 1923, aged 85) & d. in Queensland, 16 November 1920, having had issue,

1d. Smith Edmund Warwick Jephson, b. 1870

2d. Cecil William Mountenay, b. 1872, d. 1919

3d. Walter Lockwood St John, b. 1874, d. in Western Australia in 1901

1d. Mary Caroline, b. 1868

2d. Beatrice Katherine, b. 6 July 1877 in Jerry's Plains, NSW, m. 9 August 1910, Allan Ewen Cameron & had issue,

1e. Jephson Beauchamp, m. Millie Doris Hall Bentley

2e. Allan Cecil

1e. Beatrice Patricia

2e. Elizabeth Caroline

3e. Helen Husband

4b. Eliza Brooke, b. in Hull in 1816, m. in St Pancras Old Church, 16 August 1845, Caleb Thomas Rouse (d. 1900, aged 86) & had issue,

---

[431] Before her marriage, as May Laffan, she published several novels about Irish life – and is considered a pioneer of "slum fiction". She had mental problems and died in a psychiatric hospital.

       1c. John Lockwood, b. in Islington, 31 May 1846, m. Mary Jane Kenny & d. in Ontario, Canade in 1926, having had issue,

          1d. Percy Lockwood, b. 20 April 1890, d. 21 May 1911

          2d. Norman Allan, b. 4 February 1893, d. 3 June 1966

          1d. Mabel, b. 29 November 1886

          2d. Irene, b. 11 June 1888

       2c. Norman Dewe, b. 1848, m. 1890 Jane Elizabeth, dau. of Thomas Mills

       3c. Harold Cotton, b. 1853, m. 27 July 1878, Elizabeth Catherine, dau. of William Tyrie Saunders & d. in Leytonstone, 3 May 1894, having had issue,

    1a. Elizabeth, b. 23 March, 1779, m. 18 June, 1814 Stephen Rose Haworth (d. in Hull, in 1845, aged 62), and d. in Nottingham, 10 July, 1816[432], having had issue,

       1b. James King, a pharmaceutical chemist, who lost his business, b. 10 July, 1816, m. Sept 1848, Ellen Fuller (d. 1874) and d. June 1903, having had issue,

          1c. Emily Maria, d. young in 1855

          2c. Ellen Rebecca, b. 1853

          3c. Ada Jane, m. Thomas Wilson & had issue,

             1d. George

             2d. Alfred

       1b. Henrietta Jane, b. 29 March 1815.

  (2) Thomas, b. in Kirkgate, Leeds, 25 Aug. 1754, d. young.

  (3) Thomas, b. 1 March 1759

  (4) James, b. 19 Dec. 1761

  (5) John, b. 19 Dec. 1761

  (1) Elizabeth, b. 2 July 1751, m. in Gilling-by-Richmond, 1 May, 1793, Edward Ditchburn, & d. at Easingwold, 17 May, 1828.

  (2) Jane, b. in Kirkgate, Leeds, 17 July 1756,

    4. Mary bapt. at Kirkby Malham, 18 Oct. 1724, d. 23 Oct. 1729

Thomas King was bur at Kirkby Malham 12 Feb 1727/8[433]

The elder son,

The Very Rev James King, D.D.[434], of Skellands, Perpetual Curate of Clitheroe, 1743-74, with Downham, Lancs; Chaplain to the House of Commons & vicar of

---

[432] Described by her great niece, Mortimer Sarah Lockwood, as "a handsome, clever, but self-willed young woman", whose father did not wish her to marry Stephen Haworth, whose sister was married to her younger brother. She named her son after the dean, who was her great uncle.

[433] His will was made 20 January 1727/8 and proved at the York Registry 19 August 1728. He named as guardians of his children John Walker of Hungerhill, John Serjeantson of Hanlith, Charles Nowell of Capelside, Giggleswick and Henry Wilcock of Thornton

[434] He took his BA in 1737, his MA in 1741, and his DD in 1771.

Holy Trinity w. St Mary, Guildford, Rector of Dunsfold, Canon of Windsor, Dean of Raphoe from 1776. bapt at Kirkby Malham 5 April 1715, educ Ripon Grammar School & St John's Coll. Cambridge, m. at Bolton-by-Bolland 26 Dec 1743, Ann (d. 4 Nov 1794 aged 80), dau. & coh. of John Walker, of Hungerhill, Yorks. and d. 24 April 1795[435] having had issue

1. Thomas (Rev) D.D.[436], Domestic Chaplain to the Duke of Marlborough & Rector of Bladon w Woodstock, Oxon. from 1778, Prebendary of Canterbury from April, 1786 - 1795, Chancellor of Lincoln from 1795, formerly tutor to the son of Edmund Burke, bapt. at Bolton-by-Bolland 26 Feb 1744/5, educ. Clitheroe & Christ Church, Oxford, m. at Eton, 19 April, 1781 Mary[437], dau. of Edward Manby, of Agmondesham, Bucks. and d. 29 July 1801, having had issue

  1a. Ann, b. at Bladon 6 April 1782

  2a. Mary

   3a. Frances, bur. at Bolton-by-Bolland 22 Oct 1787

  4a. Caroline, b. 1795

2. James, Capt. R.N., LL.D., F.R.S., mathematical adviser on Capt Cook's last voyage 1776-1780, bapt. 13 July 1750, d. unm. at Nice 16 November 1784[438]

3. Walker (Rt Rev) Private Sec. to the Marquess of Rockingham as Prime Minister 1782, Fellow of Corpus Christi Coll. Oxford, Preacher of Gray's Inn from 1787, Prebendary of Peterborough from 1794, Prebendary & Canon of Wells 1796-1827, Vicar of Burnham-on-Sea, Somerset, 1799-1827[439], Easington w Aller, Somerset, 1799-1809, Prebendary of Canterbury from 1803, Prebendary of Westminster from 1808, Bishop of Rochester from Jan. 1809, an intimate of Edmund Burke, whose literary executor he became, b. 1751, educ. Clitheroe & Corpus Christi Coll. Oxford, m. from the Burkes' house at Beaconsfield[440], 21

---

[435] His will, made 15 February 1786, left £1,000 to his daughter and each of his younger sons and all his real and personal estate to his eldest son, Dr Thomas King. He added a codicil in 1790, leaving £100 to his (wife's?) niece, Lettice Hanson.

[436] He took his BA in 1768, his MA in 1772, his BD in 1783, and his DD in 1785.

[437] It was said that she was the sister of James Manby, who taught at Eton. She is also likely to have been the sister of Rev John Manby (1763-1844), who served as a curate at Bladon in 1790 and who was presented to the parish of Lancaster in 1806 – presumably through the influence of Edward King, his sister's brother-in-law. John Manby's wife, Elizabeth Margaret, died in Lancaster on 21 March 1821, aged 39.

[438] Not in October, as stated on his father's memorial in Woodstock Church.

[439] Rochester was a poor diocese, which had previously been held with the deanery of Westminster. This link was broken on his predecessor's death, but Walker King kept his stall at Wells (and maybe his other stalls too) to supplement his income. His vicarage at Burnham – just south of Weston-super-Mare – was in the gift of Wells Cathedral. Burnham Church is distinguished by some marbles, designed by Sir Christopher Wren for the Palace of Westminster, which were removed from Westminster Abbey and installed in Burnham by Bishop Walker in 1820.

[440] On 21 July 1792, Sir Joshua Reynolds' niece and heiress, Mary Palmer, married Lord Inchiquin from the Burke's house – but Walker's marriage was less than three weeks after the devastating death of the Burkes' only son. Probably the Burkes were not at home.

Aug., 1794 Sarah (d. at Burnham-on-Sea, January 1852, aged 78), only dau. of Edward Dawson, of Long Whetton, Leics., and d. 22 Feb 1827 having had issue,

1a. Walker (Rev), of Stone Park, Kent, Archdeacon & Canon of Rochester[441], Rector of Stone from 1822, b. 3 May & bapt. at St Marylebone 31 May 1798, educ Westminster (1811-16) & Trinity Coll., Cambridge (matric. 1816), m. at St James, Piccadilly, 15 May 1823 Anne (d. 3 April 1883), dau of Dr William Heberden, Physician to George III[442], and d. 13 March 1859, having had issue,

1b. Walker (Rev), Canon of St Albans, Rector of Leigh-on-Sea, Essex from 1859, b 21 Dec 1827 & bapt. at Stone 16 July 1828, educ. Westminster (1839-40) & Oriel Coll, Oxford (matric. 1846), m. 28 Dec 1850 Juliana (d. 1896, aged 71), dau. of Capt. Henry Stuart, 68th Regt[443], and d. 20 July 1892, having had issue,

1c. Walker Stuart, Capt R.N., b. at Stone 1 October 1851, d. unm. at Lower Hensleigh, Withleigh, Tiverton, Devon, 8 February, 1903

2c. Henry Stuart (Rev), Vicar of Tatworth, near Chard, Somerset from 1887, b. at Stone 1854, educ. Felsted & Clare Coll, Cambridge, d. unm. in Chard, 2 April 1927

Richard had died in London.

[3] He was made deacon by his father on 28 March 1822 and a few weeks later instituted to the living of Frindsbury in Kent, together with the living of Stone. In August, 1825 he handed Frindsbury over to his younger brother, James – having also received the parish of Dartford (which he only kept for a few months). Archdeacon John Law died on 5 Feb 1827, seventeen days before the Bishop. He had been Archdeacon of Rochester for sixty years and ex officio holder of the sixth prebend. It appears that the Bishop then made a deathbed request for his son to be appointed to the vacant archdeaconry – which he duly was in June, before the next Bishop was appointed. However, just before young Walker was instituted as Archdeacon, another person was admitted to the prebendal stall. The Archdeacon took the matter to court and in 1832 he was duly admitted to the prebend. The archdeaconry of Rochester was suspended on his death.

[442] On the death of Sir George Baker in June 1809, Dr William Heberden joined Sir Lucas Pepys, Sir Francis Milman and Dr Reynolds as one of the four Physicians to the Person – the senior physicians attendant on the King. He had been a Physician Extraordinary since 1801. He had specialized in psychiatric medicine and was known as the physician who dealt most kindly with the unfortunate King. His sister Mary was married to Rev George Jenyns of Bottisham Hall, who held a canonry at Ely (and lived at the Priory when in residence). His father, also Dr William Heberden, was a very distinguished physician – known as the 'father of rheumatology' and as the first physician to describe angina. Dr. Heberden senr. built a house for himself in Pall Mall, which his son inherited, but sold in 1814.

[443] Juliana's descendants have all added her surname. Her father, Capt Henry Stuart (1804-1835) was a soldier – one of the thirteen children of Thomas Stuart (1780-1826). Stuart was a Limerick gentleman whose father, Thomas Smyth (1740-85), had changed his name on marrying a Miss Stuart. The Smyths were an Anglo-Irish family. Thomas Smyth's younger brother had inherited from an uncle and was created Viscount Gort in 1816. Gort was unmarried, but engineered a special remainder of the peerage in favour of a younger son of one of his sisters, Juliana Vereker.

3c. Edward, d. an inf.

4c. Edward William Stuart, b. in Stone 1859, educ. Felsted, m. 1894, Lizzie Milburn Marriott (d. in Tunbridge Wells, 21 July 1957, aged 91), and d. at Tanglewood, Brenchley, Kent, 30 Nov 1936[444] having had issue,

  1d. Walker Stuart, b. in Broadembury, Honiton, 1902, d. in Crowborough, Sussex, 2 March 1963 (?unm)

  1d. Julia Milburn, b. in Minnesota 27 March 1899, m. 1922 George Vernon Hinds (d. in Goldhurst, Kent 3 July 1963, aged 68) and d. in Tunbridge Wells, 15 February 1983, having had issue

    1e. George Mervyn, b. in the Cranbrook Reg. District, 1927

    1e.Susan E., b. in the Cranbrook Reg. District, 1923, m. in the Maidstone Reg. District in 1952, Richard T. Wickenden

5c. Charles James Stuart, of Chard, Devon, b. 1860, educ. Felsted & Hertford Coll., Oxford (matric. 15 Oct 1879), m. 1888, Violet Hankin (d. 12 December 1904, aged 42), & d. at Chardstock, Devon 23 April 1928, having had issue[445],

  1d. (Edward) Leigh Stuart (Adm.), C.B., M.V.O., b. 22 February 1889, m. 1917 Lilian, dau. of Edward Strickland, of Clifton, and d.s.p. 8 May 1971.

  2d. Charles John Stuart (Lieut. Gen. Sir), Engineer in Chief, War Office 1941-44, b. in the U.S.A. in 1890, educ. Felsted & R.M.A., Woolwich, m. 1920, Kathleen, dau. of Col. T.W. Rudd, and d. 1967, having had issue

    1e. John Michael Stuart (Rev.), b 1922, educ. Felsted & St Edmund Hall, Oxford, Vicar of Hibaldstow, Lincs. 1970-88, m. 1962, Margret Brand, and d. 12 Oct 2003, having had issue,

      1f. Andreas Charles Stuart, of Streatham, SW16, b. 1963, m. & div., s.p.

      1f. Joy (adopted), b. 1968

      2f. Nicola Carol Stuart, of Gateshead, Tyne & Wear, b. 1969, unm.

    2e. Simon Charles Stuart, Lt. Col., b. 25 Aug. 1924, educ. Felsted, m. Priscilla Coppinger & d. 15 July 2002, having had issue,

      1f. Jeremy, London banker, unm.

      1f. Annabel, m. N.. Knox, but s.p.

    3e. Richard Anthony Stuart, b. 1937, educ. Felsted, m. in Spain & had issue, 3 sons

      1f. Charles, clinical psychologist, Oxfordshire & Buckinghamshire NHS Trust, m. with two adopted daughters

      2f. N.. in Spain

      3f. N.. in Spain

---

[444] He emigrated to the U.S.A. in the 1890s and was a rancher in Minnesota, but it didn't work out. He came back and farmed on a small scale in Kent.

[445] Early in life he went to Minnesota with his wife and children to make his fortune – which he didn't manage to do.

3d. Geoffrey Stuart, KCB, KBE, MC, educ. Felsted, m. 1920 Ethel, dau of D.C.M. Tuke, of Chiswick and d. 1981[446], having had issue,

  1e. James Stuart, emigrated to New Zealand, m. Isabel Woods & had issue,

    1f. Simon, m. Andrea Middleton Smith & had issue,

      1g. Isabella, b. 17 July 1998

      2g. Georgia, b. 25 March 2000

    2f. Mark, m. Lynn Sullivan

  2e. David Clive Stuart, Children's Author[447], b.1924, educ. King's School, Rochester, Downing College, Cambridge & SOAS, m. 1stly, Jane Tuke (div.), and had issue,

    1f. Charles, m. Monica Geary, and has issue,

      1g. Georgina

      2g. Jennifer

    1f. Susan, m. 1stly Ilias Sikiniotis (div.) & had issue

      1g. Alexandra, who has issue,

        1h. Chloe

        2h. Dea Danielle Sacco, b. 28 Aug. 2011

    She had further issue,

      1g. Jeremy

    She m. 2ndly, Tim Grimshaw (div.) and has further issue,

      2g. Toby

      3g. Theo

      2g. Jemima

    She m. 3rdly, Kevin Burke

  He m. 2ndly, Penny Tummins, and d. 9 July 2018, having had further issue,

    2f. Emma, m. & has issue

  3e. Robin Stuart, Capt., Mary Louise Collins of the U.S.A. & had issue,

    1f. Christopher Leigh Stuart, m. Caroline Bergland & had issue,

      1g. Stuart Ramsey

      1g. Lilian

    1f. Teresa, m. & div, s.p.

  4e. Richard Stuart, m. Janet & d. 2008, having had issue,

    1f. Marcus

    1f. Fiona

6c. Geoffrey

7c. Robert Stuart (Rev), Canon of Chelmsford, Rector of Leigh from 1892, b. 1862, educ. Felsted & Keble Coll., Oxford, m. 1904 Ruby Dando, & d. 4 March 1950, having had issue

---

[446] A childhood illness left him almost stone deaf, and yet he became a senior civil servant. A remarkable man.

[447] "Stig of the Dump" is his best-known book.

1d. Noel Leigh Stuart, a Schoolmaster, b. at Leigh 23 December 1903, educ. Felsted & Hertford Coll., Oxford, d. unm. in Bedford, 17 June 1986.

2d. (Robert) Jasper Stuart, Solicitor, b. 10 May 1909, educ. Felsted, m. Josephine Turner and d. 11 May 1992 at Westcliff-on-Sea, having had issue,

  1e. Brian Robert Stuart, tax accountant, b. 1943, educ. Felsted & Lincoln Coll. Oxford, m. Lynette Ramsey (div.) & has issue,

    1f. Richard, b. 1977, educ. Felsted & Edinburgh Univ.

    1f. Lorna, b. 1973, m. Neil Bidgood

    2f. Susan, b. 1973, Ph.D. Manchester Univ., immunologist.

  2e. David John Stuart, b. 1945, educ. Felsted, m. Janice & has issue,

    1f. N...

3d. Denys Stuart, b. 1910, educ. Marlborough, Mining Engineer in Nigeria, d. unm.

4d. Anthony Stuart, MRCVS, D.Sc (London), D.Sc (Khartoum), Professor of Veterinary Anatomy at the University of Liverpool 1962-1987 & Pro-Vice Chancellor, b. at Leigh, 4 April 1922, educ. Felsted & Royal Vet. Coll., London, m. Zoe....., & d. 13 October 2012, having had issue

  1e. Janice, m. & has issue

  2e. Sarah, m. & has issue.

1d. Beryl, LRAM, b. 27 December 1906, d. unm. 1982

1c. Annie Stuart[448], b at Stone, 1852, m. at Leigh in 1879, as his second wife, her cousin, Edward Stanhope Rodd (d. 9 June 1928, aged 80), of Chardstock House, second son of Francis Rodd of Trebartha Hall, Launceston, and d. at Trebartha Hall, 13 December 1938, having had issue,

  1d. Edward Francis Stanhope, of Trebartha Hall, b. at Chardstock House, 1886, m. 1919 his cousin, Florence Maria (d. at East Johnstone, South Molton, 11 November 1952, aged 65), dau. of Charles Wynne Pride, of Horton Kirby, by his wife Edith, dau. of Rev. H.B. Rashleigh, by his wife Sarah Maria, dau. of Rev James King, vicar of Longfield (see below) and d. at East Johnstone, South Molton, 30 November 1947[449], having had issue,

---

[448] Annie Stuart Rodd was a family historian. Her account of the medieval origins of the King family has been generally discounted by other researchers. She – with her sisters – gave a home to the children of her brother Charlie after their mother's death in 1904. Her husband eventually inherited Trebartha Hall on Bodmin Moor from a bachelor brother.

[449] He sold Trebartha Hall to Bryan Lathom in 1940 and he demolished the house in 1949. A newspaper report lamenting the demolition said, "There are few great houses in Cornwall which can boast such a charming natural setting as Trebartha". It had fifty rooms. It had descended from the medieval Trebartha family through the Spoures to Capt Francis Rodd of Herefordshire, who was due to marry the Spoure heiress in 1730 when she died, leaving him her estate. Mrs Mann and her sister lodged many family papers in the Cornwall Record Office.

1e. Evelyn Mary Stanhope, b. at Chardstock House, 1920, m. 1946 William Mann

2e. Anne Frances Hope, b. at Chardstock House, 1922, m. 1950 Christopher Morshead & d. 1991

3e. Elinor Mary Wynn, b. at Trebartha Hall, 1923, m. 1951, Eric Richard Lloyd

4e. Diana Edith Alicia, b., at Trebartha Hall, 1927

2c. Emily Stuart, b. at Stone 1856, d. unm. at Church Hill, Honiton, 6 May 1934

3c. Juliana Stuart, b. 1857, m. at St Clements, Leigh in 1893, Dr Charles Stanley Kirton (d. in Dawlish, 3 December 1897, aged 28), and d. at Church Hill, Honiton, 21 June 1934, having had issue,

1d. Kenneth Stanley, of Honiton, b. at Leigh Rectory in 1896,

1d. Winifred Kathleen, b. at Leigh Rectory in 1894, d. unm. at Church Hill, Honiton 25 April 1936.

2b. Edward (Rt. Rev.), Bishop of Lincoln from 1885, Principal of Cuddesdon Theological Coll., Professor of Moral & Pastoral Theology, Univ of Oxford, b 29 Dec 1829 & bapt. at Stone 17 Aug. 1830, educ. privately & at Oriel Coll., Oxford, d. unm. 8 March 1910

3b. Henry, Capt 21st Fusiliers, bapt. at Stone, 29 July 1833, educ. Harrow, drowned in Malta, 28 March 1857, unm.

4b. William, 58th Regt., bapt. at Stone 19 Oct 1837, educ. Oriel Col, Oxford (matric. 1855), m. at Curry Rivel, Somerset, 20 August 1868, Frances Isabella Juliana Speke, dau. of Dr C.H. Marword Mules, of Ilminster and had issue,

1c. Marword Edward Rex, Capt., D.S.O., b. 13 Nov. 1869, & baptized at Cricket Malherbie, 28 December 1869, educ. Winchester, 3rd Batt. Royal Scots 1887-91, in the U.S.A. 1891-98, in South Africa from 1900. Capt in the South African Constabulary, A.D.C. to the Governor of Transvaal, and d. unm in Transvaal, 21 June 1906.

2c. William Henry, Maj. 6th Dragoons, bapt at Angersleigh, Somerset, 19 October 1871, m. Mary Violet O'Connor and had issue,

1d. Edward Rex

2d.Desmond

1d. Violet Lilian, b. 1908 – living with her parents in Donegal in 1911

5b. Charles James, bapt. at Stone, 8 Sept. 1844, m. in London in 1865 Marie Anne Theresa Batchelor (who m. 2ndy in 1876 in Melbourne, William Arthur Brins Tobin). They emigrated to Australia in 1866 and he d. in Queensland, Australia, 30 October 1872.

1b. Anne, d. young

2b. Anne, b. at Stone Park, 22 June 1831, d. unm. at Stone 1858

3b. Mary, b. 1835, m. 6 March 1864, Rev George Frederick Wilgress (d. 1878, aged 50), and d. in Bath, 21 May 1922, having had issue,

1c. George Frederick, (Rev. Prebendary), b. Aug. 1868, educ. Lancing & Keble Coll. Oxford, Domestic Chaplain to Bishop King, 1894-1910, Rector of Elm, Somerset, d. unm. in Stamford, Linc. 21 September 1953

2c. Edward Heberden (Rev.), Rector of Carlton Scroop, b. at Cuddesdon, 1871, educ. St Edward's School, Oxford & Keble Coll. Oxford, m. Florence Margaret... & d. at Sutton Veny, Warminster, 4 September 1934

   3c. John Henry Farquhar, b. 8 March 1876, m. 23 October 1905, Florence Edith, dau. of Thomas Woodward of Feltham, Middlesex & d. in Folkestone, 12 June 1921, having had issue,

      1d. Mary, b. in Folkestone, 1907

1c. Mary Frances, b. 1866, d. unm. in Bath 7 December 1939

2c. Elizabeth Catherine, b. 1870, k'd in a bombing raid in Exeter, 25 April 1942, unm.

   3c. Anne Henrietta, b. 1872, k'd in a bombing raid in Exeter, 25 April 1942, unm.

4c. Emily Barbara, b. 1874, d. unm. in Bath, 5 November 1937

4b. (Sarah) Frances, b. 1836, m. 1868, Rev. Stephen Fox Nicholl (d. 31 July 1920, aged 85), 4th son of Rt. Hon. Sir John Nicholl, of Merthyr Mawr, Glamorganshire[450], and had issue,

1c. Henry Stephen (Rev.), b. at Llandough 13 April 1869, m. 1stly Etheldreda Elizabeth (d. 1917), dau. of Rev Arthur L'Argent Bell, and had issue,

      1d. Irene Marjorie Fox, b. in Leigh, 1898, d. unm. in Carmarthen, Dfyd, in 1976.

He m. 2ndly, 21 January 1919 Frances Edith (d. 1962), dau. of Charles William Sellar, and d. 11 April 1954

2c. Christopher Edward, Master at Bradfield School, Berks., b. 1871, d. unm. at Llandough, 24 July 1960

3c. Rice Mansel Dillwyn, mining engineer & surveyor, b. at Merthyr Mawr 1875,

4c. Archibald Michael Cyprian, Master at the Royal Naval College, Osborne, b. at Llandough 22 September 1879, m. 1906, Ethel Beatrice (d. 1964, aged 87), dau. of John Heberden, and d. in Falmouth, Cornwall in 1975, having had issue,

   1d. Stanley John Archibald, b. 1911, m. 1940, Enid Ellen (d. 2001, aged 86), dau. of Capt. William Lloyd Jenkins, and d. in Pembrokeshire in 1983, having had issue,

      1e. David John Alan, b. 1943

      1e. Janet Yvonne, b. 1948

   1d. Catherine Gwendolin, b. 1908, d. unm in Truro in 2001

---

[450] He was M.P. for Cardiff Borough for twenty years from 1832, Lord of a Treasury under Lord Grey and Judge Advocate General under Peel.

5b. Elizabeth Catherine, b. 1839, m. 1860, Rev. Charles Gerrard Andrewes (d. 1892, aged 64), Rector of Wouldham, Kent, and d. in Bouverie Square, Folkestone, 29 May 1902, having had issue,

    1c. Charles Gerrard, of Ramsgate, b. at Ickleford, Herts. 1863, m. in Auckland, Durham, 1889, Lucy Ethel Leigh (d. 1931, aged 63) & d. in Ramsgate 27 August 1933, having had issue,

        1d. Marjorie Anne, b. at Wouldham, 21 August 1890, d. unm. in Thanet in 1977

        2d. Jessie Madeline, b. at Wouldham, 9 September 1891, d. unm. in Thanet in 1977

    2c. William Gerrard, b. at Wouldham, 1870, d. in Folkestone 1872

    1c. Elizabeth Catherine, b. in Ickleford in 1864, d. unm. in Hastings, 12 March 1917

    2c. Annie, b. in Ickleford, 1866, d. unm. in Bouverie Square. Folkestone 27 March 1906.

    3c. Mary, b. at Wouldham in 1874, d. unm. in Wouldham, 1890,

    4c. Sarah, b. at Wouldham in 1877, d. unm. in Wouldham, 1888

2a. Edward Dawson, b. 17 June 1799 & bapt at St Marylebone 21 July 1799, d. 15 May 1815, aged 16 & is buried in Bromley Church.

3a. James (Rev), of Longfield Court, Kent, Rector of Longfield from 1825[451], and of Henley-on-Thames   1825-52[452], b. 1801, educ Westminster (1814-16) & Oriel Coll, Oxford (matric 1818), m 13 July 1825 his cousin, Maria (d. 5 May 1841, aged 35), dau of Lt. Col. Hon. George Carleton, by Henrietta, eldest dau. of Edward King, of Askham Hall (see below), and d. 21 June 1864, having had issue,

    1b. James Carleton (Rev), Vicar of Bury, Sussex from 1856[453], b 1830, educ Balliol Coll & St Mary Hall, Oxford, m. at Stone, 13 April 1852, his cousin Anne (d 25 May 1911), dau of Rev. Canon Thomas Wodehouse, by his wife

---

[451] Rev John Currey, the ancient rector of Longfield, with Dartford, died on 9 April 1825. He had been in post for nearly 50 years. On 18 June, James was ordained by Bishop Law of Bath & Wells and was then presented by his father to Longfield (24 June 1825) while his brother gave him Frindsbury (31 August 1825) in exchange for Dartford. James handed over Frindsbury a few months later (27 February 1826) to his cousin, James Formby, having received Henley-on-Thames in Oxfordshire (18 December 1825).

[452] James King's tenure at Henley did not long survive the arrival of Samuel Wilberforce as Bishop of Oxford. In February 1846, Wilberforce wrote 'I am anxious to draw your most serious and earnest attention to the state of your important parish of Henley. It is overrun with Dissent and Godlessness.' A second curate was needed and a contribution to the establishment of a district chapel at Rotherfield Grey. Six years later, the Bishop was writing again – in effect requiring residence or resignation. James had intended to put his son in as curate, when he was old enough, but the Bishop did not think this would answer. James junr. was presented to Bury by Bishop Wilberforce as a sort of *quid pro quo*.

[453] Seymour & Rhona Tuck were living in Bury at the time of my ordination in 1974. There were still memories of James King around and prayers were offered for me in Bury Church.

Anne, dau. of Rt. Rev. Walker King, Bishop of Rochester (see above),and
d.s.p. 14 Jan 1887

2b. Carleton, b. at Henley, 25 March 1841, *living* 1861

1b. Sarah Maria, b. 1828, m. at Longfield, 14 Sept 1847 Rev. Henry Burvill
Rashleigh (d. 13 Jan 1916, aged 95), Vicar of Horton Kirby, near Dartford,
eldest son of Rev. George Rashleigh, vicar of Horton Kirby. and d. 24 June
1923, leaving issue,

  1c. George Burvill, of Horton Kirby, Chairman of the Parish Council there
  for 22 years, b. at Horton Kirby, 31 Aug. 1848, educ. Oxford, m. 17 Aug.
  1882, Lady Edith Louisa Mary (d. 20 June 1904, aged 50), eldest dau. of
  John Bligh, 6th Earl of Darnley & d. 7 April 1916, having had issue,

    1d. Henry Pelham, b. 21 June 1883, d. 2 Dec. 1954

    1d. Isabel Mary, b. 20 Aug. 1884, m. 31 Aug. 1911, Francis Gawayne
    Champernowne, Bursar of Keble Coll., Oxford (d. 29 May 1921, aged 56),
    3rd son of Rev. Richard Champernowne, Rector of Dartington, by his
    wife Elizabeth, dau. of Rev. Thomas Keble & niece of Rev. John Keble, the
    churchman & poet, & had issue,

      1e. David Gawen, b. 9 July 1912, Professor of Statistics at Oxford, 1948-
      1959, educ. Winchester & King's Coll., Cambridge, m. 30 March 1948,
      Wilhelmina Barbara Maria, dau. of Petrus Ludovicus Dullaert, of the
      Netherlands, & had issue,

        1f. Arthur Francis, b. 1 June 1949, educ. Bedales & Churchill Coll.,
        Cambridge, m. in Leeds in 1976, Ellen M. Taft, & had issue,

          1g. Sarah Margaret Taft, b. 1990

          2g. Clare Marie Taft, b. 1996

        2f. Richard Peter, b. 19 June 1953, m. at Exeter in 1986, Jacqueline
        Mary, dau. of William F. Wills, of Petersfield, & had issue,

          1g. Alison Clare, b. 1991

    2d. Beatrice Mary, b. 26 Nov. 1885

    3d. Mary Elizabeth Joan, b. 22 March 1887, m. 1908, Hugh Barrington
    Worsley, & had issue,

      1e. Eleanor Edith Joan, b. 1909

    4d. Katherine Maria Theodosia, b. 13 May 1888, m. 1stly, 4 April 1910,
    Evelyn Godfrey Worsley (k'd. in Flanders 17 Sept. 1916) & had issue,

      1e. Margaret Katherine, b. 14 May 1911, m. 1935 Maj. Mark Harold
      Collet, & had issue,

        1f. Mark Evelyn Worsley, b. 1937

        1f. Veronica Margaret Rose, b. 1941,

      2e. Diana Mary, b. 26 Feb. 1914, m. 1938 John Gutch & had issue,

        1f. Christopher John Worsley, b. 1941

        2f. Timothy Clement, b. 1943

        3f. Richard Evelyn, b. 1946

    She m. 2ndly, 22 July 1919, her cousin, Rev. William Rashleigh & d. 1974,
having had further issue (*see below*)

2c. Carleton (Revd), some time curate to his father at Horton Kirby, b. 11 Nov. 1851, educ. Charterhouse, m. 1 June 1886, Florence Wyndham (d. 10 May 1906), dau. of Capt. Hervey George St John-Mildmay, of Hazelgrove, Somerset, & d. 29 April 1938, having had issue,

    1d. Rosamund

    2d. Muriel

    3d. Ethel

1c. Mary Georgina, b. at Horton Kirby, 1850, m....Hale & had issue

    1d. James R. b. 1874

    1d. Mary Evelyn, b. at Rusthall, Kent, 1873, living unmarried with her mother and grandparents at Horton Kirby Vicarage from the 1881 census onwards

    2d. Annie M. b. 1876

2c. Edith, b. at Horton Kirby, 1859, m. 1stly Charles Wynne Pride, of Horton Kirby, & had issue,

    1d. Florence, b. 1888, m. her cousin, Edward Rodd, son of Edward Stanhope Rodd, by his wife Annie, dau. of Rev Walker King, Rector of Leigh (see above)

She m. 2ndly 1905 her cousin, Walker King, of Barley House, Exeter (see below), & d. 1910

2b. Henrietta Maria, b. 1829, d unm 1906

3b. Mary Georgiana, b. 1831, m. at Longfield, 28 Jun 1865, her cousin, John Myers King, of Minehead, Somerset (see below), and d.s.p. 14 May 1912.

4b. (Frances) Portia, b. 1836, m 2 July 1863 William Boys Rashleigh, of Farningham Manor, Kent, and d 15 Dec 1906, leaving issue

    1c. William (Revd), vicar of Horton Kirby, b. 7 March 1867, m. 1stly 1902 Harriet Eddowes (d. 26 Feb. 1919) and had issue,

        1d. William Eddowes, b. 17 Dec. 1904, m. 24 July 1931, Joan Arbuthnot Scott & had issue,

            1e. William George Timothy, b. 30 October 1936

        2d. Jonathan, b. 13 July 1913

        1d. Marjorie Frances, b. 5 May 1903, m. 4 April 1923, Quintin Bernard-Thomas & had issue,

            1e. Hugh, (Ph.D. Bristol) b. 26 Dec. 1923

            2e. Colin Barnabas Rashleigh (Rev.), Rector of Rosyth in 1960, b. 11 June 1928

            1e. Elizabeth, (Ch.B., Bristol, 1948) b. 22 Dec. 1924

        2d. Phyllis Mary, b. 22 Sept. 1906, m. 26 April 1929, John Rashleigh Low & had issue,

            1e. Robert John Rashleigh, b. 5 Nov. 1931

            2e. Peter William, b. 13 Nov. 1936

            3e. James Edward, b., 1 July 1943

        3d. Ruth Portia, b. 12 Dec. 1908, m. 9 April 1931 Frank Grant Burslem & had issue,

1e. Michael Rashleigh Grant, b. 7 Feb. 1933

2e. Christopher David Jeremy Grant, b. 27 Jan. 1935

3e. Quintin Nathaniel Grant, b. 1 May 1936,

4d. Katharine b. 1 Nov. 1911, m. 2 Nov. 1932 Curtis William Folliott Scott & had issue,

1e. Richard Rashleigh Folliott, b. 2 Oct. 1934

1e. Eleanor Marion, b. 20 Oct. 1933

Rev. William Rashleigh married 2ndly, 22 July 1919, his cousin, Katherine Maria Theodosia (d. 1974, aged 86), widow of Evelyn Godfrey Worsley & dau. of George Burvill Rashleigh & had further issue,

3d. Francis Evelyn George, b. at Horton Kirby, 19 July 1920, m. Ann, dau. of Wilkinson Hartley & was killed near Leros, 30 Sept. 1943, having had issue,

1e. Anthony, b. 17 July 1942, m. 1stly, at Aspley Guise, 6 Oct. 1962, Annette, dau., of Donald Butcher, & had issue,

1f. David Teasdel, b. in Bedford, 29 May 1963

He m. 2ndly in Bedford, 26 Feb. 1967, Christina Mary Powons & had further issue,

1f. Kathy, b. in Bedford, 5 Aug. 1967

2f. Michelle, b. in Bedford

5d. Jean Marion, b. at Horton Kirby, 27 June 1922, m. 22 Jan. 1946, Clive Walter Collyer Beasley & had issue,

1e. Michael Clive Rashleigh, b. 5 July 1948

2e. Richard King, b. 4 May 1950

1e. Judith Margaret, b. 27 Dec. 1951

6d. Portia, b. 26 Oct. 1923, m. 30 April 1948, George Milton, son of George Edward Kelly & had issue,

1e. Jonathan Christopher George Rashleigh, b. 19 April 1954

1e. Barbara Jane Alison, b. 1 May 1950

2e. Philippa Frances Portia, b. 15 July 1952

3e. Deborah Jean Cecilia, b. 1 Oct. 1955

7d. Alison Clare, b. in Ridgmont, Bedfordshire, 10 Sept. 1930

2c. Hugh George, b. at Farningham, 8 June 1876, d. 29 Aug. 1948

1c. Portia Maud, b. at Farningham in 1866, d. 24 Aug. 1912

2c. Eva Mary, b. at Farningham in 1869, d. 1947

3c. Clara, b. at Farningham in 1871, d. 1926

4c. Agnes Lilian, b. at Farningham in 1873, d. 13 March 1952

5c. Blanch, b. at Farningham, 2 Oct 1874, m. 14 July, 1915, as his second wife, her cousin, Walker King, of Barley House, Exeter, & had issue (see below)

5b. Georgiana Anne, b. 1840, m. at Longfield, on the same day as her sister, 28 June 1865 her cousin, Rev Walker King, Rector of Huish Champflower, and had issue (see below)

1a. Mary, b. in London, 28 June 1795, d. 22 Feb 1817, aged 21, and is buried in Bromley Church.

2a. Anne, b. 1 December & bapt at St Marylebone, 31 December 1796, m. at Norton, 3 June 1817, Rev. Thomas Wodehouse (d. 22 March 1840, aged 52), Rector of Norton, Kent from 1816, Rector of Stourmouth, Kent, Prebendary & Canon of Wells from 1817, second son of Thomas Wodehouse[454], of Sennow, Norfolk and grandson of Col. Sir Armine Wodehouse, 5th Bt, of Kimberley, Norfolk, and d. 6 March 1854, leaving issue,

    1b.Thomas (Rev), b.22 May, 1818, assistant chaplain at the Savoy Chapel, d. unm. 15 Feb., 1905

    2b. Walker (Rev), b. 31 Aug. 1819, vicar of Elham, Kent, d unm. at Elham 24 December 1899[455]

    3b. James, b. 25 October 1829, d. at sea 11 January 1866

    4b. Francis Arthur, of Edenbridge, Kent, b. in Wells, 18 June, 1831, m. 1879, his cousin Frances (d. 13 June 1928, aged 89), dau of Rev Nathaniel Wodehouse, vicar of Dulverton[456], and d.s.p. 30 Dec. 1891

    5b. Armine, b.1832, d. young

    6b. George Carleton, bapt at Norton 23 April 1834 & bur. there 22 August 1834

    7b. Edmond Henry, CB, b. at Norton, Kent, 17 Feb. 1837, Barrister-at-law, Commissioner of the Inland Revenue 1891-1902, m. 26 May, 1864 his cousin, Louisa Clara (d. at Plomer Hill, 18 Jan 1920), dau of Rev Nathaniel Wodehouse, vicar of Dulverton, & d.s.p. at Plomer Hill, High Wycombe, 23 March, 1923.

    8b. Octavius, b. at Norton 1838, d. at Wells, 1838

    1b. Sarah Frances, b. at Wells, 1821, m. 15 May, 1850 her mother's first cousin, William Spencer Dawson (d. at Cobham 6 March 1887, aged 71), of Meadow House, Cobham, Kent, youngest son of Edward Dawson, of Whatton House, Leics.[457] & d.s.p. at Cobham, 27 April 1909

---

[454] Thomas Wodehouse was a barrister. His eldest brother became Lord Wodehouse, and his second brother was a Prebendary of Norwich Cathedral. His mother, Sarah Campbell, was the sister of the 1st Lord Cawdor.

[455] A picturesque village on the way to Folkestone.

[456] Francis Wodehouse described himself as a 'glass painter' – which didn't bring in much money. He was not well off. Georgiana Wodehouse, the mother of Frances and Louisa, was the daughter of the Hon. & Rev. Henry Capel, a rather eccentric vicar of Watford. Capel was a younger son of the 3rd Earl of Essex, a M.F.H. and keen cricketer, who was had up by Bishop Bloomfield for neglecting his parish duties.

[457] Edward Dawson (1778-1815) of Whatton House married Susan March Phillips (1778-1853), whose nephew was the famous Catholic convert, Ambrose March Phillips de Lisle of Garendon Park, who founded Mount St Bernard Abbey. Spencer Dawson's elder brother sold Whatton House in the 1870s (it was soon afterwards burnt down) and moved to Launde Abbey.

2b. Anne, b. 1823, m. 13 April, 1852 her cousin Rev James Carleton King *(see above)* & d.s.p. 25 May 1911

3b. Mary Dulcibella, b. 1824, d. unm. in Stone, February 1847

4b. Blanch, b. 1826, d. unm. in Stone, October 1850

5b. Agnes, b. at Norton, 1828, m. 11 Feb. 1865 George Sanders Williams (d. in Kensington, 4 April 1903, aged 64), Ceylon C.S., and had issue,

  1c. John Wodehouse, of Wadhurst, b. in Ceylon in 1869, m. 1stly in 1893 his cousin, Eliza Frances (d. in Wadhurst, 14 September 1906, aged 41), dau. of Rev W.C. Fox by Georgina Sarah Wodehouse, and had issue,

    1d. Thomas Wodehouse, b. in Wadhurst 1895, educ. Wellington, k'd in France 9 May 1915

    2d. Charles Wodehouse, b. in Wadhurst 1899, m. Sheila.... & d. in London, 1957, having had issue,

      1e. Gary Allen, b 1939, d. 2009

    1d. Agnes, b. 1903

    2d. Georgina Elsie, b. 27 August 1906, d. unm. in Salisbury, 19 May 1988

  He m. 2ndly 12 November 1910, Mildred Caroline (d. in Wadhurst, 25 June 1930, aged 59), dau. of Dr Arthur Watson of Harrow School, & d. at Wadhurst, 2 September 1929, having had further issue,

    2d. Edmond George, b. 14 February 1912, d. 25 March 1972

    3d. Elizabeth Digby, b. in Wadhurst, 7 April 1913, m. in 1939, Alexander Meadows Rendel (d. in Salisbury, 1991, aged 81) & d. in Barnes, London in 2006, having had issue[458]

2a. Sarah Frances, m. 9 June, 1827, her cousin, Rev John Myers King, Vicar of Cutcombe, Somerset (see below)[459], and d 11 March 1886, leaving issue *(see below)*

5. Edward, of whom presently

6. Edmund, baptized at Clitheroe, 14 May 1756, d.an inf

7. John, of Aldenham House, Herts.[460], Permanent Under-Secretary at the Home Dept 1792-1806, MP for Enniskillen & Joint-Secretary at the Treasury, 1806-7 in the ministry of his patron Lord Grenville, b 1759, educ Eton & Christ Church, Oxford[461], m. 9 April 1792 Harriot Margaret (d 1841[462]), only dau of Rt Rev

---

[458] Lane, MR (1989). *The Rendel Connection: a dynasty of engineers.*

[459] It said somewhere that John's elder brother, Bolton King, had hoped to marry Sarah but that "she jilted him" in favour of his younger brother.

[460] This was rather a grand house that was later sold to the banker, Vicary Gibbs (Lord Aldenham).

[461] He matriculated on 16 July 1777, took his BA in 1781 and his MA in 1784. He was a Student of Lincoln's Inn in 1781, but migrated to Gray's Inn on 4 June 1790 and was called to the bar five days later. He was Bencher of Gray's Inn 10 Feb 1813 and Treasurer in 1815.

[462] John King's will, dated 21 Nov 1818 and proved 10 March 1830 left everything to his wife. Her will stated that Mary Anne had had £10,000 on her marriage and that Caroline had had £5,000 on hers. £6,000 was left to Rev W M King and £4,000 to Robert.

Charles Moss, Bishop of Bath & Wells, and sister of Rt Rev William Moss, Bishop of Oxford, and d. at Grosvenor Place, 30 March 1830, having had issue,

1a. John James, of Coates Castle, Sussex and afterwards of Preston Candover House, Hants[463], D.L & J.P., 13 Dec 1794, educ. Eton & Christ Church, Oxford, m. at St George's, Hanover Square, 29 July 1823, Charlotte (d. 1870, aged 75), natural dau. of William Wyndham, 3rd Earl of Egremont and d. 19 July 1867, having had issue,

1b. John Henry Wyndham, of Preston Candover House, Hants[464], DL & JP, b. April 1825, m. Dec. 1852, Emily, dau of Hon Lionel Charles Dawson, and d.s.p 7 Nov 1889

1b. Charlotte, b. 1826, m. at St Peter's, Eaton Square 12 July 1856 Philippe Marie de Gilibert (d. in Haywards Heath, Sussex 4 January 1889), of Breye Cortese, France, and Brighton & d. in Brighton, 16 August 1900, having had issue

1c. Emily Mary, b. 1860, m. 21 April 1881 William Dundas Scott Moncrieff (d. 1 December 1924, aged 78), civil engineer & inventor & d 1929, having had issue,

1d. Philip David, Asst Keeper of Egyptian & Assyrian Antiquities, British Museum, b. 27 February 1882, m. 3 February 1906 Grace Isabella Florence Josephine (d 22 December 1953, aged 86), dau. of Col. Hardy Eustace, of Castlemore, co. Carlow & d. 8 February 1911 leaving issue[465],

1e. David William Hardy "Bunty", of Kirkton House Forfar, b. 1 July 1907, m. 3 May 1941, Averill Marion Anne (d. 9 March 2006, aged 90), of Basford Hall, Staffs., only child of Capt. Thomas Humphrey Sneyd[466] & d. 1987, having had issue

1f. Humphrey David Sneyd, of Basford Hall, Lord Lieut. of Staffordshire from 2009, b. 28 December 1945, educ. Wellington, m. Judy Prince

2f. Ambrose Patrick Eustace, b. 4 March 1947, educ. Wellington, m. 1971 Claudia Mary Delphine, dau. of Maj Robert Charles (Bobby) Petre & has issue,

1g. Chloe, b. 1976

2d. William Walter, M.C., ARIBA, FRIBA, of Horham, Diss, b. 8 March 1886, m. 18 August 1938 Kirsten, dau of Axel Ingworsen of Copenhagen.

3d. Gilbert, b. 31 August 1891, d unm. 4 July 1949

---

[463] He built Coates Castle, near Pulborough, in 1829 presumably so that Charlotte could stay close to her father. They were much involved with Petworth during the old Lord's lifetime. A portrait of Mrs King hangs there. He sold Coates in 1858.
[464] He sold the estate to Lord Templemore in 1873.
[465] Philip & his brothers were second cousins of Charles K. Scott-Moncrieff, the translator of Proust
[466] Bunty & Averill Scott-Moncrieff were heavily into motor-racing.

1d. Madeleine Zoe, b. 31 August 1891, m. 1stly 24 December 1914, Capt Harold Gilead Smith (d. 2 July 1941), of Philadelphia. She m. 2ndly 4 June 1953 Maj. William McCall (d. 16 April 1959) & d. 1980

2c. Mildred Jeanne, b 1865, m 1902 Lt Col Arthur Joseph Berkeley Addison (k'd on the Somme, 1 July 1916, aged 49) & d. 13 April 1961, having had issue

    1d. Marie Josephine de Gilibert, b. 1 November 1902 & baptized on 26 November 1902 at Holy Trinity, Sloane Street, m. 1 November 1928 Col. Henry Somerset Parnell Hopkinson (d. 6 November 1988, aged 89) of Llanvihangel Court, Abergavenny, and d. 27 July 1989, having had issue,

        1e. Carola Blanche de Gilibert, b. 9 April 1932, d. 15 November 1956

        2e. Julia Clare Addison, of Llanvihangel Court, Abergavenny, b. 14 November 1940, m. 1968 David B. Johnson, and has issue

2b. Harriet Elizabeth[467], b. 26 November 1831, m. April 1860, Vicomte Charles Rousseau de Labrosse (d. in Bembridge, I. of W., 18 September 1903, aged 83), of Chateau de Varennes-sur-Allier, Brittany, and d. in Cannes 29 November 1902, having had issue,

    1c. Henriette Rousseau, Lady of Grace, St John of Jerusalem, b. at 20 Grosvenor Square, 20 February 1861, d. unm. in Chelsea 15 June 1933.

    2c. Leila Josephine Rousseau, b. in Savennieres, Maine-et-Loire, 17 August 1862, m. at St Paul's, Knightsbridge, 17 June 1906 Charles Stanislaus Stafford (d. 8 May 1938) & d.s.p. in Windsor 8 April 1940.

    3c. Aimie Marguerite Rousseau, b. in Savennieres, Maine-et-Loire, 31 May 1869, m. 1stly in St Paul's, Knightsbridge, 3 January 1894, William Reginald Cookson, of Binfield Park, near Windsor (d. 23 February 1905, aged 38) & had issue,

        1d. Robert Reginald Freville, b. in Chelsea 25 October 1895 & baptized at St Paul's, Knightsbridge. He d. *post* 1959

        2d. John Wyndham, Commander, R.N., b. in London in 1897, m. at St George's, Hanover Square, 23 June 1922, Mary (d. 30 March 1963, aged 67), dau. of Sir Alan John Colquhoun, 6th Bt of Luss & d. in Hastings 29 September 1958, having had issue,

            1e. Leila Mary, m. 1stly 31 October 1942, Hugh William Jardine Ethelstan Peel (k'd in action, 17 February 1945, aged 25)[468] & had issue,

                1f. Sarah Anne Ethelstan[469], b. 14 September 1943, m. Peter Rosselli & had issue

                    1g. Simon

                    2g. Timothy James

---

[467] There is a picture of her at Petworth with her grandfather, Lord Egremont.

[468] His great-grandfather, Edmund Peel, married (as his first wife) my father's great aunt, Anna Lethbridge.

[469] Said to have inherited some £350,000 – quite a sum in those days.

She m. 2ndly Lloyd Tyrell-Kenyon, 5th Lord Kenyon (d. 16 May 1993, aged 76)[470] & had further issue,

    1f. Lloyd, 6th Lord Kenyon, of Gredington, Whitchurch, b. 13 July 1947, educ. Eton & Magdalene College, Cambridge, m. Sally Carolyn, dau. of Jack Frank Page Matthews, of Bury St Edmunds, & d. 17 August 2019, having had issue

        1g. Lloyd Nicholas, 7th Lord Kenyon, b. 9 April 1972

        2g. Alexander Simon (Hon), b. 29 November 1975

    2f. Richard (Hon), b. 26 November 1948, m. 1stly, 7 October 1970 (div. 1977), Davina Jane Jessel (who m. 2ndly Charlie Phillips of Whitchurch, Hants) & had issue,

        1g. Vanessa Zoe, b. 29 March 1974, m. 2004 Luke de Haan

    He m. 2ndly, 1980, Janet Nelson & d. 1982

    3f. Thomas (Hon), b. 14 March 1954, d. 1993[471]

    1f. Katherine (Hon), b. 21 April 1959, m. 1985, Nigel David Vardon Churton[472] & had issue,

        1g. Oscar Vardon, b. 1987

        2g. Rollo Crispin, b. 1989

        1g. Zara Fleur, b. 1991

Mrs Cookson m 2ndly at Aston, 1 March 1906 Edward Charles Shuttleworth Holden, J.P. (d. 19 May 1916, aged 51) of Aston, Derbyshire & d. on the Isle of Wight in 1913.

3b. Elizabeth (Lilla), b. 1836, m. 1stly, 31 Aug 1854, Capt George Frederick Dawson (k'd at Sevastopol, 5 June 1855), only son of Hon. Lionel Charles Dawson (youngest son of the 1st Earl of Portarlington), and had issue,

    1c. Georgina Frederica, b. 6 Oct. 1855, m. Feb. 1875 Arthur Henry Mure (d. in Onslow Gardens, Kensington, 12 Feb. 1931, aged 83) and d. 12 April 1944, having had issue,

        1d. Godfrey Arthur Stanhope (Jock), b. 1880, k'd. 3 January 1917

        2d. James George Dawson, a brewer, Mure & Co. Hampstead Brewery, b. 19 Oct. 1883, m. 1914, Muriel Decima Horne (d. 29 Jan. 1965, aged 80) & d. 28 June 1966, having had issue,

---

[470] Provincial Grand Master of the North Wales Province in the 1980s – which was the cause of rumours that freemasons were involved in the abuse that took place in the children's homes.

[471] Died of AIDS. In 1977 he was convicted of arson while living in the Birmingham YMCA. Said to have been involved in the North Wales Children's Homes scandal. In 1979 he accused a former Bryn Estyn Children's Home resident (then aged 16) of theft while they were both staying in a flat in Wrexham. During the investigation, the owner of the flat was found to have a collection of indecent photographs and was jailed. Kenyon was not prosecuted. He spent his life among the "low life" of Wrexham, haunting public lavatories and having sex with boys.

[472] Successful businessman, member of the Jockey Club

1f.

1e. Alexander David Evelyn, b. 27 December 1916, m. 8 May 1968, Mrs
Bridget Alice Wickham (née Colfox)
1e. Pamela Frederica, b. 28 September 1919
1d. Marjorie Mary, b. 25 June 1876, m. 30 April 1902, her cousin, William
Addington Venables, son of Rt Rev Addington Venables, Bishop of
Nassau, and d. May 1945, having had issue (see below)
She m. 2ndly Jan. 1859 Roddam Spencer Stanhope (d. 1908 aged 79), of
Bellosquardo, Florence[473], yr son of J.Spencer Stanhope, of Cannon Hall,
Yorks. and d. 1920, having had further issue,
2c. Mary, b. 9 November 1859, d. in Florence, 23 February 1867
2a. (William) Moss (Rev), Rector of Long Crichel, Dorset from 1823[474] & JP, b.
1795, educ. Eton & Christ Church, Oxford, m. 9 March 1825 Elizabeth
Margaret (d. at 82 Gloucester Place, London, 5 Feb 1880, aged 80), dau of
Very Rev Latham Coddington, Dean of Kilfenora, and d 14 July 1864[475], having
had issue,
1b. James, b. 1826, d. unm. 1843, and bur. at Coates, Sussex
2b. Charles John, a merchant in China, b. 1831 & baptized at Coates 29 Nov.
1832, educ. King Edward VI School, Bruton & Merton Coll., Oxford, m. 1stly
at Fuchow, 1 April 1856 (div. 1863[476]), Fanny Rosina, dau. of George Grey
Sullivan, R.N., Consul at Amoy, China, and had issue
1c. (a son) b. & d. 1856
2c. William Henry Raymond, b. April 1858 & bapt. at Long Crichel on 6
June 1858, d. Sept. 1858.
1c. (Elizabeth) Margaret[477], b. Oct. 1859 & bapt. at Long Crichel 5 Nov.
1859, m. 1878, William Donaldson Rawlins K.C. (d. 21 May 1920, aged 74),
of White Waltham Grove, Maidenhead[478], and had issue

---

[473] He was a painter of some note. Cannon Hall is near Barnsley, and is now a recreation
centre, owned by the Borough Council. Roddy's sister, Anna Maria, married Percival
Pickering QC, and was the mother of Mrs Wilhelmina Stirling (1865-1965) who got Aunt
Ethel to leave her pictures to Old Battersea House. Mr Stirling mentioned the relationship
when encouraging Dollman & Pritchard to release the pictures to her. Mrs Stirling's sister
Evelyn (1855-1919) was married to William de Morgan, and was a talented painter in her
own right. William's mother, Sophia de Morgan, wrote the seminal Victorian spiritualist
tract, "From Matter to Spirit" (1863) and William and Evelyn were both into spiritualism.
[474] Long Crichel church was made redundant in 2003, and taken on by the Friends of
Friendless Churches in 2010.
[475] "The late rector was greatly beloved by his parishioners and neighbours, and was
eminently a good preacher and an exemplary Christian." *Dorset County Chronicle* 28 July
1864
[476] On 12 June 1862, Charles petitioned for divorce on the grounds of his wife's adultery
with a William Dent, which he alleged had begun in 1857. Rosina then went on to marry
William Life at St George's, Hanover Square, on 24 September 1864. This marriage wasn't
happy either and she got a divorce on the grounds of cruelty and his adultery in November
1880, by which time she had married for a third time, to Cornelius Thompson, who worked
at the Admiralty. She died in 1900.

1d. Stuart William Hughes, Col., R.M.A., b. 27 May 1880, m. at All Saints', Clapton Park, 22 November 1910 Dorothy Pepys Cockerill & d. 16 December 1927, having had issue

  1e. John Stuart Pepys, KBE, FRCP, FRAeS, Surgeon Vice-Adm., Royal Navy Medical Director General, 1977-80, b. 12 May 1922, educ. Wellington & University Coll., Oxford, m. in Oxford in 1944, Diana Margaret Freshney Colbeck (d. at Little Cross, Holne, Newton Abbot, 20 May 1992, aged 70) & d. 27 July 2011[479]

2d. Evelyn Charles Donaldson, a diplomat, Minister in Bolivia 1937-9, C.M.G., C.B.E., b. 29 March 1884, educ. Eton & Trinity Coll. Cambridge, m. 1909, Matilda Adele Susanne Kapper[480] & had issue,

  1e. Ralph Ian Donaldson, b. 1920

  1e. Lilian Margaret Donaldson, b. 1910, d. 10 January 1912 & bur, in the Suda Bay War Cemetery, Crete

3d. Francis Ian Gregory, CBE, FRSE, FSA, FIP, Physicist & Crystallographer, Deputy Keeper of & Scientific Adviser to the National Gallery, b. 5 August 1895, d. 2 March 1969.

He m. 2ndly 5 May 1870, Frederica Frances (d.s.p. 6 July 1933, aged 87), dau of Col. James Mure, of 20 Gloucester Place, London & d. at 10 Westbourne Place, London, 25 May 1886.

3b. Robert Moss, I.C.S, of Aschott Hill, Bridgwater, b 1834, educ Eton & Merton Coll, Oxford, m. at Swanley, Kent, 5 Aug 1869, (Elizabeth) Augusta (d 22 July 1917, aged 74)[481], dau of Rev John Egerton, Vicar of Hextable, Kent, and d. at Aschott Hill, 7 July 1903 having had issue

  1c. Gerald Curzon Moss, b. 1870, d. 1871 in India

  2c. Robert Curzon Henry Moss, I.C.S., Commissioner of Nagpur, and latterly of Harcourt House, Camberley, b, at Lucknow, 26 July 1871, educ Eton & Merton Coll, Oxford, m. at Nagpur, India, 9 Dec 1895, Catherine (who 2ndly 12 Dec 1934, Capt H.R.M. Hawkins J.P. (d 1946), only son of

---

[477] From 1862, she was brought up by her grandparents at Long Crichel Rectory. A beautiful portrait of her, painted by Evelyn de Morgan in 1883, was sold at Christie's in 1999, by one of her descendants for £34,500. Evelyn was only 28, and was the niece of Roddam Spencer Stanhope, who was married to a first cousin of Margaret's father's.

[478] His brother, Francis Hay Rawlins, was Vice-Provost of Eton from 1916 until his death in 1920. He is said to have chosen the motto for the R.A.F. - *Per Ardua ad Astra*.

[479] Honorary Member of the British Sub-Acqua Club, President of the Historical Diving Society and the Association of RN First Class Divers. He was also Oxford University Judo Club President in 1941-2.

[480] He was a judo enthusiast, founding the first tojo to be set up in the U.K. at Trinity College, Cambridge in 1906.

[481] According to Oliver Bolton King, this Mrs King did a great deal of research into the King family history, which was continued by her son Sir Carleton King. She wrote *Diary of a Civilian's Wife in India, 1877-1882*. Her brother, Rev Philip Egerton, founded Bloxham School

James Staples Hawkins, of St Fentons, co. Dublin & died 15 May 1952), elder dau of Col James Edward Kitson, C.B., 21st Hussars, and d. at the Bull Hotel, Rochester, 14 Sept 1929, having had issue

  1d. Gerald Carleton, b. 7 Dec 1899, educ Haileybury, d. unm. 21 June 1966

  2d. Robert Charles Moss (Maj.Gen.), C.B., D.S.O., O.B.E., late W. Yorks. Regt., b. at Coonoor, India, 6 June 1904, educ. Clifton & R.M.C. Sandhurst, m. 15 June 1940 Grizel (d. 1 Aug 1966, aged 57), dau. of Donald Stuart Mackay, of Cheyne Court, London SW3, and d. 1983, having had issue,

    1e. Annabel Jane, b 13 Dec 1945

    2e. Rosalind Mary, b 29 March 1949

  1d Lilla Muriel Moss, b. 1903, m. 1stly 5 Dec 1923 Lt. I.C.C. Greenlees, R.N. (d 1925) & had issue,

    1e. Ian, m Anne Rodd, and had issue,

      1f. Andrew Coleville, b 1940

She m 2ndly 1927 Capt J.H. Lewes. CBE, DSC, RN, of White Willows, Yelverton (d. 3 May 1961, aged 61) & d. in 1978, having had further issue,

    2e. John Richard, b. 1930, m. 1stly 6 May 1954, Lady Maria Coventry (div. 1968 & d. 17 Nov. 2007), dau. of 10th Earl of Coventry. He m. 2ndly in 19869, Hermione Anderson & d. in Bristol in December 2002.

    3e. Robin Hugh, b. at Pencarwick, Exmouth, 2 June 1932, m. Daphne Deidre, dau. of Maj. Hon. James Philipps & d. 15 April 1969, having had issue,

      1f. James Hugh, b,. 30 June 1967

      1f. Katherine Mary, b. 18 September 1968

      2f. Sarah Jane, b. 18 September 1968

  2d. a dau. b. in Simla, India, 29 August 1910

3c. Bertram Egerton Moss, b. 1873, d. at Villa d'Este, Lake Como 1876

4c. Carleton Moss, KB, CIE, ICS, Chief Justice of the Chief Court of Oudh, b. at Meerut, India, 17 July 1878, educ. Brighton Coll. & Balliol Coll. Oxford, m. at St Stephen's, Gloucester Road, 11 Nov 1909 Fanny Helen (Nell) (d. 7 July 1962), dau. of Alexander Walmeseley Cruikshank, I.C.S., of Crowborough, and d. at Wildacres, Fleet, Hants., 26 Nov 1954, having had issue,

  1d. Margaret Moss, m. 1932 Frank Norman Crofts, I.C.S., Chief Film Censor in 1953, & had issue,

    1e.James Norman, b 1936

    2e. Robert Frank, b 1938

    1e. Susan Elizabeth, b 1935

  2d. Helen Elizabeth Moss, b. 1912, m. 1935 John E. Smith, and had issue,

    1e. John William, b 1941

    2e. Benjamin, b 1945

1e. Prudence, b 1938

3d. Cecily Moss, b. 14 January 1914, m 1943 S/L Francis Michael Doran, F.R.C.S., R.A.F.V.R. (d. 1995, aged 85) and d in Hereford in 1988. had issue,

1e. Gillian Frances, solicitor, b. 28 September 1949,

1c. Geraldine Augusta, b. 1872, d. at Aschott Hill, Bridgwater, 1888

2c. Lucy Campbell, b 1874, m. as his second wife in 1903, Lt. Col. Layard Livingstone Fenton, I.C.S. (d. 14 October 1921, aged 72) of Marsh Hall, North Molton, Devon, and d.s.p. at Marsh Hall, 22 February 1937[482]

3c. Margaret D'Este, b. at the Villa D'Este, Lake Como, 1876, m. at the Garrision Chapel, Rangoon, Burma, 14 December 1925, her first cousin, Charles Hertel Egerton (d. 1951, aged 67) and d.s.p. at Great Bedwyn, Wilts in 1930.

4b. Walter Edward, Consul in China, & latterly of Donhead Lodge, Shaftesbury[483], b 1837, m. 1875 Isabella (d. 1878) dau. of Henry Iltud Nicholl of Llanmaes[484] & d. 1917, having had issue

1c. Lilla Marian, of Roland Gardens, London, S.W.7, d. unm. 16 Dec 1943

5b. William Francis Henry (Rev), b. 1843, educ. Marlborough & Christ Church, Oxford, d. unm. 1909, having entered the Roman Catholic Church[485]. Author of *Classical & Foreign Quotations*

1b. Florentia Martha, b. in Nice, 1828, d. unm. 1884 & bur. in Bournemouth Cemetery

2b. Harriet Penelope, b. 1829, d. unm. 3 October 1891 & bur. at Wokingham[486]

3b. Caroline Jane, b. 1834, d. unm. 23 November 1890 & bur. at Wokingham

4b. Elizabeth Anne (Lilla), b. 1835, m. 1stly at Long Critchel, 1 July 1862, her cousin, Rt. Revd. Addington Venables, Bishop of Nassau (d. 8 October 1876, aged 49), son of Thomas Venables, by his 1st wife Anne, dau. of John King,

---

[482] Col. Fenton wrote *The Rifle in India: being the Sporting Experiences of an Indian Officer*, which was published posthumously. Mrs Fenton left her husband's collection of hunting trophies to South Molton, and they were hung in the Town Hall. I doubt that they are still there! She was well-known as a breeder of dogs.

[483] The house is still there in Donhead St Andrew, with the King family motto above the gates, "*Rex Rege Beatior*". There is a memorial to Isabella King in the church. He did some research into the history of the King family

[484] The Nicholl family were an extensive landed family in and around Cardiff. Walter King's second cousin, Sarah (daughter of Archdeacon Walker), married Rev Stephen Fox Nicholl – from the same family.

[485] He acted as executor to his brother-in-law & cousin, Addington Venables, Bishop of Nassau, and wrote his biography, *Addington Venables, Bishop of Nassau* (1877)

[486] She was one of the witnesses at the wedding in 1862 at Long Crichel of her sister Elizabeth to Addington Venables. The service was taken by Rev Edward Harford, cousin of the bride and groom. At the time of her mother's death, she and her sister Caroline were living with her in Gloucester Place. She died at Pamphill Manor, Wimborne, the home of her sister, Mrs Smith, but her home had been at Shute End, Wokingham.

of Coats Castle & had issue (see below). She married 2ndly 12 June 1883, Maj.-Gen. C. E. Cumberland, C.B. (d. 1920) of Manor House, Maidstone, and d. 14 Jan 1891.

5b. Elinor Mary Frances, of Newton House, Sturminster, b. 1846, m. at St Mary's, Bryanston Square, 14 January 1868, Rev. Francis Alfred Smith, Rector of Tarrant Rushton, Dorset (who d. 15 July 1877, aged 35[487]), grandson of Sir Reginald Wildbore Smith, 2nd Bt. & & d. 28 March 1913, having had issue

  1c. Hugh Francis Wyldbore, of Marston Lodge, Broadstone, Dorset, Capt. R.N., b. 13 Feb. 1869, m. 19 November 1903 Kate Beatrice, dau, of William Henry Deane (d. in Uckfield, Sussex in 1959) & d. 8 May, 1919[488] having had issue,

    1d. Hugh Deane, Lt. Cmdr. R.N. b. 1907, m. in Bombay, 5 June 1937, Rachel, dau. of Rev. E.G. Orlebar, & d. in H.M.S. "Hood", 24 May 1941, having had issue,

      1e. Nicolas Hugh Wyldbore, of Clifton Hampden, Oxfordshire, Director of Ind Coope, b. 23 May 1938, educ. Wellington, m. 18 July 1964 Gillian Mary, dau. of Leslie Boland Carman & had issue,

        1f. Alexander Hugh Nicholas Wyldbore, b. 9 August 1969, educ. Bryanston & Oxford Brookes

        2f. James William Wyldbore, b. 29 October 1971, educ Radley & Bristol University

      2e. Piers Wyldbore, Schoolmaster, b. 22 July 1939, educ Eton & New College, Oxford, d. unm. 28 December 1987

    2d. Alfred Reginald, b. 16 July 1910, d. 13 April 1911

    3d. John Henry Wyldbore, Stockbroker, b. 11 September 1916, educ. Charterhouse, m. 15 April 1939, Robina, dau. of Capt Francis Welsford Ward & d. 4 May 1982, having had issue,

      1e. William Francis, of Bremhill Manor, Calne, b. 15 January 1948, educ. Marlborough, m. 27 December 1974 Mrs Prisca Faith Jenney, dau. of Rev Peter Nourse & had issue,

        1f. Philippa, b. 15 April 1977, m. 2009, Thomas Leon Siegler & has issue,

          1g. Ralph Leon Wyldbore, b. 12 September 2010

          2g. Olivia Isabel Wyldbore, b. 7 May 2012

      1e. Robina Ann, b. 3 October 1943, m. 25 June 1977 (Richard Robert) Bindon Plowman & had issue,

        1f. Andrew John Napier, b. 11 January 1979, d. 8 July 1989

        1f. Felicity Frances Robina, b. 1980

---

[487] He collapsed and died after Evensong – memorial in Rushton Church.
[488] He appears on the village Roll of Honour, so he obviously died as a result of war wounds

2e. Susan Elizabeth, b. 15 August 1950, m. 4 November 2000, Michael Clode

1d. Katherine Elinor, b. 1905, m. 3 June 1936, Algernon Spencer (d. 1965), of The Mount, Stanstead & South Africa and had issue,

    1e. (Charles) Peter, of Johannesburg, South Africa, b. 20 March 1937, m. 27 Sept 1960, Charlotte Ann, dau of Elwyn Lind & had issue,

        1f. Michael John, b. 24 Set 1961, m. Megan Saegar & had issue,

            1g. Joshua, b. 1987

            1g. Samantha, b. 1990

        2f. Gregory, b. 23 October 1966, m. Caryn... & had issue,

            1g. Garrick, b. 1995

            2g. Jarred, b. 1999

        1f. Claire Anne, b. 23 August 1962, m. Chris Britz & had issue,

            1g. Vincent, b 1991

            2g. Ryan, b. 1995

        2f. Lindsay Anne, b. 19 October 1964, m. Martin Shackley & had issue,

            1g. Cameron, b. 1992

            1g. Leila, b. 1997

    2e. David Wyldbore, of Johannesburg, South Africa, b. 1939, m. 1965, Cynthia Raulo & had issue,

        1f. Paul Gregory, m. Melica... & had issue,

            1g. Katarina

        2f. Leila Carinne, m Martin Kuhlmann & had issue,

            1g. Tania

            2g. Chantal

    3e. Hugh Mark, of Johannesburg, South Africa, b. 1941, m. 1stly Elsobie Robbertse & had issue,

        1f. Marten

        1f. Susan

    He m. 2ndly Pamela....

    4e. Simon Francis, of Johannesburg, South Africa, b. 1941

    5e. Christopher Audley, of Johannesburg, South Africa, b. 1948, m. Moira Spier & had issue,

        1f. Neale

        1f. Jenny

2c. (William) Reginald Wildbore (Rev), Vicar of Coleshill, Warwicks., b. 26 March, 1874, m. 20 June 1905, Dorothy (d. 13 June 1969, aged 92), dau. of George Green[489], of Watford House, Watford & d. at Holly House, Berkswell, 26 June 1943, having had issue

---

[489] She was a brewing heiress.

1d. Anthony Reginald, of Elmcroft, Berkswell, m. 30 Sept 1933 Honor Christine Dyott (d. 1984, aged 77), dau. of George Dyott Willmott & d. 1987 having had issue,

1e. Michael Anthony, b. 6 September 1944, m. 24 June 1967 Sheila Margaret, dau, of Ewart Charles Harold Organ & had issue,

1f. Sarah, b. 5 July 1969

2f. Nicola, b. 27 April 1971

3f. Claire, b. 26 April 1977

2d. Francis Brian, Maj. Gen. Sir, C.B., D.S.O., O.B.E. b. 10 July, 1913, of Grantham House, Lincs., m. 1 April 1944, Hon. Molly Angela Cayzer (d. Sept 2001, aged 84), dau. of the 1st Lord Rotherwick & d. at Grantham, Lincs., 6 Dec. 2005, having had issue,

1e. Robin Brian, 4 September 1957, m. 4 September 1999, Philippa Scott & d. 16 August 2001[490]

1e. Carolyn Molly, b. 11 December 1944, m. 2 December 1968, Harry O. Ditson & had issue,

1f. Sam Lennie, b. 1984

1f. Lucy Rebecca, b. 1975

2f. Melissa Martha, b. 1978

2e. Angela Maureen, b. 24 February 1947, m. 1975 Barrie Giffard-Taylor, an accountant, & had issue,

1f. James William, b. 1982

1f. Jemima Alice, b. 1977

2f. Emily Victoria, b. 197

3e. Penelope Ann, of Grantham House, Lincs., b. 2 May 1948, m. 18 October 1973, James Emerson   Herdman & had issue,

1f. Emerson John, b. 1979

1f. Katherine Louise, b. 1977

4e. Nicola Jane, b. 22 August 1952, d. unm. 30 June 1996[491]

3c. Edmond Charles Wildbore, (Sir), of Stoke D'Abernon, Surrey, Chairman of Thomas Cook, Vice-President of the F.B.I., b. 15 Jan. 1877, educ. Haileybury, m. 1901, Evadne Maude (d. 28 April 1960), dau of John Talbot Kellet & d. 18 October, 1938, having had issue,

1d. Monica Elizabeth, m. 1stly 28 April 1930 Capt. Evan Llewelyn Gibbs, Coldstream Guards (k'd at Dunkirk, 1 June 1940, aged 34), a stockbroker & had issue,

1e. Michael Edmund Hubert, of Caroline Place, London, b. 31 March 1932, educ Eton & Christ Church, Oxford, m. 31 March 1960 Helena Antonia dau of Commander Edward Edmonstone & d. 27 March 2016, having had issue,

---

[490] He was an alcoholic, and was found dead in his bed.

[491] She was addicted to drink and drugs and was found dead in the street, after falling from the window of a council flat in west London.

1f. Patrick Michael Evan, b. 1962, m. 1989 Catherine Barroll & had issue,

   1g. Rufus Michael John, b. 1994

   1g. Clemency Columba Alice, b. 1992

2f. Edward Michael John, b. 1964, m. 1999 Henriette Manon Margarete Maren & had issue,

   1g. Manon Sophia Antonia Grisebach, b. 1999

   2g. Anastasia Henriette Eveline Grisebach, b. 2002

3f. Adrian Michael Philip, b. 1967

1f. Arabella Maria Clare, b. 1969, m. 1994 Quentin John Davies & has issue,

   1g. Hugh Alexander Evan, b. 6 July 1998

   1g. Ailsa Isadora Evelyn, b. 2002

2e. Peter Evan Wyldbore, Lt Col Sir, of Leigh House, Chagford, b. 1 February 1934, educ. Eton, m. 1stly 30 January 1957 (div 1975) Jane Duncombe, dau. of Col Arthur Howell & had issue,

   1f. Nicholas Roland Anthony, b. 18 November 1957

   2f. Simon Evan Alexander, b. 8 June 1962

   1f. Camilla Jane Evadne, b. 16 July 1959

He m. 2ndly 11 June 1976 Elena Sally... and & d. 2001, having had further issue,

   3f. Evan Rupert Michael, b. 27 April 1977

1e. Evadne Jane, b. 17 May 1938, m. 17 November 1958, Sir Howard Christian Sheldon Guinness, banker and businessman, of Clyst St George, Devon & had issue,

   1f. Christopher Edward Howard, b. 9 January 1963, m. 1992 Alicia Mary, dau of Thomas Barrington Cubitt & had issue,

      1g. James Edward Chaytor, b. 1997

      1g. Tatiana Emily, b. 1995

      2g. Fenella Evadne, b. 2002

   2f. Dominic Evan Mark, b. 20 June 1966, m. 1994 Amanda Claire Blunt & had issue

      1g. Edward Patrick Walter, b. 1998

      1g. Sophia Fenella, b. 1998

   1f. Annabel Evadne, b. 20 September 1959, m. 1987 Lt Gen Sir William Raoul Rollo, K.C.B., C.B.E. & had issue,

      1g. Andrew Patrick Hugh, b. 17 March 1996

      1g. Katherine Iona, b. 1989

      2g. Laura Evadne, b. 1991

Mrs Gibbs m. 2ndly 24 October 1957, Lt Col Walter Pearce-Serecold (d. 28 November 1994, aged 87) & d. 8 July 1973

2d. Jocelin Evadne, b. 11 November 1907, m. 11 February 1929 Sir John Duckett Floyd, Bt. (d. 1 April 1975), a solicitor, & d, in Winchester 17 January 1976, having had issue,

1e. David John Wyldbore, b. 12 November 1929, accidentally k'd on active service in Germany, 9 December 1949.

2e. Sir Giles Henry Charles, 7th Bt., of Tinwell Manor, Stamford, b. 27 February 1932, m. 23 November 1954 (div. 1975), Lady Gillian Moyra Katherine Cecil, dau. of 6th Marquess of Exeter (who m. 2ndly George Kertesz & 3rdly in 2008 Jeremy Smith) & had issue,

    1f. David Henry Cecil, F.C.A., merchant banker, of Manor Farm, Bowerchalke, Wilts., b. 2 April 1956, educ. Eton & R.M.A., Sandhurst, m. 20 June 1981 Caroline Ann, dau. of John Henry Beckly & has issue,

        1g. Suzanna Mary Caroline, b. 1983, m. William Henry Glyn & has issue,

            1h. Henry John Cecil, b. 4 March 2017

        2g. Claire, b 1986

    2f. Henry Edward Cecil, b. 3 August 1958, m. 13 April 1994 Leonor, dau of Sergio Castello, of Santiago, Chile, & d. in Chile 22 March 2013, leaving issue,

        1g. Henry William, b. 18 November 1994

        1g. Daniela Sophia, b 23 October 1996

He m. 2ndly in 1985 Judy Sophia, formerly wife of Thomas Lane & dau. of William Leonard Tregoning

1c. Ursula Gertrude Wyldbore, b. 1870, d. unm. 20 June 1922

2c. Bertha Sybil Wyldbore, b. 1872, d. unm in Dorchester in 1934 & bur at Tarrant Rushton

3a Robert, b 1805, of 28 Chester Street, Grosvenor Sq, educ. Eton, m 1stly at Henley-on-Thames, 3 May 1831 his cousin, Hon Georgiana Anne Carleton (d 28 Jan 1837, aged 23), yst. dau. of Lt. Col. the Hon. George Carleton, by Henrietta, eldest dau. of Edward King, of Askham Hall (see below), by whom he had issue,

1b. Georgiana Harriet, b. 1832, m. in Paris, 28 April 1859, Richard Waugh McArthur (who m. 2ndly 1 April 1889, Elizabeth Ogilvie Shaw & d. 1896, aged 71) of Edinburgh and d. in London, 10 August 1887 having had issue,

    1c. Richard Carleton Waugh, b. in Sussex, 1863, d. unm. in Harrow Road, Paddington, 25 Sept 1887

    2c. Kenneth Henry Waugh, b. in Hampstead, 1869, m. at St John's Hammersmith, 20 December 1894, Mrs Alice Heynes, dau. of Benjamin Richard Browning & d.s.p, in 1895

    1c. Georgiana Mary Waugh, b. in Scotland, 1862

    2c. Mildred Louisa Graham Waugh, b. 56 York Terrace, Regents Park, 21 April 1864 & bapt at St Marylebone

    3c. Lillias M. Waugh, b. in Kensington, 1866, m. 1889, Herbert Scott Bugby, of Hogarth Road, Kensington & d. 1933, having had issue,

        1d. Margaret Lillias Scott, b. 21 December 1890, m. 1912 Edmund Lavis & d. in Devizes in 1970 having had issue,

1e. Margaret Mary, b. in Godstone, Surrey 1913, d. in British Columbia in 1984

2b. Emily, b. 13 October 1833, m. 1853, a solicitor, Oliver Wimburn Lloyd (d. 1917, aged 89)[492], and d. had issue

  1c. Robert Carleton, b. 1854

  2c. Oliver John Henry Eustace, b. 22 Nov 1856 & bapt at Holy Trinity, Sloane Street 30 Dec 1856

  1c. Emily M, b. 1855

3b. Eleanor Jane, b. 3 August d. 3 September 1835.

4b. Henrietta Jane, b. 1836 & baptized at Long Critchel on 9 October 1836, m. at St James, Piccadilly, 17 February 1857 Henry Corbett (d. at Church Aston 28 April 1875, aged 52) and d. at The Hall, Church Aston, Shropshire, 11 October 1873, having had issue

  1c. (Henry) Guy, b. 1859, m Nannie, dau of William Brown, of Baltimore and d. in Charlottesville, Virginia in July 1945, having had issue,

    1d. Vincent, b 1905

    1d. Elsie, b in Virginia 1902

  2c. (Robert) Edwin, (Lt Col), b. 24 February 1860, m. 28 October 1891, at St Mary's, Newington, Cecilia Emily, dau. of Charles Read, served in the Second Boer War 1899-1902 and thereafter seems to have settled in South Africa.

  3c. Julian, b 1863, educ. Hailybury, settled in Charlottesville, Virginia, m. N.. Buckle of the U.S.A. & d. 1932

  4c. (Charles) Harold, b. 19 August 1867, k'd at Ypres, 13 May 1915

  1c. Edith, b. 1862, d. in Nancy, France in 1879

  2c. Muriel, b. 1866, m. 1891 in Presteigne, Cuthbert Buckle (d. 1934, aged 68) and d. in Virginia, U.S.A., 1946, having had issue,

    1d. C. C. Corbett ("Bertie"), b. 1892, k'd 1916

    2d. Stuart

  3c. Evelyn Mary, b. 1869, d. 1870

  4c. Hester Lilian, b. 1871, m. as his first wife, 22 Oct 1898, Aston Edward McMurdo (he was naturalized American with his family in 1920[493]) & d. in Charlottesville, Albemarle County, 22 June 1938. He m. 2ndly 30 Oct 1939 Mary Fisher Minor Miller (d. 28 May 1966, aged 86) & died in Charlottesville 2 April, 1973, aged 99, having had issue,

    1d. Cyril Edward, b. in Albemarle County, 5 September 1899, d. in Charlottesville, 8 July 1979

    2d. Montague Henry, b. in Buena Vista, Rockbridge County, 28 September 1900, d. in Charlottesville, 2 November 1989

    1d. Mary Lilian, b. in Albemarle County, 12 August 1905, d. in Charlottesville, 19 April 1994

---

[492] He was the younger brother of her stepmother's second husband.

[493] He had emigrated to Virginia with his family in 1879. He was born in Presteigne.

2d. Doris Evelyn, b. in Albemarle County, 4 December, 1909, d. in Virginia, 3 June 1983

3d. Muriel, b. in Charlottesville, 27 December 1911, d. in Keswick, Albemarle County, 23 September 2003

Robert King m 2ndly 1841 Frances Catherine Elizabeth (who m 2ndly 1852, Rev Samuel Webb Lloyd, vicar of St Thomas, Portman Square & d. 1875, aged 59, having had further issue. He d. in Braham, Kent in 1886, aged 60), elder dau. of Gen. Sir William Cornwallis Eustance, CB, KCH of Sandford Hall, Braintree by his 1st wife Catherine, dau. & heir of 2nd Lord Talbot de Malahide, and d. 1846[494] leaving further issue,

1b. Robert Eustace, b. 13 July 1842, d. 18 July 1845

2b. Talbot Henry, b. 1843, m. 1866 Fanny White, & d.s.p. in Battersea, 22 March 1873

3b. Frank, b. 1845, m. in Canada & d.s.p. in Canada, 1883

4b. John, Maj, 70th Regt, b. 1845, d.s.p. 1885[495]

4a. Thomas William, Lieut. RN, b. 1809, d. unm 1831.

1a. Marianne, b. 1795, m. at St George's, Hanover Square, 16 July 1814 Walter Campbell, of Sandilands, Lanarkshire, 3rd son of Walter Campbell, 9th of Skipnish & 3rd of Shawfield[496], and d. at 2 Lowndes Street, 23 March 1866, having had issue,

1b. Eleanora Ann, m. 14 Oct 1875 as his second wife, Sir Charles Trevelyan, 1st Bart. of Wallington, (d. 19 June 1886) & d.s.p. 1 March 1919

2b. Harriet Johanna, b. 1829, m, 16 March 1858, Richard Walter, Viscount Chetwynd (d. 1911) & d. 1898 having had issue,

1c. Richard Walter (Hon), b. 27 November 1859, m. at St Paul's, Knightsbridge, 8 January 1889 (div. 1900), Florence Mary (d. 1955, aged 92), dau of Tom Naylor-Leyland, of Nanyclwyd Hall, Denbighshire and d.v.p. 6 March 1908, leaving issue,

1d. Mary Eleanora, b. 7 March 1890, m. 6 Oct 1917, as his second wife, Robert Charles Otter (d. 1939, aged 86) of Royston Manor, Clayford, Notts & d. 30 October 1936, leaving issue,

1e. Robert Charles (Lt.), b. 2 May 1921, k'd at El Alamein, 25 October 1942

2e. John Henry, b. 2 Feb 1928, m. 3 July 1953 Monica Joan Harwood (d. 1999, aged 67) and d. 21 March 2004, having had issue.

1f. Robert Mark, b. 1955, m. 1982 Anne-Lise Catherine Pannier & had issue,

1g. Francois Jack, b. 1987

2g. Pierre Jonathan Henry, b 1989

---

[494] He was buried at St Peter's, Eaton Square.

[495] He left pictures, plate & china to his cousin, Robert Curzon Moss King.

[496] Walter Campbell senr was the grandson of Daniel Campbell of Skipish and Shawfield, a very successful Glasgow merchant, who made his fortune in slaves – amongst other things.

1g. Anne-Sophie, b. 1983

2g. Charlotte Marie, b. 1985

2f. James Anthony, b. 1957, m Hilary Chandler & had issue,

1g. Thomas, b. 1985

2g. Nicholas, b. 1990

1g. Susannah Catherine, b. 1987

3f. Hugh John, b. 1961, d. 1967

2e. Mary Constance, b. 1918, m. 1938 (div. 1959) John William Best (d. 22 April 2000, aged 87) & had issue,

1f. Robert John, b. 1946

1f. Antonia Mary, b. 1948

2d. Amélie Mary, b. 2 February 1892, m. 17 September 1912 Capt Claude Edward Reynard & had issue,

1e. Alexander Frederick, b. 1913, m. 1939 Sheila Maria Jane Ward & had issue,

1f. Edward Anthony, b. 1945

2f. John William, b. 1947

1f. Monica Mary, b. 1942

1c. Eleanora (Hon.), b. 1863, m. 29 June 1907, James Lloyd Anstruther (d. 1947, aged 95) & d.s.p. at Knapp House, Gillingham 20 February 1949

2c. Katherine Frances (Hon.), b. 1865, m. at St Peter's, Cranley Gardens, 6 June 1889, Maj George Blezard, of Cloverley Hall, Whitchurch, & d. at St James Court, Buckingham Gate, 29 June 1949, having had issue

1d. Winifred, b. 18 February 1890, m. 8 February 1912 Maj. Basil Kerr (d. 19 September 1957, aged 78) & d. 19 February 1974, having had issue,

1e. Mark George, b. 27 October 1912, k'd in Italy 13 January 1945

1e. Diana Katherine, b. 1916, m. Col. Sir Henry Nelson Clowes, K.C.V.O., O.B.E., D.S.O. & d. 19 December 2010, having had issue,

1f. Capt Andrew Henry, Scots Guards, Equerry to H.R.H. The Duke of Gloucester, b. 27 October 1942, m. 8 July 1968 Georgiana Elizabeth, dau. of Richard Cavendish, of Holker Hall, Cumbria & had issue,

1g. Richard William Andrew, b. 1971

1g. Emma Georgiana, b. 1975

2e. Elizabeth, of Wilton Street, London, b. 1919, m. 26 June 1946 Lt Col George Demetriadi, M.B.E. (d. 1991) & d. 16 February 2013

2d. Phyllis Eleanora, of Chiswick House, Pinner, b. 1892, d. unm. 18 December 1956

3d. Evelyn Mary, b. & d. 1897

4d. Ruth Gladys, b. 1901, m. 1934 Egbert Cecil Barnes (d. 1987, aged 89) & d. 15 July 1981, having had issue,

1e. Mary, b. 1 May, d. 6 May 1938

2a. Harriot, m. as his first wife, at St George, Hanover Square, 14 June 1825, William Henry Blaauw (1793-1870), of Beechland House, Newick, and d. 1828, leaving with another daughter, who d. young,

1b. Louisa Henrietta, b. 16 August 1826, d. at Beechland House in 1841

3a. Caroline Margaret, m. 1819 as his second wife, Col (later Gen Sir) William Cornwallis Eustace (d 1855) of Sandford Hall, Braintree, and d ante 1830 having had issue,

  1b. William John Walker, bapt at St George's Hanover Square, 6 January 1820 (by his uncle, Rev Moss King) d. young

  2b. Charles, b. 26 March 1821

  3b. Walter Philip, bapt at St George, Hanover Square, 30 March 1822

  4b. John Thomas, of Wynberg, S.A., Col. 60th Rifles, M.P. in the South African Parliament, b. 9 March 1825, m. 1860, in South Africa, Edith Kate, dau. of Lawrence Twentyman, of Walthamstow, and d. 25 Dec. 1919 having had issue,

    1c. John Bridges, Adm., D.L., J.P., of Denton Lodge, Wokingham, b. 20 Jan. 1861, m. Helena Kindeace Perceval Cruikshanks Charlton (d. 4 Sept 1968), dau. of Charles Robertson, 8th of Kindeace, Ross-shire, & d.s.p. 9 Aug. 1947

    2c. Robert King, b. 22 March 1862, m. Alice, dau. of Rev. N... Wiltshire & d.s.p. 1912

    3c. Maj Gen Alexander Henry, C.B., C.B.E., D.S.O., 2nd Sikh Infantry, b. 14 June 1863, educ. Felsted, m. 26 Oct. 1904, Evelyn Mary (d. 11 Dec. 1927), dau., of Samuel Stonestreet, of Kimberley, S.A., & d. 11 March 1939, having had issue,

      1d. John Curtis Wernher, C.I.E., Indian Civil Service (to 1947) and then with GKN, b. 22 Nov. 1906, educ. Wellington & Exeter Coll., Oxford, m. 9 Nov. 1937 (div. 1954), Pamela Mary, dau. of Sir Harold Glover, of Ombersley, Worcs., and d. 21 Oct. 1972, having had issue,

        1e. William John Henry, of Sale Green, Droitwich, with GKN, b. 27 Oct. 1939, educ. Wellington & R.N.C., Dartmouth,

        2e. Rowland Alexander Fitz, Marine Underwriter, Insurance Corporation of Ireland, of Lower Wissington, Herts., b. 4 Oct. 1942, educ. Wellington & Exeter Coll. Oxford, m. 1 Oct. 1966, Rosemary, dau. of Franklin Dyne, of Hampton-in-Arden, and had issue,

          1f. Edward Rowland Fitz, b. 29 Aug. 1969

          2f. Charles Henry Fitz, b. 2 Jan. 1971

        3e. Francis Edmund Portlester, b. 8 Dec. 1944

    4c. William Moss, b. 18 Jan. 1864, educ. Emmanuel Coll., Cambridge, m. 11 Dec. 1894, Elizabeth Alice, dau. of Capt Rorke & d. 1908, having had issue,

      1d. John William, d. young

      2d. Terence Henry, of Harare, Zimbabwe, South African Diplomat, b. 10 April 1899, educ. Fort Beaufort & Pretoria University, m. 6 Nov. 1935, Irene De Courcy, dau. of Maj. Herbert De Courcy Blakeney, and had issue,

        1e. Peter Blakeney, Investment Manager, of Sandton, Transvaal, b. 24 Oct. 1936, educ. King Edward School, Harare & Pretoria University, m.

18 Dec. 1965, Alison Margaret, dau. of James Coventry, of Manaton, Devon & had issue,

    1f. Caroline Anne, b. 29 Sept. 1966

    2f. Jennifer Clare, b. 14 July 1969

2e. Michael De Courcy, Investment Manager, of Johanannesburg, b. 12 April 1942, educ. Capetown University,

1e. Ann Maureen, b. 8 May 1940, m. 27 Jan. 1968, David Moss, of Harare & had issue,

    1f. John Eustace, b. 9 Jan. 1970

1d. Nora, b. 13 March 1897, m. 28 March 1921, Alfred Roy Hewitt (d. 26 July 1952), of Grahamstown, S.A. & d. 7 May 1976, leaving issue, 2 daus.

2d. Mona Alice, d. 23 March 1900, m. as his first wife, 11 June 1924, Donald Stephen Wedderburn Ogilvy & d. 12 Dec. 1925.

3d. Irene Kathleen, b. 16 Nov. 1907, m. 10 June 1933, Lt. Col. Sydney Powell Holzer, of Pretoria, and had issue,

    1e. Gillian Eustace, b. 12 Aug. 1934

    2e. Sally Eustace, b. 30 May 1938

5c. Charles Frere, b. 11 Jan. 1868, m. Lydia Lucy, dau. of Leonard Acutt 7 d. 21 Feb. 1901, having had issue,

1d. John Patrick Leonard, M.C., Lt. Col., 11th Sikhs, of Pietermaritzburg, b. 3 Aug. 1898, educ. St Andrew's Coll., Grahamstown, m. 23 July 1939, Janet Mary, dau. of Henry Ferard, C.S.I., C.I.E.

2d. Charles Frere, Capt., of Himeville, Natal, b. 11 Jan. 1901, Kathleen Violet, dau. of Rev. H.C. Orpwood,

6c. Harvey Tower, b. Nov. 1876, d. young

1c. Myra Mabel, b. 2 Sept 1866, d. unm.

2c. Edith Mary Rosalie, b. 25 June 1869, m. 22 April 1896, Walter Powrie

3c. Emily Laura Alicia, 19 Oct. 1870, m. 8 March 1893, Henry de Graeff, Baron van Polsbroek (d. 15 May 1941), of Johannesburg, & d. 1 Dec. 1941

4c. Emma Frances Stuart, b. 14 Jan. 1872, m. Dec. 1906 Capt. Alick Manson Clarke, & d.s.p. 9 Nov. 1930

5c. (Mary) Augusta, b. 21 June 1873, d. unm. March, 1896

6c. Monica Alice, b. 1 June 1875, m. 16 July 1903, her first cousin, Col. Henry Montague Eustace & d.... having had issue (see below).

7c. (Henrietta) Mildred, b. 21 May 1878, m. June 1900, Rev. Canon Enoch Jones

5b. Rev Robert Henry, Rector of Sampford, Essex, b. 1826, m. 23 Aug 1859 Emily Henrietta (d. 26 April 1915), dau. of Rev. Sir Thomas Pym Bridges & d. 27 March 1908, having had issue,

1c. Gerard John, b. 1860, d. 1872

2c. Col. Henry Montague, D.S.O. of Mountfin, Co. Wexford, b. 28 Nov. 1863, m. 16 July 1903, his first cousin, Monica Alice, dau. of Col. John Thomas Eustace, and d. 27 Feb. 1926, having had issue,

    1d. John Rowland, b. 29 Aug. 1904

2d. Robert Brook Bridges, Senior Resident for North Nigeria in 1960, b. 6 Feb. 1907, educ. Harrow & Hertford Coll., Oxford, ret'd to Ferns, co. Wexford.

3d. Gerard Henry, Lt. Col., Indian Army, b. 20 Feb. 1909, educ. Harrow & R.M.C., Sandhurst, m. 22 March 1936 Joan Norah Lakes, dau. of Lt. Col. Hugh Wesley Glenn, ret'd to Enniscorthy, co. Wexford, & had issue,

   1e. Michael Henry, Agriculturalist with I.C.I., of Hurst, Berks., b. 23 Jan. 1940, educ. Harrow, R.M.C., Sandhurst, R.M.C.S. at Shrivenham & the Royal Agricultural College, Cirencester, m. 28 July 1962, Anne Mary, dau. of Reginald Wight-Boycott, of Ascot, Berks., & had issue,

      1f. Richard Gerrard, b. 31 Dec. 1966

      1f. Mary Elizabeth, b. 30 April 1966.

   1e. Patricia Mary, of Enniscorthy, co. Wexford, b. 1 Aug. 1943, m. Hugh Trevor Wheeler

1d. Myra Caroline Henrietta, b. 7 Aug. 1905, m. as his second wife[497], Donald Stephen Wedderburn Ogilvy, M.C.S.P. (k'd in action, 8 May 1941)

3c. Louis Charles Moss, Land Agent, of Sampford Grange, Essex, b. 1866, educ. Harrow, m. 1stly Elizabeth Jane Quinton (div. & s.p.). He m. 2ndly, 3 May 1923 Marjorie Edith (d. 13 March 1967), dau., of Andrew Ross, of Ardingly, Sussex and d. 17 Dec. 1939, having had issue,

   1d. Thomas Robert Hales, Maj., of Ashford, Kent, b. 18 Feb. 1923, m.1stly 7 Feb. 1948 (div.), Pamela Venetia, dau. of Capt Hugh Browning, O.B.E., D.S.O., of Strettington, Sussex & had issue,

      1e. Rowland Desmond Browning, b. 5 Nov. 1949

      2e. Christopher Hugh, b. 19 Jan. 1952

   He m. 2ndly 23 March 1957, Hon. Dorothy Anne, dau. & coh. of Lord Eustace Percy, P.C., M.P., 1st & last Lord Percy of Newcastle[498], and had further issue,

      3e. James Maurice Percy, b. 26 March 1960, educ. Harrow

      1e. Alicia Mary, b. 30 April 1958

      2e. Katherine Anne, b. 17 March 1965

   1d. Caroline Phyllis Eleanor, b. 9 Dec. 1925, m. 25 Sept. 1954 (div. 1958), Frederick D. Dent. She m. 2ndly, 2 May 1958, Peter Alexander Baillie Crichton & had issue,

      1e. Mark Terence Ross, b. 25 Jan. 1964

      2e. Jeremy Nigel Eustace, b. 20 Oct. 1965

   2d. Alicia Emily, of Mousehole, Penzance, b. 4 Feb. 1926

   3d. Susan Fanny, of Mousehole, Penzance, b. 3 May 1929

   4d. Sarah Louisa, of Mousehole, Penzance, b. 8 Nov. 1931

---

[497] His first wife was her first & second cousin, Mona Eustace, who died in December 1925, aged 25. Mona was the daughter of Monica Eustace's brother, William Moss Eustace.
[498] A younger son of the 7th Duke of Northumberland. He was President of the Board of Education under Stanley Baldwin in 1924-1929.

1b. Harriet Sarah Frances, b. at Aldenham 3 August 1823

4a. Anne Elizabeth, m. 1821 her cousin, Thomas Venables (who m. 2ndly Jeanette Napier Sturt and d. 1837), Private Secretary to Lord Sidmouth & Sir Robert Peel, son of Thomas Venables, of Chester, by Ann, dau. of Very Revd. James King, and d. 1827, having had issue (see below)

5a. Katherine Judith, b. 3 January 1804, m. as his first wife, 24 Oct 1822 Henry John Adeane, of Babraham, Cambs (who m. 2ndly Hon. Matilda Stanley, dau. of 1st Lord Stanley of Alderley and d. 1847 leaving further issue), and d. 27 June 1825, leaving issue

    1b. Robert Jones, b. 24 June 1825, d. in 1826

    1b. Anne, b. 1824, d. unm. 1900

6a. Emily, b. 1807, m. at St George's, Hanover Square, 12 Jan 1826 William Henry Harford (d 1877), of Barley Wood, Bristol[499], yst son of J.S. Harford of Blaise Castle & d. 1832, having had issue,

    1b. William Henry, a banker, of Barley Wood, and later of Old Down Manor, Tockington, b. 4 January 1829, m. 1855 Ellen (d. 29 March 1907, aged 75), dau of Rev William Tower, of Howe Hatch, Essex and d. 2 November 1903, having had issue,

        1c. William Alfred, b. at Barley Wood 11 September 1856, m. at St Mark's, North Audley Street, 1890 Grace Mary Beata (d. 23 May 1928, aged 66), dau. of Capt. Hamilton Kinglake & d. out hunting with the Beaufort, 2 January 1925, having had issue

            1d. Jessica, b. 1892, m. 26 September 1918 Kenneth Williamson, 2nd Lord Forrees of Glenogil (d. 26 June 1954, aged 66) & d. 4 July 1972, having had issue,

                1e. John Archibald Harford, 3rd Lord Forres of Glenogil, b. 30 October 1922, m. 1stly 24 August 1945 (div. 1967), Gillian Ann, dau. of Maj. John MacLean Grant & had issue,

                    1f. Alastair Stephen Grant, 4th Lord Forres, b. 16 May 1946, m. 2 May 1969, Margaret Ann, dau., of George John Mallam, Mullumbimby, N.S.W. & has issue,

                        1g. George Archibald Mallam (Hon.), b. 16 August 1972 m. 2002, Charlotte Barrett

                        1g. Juliet Anne (Hon.), m. Nigel John Eldon Bankes & has issue

                          1h. William Nigel Wynne

                          1h. Louisa Juliet

---

[499] The Harfords were a family of substantial Bristol merchants. William and Emily Harford bought Barley Wood – a thatched cottage - from Hannah More in 1828 when she moved into Clifton. Lord Macaulay was a close friend of Miss More in her old age. In August 1852 when he was recuperating in Clifton after a heart attack, he recorded in his diary, "the Harfords of Blaise Castle called in their barouche to take Margaret and me to Barley Wood" – which held many happy memories for him. Barley Wood was later sold to H.H. Wills of the tobacco family

    1h. Fiona Gillian

   2g. Astrid Signe (Hon.), m. Peter Karl Dobrée Bell and has issue,

    1h. Hugh John

    1h. Lucy Claire

He m. 2ndly 22 September 1969 (div. 1975), Josephine, (who m. 3rdly Owen, 3rd Earl Lloyd-George of Dwyfor & d. 10 May 2012, aged 86), widow of Robert, 2nd Earl of Woolton & dau. of Sir Alexander Gordon-Cumming, 5th Bt. & d. 22 September 1978

2e. Angus Stephen (Hon.) b. 19 December 1929, d. 12 January 1988

1e. Jean Mary (Hon.), b. 17 June 1919, m. 1941 W/Cmdr William James Maitland Longmore (d. 25 September 1988, aged 70) & d. 10 December 2009, having had issue,

   1f. Virginia Marjorie, b. 17 January 1945, m. 28 November 1973, Henry D.N.B. Candy & has issue

    1g. Emma Juliet, b. 1974, m. Rupert E.C. Erskine Crum & has issue,

     1h. Isla Cerise, b. 11 February 2011

     2h. Esme Mary, b. 5 April 2014

    2g. Sophie Bridget, b. 1978

   2f. Carolyn Mary, b. 26 August 1946, m. 1stly, 6 June 1966 (div. 1976) Michael Edward Denison & has issue,

    1g. James Edward, b. 22 June 1968

    1g. Lucinda Mary, b. 1971

   She m. 2ndly, 20 February 1981, Michael Desmond Poland (d. 1982, aged 45)

   3f. Jennifer Maitland, b. 29 January 1953, m. m. 27 September 1975, Capt. Patrick J.R. Snowball, 4th/7th Royal Dragoon Guards, & had issue,

    1g. Robert Joseph Arthur, b. 1981

    2g. Thomas Edward James, b. 1984

    3g. Edward William George, b. 1990

2d. Beata (Betty), bapt at St Mark's, Swindon, 11 September 1893, d. unm. in 1982

2c. Francis Harvey, 10th Hussars, b. in Chelsea, 1858, drowned in the Kabul River, Afghanistan, 31 March 1879 unm.

3c. Arthur Edward, Cmdr., R.N., b. in Chelsea, 1859, d. unm. 22 September 1897

4c. Hugh Wyndham Lutterill, a banker, of Horton Hall, Glos., b. in Barley Wood, 2 April 1862, educ. Eton & Trinity Coll., Oxford, m. 1904, Evelyn Nora (d. 1967, aged 93), dau. of Lt Col Hon. Charles Needham & d. 20 June 1920, having had issue,

   1d. Mark William, b. 1904, m. 5 December 1945 Elizabeth (d. 2 May 2008, aged 93), dau of Col. Philip Leveson-Gower & d. 13 January 1969, having had issue,

1e. Philip Hugh, 14 August 1946, m. 1982 Willa, dau. of W.J. Franklin of Sitney, Oxon & d. 13 June 2018, having had issue,

    1f. William Scandrett, b. 1984

    1f. Harriet Kate Isabel, b. 1987

2e. Gerald Mark, b. 8 June 1948, m. 1985 Cailla Margaret, dau. of A.A. Horne & has issue,

    1f. Auriol Louise, b. 1987

    2f. Elizabeth Mida, b. 1989

2d. Arthur Hugh, The Old Rectory, Easton Grey, Malmesbury, b. 8 September 1905, m. 1947, Johneen, dau. of John Bartholomew of Rowde, Glos., & d. 28 January 1984

3d. Charles Evelyn, Ashcroft House, Kingscote, Bristol, b. 8 September 1905, m. at Hatfield in 1937, Joan Mary (d. 18 March 1973, aged 63), dau. of Hugh James Wyld, a stockbroker, & d. 10 June 1977, having had issue,

    1e. Reuben Charles, m. 1978, Georgina Jacintha, dau. of Lt Col Christopher Herbert Fleetwood Fuller & had issue,

        1f. Hugh Scandrett, b. 1980

        2f. Christopher Evelyn, b. 1985

        1f. Beatrice Louise, b. 1982

        2f. Henrietta Mary, b. 1987

4d. George Anthony, of Horton, Glos., b. 20 January 1909, m. 10 June 1933, Margaret (d. 23 September 1958, aged 49), dau. of J.B. Hotham, of Coldstream, Berwickshire & d. 9 September 1985 & had issue,

    1e. Caroline Evelyn, m. 14 July 1959 (div. 1982) Maj. Peter Lloyd-Verney & had issue,

        1f. Harry George Vivian, Upton Hill, Glos. b. 5 October 1960, m. 1stly, 1985 (div. 1989), Sarah Mary Cotteril Voelker.

        He m. 2ndly, 1992 (div.) Lavinia Mary, dau, of Maj. Sir Evelyn Delves Broughton & had issue,

            1g. Harriet Charity, b. 11 November 1992

        He m. 3rdly Sarah Cotton & has issue,

            1g. Ralph George Stanley, b. 21 March 2001

            2g. Honor, b. 17 November 2003

        1f. Louisa Margaret, b. 12 July 1962, m. 1993, Matthew Jeremy Higgs & had issue

            1g. Florence Nettle, b. 1994

        2f. Henrietta Nell, , b. 3 July 1965, m. 1987, Thomas Richard William Lapage-Norris

    2e. Henrietta Jane, m. 1965, Simon Henry Clowes & had issue,

        1f. William Nicholas, b. 1966

        1f. N..., b. 1968

1c. Ellen Harriet Maria, b. Barley Wood, 28 May 1860, m. 12 July 1882, as his first wife, George Capell, 7th Earl of Essex & d. in Cannes 31 December 1885, having had issue,

   1d. Algernon George de Vere, 8th Earl of Essex, b. 21 February 1884, m. 1stly 28 September 1905 (div. 1926), Mary Eveline Stewart Freeman (d. 30 October 1955), & had issue,

      1e. Reginald George de Vere, 9th Earl of Essex, Hon. Col., T.A., b. 9 October 1906, He m. 1stly 2nd March 1937 (div. 1957), Mary Reeve, dau, of F. Gibson Ward. He m. 2ndly 14 November 1957, Nona Isobel (d. 1997, aged 90), dau. of David Wilson Miller & d.s.p. 18 May 1981

   He m. 2ndly, 10 February 1926 (div. 1950) Alice Montgomery, dau. of Robert Hays Falkiner. He m. 3rdly, 10 December 1950 (div. 1956), Mildred Carson. He m. 4thly in 1957, Christine Mary Davis, and d. 8 December 1966.

2c. Louise Emily, b. 21 Sept 1864, m. 1stly Baron Carlo de Tuyll[500](d. 2 June 1893, aged 34) and had issue,

   1d. Francis Charles Owen, Baron de Tuyll, of Little Sodbury Manor, Glos. b. 21 May 1885, d. unm. 27 June 1952

   2d. Maurice Arthur, Baron de Tuyll, Capt. 10th Hussars, b. 1 November 1888, k'd at Ypres 13 May 1915, unm.

She m. 2ndly 9 Oct 1895, Henry Somerset, 9th Duke of Beaufort (d. 1924, aged 77), and d. 1945, having had further issue,

   3d. Henry Hugh Arthur Fitzroy, 10th Duke of Beaufort, b. 4 April 1900, m. 14 June 1923, Lady Mary Cambridge (d. 23 June 1987, aged 90), dau. of the 1st Marquess of Cambridge, and d.s.p. 5 February 1984

   1d. Blanche Linnie, b. 15 April 1897, m. John Eliot, 6th Earl of St Germans (d. 31 March 1922, aged 31) & had issue,

      1e. Rosemary Alexandra, b. 26 February 1919, m. 1stly 2 Sept 1939 Edward Christian Frederick Nutting, (k'd in the Middle East, January 1943, aged 25), eldest surviving son of Sir Harold Nutting, 2nd Bt. & had issue,

         1f. Davina, b. 8 August 1940, m. 29 May 1960, John Martin Brentnall Cope & was k'd in a car crash, 6 August 1976, having had issue,

            1g. Jonathan Edric, b. 1961, k'd in a car crash with his mother, 6 Aug 1976

            1g. Frederica Samantha Mary, b. 23 September 1963, m. Aug. 1999, David Arthur Thomas & has issue,

               1h. Davina May Mauritius, b. September 1999

---

[500] They were a Dutch family. His eldest brother, Baron Reginald Van Tuyll (1845-1903) married Countess Mathilde van Limburg-Stirum, who was thought to be the illegitimate daughter William III of the Netherlands. Prince William of the Netherlands fell in love with her but was steered away in case he married his half-sister. Their daughter, Julia Van Tuyll, married Sir Berkeley Sheffield and was the great-grandmother of Samantha Cameron.

Lady Rosemary Nutting m. 2ndly 1945 (marriage annulled 1948) David Frederick Hew Dunn. She m. 3rdly 22 Dec 1949 Col. Ralph Alexander Rubens (d. 1995) & d. 20 April 1963, having had further issue,

2f. Alexandra Louise, b. 9 Oct. 1951, m. 1976, Daniel Augusto Peyronel & has issue,

1g. Jesse Alexander, b. 1977

2e. Catherine Blanche Lily, b. 29 July 1921, m. 1stly 15 Nov. 1946 (div. 1956), John Beeton Seyfried & had issue,

1f. David John (assumed name of Seyfried Herbert & the title 19th Lord Herbert in 2002[501]), b. 3 March 1952, educ. Harrow, m. Jane Angela, dau. of Dr Ian Francis Bishop, and has issue,

1g. Oliver Richard (Hon.), M.D., b. 17 June 1976, educ Harrow, m. Sarah Victoria Fergusson & has issue,

1h. Oscar James, b. 27 November 2004

1h. Coco Florence, b. 23 July 2007

2h. Phoebe Sophia, b. 12 June 2008.

1g. Charlotte Sophia Caroline (Hon.), b. 27 October 1977, educ Wycombe Abbey & Oriel College, Oxford, m. 2007, Julian Collett & has issue,

1h. Rollo Huxley Herbert, b. 14 July 2008

2h. Caspian Huxley Herbert, b. November 2009.

1f. Sarah Diana, b. 6 April 1949, m. 1stly 1975, Peter Michael Smith & had issue.

1g. Benjamin Peter Havelock, b. 1977

2g. Matthew William Eliot, b. 1981

She m. 2ndly, as his second wife, Sir Michael Ferguson-Davie, 8th Bt, of Evercreech, Somnerset

Lady Catherine Seyfried m. 2ndly, as his second wife, 7 January 1957, Sir Havelock Henry Trevor Hudson, Chairman of Lloyds, & d. 1994, having had further issue,

2f. Michael Guy Havelock, b. 14 March 1962, m. 1992 Sarah Heidi Ehler & has issue,

1g. Havelock Henry Eliot, b. 1996

2g. Christian Alexander Havelock, b. 1998

---

[501] His great uncle, the 10th Duke of Beaufort, was also Baron Herbert & Baron Botetourt. The barony of Herbert (& Raglan Castle, which was the family's original seat) had come to the Somerset family through the marriage of Elizabeth Herbert, *suo jure* Baroness Herbert in about 1495. On the death of the 10th Duke, the barony was vested in Lady Rosemary Rubens and Lady Catherine Hudson - the daughters of his late sister, Lady Blanche Scott-Douglas. Lady Rosemary had died in 1963, leaving two daughters. Lady Catherine died in 1994 leaving two sons and two daughters. The Queen agreed to call the barony of Herbert out of abeyance in favour of the elder son of the younger daughter. The barony of Botetourt remains in abeyance between the present Lord Herbert, Lady Rosemary's younger daughter, Alexandra Peyronel, and her granddaughter, Frederica Thomas.

1f. Louise Deborah, b. 2 Dec. 1958, and has issue,

    1g. Jonathan Hudson Jones

    2g. Eliot Hudson Jones

Lady St Germains m. 2ndly 15 July 1924, Capt. George Francis Valentine Scott Douglas (d. 12 June 1930, aged 32) & d. 30 August 1968, having had further issue,

    1e. Sir James Louis Fitzroy, 6th Bt., b. 24 October 1930, d. unm. 16 July 1969

2d. Diana Maud Nina, b. 12 September 1898, m. 19 September 1925 Capt Lindsey Harry Compton Sheddon (d. 1971, aged 90) & d.s.p. 6 May 1935

2b. Edward John (Rev), Rector of Marston, Somerset & Canon of Wells, b. 1832, m. 1864 Georgiana Pym Bridges, dau of the Rector of Danbury, Essex & d. in Bath, 1917, having had issue,

1c. Edward Bridges, b. 1872, m. Violet Audrey, dau. of Lt. Col. Gore Little & had issue,

    1d. Christopher Edward Audley, b. 1907

    2d. Anthony Francis, b. 1908

1c. Edith Emily

2c. Gertrude Margaret

3c. Marion Louisa Harriet

4c. Evelyn Sophia, m. 5 April 1899, Alfred Digby Pelly (d. 20 January 1940, aged 77) & d. 27 March 1970, having had issue,

1d. Richard Edward, b. 29 May 1905, m. 29 April 1941, Diana Marthe Desgrand Mitchell (d. 1991) & d. 28 November 2002, having had issue,

    1e. Louise Sophia *Pelly*, Q.C., of Toronto, Canada, b. 27 October 1943, m. 1967 (div. 1973) Donald John Mactaggart & has issue,

        1f. Alexandra Caroline Diana *Pelly*, b. 1985

    2e. Harriet Elizabeth Annabel, of Victoria, B.C., Canada, b. 5 May 1948, m. 1stly 1984 (div. 1988), Francis Roland Stark. She m. 2ndly, 1991, Dr Gerald Pelly-Graham

1d. Violet Evelyn, b. 11 June 1900, m. February 1923, Henry, Marquis de Ruvigny (d. 10 May 1941, aged 44) & d. in 1996, having had issue,

1e. Michael Francis Wriothesley, Marquis de Ruvigny, b. 11 February 1927, m. 26 January 1956, Patricia Kirkpatrick Pile & d. in Eastbourne, 19 October 2016, having had issue,

    1f. Rupert Francis James Henry, b. 19 July 1959, m.1987, Kumudini Nelun, dau. of Dr C.S. Ratnatunga & has issue,

        1g. Annabelle

    1f. Rachel Anne, b. 2 November 1956, m. 1976, Philip Alan Rubery & has issue,

        1g. Henry Philip Michael Nicholas, b. 1984

        2g. Georgina Rachel Eugenie, b. 1983

5c. Katharine Adelaide Mary, m.1904, Philip Wilmot Dashwood (d. 8 July 1956, aged 93) & d. 21 April 1953, having had issue,

    1d. Millicent Katharine, b. 12 November 1906, d. unm. 14 March 1963

1b. Harriet Margaret, b. 1827, m. at Wrington, 29 September 1853, as his first wife, William Willoughby George Hurt Sitwell (d. 1909, aged 81), of Ferney Hall, Shropshire and d. 1855, leaving issue,

    1c. Willoughby Harford Hurt, of Ferney Hall, b. 18 May 1855, m. 1880 Rose Augusta Cecil, dau of J.H. Brabazon, of Mornington House, co Meath, and d. 28 June 1913 & had issue,

        1d. Willoughby *Hurt-Sitwell*, of Ferney Hall, b. 30 April 1881, m. 1939, Alice Edith Maud Cassin (d. 1957, aged 78) & d.s.p. in Penzance, 28 June 1942

2b. Emily Mary, b. 1830, d.1831

7a. Elizabeth, b. 1807, d. at Aldenham, 16 July 1826, when engaged to be married to (Brook) Henry Bridges, elder son of Rev Brook Henry Bridges, rector of Danbury, Essex[502].

8a. Georgiana, b. at Aldenham, 4 June 1810, d. young

9a. Eleanor Sophia, b. at Aldenham 10 November 1811, d. young

1. Ann, bapt. at Clitheroe, 17 April 1746, m. Thomas Venables (d 1803, aged 75), of Chester, eldest son of Peter Venables, of Bolton-by-Bowland[503], & d. at Buckland Newton, Dorset, 17 Nov. 1817, leaving issue,

1a. Thomas, bapt at Church Lawton, Cheshire, 4 May 1768, bur. at Middlewich, 8 July 1772

2a. James (Rev), Vicar of Buckland Newton from 1805[504], Prebendary of Wells, Canon of Salisbury from 1841, b. 1775, educ. Worcester Coll., Oxford, m. 15 July 1821, Mary Caroline, dau. of J. Lewis & d. 18 Dec 1851, having had issue,

---

[502] On her death, Elizabeth was described in the Gentleman's Magazine as "youngest daughter", but maybe "youngest surviving daughter was meant". Henry was a barrister and also died young, in 1829, aged 30. His uncle was Sir Brook Bridges, Bt, of Goodnestone, Kent. His aunt, Elizabeth Bridges, was married to Jane Austen's brother, Edward Knight, of Godmersham. Emily and Georgiana Bridges, the daughters of Henry's younger brother, Rev Thomas Pym Bridges, also rector of Danbury, later married two of Elizabeth's nephews, Rev Robert Eustace and Rev Canon Edward Harford.

[503] On ancestry.com Peter Venables (1679-1747) is said to be the son of Peter Venables, of Kinderton, Cheshire. He was not. Peter Venables of Kinderton was the last of a long line of Cheshire gentry that dated back to the 12th century. He left two daughters: Lady Ferrars and Lady Abingdon. Neither had children, so that the eventual heir was the grandson of Peter's sister, George Venables Vernon, later Lord Vernon (1710-1780).

[504] The beautiful eighteenth century rectory was on the market in 2007 for a huge sum. In James Venables' day, the living was in the gift of the Dean and Chapter of Wells. Apparently, in 1819, James Venables was summoned before the Dorset Assizes because he had entered the house of one of his parishioners to take a book he thought was likely to corrupt the morals of the man's wife. The magistrate found against him.

1b. James Lewis Walker (Rev.), of Shenley Lodge, Hertford, bapt at Buckland Newton 27 January 1822, educ. Wadham College, Oxford, was acting as his father's curate at Buckland Newton in the late 1840s and at the time of his marriage, m. at All Souls, Langham Place, 7 February 1850[505], Ellen (who m. 2ndly, at Holy Trinity, Marylebone, 23 Oct 1856, as his second wife, Henry Edward Cheywynd Stapylton & d. 27 Feb. 1870, having had issue. He d. 1900), dau. of Henry Hoyle, of Colney House, Herts., & d.s.p. 8 Jan. 1852.

2b. Edmund Burke (Rev.), later Whyte-Venables, bapt. at Buckland Newton, 15 February 1823, educ. Wadham Coll. Oxford, m. Miss Whyte, heiress of Redhills, co Cavan, and d.s.p. 1894

3b. Thomas, Maj. 83rd Regt., of Bareleigh House, Aston, Herts., b. 18 October 1824 & bapt. at Buckland Newton 6 January 1825, m. at Shephall, 10 July 1862, Elizabeth Anne Unwin Heathcote (d. 1865) & d. 22 February 1890, having had issue,

  1c. Eleanor Caroline, b. 1864, m. at Aston 6 October 1885, the brother of her cousin's wife, Capt. Frederick William Scudamore (who m. 2ndly Cara Helen Moore (d. 25 February 1924, aged 48, having had issue by him) & d. 7 January 1919, aged 62), of the Clock House, Farnborough, & d. at sea 29 November 1897, having had issue,

    1d. Frederick Venables, b. 1888, d. an inf

    2d. Thomas Venables, Lt.Col. b.1889, emigrated to Canada & served in the Canadian Army in WWI, m. Joyce Carr (d, in Poole, 22 June 1977, aged 85), dau. of Francis George Shields, & d. in Poole, 10 November 1951, having had issue,

      1e. Amoret Venables, b. 1928, m. 1stly in 1955 Christopher Scott. She m. 2ndly Dr Ralph Esmond Selby Tanner (d. at Padworth Common, Berks. 8 January 2017, aged 96)

      2e. Catherine, b. November 1933

    3d. John, Lieut., b. 3 August 1892, k'd at Gallipoli, 28 Aoril 1915.

    1d. Winifred Heathcote, b. 1886, m. in London 1911, Robert Henry Mitchell & d. in Cuckfield, Sussex, 28 June 1960, having had issue,

      1e. William Scudamore, M.B.E., publicity manager, b. 6 February 1912, d. in West Clandon, Surrey, 3 March 1987

      2e. Michael Richard Scudamore, banker, b. 29 October 1925, educ. Eton, m. 1958 Patricia A.M. Murray & d. in Aldham, Essex, 15 December 2005

      1e. Barbara Scudamore, b.29 January 1915, m. 1951, Anthony James Arnaud Watson (d. in London in 1970, aged 60)

    2d. Elizabeth May, b. 1890, m. 1919, George Clifton Oakes (d. 6 March 1933, aged 43), a landowner of Nowton Court, Bury St Edmunds & d. in Bury St Edmunds, 1970, having had issue

---

[505] The witnesses were his mother, Georgiana Mary Venables (?), her father and Anne Oddie. The service was taken by Rev G.A, Oddie, Rector of Aston.

1e. Orbell Ray, of Nowton, Bury St Edmunds, b. in Kenya, 24 July 1920, m. in Sunderland, co. Durham, 1945 Joyce Pickersgill & d. 29 December 1988, having had issue

2e. John Pamplin, b. 1922, k'd in Italy 8 August 1944

3e. Peter C. b. & d., in Bury St Edmunds in 1931

4b. John, bapt. at Buckland Newton, 3 April 1827

1b. Caroline Maria, bapt. at Buckland Newton 28 December 1823, unm.

2b. Ann, bapt. at Buckland Newton 5 February 1826, m. in Dorchester in 1848, Rev. George Augustus Oddie (d. 1877), Rector of Aston, Herts. & d. 1876, having had issue

1c. George Venables (Rev), Rector of Aston, Herts., b. in Colney House, St Albans, 1850, educ. Haileybury, m. in Maidstone, 1878 Frances Eliza (d. in Eastbourne, 12 November 1939, aged 84), dau. of William Scudamore, attorney & solicitor in Maidstone & d. 1 September 1919, having had issue,

1d. George Scudamore, b. 1882

1d. Annie Marguerite, b. 1879 & baptized at Aston on 2 November 1879, d. unm. in Hillingdon, 1968

2d. Sybil Frances, b. 1885, & baptized at Aston on 4 October 1885, d. unm.

3d. Joan Evelyn, b. 1893, d. unm. in Clifton, Bristol, 23 December 1969

2c. Arthur Thellusson (Rev), Vicar of Glen Magna w. Stretton Magna, took the name of Whyte-Venables in 1905 on succeeding to Redhills, b. in Aston, 7 September 1851, educ. Haileybury & St John's Coll. Cambridge, m. at St Mary's, Newington, 27 July 1886 Alice Blair, dau. of Rev. Canon George Thomas Palmer, Rector of Newington & d. 13 February 1929 having had issue,

1d. Harold Arthur *Whyte-Venables*, M.D., of Pulborough, W. Sussex, b. 1891, educ. Queen's Coll. Cambridge, m. 1924 Eileen Christian (d. 1983, aged 84), only dau, of Maj. Claud Garrard & d. in 1961, having had issue,

1e. Gilbert Arthur, b. 1925, m. Mary Munro... (d. 1987, aged 59) & d. in Pulborough, in 2011

2e. Francis Thellusson, M.D., b. 8 June 1927, m. 1957, Gillian Elaine (d. 1982, aged 46), dau. of Arthur Tippetts & d. in Pulborough in 2001, having had issue (with 2 others),

1f. Andrew George, b. July 1965, d. 2019

2f. Francis Thelluson,

3f. Henry Thelluson, b. 1971, d. in 2007 & was bur. in Pulborough.

3e. David Henry, M.B., B.Ch., of Hampton, Middlesex, b. 1932, educ. Epsom College, & Queen's Coll., Cambridge, m. & had issue

1d. Dorothy, b. 1888

2d. Gladys, b. 1889

3c. Henry James, b. in Aston, 1853, educ Haileybury & The Royal India Engineering College, Cooper's Hill, m. 1885 Ella Grace (d. 1 January 1906, aged 43), dau. of H. R. Goodhall, Barrister-at-law, & d. in Bedford, 21 January 1924

4c. Charles Walter, solicitor, b. in Aston, 1855, educ. Haileybury, m. 4 August 1888 Emily Caroline (d. 13 January 1941, aged 90) dau. of Gen. Sir Arthur Thurlow Cunynghame & d.s.p. in Winchester, 12 November 1920

5c. Thomas Edmund, b. in London, 1856, educ. Haileybury, m. at St Jude's, Courtfield Gardens, 26 March 1887 Julia Annie (who m. 2ndly in 1893 Harry Delacombe, a journalist, who d. 1959, aged 87) dau. of Dr William Towers Smith and d. 1892

6c. Algernon, b. 1858, educ. Haileybury, d. unm

7c. Reginald Augustus, b. 1863, educ. Haileybury, d. in an asylum in Singapore, 11 June 1918

8c. Lewis Gilbert, solicitor, b. in Aston July 1866, educ. Haileybury & d. 1911

1c. Mary Caroline, of The Cottage, Aston, b. in West Hills, Putney 1849, d. unm. 22 May 1939

2c. Annie Gertrude, of The Cottage, Aston, b. 1852, d.unm. 15 July 1908

3c. Georgiana Ellen, b. in West Upper Brook Street, London, 1857, d. unm. in Aboyne, 4 January 1910

4c. Mary Isabella, b. July 1859, d. 1864

3a. Thomas, Clerk at the Home Office (Senior Clerk from 1834), Private Sec to Lord Sidmouth (1820-2) and Sir Robert Peel (1822-30) when Home Secretaries, bapt at Whitchurch, Salop 27 Jan 1788, m 1stly 1821, his cousin Anne (d. 1828), dau. of John King of Coates Castle, and had issue,

1b. Addington Robert Peel, Rt Revd., Bishop of Nassau from 1863, b. July 1827 & bapt. at Aldenham, 16 September 1827, educ. Eton & Exeter Coll. Oxford, m. 1st July 1862 at Long Critchel, his cousin, Elizabeth Ann Venables, dau of Rev. William Moss King (who m. 2ndly 12 June 1883, Maj.-Gen. C. E. Cumberland, C.B. (d 1920) of Manor House, Maidstone, and d. 14 Jan 1891) and d. in Hartford, Connecticut, 8 October 1876, leaving issue,

1c. Thomas, b. & d. 1863, & is buried in St Sepulchre's Cemetery, Oxford

2c. Charles John, Major, Glos. Regt.,D.S.O., b. on New Providence Island, 21 Jan. 1865, educ. Charterhouse & R.M.C., Sandhurst, m. 21 March 1896 Helen Margaret, dau. of Robert Terry, k'd at Gallipoli 8 August 1915, having had issue,

1d. Lilla Anne, b. 21 January 1897, m. 8 November 1931, William Arnold Edwardes

2d. Joane Margaret, b, 13 April 1903, m. 18 May 1924, Harold Stanley Edwards

3c. Walter, d. young

4c. Henry, d. 1870

5c. Robert, d. 1871

6c. William Alfred, Capt., Glos. Regt., b. in New York, 21 Oct. 1872, educ. Charterhouse & Magdalen College, Oxford, m. 30 April 1902, his second cousin (once removed), Marjorie Mary (d. May 1945, aged 68), dau. of Arthur Henry Mure by his wife, Georgina Dawson (dau. of the Hon. George Dawson by his wife Elizabeth, dau. of John James King of Preston Candover) & d. at Fords Farm, Purbright, Surrey, 4 March 1920, having had issue,

    1d. Peter Addington (Rev), Roman Catholic Priest, b. 9 Feb. 1905[506], educ. Winchester & Christ Church, Oxford, d. unm 24 August 1969

    2d. John Michael, b. 8 Dec. 1910, educ. Charterhouse & Christ Church, Oxford, m. 8 Oct. 1950 Kathleen O'Morrison and d. 1994

    1d. Elizabeth Hope, b. 7 Feb. 1908, d. unm 22 June 1984

  7c. James Geoffrey, b. 23 July 1875, d. 17 December 1887

  1c. Anne Catherine, b. 5 October 1866, d. in London, 8 December 1875.

He m 2ndly 28 September 1828, Jeanette (d. 1885, aged 83) dau of T.L. Napier Sturt, Puisne Judge in India, and d. 25 June 1837, having had further issue,

  2b. Henry Pares, emigrated to Australia, Permanent Head of Education Dept in Victoria State, b. 1831, bapt. at Buckland Newton 18 September 1831, educ. Eton & Exeter Coll., Oxford, m. in Australia in 27 June 1867, Mary Christian, dau of Robert Bartlett Burke, of St Kilda, Melbourne, and d. in Fordingbridge, Hants. December 1890, having had issue,

    1c. Henry Cavendish, British Consular Service, in Varna 1908-13 & New Caledonia 1913-18, b. 16 October 1871, educ. Univ. of Melbourne, m. 11 April 1910 Emira, dau of Cav. Pietro Terzetta of Antivari, Jugoslavia, and d. in Singapore, 30 August 1919, having had issue,

      1d. Roger (Evelyn Cavendish), b 4 March 1911, educ. Beaumont College & Christ Church, Oxford, Lecturer at The Army Coll, Welbeck Abbey[507]

    2c. Charles Napier Burke, b. 1881, emigrated to Rhodesia

  3b. Cavendish, Capt. 74th (Highland) Regt., b. 14 February 1833, d.s.p 1865

  4b. Thomas Evelyn, b. 24 November 1835, educ. Charterhouse, d.s.p. 1885

  1b. Anne, b. 29 September 1834 & bapt. at Buckland Newton 30 November 1834, d. 20 October 1907

2. Lettice, bapt at Clitheroe 23 June 1747, bur at Bolton-by-Bolland 17 Sept 1759

3. Marianna, bapt. at Clitheroe, 23 January 1748, bur at Bolton-by-Bolland 18 Oct 1750

The 4th son,
Edward King, of Hungerhill, Bolton-by-Bowland, Askham Hall, Westmoreland, and latterly of Kirkham, Lancashire, Vice-Chancellor of the County Palatine of

---

[506] He was baptized at St Luke's, Chelsea on 20 March 1905, when his parents were living at 74 Oakley Street. His father was in the War Office. In 1933 he was at the Brompton Oratory.

[507] Published *Forebodings,* a collection of poems, in 1963 and *"D": Portrait of a Don* in 1967.

Lancaster, baptized at Clitheroe 15 June 1753, m 1stly 2 March 1777 at Sefton, Lancs., Henrietta (d. 11 May 1796, aged 42 and was buried in the churchyard of St Mary's, Lewisham), dau. of Robert Lang of Leyland, Lancs[508], and had issue,

1. James, b. 22 October 1781 & baptized at St Clement Danes 15 November 1781, d. 13 November 1797 and was buried in the churchyard at St Mary's, Lewisham.

2. Edward, b. 1787, d. at Ruthin School, Denbighshire 11 March 1796

1. Lettice, bapt. at St Clement Danes 9 October 1778, d. 26 October 1794 and was buried in Lewisham churchyard.

2. Henrietta, bapt. at St Clement Danes in March, 1780, m. 1stly at Askham, 19 Sept 1805, Lt. Col. Hon. George Carleton (k'd. at Bergen-op-Zoom, 18 March 1814), 2nd surviving son of Sir Guy Carleton, 1st Lord Dorchester, and had issue,

    1a. Guy, bapt. in Quebec, 27 Feb. 1809, d. 8 Sept. 1811

    2a. Guy, of Greywell Hill, Hants., b 25 Oct. 1811, succeeded a cousin as 3rd Lord Dorchester in June 1826, m 1837, Anne (d 1861), dau. of T. W. J. Wauchope, and d. 1875, leaving issue,

        1b. Henrietta Anne (Hon.), of Greywell Hill, cr. 1899 Baroness Dorchester & resumed the name of Carleton, b. 25 May 1846, m. 1stly 14 June 1864, Francis Paynton Pigott (d. 7 April 1883, aged 46) & had issue,

            1c. Guy Francis *Pigott-Carleton*, b. 8 March 1875, d. 21 Nov. 1892.

            2c. Dudley Massey *Carleton*, Lt. Col., 2nd Lord Dorchester, b. 28 Feb. 1876, m. 21 Sept. 1911, Kathleen, dau. of the 6th Lord de Blaquière & d. 20 Jan. 1963 having had issue,

                1d. Diana Claudia Patricia, of Greywell Hill, b. 2 July 1912, m. 7 July 1932, as his first wife, William Harris, 6th Earl of Malmesbury (who m. 2ndly 1991, Margaret, O.B.E. (d 25 December 1994, aged 78), widow of Raymond Baring & dau. Col. Robert Campbell-Preston & 3rdly, 5 July 1996, Mrs Bridget Hawkings & d. 11 November 2000, aged 92) & d. 19 March 1990, having had issue,

                    1e. James Carleton, 7th Earl of Malmesbury, of Greywell Hill, b. 19 June 1946, educ,. Eton & St Andrew's, m. 14 June 1969, Sally Ann, dau. of Sir Richard Rycroft, 7th Bt., & has issue,

---

[508] Robert Lang, of Leyland, married at St Helen's, Sefton on 7 July 1748, Mrs Henrietta Fleetwood, widow, of Liverpool. They had a daughter, Henrietta (b. 1754), and a son, John, who died on 19 July 1816, leaving issue. From the early 1780s, Edward and Henrietta lived at Perry Hill, Sydenham Road in the parish of St Mary's, Lewisham. "In the eighteenth century the old farming community of Sydenham developed into an area of small country houses, many occupied by City merchants and bankers. Their private parks off Perry Hill, Sydenham Road, and Westwood Hill are marked in pink on this map. Several of the houses were built on the edge of the Common, which continued to account for a third of Sydenham's land until 1810". http://www.ideal-homes.org.uk/lewisham/assets/maps/sydenham/1797

1f. James Hugh Carleton, Viscount Fitzharris, b. 29 April 1970, m. 1 June 1997, Jemima Nancy, dau. of Capt. Michael Fulford-Dobson & has issue,

    1g. James Michael Oswald, b. 26 April 1999

    2g. Fiennes Gilbert, b. 2005

    1g. Letitia Barbara, b. 2000

2f. Charles Edward (Hon.), b. 26 April 1972

3f. Guy Richard (Hon.), b. 28 April 1975

1f. Frances Maria (Lady), b. 1979

2f. Daisy Catherine (Lady), b. 1981

1e Sylvia Veronica Anthea (Lady), b. 17 May 1934, m. 28 July 1956, John Newcombe Maltby & has issue,

    1f. William John, b. 5 September 1959, m. 1985, Sarah Catherine, dau. of Cmdr. James Ekins & has issue,

        1g. George de Blacquiere, b. 1989

        1g. Alice Diana, b. 1992

        2g. Poppy Elizabeth b. 1994

    1f. Caroline Jane, b. 14 May 1957, m. 1990, Alexander Roe & has issue,

        1g. Edward Frederick John, b. 1994

        2g. James, b. 1996

        1g. Charlotte Louise, b. 1992,

    2f. Sophie Louise, b. 11 November 1963, m. 23 September 1995, Alexander Ross & has issue,

        1g. Jasper David, b. 1996

        2g. Geordie, b. 1999

        1g. Natasha Sylvia, b. 1996

2e. Nell Carleton (Lady), b. 3 July 1937, m. 28 July 1962 (div. 1995) Michael Patrick Radcliffe Boyle & has issue,

    1f. Robert Algernon Radcliffe, Maj., Irish Guards, b. 10 January 1963, m. 1987, Fiona Elizabeth, dau. of Col. George Maule Ramsey

    2f. Rupert, b. 10 February 1968, m. 31 May 2003, Caroline dau. of Friedrich-Wilhelm Gutbrod & has issue,

        1g. Henrietta Eugénie Dieudonné, b. 13 January 2005

        2g. Catherine Charlotte Carleton, b. 16 September 2008

    1f. Maria, b. 26 October 1964

2d. Lorraine Charmian Gabrielle (Hon.), b. 29 Dec. 1919, m. 21 March 1947, James Metcalfe Knowles & d. 14 November 2010, having had issue,

    1e. Thomas James Metcalfe, b. 8 January 1952

    1e. Elizabeth Charmian Carleton, b. 8 March 1949

1c. Daisy Carleton (Hon.), b. 23 October 1873, m. 5 July 1904, Brig. Gen. Vesey Thomas Bunbury, CB, CMG, DSO (d. 2 April 1934, aged 74) , of The Red House, Hook, & d.s.p. 15 Nov. 1936

She m. 2ndly 10 Nov. 1887, Maj. Gen. Richard Langford Leir (d. 18 Dec. 1933, aged 91), and d. 3 March 1925.

2b. Maria Georgiana, m. 4 July 1865, Timothy Fetherstonehaugh & d. 3 Aug. 1918, having had issue,

    1c. Mabel, m. 13 April 1898, Adm. Sir Rudolf Walter Bentinck (d. 31 March 1947, aged 78), & d. 14 Feb. 1948, having had issue,

        1d. Wolf Walter Rudolf, O.B.E., R.N., b. 28 Nov. 1903, m. 19 April 1940, Yvonne Barbara Wakefield (d. 16 July 1986, aged 76), dau. of Col. Harold Street & d. at Woodfalls, Wilts., 6 December 1992, having had issue,

            1e. Vivian Mark, Maj., Royal Marines, b. 1945, m. Dr Miranda Whitehead & had issue,

                1f. Alice, CPO Entrepreneur First & co-founder Code First:Girls b. 23 June 1986, educ. Godolphin School, Salisbury & Nottingham University Business School,

        1d. Renera, b. 19 January 1899, m. 10 Oct. 1931, Lt. Col. Walter John Stopford, M.C. (d. in Poole, 30 November 1982, aged 85) & d. 18 September 1983

1a. Hon. Maria, b. 1806 in Gibraltar, m 13 July, 1825 her cousin, Revd James King, rector of Longfield, younger son of Rt Revd Walker King, Bishop of Rochester, and d. 5 May 1841, leaving issue (see above)

2a. Hon. Henrietta Priscilla, bapt. in Quebec, 8 June, 1810, m. Oct. 1836, as his second wife, Henry Jeremiah Smith (d. 13 March 1877, aged 74), of Beabeg, near Drogheda, and d. in Bath, 20 Oct 1892 having had issue,

    1b. Carleton, Lt. Col., 3rd Battn., East Surrey Regt (ret'd 1883), b. ca. 1837, m. 12 Oct 1865, Alice Anna (d. 27 June 1902, aged 56), dau. of Charles Kaye Freshfield, M.P., of Brighton[509] & d. in Swindon in 1910, having had issue,

        1c. Edward Guy Carleton, b. in Brighton, January 1868, d. in Queensland, Australia, 7 November 1889.

        2c. Charles Dudley Carleton, Major, West Somerset Imperial Yeomanry, served in the Boer War as a Honorary Captain, b. at Upper Gatton, Surrey, 1869, m. at St Mary's Reading, 3 Dec 1891 Henrietta Dowson (who obtained a judicial separation, 1911 & d. 1948, aged 78)[510] & had issue,

            1d. Dudley Lancelot Guy Carleton, Lt.Col. 1st King's Dragoon Guards, in S.O.E. 1939-1946, Croix de Chevalier de la Legion d'Honneur (10 May 1940), b. 8 Sept 1892, educ. Radley & RMC, Sandhurst, m. 1stly, at St Martin's in the Field, London, Dec 1928, Barbara Letitia Camilla (d. 1980, aged 78)[511], only dau of Alexander Popham, of Carlton Mansions, Maida Vale & d. in Corby, Northants. 26 Nov 1984 having had issue,

---

[509] He was solicitor to the Bank of England and M.P. for Dover in 1865-8 and 1874-1886.

[510] At the time of the 1911 census, he was living with his brother ("of no occupation") and wife at 58 Fitzgeorge Avenue, Kensington. He was described as "reserve officer".

[511] The Online Peerage says that he married– and that they were divorced in 1968.

1e. Michael Edward, Maj Gen. Sir, CBE, b. 1931, m. 1stly Helga Kaya Stoss (d. 1993, aged 52) & had issue,

    1f. Mark Alexander Popham, Gen. Sir, CBE, Chief of General Staff from 2018, b. 9 February 1964, educ. Eton, m. 1991 Catherine Nalder & has issue

    2f. Andreas Martin F., M.C., former SAS officer, b. 1967, m. 1stly 1994 Camilla, dau. of Henry Crichton-Stuart[512] & has issue,

    He m. 2ndly at St Margaret's Westminster, 18 September 2015 Emma, dau. of Broderick Munro- Wilson, of Little Venice.

Sir Michael Carleton Smith m. 2ndly 17 December 2011 at St John the Divine, Richmond, Penny, Lady Francis

2e. Martin Vyvyan Carleton, Maj., Irish Guards, m. 10 Dec 1968 (div.), Eleanor Ivy (who m. 2ndly Ian V. Fletcher, of Johannesburg), dau. of S/Ldr Nigel Seely & had issue,

    1f. Robin Francis Popham, b. 1972, d. 2001

    1f. Camilla Alison, b. 11 December 1969

He m. 2ndly 1960 (div. 1968) Caroline Anne, daughter of Charles Rodolph d'Anyers Willis

2d. Henry Pendlebury Wilton Carleton, b. 3 May 1894, d. 16 June 1961

3c. Henry, unm.

1c. Henrietta Christina Carleton, b. in Brighton, 18 August 1866, m. 1903 as his first wife, Ernest Alexander (d. in Camberley 27 March 1960), a butcher of Camberley, & d. in Camberley 12 September 1908.

2c. Emilie Violet Carleton, b. in Gatton, 1872, m. in Bath, 1896, as his second wife, George Patrick Smith (d. 20 July 1936, aged 70), a bank manager & d. in Bath, 3 April 1938, having had issue.

    1d Arthur Carleton, b. 1897

    1d Lily Violet, b. 1898

3c. Constance Mary Carleton, b. in Gatton, 1874, m. in Corsham, Wilts. 15 Aug. 1896, Charles Joseph Mayo & d. in Tavistock in 1900.

2b. George, b. ca. 1838, emigrated to Manitoba, Canada.

3b. Dudley Henry Jeremiah, of Manitoba, Canada, b. ca. 1840, m. in Manitoba, 3 May 1883, Jane McTaggart and d. 30 May 1923

1b. Georgina, b. ca. 1842, m. at St Martin's in the Fields, 13 September 1859 Capt Marcus Davies, Essex Rifles, emigrated to Manitoba in the 1870s and thence to Tacoma, Washington, USA where she died 25 July 1904, having had issue,[513]

---

[512] She is a great-grand daughter of the 4th Marquess of Bute

[513] Capt Davies was to be the best man at her wedding to someone else, but apparently she ran off and married him. See 'The Smith Family of Maine, Greenhill, & Piperstown, county Louth and Beabeg & Annesbrook, co. Meath', John McCullen, *Journal of the County Louth Archaeological & Historical Society*, Vol. 27, No. 3 (2011) pp, 379-409.

1c. Harry Walton, b. in co. Mayo 15 August 1866, m. in Oregon, Susan Ida Stimpson (d. in Tacoma, 11   February 1958, aged 80) and d. in Tacoma, 1924

2c Marcus Carleton, b. in co. Mayo 7 January 1869, d. in Tacoma, 20 August 1929

1c. Georgina Henrietta Elizabeth, b. in co. Mayo 11 October 1870, d. in Tacoma 5 December 1937

2c. Alice Mabel, b. in co. Mayo, 17 November 1873, d. an inf.

3a. Georgiana Anne, b 17 August 1813, m 3 May, 1831, her cousin, Robert King, 3rd son of John King, of Coates Castle, and d. 28 January, 1837, leaving issue (see above)

Mrs Carleton m 2ndly 23 Jan 1818 Rear Adm. James Macnamara (d.s.p. at Clifton, 15 January 1826, aged 57) and d 30 Dec 1855.

3. Ann, b. 26 April 1783 & baptized at St Clements Dane in May 1783, d. 20 Nov 1783 and was buried in Lewisham churchyard.

4. Ann, bapt at St Mary's, Lewisham 9 August 1784, m. at Askham 17 Dec 1806, as his 1st wife, Rev John Sunderland (d. 23 Dec 1837, aged 69), vicar of Ulverston with Pennington, Lancs from 1807, vicar of Wiveliscombe, Somerset from 1813, eldest son of Col. Thomas Sunderland, of Ulverston, and was bur. at Ulverston, 7 Feb. 1816, having had issue,

1a. Thomas, b 1807, educ Rugby & Trinity Coll, Cambridge[514], d. unm 1867

2a. Edward, Lt. Col. Royal Artillery, b 1808 & bapt. at Ulverston 6 Feb. 1809, m. Frances Austin, of Dublin, & d. in Folkestone, 9 October 1885, having had issue,

1b. Mary Henrietta, b. in India, 2 February 1838, m. 23 February 1857, Lt Col John Philip Anthony Theobald,   Bengal Cavalry (d. in India, 1 June 1872, aged 47) & had issue,

1c. Edward James, Coffee Planter, b. in Calcutta 6 July 1858,m. 1stly at St Luke's, Cheltenham, 30 November 1887, Frances Georgiana Rodney Chesney Floyd, dau, of David Wilson, of Cheltenham d in London 7 March 1938

1c. Fanny Lavinia, b. in Marylebone, 1861, d. 1877

2c. Theodosia Mary, b. in Ryde, 1862

3c. Annette Caroline Maud, b. in Matlock, 1866, d. 14 April 1886

2b. Anne Eliza Plantagenet, b. 1845, d. unm in Folkestone 1868

3b. Catherine, b. 1846

---

[514] He was a friend of the Tennysons, Monckton Milnes and Arthur Hallam at Cambridge and was considered by them and their contemporaries at Trinity to be the most brilliant of their generation. He was part of the group that went to Oxford to debate the merits of Shelley over Byron. They were opposed by the future Cardinal Manning! He is the subject of Tennyson's poem *A Character*. Soon after going down, he suffered a mental breakdown from which he never recovered (see T.W. Reid's *Life of Lord Houghton*, vol 1, pp 74-6 and also James Pope-Hennessy's *The Years of Promise*, pp. 13-15).

4b. Charlotte Augusta Maria, b. 1847, d. unm in Tunbridge Wells, 11 July 1923

3a. John, b. 5 Dec. 1812, and bapt. at Ulverston 29 Jan. 1813, d. February 1813 & bur. at Ulverston

4a. George Henry Carleton, Commander (R.N., ret'd 1864), D.L., Lancs. (22 Nov 1852) b. 3 May 1814, and bapt. at Ulverston, 8 May 1814, m. Margaret (d. 1856), dau. & coh. of Lt. Col. Story & d. at Swarthdale, Ulverston, Dec. 1876, having had issue,

1b. John William, Lieut., R.N., of Swarthdale, Ulverston & Swarthmoor, Patutahi, Gisburne, N.Z. b. 1846, m. Agnes Henrietta (d. in London, 7 January 1926, aged 68), dau. of Rev Robert Davies, Rector of Chelsea Old Church, & had issue,

1c. Henry, b. 1882

2c. John, b. 1884

3c. Marmaduke Langdale, b. in New Zealand, 1887, d. in Stamford, Lincs 1969

4c. Richard, b. 25 July 1889

5c. Geoffrey, Capt. Royal Sussex Regt. b. in New Zealand 1890, volunteered as an ordinand in 1914, killed in action, 24 September 1918

1c. Joan, b. in New Zealand, 1883, k'd in an air raid at 67 Warwick Square, Kensington 26 September 1940.

2c. Agnes, b. 18 August 1885, m. 29 February 1912, Noel Gray Frere, C.M.G. (d. 14 Oct 1955) Colonial Service, and d. in Stamford, 25 July 1986, having had issue,

1d. Sheppard Sunderland, Professor of the Archaeology of the Roman Empire, & Fellow of All Souls, University of Oxford, b. 23 August 1916, educ. Lancing & Magdalen College, m. 3 July 1961, Janet Cecily, dau of Edward Graham Hoare, and had issue,

1e. Bartle Henry David Hoare, b. 7 Dec 1963

1e. Sarah Barbara Ruth, b. 11 April 1962

2d. Bartle Sunderland, Master at Stamford School, b. 1 Dec 1919, educ Lancing & Pembroke College, Oxford, d. unm. 10 January 2002

3d. David Henry Sunderland, Colonial Service, b. 14 March 1921, educ Lancing & Magdalene Coll. Oxford, d.s.p. at St Bartholomew's Hospital, 13 December 1947

3c. Ruth, b. in New Zealand 1888, k'd in an air raid at 67 Warwick Square, Kensington 26 September 1940

1b. Mary Eleanora[515], b. 1845, d. unm 26 July 1877

---

[515] Listed as one of Charlotte Mary Yonge's 'Goslings' in 1867-9, when she was living at Swarthdale. This was society for young girls at home who wrote two essays a month for Miss Yonge, to give them some mental stimulation.

2b. (Edith) Anne Lucy, b. 28 June 1848, m. at Ulverston, 17 May 1871 (Richard) James Reynolds, with whom she emigrated to Gisburn, Poverty Bay, New Zealand around 1878 & by whom she had issue,

1c. George Henry, b. 1872

2c. George Morris, Sheep Farmer, b. in Uverston 1878, m. 1stly in Gisburn, N.Z. in 1908, Eva (d. 12 August 1939, aged 55), dau. of John Clark & had issue. He m. 2ndly in 1943 Florence May (d. 11 August 1963, aged 80), dau. of James Orr of Turanga, N.Z. and d. in Gisburn 6 June 1959.

3c. Ralph, b. 1881

1c. Margaret, b. 1872

2c. Alice Leonora, b. 1874

3c. Mary, b. 1875

4c. Edith Rosamund, b. 1876

5c. Eleanor, b. 1877

6c. Constance Mary, b. 1879

7c. Winifred, b. in Gisburn, 1883, m. Robert Ulick Burke (d. 1965, aged 88)

3b. Constance Henrietta b. 1851, m. Rev James Moore (d. 23 July 1893, aged 44), vicar of Pennington, Lancs & d. in Lowick, Ulverston 27 September 1919 having had issue,

1c. Constance Sunderland, of Cowmire Hall, Crosthwaite, Lancs. b. 1885, m. 1919 Harry S. Spicer & d. 15 Oct 1959

2c. Mabel Sunderland, b. 1887, d. unm in Gisburn, N.Z. 12 Oct 1906

3c. Edith Rosalie Sunderland, b. 1889, m. at Ulverston in 1919 Michael Gordon

1a. Ann, b. 20 October 1811 & bapt. at Ulverston, 26 Nov. 1811, bur. at Ulverston, 2 May 1820

5. Mary, b. 1786, d. 30 May 1788 and was buried in Lewisham churchyard.

6. Mary Elizabeth, bapt at St Mary's, Lewisham 20 April 1789, m. at Kirkham 7 March 1826[516], Rev James Radcliffe (d. at Kirkham, 11 February 1836, aged 46)[517], of The Ashes, Goosnargh, perpetual curate of Whitechapel 1815-36, Headmaster of Kirkham Grammar School, son of John Radcliffe of Worcester, and d. in New Bromley, Kent, 3 January 1870, having had issue,

1a. James, b. at Kirkham, 10 November 1831, matric. at Queen's Coll., Oxford, 14 March 1850, m. Susannah ….[518]

---

[516] The witnesses from her family were her stepmother, Dorothea King, her half-brother Edward Bolton King, and her half-sister's husband, Edward Williams Hasell.

[517] He graduated from Christ Church Oxford, was licensed by Bishop Law of Chester on 24 August 1815, and held this post with a curacy at Kirkham – both in the patronage of Rev John Webber, the vicar of Kirkham. The church at Newchapel was extensively rebuilt in 1818, and the independent registers date from that year. He bought *The Ashes* in 1830. In his *History of the Parish of Kirkham*, Henry Fishwick says, 'He was a man of considerable ability, of a reserved manner, and as a schoolmaster a strict disciplinarian."

[518] James Racliffe's life seems to have been a disaster. Despite having been at Oxford, and first cousin to a peer and other rich people, by the time of his mother's death he was living

2a. John Edward, b. 1833

He m 2ndly at Croston, Lancs. 11 Oct. 1798, Dorothea (d. 1846, aged 79), only child of John Myers, sometime Mayor of Preston, by Alice, sister of Edward Bolton of Askham Hall, Westmoreland. He d.in Kirkham 2 November 1824, having had further issue,

3. **Edward Bolton**, of whom presently

4. John Myers (Rev), vicar of Cutcombe with Luxborough, Somerset from 1832, author of "The Parson's Home" and several translation of Vergil, b. 16 Feb 1804, bapt. at Askham 21 March 1804, educ Balliol Coll Oxford (matric. 12 June 1820), Scholar 1821-7, B.A. 1824, M.A. 1827, m. at St Mary's, Norton, 9 June 1827[519], his cousin, Sarah Frances, (d. 11 March 1886), younger dau. of Rt. Revd. Walker King, Bishop of Rochester (see above), and d. 25 May 1887, having had issue,

1a. John Myers, of Minehead, Somerset, b. at Badgworth, 1832, m. at Longfield, 28 June 1865, his cousin, Mary Georgiana (d. 14 May 1912), dau. of Rev James King, Rector of Longfield, and d.s.p. 1 July 1896[520].

2a.Walker (Revd), Rector of Huish Champflower, 1873-1893, b. 9 July 1834, educ. Harrow & Emmanuel Coll Cambridge, m. at Longfield, 28 June 1865, his cousin, Georgiana, dau. of Rev. James King, Rector of Longfield, and d 23 April 1914, having had issue,

1b. Walker, of Barley House, Exeter[521], b. 1866, m 1stly 1905 his cousin, Edith (d. 9 Feb 1910, aged 50) widow of Charles Wynne Pride of Horton

---

in reduced circumstances in Bromley. At the time of the 1891 census, he was living with his wife in two rooms in Tottenham, and described himself as a tea-seller. Ten years later he was in four rooms in Danbury, and describes himself as an insurance commission agent.
[519] This was just three months after her father's death, when she was living with her sister at Norton Rectory, near Faversham. The witnesses were her sister & brother-in-law, Anne & Thomas Wodehouse, and her brother, James King. John King was still a deacon. Less than a month after his marriage, on 5 July 1827, he was ordained by Bishop Law of Bath & Wells to a curacy at Chilton Polden, near Bridgwater. Two years later, on 8 June 1829, he also took responsibility for the neighbouring village of Edington. However, he resigned that on 12 July 1830, and on 15 October 1831 he was licensed to a curacy at Badgworth, near Axbridge – on the A38 just east of the M5. Then, on 8 December 1832, he was instituted to the parish of Cutcombe, in the Exmoor National Park, off the A396 near Dunster. He built the modest house at Cutcombe that was used as the vicarage until the early 1970s – and extended & 'improved' the little church. It is a tiny village. The lord of the manor in his time was Philip Pleydell-Bouverie of Brymore. Luxborough was nearby. In the 1820s John Lethbridge lived there - at Chargott Lodge – when the village was owned by his father. I'm not sure that he still owned it in John King's time. John King was a founder member and enthusiastic supporter of the Dunster show. He was also a noted speaker – a colleague remembering him some thirty years after his death 'there came from his lips such a burst of oratory as he had never heard before or since'.
[520] He was engaged in the local political scene – and (like his father) feared for the lives of the industrial poor ."......in those busy hives of men, where day and night, the roar of the engine and the whirl of the shuttle spoke of incessant toil and incessant money-making...
[521] He was blind from an early age. He nevertheless learned to ride and to use a

Kirby, and dau. of Rev. H.B. Rashleigh, vicar of Horton Kirby by his wife, Sarah Maria, dau. of Rev. James King, Rector of Longfield. He m. 2ndly 14 July 1915, his cousin, Blanch, yst. dau. of W.B. Rashleigh, of Farningham Manor, Kent by his wife, Frances Portia, dau. of Rev. James King, Rector of Longfield, and d. 14 June 1931, leaving issue,

    1c. John Rashleigh Walker, b. 2 Sept 1916, m. 27 Sept 1941 Dorothy Milligan, & d. in St Austell, 1992 having had issue,

        1d. Malcolm John Redvers, b. 21 Oct 1944

    1b. Sarah Frances, b. 1829, d. unm. in Minehead, 26 February 1912

    2b. Alice Ann Dorothea[522], b. 28 March, 1839, author of *The Lady of Winburne*, *The Woman with a Secret*, *Twice Loved*, etc. d. unm. 26 April 1894.

7. Susan Alice, b. 1799 & baptized at St Mary's, Tarleton 1 September 1799, m. at Kirkham, 30 July 1821, Revd James Formby (d 14 Feb 1881), vicar of Frindsbury, Kent from 1826[523], yst. son of Rev. Richard Formby, of Formby Hall, Lancs, and d. Aug. 1872[524] leaving issue,

    1a. Richard Edward (Rev), b 1823, educ. Charterhouse & Brasenose College, Oxford[525], rector of Latchington, Essex from 1859, m. at St Mary Magdalene, Richmond, Surrey[526], 21 August 1849, Phoebe (d. 27 July 1887, aged 63), dau. of James Back, of Richmond, and d. 8 November 1894, leaving issue,

        1b. Edward Hesketh, b. 1850, educ. Haileybury and St Mary Hall, Oxford, m. at St Luke's, Liverpool 5 June 1879, Ada Mary (d. 25 March 1918, aged 66), dau. of Thomas Stamford Raffles, of Liverpool[527] & d. at Glandenys, 2 September 1926[528], having had issue,

---

typewriter. He was active in politics and in 1910 stood as the Liberal candidate for the West Somerset division. He was also a noted campaigner against blood sports, which didn't go down well in that part of the world. He left an estate valued at £44,000. His widow moved to Folkestone, and was interested in family history.

[522] She went blind at the age of seven & was educated by her mother. She learned seven languages and contributed to the *Argosy* and the *Quiver,* journals largely devoted to fiction and associated with Mrs Henry Wood. She also wrote 11 three decker novels between 1861 and 1887.

[523] The service was taken by his father. Her brother, Edward Bolton King, was one of the witnesses Cecily Hornby was another. Formby was appointed to the living on 28 February, 1826 by his wife's uncle, Bishop Walker King. The living had previously been held by his wife's cousins, Walker King (1822-5) and James King (1825-6). On 21 March 1826, he was also appointed curate at Lydney with Aylburton in Gloucestershire, with the right to live in the vicarage – and his sister-in-law, Dorothea, was married from Lydney that July.

[524] Causing her brother to write the charming poem that Oliver Bolton King reproduces in his History.

[525] His father had been there.

[526] His father took the service. His brother Charles was one of the witnesses.

[527] He was the stipendiary magistrate in Liverpool, a son of Rev Thomas Raffles, a distinguished Congregationalist Minister at the Great George Street Chapel and a cousin of Sir Thomas Stamford Raffles.

1c. Hesketh, Commander, R.N., b. in South Weald, Essex, 1881, m. 1stly 1909 Gwladys (d. 23 March 1919, aged 35), dau. of William Richard Hurford & had issue,

    1d. Myles Hesketh, b. 1910, m. Diana Joan (d. 1998, aged 86), dau. of George Robert Sanderson & had issue,

    2d. John Hesketh, Sub-Lieut. Fleet Air Arm, b. 21 January 1918, k'd while flying, 30 May 1941

He m. 2ndly 1927, Kathleen Estelle Higgin-Birket, of Windermere & d. in the New Forest, 27 November 1952

2b. Richard (Rev), Rector of Hartfield, Sussex, b. 1851, educ. St Edmund Hall, Oxford, m. 1894, Emily Charlotte (d. 5 October 1959, aged 100), dau. of Rev Charles Leigh, Rector of Goldhanger, Essex, & d. 21 March 1905, having had issue,

    1c. Eric Lonsdale, Lt Col, of Ashdown House, Forest Row, Sussex, b. in Hartfield, 1896, educ. Marlborough, m. in Winchester in 1928, Eileen Edith (d. 2001, aged 98), dau. of Rev W.P. Hanks, Vicar of St John's, Notting Hill, and d. in Forest Row in 1968.

3b. Arthur Mawdesley, b. 1859, educ. Haileybury, d.unm. in Lossiemouth 19 December 1943

4b. Hugh Carleton, J.P., of Shipton Bellinger, Hants. b. Oct. 1862, educ. Haileybury, m. 16 October 1900, Isobel Myrtle (d. 19 February 1971, aged 90), dau of Col. Henry Wood & d. 5 Aug. 1940, having had issue,

    1c. Richard, of Shipton Bellinger, b. 31 March 1913, educ. Marlborough, d. 8 June 1958

    1c. Olive Zoe, b. 1904, m. 4 January 1928 (div.), as his first wife, Maj. Richard Clive Strachey, M.C. (d. 1979, aged 82) & had issue,

        1d. Anne Julia, b. 30 July 1930, m. 24 January 1953, John Branfoot Simpson-Pedler (d. in Perigueux, France, 11 November 2018, aged 90), diplomat & war correspondent, & had issue,

            1e. Dominic Julian Simpson, Freelance writer, author & musicologist, b. 19 December 1959

            1e. Francesca Julia Therese Simpson, b. 6 June 1954

5b. Charles Wykeham (Rev), Rector of Bix, near Henley 1924-37, b. 1865, educ Haileybury and Keble Coll, Oxford, m. 23 September 1903 Doris Marjorie (d. 24 September 1955), dau of H.M. Woodhouse of Brackenhurst, Woodbridge and d. 1947[529], having had issue,

---

[528] In 1892, he fell in love and moved in with Ann Jones (1854-1929), the wife of William Jones (1812-1897) a rich banker of Glandenys, near Lampeter. Their affair scandalized local people. The story makes him 18 years younger than he really was – to make it even more scandalous!

[529] He published various books, including "The Unveiling of the Fall", "Why did God allow the War?" and others.

1c. Iris May, b. 31 May 1915, m. 1936, a journalist, Arthur Robert Cousins (d. in Tarlton, Glos. 6 December 1990, aged 79) & d. 1985

1b. Henrietta Gertrude, b. 1855, d. unm in Eastbourne 28 November 1948

2a. Charles, Lime and Cement Merchant, of Chelsea, b. 8 June 1828, m. in Brighton, 26 August 1869 Caroline, dau. of George Shrubsole, a blacksmith of Maidstone and d. 1880, having had issue (out of wedlock),

1b. Henry L.., a solicitor in Chelsea, b. 1854, m. Alice…

1b. Florence, b. 1856

3a. James Marshall, b. 1836, m. 1861, his cousin, Alice (d. in Penrith, 27 March 1915, aged 82), dau. of E. W. Hasell, of Dalemain, Cumberland, and d.s.p. in Halling, Kent, 16 October 1898

1a. Dorothea Myers, b. 1827, m. Richard Moore, solicitor of Kirkham, Lancs (d. 1870), son of Rev Richard Moore, vicar of Lund and d.s.p. at Kirkham House, Rochester, 6 April 1906.

2a. Susan Alice, b. 1838, m. at St George's, Hanover Square in 1883, Samuel Sayer (d. 13 February 1903, aged 65), and d.s.p. in Frindsbury, Kent d. 1 June 1925

3a. Fanny Douglas, b. 1842, d. unm. in Frindsbury, 26 June 1932

4a. Jane, b. 1842 d. unm. in Rochester, 13 May 1936

7. Dorothea, b. 24 November 1805, bapt at Askham 21 December 1805, m. at Lydney, Glos. 12 July 1826 Lt Col Edward Williams Hasell of Dalemain, Cumberland (d 7 April 1872) & d 15 June 1885[530], having had issue,

1a. Edward, b 1828, d 1833

2a. Williams, b 1836, d unm 1870

3a. John Edward, b. 19 September 1839, of Dalemain, D.L., J.P., educ Harrow & Trinity Coll, Oxford, m. in Paris 4 July. 1877 Frances Maud (d. 1911), granddau of Henry Flood, of Paulstown Castle, Kilkenny, and d. 16 Jan 1910, having had issue,

1b. Dorothy Julia, b. 1883, d. unm 1936

2b. (Frances Hatton) Eva, b. 1887, d. unm. 1974

4a. George Edmund (Rev), rector of Aikton, Cumberland, and latterly of Dalemain, b 1847, m. 27 October 1880 Helen (d. 1919), dau of Rev. Prebendary William Sinclair, and d 1932, leaving issue,

1b. Edward William, of Dalemain, b. 16 January 1888, m. Gertrude Stroyan and d. 1972, having had issue,

1c. Sylvia Mary, of Dalemain, b. 8 November 1922, m. 1stly, 7 June 1944, Henry William Somerville Marshall, Scots Guards (k'd at Tiernay, 6 November 1944, aged 21). She m.2ndly, 22 April 1948, Bryce Knox

---

[530] There is a picture of her at Dalemain - where her descendants still live and which is open to the public. Pictures of E. W. Hasell hang at Dalemain and in the Grand Jury Room in the Citadel at Carlisle. There is a silver fir at Dalemain – the largest in the UK – said to have been planted by Dorothea Hasell from a seedling brought back by her uncle, Capt. James King.

McCosh, of Huntfield, later *Hasell-McCosh* & d. 17 August 1991, having had, with other issue

  1d. Robert *Hasell-McCosh*, of Dalemain, m. Jane & has issue,

    1e. George

    1e. Hermione

    2e. Beatrice

  2d. Andrew Knox *McCosh,* of Huntfield, m & had issue,

    1e. David Andrew Hesketh, m. Emily, dau. of Alistair Kendon, of Fryerning, Essex

    2e. Peter, m. Katherine, dau . Hugh Dodd, of Tyninghame, East Lothian

 2c. Margaret Helen, m. 10 July 1956, Timothy John Clulow Washington & had issue

2b. Godfrey Sinclair, b. 2 November 1889, m. 1929 Mrs Ethel Dorothy Micklem (d. 1971, aged 79) & d. 1977, having had issue

1a. Dorothea, b. 1827, d. unm. at St Leonards-on-Sea, 14 Feb 1898,

2a. Elizabeth Julia, b. 1830, d. unm. at Dalemain, 14 Nov 1887[531]

3a. Alice Jane, b. 1833, m. 1861, her cousin, James Marshall Formby, youngest son of Rev James Formby by his wife Susan Alice, dau. of Edward King of Askham (see above) and d.s.p. in Penrith, 27 March 1915

4a. Mary, b. 1834, m. 28 September 1854, William Parker, J.P. (d. 1892, aged 72) of Carlton Hill, Penrith and d. 1911, having had issue,

 1b. William Hasell, (Rev), Vicar of Cockermouth from 1881, b. 1855, d. unm. 3 January 1935

 2b. Christopher John, Solicitor, of The Laithes, Penrith, b. 22 March 1859, m. 29 October 1882 Alice Mary (d. 31 December 1923, aged 66), dau. of Samuel Radcliffe of Werneth Park, Lancs. & d. 17 September 1932, having had issue

  1c. Christopher Miles, farmer of Hawksdale Lodge, Dalston & later of Skelton, Penrith, b. in Oldham, Lancs. 9 February 1866, m. 1stly 1911 Mary Ella Marjorie Carleton Cowper (d. 1980, aged 89) & had issue,

    1d. Anne Marjorie Alice, b. 22 December 1912, m.as his third wife, in Wallingford, 1938, Frederick Reginald Parkes Dexter (d. in Leeds, 1969, aged 80) & d. in Droitwich, Worcs. 10 September 2001, having had issue,

      1e. Ann,

    2d. Nancy Ellen, Huntsman of Bleasdale Beagles, b. 29 September 1915, m. 1941 Rupert Anthony Metcalfe-Gibson (d. 27 January 1948, aged 61), of Elm Lodge, Ravenstonedale, & d. in Kendal, Westmorland 5 December 1995

    3d. Joan Daphne, b. 17 February 1917, m. Peter Reginald Crauford Pitman (d. in Winchester, 1990 aged 78) & d. in Scotland, 23 December 1999

  He m. 2ndly 1930 Gladys Parker (d. 1983, aged 76) & d. in Penrith, 22 November 1959, having had further issue,

---

[531] She published devotional works and others on Calderon and Tasso

4d. Gladys M.. b. 28 July 1932, d. 1941

5d. Ruth, b. 13 September 1936

3b. Edward Thomas, Land Agent & Farmer, b. 1862, d. unm. 20 June 1942

1b. Mary Dorothea, b. 1858, unm in 1911

2b. Alice Margaret, b. 8 July 1860, m. 23 July 1884, Rev William Foster Gilbanks (d. in Cuckfield, Sussex, 20 May 1945, aged 86) Rector of Great Orton, Cumberland & d. at Great Orton, 3 December 1932, having had issue,

1c. George William, b. 21 July 1885, m. 19 April 1911, Mary Todd (d. in Allonby, Cumberland 21 April 1965, aged 83) & d. in North Vancouver, B.C., 5 November 1968, having had issue,

2d. George William Todd, electrician, b. in Penrith, 23 January 1912, m. 1938, Grace Southwood & d. In Coulsdon, Surrey, 7 August 1973

1d. Mary Todd, b. 4 April 1915, m. in 1948, John Brockbank (d. 1975, aged 92) , a farmer of Heathfield, Bromfield, Cumbria & d. 12 January 2002.

2c. Christopher Ernest, b. 29 October & d. 29 November 1886

3c. Edward Francis, b. 1889, m 23 February 1921 Eleanor Margaret Keys-Wells (d. 14 October 1986, aged 85) and d. in Crawley, West Sussex, 20 February 1979, having had issue,

1d. Margaret Patricia, b. 20 September 1924, m. 1947, Thomas G. Bowman

4c. Richard Parker, Lieut., Border Regt., b. 18 April 1892, educ. Carlisle Grammar School, Rossall & Trinity Coll., Oxford, k'd at Suvla Bay, Gallipoli, 9 August 1915[532]

5c. Philip Nelson, b. 1 April 1895, m. 1stly in 1920, Martha J. Stordy & had issue,

1d. Philip Richard Howard, gas board employee, b. 1924, m. in 1951, June J.R. Macmillan & had issue,

1e. Philip E..., b. 1956

1d. Alice Martha, d. unm.

2d. Elizabeth Mary, m. N.. Routledge

He m. 2ndly in 1952, Anne Elizabeth Noble & d. in Thurstonfield, Carlisle, 4 April 1965

1c. Dorothy Alice, b. 20 October 1900, m. 1925, Hamilton C. Allen & d. in Hursterpoint, W Sussex, 14 January 1980

2b. Cicely, b. 1865, d. unm. at Carlton Hill, 20 July 1918

3b. Mabel, b. 1868, d. unm 1923

4b. Amy, b. 1870, d. 1955

5b. Sybil, of Carleton Cottage, Penrith, b. 1874, m. 1898 ..... O'Neill & had issue

1c. Roderick Nigel, b. 1900

---

[532] He was in training for the ministry when war broke out.

5a. Henrietta Marie, b. 1837, m. 1876 Sir Henry Verey, J.P. (d. 1920) of Bridge House, Hurst, Berks. & had issue,

    1b. Henry Edward, a solicitor, of Bridge House, Hurst, b. 8 May 1877, educ. Eton & Trinity Coll. Cambridge, m. Lucy Alice, dau of Judge Amyas Philip Longstaff Atkinson & had issue

    1b. Dorothy Parnell, b. 1880

6a. Frances Anne, b. 1841, d. unm. at Dacre Lodge, Penrith, December 1917

The elder son,

Edward Bolton King, D.L., J.P., of Umberslade, Warwickshire and latterly of Chadshunt. M.P. for Warwick 1831-7 and afterwards for the co. of Warwick 1857-9, High Sheriff 1830. b. 15 July 1801, educ. Corpus Christi Coll, Oxford & Lincoln's Inn, m. 1stly 7 Feb 1828, Georgiana (d. 6 May 1858), yr. dau. of Robert Knight, D.L., J.P. of Barrells, Warwicks., and had issue,

1. Bolton, b. Jan 1829, d. at school in Bray, Berkshire, 7 Nov 1840, aged 11.

2. Raleigh, b. 10 June 1831 & baptized at St George's. Hanover Square, 10 July 1831, d. 19 March 1832, aged 9 months.

3. **Edward Raleigh,** of whom presently

4. Walter, b. 4 July 1836, d. 11 Jan 1837, aged 6 months.

1. Georgiana, b. 19 Feb 1830, m. 14 March 1856 Capt. Henry Cotton, 21st Royal Scots Fusiliers, of Shrewsbury, only son of Rev. Henry Calveley Cotton. He d. 16 Dec. 1909. She d. in London, 24 July 1914, leaving issue[533]

    1a. Henry Robert Stapleton*, Dodbrooke Manor, Kingsbridge & formerly of Wem, Capt 1st Bn, Oxfordshire L.I., b. 8 June 1859, m. 12 Sept. 1900, Isabella (Ella) (d. 1 April 1953), widow of Arthur Lyon & dau of John Johnstone, of Halleath, Dumfries, & d.s.p. 25 Jan. 1946

    2a. Willoughby Lynch, Capt 3rd Bn Shrops L.I., b. 22 Aug. 1863, m 1stly 1888, Rosina Mary Adelaide (d. 29 Jan. 1914), dau of Andrew Jones, of Shelton, Salop, and had issue,

        1b. Vyvian Stapleton, Clifton College, Bristol, b. 1889, d. unm. 23 April 1973. He m 2ndly, April, 1916, (Eleanor) Mary, widow of Walter Sutton Salt and dau. of James Henry Sprott, and d. 6 January 1918.

    1a. Frances Georgiana, d. unm. 11 Nov. 1936

    2a. Eloisa Alice, d. unm. 2 Nov. 1906

2. Frances Dorothea, b. 27 Aug 1832, m. 26 April 1860 Hon. John Stapleton, M.P. for Berwick-on-Tweed[534], of Berwick Hill, Northumberland & 31 Campden

---

[533] Papa said that he had never met Mrs Stapleton – unsurprisingly since she had died when he was five years old. But he also said that he had never met Mrs Cotton. I suppose that she was based in Shropshire, but papa was 20 when she died. You would have thought that there might have been some contact, but maybe his father had no desire to foster relations.

[534] He was a barrister. He won Berwick for the Liberals in 1852, but was unseated on petition. He sat for Berwick in 1857-9, was defeated and sat again in 1868-74.

Grove, London, W., 4th son of Thomas Stapleton, of Carlton Hill, Yorks. and brother of the 8th Lord Beaumont (*see Burke's Peerage, Beaumont B),* and d. 8 May 1899, leaving issue. He d. 25 Dec 1891 aged 81.

1a. Gilbert (Rev)*, of Berwick Hill, b. 1862, educ. Haileybury & Oriel Coll. Oxford, Rector of Rotherwick, Hants 1896-1933, m 1stly 1891 Anna, eldest dau of Rev Thomas Langshaw, of Silchester. She d. 1891. He m 2ndly Jan 1894 Eleanor, only child of Rev Gibbes Jordan, rector of Tunworth, and d. 19 July 1949, having had issue. She d. 18 Jan 1947.

1b. Katherine Anna*, of Yately Hill, Hants. b. 14 June 1895, d unm. at Yately Hill, 6 August 1987

2b Margaret Alianora (Nora)*, b. 20 August 1897, murdered in Bermuda 6 July 1941 unm.

2a. Cuthbert, b. at Queen's Gate Terrace, 25 April 1863, living in George Town, Queensland in 1892[535], m. 1899 Mrs Amelia Grainer, and d.s.p. at Gilbert River, Queensland, 10 July 1906

3a. Thomas, b. 1869, served in the First World War in the 1st Battalion, The Rifle Brigade, k'd in Flanders 19 December, 1914

4a. Bryan, Public Works Dept (State Railways) in India, b. 1871, m. 1stly 1912 Geraldine Emma (d. 1916), dau. of Col. Crowdy, R.E. & had issue,

1b. Miles Henry, Lieut. Fleet Air Arm, b. 1915, k'd. in action off Malta, 21 January 1943

2b. Anne Dunscomb, of Wellington, New Zealand, b. 1914, m. David Colwyn Clark (d. 1987), Colonial Service, son of William H. Clark, of Pretoria and had issue,

1c. Anthony Miles Stapleton (Dr.), Geologist, of Coquitlam, B.C., Canada, b. 15 March 1941, m. 1970, Ruth Christine, dau. of Frederick Guy Harrison, of Appleton, Roebuck, Yorks. & had issue,

1d. David Crispin Stapleton, b. 1973, & has issue by Jennifer Lee, dau. of Lloyd King,

1e. Aiden Natis Miles, b. 1993

1d. Natasha Alexandra, b. 1971, m. 1993 Scott Dean Charpentier

2c. Bryan Stapleton, of Wellington, New Zealand, b. 4 April, 1944, m. 1971 Nicolian, dau. of Leslie Lulofs, of Johannesburg, S. Africa & has issue,

1d. Graham Leslie, b. 1975

1d. Bronwyn, b. 1972, m. Cameron Gough & has issue,

1e. Hannah Nicolian

1c. Geraldine Anne, of Toronto, Ontario, b. 1947

He m 2ndly 1918, Ruth Jane (d. 1954), dau., of Richard James Friel, of Waterford, and had further issue,

---

[535] George Town began its life during the 1870s Australian gold rush. It is surrounded by good grazing land.

2b. Thomas, B.A., B.M., B.Ch. M.R.C.P., b. 1920, educ. King's School, Canterbury & University Coll. Oxford, Professor of Paediatrics, University of Sydney, Sec. International Paediatric Association, d. unm. 16 Dec. 2007.

5a. Louis Henry, of Sonning Common, Oxon, served in the Matabele War 1893, Jamieson Raid 1895, S. African War & Great War, b. 1874, m. in Kimberley, South Africa, 2 July 1908 Annetta Lima (d. 1956), formerly wife of N... Smith, & dau. of Achille Perossi, and d. 1949, having had issue,

  1b. Diana Enid Violet Dorothea, of Sonning Common, Oxon. b. 21 May 1911, m 30 September 1939, Dr Allan William Vaughan Eley (d. Sonning Common, 12 June 1965, aged 52) and d. 2005, having had issue,

    1c. Ian Miles Stanley Vaughan, b. 18 June 1944, d. in Goring on Thames, 3 September 1983

    2c. Nigel Louis Allan, b. 1949

    1c. Bridget Diana Lilian Annetta, b. 1940, m. 1965, Derek Frank Gardner & d. 1966

1a. Monica, of Warwick Gardens, Kensington, b. at Queen's Gate Terrace, 3 February 1861, d. unm. at Tenterden, Kent, 3 June 1936

2a. Frances, b. in Kensington, 15 May 1864, m. 1894 Thomas W. St Lawrence Lush (d. 1948), of Silchester, nr. Reading and d.s.p. in Surbiton 19 December 1943

3a. Dorothea, b. in Kensington, 9 April 1867, d. 17 January 1875

4a. Georgiana Maria, b. in Kensington, 16 April 1868, m. December 1891 Rev Edwin John Frayling, rector of Harwich (d. 1907) and d. at St Germans, Cornwall, 23 November 1922[536], having had issue,

  1b. Bryan Edwin, C.B.E., b.in Singapore, 5 August 1893, m. 1stly 25 January 1926, Jean Dick, M.B.E., & had issue,

    1c. Michael Alastair William, m. 1952 Ann Gray Thompson & had issue,

      1d. Andrew

      2d. Alisdair

      1d. Allison

    1c. Judith Aline, b. 19 December 1931 m. 1953 John Keith Holesworth, O.B.E., & d. in Melbourne, Australia, 5 May 2011, having had issue,

      1d. Keith Mark, b. 1958

    2c. (Rosemary) Shiona, b. 1931, m. 1952 Richard Neville Jackson

He m. 2ndly 1946 Mary Adela Leaning & d. in Tunbridge Wells, 23 December 1987

2b. Michael Stapleton, 2nd Lieut., Royal Field Artillery, b. in Birtsmorton Rectory, April 1898, k'd. in the Battle of the Somme, 16 September 1916

3b. John Cuthbert, b. at Birtsmorton Rectory, 1 July 1899, m. 1937 Wendy Ford and d. on Waiheke Island, Auckland, New Zealand, 6 August 1981, having had issue,

---

[536] After her husband's death, she retired to Broadstairs with her youngest sister – which is presumably where the children were brought up.

1c. David John, b 1938, m 1 July 1961 Jacqueline Maria Crawford & has issue,

1d Miles Brandon, b. 1967

2d. Nigel, b. 1968

1d. Kim Antoinette, b 1963

2d. Hilary Adair, b. 1967

4b. Gerard Dunstan Warren, b. at Birtsmorton Rectory, 19 September 1900, d. unm. 1970[537]

1b. Eve Georgiana, b. in Singapore, 3 January 1895, d. unm. in Bath December 1984

2b. Patricia Mary, b. in Harwich Vicarage 18 September 1906, m 1937 John George Bela (Janci) Alekxander Simon, an artist & d.s.p. in Oxford, 30 May 2000.

5a. Joan Henrietta Dorothea*, b. in Kensington 1873, d. unm. in Harrogate, Sept 1952

3. Jane, b. 1835, m. 2 Oct 1855 at St James, Piccadilly, Capt Charles Wilson Carden, 36th Regt[538], 5th son of John Wilson Carden, of Barnane, co. Tipperary, and d. 5 Sept 1903 having had issue. He d. 24 Nov 1894, aged 76.

1a. Charles Edward, Engineer & Contractor, b. 3 August 1856, m. 1880 Eliza Wyvill (d. 18 April 1952, aged 97), and d. 1925, having had issue,

1b. Charles William, b. 9 January 1882, d. unm. 8 October 1930[539]

2b. John King, b. 1885, emigrated to Argentina, m. 19 September 1921 Emelinda Maria Dionisi (d. 1965, aged 63), and d. 1963, having had issue,

1c. Arnold Frederick, of Mendoza, Argentina, b. 15 July 1922, an engineer, m. 17 March 1949, Josefine Solans & had issue,

1d. Monica Eliza, b. 16 December 1949

2d. Patricia Irene, b. 1 December 1951

3d. Claudia Marguerite, b. 11 January 1956

2c. Charles Edward, of Buenos Aires, b. 19 Nov 1924, m. 28 April 1949, Clotilde Voget & had issue

1d. Andrew Edward, 4 February 1950

2d. Frederick Arthur, b. 3 November 1952

3d. Charles William, 14 September 1955

1d. Elizabeth, b. 3 February 1969

---

[537] He suffered from shell shock after WW1 and latterly lived in a sanatorium, where he committed suicide.

[538] He retired on his marriage, since Jane's father did not approve of his daughter following ' a marching regiment' (see Octavia Higgon's Memoirs). They moved from Stratford-on-Avon to Southam Hall around 1867, to Heyford Manor in Upper Heyford in 1875, and to The Rookery, Brixworth in 1882. They seem to have spent most of their time hunting. He died suddenly, after a good day's hunting, while driving with his wife.

[539] He died from the effects of his wounds in the First World War.

1c. Hilda Estelle, b. 9 Jan 1932, m. 26 July 1957, Nicholas Gomez & had issue,

    1d. Nicholas, b. 10 February 1961

    1d. Maria Laura, b. 26 May 1958

3b. Frederick*, electrical engineer, b. 5 February 1887, d. unm. in Bath, 24 March 1970

4b. Edward Percy, local government official, b. 28 April 1888, m. 9 July 1919 Constance Evelyn, dau. of Arthur Robinson, and d. 20 June1963, having had issue,

    1c. Robert Arthur, b 14 October 1923

    1c. Constance Margaret, b 28 May 1922, m. 20 September 1947, Ingram Edward Wright, M.M., of Colchester & had issue,

        1d. David Edward, ceramist,b. 20 November 1948 educ. Colchester Grammar School & Birmingham Univ., m. 30 December 1972, Mary Rose, dau, of Edmund Riley, of Colchester

        2d. Michael Charles, b. 1 January 1952

        3d. Richard John, b. 4 August 1953

    2c. Caroline Eliza, b. 4 September 1926, m. 3 July 1948, Ronald Thomas Ward, of Grays, Essex & had issue,

        1d. Susan, b. 10 January 1950, m. 28 July 1968, Michael Vincent, of Corringham, Essex & had issue,

          1e. Shaun, b. 10 November 1968

          1e. Tracy, b. 9 September 1971

        2d. Anne, b. 9 August 1952, m. 22 September 1974, Raymond Ewing, of Grays, Essex

    3c. Kathleen Mary, of Grays, Essex, S.R.N., S.C.M., b 28 July 1928

5b. Arnold, b. 26 November1890, k'd. in Palestine, 7 November 1917[540]

1b. Jane Dorothea*, b. 5 June 1883, m. 17 April 1906 Charles Henry Cadwallader (d. 17 December1954) & d. 2 September 1966, having had issue,

    1c. Amy Dorothea*, b. 1909, d. unm. *post* 1987

    2c. Gwyneth Maria Carden*, b. 1920, m. 1943 Richard Sidney Watts (d. 1956), and had issue,

        1d. John Richard, b. 13 March 1944

        1d. Mary Elizabeth, b 22 Feb 1947, d. an inf.

        2d. Ann Mary, b. 9 May 1954

She had further issue,

        2d. Michael Seeley[541], b. 15 Feb 1960, m. 1981, Chloe Esther Walker & has issue,

          1e. Amy, b. 1984

---

[540] 'A very quiet young fellow' (Mrs Higgon)

[541] He has the photo album that belonged to his great-great-grandmother, Mrs Charles Carden, and showed it to Arthur Carden in 2010. He sent me copies of the photos.

    2e. Emma, b. 1986

    3e. Alice, b. 1993

  2b. Margaret Wyvill*, of Bath, b. 1894, d. unm. *post* 1988

2a. Alfred, Lieut., 2nd West Indies Regt., b. 11 June 1859, at Sandhurst. Lost at sea from H.M.S. Tyne, off Barbados on his way to join his regiment, 1883[542].

3a. Eustace, First Officer P. & O., b. 29 December 1863, m. 6 February 1893, Lilias Agatha Mary Racester (d. 1 April 1935, aged 72), dau. of Henry Philip Markham, of Sedgebrook, Northants., and was lost at sea in the wreck of the Aden, 9 June 1897, having had issue,

  1b. Eustace*, A.M.I.Mech.E., b. 17 May 1895, m. 29 December 1924, Dr Lucy Theodosia Badcock, dau. of Rev. Thomas Badcock, Rector of Walgrave, Northants., and d. 9 September 1959 having had issue. She d. 1977, aged 86

    1c. Arthur Eustace*, b. 28 June 1929, educ. Sherborne & Corpus Christi, College, Cambridge, m. 1955 Albertine (Atty) Voss (d. January 2016) & has issue

      1d. Mark Thomas Jan, b. 15 October 1958, educ. Sherborne, m. 1990 Kathryn Bishop & has issue

        1e. Alexander

        2e. Charles

      1d. Kirsten Isabella, b. 26 November 1956, m. 1977 Nelson McCorkell & has issue

        1e. Thomas, b. 1986

        1e. Tamsin, b. 1984

    2c. Michael Terence, A.R.I.B.A., b. 18 February 1934, educ. Sherborne, m. 10 August 1957, Shione, dau. of William Gilbert Pirrie, & has issue

      1d. Matthew Pirrie, b. 18 May 1960, educ. Sherborne, m. Carol Curvin & has issue,

        1e. Adam, b. 1998

        2e. Giles, b. 2004

      1d. Melanie Markham, b. 29 March 1962, m. Jonathan Kelly, & has issue,

        1e. Benjamin, b. 2004

        1e. Olivia, b. 2002

    1c. Audrey Theodosia*, b. 10 December 1927, m. 19 January 1952 Terl Malcolm Bryant (div. & d. 2005) & d. 10 April 2015, and was buried at Walgrave, having had issue

      1d. Terl Timothy Carden, drummer & precussionist, b. 2 May 1961, m. Juliet Hodges & has issue,

        1e. Louis

        2e. Gabriel

        3e. Inigo

        4e. Oscar

        1e. Cecily

---

[542] 'Poor Alfred, handsome and smart and always in debt' (Mrs Higgon's memoirs)

2e. Honor

1d. Shane Theodosia, b. 1 November 1956, m. Stuart James & has issue,

  1e. Henry Stuart Bryant, b. 1988

  2e. Charles Terl George, b. 1991

  1e. Arabella Theodosia, b. 1987

2d. Virginia Tarrant, in California, b. 16 May 1958, unm.

3d. Suzanna Baynes, b. 25 March 1963, m. Mark Owen & has issue,

  1e. Declan, b. 1997

  1e. Martha, b. 1999

2c. Marion Edith, b. & d. 1931

4a. John, Lt Col., C.M.G., Commissioner, Northern Rhodesian Police, b. 13 May 1870, m. 25 October 1909 Susan Ellen (d. 26 April 1961, aged 82), dau. of Drury Wake[543], of Pitsford House, Northants., and was k'd. at Gallipoli, 10 August 1915, having had issue,

1b. Andrew, A.R.I.B.A., b. 4 August 1910, educ. Stowe, m. 1stly 19 June 1937 Katherine Hugo, dau. of Capt. Cross and had issue,

  1c. Andrew Murray Hugo, Ph.D., b. 2 March 1948, educ. Malden Grammar School & Sheffield University, m. & s.p.

  1c. Vanessa Hugo, Housing Manager in Kennington, b. 16 Nov 1946, educ. Girton Coll., Cambridge, d. unm. 2003

He m. 2ndly 18 April 1973, Mrs Elizabeth Kendall, M.R.C.S., and d. in Woodham Mortimer, Essex, in July 1996

1a. Eveleen*[544], b. 26 November 1860, d. unm. 4 Jan 1941 at Withycombe Rectory

2a. Georgiana Anne, b. 3 April 1862, d. 26 April 1886[545]

3a. Bertha*, b. 4 June 1865, d. unm. at Stoke Poges, 21 January 1948

4a. Maud*, b. 3 December 1866, m. 13 July 1897 William Thurnall, Solicitor of Kettering (who d. 1903)[546], and d. 22 March 1947 at White Bays, Stoke Poges, leaving issue,

1b. William Valentine, 2nd Lieut. Royal Marines, b 1903, d. unm. 1921

1b Dorothy Maud[547]*, b 1899, m 1920 Douglas Myddleton Morriss, Barn Cottage, Great Kingshill, High Wycombe (who d 5 Oct ??), and d.s.p. at Windsor Forest Stud, Ascot, 20 Nov 1983

5a. (Catherine) Octavia, M.B.E., J.P., b. 22 March 1868, m 1stly 7 October 1888, Capt. C.G.W.E. Edwardes, of

---

[543] He was the third son of Sir Charles Wake, Bt by Charlotte Tait, the sister of Archibald Campbell Tait, Archbishop of Canterbury.

[544] Known as Eva.

[545] Of a chill, caught after a long day's hunting on a cold, rainy day.

[546] Maud and Bill met on the hunting field – he was 'a first rate performer with the Woodland Pytchley'.

[547] Cousin Dolly Morriss was a noted breeder of Welsh Springer Spaniels

Sealyham, Pembrokeshire[548], J.P., Northamptonshire Regt (d.s.p. 1902, aged 52). She m 2ndly, 4 Oct 1905, Victor James Higgon, M.B.E., J.P., Trefgarne Hall, Pembrokeshire, and d. 18 November 1954, having had issue,

    1b. Frances Carden*, b 1907, m 31 Jan 1940 at Winchfield Church, Hants. Capt P. Michael Hill, Royal Fusiliers, and had issue,

        1c. John, b & d 11 Nov 1940 at Aldershot.

4. Catherine, b. 1 Feb 1838, of 16 Brompton Sq, London S.W., d .unm. 4 Jan 1923

5. Isabella, b. 19 April 1839, author of "Helpful Half Hours", "A Children's Guide to the New Testament Stories" etc. m 12 Dec 1865 as his second wife Rev Christopher Dunkin Francis, vicar of Tysoe, with Compton Wynyates[549], and d. 10 April 1922, leaving issue. He d 29 August 1895, aged 80 and is bur at Compton Wynyates.

    1a. Murray King,a farmer in Rosario, Sante Fe, Argentina, bapt at Tysoe 29 August 1869, m. 1stly, Lucy Cuilson of Buenos Aires & had issue,

        1b. R..., b. 1908

        1b. P... b. 1911

He m. 2ndly in Salisbury, 17 May 1914, Ethel Mary, dau. of James Barclay, & d. in Battle, Sussex in 1939

    2a. Geoffrey Christopher, a rancher in Argentina, bapt at Tysoe 30 April 1871, m. 1910 Blanche Kathleen (d. 1957, aged 71), dau. of Alexander Traill & d. in Thakeham, Storrington, Sussex 7 April 1946

    3a. Edward Tyrrell Dunkin*, Crawford Bay, British Columbia, b. at Tysoe, 11 August 1883, served in the Canadian Army in World War I, m. 1915 Susan S., dau of Maj Gen A. Hales & d. in Nelson, B.C., Canada 17 March 1946

    1a. Muriel[550]*, b. 1866 & bapt at Tysoe, 27 Jan. 1867, m. at Tysoe, 30 December 1890. Rev. Edward Taswell Richardson (d. 1957, aged 97), vicar of Great Easton, Essex, and had d. in Bude, Cornwall in 1952, having had issue,

---

[548] He was in Malaysia and Singapore until 1891 when he was invalided home after a riding accident. They eventually settled at the denuded family estate – which he inherited after a string of drunken heirs had died. He developed epilepsy as a result of the accident and died after a long illness. Octavia inherited the house but not much else.

[549] He had had six children by his first wife. There is a stained glass window of St Christopher in his memory in Tysoe church, and another that commemorates Queen Victoria's golden Jubilee and his own 35 years in the parish. It has two lights – one showing St Francis and one himself in Eucharistic robes. It shows him as a fine looking man – perhaps self-consciously so!

[550] Muriel Richardson gave Octavia Higgon the Knight family letters. Her mother was "the family historian of her generation" and had treasured them - handing them on to her daughter. Mrs Higgon, with Mrs Richardson's agreement, gave them to the British Museum in 1943 - where they remain. Thank goodness for these three ladies. Without their concern, some key resources for the life of Lord Bolingbroke would have been lost, besides what we know of the Knights themselves.

1b. (Richard) Francis, Lieut, Royal Warwickshire Regt., bapt at Moreton Morrell, Warwicks. 10 December 1893, died of wounds received in the Battle of Loos, 30 September 1915

2b. Geoffrey Taswell, served in WW1 as Lieut. in the R.F.C. & in WWII as Major, T.A., b. in Warwick April 1897, educ. Rugby School, m.1920, Gwendoline Mary Hedges & d. in Gwanda, Rhodesia 31 December 1974

3b. Eric

1b. Muriel Anne, b. at Moreton Morrell, 1892

2b. Eve, b. in Vevey, Vaux, Switzerland 24 December 1905, m. at Weymouth, June 1940, Wentworth Godfrey and d. in Stratton, Cornwall in 1995

2b. Helen, d. unm. 5 February 1963

3b. Katherine

2a. Sybil Octavia*, bapt at Tysoe, 23 February 1868, m. at St Mary's, Warwick, 17 April 1895, William Godfrey Dickens (who d 26 Jan 1938, aged 68), son of William Park Dickens, of Cherington, Warwickshire, and d. at Hardham Green, Sussex, 17 January 1957, having had issue,

   1b. William Anthony, b in Edgbaston, Birmingham, 8 March 1896, m. in Ulverston in 1932, Edith Alice Barnes, and d. at Little Compton, Tisbury, 15 November 1964, having had issue,

      1c. William, b 1934

   2b. Godfrey Christopher, b 1902, m Jeanne Kenyon and had issue,

      1c. Hugh, b 1929

   1b. Hilda Sybil, b 1897, m Samuel Bridell and had issue,

      1c. Christopher, b 1925

      2c. David, b 1927

   2b. Gillian Ruth, b 1909, m Anthony Ryden, and had issue

      1c. Jonathan, b 1934

      1c. Joanna, b 1937

3a. Isobel, b 1873, m Robert Mackintosh (d. 1949) and had issue,

   1b. Donald, b 1904, m Barbara Phillips

   1b. Elspeth, b 1906

   2b. Jean, b. in Argentina 23 Jan 1911, m. in Storrington, Sussex, Arthur Bradley   (d. in Cornwall, June 1975, aged 76), and d. 17 Nov 1997, having had issue

      1c. Jean Mary, b 1936

      2c. Sarah, b. 2 Jan 1945, m. Richard Weller & had issue,

         1d. Jane

         2d. Sally

   3b. Margaret, b 1911

   4b. Moira Agnes, b in Rosario, Argentina, 11 September 1912, m. N…. Crapp & d. in Pabu, France, 19 June 2000

4a. Marjorie, an Anglican nun. b. 1876, d. 1921

5a. Bridget, b. 1879, m. at St Mary's, Warwick, 25 August 1906 Maj. Philip Joseph Locke (d. in Vancouver), a farmer of Vancouver, British Columbia, and had issue,

    1b. Richard Philip, P/O, R.C.A.F., b 1911, k'd 8 April 1942, s.p.

6. Maria, b 20 Jan & d 24 June 1841, aged 6 months.

7. Henrietta, b. 1842, m. 18 June 1862, George Hyde Granville, 3rd son of Bernard Granville, of Wellesbourne, Warwickshire, and d. 28 Feb 1920, having had issue. He d. 13 Dec 1903.

    1a. Dennis, M.V.O., O.B.E., of Somerleigh Gate, Dorchester, b. 14 April, 1863, Capt. Royal Warwickshire Regt., Chief Constable of Dorset 1898-1924, m. 1895, Margaret Beatrice (d. 1929), dau of Sir George Waller, 3rd Bt, of Woodcote, Warwicks.[551], and d. 29 Aug. 1929, having had issue,

        1b. Judith Margaret, b. 1896, m. 1930 George Vivian Cole, of Vancouver, B.C., son of Ernest Henry Cole & had issue (two or three children).

    2a. Robert, Sherwood Foresters, b. 26 Oct. 1864, d. in Jubblepore, India, 24 May, 1892, unm.

    1a. Mabel Georgiana Lucy, b. 29 May, 1868, m. Maj. Henry Clerk, Queen's Bays (d. 29 Feb 1924, aged 68), of Wellesbourne, Warwicks. and had issue,

        1b. Mary Conyers, b. 5 Aug. 1898, m. 1929, Lt. Col. William James Riland Bedford, Royal Artillery, of Manor Farm House, Bishopstone, only son of Canon W.C. Riland Bedford, Rector of Sutton Coldfield (1892-1908)[552]. He was killed in Tunisia in April, 1943, aged 45. She died in 1968.

        2b. Valmai, b. 11 Oct. 1899 d. unm. in Swindon, 30 July 1973

        3b. Letitia, b. 29 Aug. 1904, m. 1930, as his first wife, Capt. George Douglas James McMurtrie, Somerset L.I. (d. at Fordingbridge, 31 July 1994, aged 95), and d. 8 September 1931, having had issue,

            1c. David Henry, b. 1931, educ. R.M.C., Sandhurst

        4b. Georgiana*, b. 26 July, 1909, m. 1934 Col. Edward Jenner Jerram, M.C. (d. 1992, aged 89), Royal Warwickshire Regt., of Evenlode, Glos[553] & d. in Midhurst, Sussex in 1963 having had issue,

            1c. Christopher Edward Jenner, b. December 1953, m. 1stly in May 1982, Fiona Caroline (d. Dec. 1982, aged 25), dau. of Sir Robert Black, 3rd Bt. He

---

[551] General Sir George Waller had died in 1892 (His grandfather – who was oculist to George III and a groom of the bedchamber to William IV – had been made a baronet in 1814). Margaret's elder brother, who succeeded as 4th Baronet, was killed during the first Battle of Ypres in October 1914. Her younger brother then succeeded, but died s.p. in 1947.

[552] He seems to have retired to Leamington Spa, where he died in 1922, at the age of about 70.

[553] His diary of his experiences in the retreat from Dunkirk were included in Hugh Sebag-Montefiore's *Dunkirk: Fight To The Last Man*, Penguin, 2007. But was he Edward Jerram or the Capt. J.F.K. Jerram, also of the Warwickshire, who was involved in the D-Day landings.

m. 2ndly in 1985 Caroline Margaret, dau,. of Maj. George Arthur Bulwer Jenyns & had issue,

    1d. George Edward Jenner, b. 1986

Col. Bolton King married 2ndly, 1859, Louisa (d. 15 Aug. 1920, aged 96), dau. of Rev. Charles Palmer by Lady Charlotte Finch, dau. of the 4th Earl of Aylesford, and d. 23 March, 1878, having had further issue,

    5. Bolton, First Secretary of Toynbee Hall, Director of Education, Warwickshire County Council, author of *A History of Italian Unity, Mazzini,* etc. b 8 May, 1860, educ. Eton & Balliol Coll. Oxford, m. 8 May, 1895 Lydia (d. in Warwick, 2 February 1965, aged 89), dau. of George Arnold, an agricultural labourer, of Gaydon, and d. 15 May, 1937 having had issue,

    1a. Oliver Bolton, b. 24 Nov. 1896, educ. Warwick School & Manchester University, m. 2 April, 1926 Idina Sybil (d. 21 Jan. 1962), dau. of Philip Hardinge Papillon[554], of Westerham, Kent & d. in High Wycombe, 15 Nov. 1964 having had issue,

    1b. John Oliver Bolton, Estate Agent in Berkhamsted (Brown & Merry), b. 1927, m. 1953 Margaret Copp, and d. 10 December 2008, having had issue,

    1c. Peter John Bolton, of Leamington Spa, Chief Executive of the National Association of Estate Agents, b. 1955, m. 1978 Laura Munyard, and had issue,

    1d. Christopher Bolton, b. 1983, educ. King's School. Ely

    2d. Alexander Bolton, b. 1987

    2c. David Bolton, Estate Agent in Banbury, b. 1960, m. 1986 Celia Noakes & had issue,

    1d. Edward Bolton, b. 1988

    2d. James Bolton, b. 1990

    3d. Thomas Bolton, b. 1996

    1d. Frances Bolton, b. 1992

    1c. Jenny Bolton, b. 1957, m. 1stly 1978 Edward Steele (div. 1982). She m 2ndly 1982, Rev Michael Eggleton & had issue,

    1d. Richard, b. 1983[555]

    2d. Oliver, b. 1984

    1d. Lucy, b. 1991

    1b. Joan Patricia Bolton, b. 1930, unm.

2a.Edward Bolton, Student of Christ Church, Oxford, b. 21 May, 1900, m. 1945 Ardis, dau, of Joseph Thompson (d. 1985, aged 65) & d. March, 1974, having had issue,

    1b. Ann Bolton, b. 1946, m. 1972 (Dacre) Russell Watson & had issue,

    1c. Alexandra, b. 1974

---

[554] He was the youngest son of Philip Papillon of Crowhurst Park in Sussex. His elder brother sold the estate during the Second World War, and it is now a caravan park. The Healing Centre is housed in the Old Rectory in the same village.

[555] On Facebook. Lives at Fishbourne, on the outskirts of Chichester.

2c. Abigail, b. 1978

3a. Ralph Bolton, Headmaster of Buxton College, b. 10 Aug. 1906, m. 4 April, 1934 Evelyn, dau. of Caleb Coy, of The Manse, Tintern, and d. 1989, having had issue,

    1b. James Bolton, of Preston, Lancs., b. 1936, m. 1963 Inger Valebjorg (div. 1971), and had issue,

        1c. Charlotte Bolton, b. 1967

        2c. Ellen Bolton, b. 1970

    He m. 2ndly Marjorie Tralower (div.), and had further issue,

        1c. Peregrine, b. 1972

    He m. 3rdly, 1981, Vivienne Sellars, and further issue,

2c. Mark Bolton, b. 1985

        3c. Jenny Bolton, b. 1988

    2b. Robert Bolton, b. 1940, n. 1967 Ann Coulter, and had issue,

        1c. Guy Bolton, b. 1971

        1c. Georgina Bolton, b. 1977

    3b. Francis Bolton, b. 1948, m. 1977 Wendy Dicks (div. 1989), and had issue

        1c. Oliver Bolton, b. 1980[556]

        1c. Emma Bolton, b. 1978[557]

    1a. Lettice Bolton, b. 10 August 1906, educ. King's High School, Warwick, d. unm. 1991

  7. Charlotte Bolton, b. 1862, d. unm. in Minehead, Somerset, 1 February 1942

  8. Louisa Bolton, b. 1867, d. unm in Minehead, Somerset, 6 February 1951[558]

The elder surviving son,

Edward Raleigh King, of Chadshunt, Warwickshire & latterly of Brompton Square & Egerton Crescent, London S.W., D.L., J.P., Capt. 13th Light Dragoons and latterly Maj. Warwickshire Yeo, b. at Umberslade, 21 Dec. 1833, educ. Eton, m. at Bishops Lydeard, Somerset, 1 July 1861 Susanna Octavia (d. at 43 Brompton Square, 14 June, 1920, aged 76), 12th & youngest dau. of Sir John Hesketh Lethbridge, 3rd Bt. of Sandhill Park, Somerset, and d. 14 March, 1900, leaving issue,

  1.Ernest Raleigh Bolton King, of whom presently.

  1. Violet Frances Raleigh, b. in Torquay, 1864, d. unm. at 43 Brompton Square, 27 March, 1915

  2. Adeline Agnes, b. in Melcombe Regis & baptized at St John's Church there on 5 Feb 1866, d. at Lillington April/June 1868.

---

[556] He was on Facebook in '08, with his cousin Jenny Bolton King – and is clearly a keen carp fisherman.

[557] In '08 was Promotional Planning & Strategy Manager for Argos

[558] Her estate was valued at nearly £45,000, which was not bad – considering that they were left £8000 each by their father.

3. Ethel Mary Raleigh, of Tedworth Square, London, S.W., b. at Lillington 21 January & baptized there 25 February 1871, d. unm. in Featherstone Lodge Nursing Home, Sydenham, 21 January, 1946

The only son,

Ernest Raleigh (Bolton) King, of Appletree, Byfield & latterly of Egerton Gardens, London, S.W., b. in Weymouth, 2 June, 1862, m. at St Mary's, Bourne Street[559], 18 October, 1892, Dorothy Mildmay (d. in Winchester, 26 Feb. 1915, aged 46[560]), younger dau. of Victor Buckley, of Stanhope Gardens, London, S.W. & and granddau. of General Edward & Lady Catherine Buckley, of New Hall, Salisbury, & d. in London, 2 February, 1920, having had issue,

    1. Roderick Noel Raleigh, of whom presently.

The only child,

Roderick Noel Raleigh King, Capt., Actor, Author & Film Producer, b. in London, 25 December 1893, educ. Repton, m. 1stly at St Michael's, Chester Square, 31 December 1919 (div. 1934), Leila Sybil (d. in Majorca, 1959, aged 58), dau. of Cuthbert Harrison, of Jersey, C.I.[561], and had issue,

    1. Robin Victor Lethbridge Raleigh, author & journalist, b. in Bangalore, 25 November 1920, educ. Victoria Coll., Jersey, m. at Kensington Register Office, 22 June, 1950 Luisa (d. in Turin, 19 February 1990, aged 83) dau. of Ercole Manfredi, and d.s.p. in Majorca, 26 Nov. 1961[562].

    2. Edward James Raleigh, of Los Angeles, b. in Leamington, 15 July 1923, educ. Elizabeth Coll., Guernsey, d. unm. in Los Angeles, 25 October, 1994[563]

    1. Pamela Violet Mary Raleigh, b. in London, 27 April, 1922, d. unm. at Clare Hall Hospital, South Mimms[564], 15 December 1940.

He m. 2ndly at Caxton Hall Registry Office, 18 March 1939 (div. 1950), Dorothy Seaber (d. 25 May, 1998, aged 94), yst. dau. of James Seaber Pratt, J.P., of Sextry House, Ely, and d. in Dieppe, 24 May 1967, having had further issue,

---

[559] They were married by her uncle, Canon Felix Buckley, assisted by Rev James Baden Powell, one of the curates.

[560] She was working as a nurse at a military hospital there and caught meningitis.

[561] She had a younger sister Jean Patten, who lived in Edinburgh. Her father was in the Colonial Service. Her mother, Sybil, was the daughter of William Thomas Wailes, whose father made a fortune in Gateshead by the manufacture of stained glass. The great west window at Gloucester Cathedral is one of his. Saltwell Park, his house and grounds at Gateshead, is now a public space. W.T. Wailes continued his father's business and then retired to Bath.

[562] Dollmann & Pritchard put a notice in the paper listing his addresses as Calle Mas 4, Son Espanolet, Palma de Mallorca, Flat 2, Portland Lodge, Midvale Road, St Helier, and 124 Clare Court, Judd Street, London WC1

[563] For fifty years he lived with Bill Reilly, who died of AIDS on 24 April 1995.

[564] This was a TB hospital, and Pamela died of tuberculous meningitis that she caught nursing there

1f.

    3. **Walter Raleigh,** of whom presently

    2. Susan Audrey Raleigh, of Palace Green Cottage, Ely, b. 29 Oct. 1943

The third son,

Walter Raleigh King, Rev. Canon, b. in Cambridge, 12 Jan 1945, educ. Christ's Hospital & New Coll., Oxford, m. at Holy Trinity, Brompton, 9 Sept. 1975, Pamela Kirsten, dau. of Alasdair Garrett, of Wincanton, and has issue,

    1. Cecily Georgiana Raleigh, b. in Wisbech, 16 June 1976, m. at St James the Less, Vauxhall Bridge Road, 19 May 2007, Calvin, yst. son of Arthur Hollingworth, of Sutton Coldfield, and has issue,

        1a. Alfred Edward, b. in Sutton Coldfield 13 May 2011

        2a. Laurie Ralph, b. in Sutton Coldfield, 16 March 2013

    2. Imogen Frances Raleigh, b. in Barrow-in-Furness, 27 January 1978, m. at the Church of the Immaculate Conception, Farm Street, 20 Sept. 2008, Alexander Humphrey, only son of Sir John de Trafford, 7th Bt. & has issue,

        1a. Max Humphrey, b. in London, 21 Dec. 2010

        1a. Vivienne Inès, b. at Stowe, 17 Jan. 2013

    3. Alice Jane Raleigh, b. in Barrow-in-Furness, 16 July 1979, m. at the Century Club, Shaftesbury Avenue, 24 Nov. 2012, Michael, stepson of Maurice Pote, of Earlsfield, London, S.W. and has issue,

        1a. Casper Maurice, b. in London, 3 September 2016

        1a. Ottilie Pamela, b. in London, 22 September 2013

GENEALOGY OF KNIGHT

NICHOLAS KNIGHT, of Beoley, Worcs., liv. 1484, m. Agnes (liv 1535), and had issue,
1. Thomas
2. ROBERT of whom presently.

The younger son,
ROBERT KNIGHT, of Beoley, m. Marjerie, and d. 1558, leaving issue,
1. Nicholas, d.s.p. 1559
2. Thomas, d.s.p. 1558
3. WILLIAM, whom presently
4. Ralph, d.s.p. 1558
1. Alice, m. 1stly, George Paine, & 2ndly, John Addenbroke

The third son,
WILLIAM KNIGHT, who purchased Barrells Green, Warks. from the Bolton family in 1554, m.1stly, N..., and had issue,
1. Richard, d.s.p.
1 Mary, m. John Mills, of Crimscott
2. Isabell, m. John Cullabine
3 Alice, m. William Palmer
4 Elizabeth, m.1stly, William Pain, and 2ndly, William Moore
He m. 2ndly, Elizabeth (whom. 2ndly, Thomas Court), dau. of William Cookes of Norgrave, Worcs., and d. 1580, having had further issue,
2. NICHOLAS, of whom presently.
3. John, d.s.p.
4. Thomas, d.s.p.
5. Edward (Rev.), m. Susanna Basset, and had issue,
    (1) Richard
    (2) Thomas, d.unm.
    (3) George

The second son,
NICHOLAS KNIGHT, of Barrells Green, m. 1593, Margaret (d.1650), dau. of George Townes, of Stoke Prior, Worcs., and d. 1652, having had issue,
1. William, b. 1594, m. 1stly, 1622, Agnes (d. 1639), dau. of John Randell, of Barrells, and had issue,
    (1) John, of Barrells Green, bapt at Ullenhall, 28 Apr., 1623, m. 1651, Johanna (d. Apr. 1664), dau. of Edmund Rawlins, of Dunnington, Warks., and d. 23 Aug., 1681, leaving issue,

1a. William, of Barrells, Barrister-at-law, bapt. at Ullenhall, 6th Nov., 1657, m. July, 1685, Anne (bur. at Ullenhall, 29th June, 1706, aged 48), yst. dau. & co-heir of Sir Walter Raleigh, of Sandiwell, Glos., and was bur. at Wootton Wawen, 23rd Oct., 1733, having had issue,

1b. Raleigh, of Barrells (which he sold in 1730 to his cousin, Robert Knight, Earl of Catherlough), and later of Henley-in-Arden, b. 7 Sept & bapt. at Ullenhall, 12th Sept., 1688, m. 1stly 17th Oct., 1710, Mary, dau. of Joseph Hunt, of Stratford-on-Avon, and had issue,

1c. John, bur. at Wootton Wawen, 1st Oct., 1716

1c. Mary, bapt. at Ullenhall, 8th Feb., 1716, m. at Oldberrow, 15 June 1745 James Davis (who died in London, Nov. 1749), apothecary, of Great Pulteney Street, London, ?son of Rev. Edward Davies, vicar of Dunchurch

2c. Anne, bapt. at Ullenhall, 22nd Sept., 1721,

He m. 2ndly, Elizabeth (d.s.p. 1767), dau. of N...[565], and d.s.p.s. 1760, bur. at Oldberrow, 11 May 1760[566].

2b. Carew, a Joiner of Bread Street, London, bapt. at Ullenhall, 12th June, 1699, m. at the Fleet, 29 May 1719 Sarah Jones, and had issue[567],

1c. James, bapt. at All Hallows the Great, London, 7 July 1720

2c. Rawleigh, bapt. at St Michael's, Queenhithe, London, 20 January 1731

3c. Martin, b. 26 March & baptized 28 March 1739 at St Mary Magdalene, Old Fish Street, London, bur. there 22 July 1740[568]

1c. Henrietta, bapt. 29 January 1723 at St Giles in the Fields, London

---

[565] Elizabeth Knight had a nephew called Robert Askew (to whom Mrs Wilson left £50) and two nieces Elizabeth Askew (left £40) and Mrs Ann Field (left £50). Mrs Field's son, Robert Field, was left £10.

[566] His will was signed on 24 March 1750 and sworn on 22October 1760. '..and as to my estate and small things that I have, whereas I stand indebted to Mrs Mary Wilson in the sum of six hundred and fifty pounds, she lending me the same when I was in the greatest want to pay my debts', so he requires his dearly beloved wife Elizabeth Knight to sell Crowleys Farm in Ullenhall to pay the debt. Mrs Knight in fact left Crowleys to Mrs Wilson in her will, dated 10 June 1760. Mrs Wilson was aunt to Rev Richard Jago's second wife, Margaret Underwood. Jago was vicar of Snitterfield and a poet. He didn't think that Mrs Wilson's estate amounted to more than £100, so the legacies were pretty worthless.

[567] I haven't yet found any of the family who left either Carew or Raleigh Knight even a guinea in his or her will. It is as if they didn't exist.

[568] No doubt named for his father's rich cousins, the Martin brothers of the bank.

2c. Anne, bapt. at St Michael's, Queenhithe, London 2 July 1729, m. at St Mary Magdalene, Old Fish Street, 1 January 1752, John Parrell, of Tottenham High Cross & had issue,

 1d. Mary, bapt. at All Hallows, Tottenham, 6 November 1752

 2d. Anne, bapt. at All Hallows, Tottenham, 17 May 1755, d. an inf.

 3d. Anne, bapt. at All Hallows, Tottenham 18 August 1760

3c. Elizabeth, b. 17 March & baptized 28 March at St Mary Magdalene, Old Fish Street, 1742, d. 1 April 1746

2a. John, d. an inf.

3a. Edmund, b. 1662, a mercer in London (apprenticed to John Came, citizen & mercer, in 1679)

1a. Elizabeth, b. 1653, m. 1678, William Martin, of Evesham & had issue,

 1b. Thomas, of Clapham, entered the firm of Smith & Stone, bankers of Lombard Street in 1699, becoming a partner in 1703 and sole partner in 1711, M.P. for Wilton 1727-1734, b. 1680, m. Elizabeth, dau. of Richard Lowe of Cheshunt and d.s.p. 21 April 1765[569]

 2b. William, a barrister, M.P. for Gowran, co. Kilkenny, b. 1684, m. at St Mary, Woolnoth in 1715, Laura, dau. of I Mirrelli, and d. 1757, had issue,

  1c. William, b. 1716, d. an inf. 1718

  2c. Thomas, b. 1725, d. young in 1741

 3b. John, of Overbury, Worcs. & Quy Hall, Cambs., senior partner in the bank from 1741-1761, M.P. for Tewkesbury 1741-1747, b. 1687, m. 1stly at Bourton-on-the-Hill, Glos., 13 August 1720, Katherine (d. 1762), da. of Joseph Jackson of Sneed Park, Glos., He m. 2ndly at Overbury, 20 July 1763, his kinswoman Anna Kinloch (d. 1765), widow, of Chipping Norton, Oxon. He d. 7 March 1767, having had issue by his first wife,

  1c. John, of Overbury, Worcs., M.P. for Tewkesbury 1754-61, b. 1724, m. 3 Dec. 1761, Judith (who m. 2nd Thomas Bland & d. 1809), da. and h. of William Bromley of Ham Court, Worcs., & d.s.p. 28 May 1794.

  2c. Joseph, senior partner at Martin's Bank from 1761, M.P. for Gatton 1768-1774 and for Tewkesbury 1774-1776, b. 19 January 1726, m. 6 Feb. 1749, Eleanor, da. of Sir John Torriano of College Hill, London, by Eleanor, sister of Sir Horace Mann, British Envoy in Florence, & d. 30 March 1776, having had issue,

   1d. Thomas, of Quy Hall, d. 11 July 1821

---

[569] The main beneficiary of his will was Joseph Martin, the senior partner at the bank. His niece, Anna Herbert, was to have interest on £5000 for her own use, and James was to have £6000.

2d. Joseph, Rev., of Ham Court, Worcs.(which he inherited from his aunt, Judith Bland), rector of Bourton-on-the-Hill, Glos., Canon of Exeter, m. 1786 Isabella Margaret, dau. of Rev John Sturges, Prebendary & Chancellor of Winchester & sister of the Rt Hon William Sturges Bourne & had issue,

    1e. Joseph John, Maj., of Ham Court,

    2e. George, Rev., Canon & Chancellor of Exeter & vicar of Harberton, m. 1st 26 July 1825, Lady Charlotte Sophia Eliot (d,. 1839), youngest dau. of 2nd Earl of St Germans & d. 11 August 1860, having had issue,

      1f. George Edward *Bromley-Martin*, of Ham Court, Worcs,, m. Maria Henrietta & d. 1905, having had issue,

        1g. Eliot George *Bromley-Martin,* Maj. of Ham Court (which he let) b. 2 Oct. 1866, m. 26 January 1899 Katherine Emily, dau,. of Andrew Rouse-Boughton-Knight & d. 23 January 1946, having had issue,

          1h. Peter Edward *Bromley-Martin*, m. Hon. Anne Walsh (d. 8 December 2006, aged 95), dau. of the 5th Baron Ormathwaite & d. 1968

        2g. Granville Edward *Bromley-Martin*, b. 1875, m. 17 July 1913, Olivia May, dau. of Hon. Richard Strutt & d. 31 May 1941, having had issue,

          1h. David Eliot, b. 1914, m. 1949 Angela Felicity, dau. of Sydney Hampden-Ross & d. 2002, having had issue,

            1i. Robin, m. Lorna & had issue

              1j. Timothy

              2j. Edward C..

            2i. Michael

          2h. Giles Neville

          1h. Judith Eleanor, m. N.. Graves & had issue,

            1i. Julia, m. N.. Shaw

          2h. Catriona Mary, m. 9 July 1946, Brig. Sidney Wilford-Thomson (d. 8 November 2008, aged 93) & d. in British Columbia in 2000, having had issue,

            1i. Linda, m. Michael Franklin & had issue,

              1j. Melissa

              2j. Zoe

              3j. Jayme

            2i. Jacqueline, m. 1st Nigel Killick (div.) & had issue,

              1j. Samantha Jane, m. 2nd Randall Taylor Jordan & had issue,

                1k. Will Maxton, b. 25 December 2009

Jacqueline Killick m. 2nd Ian Maxton
  3i. Terry, m. McGreggor McDiardmid & had issue,
    1j. Ian
    2j. Christophe
3h. Genifer Anabel, b. 26 November 1926, m. January 1951, Roger William Malden & d. 11 January 2012, having had issue,
  1i. Martin Christopher, b. 27 December 1952
  2i. Robert Charles, b. 16 April 1955, m. May 1992, Caroline Mary Miranda Allen & has issue,
    1j. Benedict Henry William, b. 17 April 1997
    1j. Kate Olivia Gemma, b. 12 December 1998
1g. Eleanor Mary, b. 14 November 1869, m. her cousin, Robert Holland-Martin, C.B., of Overbury Court & d. 14 April 1955 having had issue *(see below)*
2g. Annora Margaret Bromley, b. 7 April 1872, m. 23 August 1905, Hon. Victor Russell, son of the 1st Lord Ampthill & d. 21 June 1949 having had issue,
  1h. Avril, O.B.E., b. 24 July 1906, d. unm. 15 August 1963
  2h. Rosemary, b. 3 October 1907, m. 12 December 1935, Lt Col William Douglas Gosling, M.B.E. of Thrimley House, Farnham & had issue
    1i. Petronella Margaret, b. 27 December 1936, m. 20 February 1965, Charles William Humphreys & had issue,
      1j. Charles, b. 27 January 1968
      2j. Thomas William, b. 1972
      1j. Lucinda Ferelith, b. 28 October 1966, m. 29 December 1995 Stuart David Smith & had issue,
        1k. George Robert, b. 10 October 1999
        2k. Alfred Alexander, b. 12 August 2001
        3k. Edmund David, b. 25 April 2006
      2j. Susanna Rosemary, b. 1970, m. 10 May 1997 Edward Michael Dutton & has issue,
        1k. Ella Elizabeth, b. 27 August 2000
        2k. Sophie Rosemary, b. 14 May 2001
    2i. Lucy Annora, m. N... Murphy
    3i. Gwendolin Frances, b. 30 June 1946
3h. Angela Irene, b. 29 September 1912, m. 19 July 1938 Robert Alexander Bennett (Robin) Gosling (d. 31 August 1994, aged 91) & d. in 1996, having had issue,

1f.

1i. Alexander Bennett, b. 10 June 1940, educ,.
Eton 7 King's Coll., Cambridge, m. 1st (div 1987) 11
June 1963, Mary Fiona, dau. of Duncan MacRae &
had issue,
> 1j. Henrietta Mary, b. 8 June 1966, m. 1990
> Nicholas R. Worthington & has issue,
>> 1k. Victoria Mary, b. 1994
> 2j. Louisa Catherine, b. 22 April 1968

He m. 2ndly Wirat Sukprem

2i. Andrew Edward, b,. 26 October 1944, educ.
Eton, m. 1st in 1966 (div.), Rosemary Ailsa, dau, of
Col. John Corbett-Winder & has issue,
> 1j. Amanda Sophia, b. 30 May 1968
> 2j. Catherine Angela Rose, b. 1970

He m. 2ndly in 1977 Imogen Margaret, dau, of
Humphrey Halahan & has further issue,
> 3j. Matilda Anne, b. 1979

3i. Robert Anthony, b. 1 April 1948, educ. Eton, m.
12 July 1969, Clarissa Beatrice, dau. of Maj. John
Whitcombe & has issue,
> 1j. Richard Bennett, b. 17 March 1972, educ.
> Eton & Cambrdge, m. 1st in 1998 (div. 2014),
> Nicola Jane Robb & has issue,
>> 1k. Cameron Robert, b. 3 May 2002
>> 2k. Marcus Bennett, b. 19 June 2005
>> 1k. Flora Kirsten, b. 14 September 1999
> He m. 2ndly 14 February 2015, Heather
> Frances, dau. of William   Buchanan, and has
> further issue,
>> 3k. Frederick William, b. 10 June 2015
> 1j. Charlotte Arabella Ida, b. 1974, educ.
> Downe House & Cambridge

1i. Annabel Victoria, b. 1942, m. 25 October 1965,
Nathaniel Charles Sebag-Montefiore & has issue,
> 1j, Matthew Oliver, b. 1971, educ. Eton,
> Cambridge & the L.S.E., m. 18 November 2000,
> Jessica Desirée Porsgren & has issue,
>> 1k. Ivan Nathaniel Marne, b. 13 November
>> 2001
>> 1k. Harriette Annora Desirée, b. 11
>> February 2004
> 1j. Victoria Alice, b, 1969, educ. at Benenden &
> Bryanston Schools & The Slade, m. 15 May

1999 James Matthew William Alexander & has issue,

        1k. Louis Bennett William, b. 12 May 2001

        2k. Robin Matthew William, b. 30 June 2003

2f. Henry Arthur, Rev., vicar of Laxton, Notts.

1f. Georgina

2f. Susan Isabella

3f. Charlotte Harriet, of The Hill, Worcs., unm.

4f. Jemima Anne Frances, m. 1860 Col. Sir Charles Cooper Johnson (d.at The Hill, Dec. 1905), K.C.B. & had issue,

        1g. Percy, b. 1869, d. 1877

Rev. George Martin m. 2nd Renura Hebrietta Aldenburg (d 10 Jan 1868), dau of Admiral William Bentinck & had further issue,

3f. Albert Bentinck, b, 16 December 1843, d. 9 May 1886

4f. Evelyn Charles, Capt. 87th Royal Irish Fusiliers, b, 5 July 1847, m. 3 June 1880 Edith Hamilton, dau. of John Martin, of Upper Hall, Ledbury & had issue,

        1g. Evelyn George, b. 6 March 1881

        2g. John Bentinck, b. January 1883

        1g. Edith Henrietta Dorothea, b. 25 May 1885

5f. Renira Isabella

6f. Lucy Annora, m. 16 Sept. 1879 Arthur Charles Cherry, of Hanwick Hall, Worcs & had issue

3e. Henry, d. 1843

4e. William, Rev., vicar of Staverton, Devon, m. Jane, dau. of Arthur Champernowne, & d. 10 April 1850, having had issue,

1f. William, Rev., b. January 1831, m. 10 February 1886, Mary, dau,. of Richard Luxton & d. 7 Sept. 1890 having had issue,

        1g. William Arthur, b. 2 December 1886

2f. Arthur

3f. Richard, Rev., vicar of Ilfracombe, m. Eliza Rose, dau. of Rev. Daniel Rose Fearon, vicar of St Mary's Church, Devon

4f. Francis

5f. Charles, Rev., rector of Dartington, m. Dora Frances, dau, of Rt Rev George Moberly, Bishop of Salisbury & had issue,

6f. Alfred John

7f. Charles Harington, Capt. R.N.

8f. Reginald

1f. Caroline

2f. Frances, m. 1852, Rev. Joseph Lloyd Brereton,
Prebendary of Exeter & rector of Little Massingham,
Norfolk & d, having had issue

3f. Mary Isabella

4f. Anne

5f. Louise Renira, of The Hill, Worcs. unm.

5e. Francis, d. unm. 24 February 1810

6e. Richard, Rev., Canon of Truro, vicar of Menheniot,
Cornwall, m. Charlotte (d. January 1882), dau. of Rev. J.W.
Baugh, rector of Ripple, Worcs. & d. 3 Feb 1888

7e. John Sturges, d. unm. 9 August 1839

1e. Isabella Margaret

2e. Eleanor

3e. Anne

4e. Frances

3d. Charles, Lt. Col. m. Elizabeth, dau. of Solomon Williams, of
Dublin, and d. 1827, having had issue,

1e. Charles Herbert, Rev. rector of Maisemore, Glos., m.
1stly 1815, Eliza Porter, dau. of William Sloane, of Tobago, &
had issue,

1f. Henrietta Ann Bidgood, m. 3 August 1843, Sir Samuel
White Baker, of Lypiatt Park, Glos. & d. 29 December
1855, having had issue,

1g. Agnes Charlotte Mary, m. 2 July 1889 Anthony
Crawley-Boevey & d.s.p. 8 April 1890.

2f. Eliza Heberden, m. 3 August 1843, John Garland Baker

3f. Charlotte Louisa

He m. 2ndly Frances Anne, dau. of Joseph Goodwin & d. 16
November 1865, having had further issue,

1f. Charles Frederick

4f. Gertrude Eleanor Frances,

2e. John Williams, of Twinning, Glos., J.P., m. 1stly Jane
Clarke (d.s.p.) He m. 2ndly 1841, Sophia Bashford, dau. of
William Whitehouse and d. January 1859, having had issue,

1f. Charles Stanhope

1e. Eliza, m. Dr James M. Cabe & had issue

4d. George, Rev., vicar of Overbury & afterwards of Broad
Windsor, m. Maria, dau,. of Richard Clarke & d. in 1796,
having had issue,

1e. Maria, m. William Hill Buckle, of Chaceley, Tewkesbury &
had issue

1d. Eleanor, m. J. Foote & d. 12 May 1831, having had issue

2d. Mary, m. her first cousin, Rev Thomas Heberden, Canon of Exeter, son of Dr William Heberden, by Elizabeth, dau of John Martin *(see below)* & d. 29 November 1849, having had issue

3d. Anna, m. Joseph Smith, Private Secretary to William Pitt & d. 13 August 1791

3c. Thomas, d. an inf. 1732

4c. James, d. an inf. 1733

5c. James, of Overbury, Worcs., banker with Martin's Bank, M.P. for Tewkesbury 1776-1807, b. 4 June 1738, *m.* 17 Feb. 1774, Penelope, dau. of Joseph Skipp of Upper Hall, Ledbury, Herefs. & d. 26 January 1810, having had issue,

1d. John, of Overbury, Worcs., Senior Partner in Martin's Bank from 1807, M.P. for Tewkesbury 1812-1832, b. 27 November 1774, m. 5 March 1803, Frances (d. 3 May 1862), da. of Richard Stone, banker, of Lombard Street and Chislehurst, Kent, & d. 4 January 1832, having had issue,

1e. John, of the Upper Hall, Ledbury, J.P., M.P. for Tewkesbury 1832-5 & 1837-59, b. 2 February 1805, m. 1stly 1 October 1837 Mary (d. 27 July 1843) dau. of Capt. Thomas Aubrey Morse & had issue,

1f. Elinor Traherne, m. Oct 1875 as his 2nd wife, Rev Frederick Whitmore Holland, vicar of Evesham (previously married to her cousin, Penelope Martin, of Overbury) and had issue,

1g. Edward, M.C., b. 1877, killed in action 13 September 1916

He m. 2ndly 7 June 1847 Maria Henrietta (d. 15 February 1865), dau. of Evan Hamilton Baillie & d. 7 March 1880, having had further issue,

1f. John Hamilton, b. 23 April 1850, d. 18 March 1851

2f. Waldyve Alexander Hamilton, formerly of The Upper Hall, Ledbury & afterwards of Byams, Marchwood, Hants., D.L., J.P., b. 22 September 1854, m. 1stly 28 August 1877, Georgia Maude (d. 19 December 1883), dau of Col. Gregory Haines, Madras Army & had issue,

1g. Hugh Waldyve, Maj. 59th Scinde Rifles, b, 8 July 1878, d. of wounds 2 June 1918

2g. George Dermot, Lt. 1st Warwickshire Regt., b. 2 March 1880, d of wounds 24 April 1918

3g. Alick Gregory, M.C., Capt. Princess Patricia's Canadian L.I., b. 4 October 1882, m. 19 September 1910, Louisa Helen, dau of Capt Frederick J.Mackenzie Grieve, R.N. & was killed in 1918, having had issue,

1h Dermot Frederick, of Miami, Florida, b. 3 July 1911

2h. Patrick Waldyve, of Vancouver, B.C., b. 12 May 1915

4g. Evan Hamilton, Cdr. R.N., b. 8 December 1883, m. 4 February 1913, Bertha, dau. of Capt Hugh Fallowfield, Argyll & Sutherland Highlanders & d. 1946

Mr W.A.H. Martin m. 2ndly 30 December 1886 Frances (d. June 1948) dau. of Ferdinand Hanbury Williams, of Coldbrook Park, Mon. & d. 25 February 1929, having had further issue,

5g. John Hanbury, M.P. for Southwark 1939-1948, b. 4 April 1892, m. 1stly 1934 (div. 1938) Avice Blanaid, dau of Frederick Trench. He m. 2ndly 1951, Dorothy Helen, dau, of Lloyd Jones of Pas Mancot, Flintshire.

1g. Frances Penelope, b & d 14 Nov 1887

3f. Hugo Hamilton, of Oakwood, West Malvern, Worcs., J.P., b. 20 June 1858, m. 2 August 1893 Mary Cecilia (d. 31 December 1946), dau, of W.G. Coventry & d, 29 December 1936, leaving issue,

1g. James Hamilton, explorer, went to Antarctic in Discovery 1929-30 and 1934-37, had two Polar Medals, Lt RNVR, served in WW II, served in WW I with 2nd Bn Gren Gds; b 25 June, 1899; educ Harrow; m Sept 1939, Lynda Lucie (who m 3rd, 2 Oct 1947, Cdr Christopher Simpson, RN), formerly wife of Maurice Bernhard Baron, and 3rd dau of late Lt-Col Robert Loftus Tottenham, IA & d. on active service, 29 June, 1940.

1g. Mary Hamilton, b 11 Oct 1895; m 26 Feb 1924, Lt-Col Roger Edward Harenc, Indian Cav, s. of late Lt-Col Charles Edward Harenc, of Dila Ram, Bedford. He d. 24 Aug 1959.

4f. John Evan Hamilton, b 19 Sept 1863; educ Wellington; m 31 Jan 1889, Charlotte Ethel (d 5 Feb 1936), 3rd dau of Richard Penruddocke Long, of Rood Ashton, Trowbridge, Wilts, and sister of 1st Viscount Long of Wraxall and d 20 Nov 1918, leaving issue,

1g Jack; b 31 March, 1890; m 28 July, 1928, Kathleen Ellen Valentia, dau of William Arthur Pethick, of Lanoy, Launceston, Cornwall, and d 7 June, 1959.

2g Richard Hugo Walter Robert, b 21 May, 1891; d unm 9 Feb 1931.

1g. Margaret Frances Maud, b 10 July, 1895.

1f. Edith Hamilton; m 3 June, 1880, her cousin, Lt-Col Evelyn Charles Martin (d. 1904), Roy Scots, and d 27 March, 1935, having had issue

2f. Ada Hamilton; m 7 Oct 1880, Gerald Edward Wellesley (d. 13 January 1915), 2nd s of Capt. Hon. William Henry George Wellesley, RN, yr. bro. of 1st Earl Cowley, and d. 18 Dec 1933, leaving issue.

3f. Dora Hamilton, d. unm. 15 Sept 1872.

4f. Nora Hamilton, m 4 Feb 1888, Capt Charles Harvey Palairet (d. 27 February 1905), 9th Lancers, of West Hill, Ledbury, and had issue.

5f. Frances Hamilton; m 7 Aug 1884, Alexander Baillie, only son of Evan Baillie, of Filleigh, Devon, and d 1885.

2e. Richard, b. 13 May 1806, d. unm. 5 June 1829

3e. James, b. 1807, d. unm. 1878

4e. Robert, of Overbury Court, Worcs., J.P., Hugh Sheriff 1877, b. 14 August 1808, m. 20 April 1837, Mary Anne (d. 24 November 1892) dau. of John Biddulph, of Ledbury & d. 18 March 1897, having had issue,

1f. Sir Richard Biddulph, 1st Bt., of Overbury Court, F.R.G.S., J.P., M.P. for Tewkesbury 1880-5, and for Droitwich 1892-1906,b. 12 May 1838, m. 1864 Mary Frances, dau. of Admiral Richard Crozier, of West Hill, Isle of Wight & d.s.p. 26 August 1916

2f. John Biddulph, F.Z.S., F.S.S., b. 10 June 1841, m. 1881, Victoria, dau. of R.B. Claflin of Horner, Ohio, U.S.A. & d. 20 March 1897.

1f. Julia, m. Douglas Henty, of Westgate, Sussex

2f. Penelope, m. Rev Frederick Whitmore Holland, vicar of Evesham & d. 7 December 1873, having had issue,

1g. Robert Martin, from 1917 *Holland-Martin*, of Overbury Court, Chairman of Martin's Bank, b. 10 October 1872, m. his cousin, Eleanor Mary (d. 14 April 1955, aged 85), dau. of George Bromley-Martin, of Ham Court & had issue,

1h. Geoffrey Robert, b. 3 August 1898, k'd in action 26 March 1918

2h. Edward Ruby, of Overbury Court, Governor of the Bank of England, Steeplechase jockey & founder of the Overbury Stud, b. 1900, m. 28 December

1955, Dagny Mary MacLean (d. 10 April 2019, aged 94), dau, of Maj. John MacLean Grant & d. 1981 having had issue,

- 1i. Penelope Jane, of Overbury Court, b. 1960, m. 27 October 1985, Sir Bruce Bossom, 3rd Bt. & has issue,
    - 1j. George Edward Martin, b. 21 February 1992
    - 1j. Rosanna Emily, b. 1986
    - 2j. Amanda Lucy, b. 1988

3h. Cyril George, b. 1902, m. Rosa Mary Philippa, dau, of Sir Gerald Chadwyck-Healey 2nd Bt & d. 12 April 1983 having had issue,

- 1i. Geoffrey Edward, Lieut., R.N., b. 6 May 1934, educ. Eton, k'd in a motor accident, 7 June 1958
- 2i. Timothy David, b. 6 October 1936, educ. Eton, m. 1977 Caroline Mary, dau, of Thomas Blackwell, of Langham Hall, Bury St Edmunds (div. 1988)
- 3i. Robert George, partner at Cazenove & Co. b. 6 July 1939, educ. Eton, m. Dominique, dau, of Maurice Fromaget & has issue,
    - 1j. Emily Mary, b. 1978
    - 2j. Tamara Sophie, b. 1980
- 1i. Faith Mary, b. 15 March 1949, m. 1972 Capt. Anthony Philip Hallett & has issue,
    - 1j. James Anthony, b,. 1976
    - 2j. Edward George, b. 1978
    - 3j. Thomas Alexander Pitfield, b. 1981

4h. Adm. Sir Deric, G.C.B., D.S.O., D.S.C & bar, Second Sea Lord, , b. 10 April 1906, m. 1951, Rosamund Mary. M.B.E. dau. of St John Hornby & d. 1977, having had issue,

- 1i. Benjamin Guy, b. 11 July 1955[570]
- 1i. Emma Rose, b. 5 September 1953, m. Timothy B. Cobb & has issue,
    - 1j. Harry Timothy, b. 1985, m. 2 September 2017, Elizabeth, dau, of Brigadier Ronald Ferguson (and half-sister of Sarah, Duchess of York)

---

[570] Described as "a businessman and friend of Princess Margaret", when he suffered a violent burglary at his home in South Kensington in 1996. Princess Margaret and her family were at his 40th birthday party

5h. Richard Thurstan, Chairman of the Tewkesbury Abbey Lawn Trust, b. 26 December 1907, m.(& div. in 1966) 7 August 1951 Anne Diana Frances Ayesha (d. 4 May 2008, aged 89), formerly wife of Viscount Ward of Witley & later (1972) wife of Peter Higgins, dau. of Capt. Arthur Capel & d. 24 January 1968, having had issue,

> 1i. Barnaby Robert, b. 1952
>
> 2i. Giles Thurstan, b., 1955, d. in the U.S.A. 4 May 2008

6h. Christopher, Director of Martin's Bank, M.P. for Ludlow 1951-1960, b. 5 April 1910, m. 1949, Lady Anne Hunloke (d. 1981), formerly wife of Lt Col Henry Hunloke (and in 1962 wife of Viscount Hinchingbroke, though the marriage was annulled in 1965) dau. of the 9th Duke of Devonshire, and d.s.p. 5 April 1960.

1g. Julia. b. 28 November 1873, m. 30 August 1923, Algernon Cockburn Rayner-Wood & d. 1955

5e. Henry, d. unm

1e. Frances Penelope, b. 19 December 1803

2e. Emily, m. June 1830, Robert Cumming Norman (d. at Hucclecote, Glos., 13 June 1875, aged 70)[571], of Hucclecote & d. 25 October 1842, having had issue,

> 1f. Martin, I.C.S., b. 1831, educ. East India College, Herts., d. unm. at Camden Place, Chislehurst, 16 October 1859
>
> 2f. Francis Martin, Cmdr., R.N., of Cheviot House, Berwick-upon-Tweed, b. 19 December 1833, d. unm. 6 October 1918[572]
>
> 3f. Henry Martin, b. 1837, d. unm. at Hucclecote, Glos., 29 January 1860 & bur. at Chislehurst.
>
> 1f. Frances Martin, b. 1840, d, unm. 6 May 1866 & bur. at Chislehurst

2d. Joseph, b. 1776, m. Sarah Harriett, dau. of Robert Hewitt, of Whitehaven, Cumberland & d, 20 December 1856

3d. James, b. 1778, m. 20 September 1819, Julia, dau, of Rev John Vignoles, of Portarlington, co Leix & d. 1870

---

[571] A member of the Norman banking family – Montague Norman, Governor of the Bank of England from 1920-1944 was his great nephew.

[572] There is a memorial plaque to him in the parish church, "a leader and supporter of all good works in the town". He was mayor, alderman and sheriff of Berwick. He presented a memorial fountain to the town to mark the Diamond Jubilee of Queen Victoria's accession. He also published two volumes of naval reminiscence and a history of Berwick's defences!

1d. dau. unm.

2d. dau. unm.

3d. Elizabeth, m. Charles Edward Hanford – a Roman Catholic - (d. 1854) of Woollas Hall, Eckington & d. 1844, having had issue,

> 1e. Compton, of Woollas Hall, also R.C. d. unm. 1860
>
> 1e. Frances, of Woollas Hall, m. William Lloyd Flood, later Hanford-Flood (d. 3 May 1892), of Farmley, co. Kilkenny & d. 21 February 1875 & had issue,
>
>> 1f. John Compton *Hanford*, Col., of Woollas Hall, d. unm. 1911
>>
>> 2f. Robert Thomas *Hanford*, of Woollas Hall
>
> 1f. Mary Frances, m. 12 August 1886 Col. Constantine Rodney William Hervey (d. 9 July 1949, aged 98), son of the Rt Rev Lord Arthur Hervey, Bishop of Bath & Wells, & d. 9 July 1937, having had issue,
>
>> 1g. Alice Lucy Patience, of Woolas Hall, b. 9 July 1887, m. 21 December 1912, Aymer William Whitworth (d. 1976, aged 99), a master at Eton, and had issue,
>>
>>> 1h. (John) Compton Aymer, of Moor Hall, Thorley, Herts., b. 1914, m. 1944, Isobel (d. 1977, aged 61), dau. of Very Rev. Harold -White, Dean of Gloucester & d. 23 August 2006, having had issue,
>>>
>>>> 1i. James
>>>>
>>>> 2i. Rodney Compton, b. 1946, d. unm. 4 July 2018
>>>
>>> 2h. Reginald Henry, Maj. Gen. b. 27 August 1916, educ. Eton & Balliol Coll. Oxford, m. 1st in 1946, June, only dau. of Lt Col Sir Bartle Edwards, C.V.O., M.C., of Hardingham Hall, Norfolk & had issue,
>>>
>>>> 1i. Charles
>>>>
>>>> 2i. Patrick, Rev., m. 1979, Olivia, dau. of Sir Michael Colman, 3rd Bt. & has issue,
>>>>
>>>>> 1j. David John William, b. 1990
>>>>>
>>>>> 1j. Emma Rachel, b. 1982
>>>>>
>>>>> 2j. Louisa Judith, b. 1984
>>>>>
>>>>> 3j. Sophia Rose, b. 1987
>>>>
>>>> 1i. Teresa, m. 30 June 1979, Roger Palmer (d. 6 March 2004, aged 54) & has issue,
>>>>
>>>>> 1j. Johnny
>>>>>
>>>>> 1j. Zana
>>>>>
>>>>> 2j. Lara

Gen. Whitworth m. 2ndly in 1999, Victoria, widow of Maj. David Faukner & dau of Maj. Robert Buxton & d. 22 May 2004.

    1h. Ursula Joan, m. 10 January 1946, Capt. Roderic Thesiger & had issue,

        1i. Simon Dermot, b. 25 May 1950, m. 27 July 1973, Concepción Pérez-Palacios & had issue,

            1j. Rebecca Maria, b. 16 September 1980

        2i. Sarah Elizabeth, b. 12 April 1947

    4d. dau. unm.

1c. Anne, b. 1721, m. 1755 Henry Herbert, of Muckross, Killarney & d. 1774, having had issue

2c. Catherine, bapt. at St Martin Outwich, 12 January 1722, m. April 1741 Sir Nicholas Hackett Carew, 2nd Bt. (d. 19 August 1762, aged 46) of Beddington, Surrey & d. 18 March 1762

    1d. Elizabeth, d. an inf.

    2d. Catherine, of Beddington, d. unm. 3 March 1769[573]

3c. Elizabeth, b. 1722, d,., an inf. 1723

4c. Margaret, b. 1727, d. an inf.

5c. Mary, d. an inf. 1727

6c. Margaret, b. 1728, m. Rev. Dr Treadway Russell Nash, of Bevere House, Worcs. (d. 1811, aged 86) & d. 21 May 1811, having had issue,

    1d. Margaret, m. 19 March 1785, James Somers, 1st Earl Somers (d. 5 January 1841, aged 80) of Eastnor Castle, & d. February 1831, having had issue,

        1e. Edward Charles, Major, M.P., for Reigate 1806-1812, b. 27 July 1786, killed at the siege of Burgos, 8 October 1812

        2e. John *Somers-Cocks*, 2nd Earl Somers, of Eastnor Castle, b. 19 March 1788, m. Lady Caroline Yorke, daughter of Philip, 3rd Earl of Hardwicke & d. 5 October 1852, having had issue

            1f. Charles Somers *Somers-Cocks*, 3rd Earl Somers, b. 14 July 1819, m. 2 October 1850, Virginia (d. 29 September

---

[573] She was the last of the Carews of Beddington, and descended from Lady Raleigh's brother, Nicholas Throckmorton, later Carew, who inherited Beddington from his uncle. Miss Carew left Beddington to her father's second cousin, Richard Gee, who took the name of Carew but d. unm. in 1816. He left Beddington to his brother's widow, Mrs Ann Paston Gee. She d. unm. in 1828, leaving Beddington to her cousin, Admiral Sir Benjamin Hallowell, who took the name of Carew (despite having no Carew blood). His grandson, Charles Hallowell-Carew was a gambler and had to hand Beddington over to William Ford, the son of a notorious money-lender. William's son was Lionel Ford, headmaster of Repton when papa was there, and later Dean of York!

1920, aged 83), dau. of James Pattle, H.E.I.C., & d. 26 September 1883, having had issue,

    1g. Isabella Caroline, b. 1851, m. 6 February 1872, Lord Henry Somerset (d. 10 October 1932, aged 82), 2nd son of the 8th Duke of Beaufort, and d. 12 March 1921, having had issue,

    1h. Henry Charles Somers Augustus, b. 18 May 1874, m.1st 23 January 1896 (div. 1920), Lady Katherine de Vere Beauclerk (who m. 2nd Maj Gen the Hon. Sir William Lambton & d. 1 February 1958, aged 80), dau of the 10th Duke of St Albans & had issue,

      1i. Henry Robert Somers Fitzroy de Vere, b. 3 March 1898, m. 2 December 1922, Bettine Violet (d. 24 September 1973, aged 73), dau. of Maj Charles Malcolm & d. 27 February 1965, having had issue,

        1j. John Alexander, Lieut., Coldstream Guards, b. 1 January 1925, k'd in action, 15 April 1945.

        2j. David Robert, 11th Duke of Beaufort, b. 23 February 1928, m. 1st 5 July 1950, Lady Caroline Thynne (d. 22 April 1995, aged 66), dau. of the 6th Marquess of Bath & had issue,

          1k. Henry John Fitzroy, 12th Duke of Beaufort, b. 22 May 1952, m. 1st 13 June 1987 (div. 2018), Tracy Louise, dau. of Hon Peter Ward & had issue,

            1l. Robert, Marquess of Worcester, b. 20 January 1989, m. Lucy Yorke-Young

            2l. Alexander Lorne, b. 19 December 1993

            1l. Isabella Elsa, b. 3 August 2003

          He m. 2nd 3 April 2018, Georgia, formerly wife of Tobias Coke, and dau. of Tristram Powell

          2k. Edward Alexander, b. 1 May 1958, m. 2 October 1982 (div.2013), Hon Georgiana Caroline Davidson, dau. of 2nd Viscount Davidson & has issue,

            1l. Francesca, b. 1984

            2l. Rose Victoria, b. 1992

          2k. John Robert, b. 5 November 1964, m. 1990 (div. 1996) Lady Cosima Vane-Tempest-Stewart, formerly wife of Cosmo Fry & dau.

of 9th Marquess of Londonderry (or of Robin Douglas-Home) & has issue,

    1l. Lyle David, b. 1991

      1l. Romy Caroline, b. 1993

    1k. Anne Mary, b. 21 January 1955, m. 1988, Matthew (d. 23 February 2011, aged 58), son of Sir Raymond Carr & has issue,

      1l. Eleanor, b. 1992

The 11th Duke m. 2nd 11 June 2000, Miranda Elisabeth, dau. of Brig Gen Michael Morley & d. 16 August 2017.

1j. (Elizabeth) Anne, b. 1 November 1929, m. 10 November 1953, Maj. David Rasch (d. 27 November 2005, aged 83) & d. in 1995, having had issue,

    1k. Guy Martin Carne, of Middle Woodford, Wilts., b. 22 August 1959, m. November 1996, Frances, dau. of Richard Hulse

    1k. Jane Catherine, b. 3 December 1955 , m. 1976 (div. 1980), Michael Smedley

    2k. Emma Caroline, b. 3 March 1962, m. August 1996, Robert Jackson

2i. John Beauclerk, Sub.Lieut., R.N., b. 5 October 1901, d. unm. 26 September 1921

3i. Edward Victor, 2nd Lieut., Coldstream Guards, b. 2 July 1903, k'd in an aircraft accident, 23 September 1929, unm.

2g. Adeline Marie, b. 24 May 1852, m. 24 October 1876, George Russell, 10th Duke of Bedford (d. 23 March 1893, aged 40) & d.s.p. 12 April 1920.

3g. Virginia, b. 1853, d. 9 January 1859.

1f. Caroline Margaret, m. 20 June 1849, Rev.& Hon. Charles Courtenay, vicar of Bovey Tracey, Devon, son of the 10th Earl of Devon & d.s.p. 14 November 1894.

2f. Harriet Catherine, m. 22 April 1850, Francis Richard Wegg-Prosser (d. 16 August 1911, aged 87), of Belmont, Herefordshire, & d. 6 May 1893, having had issue (with 2 daus.),

    1g. John Francis, Maj., of Belmont, b. 21 September 1854, m. 16 July 1891, Florence Isabel Brooke (d. 1952, aged 88) & d. 30 November 1948, having had issue,

      1h. Cecil Francis Joseph, 2nd Lieut., b. 22 November 1893, m. 14 June 1915, Emmeline

Josephine Sleeman (d. 4 February 1973, aged 83) & was k'd at the Somme, 3 September 1916, having had issue,

    1i. Sonia Marie Katherine, of Belmont House, Hereford, b. 1916, m. 26 August 1941 Lt Col Arthur Edward Raleigh Chichester & d. in Hereford in 1977, having had issue,

        1j. Raleigh Cecil Arthur, b. 31 July 1942, d. 1961

        2j. William Henry James John, b. 27 December 1946

        3j. Philip Nugent Cresswell, b. 23 May 1948

        1j. Evelyn Mary Josephine, b. 8 October 1943

        2j. Nina Cecilia Isabel, b. 23 February 1945, m. 1964, Christopher J.R. Friend

2g. Charles Edward, Maj., Labour M.P. & former member of the B.U.F., b. 26 September 1859, m. Mary Fane (d. 17 May 1950) & d. 28 November 1925 & had issue,

    1h. Charles Francis Haggitt, b. 18 August 1910, m. 19 June 1940, Betty Shapiro & d. 7 October 1996, having had issue,

        1i. Stephen Brian, a solicitor, b. 26 November 1946, m. Victoria Bird, a producer at the BBC, & has issue,

            1j. Benjamin, Managing Director, Global Council, formerly Director of Strategic Communications under Tony Blair, b. 11 June 1974, m. 2004, Yulia Khabibullina & has issue (with another son & 1 dau.).

                1k. Alexander

                2k. Feodor, b. 13 June 2009

                1k. Sybil

        1i. Anne, b. 12 May 1941, m. 1971 Patrick J. Gibbins

    1h. Cecily Mary Haggitt, b. 19 March 1913

    2h. Christine Mary Odile, b. 23 August 1914

    3h. Joan Pauline Mary, b. 15 February 1916, unm.

1g. Cecilia Lucy, b. 22 November 1851, d. unm. 17 June 1905

2g. Catherine Mary b. 3 May 1863, d. unm. 7 June 1919.

7c. Mary Ann, b. 1733, d.an inf 1735

8c. Elizabeth, b. 1736, m. 1752 as his first wife, Dr William
Heberden (d. 17 May 1801, aged 80) & d. 24 November 1754,
having had issue,

    1d. Thomas, Rev., Canon of Exeter, b. 1754, m. his first cousin,
Mary, dau. of Joseph Martin *(see above)* & d. 1843

4b. James, of Quy Hall, Cambs., partner with his brother Thomas in
1714, senior partner from 1727-44, M.P. for Cambridge from 1741, b.
1692, d. unm. 15 December 1744

1b. Mary, b. 1681, d. at Evesham 1686

2b. Elizabeth, b. 1682

3b. Anna, b. 1685, d. 1688

4b. Anna, b. 1689, d. 1692

(2) William, bapt. at Wootton Wawen 22 March 1628, d. unm. 1647.

(3) ROBERT, of whom presently

(4) Thomas, d. unm. 1664

(1) Mary, bapt. at Wootton Wawen, 21 Nov 1623,

(2) Elizabeth, bapt at Wootton Wawen, 6 Jan 1624, m. Thomas (who d. 11
Sept., 1668), son of Henry Hanbury, of Dodderhill, Worcs., and d. 1651,
leaving issue,

    1a. Sarah, d. unm. 1657

    2a. Elizabeth, b. 1649, d. unm. 1667

    3a. Anne, b. 1650, d. unm. 1668

William Knight m. 2ndly, 1641, Johanna (d. 1655), widow of Clement Parker, of
Rowington, and d.v.p.   1651

2. Nicholas, d.unm. 1630

3. Robert, m. Elizabeth, dau. of Edward Waring, of Worcester, and d.s.p. 1654.

4. John, bapt at Wootton Wawen 17 June 1607,

1. Mary, m. Robert Adams, of Ullenhall.

2. Jane, m. Hugh Hopkins, of Pinley

3. Elizabeth, m. Thomas Lea, of Ullenhall.

4. Agnes, m. George Brocke, of Farnborough

5. Margaret, d. an inf.

His grandson,

ROBERT KNIGHT, citizen of London, admitted member of the Grocers' Company,
1658, warden, 1687, bapt at Ullenhall, 14th April, 1632, m. 1stly, his first cousin,
Elizabeth (d. 1684[574]), dau. of Major Thomas (or John) Randoll, citizen of London,
and had issue,

---

[574] Joan Sato has discovered that an Elizabeth Knight, "a woman from Holborne" was
buried on 31 January 1685 in the parish graveyard of St Andrew, Holborn. This may have
been our Elizabeth Knight - though the family were living in Bread Street and had a strong
link with the destroyed St Mildred's. Nonetheless, the dates coincide.

1. Thomas, of West Ham, citizen of London, b. 1664, m. Sarah, dau. of Sir Leonard Robinson, Chamberlain of the City of London[575], and d. leaving issue,

    (1) Robinson, a goldsmith/banker of West Ham, Essex, m. Sarah … and d. 1780[576], leaving issue,

        1a. Robert, living 1763

        1a. Sarah, bapt at St Katherine Cree, 10 December 1724, m. Rev Thomas Foxley (d. 26 November 1761), vicar of St Mary's, Stratford Bow & Fellow of the Collegiate Church & Rector of St Mary's, Manchester from 1756, & had issue,

            1b. Thomas, Rev., Unsworth Lodge, Radcliffe, b. 1749, Perpetual Curate of Atherton from 1777, Vicar of Radcliffe from 1784 and Vicar of Batley from 1798, d. unm. 13 December 1839

        2a. Katherine , b. 13 October 1730 & bapt. at St Mary Woolnoth 29 October 1730, d. young

        3a. Ann

        4a. Catherine, bapt. at St Mary, Woolnoth, 27 February 1740, m. N… Dennis, of West Ham

    (1) Deborah, m. at St Olave's, Bermondsey, 24 July 1713, Dr William Cheseldon, surgeon at St Thomas' Hospital & to Queen Caroline (d. 10 April 1752, aged 63) & d. in 1754, having had issue,

        1a. Wilhelmina Deborah, m. 2 September 1736, Dr Charles Cotes, M.D., F.R.C.P. (d. 17 March 1748, aged 43), of Woodcote, Shropshire, M.P. for Tamworth & d.s.p. in 1763 at Greenhithe, Swanscombe, Kent[577]

    (2) Sarah, d. unm?

---

[575] The younger brother of William Robinson, of Rokeby, Yorks. He had a son, Thomas, & five daughters. In his will, Robert Knight gives a legacy to his granddaughter Deborah and her husband, and also £10 for mourning to Sarah, Robinson & James Knight. Who is James Knight? Was there another son?

[576] Robinson Knight was declared bankrupt in 1755 and his estate and effects assigned to Sir Henry Blunt, Bt., Michael Impey & John Fremantle. When his sister made her will, she directed that her daughter should remember her uncle Robinson and his wife and leave them the interest on £2000. He was living in the family house in West Ham when he made his will, leaving a life interest in the house and his other property to 'my sister Ann Capell'. Ann was unmarried, so must have been the child of Robinson's mother by another husband. On Ann's death, the property went to his two daughters but there is a curious note from 1818 which refers to an indenture of 6 May 1745 in respect of the manor of Edstone in Warwickshire, and other land in Beoley, Wootton Wawen and elsewhere in Warwickshire which eventually was vested in the deceased. Robert Knight of Barrells appointed someone to look into the business for him. Ann died intestate.

[577] In her will, she left various legacies, including a legacy of £2000, which was at her late mother's request, to Lord Luxborough and his son, Henry Knight, as trustees, to her uncle Robinson Knight and his wife Sarah – and on their deaths, to their three daughters, Sarah, Ann & Catherine. She also left £1000 to her cousin, Sarah Surman. If Sarah was to die childless before her, then the £1000 would go to Robinson's son, Robert. However, she later revoked the legacy to Robert – who had clearly displeased her!

2. William, bur. 29 Aug. 1671 at St Mildred's[578]

3. ROBERT, of whom presently.

1. Sarah, bapt at the Collegiate Church of St Katherine by the Tower, 17 Sept. 1666[579], m. in Tunbridge Wells, 4 Aug. 1690, Philip Surman (d. 27 July 1722), citizen of London, member of the Haberdashers' Company, and d. Nov. 1744[580], having had issue,

> (1) Robert, of Valentine House[581], West Ham, Partner in Martin's & the Sword Blade Banks, Deputy Cashier of the South Sea Company 1718-21. Senior Partner at Surman, Dinely & Cliff, b. ca. 1693, m. Thomasin... (who d. 26 Nov. 1734, aged 41) & died 14 June 1759, having had issue,
>
>> 1a. Thomasin, b. 1719, m. 29 Dec. 1748, Maj. Gen. the Hon. John Boscawen (d. 30 April 1767, aged 53), 45th Foot, M. P for Truro from 1747, 4th son of Hugh Boscawen, 1st Viscount Falmouth, and d.v.p. Jan. 1750, leaving issue,
>>
>>> 1b. William Augustus Spencer, Lt Col Foot Guards, M.P. for Truro 1784-1792, b. 6 Jan. 1750, m. & d. 13 June 1828, having had issue,
>>>
>>>> 1c. George Spencer, Capt R.E., b. 1802, d. 1832
>>>>
>>>> 2c. Evelyn Spencer, Capt., b. 1803, d. 1845
>>>>
>>>> 1c. Mary Spencer, m. 1stly 1827, Maj. W.H. Foy (d. 1838) & had issue,
>>>>
>>>>> 1d. a dau., b. at Cheltenham, 19 Nov. 1827.
>>>>
>>>> She m 2ndly 1840, William Newneham
>>>>
>>>> 2c. Elizabeth Spencer, m. 1829, Hugh Foy
>>
>> 2a. Sarah, b. 31 March & baptised at St Dionis, Backchurch on 26 April 1721, d. unm. 1779, will proved at PCC, 1 July, 1779, and buried with her parents and sister in Barking Parish Church.
>
> (1) Sarah, m. 1stly Nathaniel Cliffe[582] and had issue,
>
>> 1a. Robert, of Lombard Street, partner in his uncle's bank – Surman, Dinely & Cliffe (est. 1749)[583] until 1769. He m. a widow, Joanna .... (d. 1786) & d.s.p. in Worcester in 1787.

---

[578] via Joan Sato.

[579] date of baptism & marriage via Joan Sato, The Great Fire raged from 2-5 Sept 1666, during which St Mildred's, Bread Street was destroyed.

[580] Her will was drawn up on 26 June 1744, showing her to be an affectionate mother and grandmother. A note from September 1736 to her 'dear Bobb', asking him to 'have regard to poor Bob Cliff who has not met with his just reward from any but yourself for the whole time of his service which I am sure has been very faithful and just to the ...... and don't forget your poor sister.'

[581] "Robert Surman of Valentines" by Georgina Green, price £4.50. Copies can be ordered by post from Mrs Cherry Hooker, 115 The Drive, Ilford, IG1 3JD enclosing a cheque or postal order for £5.00 per copy (including postage) made payable to "Friends of Valentines Mansion"

[582] He was buried in Tindal's Burial Grounds (Bunhill Fields) – see Mrs Sarah Surman's will – which was mainly used by non-conformists.

[583] He was clearly close to his uncle, Robert Surman, who (in his will) named him his

      1a. Mary, m. *Howling Anson* ?

She m. 2ndly in the Chapel of St Aske's Hospital, Hoxton, 3 September 1716, Robert Cruttenden (d. 23 June 1763, aged 73) & was living in 1750, having had further issue,

      2a. Joseph, secretary of the Royal College of Surgeons, and latterly of Switzerland. He m. & d. 1796, having had issue,[584]

          1b. George

          1b. Sarah

          2b. Elizabeth

      3a. Edward Holden, Director of the E.I.C., Member of the Council of Calcutta, Lieut. Governor of Fort William, Bengal, b. 1717, m. at St Anne's Church, Calcutta, 7 April 1746, Elizabeth Jedderee (d. at Phulta in the flight from Calcutta in 1756) & d. 19 June 1771, having had issue,

          1b. Edward Holden, , b. in Calcutta 1756[585], m. St George's, Bloomsbury, 24 July 1783, Harriet Jones & d. in 1832 (bur. in All Saints', Weston, Somerset), having had issue

               1c. Edward Holden, Judge in the Tiruchirappalli station, Tamil Nadu, b. 2 February & bapt at St Marylebone 14 March 1786, m. in Madras, 1 March 1819, Charlotte Taylor (d. in Cheltenham in 1856, aged 59) & d.s.p. on the Nilgiri hills, in Tamil Nadu, 30 March 1822[586]

               2c. William, bapt. at St Marylebone 20 March 1787

               3c. Charles, bapt at Iver, Bucks, 13 March 1790

               4c. Henry, bapt at Iver, Bucks 12 September 1797

               1c. Elizabeth, bapt at Iver, Bucks., 2 March 1789, m. at Clifton, Bristol, 15 December 1822, Col. Thomas William Ravenshaw, Royal Berkshire Regt. (d.s.p. in Wimpole Street, 14 August 1842, aged 66)[587]

---

executor and commended his daughter Sarah to his care. He was also appointed one of the executors of the will of his half-brother, Edward Holden Cruttenden, ad guardian to his infant children.

[584] He was Clerk to the Barber-Surgeon's Company and lived with his wife at the hall, though he spent the last part of his life in Switzerland – according to family papers. He did some business for Lord Catherlough, his mother's first cousin, and was a witness to the several codicils added to the will of his cousin, Wilhelmina Cotes. Anna Wastfield left him £500 in trust for his daughters. His brother left him £1500 and any debts outstanding were to be written off; his children were to have £50 each.

[585] There is a portrait by Sir Joshua Reynolds of Edward as a child, with his two sisters, Elizabeth and Sarah. They had been sent home with their Indian nurse after their mother's death. There is also a portrait of his father by Reynolds. E.H. Cruttenden senr. had made a large fortune in India, which passed to the children. His son had £18,000, and the daughters £16,000 each.

[586] There is a memorial to him in St John's Church, Tiruchirappalli, Tamil Nadu.

[587] He was the brother of the husband of her cousin, Elizabeth Purvis. There is a memorial to him in the Lady Chapel of All Saints, Fulham.

2c. Harriet Catherine, bapt at Iver, Bucks. 24 December 1794

1b. Elizabeth, bapt in Calcutta 7 February 1752, m. 29 January 1774 Charles Purvis, D.L., J.P. (d. 10 December 1808, aged 65), of Darsham, Suffolk & d. in Bath 26 March 1816, having had issue,

 1c. Charles, b. at Darsham, 19 February 1777, m. at St Marylebone, 12 February 1805, Margaret Eleanor Randall (d. 1 November 1859, aged 81) & d. in Brighton, 5 November 1859, having had issue,

  1d. Charles, b. in York, 4 February 1806, d. in Dundalk, 19 May 1808

  2d. William Wheatley, b. in York, 25 March 1808, d. in Colchester, 1815

  3d. Henry Tillard, b. in London, 29 April 1810, d. in Richmond in 1818

  4d. Arthur, Madras Civil Service, of Darsham, Suffolk, b. in Brighton 25 April 1813, m. at St George's, Hanover Square, 7 August 1847, Mary Jane (d. 17 July 1892, aged 69), dau. of General Alexander Clark Kennedy & d. in London, 1 June 1879, having had issue,

   1e. Arthur *Kennedy-Purvis,* Capt., b. in Madras, 2 December 1848, m. 29 July 1875, Alice Maud (d. 1924, aged 82), dau. of J.J. Sawyer, of Halifax, Nova Scotia, & d. in Montreux 26 January 1887, having had issue,

    1f. Maud Frances Alice *Kennedy-Purvis*, of Hove, Sussex, b. in Halifax, N.S. 12 June 1876, d. unm. 22 August 1949

    2f. Gladys Eleanor *Kennedy-Purvis*, b. in the Bahamas, 11 October 1877, d. unm. 1974

    3f. Maud Charlotte *Kennedy-Purvis*, b. in Youghal, co. Cork, 27 March 1879, d. unm. in Cuckfield, Sussex, 5 December 1955

    4f. Evelyn Lily *Kennedy-Purvis*, b. in Guernsey, 11 October 1884, d. unm. in Lewes, Sussex, 1962

   2e. Charles *Kennedy-Purvis*, Capt., R.N., b. in Madras, 26 October 1849, m. 7 August 1883, Cecilia Harriet (d. 26 January 1886, aged 38), dau. of Edward John Lloyd & had issue,

    1f. Charles Edward, Vice-Admiral, G.B.E., K.C.B., R.N., Deputy First Sea Lord, b.in Clifton, Bristol, 2 May 1884, m. 1908., Ethel May (d. 1971, aged 86), dau, of George Henry Conquest, of Newport, I.of W. & d.s.p. in Marsham Court, London, 26 May 1946

   Capt. Kennedy-Purvis m. 2ndly 19 March 1888, Jane Diana de Ricci (d. 18 November 1927) & d. at East Molesey, Surrey, 7 June 1916.

3e. Alexander *Kennedy-Purvis,* Clerk at the Charity Commission, b. in Madras, 16 January 1854, d. unm. in Newton Abbot, Devon in 1918

4e. Frank *Kennedy-Purvis,* b. in Madras, 10 May 1859, d. unm. in Natal, 27 March 1884

1e. Mary Jane *Kennedy-Purvis,* b. in Madras 2 December 1848, d. unm. 1918 & was bur. at Darsham.

2e. Mary Eleanor *Kennedy-Purvis*, b. in Madras, 17 June 1851, d. unm. in Durham Terrace, Porchester Square, London, 4 September 1909 & was bur. at Darsham.

5d. Frederick, b. in Colchester, 14 August 1815, at St Giles', Reading, 21 September 1841, his first cousin, Caroline Elizabeth (d. 4 June 1910, aged 91), dau. of Edward Purvis *(see below)* & d. in Brighton, 21 November 1859, having had issue,

1e. Charles Edward, b. 13 August 1842, d. 8 April 1847

2e. Frederick Arthur, a solicitor, b. in Reading, 14 October 1844, m. in Auckland, N.Z. 8 December 1881, Elizabeth Trimble (d. in N.Z. 13 December 1930, aged d. 75), & d. in Auckland, 10 November 1906, having had issue,

1f. Frederick Charles, b. in Tamanga, N.Z. 23 September 1884, m. 6 September 1911, Beatrice Bolton (d. 27 March 1965) & d. 25 November 1945, having had issue,

1g. Frederick Charles Mulso, b. 18 March 1922, m. & d. 1996, having had issue,

1h. Elizabeth Jean, b. 26 May 1951, d. 1990

1g. Joan Penelope, b. 29 June 1912, d. 10 January 1994

1f. Caroline Elizabeth Amy, b. in N.Z. 1 November 1886, d. in Eastbourne, Sussex, 22 October 1970

2f. Mary Catherine Grace, b. in Ealing, Middlesex, 12 May 1888, d. unm. 14 December 1967

3e. George Henry Wheatley, b. 11 March & d. 24 July 1854

4e. Edward Charles, b. & d. 1857

1e. Caroline Lauretta Harriet, b. 2 March 1846, d. unm. in Eastbourne, 23 March 1896

2e. Frances Margaret, b. 23 December 1848, d. 20 March 1851.

3e. Florence Amelia, b. 20 March 1851, d. unm. in Bayswater 31 December 1929.

4e. Amy Sarah, b. 29 December 1855, d. unm. in St Leonard's-on-Sea, 2 June 1924.

6d. George John, Lieut., H.E.I.C., b. in Ipswich, 4 July 1816, d. in India, 9 May 1843

7d. Charles Alexander, b. 30 August 1819, m. at St Giles, Reading, 10 June 1851, his cousin, Jane Lauretta (d. in Bath, 20 March 1916, aged 96), dau. of Edward Purvis *(see below)* & d. in Bath, 7 September 1894, having had issue,

    1e. Charles, b. & d. in Madras, 6 March 1854

    2e. Edward Alexander, b. in Singapore, 9 December 1856, m. 27 August 1913, Madeleine Louise (d. in Cirencester, 9 October 1950, aged 69), dau. of George Wyatt, of Salisbury & d. 26 April 1936, having had issue,

        1f. Charles John Mulso, M.V.O., b. 15 March 1918, m. 4 November 1944, Janet Ross & d. in Wasperton, Warwicks., 15 March 2007

        2f. Barbara Mary Mulso, b. 14 June 1914, d. unm. 27 March 2008

1d. Charlotte Sarah, b. 27 June 1821, d. unm. in Barnet, 1891

2c. Edward, b. in Darsham, 17 April 1786, m. at Walcot, Bath, 27 July 1817, Lettice Elizabeth (d. in Ealing, 18 January 1875, aged 86), dau, of John Mulso & d. 13 April 1873, having had issue,

    1d. Edward Mulso, b. 11 February 1828, d. in Tunbridge Wells, 21 March 1879

    1d. Caroline Elizabeth, b. 12 October 1818, d. 1910

    2d. Jane Lauretta, b. in Reading, 17 March 1820, m. 10 June 1851, her cousin, Charles Alexander Purvis & d. 20 March 1916, having had issue (see above).

    3d. Eleanor Sophia, b. 12 February 1822, m. 8 January 1852, Rev. Canon Septimus Lloyd Chase (d. 1895, aged 76) & d. in Melbourne, Australia, 4 May 1866, having had issue,

        1e. Charles Lloyd Purvis, b. in Wellingborough, 15 May 1854, m. in East Melbourne, 8 August 1885, Fanny Emily Ker & had issue

            1f. Charles Mulso Compigne, b. in Melbourne, 21 January 1888

            2f. Lloyd, b. in Melbourne, 3 June 1889

            3f. Airey Ker, b. in Heidelberg, 9 September 1890

            1f. Hester Violet Airey, b. in Melbourne 7 November 1886

        2e. Arthur Pelham, b. in Melbourne, 11 March 1858, m. in Elsternwick, 12 October 1886, Marion Eliza Weigall & had issue

            1f. Theyre Pelham, b. in Sorrento, 30 January 1889

            2f. Cedric Weigall, b. in Carlton, 9 April 1894

            1f. Hilda Marian, b. in Elsternwick, b. 24 October 1888

3e. Lloyd Heber, b. in Melbourne, 17 December 1859, m. in Richmond by Nelson, South Island, New Zealand, 25 February 1891, Grace Nightingale & had issue,

    1f. Alice Eleanor, b. in Caulfield by Melbourne, 24 February 1892

4e. William St John, b. in Melbourne, 15 July 1862, m. at St Paul's Cathedral, Melbourne, 3 February 1892, Emily Selina Ethel Lawes & had issue,

1f. Catherine Phyllis, b. in Golden Square, Victoria, 11 June 1893

    2f. Eleanor Emily, b. in Whittlesea, Cambs., 15 December 1895

5e. Edward Selwyn, b. Melbourne, 21 March 1864

1e. Pauline Caroline Jessie, b. in Wellingborough, 27 October 1852

2e. Sophia Louisa, b. in Wellingborough, 16 February 1856, m. 12 July 1881, William Hutchinson (d. 13 August 1941, aged 85) & had issue

    1f. Cecil Willliam, b. 15 July 1898, m. 23 May 1924, Mercia Quinan Julian (d. 23 August 1943, aged 45) & d. in Burradoo, N.S.W., 25 April 1973

4d. Amelia, b. in Reading, 26 March 1823, m. 1stly 8 October 1846, Edward Sherwood (d. in Pangbourne, 12 March 1856, aged 48) & had issue,

    1e. Edward Purvis, b. in Purley, 17 December 1847, m. in St Peter's, Newcastle-on-Tyne, 24 August 1872, Frances James (d. 7 November 1905, aged 57), & d. in Kenilworth, 14 September 1929, having had issue,

        1f. Edward Charles, b. in Gateshead, 5 February 1873, m. in Cheltenham, in 1911, Naomi Claire Flecker (d. 1937, aged 49) & d. 20 February 1947, having had issue,

            1g. John Herman Mulso, 14 May 1913, m. & d. in Charing, Kent, 7 September 2002, having had issue.

            2g. Edward Godfrey Purvis, b. 23 May 1916, m. 1945 in the Anglican Cathedral in Naorobi, Kathleen Theodosia Onslow (d. in Lewes, 7 March 2003) & d. in Cumbria, 4 June 1989, having had issue,

                1h. Patrick, b. 1946, d,. in Africa in 1990

            1g. Frances Pardon, b. 30 May 1918, m. N.. Woods & d. 1993, having had issue

        2f. Arthur James, b. in Warrington, 1875, m. & d. 31 December 1950, having had issue.

        3f. William James Purvis, b. in Kimberworth, 19 May 1879, m. & d. 20 December 1950, having had issue

4f. Richard, Rev., vicar of Goring-on-Thames, b. in Kimberworth, 13 November 1880, m. Hilda Ward (d. 30 November 1956, aged 74) & d. in Knutsford, 27 April 1970 & had issue,

    1g. Charles Purvis, Rev., b. in Praham, Victoria, Australia, 16 October 1910, m. 11 June 1939, Kathleen Tomlinson & d. in Manchester, 14 January 1984, having had issue.

    2g. Richard, Lieut., R.A.F., b. in Melbourne, Australia, 30 May 1922, d. at R.A.F. Benson, 10 October 1946.

5f. Francis Gordon, Rev., b. 29 November 1884, m. & Kathleen Maud, dau, of N... & d. 19 June 1960, having had issue,

    1g. Humphrey Gordon, P/O, R.A.F., b. 10 January 1923, lost over Belgium, 2 February 1942

6f. Harry Purvis, b. in Rotherham, 5 July 1893, m. April 1926, Mary Kathleen Simpson (d. 1979) & d. in Conwy, Wales, 12 January 1980, having had issue,

    1g. Christopher Simpson, b. 13 February 1929, m. & d. in Sevenoaks, 9 April 2003, having had issue.

    2g. Joan Catherine, b. 3 April 1931, m. 3 April 1978, Frank Skelcy (d. in 2004, aged 87) & d. in 2005

1f. Emily Mary, b. in Warrington, 21 October 1876, d. 3 May 1961

2f. Frances Marcella, b. in Kimberworth, 12 January 1878, d. May 1966

3f. Amy, b. 24 September 1883, d. in Rugeley, in 1966

4f. Edith Grace, b. 13 March 1887, d. 24 November 1961

5f. Olive, b. 8 June 1888, d. unm. 24 September 1959

2e. Arthur Paul, M.D., b. in Pangbourne in 1852, m. 1880, Katherine Douglas Williams & had issue,

    1f. Arthur Wynne, M.D., b. in Walton-on-Thames in 1881, m. in Gore Bay, Ontario, 30 December 1909, Irene Helen (d. in Croydon 8 April 1972, aged 85), dau. of Rev. John Tate, vicar of All Saints', Gore Bay, Ontario & d. in Winnipeg, Canada 1 February 1912, having had issue

    2f. Alexander Charles, b. 1882, m. & had issue

    3f. Maxwell, b. 1884, d. 1886

    1f. Katherine Mary, b. 1887

    2f. Edith Nora, b. 1895, d. in Crawley, 30 March 1968

1e. Mary, b. in Purley in 1849, m. in Kensington in 1875, Rupert May Banks (d. 1878, aged 32) & had issue,

    1f. Delamark Joseph, b. in Walton-on-Thames, 21 December 1875, m. at Ashover, Derbyshire, 15 July 1902,

Louise de Vere (d. in Cork, 13 February 1964, aged 86), dau. of Col. Arthur John Doig, H.E.I.C. .& d. in Cork, 19 September 1947

2e. Edith Sophie, Chinese Inland Mission, b. in Purley in 1853, k' d during the Boxer rebellion, in China, 24 July 1900

3e. Edith Amelia, b, in Pangbourne, 31 March 1856, m. 16 October 1883, Rev. Joseph Frederick Cholmondeley James, vicar of St Peter's, Macclesfield, & had issue,

1f. Cholmondeley Sherwood, Rev., b. in Ventnor, I. of W. 12 December 1884, d. unm. at Bishop Heber College, Tiruchirappalli, Madras, 13 May 1931[588]

Mrs Sherwood married 2ndly Lionel D. Byron, a schoolmaster of Bath Place, Reading & d. in Macclesfield, 8 December 1916,

5d. Marcella, b. 16 May 1825, d. unm. 1888

6d. Mary, b. 24 March 1828

7d. Octavia Frederica, b. & d. 1831

1c. Elizabeth, b. 24 February 1775, m. as his first wife, 8 July 1817, Rev Edward Ravenshaw (who m. 2ndly in 1839, Jemima Charlotte, dau. of John Ibbotson, of Ealing & d. 14 December 1854, aged 72), rector of West Kington Wilts & d.s.p.

2c. Sarah Anne, d. unm. in Bath, 12 July 1797

2b. Sarah, b. in Calcutta, 9 April 1754, m. in Berhampore, West Bengal 22 May 1788, her cousin, Robert Percival Pott (*see below*)

1a. Sarah, b. 1725, m. 1746 Dr Percival Pott, F.R.S. (d. in Prince's Street, Hanover Square, London, 22 December 1788, aged 74) surgeon at St Bartholomew's Hospital from 1749, & d. in 1811, having had issue[589],

1b. Percival, banker of Lombard Street, bapt. at St Augustine's, Watling Street, 14 December 1749, d. at his brother's vicarage in Kensington, February 1833

2b. Robert Percival, b. 19 January 1756, m. in Bengal 22 May 1788, his cousin, Sarah, dau of Edward Holden Cruttendon & d. in India ca. 1794

3b. Joseph Holden, Rev. Vicar of St Martin's in the Fields, 1812-24, Archdeacon Of London 1813-42, Vicar of St Mary Abbotts, Kensington, 1824-42, Canon of St Paul's 1824-47, Canon & Chancellor of Exeter Cathedral, 1826-47, b. 27 October 1758, educ. Eton & St John's College, Cambridge, d. unm. 16 February 1847

---

[588] His executors were his cousins, Rev. Francis Gordon Sherwood & his sister, Olive Sherwood

[589] Sarah Pott was an executor and residual legatee of her cousin, Anna Wastfield. In his will, her brother, Edward Holden Cruttendon, left her and her husband £100 each, and to each of her children £50.

4b Edward Holden, Maj. Westminster Regt., Middlesex Militia, bapt 2 April 1766 at St Augustine's, Watling Street, d. in Toxteth, Liverpool in 1798

5b

1b. Sarah b. 30 March 1751, m. John Ravel Frye of Wimpole Street, and d. in Bath 27 October 1791.

2b. Elizabeth, b. 1 August & baptized at St Augustine's, Watling Street, 19 September 1752, m. at St Marylebone 14 June 1776, Samuel Potts (d. October 1815, aged 80), Comptroller of the Post Office.

3b. Mary b. 7 June 1754, m. at St George's, Hanover Square in June 1782, Sir James Earle, Surgeon Extraordinary to George III & d. in Harley Street, 16 February 1831

4b.

2. Anne, bapt. at St Mildred's, Bread Street, 12 January 1673[590], m. at St Clements Dane, in 1696, Arundell Wastfield, citizen & clothworker of London, (d. 1728, will proved at PCC), citizen of London, and d. in Clapham in 1742, having had issue,

(1) Robert, of Mile End, London, citizen & clothworker of London, b. 1702 m. at St Dunstan's, Mile End, 15 March 1736, Elizabeth Powell (monument in Bristol Cathedral), and was buried in Whitechapel Churchyard, 15 May 1776 s.p., will proved at PCC, 3 July, 1776,

(1) Anna, of Cheshunt, Herts., b. 1707, bur.in Whitechapel churchyard, 8 September 1783, unm.[591]

(2) Elizabeth, d. before 1776, unm.

3. Elizabeth, m. at St Martin's in the Fields, 5 November 1706, Edmund Bayly, citizen of London, member of the Mercers' Company, and had issue,

(1) Knight[592]

(1) Mary

Mr Knight m. 2ndly Jane, dau. of Sir Edward Barkham & 3rdly Susannah ....., and d. 1715[593].

The youngest son,

---

[590] baptism date via Joan Sato. All Hallows the Less was destroyed in the Great Fire and was never rebuilt. The parish was amalgamated with that of All Hallows the Great in Upper Thames Street – which was also destroyed but was rebuilt (though demolished and built over in 1894)

[591] Her will provided generously for her Knight cousins – including Robinson Knight (£1000), Sarah Surman (£500), Joseph Cruttenden (£500), Catherine Page (£100) – besides Sarah Pott, the main beneficiary. Like her brother and mother, she also remembered several dissenting charities.

[592] He was left £50 by his cousin, Thomas Martin.

[593] In his will dated 17 March 1714, he left (among other legacies) £10 for mourning to his granddaughter Sarah Robinson & grandson James Knight. He also mentions his 'loving wife Susanna'. None of these are identified

ROBERT KNIGHT, Cashier of the South Sea Company, 1711-21, b. 30 November, 1675, m. 1stly, 2 February, 1702 at St Michael Bassishaw, Martha (d. 27 July, 1718, aged 37), eldest dau. & coh. of Jeremiah Powell of London & Edenhope, Salop., a Director of the Bank of England, and had issue,

    1. ROBERT, of whom presently.

    1. Catherine, b. 9 August, 1704, m. 1 May, 1727 John Page (who m. 2ndly at Stockbridge, Surrey, 25 June 1741, Anne, only child of Francis Sone, of Stockbridge, near Chichester & d. 1779, aged 83), of Watergate House, Chichester, for 27 years M.P. for Chichester[594], and d. 15 October 1736, having had issue,

        (1) Catherine, d.unm.

    2. Margaretta, b. 13 March, 1713, m. at St George's, Hanover Square, 29 Feb. 1732, Hon. Morgan Vane (who m. 2ndly 19 Feb 1742, Anna Maria (d.s.p. 19 July 1756), dau. of Rt Revd Edward Fowler, Bishop of Gloucester & 3rdly 18 Dec 1759, Mary (d.s.p. 11 July 1771), dau. of William Woodyeare, of Crookhill, Yorks. & d. at Scarborough 14 Nov. 1779, aged 73), barrister, of Bilby Hall, Notts., Comptroller of the Stamp Duties, brother of Henry Vane, Earl of Darlington[595], and d. in childbirth at Bath 1 May, 1739, having had issue,

        (1) Morgan, of Bilby Hall, Notts., b 5 Dec. 1737, m. at St James, Piccadilly, 4 July 1760, Anna Maria Margaret dau. of .....Upton, of Newman Street, St Marylebone (d.s.p.s 15 July 1771 & bur. in the churchyard of St Anne's, Soho), having had issue,

            1a. a dau. b. Sept 1764[596].

    He m. 2ndly, Sarah Brookes (d.s.p. at Whitchurch, near Reading, 21 Oct. 1779). He m. 3rdly, at St George the Martyr, Queen's Square, Holborn, 9 May, 1780, his 2nd wife's niece, Catherine (who m. 2ndly, 21 May, 1791,

---

[594] He was a faithful supporter of the Duke of Newcastle until his retirement. There is a memorial to him and to his two wives in St George's Church, Donnington, near Chichester. He had a daughter, Frances, by his second wife. She married Edward White Thomas, of Watergate House, who was M.P. for Chichester from 1784-1812. Their daughter & heiress, Frances Thomas, married Maj. Gen. Crosbie.

[595] It was said in the *Universal Spectator and Weekly Journal* for 2 Jan 1731 that Margaretta Knight brought with her some £30,000. The name Morgan came through Morgan Vane's mother, the daughter of Sir Morgan Randyll, of Chilworth, Surrey. Sir Morgan's grandmother was Anne, daughter and heiress of Sir John Morgan of Chilworth. Morgan Vane's father, who succeeded as 2nd Lord Barnard, had been involved in angry disputes with his father. His sister, Anne Vane (1705-1736), had affairs with Lord Hervey and Frederick, Prince of Wales (by whom she had two children, both of whom died in infancy). He bought Bilby Hall in 1748. His third wife was painted by John Astley in 1753.

[596] Birth announced in the *Annual Register* and *The London Magazine* for 1764. She is mentioned in Kimber's *Peerage* (1766). There is a memorial to Morgan Vane's second wife in Babworth parish church (near Bilby). Morgan Vane is buried with his third wife in Chesterfield Parish Church.

John Dore, of Reading, and d. 5 Sept. 1839, aged 80), dau. of John Brookes, and d. 11 Nov. 1789[597], having had further issue,

1a. Robert Morgan (Rev), Rector of Lowick & Islip, Northants., b. at Bullmarsh, Berks. 4 Oct. 1785, m. 24 July 1832, Sarah (d. 24 Oct. 1862), dau. of Joseph Tolson, of Birdby, Cumberland & d. 27 Aug 1842, having had issue,

1b. Morgan, b. 23 May 1833, m. 8 February 1865 at Little Paxton, Hunts. Alice Elizabeth (who m. 2ndly in 1879 Harry Farquhar de Paravicini (who. d. in Hove, 28 October 1942, aged 83) and d. in Steyning, 25 May 1902, aged 58, having had by him issue), dau. of Henry William Booth, and d.s.p. 7 May 1877[598].

2a. John Henry, b. at Reading, 12 April, 1788, m. at Louth, 10 June 1808, Elizabeth (d. 19 Nov. 1865), dau. of Richard Nicholson, of Glandford Bridge, Lincs. & d. 10 Jan, 1849, having had issue,

1b. Sir Henry Morgan, barrister, b. at Wrawby, Lincs. 29 November 1808[599], m. at St James, Piccadilly, 6 July 1853, Louisa (d. 16 December 1878), dau of Rev Richard Farrer & d. 22 April 1886 & had issue,

1c. Henry de Vere, succeeded as 9th Lord Barnard in 1892, of Raby Castle, b. 10 May 1854, educ. Eton & Brasenose Coll., Oxford, m. 28 June 1881, Lady Catherine Cecil, dau. of the 3rd Marquess of Exeter & d. 28 December 1918, having had issue,

1d. Maj. Hon Henry Cecil, b. 19 September 1882, educ. Eton & Christ Church, Oxford, m. Lady Enid Fane (who m. 2ndly 1 September 1922, Maj. Herbert Broke Turnor & d. 9 September 1969, aged 75), dau. of the 13th Earl of Westmoreland & d.s.p. 9 October 1917

2d. Christopher William, 10th Lord Barnard, of Raby Castle, b. 28 October 1888, educ. Eton & Trinity Coll., Cambridge, m. 14 October

---

[597] Morgan Vane was buried in Babworth parish church, where there is a memorial. He settled everything on his third wife and, when she married again and had children, she divided the property equally with the children of her second husband. The Bilby estate was sold in 1801 and the hall has since been pulled down.

[598] He left an estate valued at "under £350,000".

[599] The last Duke of Cleveland had left Raby Castle and a considerable income to whoever was able to establish his right to the barony of Barnard. If no one was successful within five years of his death, the property would go to Capt. Forrester, his wife's great nephew. Henry Vane thereupon claimed the title, which was contested by Captain Forrester on the grounds that Harry Vane's father had been born only five months after his parents' marriage and so might not have been the father's son. The Committee of Privileges of the House of Lords could recognize that this was a ruse to extend the proceedings beyond the five year rule and gave their judgement that there were no grounds for believing Sir Henry Morgan Vane illegitimate and so Harry Vane was declared heir and so also heir to Raby Castle.

1920, Sylvia Mary (d. 1993), dau. of Herbert Straker, of Hartforth Grange, Richmond & d. 19 October 1964, having had issue,

1e. Harry John Neville, 11th Lord Barnard, b. 21 September 1923, educ. Eton & Durham Univ., m. 8 October 1952 (div. 1992), Lady Davina Cecil, dau. of 6th Marquess of Exeter & d. 3 April 2016, having had issue,

1f. Henry Francis Cecil, 12th Lord Barnard, b. 11 March 1959, m. 12 December 1998, Lydia, dau, of Christopher Robson, of Rudd Hall, Richmond, & has issue,

1g. William Henry Cecil, Hon., b. 4 June 2005

1g. Cicely Margaret, b. 20 June 2000

2g. Alice Isabella, b. 16 October 2001

1f. Caroline Mary, Hon., b. 5 June 1954, has issue,

1g. Nicola Lauren, b. 1988

2f. Elizabeth Anne, Hon., b. 17 May 1956, m. 1982 Glyn H. Deacon & has issue,

1g. Jessica Anne, b. 1982

2g. Lauren Sophie, b. 1984, m. Justin Stephenson & has issue.

1h. Megan Louise, b. 30 December 2003

3f. Sophie Rosalind, Hon., b. 24 January 1962, m. 1986 Simon B. Phillips & has issue,

1g. Oliver John, b. 1989

2g. Benjamin James, b. 1994

1g. Emily Josephine, b. 1992

4f. Louise Cicely, b. 30 May 1968

3e. Gerald Raby, Hon., b. 20 December 1926, educ. Eton & Trinity Coll., Cambridge[600], d. unm. 1993

1e. Rosemary Myra, Hon., b. 4 November 1921, m. 14 August 1948 (div.1954) Sir Angus Gore-Booth, 8th Bt. & d. 31 December 1999, having had issue,

1f. Sir Josslyn Henry Robert, 8th Bt., b. 5 October 1950, educ. Eton & Balliol Coll., Oxford, m. 15 July 1980, Jane Mary, dau, of Rt. Hon. Sir James Hovell-Thurlow-Cumming-Bruce & has issue,

1g. Mary Georgina, b. 1985

2g. Caroline Sarah, b. 1987

3d. Capt. Hon. Ralph Frederick, b. 8 June 1891, m. 5 June 1917, Kathleen Airini, dau. of Capt. Gilbert Mair & d.s.p. 6 June 1928

2c. Rev. Hon. Gilbert Holles Farrer, rector of Wem, Shropshire, b. 26 September 1856, m. 24 June 1891, Mary (d. 29 July 1921), dau. of

---

[600] In 1949, while at Cambridge, he was jailed for six months for running over & killing three women

E.B. Steadman, of High Ercall Hall, Shropshire & d. 27 June 1905, having had issue,

  1d. Mary Louisa, b. 25 March 1892, d. 29 June 1909

3c. Ralph John, b. 14 July & d. 28 July 1858

4c. Lt. Col. Hon. William Lyonel, b. 30 August 1859, m. 27 January 1904, Lady Katharine Pakenham (d. 9 March 1954), dau. of the 4th Earl of Longford & d. 23 January 1920, having had issue,

  1d. William Morgan *Fletcher-Vane*, 1st Lord Inglewood, M.P. for Westmoreland 1945-1964, b. 12 April 1909, educ. Charterhouse & Trinity Coll., Cambridge, m. 28 July 1949, Mary (d. 1982, aged 68), dau. of Sir Richard Proby, 1st Bt., & d. 22 June 198, having had issue,

    1e. (William) Richard, 2nd Lord Inglewood, M.E.P. for Cumbria & Lancashire 1989-94 & for North West England 1999-2004, b. 31 July 1951, educ. Eton & Trinity Coll., Cambridge, m. 29 August 1986, Cressida, dau, of Desmond Pemberton-Pigott, of Fawe Park, Keswick & has issue,

      1f. Henry William Frederick, Hon., b. 25 December 1990

      1f. Miranda Mary, Hon., b. 19 May 1987

      2f. Rosa Katharine, Hon., b. 25 July 1989

    2e. Christopher John, Hon., Chester Herald, b. 27 March 1953, educ. Eton & Trinity Coll., Cambridge, m. 23 June 1990, Margaret, dau, of Dr. Paul Eisenklam & has issue,

      1f. Francis William Paul, b. 1 November 1992

      2f. Arthur Wladek Jocelyn, b. 30 June 1995

      3f. Olivia Evelyn Mary, b. 19 August 1991

  1d. Katharine Selina, Hon., b. 13 July 1906, m. 1 October 1932, Hugh Bullock Hall (d. 17 June 1949, aged 47) & d. 14 April 1992, having had issue,

    1e. Alexander Bullock, of Craiglearan, Dumfriesshire, b. 11 November 1934, educ. Eton & R.A.C., Cirencester, m. 25 July 1964, Rosalind Mary, dau. of Commander Robert Halliwell, D.S.O., R.N. & has issue,

      1f. Robert Hugh Bullock, of Craiglearan, Dumfriesshire, b. 28 December 1965, m. 17 December 1994, Diane, dau. of Gerald Cheek

      2f. Richard Alexander Bullock, Rev., Army Chaplain, b. 13 June 1971, m. 29 July 1995, Anabel Barbara, dau, of David Moon & has issue

        1g. Rory

        2g. Phoebe

      1f. Rosemary Joan Catherine, b. 25 April 1967, m. 24 July 1993, Jonathan Mark Hutchinson

2e. David Bullock, b. 22 May 1936, educ. Eton, m. 22 April
1961, m. 22 April 1961, Susan Stephanie, dau. of Samuel
Perry-Aldworth., of New Romney, Kent & had issue,
> 1f. Katrina Favell, b. 16 June 1968, m. 2003 Tom
> Howard Niblett & has issue,
>> 1g. Tom Howard, b. 2003
>> 2g. Alexander Howard, b. 2005

He m. 2nd 30 December 1971, Ellen Turner & has further issue,
> 1f. Mark Bullock, b. 8 November 1973, m. 2015, Paola
> Andrea Castro Medina
> 2f. Andrew Bullock, b. 11 February 1976, m. 2014, Karin
> Luedi & ha issue,
>> 1g. Benjamin Bullock, b. 2015

2d. Margaret Cicely, Hon, b. 24 December 1910
1c. Louisa Henrietta, b. 18 October 1856, m. 10 November 1891,
William Blackstone Rennell (d. 11 December 1912, aged 66) & d. 6
December 1923, having had issue
2b. Frederick Nicholson, Maj., Clerk to the House of Lords, b. at Brigg,
Lincs. 18 December 1809, d. 10 February 1878
2a. Catherine Mary, b. 27 March 1790, d. unm. 1810
(2) Margaretta, b. 1739, d. unm. *ante* 1760.
Mr Knight m. 2ndly, 1731 Anne (who m. 2ndly, in King Henry VII's Chapel in
Westminster Abbey, 2 April 1752, James Cresset, private secretary to the Princess
Dowager of Wales & Comptroller of the Army Accounts & d. 5 June 1759, aged
59), elder daughter of Thomas Robinson, of Rokeby, Yorks. and d. 8 November,
1744, at Luxborough Hall, having had further issue,
2. William, b. 1732, m. at the English Ambassador's Chapel in Paris, Oct
1767, Isabella Panchaud (d. 1775, aged 24)[601]

The elder son,
ROBERT KNIGHT, of Barrells, cr 1745 Baron Luxborough, in the peerage of Ireland
and, in 1763, Viscount Barrells & Earl of Catherlough, K.B. , b 17 December 1702,
educ. Wadham Coll., Oxford (matric. 22 June 1719), m. 1stly 10 June 1727, at St
Mary's Church, Battersea, Hon. Henrietta St John (from whom he was separated
in 1736, and who d 26 March 1756), only dau. of Henry, 1st Viscount St John, and
had issue,
1. Henry, Hon., of Upper Brook Street, London, M.P. for Grimsby, b. 25 Feb.
1728, m. at the house of Thomas Jewell at Serjeants' Inn, Fleet Street, 21 June
1750[602], Frances (who m. 2ndly 16 Nov. 1763, Henry Scott, 4th Earl of

---

[601] Marriage reported in the Gentleman's Magazine, Nov. 1767.
[602] Marriage entry in the registers of All Hallows, London Wall, via Joan Sato. Serjeants Inn
had recently been abandoned by the Serjeants-at-Law and seems now to have been a
private house. I've no idea who Mr Jewell was.

Deloraine, and d.s.p. in a French convent in Feb. 1782), dau. and heiress of Thomas Heath of Stanstead Mount Fitchet, and d.s.p. at Peterley, Bucks. 15 Aug, and was bur. at Ullenhall 24 Aug 1762.

1. Henrietta, Hon., b. 21 Nov 1729, m. 1stly, 7 May 1748 (div. 1754) Charles (who m.

2ndly, 22 July 1763, Sarah Turnheart and d. August, 1776, aged 58), yst. son & eventual heir of Matthew Wymondesold of Lockinge, Berks. She m. 2ndly, in Paris, 7 May 1754, Hon. Josiah Child (d. at Lyons, 24 Jan. 1760), yst son of Richard, 1st Earl Tylney, and had issue,

    (1) Josiah, b. 27 Jan 1754, d. unm. in Florence, July, 1774.

    (1) a dau., b. 1755 d. 1757.

She was said to have married 3rdly in Brussels in May 1762, Col. Louis Alexandre de Grimoard de Beauvoir, Count Duroure, The King's Musketeers[603] (who m. later Jeanne de Villeneuve, Marquise de Roux, and d. in Avignon, 9 Aug 1792). She d. in Marseilles, 1 March, 1763, & was bur. at Ullenhall, having had by him further issue,

    (2) Louis Henry Scipion de Grimoard de Beauvoir, Count Duroure, writer and politician, Vice President of the Council of the Paris Commune, First Commissioner of Finance in 1793, Member of the Central Revolutionary Committee, 1793-4. b. in Marseilles 26 Feb. 1763, m. 1stly 27 Jan 1790, Adrienne Jeanne (div. 1794), dau. of Charles Philibert de Maleyssie. He m. 2ndly, 1804, Sacriste de Tobebeuf & d. in London 24 Sept. 1822[604].

Lord Catherlough m. 2ndly, at St George's, Hanover Square, 17 May, 1756 Mary (from whom he separated in 1760 and who d. 1795), widow of Sir John Lequesne, and dau. of N... Knight but had no issue by her.

In 1765/6 he took as his common law wife, Jane Davis (who assumed the name of Knight by deed poll, May 1772, d. in Holles Street, Cavendish Square, & was bur. in St Marylebone Churchyard, 9 November, 1772[605]) & d. 30 March 1772, and was bur. at Ullenhall on 15 April 1772, having had by her further issue,

    2. **ROBERT**, of whom presently

    3. Henry Raleigh[606], Lt. Gen., 31st Regt, latterly of Portman Street, London, b. at Barrels, 18 Sept & baptized at Ullenhall, 18 Oct. 1769, m. at St George's

---

[603] According to Joan Sato, he was born in Saint Roch, Paris, on 6 Oct. 1730, the son of Col. Ange-Urbain de Grimoard de Beauvoir and Jeanne-Marie-Louise le Gagneux. Col. du Roure was killed (aged 63) at the Battle of Fontenoy in 1745 – during the War of the Austrian Succession.

[604] His marriages from information from Joan Sato. He is said to have had an illegitimate son, who died with him.

[605] She signed her will on 18 October, and it was proved on 3 November. She had wanted to be buried in the mausoleum at Barrels, near Lord Catherlough, after a service in Wootton Wawen church. At this point, Marylebone church was towards the north end of the High Street. Jane was probably buried in the new graveyard in Paddington Street. Since the development undertaken by Lady Oxford and her daughter, the Duchess of Portland – the area had become seriously smart.

Bloomsbury, 1 December, 1808, Juliana (d. 1859, aged 80), dau. of Henry Boulton, of Givens Grove, Leatherhead[607]. He d. 7 Aug. & was bur. on 13 Aug. 1836 at All Souls' Cemetery, Kensal Green, having had issue,

(1) Henry Raleigh, bur. 15 Jan 1813 (?or 1812) aged 2 months, when his parents were living in St Owen Street, Hereford.

(2) Charles Raleigh, Capt. 25th Regt., bapt. 22 Dec. 1813 at St Owen's Church, Hereford, m. at Marylebone Parish Church, 6 March 1856, his cousin, Julia Sophia (d. at Charlecombe, 7 Feb. 1894, aged 76), widow of Robert Hickson, and dau. of William Sadleir Bruère of Berwick-upon-Tweed and Somerset Place, Bath[608], & d. in Charlecombe, Bath, 29 July 1901[609] having had issue,

1a. Henry Raleigh, Capt. 'The Buffs', & author of *A History of The Buffs, 3rd Foot, 1572-1704*, b. 13 Jan. & bapt at St Mary-le-Bone, 18 Feb. 1857, when his parents were living at 19 Portman Street, m. 4 Nov 1886, Constance Mary (who m. 2ndly, 1912, her first cousin, Thomas Milnes Wheat & d. at Woodhall Spa, Lincs. on 13 Aug 1934, aged 69. He d. in Lincolnshire in 1969, aged 93), dau. of Revd Christopher Wheat, vicar of Timberland, Lincs., and d. at 44 Redcliffe Square, London, W. 27 June, 1909[610], having had issue,

1b Charles Raleigh Bruère, O.B.E., Col. The Buffs, b. July 1896, m. Frances Kingsford Lethbridge, dau of H. W. Wood, of Okehampton Devon, and d.s.p. 24 Feb. 1959

---

[606] According to Aunt Catherine, and reported by Mrs Higgon, he "took part in the unfortunate expedition of the British to the Island of Walcheron in 1809, his health was ruined, and he became paralysed as a result of the unhealthy conditions and privations". A miniature, said to be of him, by Frederick Buck was sold at Christie's in 1991 for £275.

[607] Jane Fuller was a witness. Henry Boulton (1752-1828) of Givons Grove was the nephew and heir of Henry Crabbe Boulton (1709-1783), M.P. for Worcester and several times Chairman of the Court of Directors of the East India Company. They were pretty well off. Juliana's sister, Frances, married Richard Fuller, of the Rookery, whose younger brother was married to Henry's sister Jane. A younger sister, Louisa, married Col. William Raikes – younger son of Robert Raikes of Gloucester – founder of the Sunday School movement.

[608] Julia's mother, Harriet Bruère, and Charles' mother, Juliana Knight, were sisters. Julia's brother, William Sadleir Bruère (1805-44) was at Charterhouse around 1819 and in 1826 made a disastrous marriage with the daughter of a Cambridge upholsterer. Two other brothers were also at Charterhouse - James Sadleir Bruère (b. 1807) who was in the E.I.C.S., and Henry Sadleir Bruère (b.1809) who was a Captain in the 43rd Regt. She seems to have had nine brothers and three sisters.

[609] He bought the Frimley Park estate (jointly with his brother-in-law, Maj. Spring) in 1860 and developed shops and houses around Camberley during the 1860s and 1870s.

[610] He left an estate of some £20,000. He wanted to be regarded 'as far as possible as heirlooms all my silver plate, particularly those articles which belonged to my great-grandfather, the Earl of Catherlough...my grandfather Gen H.R, Knight's gold snuff box, gold medal from Egypt, and sword and scimitar he brought from Egypt..'

1b Julia Mary, of 27 Arlington Road, Eastbourne, b. 28 May 1892, m. Herbert Basil James (d. 3 May 1959, aged 72), Nigerian Civil Service, and d. in Oxford 19 March 1977, having had issue,

> 1c. Michael, b. in Tonbridge 14 November 1927, m. 12 September 1953, Marjorie Patricia Richmond, & d. in Eastbourne 26 February 1990, having had issue
>
> > 1d. Frances Catherine, b. 22 December 1961, m. in Eastbourne 1985, David C. Powney & d. in Lewes, 2005
> >
> > 2d.
>
> 2c. David, b. 30 March 1930, m. Jane Stuart (d. 14 June 1991, aged 59) & d. in Chichester 21 September 2011, having had issue.

1a Juliana Frances[611], b. in Brighton, 1859, d. unm. in Bath, 1947

(1) Juliana, b. 7 Aug. & baptized at St Martin's in the Fields on 10 Sept. 1811, m. 1840, Capt. Skeffington Bristow (d. at 1 Curzon Street, London 12 March 1883, aged 69)[612]. She d. in Rome 10 April 1854, and was buried in the Protestant cemetery there, having had issue,

> 1a. Juliana Eleanor Rose, b. 7 Aug. and bapt. at St Mary's, Bryanstone Square on 8 Sept. 1841. She died unm. in Clarges Street, London 19 July 1929[613].
>
> 2a. Caroline Jane Harriet, b. 6 Feb. and bapt. at St Mary's, Bryanstone Square on 30 March 1845, a Roman Catholic nun, professed some time between the 1871 and 1881 censuses.

(2) Caroline Emily, b. 24 July & bapt. at St Mary-le-Bone, 11 Aug. 1818, m. at St Mary's, Bryanstone Square, 7 Feb. 1850, Maj. Robert Spring (d. in Bath, 21 March 1890, aged 76), 3rd son of Lt. Col. William Collis Spring, 57th Regt[614]. She d.s.p. in Bath 1 Aug. 1893.

2. Jane[615], b. 13 Dec. 1766 & baptized as "Jane Davis" at St Mary-le-bone, 31 Dec. 1766, m. 1stly 22 Feb 1791, as his third wife, Benjamin Bond Hopkins (d. 30 Jan 1794, aged 48), of Pains Hill, Surrey and 2ndly, 22 April 1795, Col. Charles Fuller, of Philberds, Bray (d. 1 Feb. 1855)[616]. She d.s.p. in Regency Square, Brighton 7 Sept. 1861.

---

[611] Her house and contents were destroyed during the Second World War.

[612] When his daughters were married, he was living at 14 Portman Street. In the 1871 census he and his daughters were living at 43 Curzon Street. In the 1881 census he and his elder daughter were living at 1 Curzon Street.

[613] At the time of the 1891 census, after her father's death, she was living alone (apart from staff) at 43 South Street. At her death she was living at 25 Clarges Street. She left over £25,000 — it would be interesting to know who to. She was like her sister a Roman Catholic.

[614] In 1860, Maj. Spring bought the Frimley Park estate jointly with his brother-in-law, Capt. Knight.

[615] Jane was godmother to Jane Carden, to whom she left her pearls. These were left by Mrs Carden to her daughter Bertha. Fuller was, according to aunt Cat, "a scamp".

[616] So described in the announcement of his widow's death in The Times. He was living at

3. Henrietta Matilda[617], b. 15 Nov. & baptized at St. James', Piccadilly, 13 December 1770, m. 11 June, 1792, at St George's, Hanover Square, Maj Michael Impey, 64th Foot[618], (k'd. in a duel in Canada, 1 Oct 1801, aged 31) eldest son of Sir Elijah Impey, Chief Justice of the Supreme Court in Bengal[619], and had issue

    (1) Henry Raleigh, Capt., 50th Bengal Native Infantry[620], b. 28 July 1794 in St Lucia[621], & baptized at St Paul's, Birmingham (with his younger sister) on 14 July 1796, d. at Kederee 14 July 1835, leaving issue, by an Indian lady who he did not marry,

---

Philberds in 1828 according to *Paterson's Roads*. The house had apparently once been the property of Nell Gwynne – but was demolished in 1850. He was the third son of Richard Fuller, the banker, of The Rookery, Dorking. Fuller's Bank was founded in 1737 and continued until 1891, when it was taken over. It has now disappeared into the Nat West. Col. Fuller is listed among the nobility and gentry in Pigot's Directory of Brighton for 1840. He was then resident at 56 Regency Square. In the 1851 Census, Col. Fuller and his wife (at 29 Regency Square) both claim to be 80. In the 1861 Census, Jane Fuller (describing herself as a widow and 'fundholder') was living at 29 Regency Square, aged 93, with a butler, a housekeeper, a housemaid and a cook. She had her infant great-nephew & niece staying with her – Henry Raleigh Knight and his sister Julia (with their nurse).

[617] Married according to Aunt Cat "badly", which suggests that the Impey children were considered poor relations. She lived in South Audley Street when the children were small – close by her brother Robert in Grosvenor Square.

[618] He was educated at Westminster School. In December 1792 he was serving as a lieutenant in the 2nd Lifeguards, when Capt John Gawler was requested to relinquish his membership of the Society for Constitutional Information. When he refused, he was dismissed from the regiment. Lieut. Impey was one of three officers who refused to sign the request. On 21 January 1793 he transferred to the 6th Regiment of Foot. Questions were raised in the Commons. Fox spoke in defence of Capt. Gawler; Burke spoke in defence of the government. The fatal duel was with Lieut. Willis of the same regiment. Impey was apparently a reluctant duellist and didn't fire.

[619] See E.P. Impey, *Sir Elijah Impey*, 1846.

[620] Nepal and the E.I.C. were in stiff competition at this period, so there was quite a lot to do up there. Gorakhpur, where his elder son was born, is up by the Nepalese border. The 50th BNI was one of those that joined the rebellion of 1857.

[621] His paternal uncle, Sir Robert Affleck of Dalham Hall, was partly responsible for his education, though the family went to the Lovibonds at Maidstone when they first returned to England. He entered the Royal Military College (then in temporary lodgings at Great Marlow) on 4 August 1807, with a number of other well-born gentlemen, aged 13 (the usual age), and 5' ½" tall. He was admitted a Cadet in 1811 and arrived in Madras en route for Bengal on 14 July 1812. He was gazetted Ensign 1814, Lieut., 1817, Capt. 1829. Fought at Mukwampur in the Third Mahratta War and for his conduct there was thanked in General Orders (Gentleman's Magazine, 1816). He died on board *Shelburne,* off Kederee, at the mouth of the Hooghly River, south of Calcutta. His will, dated 9 July 1835, and proved 1835 leaves "all to my two beloved children" with "support for their mother". His executors were his sister, Frances Hearn, his brother Michael Elijah Impey, and Brevet Captain James Saunders, 50th Bengal Native Infantry (who was gazetted brevet captain on 4th March 1835 & was gazetted Major on 30 April 1844).

1a. Henry, b. 28 Sept 1828 at Gorakphur & baptised there on 30 October 1829[622]. He was brought up at the Military Orphan School after his father's death. He later moved to Jaffna in northern Sri Lanka and died either there or in Colombo ca. 1859. He had issue by a Tamil woman whom he subsequently married,

    1b. Francis Wellington, (known as Johnny), b. in January 1845, implicated in the murder of his mother's partner in February 1867[623].

    1b. Cecilia Penelope Caroline, m. 1865, Juan Perara

2a. Michael, b. 23 December 1831 at Khidirpur, Calcutta. He was baptised 7 Aug 1836[624] and d. 19 Jan. 1839. He was bur. at Khidirpur.

1a. Matilda, b. Jan. 1824, d. at Allahabad, & was bur. there 2 Sep. 1827.

(2) John Sawrey, Capt. Madras Infantry, b. 12 Jan. 1798, educ. at Blundells School, Tiverton, Cadet 1819 in the E.I.C., Ensign 1820, Lieut. 1824 8th Madras Native Infantry, Nagpore Subsidiary Force, Postmaster at Nagpore 1825, Capt. 1829. m. at St Cuthbert's, Midlothian, 1 April 1818, Barbara (who d. 1 April 1870, aged 75[625]), dau. of Robert Fenwick, of Edinburgh. He was invalided in Dec. 1829 and d. 2 Nov. 1831 at Visakhapatam, having had issue,

1a. John Fenwick, b. in Prospect Place, St George's Fields, Southwark, 2 March 1820, d an inf. at sea on *Lady Carrington,* 12 May 1820.

2a. Robert John Palmer, b. in India, 10 Sept. 1821, baptised at Nagpur, 3 Nov. 1821[626], d. in Madras, 25 May 1824

---

[622] Henry's prospects were not good. Discriminatory legislation against Anglo-Indians had been introduced from the 1780s. As mixed-race orphans, they could not be returned to the UK. They could not serve in the EIC military, they could not own land, they were not to be employed by the EIC. They had no access to European civil law. There is Item reference TS 11/830 in the National Archives at Kew - Henry IMPEY v Michael Elijah IMPEY and others re will of Henry Raleigh Impey dated 9 July 1835: came before Chancery, 14 Oct 1842. There was settlement by December 1845, because the creditors were required to submit their claims by Christmas 1845.

[623] Henry Impey left his estate of just over £1000 in trust for his children, with his widow having a life interest. After his death, his widow lived in Colombo with a Tamil man, Simeon Sedemberen. Her children and her son-in-law wanted her to divide the capital with them, but Sedemberen refused to let her. Thereupon they hired some men to murder him, which they duly did. They were caught. Two of the men died in prison, but Cecilia's husband and another man were hanged (Colombo Observer, 25 Feb. 1867, reported in the Hobart Mercury on 29 April). Johnny seemed to get off.

[624] He was baptised at the Military Orphan School in Khidirpur by Rev John McQueen, headmaster and chaplain – when it was noted that he was illegitimate. At his burial he was described as a ward of the Khidirpur School.

[625] She was living with her son and his wife in Oxford at the time the 1851 census. After her son's death, she lived with her sister (Mrs Ball) and her sister's daughter's family at Boddington Manor, near Cheltenham. Her sister's daughter was married to, Rev Thomas Purnell, vicar of Staverton with Boddington from 1841-1892. .

[626] An infant son of J.S. Impey died 25 May 1824 – which could have been Robert, or his

3a. N... b. in Madras, 10 July 1823, d. in Madras 25 May 1824

4a. Archibald Lovibond, b. in India, 6 June 1825 at Nagpur, educ. Rugby School[627], Gonville & Caius Coll. Cambridge & New Inn Hall, Oxford, m. at St Pancras Parish Church, 6 Oct. 1846, Emma, dau. of John Harvey, of Doddington, Cambs. He d.s.p. in Oxford, 11 Jan. 1853 from the effects of epilepsy.

5a. N... b. still-born in Madras, 9 Dec. 1826.

(3) Michael Elijah[628], of The Elms, Mortlake, b. posthumously at Bexley in Kent 3 May 1802, educ. Blundells School & Bagshot Military School. By 1846 until sometime before 1870 he was company secretary to the Universal Life Assurance Society[629], m. at Harpsden, Oxfordshire, 6 October 1830, Elizabeth (d. 16 December 1886, aged 74), eldest dau. of Maj. Gen. William Mayne of Boulney Court, near Henley[630], and d. 30 January 1880, having had issue, with two other sons (who d. in infancy)

1a. Armstrong Arthur, b. 23 Feb. & bapt at St Mary-le-Bone, 8 July 1835, when his parents were living at 49, Charlotte Street, d. 18 August 1835

2a. Richard Charles, b. 2 May & bapt at St Mary-le-Bone, 6 July 1836, when his parents were still in Charlotte Street, bur. in All Souls Cemetery, at Kensal Green, 4 May 1837.

---

un-named younger brother.

[627] From 1839-43 – his first two years being under the great Thomas Arnold. Mrs Arnold was the dau. of Rev John Penrose of Penrhyn – so there may have been a family link. Why did he interrupt his university career to marry at the age of 21? Letters to his tutor at Caius, dated December 1846, show that he wanted to take his degree and to be ordained. When he matriculated at Oxford in February 1849, perhaps that was his intention. He was still at Oxford – un-ordained – four years later. Maybe his epilepsy prevented him proceeding.

[628] He bore the brunt of his mother's disastrous second marriage. At the census of 1861 he was living at The Elms, Ship Lane, Mortlake – with a resident cook and housemaid. He described himself as 'Esquire'. The younger children were born in the parish of Marylebone. Mrs E. M. Impey says that he practised as a solicitor in East Ham, and had interests in the E.I.C. His death is recorded in the district of Richmond, Surrey. The surviving family were still at The Elms in 1881, except for Victoria.

[629] The company was established in 1834 with a particular interest in people serving in India. Impey was its second company secretary. It was later taken over several times and is now subsumed in Aviva.

[630] General Mayne was the son of Robert Mayne, M.P., a banker who went bankrupt in 1782 and committed suicide. He served as a Captain in the Life Guards at Waterloo and was known as "Waterloo Bill". His older brother William Mayne M.P. was created Lord Newhaven in 1776. In 1805, General Mayne had married Elizabeth Taylor, dau. of Sir John Taylor, Bt. who (with his bachelor brother Simon) owned extensive estates in Jamaica. Elizabeth had been disowned by her family on her marriage and the considerable Taylor family fortune went instead to her elder sister. This didn't prevent Michael Impey making an (unsuccessful) claim for compensation from the Jamaica estates when slavery was abolished in 1833. The Mayne family had strong connections with the HEIC.

3a. Charles Hastings, b. 31 Jan. & bapt. at St Mary-le-Bone, 27 Aug. 1839, when his parents were living at 1a Devonshire Street, d. an inf.

4a. Percy Roberts, an East India Merchant, b. 10 Aug. & bapt at St Mary-le-Bone, 25 Oct 1848, when his parents were living at 4 Duchess Street, m. in Conway, Caernarvonshire, 11 December 1886, Esther Alice Kemp, formerly Meek (d. in West Derby 16 Dec. 1889, aged 24), and d. in New York, 23 May 1910, having had issue[631],

    1b. Percy Michael Elijah, Capt. R.F.C., of Salterns House, Parkstone, b. 10 Feb & bapt. at St Anne's, Stanley, Lancs. 14 July, 1888, educ. Merchant Taylors School, m. at St Paul's, Kingston Hill, 17 August 1912, Kathleen Olinda (d. 19 October 1957, aged 71), dau. of Johnston Montgomery & d. at the Star & Garter Home, Richmond, 23 August, 1929[632], leaving issue,

        1c. Michael Elijah, Commander, R.N., D.S.C. (March 1942 & bar June 1942), D.S.O. (Sept 1943), b. 8 Nov. 1915, and baptized at St Mary's, Osterley, 5 December 1915, Midshipman, 1933; Sub-Lieutenant, 1936; Lieutenant, 1938, Lieut. Commander, 1946; Commander, 1950, ret'd 1958, d. in Poole, 15 March 1986.

        1c. Maisie Evelyn Montgomery, b. 4 October 1914, m. December 1945 Jan M. I. Wroblewski & d. in Dorchester 27 April 2003

    1b. Alice Henrietta Eveline, a nurse, b. 7 Dec. 1889, m. at Maidenhead in June 1924, Charles Blake Coleman and emigrated to Kew, Victoria, Australia where she d. in 1968.

1a (Elizabeth) Victoria, b. at Peppard Common, near Henley-on-Thames, 1831 & baptized there on 24 August 1831, m. 1stly at Mortlake, 4 Feb 1874, Frederick Croshaw (d. 1880, aged 54), of Richmond, Surrey. She m. 2ndly at Christ Church, Mayfair, 14 September 1882, George Smyth of Lewisham and d.s.p. in January 1904, and was buried in Norwood Cemetery.

2a. Henrietta Matilda, b. in St Mary-le-Bone, 30 March 1841, adoptive mother of her nephew and niece, d. unm. Apr-June 1919 at 20, Sheen Lane, Mortlake.

3a. Frances Anna, b. 8 June & bapt. at St Mary-le-Bone, 26 July 1843, when her parents were living at 1a Devonshire Street, m. at Mortlake, 8 September 1887, Edward Charles Griffiths, a Shropshire corn merchant & surveyor (who married again and d. at Church Cottage, 22 April 1917,

---

[631] He apparently imported carpets, but was declared bankrupt in 1886 and absconded. He settled in Liverpool, married and took his wife's name. His sister Henrietta took the boy and the girl also and adopted them – though Percy kept in touch (by letter after he emigrated). Alice Impey had to go to law in 1919 to establish her legitimacy since she had been registered under her mother's name, and her father had registered her mother's death under her maiden name.

[632] For disabled ex-service men, established in 1916.

leaving issue). She d.s.p. at Church Cottage, Gnosall, Staffs. 27 January 1892.

(1) Henrietta (Matilda), b. 3 April & baptized at St Mary-le-Bone 29 April 1793, m. 12 Aug. 1813 at St Gluvias, Penrhyn, Maj. Richard Treeve, Royal Welch Fusiliers, Brigade Major to the Forces in Jersey, Barrack Master 1825-1852, elder son of John Treeve, of St Gluvais[633]. He died in Jersey, September, 1860, aged 79. She d. in Coie House Jersey 14 Sept. 1844, having had issue,

    1a. John Richard Henry, Capt., of St Saviour, Jersey, b. in Barn Hall, Colchester, 30 May 1814[634], cadet at the R.M.A., Sandhurst, 1827-1832, m. at St Mary's, Melcombe Regis, 22 Oct. 1834, Margaret Emma Logan[635] (with whom he was living at Old Coie House, in the parish of St Saviour, Jersey, in the census of 1851. He then described himself as a "landed proprietor"). He had issue,

        1b. Henry Richard, Lt. Col., b. in France, 1840, m. at Holy Trinity Church, Marylebone Road, 9 August 1862, Fanny (d. Oct-Dec 1900), dau. of Charles Tayler, of Ryde, Isle of Wight[636]. He presumably m. 2ndly his sister-in-law, Rose Tayler, and d. in Bedhampton, Hants in 1911[637].

---

[633] The Treeve family seem to have come from Cornwall. He was severely wounded in the foot at Albuera and received a pension of £100 a year. The garrison at Jersey was home to a number of recuperating or disabled soldiers. 'Henriette' claimed to be 40 in the 1841 census! In the 1851 census, Richard lived in St Helier. By the 1881 Census, there were no Treeves in the Channel Islands.

[634] Colchester was a major garrison town during the Napoleonic War.

[635] They both of them were described as "sojourner" in the marriage record, so neither came from Weymouth. He was only twenty and she a little older. Who was she? On 4 Dec. 1857, when Capt. John R. H. Treeve was appointed Paymaster of the 4th Royal Jersey Militia, he was said to be "late of the 4th Royal Jersey Militia". A Margaret Treeve (who was born in Jersey) was in lodgings in Bermondsey at the time of the 1871 census. She was described as "married" but her husband was not with her. She died in the Bermondsey area the following year. Since the dates fit, this seems most likely to be her. The St Olave's district – between London Bridge and Tower Bridge – was not a very prosperous area.

[636] H.R. Treeve was described in the marriage register as "Lieut. H.M. 28th Regt." He was apparently a resident of the parish – as was his wife. Her father was described as "Esquire". H.R. Treeve's father was present and signed the register. Curiously Fanny's witness, Dinah Cheshire, was illiterate. According to the 1891 census, Fanny was born in Ryde in the Isle of Wight and was two years older than her husband. Her mother and sister (who were both born in Ryde) were living with them – at 26 Nelson Road, Portsea (in what is now Southsea) with one live-in servant. H.R. Treeve was by now a retired Lt. Colonel. By the 1901 census, Mrs Tayler and Mrs Fanny Treeve were both dead and Col. Treeve and his sister-in-law had moved to 32 Nelson Road.

[637] In the 1901 census, a Richard Montague Tayler (aged 9), described as his nephew, is living with him. By the time of the 1911 census, Richard Montague Tayler has become Richard Montague Treeve and is described as his son. He served in World War I from Dec. 1915 (when he was described as a fitter & when he was still living at the house in Bedhampton). He married in the Gosport area Jan-March 1936, Minnie Agnes Langrish (d.

2a. (Michael) Elijah, of 29 Edwardes Square, Kensington, b. in Jersey, 23 Oct 1815, m. in Jersey, 19 Nov. 1844, Eliza Cecilia (d. 27 Nov 1891, aged 85), dau. of Hon. Peter de Blaqueire & d.s.p. 29 Sept. 1888[638].

3a. George Lovibond, b. 17 Aug. 1817 & baptized at St Saviours, 25 September 1817, at the R.M.A. Sandhurst, 1832-3, m. in Guernsey in 1843

4a. Frederick William, b. 10 May 1819 & baptized at St Saviour's 30 May 1819 (Henrietta Nicholson & Michael Elijah Impey were his godparents)

5a. Charles Hastings, b. in Jersey, 1821, & baptized at St Saviours 30 May 1821, m. in Grouville, 1 Aug. 1842, Harriet Marsh, dau. of Lieut. George Renwick, of Grouville[639] (d. at Beechworth Hospital, Victoria, 20 June 1859) & d. at Adelong, New South Wales 23 June, 1863[640], having had issue,

    1b. George, b. in Jersey, 1843, d.s.p. in Liverpool, N.S.W. in 1918[641].

    2b. James Charles, b. at sea 1849, m. 4 March, 1892 at St Joseph's R.C. Church, Beechworth, Victoria, Sarah Ann, dau. of Thomas Harvey, of Yackandandah[642], & d. in Fitzroy, Victoria in 1895. (She m. 2ndly, in 1897 at Albury N.S.W., Richard Swasbrick, who married 2ndly, Rosina Cook

---

in the Portsmouth area, Dec. 1984, aged 84) & d. in the Gosport area Oct-Dec 1967.

[638] Michael Elijah was named for his young uncle and godfather, Michael Elijah Impey, who was present at his baptism. She was a granddaughter of John de Blaquiere, who was given a peerage by Pitt in 1800 for his work on behalf of the Union. In the 1851 census they were living at 9 Edward Street (just off Deptford High Street), and Elijah Treeve is described as a "fundholder" – i.e. living on the interest of his (and/or his wife's) capital. By 1861 they had moved to 29 Edwardes Square, Kensington, where they stayed put. It is now regarded as the most beautiful square in Kensington. In 1871 he described himself as "engaged with the press" and in 1881 as "literary".

[639] Described in the 1841 census (when he was 65) as "Army, H.P.". Probably he was the Lieut. George Renwick, 6th Regt of Foot, who was promoted Lieut. during the Napoleonic Wars in July 1810 (aged 34), but was put on half-pay (in 1817) after the war had ended. There were plenty of men like him, who (despite slender means) had managed to make a career in the army. They had managed to avoid purchasing their commission because of casualties, but were later left high and dry. Young Charles Treeve was staying with his uncle, Lieut. John Treeve, R.N., at the Fort Henry Barracks at Grouville at the time of the 1841 census – so that is how he met Harriet Renwick.

[640] Charles & his family arrived in Melbourne, Australia in January 1850. He established a grocer's business in Lonsdale Street, Melbourne, but it soon folded. At the time of his death he was in Adelong – some 500 miles north east of Melbourne. It was a major centre in the Australian 'Gold Rush', which began in 1857. Charles was described as a "tutor", so maybe he wasn't actually digging.

[641] On 30 April 1869, the Victoria Government Gazette announced that the license granted to George Treeves (they were spelling the name with an 's' now) of 20 acres in the Beechworth district was revoked because of non-performance. Maybe he thought he would do a bit of farming and then didn't.

[642] He had emigrated to Australia from Western-super-Mare in the 1850s and married an Irish Catholic girl. Yackandandah was some 20 miles from Beechworth and also part of the gold mining area.

and d. 2 June 1953, aged 80, and d. in Albury, 25 Oct 1908, aged 43, having had further issue.) Her issue by her first husband,

    1c. James Thomas, a miner and horse breaker of Rowdy Flat, Yackandandah, b. in Mitta Mitta, Victoria, 1893, d.s.p. in Wangaratta, 1942.

    2c. George Henry, labourer, of Pentland Avenue, Punchbowl, N.S.W., b. 8 Nov 1894, m. in Canterbury, N.S.W., 1920, Ellen Lydia Sarah (d. 23 April 1986, aged 89), dau. of Mary Ann Harriet Swasbrick, and granddaughter of John & Lydia Swasbrick & d. 6 Aug. 1954, having had issue,

        1d. William James Henry, OIC, Chullora Motor Registry, of Mount Avenue, Punchbowl, b. 26 Aug. 1920, m. Ione Margaret... and d. 6 May 1993, having had issue

        2d. Herbert John ('Jack'), b. 13 Sept. 1923, m. Hazel Holly (d. 21 July 2002, aged 84), dau. of Berkeley Harcourt Smith, of Richmond, Queensland & d. in Sydney, 22 Nov 2006.

        1d. dau., m. 1953 John Christopher Gray (d. in Penrith, N.S.W. 2003, aged 83) & has issue

        2d. Rita Ellen, of Munro Street, Sefton, N.S.W., b. 7 Feb 1926, m. ... Forrest & d. 2008

        3d. Marie Lucy, b. 1928, d. 1943

6a. Adolphus Cornelius, b. in England, 1826 & baptized at St Saviours 10 December 1831, d. in Kolkata, West Bengal, 19 April 1848.

1a. (Amelia Georgiana) Matilda, b. 31 May 1823 & baptized at St Saviours, 6 July 1823, m. Robert George Adams Welsford Lillicrap (d. in Plymouth, 9 Oct. 1850), Paymaster in the R.N., 6th child of Rear Adm. James Lillicrap & d. 1860 having had issue an only daughter[643],

    1b. Matilda (Frances Adelaide), b. in St Saviours, Jersey in 1846[644], m. at St Brelade, Jersey, 16 October 1866, Francis William Fielding, a solicitor's clerk, of St Helier, Jersey & had issue,

        1c. Clarence Hastings[645], of St Helier, b. in Brighton, 14 July 1868, m. at St Luke's, St Helier, 22 July 1903, Elise Ann L'Amy (d. in St Helier 25 April 1935, aged 62) & had issue,

---

[643] She was living with her parents and her brother Elijah in the 1841 census (though none of her other brothers and sisters are mentioned). Her will was dated 1860, leaving everything to her daughter and, failing her, to her sister Marian and her children by John Philip Searle.

[644] In 1861, after her parents' deaths & at the time of the census, she was living at Bayview Villa, St Lawrence, Jersey – the house of John Underwood Searle – and she is described as his niece. Francis Fielding was a clerk in a solicitor's office – the Muncipal Registry of Deeds in St Helier. In 1911 they shared a house in New Street, Jersey with their son, Clarence.

[645] He was already "living on his own means" at the time of the 1891 census and was still

1d. Charles, b. 20 December 1904, m. Doris M...

1d. Dorothy Adelaide, b. 1905

2d. Evelyn, b. 1909

2a. Marianne Impey, b. 29 Oct 1831, & baptized 25 January 1832 at St Saviour's, Jersey & had issue,

1b. Barbara Emma Impey[646], b. in England, 13 Aug 1849 & baptized at St Pancras Church, London on 24 Sept 1852, arrived in Moreton Bay 15 Nov 1873, d. unm. in Sydney, N.S.W., 28 July 1926

She m. 28 July 1859, John Philip Searle (1833-1873), of St Helier[647], and d. in Mitcham Lane, Streatham, 31 Dec 1906[648], having had issue by him,

1b. John Richard Impey Thomas, b. in Jersey, 15 Aug. 1860, d. an inf.

2b. John Impey, b. in Jersey, 1864, m. at Christ Church, Croydon, 26 Aug 1885, Alice (d. in the Lambeth Infirmary, and was bur at Norwood Cemetery 15 May 1897, aged 37), dau. of Frederick James Hatley & d. in 1906[649], aged 42, having had issue,

---

doing so in 1911, but they were living in small flats and he was a sort of clerk – like his father

[646] It seems possible that the seventeen year old Marian left Jersey when the pregnancy was discovered and went to Oxford, to her aunt, Barbara Impey, and her cousins, Archibald and Emma Impey. Since the child was named Barbara Emma, it may be that the childless Archibald and Emma were intending to adopt her – or at least care for her. By the time of the 1851 census, Marion was back in Jersey, living with her widowed father and sister, but without Barbara. In September 1852, Barbara was baptized at St Pancras Parish Church, in London, where Archibald and Emma had been married in 1846. She was said there to be the dau. of Archibald Lovibond Impey, of High Street, Oxford and Marian Impey. Then, in 1853, Archibald died. By the time of the 1861 census, Barbara is listed as "Barbara Impey" in the household of John Underwood Searle of Bayview Villa, and said to be his niece. By the time of the 1871 census, she is called "Barbara Impey Searle" and is said to be his daughter.

A version of her story is told in *About the Impeys*. Barbara was devoted to her mother, but feared her stepfather. She said that her father was a clergyman in Jersey. In 1873, her mother sent her to Australia with £1000 and told her not to come back. She lived – very poor - by doing washing and selling magazines. Given his reputation, it is probable that her father was Rev William Corbet le Breton (1815-1887), who became vicar of St Saviour's Jersey from some time in the 1840s until 1875, when he transferred to St Helier until he was deprived in 1883. He served as Dean of Jersey from 1850-1883. He was given a parish in Kennington, where he died. His wife had left him by then. This would make poor Marion Lily Langtry's half-sister. Lily didn't become famous until 1877, after Marion's departure.

[647] In the 1881 census she was described as a widow and was working as a 'nurse and lady help' to Frederick Ford, a stockbroker's clerk, his wife Florence, a 'lecturer in psychology and literature', and their infant daughter, Irene, at 18 Grosvenor Road, Islington. Ten years later she was living with Emma at 36 Friern Road, a small house in Camberwell. In 1901 she and Emma were in lodgings in Devonshire Road, Lewisham.

[648] On 21 February 1902, she was granted administration of the estate of her brother, M.E. Impey who had died in 1888 – to the value of £5!

1c. Willie Walter John, b. 1888[650], joined the army in 1907, and served in World War I in the Worcestershire Regt (discharged Dec 1918). He died in Colchester in 1921.

3b. William, b. 28 March 1867 – at Bay View Villa in the 1871 census

1b. Marion Thomas, b. in Jersey, 29 December 1861 & baptized at St Lawrence, - d. in 1879, being buried in the St Helier cemetery.

3a. Emma Octavia Augusta, b. 1832, & baptized with her sister at St Saviour's, Jersey, 25 January 1832, m. 28 April 1859, as his second wife, John Underwood Searle (d. in St Helier, 28 January 1878, aged 68), a spirit merchant[651] & d. at 77 Caithness Road, Streatham on 25 Nov 1916, having had issue,

1b. Richard John, b. 29 November 1859.

(2) Frances, b. 30 May & bapt. 14 July 1796 at St Paul's, Birmingham. m. 10 Sept 1814 at West Teignmouth, William Hearn, late of Hampshire. In 1835, she acted as an executor to the will of her elder brother, Capt H. R. Impey. She d. at Richmond Place, Brighton in Oct. 1854[652], having had issue,

1a. Michael Elijah (Rev.), Curate of Miningsby, & later Rector of Martin, near Horncastle, Lincs., b. in Jersey in 1816, m. 1stly, in 1838 from his grandmother's house in Brislington, Elizabeth Emily (d. at Wiggenhall St Mary Magdalene Vicarage, Norfolk, 7 May 1855, aged 40), dau. of Lt.Col. Richard Lang, South Devon Militia, of Broad Clyst, Devon, and had issue,

1b. Sarah

2b. Ada, born in Worthing, ca. 1847,

He m. 2ndly, 21 Aug. 1855, at St Mary's Lewisham, Henrietta Baker (d. 13 Oct. 1892 at Maze Lodge, Priory Park, Kew, aged 76), dau. of George Sanders, of Lewisham, and d. 29 Sept. 1875[653], having had further issue,

3b. Florence Amelia, b. 1857

4b. Eveline (Maud Augusta), b. 1858, m. Rev. George Rawlinson (d. in Middlesborough, 1911, aged 65), Vicar of Whiston, nr. Northampton. & later of Shenton, Leics. & d. at Fairfield House, Yardley, Birmingham, 7 Feb. 1938[654], having had issue,

---

[649] In the 1891 census he and Alice had four rooms at 26 Lowdon Road, a small terraced house in Brixton. The Lambeth Infirmary was next to the workhouse where Charlie Chaplin was placed for a short while. In 1901 John was lodging at 144 Westminster Bridge Road, in Lambeth

[650] In the 1901 census, he was on the Training Ship at Mount Edgcumbe – which was where boys were sent who were "found wandering" or in need of care and protection or had been involved in minor criminality.

[651] In 1861 they were living at Bay View Villa with John Philip & Marion Searle and with Amelia, J. U. Searle's daughter by his first marriage, with Matilda Lillicrap and with Barbara Impey (described as niece); by 1871 they were living in Whitchurch, on the outskirts of Bristol – where Searle was born.

[652] Info from Joan Sato.

[653] He left an estate of some £10,000.

1c. Hugh George, in the Indian Educational Service, 1908-1933, author of many books on India, b. 1880, d. in the Isle of Wight in 1957.

2c. Basil Lethbridge, b. 19 Nov. 1882, described himself as a farmer when he arrived with $2 in his pocket in Winnipeg in 1903, from St Albans in Vermont, *en route* for Langdon, in Saskatchewan.

3c. Colin Sidney, a schoolmaster, b. 28 May 1886, served in the Royal Engineers in World War I, m. & d. in Warwickshire in 1981, aged 94.

4c. William Julius Stephen, b. 1 Sept. 1890, in 1911 was a general labourer at the steel works in Middlesborough, m. 1 Dec. 1914 & d. in Queensland, Australia 9 Dec 1961.

5c. George Lancelot Herbert, 4th Batt., Grenadier Guards, b. in Tysoe, 1892, was a lathe turner at the steelworks in Middlesborough in 1911, d. in Middlesborough of cerebro-spinal meningitis, 10 Feb 1915 and was bur. in Linthorpe cemetery.

1c. Winifred Maud, b. 4 Aug. 1884, m. a Mr Wilson & d. in the Blackpool district in 1975.

2c. Sybil Edith, b. 20 Oct 1887, m. Edwin H. Johnson & d. Sept 1979 in Leeds.

3c. Doris Ethel Amelia, b. 29 March 1894, m. in Middlesborough in 1914, Edward Fleetwood C. Rynd[655], and d. in New Zealand, *post* 1981

4c. Muriel, b. 11 June 1899, m. Norman Rushford (d. 1958, aged 60), of Middlesborough & d. Oct. 1985.

   5b. Irene Agatha, b. 1860, m. 1882, N.....

(1) Maria, b. 1800, d. 26 December 1806 in South Audley Street, as a result of her clothes catching fire[656].

Mrs Impey m. 2ndly, 13 May 1816, at St Helen's, Jersey, Lieut. Adj. George Nicholson 8th Royal Veteran Battalion (from whom she was granted a separation in February, 1823) and d. his widow in Ilfracombe, April-June 1841[657].

3. Caroline, b 20 July 1772 and was bur at Ullenhall, 22 Aug. 1772.

---

[654] In 1915, when George Lancelot enlisted, she was living at 24 Ayresome Street in Middlesborough, so George appears on the Middlesborough War Memorial.

[655] In 1938 (aged 60) he and his wife are listed as living in Endeavour Avenue, Wellington. He is described as a bank employee. In 1957 they were at 22 Ferry Street.

[656] Gentleman's Magazine, Jan 1807.

[657] She married according to Aunt Cat "badly" – which must have referred to the marriage with Nicholson. It suggests that the Impey children were known as poor relations. In 1819, young Michael Impey took Nicholson to court for assault and, in February 1823, Mrs Nicholson, then of Waterloo House, Guernsey, was granted a separation. In 1836 Mrs Nicholson received a small legacy under her brother's will. In 1838, she was living as a widow in Brislington, just outside Bristol (then known as a beautiful, rural village, much favoured by the prosperous merchants of Bristol) when she made a declaration that Michael was her first husband's youngest son – apparently in respect of some contested property in Chiswick.. Death reference: Barnstaple District, Vol. 10, p. 27.

Lord Catherlough died in Golden Square, London 30 March, 1772, when his titles became extinct, but his estates devolved on his elder illegitimate son,

ROBERT KNIGHT, of Barrells, M.P. for Wootton Basset 1806-7 & 1811-12, Rye 1823-6 & Wallingford 1826-32, b. 3 March 1768, & bapt. at St James', Piccadilly, 9 April 1768[658], educ. Queen's College, Cambridge, m. at Lord Dormer's House in Dean Street on 12 June 1791, Hon. Frances Dormer[659], yst. dau. of Charles, 8th Lord Dormer & d. in Grosvenor Square 5 Jan. 1855, having had issue,

1. Henry, b. 24 May 1795 & baptized at St Marylebone, 10 June 1795. He died in France, 14 Nov. 1800 & was bur. at Ullenhall, 7 December 1800.

1. Frances Elizabeth, bapt. at Ullenhall, 22 Aug. 1793, m. 23 Jan. 1857 at St James', Piccadilly, Lt. Col. Henry Edward Gooch (d. 18 Jan. 1867, aged 73)[660], elder son of Ven. John Gooch, Archdeacon of Sudbury & Rector of Benacre & grandson of Sir Thomas Gooch, Bt., of Benacre Hall, Suffolk, and d.s.p. at Melbourne Hall, Derbyshire, 18 Nov. 1874[661].

2. Georgiana, b. 13 July, 1801, and bapt. at St George's, Hanover Square, 22 Oct 1801, m. at St George's Hanover Square, 7 Feb. 1828, Edward Bolton King, of Umberslade and d. 6 May 1858, having had issue (*see lineage of King*)

---

[658] baptism info via Joan Sato.

[659] She was baptized in the parish church at Great Missenden on 9 Aug 1774. She and her husband separated in 1802 and never saw each other again. In April, 1805 her husband brought a case of criminal conversation against Col. Joseph Fuller, his sister Jane's brother-in-law and was awarded damages of £7,000. When Mrs Knight gave birth to a son in 1813, on whose behalf she intended to claim the Barrells estate, depositions were taken to prove the child's illegitimacy. However, after Mrs Knight's death in 1842, when it was clear that airing the rival claims would revive the old scandal, her son finally agreed to divide the estate on Mr Knight's death.

[660] A Waterloo veteran. Col. Macdonell's gallant defence of Hougomont is a matter of history. More than once was the place nearly taken by the French. "The French, however," says Siborne, in his graphic account of the battle of Waterloo, " succeeded in forcing the gate ; but the defenders betook themselves to the nearest cover, whence they poured a fire upon the intruders, and then rushing forward a struggle ensued which was distinguished by the most intrepid courage on both sides. At length Lt.-Col. Macdonell, Capt. Wyndham, Ensigns Gooch and Hervey, and Sergt. Graham, of the Coldstream Guards, by dint of great personal strength and exertions, combined with extraordinary bravery and perseverance, succeeded in closing the gate against their intruders."

[661] She and Colonel Gooch rented Melbourne Hall. On Colonel Gooch's death, Catherine Bolton King went to live with her aunt and became her heir (though the family silver was left to my great-grandfather).

THE POWELL FAMILY

Jeremiah Powell (d. 1725), of Edenhope, Salop, m. Martha, dau. & coh. of Robert Barrington, of Stalisfield, Kent, and had issue,

1. Martha, b. 1681, m. 2 Feb 1702, Robert Knight & d. 1718, having had issue.
2. Catherine, m. Benjamin (d. 19 November 1746), son of Benjamin Collier, M.P., for Great Grimsby 1722-27, who bought Ruckholts, Essex in 1720, and had issue, an only child,
    1a. Catherine, b. 1718, m. 26 May, 1736, Edmund Malone (d. 22 April 1774, aged 70), Judge of the Court of the Common Pleas in Ireland[662], and d. in Bath in January 1765[663], having had had issue,
      1b. Richard, of Baronston, co. Westmeath, M.P. for Westmeath, cr. 1785, Lord Sunderlin, b. 1738, m. 1778, Philippa, eldest dau. of Godolphin Rooper, of Great Berkhampstead, and d.s.p. 14 April, 1816
      2b. Edmond, Shakespearean Scholar & friend of Johnson & Burke, b. 4 Oct. 1741, d. unm. 1812.
      3b. Anthony, d. young
      4b. Benjamin, d. young
      1b. Henrietta, d. *post* 1816, unm.
      2b. Catherine, d. unm. in 1831
3. Margaret, m. 1720, as his first wife, Michael Impey (d.s.p in 1765, aged 84), of Richmond, Surrey[664]
4. Elizabeth, m. John Weaver (d. 1747), of Morville, Salop, M.P. for Bridgnorth, 1713-34. She was bur. at Wooten Wawen, 19 March 1765, having had issue,

---

[662] In his *Life of Malone,* Sir James Prior tells the story of the wedding, which in 1788 was told Edmond Malone by Dr Taylor of Isleworth, who performed the wedding. "Old Mr Collier was a very vain man who had made his fortune in the South Sea year and, having been originally a merchant, was fond, after he retired to live upon his fortune, of a great deal of display and parade. On his daughter's wedding therefore he invited nearly fifty persons and got two or three capital cooks down from London to prepare a magnificent entertainment in honour of the day". At the end of the day, the bride and groom were required to retire to bed and each of the guests visited them to wish them a good night.
[663] Lord Catherlough sent Mr Malone a letter of condolence, saying how fond he had been of her.
[664] Michael was the elder brother of Elijah Impey (1683-1756), of Butterwick House, Hammersmith, who was the father of Sir Elijah Impey, the Chief Justice of Bengal. His widow was called Anne. He left his property to his nephews Michael & Elijah Impey (father of Michael Impey, who marred Henrietta Knight in 1792).

1a. Arthur, of Morville, d. unm in Hammersmith, 6 April 1759.[665]

5. Mary, m. at St Peter le Poer, London, 3 December 1720, Rowland (d. 1774, aged 71), younger son of Sir Rowland Aynsworth, a Turkey merchant of Basinghall Street & was bur. at St Michael Bassishaw, 10 November 1721, s.p

---

[665] He left the Morville estate (after a bachelor uncle's life interest) to his cousin, Arthur Blayney (1716-1795), who – dying unmarried - then left it to Susanna Weaver, the daughter of Arthur Weaver's uncle, Anthony Weaver. She married Lord Tracy and had an only daughter, Henrietta (d. 1839), who married Charles Hanbury. Their descendants were called Hanbury-Tracy. A letter of 2 March 1765 from Edmond Malone in London says sadly that he has heard nothing from Lord Catherlough of Mrs Weaver's personal estate (which he estimates at around £6000) and therefore assumes that they will not benefit.

Printed in Great Britain
by Amazon

35177959R00274